Better Homes and G

NEW
COOK
BOOK

BETTER HOMES AND GARDENS® BOOKS

Editor: Gerald M. Knox
Art Director: Ernest Shelton
Managing Editor: David A. Kirchner
Editorial Project Managers: Liz Anderson, James D. Blume, Marsha Jahns,
    Rosanne Weber Mattson, Jennifer Speer Ramundt, Angela K. Renkoski

Department Head, Cook Books: Sharyl Heiken
Associate Department Heads: Sandra Granseth, Rosemary C. Hutchinson,
    Elizabeth Woolever
Senior Food Editors: Linda Henry, Marcia Stanley, Joyce Trollope
Associate Food Editors: Jennifer Darling, Heather M. Hephner,
    Mary Major, Shelli McConnell, Mary Jo Plutt
Test Kitchen: Director, Sharon Stilwell; Photo Studio Director,
    Janet Herwig; Home Economists: Jean Brekke, Kay Cargill, Marilyn
    Cornelius, Maryellyn Krantz, Lynelle Munn, Dianna Nolin,
    Marge Steenson

Associate Art Directors: Neoma Thomas, Linda Ford Vermie,
    Randall Yontz
Assistant Art Directors: Lynda Haupert, Harijs Priekulis, Tom Wegner
Graphic Designers: Mary Schlueter Bendgen, Mike Burns, Brian Wignall
Art Production: Director, John Berg; Associate, Joe Heuer;
    Office Manager, Michaela Lester

President, Book Group: Jeramy Lanigan
Vice President, Retail Marketing: Jamie L. Martin
Vice President, Administrative Services: Rick Rundall

BETTER HOMES AND GARDENS® MAGAZINE
President, Magazine Group: James A. Autry
Editorial Director: Doris Eby
Editorial Services Director: Duane L. Gregg
Food and Nutrition Editor: Nancy Byal

MEREDITH CORPORATION OFFICERS
Chairman of the Executive Committee: E. T. Meredith III
Chairman of the Board: Robert A. Burnett
President: Jack D. Rehm

NEW COOK BOOK

Editors: Jennifer Darling, Linda Henry, Rosemary C. Hutchinson,
    Mary Major
Editorial Project Managers: James D. Blume, Jennifer Speer Ramundt
Graphic Designer: Lynda Haupert
Electronic Text Processor: Paula Forest
Food Stylists: Marilyn Cornelius, Jennifer Darling, Janet Herwig,
    Dianna Nolin
Contributing Editors: Julia Malloy, Sandra Mosley, Martha Schiel,
    Linda Foley Woodrum
Contributing Food Stylist: Judy Tills
Contributing Photographers: Mike Dieter; M. Jensen Photography, Inc.;
    Scott Little
Contributing Illustrator: Thomas Rosborough

Our seal assures you that every recipe in the *New Cook Book* has been tested in the Better Homes and Gardens® Test Kitchen. This means that each recipe is practical and reliable, and meets pur high standards of taste appeal.

Contents

For the Way You Cook Today

Every page of this revised edition of the Better Homes and Gardens.
New Cook Book is designed with you, the cook of the '90s, in mind. All
of the recipes, meal-planning hints, and cooking tips have been updated
to fit the hurried life you lead. Whether you're a pro in the kitchen or just
starting out, you'll find everything you need to serve delicious meals.

Both Old and New

When we sat down to choose the very best recipes for this tenth edition of the *New Cook Book,* we worked hard to find just the right mix of old standbys and modern favorites. That's why you'll see many of the recipes you remember from your childhood, such as Beef Pot Roast and Chicken and Dumplings, right alongside relative newcomers like Taco Salad and Turkey Manicotti.

Also important as we selected recipes were recent changes in food tastes and attitudes, as well as the many new food products available. Taken together, these factors became a formidable yardstick with which to measure each of the recipes in the previous edition, as well as those we developed new. The result is *the* cook book for the '90s—complete with the best of both the past and the present.

Changing Tastes

Just think about the way most of us cook today, versus how we cooked 15 years ago. We're frequently serving light meals with just one or two courses to a few people instead of big meals to a bunch. We're also preparing more ethnic and regional favorites, such as stir-fries and gumbos, instead of standard meat-and-potatoes fare. And we're serving a lot more poultry, fish, and salads.

All of these changes are reflected in this book. You'll find that most of our recipes now serve four people instead of six or eight. You'll also find more recipes for poultry, fish and seafood, main-dish salads, and vegetables, as well as a good selection of regional American and ethnic favorites. Finally, we included more recipes with whole grains, and several recipes for meatless main dishes. Whatever your preference, this edition of the *New Cook Book* has it.

Saving Time

Whether you cook because you love to or because you have to, you want your time in the kitchen to be worth the effort. We agree. So we designed our recipes to help you get the most from every cooking minute.

First, we added even more quick recipes. Just look for the symbol **FAST** at right. This symbol means that you can prepare main dishes or desserts in 30 minutes or less from the time you step into the kitchen to the time the dish is on the table. Or, if the recipe is a snack, beverage, or side dish, you can do it in under 20 minutes.

Next, we increased the number of recipes with optional microwave and crockery-cooker directions by more than a hundred. Now it's easier than ever to choose the cooking method that best suits your schedule.

Third, we improved our charts so you can tell in a glance how long to broil a steak, roast a bird, or cook green beans.

Finally and most importantly, we scrutinized every recipe to eliminate unnecessary steps and to guarantee that you will get quality results in the least amount of time possible.

Saving Effort

Next to saving time, what cooks want most is to save effort. So we looked for ways to cook easier and smarter. Take the "Cakes" chapter, for example. We developed a new way to whip cakes up from scratch that makes them almost as easy as cake mixes. For cookies, our one-bowl method saves you preparation and dishwashing time. And, in the "Breads" chapter, we show you how to make croissants in just a fraction of the time of traditional recipes.

Besides developing new ways to prepare our recipes, we also did everything possible to make them easier to understand and to use. The easiest ones are marked (EASY) with the symbol at right. These recipes are easy for their type. A bread recipe that carries this symbol, for example, will not necessarily be fast, but it will be easier to make than most other breads. What's more, we kept a close eye on the number of dishes, pots, and pans we call for so dishwashing will be easy, too.

Another way we tried to save you work was to develop as many easy flavor alternatives to the recipes as we could. Just one muffin recipe, for example, will enable you to make ten different flavor combinations, everything from blueberry to banana. You also have a choice of grilling or oven-cooking many of our meat, fish, and poultry dishes. If it rains, you can move your meal inside. Finally, we added how-to photographs. No more fumbling over difficult steps. We show you what to do at a glance.

Helpful Hints

Because cooking is more than just following a recipe, we present cooking advice throughout the book. You'll discover dozens of cooking tips in all of the chapters, and in a "Special Helps" chapter at the back of the book, to answer your questions on meal planning, shopping, nutrition, calorie counts, food storage, equipment, microwave cooking, cooking terms, garnishing, and much, much more.

No matter what your culinary style or experience, you can count on the recipes, photos, and information in the Better Homes and Gardens. *New Cook Book* to make cooking easier, faster, and more fun. Just try a few of the delicious recipes and see if you don't agree with us that this new edition is the best ever.

Eating Right

Today's cooks want the meals they serve to be not only attractive and delicious, but nutritious as well. That's why when we tested the recipes for this book, we looked for ways to reduce salt, sugar, and fat. Although good flavor and ease of preparation remained our first objectives, we also were able to make many of our recipes even more healthful than they were before.

To help you keep tabs on the quality of your diet, we continued our long-standing practice of publishing nutrition information for our recipes. In this edition, to make our information even more complete, we also tell you the amount of cholesterol in each serving. As before, you'll find our easy-to-read nutrition charts at the beginning of each chapter. Use these charts to compare the nutritional values of different recipes.

For example, look at the nutrition analyses of the recipes Ginger-Beef Stir-Fry and Herbed Rump Roast on pages 206–207. The analyses show that each recipe contains more than a third of the protein you need each day at under 300 calories per serving. But the cholesterol and sodium levels differ. Herbed Rump Roast is higher in cholesterol, but Ginger-Beef Stir-Fry has more sodium. If sodium is of concern to you, choose Herbed Rump Roast. If you're watching your cholesterol intake, try Ginger-Beef Stir-Fry.

Taste panel (above): Our Test Kitchen puts every recipe Better Homes and Gardens® Books publishes through its paces. A panel of experts including editors, designers, and Test Kitchen home economists judges each recipe for ease of preparation, texture, appeal, and flavor. No recipe receives the Test Kitchen Seal of Approval unless it meets our high standards.

Photo session (below): All the photographs in the Better Homes and Gardens® *New Cook Book* were shot by a photo team that includes an editor, designer, food stylist, and photographer. Here, our staff food stylist works with a photographer to put the final touches on a cheesecake. These pros work hard to make all of our foods as beautiful and true to life as possible.

Appetizers & Snacks

Nutrition Analysis

	Per Serving								Percent U.S. RDA Per Serving							
	Servings Per Recipe	Calories	Protein (g)	Carbohydrate (g)	Fat (g)	Cholesterol (mg)	Sodium (mg)	Potassium (mg)	Protein	Vitamin A	Vitamin C	Thiamine	Riboflavin	Niacin	Calcium	Iron
Avocado Pita Wedges (p. 15)	12	59	2	5	4	3	27	71	3	9	2	2	2	3	2	2
Bacon-Stuffed Slices (p. 14)	30	59	2	5	4	11	84	38	3	5	4	3	2	2	2	3
Barbecue-Style Chicken Wings (p. 17)	16	42	4	4	1	12	102	66	7	3	3	1	1	6	1	1
Batter-Fried Vegetables (p. 21)	8	151	4	17	7	34	537	233	7	6	52	11	10	9	2	9
Blue Cheese Ball (p. 14)	12	124	5	2	11	20	148	80	7	8	3	1	6	1	11	3
Cajun-Style Party Mix (p. 10)	40	200	3	23	11	0	445	85	5	6	6	13	4	9	1	9
Cajun-Style Popcorn (p. 11)	20	33	4	2	2	0	74	12	1	3	0	1	0	0	0	2
Cheddar Cheese Ball (p. 14)	12	82	3	1	8	18	109	35	5	8	4	0	3	0	8	2
Cheese and Pesto Spread (p. 13)	24	105	3	1	10	24	103	53	5	9	6	1	4	1	5	3
Cheese Twists (p. 17)	40	37	1	3	2	10	40	10	2	2	0	2	2	1	2	1
Chicken Liver Pâté (p. 22)	8	83	6	2	6	130	118	99	9	117	18	4	34	14	1	14
Chili con Queso (p. 12)	14	75	4	2	6	15	171	69	6	8	12	1	4	1	11	1
Cocktail Meatballs w/ Dill Sauce (p. 16)	10	177	10	4	13	71	170	142	15	6	1	4	8	10	4	8
Cocktail Meatballs with Polynesian Sauce (p. 16)	10	149	9	11	7	59	249	191	14	3	6	6	7	10	3	9
Cocktail Meatballs with Tangy Cranberry Sauce (p. 16)	10	157	9	13	7	59	163	134	14	2	2	3	6	10	2	8
Codfish Balls (p. 20)	15	49	3	3	3	25	640	107	5	2	4	2	3	5	3	3
Crab Cocktail (p. 20)	6	92	11	9	1	57	607	354	16	34	19	7	4	9	4	4
Cream-Cheese-Stuffed Slices (p. 14)	30	54	2	5	3	9	95	35	2	5	5	2	2	1	2	3
Creamy Blue Cheese Dip (p. 12)	16	111	3	2	11	25	109	63	4	10	1	1	4	0	5	1
Creamy Dill Dip (p. 12)	16	81	2	1	8	22	100	44	2	6	0	1	3	0	3	1
Creamy Onion Dip (p. 12)	16	82	2	1	8	22	128	43	2	6	0	1	3	0	3	1
Creamy Seafood Dip (p. 12)	16	87	2	1	8	26	107	52	4	6	0	1	3	0	3	3
Creamy Tarragon Dip (p. 12)	16	81	2	1	8	22	112	49	3	8	2	1	3	0	3	1
Crunchy Party Mix (p. 10)	40	202	4	23	11	0	444	105	6	6	6	11	5	11	2	10
Curried Chicken Spread (p. 15)	12	70	3	4	5	10	89	42	5	1	0	2	2	4	1	2
Deviled-Ham-and-Cheese Ball (p. 14)	12	98	4	1	8	26	158	49	7	6	5	4	4	2	10	1
Egg Rolls with Crab Filling (p. 18)	8	156	6	13	10	16	624	131	9	7	7	5	5	5	3	4
Egg Rolls with Ham-Orange Filling (p. 18)	8	134	5	11	8	7	363	181	8	2	13	12	5	5	2	4
Egg Rolls with Pork and Shrimp Filling (p. 18)	8	158	10	10	9	51	514	181	16	0	3	9	7	9	2	7
Egg Rolls with Vegetable Filling (p. 18)	8	121	3	12	8	0	471	205	5	87	6	6	7	6	2	5
Eight-Layer Spread (p. 14)	16	98	4	6	7	13	218	133	6	7	6	2	4	1	8	3
Feta Cheese Ball (p. 14)	16	98	2	1	10	22	178	31	3	8	2	1	5	0	5	2
Fried Cheese (p. 21)	20	76	4	3	5	39	117	21	6	6	3	3	6	3	8	2
Fried Potato Skins (p. 11)	48	54	2	6	3	5	36	99	3	1	3	2	2	2	4	2
Fruit Shrimp Cocktail (p. 20)	6	138	9	12	6	74	315	460	15	11	54	6	5	9	3	9
Guacamole (p. 13)	16	47	1	2	4	0	36	180	1	4	10	2	2	3	0	2
Ham-Stuffed Mushrooms (p. 11)	24	39	1	3	3	1	77	82	2	2	2	3	6	5	1	2
Herbed Parmesan Twists (p. 17)	40	37	2	2	2	10	48	9	2	2	0	1	2	1	3	1
Hot Cheese Dip (p. 12)	16	84	4	1	7	19	227	39	6	6	0	0	4	0	9	1
Italian-Style Party Mix (p. 10)	40	208	5	23	11	1	467	108	7	6	6	11	5	11	4	10
Italian-Style Popcorn (p. 11)	20	40	1	2	3	1	58	12	2	2	0	1	1	0	2	1
Lemon and Herb Mushrooms (p. 22)	6	23	1	3	1	0	22	149	1	0	4	3	10	8	0	3
Marinated Cheese and Olives (p. 22)	16	87	4	0	8	18	191	29	7	3	0	1	4	1	11	1
Melon and Prosciutto (p. 22)	36	9	1	1	0	1	30	53	1	10	11	2	0	1	0	0
Mustard-Glazed Ribs (p. 16)	6	373	22	18	23	91	377	332	35	4	2	21	18	21	6	13
Nachos (p. 8)	8	308	14	26	16	33	736	354	21	6	22	9	9	6	20	9
Nutty Cheese Spread (p. 15)	24	59	2	1	6	13	34	32	3	4	1	1	2	0	4	1
Oriental-Style Party Mix (p. 10)	40	165	3	14	11	0	279	94	5	6	6	12	5	11	2	9

On the divider: Cocktail Meatballs with Tangy Cranberry Sauce (p. 16), Potato Skins (p. 11), and Cheddar Cheese Ball (p. 14).

Nutrition Analysis

Nutrition Analysis	Servings Per Recipe	Per Serving							Percent U.S. RDA Per Serving							
		Calories	Protein (g)	Carbohydrate (g)	Fat (g)	Cholesterol (mg)	Sodium (mg)	Potassium (mg)	Protein	Vitamin A	Vitamin C	Thiamine	Riboflavin	Niacin	Calcium	Iron
Oysters Rockefeller (p. 20)	8	78	4	3	5	21	110	145	7	26	21	5	6	6	6	16
Pastry-Wrapped Olives (p. 17)	30	40	1	3	3	2	80	7	1	0	0	2	1	1	2	1
Pepperoni Bites (p. 9)	20	126	4	13	6	6	439	39	7	2	1	7	6	6	6	4
Pepperoni-Stuffed Mushrooms (p. 11)	24	41	1	3	3	1	76	81	2	2	0	1	2	6	5	0
Potato Skins (p. 11)	48	61	2	6	3	5	58	100	3	3	3	2	2	2	4	2
Rumaki (p. 17)	24	45	4	1	3	65	114	57	6	58	7	3	17	8	0	7
Salmon Mousse (p. 20)	24	73	3	1	7	35	94	51	4	3	1	1	2	3	3	1
Sausage-Stuffed Mushrooms (p. 11)	24	24	2	1	1	4	55	85	2	0	2	3	6	5	1	2
Shrimp Cocktail (p. 20)	6	54	8	4	1	74	311	138	13	4	6	1	1	5	2	7
Shrimp-Cucumber Spread (p. 15)	20	33	2	1	3	14	45	19	3	2	0	0	1	1	1	1
Sour Cream Fruit Dip (p. 12)	8	86	1	8	6	13	16	49	1	5	1	1	3	0	4	1
Spinach Phyllo Triangles (p. 19)	24	85	2	7	32	6	196	66	3	19	2	4	6	2	5	4
Spinach-Stuffed Mushrooms (p. 11)	24	38	1	3	2	1	65	89	2	5	2	2	6	4	2	2
Stuffed Cherry Tomatoes (p. 21)	24	36	1	1	3	10	29	40	1	6	4	1	2	0	1	1
Stuffed Mushrooms (p. 11)	24	43	2	3	3	2	58	77	2	2	1	2	6	4	2	2
Sweet-and-Sour Franks (p. 16)	16	132	4	11	8	14	299	117	5	0	14	3	2	4	2	3
Swiss-Caraway Twists (p. 17)	40	35	1	3	2	9	29	13	2	2	0	2	2	1	3	1
Toasted Chili Nuts (p. 10)	16	111	2	3	11	0	65	80	3	3	1	4	1	1	2	2
Wontons with Crab Filling (p. 18)	40	37	1	3	2	3	135	29	2	1	1	1	1	1	1	1
Wontons with Ham-Orange Filling (p. 18)	40	32	1	3	2	1	83	39	2	0	3	2	1	1	0	1
Wontons with Pork and Shrimp Filling (p. 18)	40	37	2	2	2	10	113	39	3	0	1	2	2	2	0	2
Wontons with Vegetable Filling (p. 18)	40	30	1	3	2	0	104	44	1	17	1	1	2	1	0	1

Appetizers And Snacks

No matter what you need—a meal opener, a party food, or an afternoon nibble—you'll find plenty of options here. For a first course, choose Oysters Rockefeller or Shrimp Cocktail. For a party menu, select appetizers that complement each other. For example, team cheesy Potato Skins with tangy Barbecue-Style Chicken Wings. For snacks, anything goes. Toasted Chili Nuts and Italian-Style Popcorn are always popular.

Just remember to always serve your hot appetizers hot and your cold ones cold. An electric skillet, hot tray, griddle, bun warmer, fondue pot, or crockery cooker is handy for keeping appetizers hot. Cold appetizers require less last-minute attention and most can be made up to 24 hours ahead. Follow the minimum and maximum chilling times in the recipes for best flavor and quality.

Pepperoni Bites

Sink your teeth into these golden biscuits and savor the saucy pizza filling inside.

> 1 cup shredded mozzarella cheese
> ½ cup chopped pepperoni
> ½ cup pizza sauce
> 2 packages (10 each) refrigerated biscuits
> 1 tablespoon milk
> ¼ cup grated Parmesan cheese   Oven 350°

For filling, in a bowl combine mozzarella cheese, pepperoni, and pizza sauce. Set aside.

Separate biscuits. Flatten biscuits to 3-inch circles. Place about *1 rounded tablespoon* filling in the center of *each* circle. Bring edges of dough together. Pinch to seal. Place, seam side down, on greased baking sheets. Brush with milk. Sprinkle with Parmesan. Bake in a 350° oven for 12 to 15 minutes or till golden. Serve warm. Makes 20.

Crunchy Party Mix

Odds are, you won't have any of this crispy snack left, but if you do, freeze it for up to four months.

1 **cup margarine *or* butter**
3 **tablespoons Worcestershire sauce**
½ **teaspoon garlic powder**
 Several drops bottled hot pepper sauce
5 **cups small pretzels *or* pretzel sticks**
4 **cups round toasted oat cereal**
4 **cups bite-size wheat *or* bran square cereal**
4 **cups bite-size rice *or* corn square cereal *or* bite-size shredded wheat biscuits**
3 **cups mixed nuts** Oven 300°

In a saucepan mix margarine, Worcestershire sauce, garlic powder, and pepper sauce. Heat and stir till margarine melts. In a large roasting pan mix pretzels, cereals, and nuts. Drizzle margarine mixture over cereal mixture; toss to coat.

Bake in a 300° oven for 45 minutes, stirring every 15 minutes. Spread on foil to cool. Store in airtight container. Makes 20 cups (40 servings).

Microwave directions: In a 2-cup measure combine the margarine or butter, Worcestershire sauce, garlic powder, and hot pepper sauce. Micro-cook, uncovered, on 100% power (high) for 1½ to 2 minutes or till margarine melts, stirring once. In a 3-quart casserole combine *half* of the pretzels, cereals, and nuts. Drizzle *half* of the margarine mixture over cereal mixture, tossing to coat evenly. Cook, uncovered, on high for 5½ to 6 minutes or till hot, stirring three times. Spread on foil to cool (mix will become crisp on standing). Repeat with remaining ingredients.

Oriental-Style Party Mix: Prepare as above, *except* omit Worcestershire sauce and pretzels. Add 3 tablespoons *soy sauce* and 2 teaspoons *five-spice powder* to margarine mixture. Add one 5-ounce can *chow mein noodles* and 2 cups *bite-size fish-shape crackers* to cereal.

Italian-Style Party Mix: Prepare as above, *except* omit hot pepper sauce and increase garlic powder to *1 teaspoon.* Add 2 teaspoons dried *Italian seasoning* to the margarine mixture. Immediately after baking, toss the warm cereal mixture with ½ cup grated *Parmesan cheese.*

Cajun-Style Party Mix: Prepare as above, *except* increase hot pepper sauce to *1 tablespoon* and substitute 3 cups *pecan halves* for nuts.

Toasted Chili Nuts

2 **tablespoons margarine *or* butter**
2 **tablespoons Worcestershire sauce**
1 **teaspoon chili powder**
¼ **teaspoon onion salt**
¼ **teaspoon ground red pepper**
2 **cups walnut *or* pecan halves *or* pieces** Oven 350°

In a saucepan combine margarine, Worcestershire sauce, chili powder, onion salt, and red pepper. Heat and stir till margarine melts. Spread nuts in a 9x9x2-inch baking pan. Toss with margarine mixture. Bake in a 350° oven for 12 to 15 minutes or till toasted, stirring occasionally. Spread on foil; cool. Store in an airtight container. Makes 2 cups (16 servings).

Nachos

Build this spicy snack up to seven layers high.

½ **pound bulk pork sausage *or* ground beef**
½ **cup chopped onion**
2 **cloves garlic, minced**
1 **16-ounce can refried beans**
6 **cups tortilla chips**
½ **cup sliced pitted ripe olives**
1 **4-ounce can diced green chili peppers, drained**
1½ **cups shredded cheddar cheese** Oven 350°

Cook meat, onion, and garlic till meat is brown. Drain. Stir in beans. Arrange *half* of the chips on each of two 12-inch ovenproof platters. Layer *half* of the meat-bean mixture, olives, chili peppers, and cheese on each platter. Bake in a 350° oven for 5 to 7 minutes or till cheese melts. Serve with avocado dip, dairy sour cream, and salsa, if desired. Makes 8 servings.

Microwave directions: In a 2-quart casserole micro-cook meat, onion, and garlic, covered, on 100% power (high) for 3 to 5 minutes or till no pink remains; stir once. Drain well. Stir in beans. Assemble as above. Cook on high for 2 to 3 minutes. Serve as above.

Italian-Style Popcorn

Great to munch in front of the TV.

 ¼ **cup margarine *or* butter**
 ½ **teaspoon dried Italian seasoning**
 ¼ **teaspoon garlic powder**
 10 **cups warm popped popcorn**
 ⅓ **cup grated Parmesan cheese**

In a saucepan cook and stir margarine, Italian seasoning, and garlic powder till margarine melts. Toss with popcorn, coating evenly. Toss with cheese. Makes 10 cups (20 servings).
 Cajun-Style Popcorn: Prepare as above, *except* omit dried Italian seasoning, garlic powder, and Parmesan cheese. Combine 1 teaspoon *paprika,* ½ teaspoon *garlic salt,* and ⅛ teaspoon *each* of ground *white, red, and black pepper* with the margarine.

Potato Skins

Make the potato shells ahead. Then bake or fry them just before serving. (Pictured on page 7.)

 12 **medium baking potatoes**
 ½ **cup margarine *or* butter, melted**
 2 **cups shredded cheddar *or***
     Monterey Jack cheese (8 ounces)
     Garlic *or* seasoned salt
     (optional)
     Salsa
     Sliced green onion   Oven 425°

Prick potatoes with a fork. Bake in a 425° oven for 40 to 50 minutes or till tender. Cut into quarters. Scoop out the insides (reserve for another use), leaving ½-inch-thick shells.
 Brush both sides of potato skins with margarine. Place, cut side up, on a large baking sheet. Bake in a 425° oven for 10 to 15 minutes or till crisp. Sprinkle with cheese and, if desired, salt. Bake about 2 minutes more or till cheese melts. Serve with salsa and green onion. Makes 48.
 Fried Potato Skins: Prepare as above, *except* omit margarine and do not bake a second time. In a heavy saucepan or deep-fat fryer heat 2 inches melted *shortening or cooking oil* for deep-fat frying to 375°. Fry shells, a few at a time, for 1 to 2 minutes or till golden. Drain on paper towels. Place on a large baking sheet. Sprinkle with cheese. Bake in a 425° oven about 2 minutes.

Stuffed Mushrooms

These delectable morsels hold plenty of cheddar or blue cheese.

 24 **large fresh mushrooms, 1½ to 2**
     inches in diameter
 ¼ **cup sliced green onion**
 1 **clove garlic, minced**
 ¼ **cup margarine *or* butter**
 ⅔ **cup fine dry bread crumbs**
 ½ **cup shredded cheddar *or* crumbled**
     blue cheese (2 ounces)   Oven 425°

Wash and drain mushrooms. Remove stems. Reserve caps. Chop enough stems to make *1 cup.*
 In a medium saucepan cook stems, onion, and garlic in margarine or butter till tender. Stir in bread crumbs and cheese. Spoon crumb mixture into mushroom caps. Arrange mushrooms in a 15x10x1-inch baking pan. Bake in a 425° oven 8 to 10 minutes or till heated through. Makes 24.
 Microwave directions: Prepare mushroom stems and caps as above. In a 1-quart casserole micro-cook stems, onion, and garlic in margarine or butter, uncovered, on 100% power (high) for 2 to 4 minutes or till tender. Stir in bread crumbs and cheese. Spoon crumb mixture into mushroom caps. Arrange *half* of the caps on a 10-inch-round plate, leaving the center open. Cook, uncovered, on high for 4 to 5 minutes or till heated through. Repeat with remaining caps. Do not micro-cook the recipes below.
 Spinach-Stuffed Mushrooms: Prepare as above, *except* omit cheese. Cook 1 cup chopped fresh *spinach* with the stem mixture. Stir ¼ cup grated *Parmesan cheese* and ½ teaspoon crushed dried *marjoram* into crumb mixture.
 Sausage-Stuffed Mushrooms: Prepare as above, *except* omit margarine or butter and cheese. Reduce bread crumbs to *2 tablespoons.* Cook ½ pound *bulk Italian sausage* with stem mixture till sausage is brown. Drain fat. Stir 2 tablespoons grated *Parmesan cheese* and bread crumbs into sausage mixture.
 Pepperoni-Stuffed Mushrooms: Prepare as above, *except* omit cheese. Stir ¼ cup chopped *pepperoni* and ½ teaspoon dried *Italian seasoning* into the crumb mixture.
 Ham-Stuffed Mushrooms: Prepare as above, *except* substitute crushed *corn bread stuffing mix* for bread crumbs and omit cheese. Stir ¼ cup finely chopped fully cooked *ham* and 2 tablespoons chopped *pecans* into stuffing mixture.

Creamy Dill Dip

For colorful dippers, serve carrot sticks, broccoli or cauliflower flowerets, and mushrooms.

- 1 **8-ounce package cream cheese, softened**
- 1 **8-ounce carton dairy sour cream**
- 2 **tablespoons finely chopped green onion**
- 2 **teaspoons dried dillweed**
- ½ **teaspoon seasoned salt or salt Vegetable dippers, assorted crackers, or chips**

In a mixing bowl beat cream cheese, sour cream, onion, dillweed, and seasoned salt with an electric mixer till fluffy. Chill up to 24 hours. If dip thickens after chilling, stir in 1 or 2 tablespoons *milk.* Serve with vegetable dippers, crackers, or chips. Makes 2 cups (16 servings).

Creamy Onion Dip: Prepare as above, *except* omit onion, dillweed, and seasoned salt. Stir 2 tablespoons (⅓ of an envelope) *regular onion soup mix* into beaten cream cheese mixture.

Creamy Blue Cheese Dip: Prepare as above, *except* omit dillweed and seasoned salt. Stir ½ cup crumbled *blue cheese* and ⅓ cup finely chopped *walnuts* into the beaten cream cheese mixture.

Creamy Seafood Dip: Prepare as above, *except* stir one 6½-ounce can minced *clams,* drained, or *crabmeat,* drained, flaked, and cartilage removed, into beaten cheese mixture.

Creamy Tarragon Dip: Prepare as above, *except* omit dillweed and seasoned salt. Stir ½ cup finely chopped *watercress or parsley,* 1 tablespoon *lemon juice,* 1 teaspoon *anchovy paste,* and ½ teaspoon crushed dried *tarragon* into the beaten cream cheese mixture.

Sour Cream Fruit Dip

To keep the fruit looking just-picked, brush it with lemon juice.

- 1 **8-ounce carton dairy sour cream or plain yogurt**
- ¼ **cup apricot or peach preserves**
- ⅛ **teaspoon ground cinnamon Apple, pear, or peach slices**

Stir together sour cream, preserves (cut up large pieces of fruit), and cinnamon. Chill up to 24 hours. Serve with fruit. Makes 1 cup (8 servings).

Chili con Queso

- ½ **cup finely chopped onion**
- 1 **tablespoon margarine or butter**
- 2 **medium tomatoes, seeded and chopped**
- 1 **4-ounce can diced green chili peppers, drained**
- 1 **cup shredded American cheese**
- 1 **cup shredded Monterey Jack cheese**
- 1 **teaspoon cornstarch**
- 1 **teaspoon bottled hot pepper sauce Tortilla or corn chips**

In a saucepan cook onion in margarine till tender. Stir in tomatoes and peppers. Simmer, uncovered, 10 minutes. Toss cheeses with cornstarch. Gradually add to saucepan, stirring till melted. Stir in hot sauce. Heat through. Serve with chips. Makes 1¾ cups (14 servings).

Microwave directions: In a 1½-quart casserole micro-cook onion and margarine, covered, on 100% power (high) for 1½ to 2½ minutes. Add tomatoes and peppers. Cook, covered, on high 2 to 4 minutes or till tender. Toss cheeses with cornstarch. Gradually add to casserole, stirring till melted. Stir in hot sauce. Cook, uncovered, on high 2 minutes or till heated; stir twice. Serve with chips.

Hot Cheese Dip

- ¼ **cup finely chopped green onion**
- 1 **clove garlic, minced**
- ½ **teaspoon dried tarragon, crushed**
- 1 **tablespoon margarine or butter**
- 1 **teaspoon cornstarch**
- ¾ **cup beer or milk**
- 2 **cups shredded American cheese**
- 1 **3-ounce package cream cheese, cut up French bread cubes or tortilla chips**

In a saucepan cook onion, garlic, and tarragon in margarine. Stir in cornstarch. Add beer all at once. Cook and stir till thickened and bubbly. Gradually add cheeses, stirring till melted. Serve with bread or chips. Makes 2 cups (16 servings).

Guacamole

Fiery chili peppers and creamy, cool avocados pair up in this Mexican favorite.

2 medium very ripe avocados,
    seeded, peeled, and cut up
½ of a small onion, cut up
½ of a 4-ounce can (¼ cup) diced green
    chili peppers, drained, *or* several
    dashes bottled hot pepper sauce
1 tablespoon snipped cilantro *or*
    parsley
1 tablespoon lemon *or* lime juice
1 clove garlic, minced
¼ teaspoon salt
1 medium tomato, peeled, seeded,
    and finely chopped (optional)
    Tortilla chips

In a blender container or food processor bowl combine avocados, onion, chili peppers or hot pepper sauce, cilantro, lemon juice, garlic, and salt. Cover and blend or process till mixture is smooth, scraping sides as necessary. Stir in tomato, if desired. Transfer to a serving bowl. Cover and chill up to 24 hours. Serve with chips. Makes about 2 cups (16 servings).

Cheese and Pesto Spread

1 8-ounce package cream cheese
1 4½-ounce package Brie cheese
1 cup firmly packed fresh basil leaves
½ cup firmly packed parsley sprigs
½ cup grated Parmesan cheese
¼ cup pine nuts, walnuts, *or* almonds
2 cloves garlic, quartered
¼ cup olive oil *or* cooking oil
½ cup whipping cream
    Crackers *or* sliced French bread

Soften cream cheese and Brie cheese.

For pesto, in a blender container combine basil, parsley, Parmesan cheese, nuts, garlic, and *2 tablespoons* oil. Cover; blend with on-off turns till a paste forms. Gradually add remaining oil, blending on low speed till smooth.

Beat cream cheese and Brie together till nearly smooth. Beat whipping cream till soft peaks form. Fold whipped cream into cheese mixture.

Line a 3½- or 4-cup mold with plastic wrap. Spread *one-fourth* of cheese mixture into mold. Top with *one-third* of pesto. Repeat layers twice. Top with cheese mixture. Chill 6 to 24 hours.

To serve, unmold on plate. Remove plastic wrap. Garnish with fresh basil, if desired. Serve with crackers. Makes 3½ cups (24 servings).

Cheese and Pesto Spread

Cheddar Cheese Ball

Skip last-minute hassle by making this appetizer ahead and freezing it. (Pictured on page 7.)

- 1 **cup finely shredded cheddar cheese**
- 1 **3-ounce package cream cheese**
- 2 **tablespoons margarine *or* butter**
- 2 **tablespoons milk *or* dry white wine**
- 1 **tablespoon finely chopped green onion**
- 1 **tablespoon diced pimiento**
- 1 **teaspoon Worcestershire sauce**
  Dash bottled hot pepper sauce
- ⅓ **to ½ cup snipped parsley *or* finely chopped walnuts *or* pecans**
  Pimiento strips (optional)
  Assorted crackers

Bring cheddar cheese, cream cheese, and margarine to room temperature. Add milk, onion, pimiento, Worcestershire sauce, and hot sauce. Beat till combined. Cover and chill 4 to 24 hours.

To serve, shape mixture into a ball. Roll in parsley or nuts. Let stand 15 minutes. Garnish with pimiento strips, if desired. Serve with crackers. Makes about 1½ cups (12 servings).

Blue Cheese Ball: Prepare as above, *except* omit diced pimiento and parsley, walnuts or pecans. Add ¼ cup crumbled *blue cheese* to cheese mixture. Roll in chopped toasted *almonds*.

Deviled-Ham-and-Cheese Ball: Prepare as above, *except* substitute *Swiss cheese* for cheddar cheese and omit Worcestershire sauce. Add one 3-ounce can *deviled ham* to cheese mixture.

Feta Cheese Ball

- 1 **8-ounce package cream cheese**
- 1 **4-ounce package feta cheese, crumbled**
- ¼ **cup margarine *or* butter**
- ⅓ **cup chopped ripe olives**
- 2 **tablespoons finely chopped green onion**
- ¼ **cup snipped parsley *or* finely chopped toasted almonds**
  Assorted crackers

Bring cheeses and margarine to room temperature. Beat till combined. Stir in olives and onion. Cover and chill 4 to 24 hours. To serve, shape into a ball. Roll in parsley or almonds. Serve with crackers. Makes 2 cups (16 servings).

Eight-Layer Spread

For variety, add a ninth layer of alfalfa sprouts.

- 1 **8¼-ounce can refried beans**
- ¼ **cup picante *or* taco sauce**
- 1 **cup shredded lettuce**
- 1 **8-ounce carton dairy sour cream**
- 1 **6-ounce container frozen avocado dip, thawed**
- 1 **cup shredded Monterey Jack *or* cheddar cheese (4 ounces)**
- ¼ **cup sliced green onion**
- 2 **tablespoons sliced *or* chopped pitted ripe olives**
- 2 **medium tomatoes, chopped**
  Tortilla chips *or* crackers

Stir together beans and picante or taco sauce.

Arrange lettuce on a 12-inch platter, leaving a 2-inch open rim at edge of platter. Spread bean mixture over lettuce, making a layer about ¼ inch thick. Then layer sour cream and avocado dip. Top with cheese, onion, and olives. Cover and chill up to 24 hours. Before serving, arrange tomatoes on top. Arrange the chips on a platter around spread. Makes 16 servings.

Cream-Cheese-Stuffed Slices

- 3 **French-style rolls, 6 inches long**
- 1 **8-ounce package cream cheese, softened**
- ¼ **cup dairy sour cream**
- 2 **tablespoons finely chopped green onion *or* snipped chives**
- 2 **tablespoons diced pimiento**
- 2 **tablespoons snipped parsley**
- ½ **teaspoon seasoned salt or salt**

Trim ends from rolls. Carefully scoop out centers, leaving ½-inch-thick shells. Reserve centers for another use. Set bread shells aside.

In a bowl combine cream cheese, sour cream, onion or chives, pimiento, parsley, and seasoned salt. Beat with an electric mixer on medium speed till smooth. Stuff bread shells with cheese mixture, pressing firmly to prevent air pockets. Wrap in foil or plastic wrap. Chill 4 to 24 hours. To serve, cut rolls into ½-inch slices. Makes 30.

Bacon-Stuffed Slices: Prepare as above, *except* omit pimiento and seasoned salt. Stir 4 slices crumbled, cooked *bacon* into the cream cheese mixture.

Shrimp-Cucumber Spread

1 **3-ounce package cream cheese, softened**
2 **tablespoons mayonnaise *or* salad dressing**
1 **tablespoon catsup**
1 **teaspoon Dijon-style mustard *or* prepared mustard**
Dash garlic powder
1 **4½-ounce can shrimp, rinsed, drained, and chopped; *or* 1 cup cooked shrimp, peeled, deveined, and chopped**
¼ **cup finely chopped seeded cucumber**
1 **tablespoon finely chopped onion**
Melba toast rounds *or* assorted crackers *or* bread*

In a mixing bowl stir together cream cheese, mayonnaise or salad dressing, catsup, mustard, and garlic powder. Stir in shrimp, cucumber, and onion. Spread mixture over melba toast or crackers. Makes 1¼ cups spread (20 servings).

***Note:** Cut white, wheat, or rye bread into decorative shapes with small cookie or hors d'oeuvres cutters, if desired.

Nutty Cheese Spread

Stuff some celery sticks with this creamy spread and add them to a relish tray.

1 **8-ounce package cream cheese**
½ **cup shredded Swiss *or* cheddar cheese (2 ounces)**
½ **cup chopped walnuts**
¼ **cup milk**
2 **tablespoons snipped parsley**
⅛ **teaspoon onion powder**
Celery sticks, apple slices,* assorted crackers, *or* melba toast rounds

In a mixing bowl bring cream cheese and Swiss or cheddar cheese to room temperature. Add walnuts, milk, parsley, and onion powder. Stir till combined. Cover and chill up to 24 hours.

To serve, spread on celery sticks, apple slices, crackers, or melba toast rounds. Makes 1½ cups spread (24 servings).

***Note:** Brush apple slices with lemon juice or ascorbic-acid color keeper, if desired.

Curried Chicken Spread

Curry powder and sour cream turn ordinary chicken salad into a tasty topping for party bread.

3 **tablespoons mayonnaise *or* salad dressing**
2 **tablespoons dairy sour cream**
2 **tablespoons finely chopped green onion**
2 **tablespoons finely chopped nuts**
¼ **teaspoon curry powder**
⅛ **teaspoon salt**
½ **cup finely chopped cooked chicken (about 3 ounces)**
12 **slices party rye *or* pumpernickel bread**
Snipped parsley (optional)

In a medium mixing bowl combine mayonnaise or salad dressing, sour cream, green onion, nuts, curry powder, and salt. Stir in chicken. Spread chicken mixture over bread (or chill up to 24 hours before spreading). Sprinkle with parsley, if desired. Makes ⅔ cup spread (12 servings).

Avocado Pita Wedges

Avocado and mozzarella cheese make a great team in these minisandwiches.

3 **small whole wheat *or* white pita bread rounds**
⅓ **cup mayonnaise *or* salad dressing**
1 **medium avocado**
¼ **cup shredded mozzarella cheese (1 ounce)**
½ **of a small tomato, chopped**
2 **tablespoons shredded carrot**
¼ **cup alfalfa sprouts**

Cut each pita bread round into quarters. Spread the inside of each with mayonnaise.

Peel and seed avocado. Cut *half* of the avocado into 6 slices. (Reserve remaining avocado for another use.) Cut each slice in half crosswise. Toss together cheese, tomato, and carrot. Spoon into each pita quarter. Place an avocado piece in each. Top with alfalfa sprouts. Secure with toothpicks, if necessary. Makes 12.

Cocktail Meatballs

Cocktail Meatballs with Tangy Cranberry Sauce are pictured on page 7.

    1   beaten egg
    ¼   cup fine dry bread crumbs
    ¼   cup milk
    2   tablespoons snipped parsley
    1   teaspoon dry mustard
    ¼   teaspoon salt
        Dash pepper
    1   pound ground beef
        Tangy Cranberry Sauce, Dill Sauce,
          or Polynesian Sauce   Oven 350°

In a bowl combine egg, bread crumbs, milk, parsley, mustard, salt, and pepper. Add beef. Mix well. Shape into 1-inch meatballs. Place in a 15x10x1-inch baking pan. Bake in a 350° oven for 15 to 18 minutes or till done. Drain.

Meanwhile, prepare Tangy Cranberry Sauce, Dill Sauce, or Polynesian Sauce. Add meatballs; heat through. Makes 10 servings.

Microwave directions: Assemble meatballs as above. Arrange *half* of the meatballs in an 8x8x2-inch baking dish. Cover with waxed paper. Cook on 100% power (high) 3½ to 5½ minutes or till no pink remains, rearranging and turning meatballs once. Drain. Pat dry. Repeat with remaining meatballs. Prepare Tangy Cranberry Sauce, Dill Sauce, or Polynesian Sauce. Add meatballs to sauce and heat through.

Tangy Cranberry Sauce: In a saucepan combine one 8-ounce can *jellied cranberry sauce,* 2 tablespoons *steak sauce,* and 1 tablespoon *brown sugar.* Heat, stirring occasionally.

Dill Sauce: In a saucepan melt 2 tablespoons *margarine or butter.* Stir in 2 tablespoons *all-purpose flour,* 1 teaspoon *instant beef bouillon granules,* dash ground *nutmeg,* and dash *pepper.* Add ¾ cup *water.* Cook and stir till thickened and bubbly. Stir in ¾ cup *light cream* and 1 teaspoon dried *dillweed.*

Polynesian Sauce: Drain one 15¼-ounce can *pineapple chunks,* reserving juice. Add water to juice to make *1 cup.* In a saucepan combine juice mixture, 2 tablespoons *catsup,* 2 tablespoons *vinegar,* 1 tablespoon *cornstarch,* 1 tablespoon *brown sugar,* 1 tablespoon *soy sauce,* ½ teaspoon *instant beef bouillon granules,* and dash ground *red pepper.* Cook and stir till thickened and bubbly. Add pineapple and 1 green *or* sweet red *pepper,* cut into 1-inch pieces.

Sweet-and-Sour Franks

    ½   cup maple-flavored syrup
    ½   cup orange *or* pineapple juice
    3   tablespoons vinegar
    2   tablespoons cornstarch
    2   teaspoons Worcestershire sauce
    1   teaspoon dry mustard
    1   16-ounce package (8 *or* 10)
          frankfurters, bias-sliced into
          1-inch pieces, *or* 1 pound
          cocktail wieners
    2   cups small frozen whole onions

In a saucepan combine syrup, juice, vinegar, cornstarch, Worcestershire sauce, and mustard. Cook and stir till thickened and bubbly. Stir in frankfurters and onions. Cook, stirring occasionally, 8 minutes or till onions are tender. Serves 16.

Microwave directions: In a 2-quart casserole micro-cook first six ingredients, uncovered, on 100% power (high) 3 to 5 minutes or till thickened and bubbly, stirring every minute. Stir in frankfurters and onions. Cook on high for 6 to 8 minutes or till onions are tender; stir once.

Mustard-Glazed Ribs

For easier eating, ask your butcher to saw the ribs in half across the bones.

    2½ to 3 pounds meaty pork
          loin back ribs *or* spareribs
    ½   cup packed brown sugar
    1   teaspoon paprika
    ½   teaspoon ground turmeric
    ¼   cup chopped onion
    ¼   cup vinegar
    ¼   cup prepared mustard
    ½   teaspoon celery seed
    ¼   teaspoon garlic powder   Oven 350°

Cut ribs into single-rib portions. In a bowl combine *2 tablespoons* brown sugar, paprika, turmeric, and ½ teaspoon *salt.* Rub mixture over ribs. Roast ribs, meaty side up, in a shallow roasting pan in a 350° oven for 1 hour.

For sauce, in a saucepan combine the remaining brown sugar, onion, vinegar, mustard, celery seed, and garlic powder. Bring to boiling, stirring till sugar dissolves.

Drain fat from pan. Brush ribs with sauce. Roast 30 to 45 minutes more or till done, brushing frequently with sauce. Makes 6 servings.

Barbecue-Style Chicken Wings

Provide lots of napkins with these saucy wings.

1½ **pounds chicken wings (about 8)**
½ **cup catsup**
¼ **cup finely chopped onion**
1 **tablespoon honey**
1 **tablespoon vinegar**
1 **clove garlic, minced** Oven 375°

Rinse chicken; pat dry. Cut off and discard wing tips. Cut each wing at joint to make 2 sections. Place the wing pieces in a single layer in a 13x9x2-inch baking pan. Bake in a 375° oven for 20 minutes. Drain fat from baking pan.

For sauce, combine remaining ingredients. Brush wings with sauce. Bake 10 minutes. Turn wings over; brush again with sauce. Bake for 5 to 10 minutes or till chicken is tender. Makes 16.

Microwave directions: Prepare the chicken wings as above. Place wing pieces in a single layer in a 12x7½x2-inch baking dish. Cover with waxed paper. Micro-cook on 100% power (high) for 5 minutes. Drain. For sauce, combine remaining ingredients. Brush wings with sauce. Turn wings over and rearrange. Brush with sauce. Cook, covered, on high for 3 to 5 minutes more or till chicken is no longer pink.

Rumaki

If you like chicken livers, you'll love these.

¼ **cup dry sherry**
¼ **cup soy sauce**
2 **tablespoons cooking oil**
1 **tablespoon sugar**
¼ **teaspoon garlic powder**
⅛ **teaspoon ground ginger**
12 **chicken livers (12 to 14 ounces), cut in half**
½ **of an 8-ounce can (24) sliced water chestnuts, drained**
12 **slices bacon, cut in half crosswise**

Combine wine, soy sauce, oil, sugar, garlic powder, ginger, and ¼ cup *water.* Stir in livers and water chestnuts. Cover; chill 4 to 24 hours.

Cook bacon slightly. Drain. Drain livers and water chestnuts. Wrap a bacon piece around a liver half and a water chestnut slice. Secure with a wooden toothpick. Broil 4 inches from heat for 6 to 8 minutes or till livers are no longer pink; turn once. Serve warm. Makes 24.

Cheese Twists

These pastry snacks go great alone or with salads.

1 **cup all-purpose flour**
¼ **teaspoon garlic powder**
⅛ **teaspoon salt**
⅛ **teaspoon ground red pepper (optional)**
1 **cup finely shredded cheddar *or* American cheese (4 ounces)**
¼ **cup margarine *or* butter**
3 **to 5 tablespoons cold water**
1 **beaten egg**
2 **tablespoons toasted sesame seed *or* poppy seed** Oven 400°

In a large mixing bowl combine flour, garlic powder, salt, and, if desired, red pepper. Cut in cheese and margarine or butter till pieces are the size of small peas. Sprinkle *1 tablespoon* of the water over part of the mixture. Gently toss with a fork. Push to side of bowl. Repeat till all of flour mixture is moistened. Shape dough into a ball.

On a lightly floured surface, flatten dough with hands. Roll out dough from center to edges, forming a 10-inch square. Brush with egg. Sprinkle with sesame seed or poppy seed. Cut dough into 5x½-inch strips. Twist each strip. Place on lightly greased baking sheets. Bake in a 400° oven for 10 to 12 minutes or till golden brown. Serve warm or cool. Makes 40.

Herbed Parmesan Twists: Prepare as above, *except* do not use red pepper, add ¼ teaspoon crushed dried *oregano* to the flour mixture, and substitute 3 tablespoons grated *Parmesan cheese* for the sesame seed or poppy seed.

Swiss-Caraway Twists: Prepare as above, *except* substitute *Swiss cheese* for the cheddar or American cheese and *caraway seed* for the sesame seed or poppy seed.

Pastry-Wrapped Olives

Oven 375°

In a large mixing bowl combine 1 stick *piecrust mix,* ½ cup shredded *cheddar cheese,* and a dash ground *red pepper.* Prepare piecrust dough according to package directions.

Pat 30 pitted *ripe or pimiento-stuffed olives* dry with paper towels. Shape about *1 teaspoon* of the dough around each olive. Place on a baking sheet. Bake in a 375° oven for 12 to 15 minutes or till golden. Serve warm. Makes 30.

Egg Rolls

These crisp, golden egg rolls make a delicious start to any meal.

>   8   **egg roll skins**
>   **Crab Filling, Pork and Shrimp**
>   **Filling, Ham-Orange Filling,** *or*
>   **Vegetable Filling (see recipes,**
>   **opposite)**
>   **Shortening** *or* **cooking oil for**
>   **deep-fat frying**
>   **Sweet-Sour Sauce (see recipe,**
>   **page 363)**
>   **Oriental-Style Mustard Sauce (see**
>   **recipe, page 365)**   Oven 300°

For each egg roll, place one egg roll skin on a flat surface with one corner toward you. Spoon about ¼ *cup* of the desired filling just below the center of egg roll skin. Fold the corner nearest you over the filling, tucking the corner under the filling. Fold side corners over top, like an envelope. Roll up toward the remaining corner. Moisten the point with water and press firmly to seal.

In a heavy saucepan or deep-fat fryer heat 2 inches of melted shortening or cooking oil to 365°. Fry the egg rolls, a few at a time, for 2 to 3 minutes or till golden brown. Drain on paper towels. Keep warm in a 300° oven while frying the remainder. Serve warm egg rolls with Sweet-Sour Sauce or Oriental-Style Mustard Sauce, or both. Makes 8 servings.

Bring the side points over the top to resemble an envelope. Then roll up and seal.

Wontons

Every bit as tasty as egg rolls, wontons are smaller and more manageable at appetizer parties. One or two bites and it's time to reach for another.

>   40   **wonton skins**
>   **Crab Filling, Pork and Shrimp**
>   **Filling, Ham-Orange Filling,** *or*
>   **Vegetable Filling (see recipes,**
>   **opposite)**
>   **Shortening** *or* **cooking oil for**
>   **deep-fat frying**
>   **Sweet-Sour Sauce (see recipe,**
>   **page 363)**
>   **Oriental-Style Mustard Sauce (see**
>   **recipe, page 365)**   Oven 300°

For each wonton, place one wonton skin on a flat surface with one corner toward you. Spoon a rounded teaspoon of desired filling just below the center of wonton skin. Fold the corner closest to you over the filling and tuck it under the filling. Roll up, leaving 1 inch unrolled at the top. Moisten the right corner with water. Grasp right and left corners and bring them over the filling, lapping the right corner over the left corner. Press firmly to seal.

In a heavy saucepan or deep-fat fryer heat 2 inches of melted shortening or oil to 365°. Fry the wontons, a few at a time, for 2 to 3 minutes or till golden brown. Drain on paper towels. Keep warm in a 300° oven while frying the remainder. Serve warm with Sweet-Sour Sauce or Oriental-Style Mustard Sauce, or both. Makes 40.

Lap the moistened right corner over the left corner. Press the ends to seal.

Crab Filling

Use this or any of the following three fillings for either Egg Rolls or Wontons.

In a skillet cook 1 cup chopped *Chinese cabbage or cabbage,* ½ cup finely chopped *pea pods,* ¼ cup chopped *water chestnuts,* 2 tablespoons finely chopped *onion,* and 1 clove *garlic,* minced, in 1 tablespoon *cooking oil* for 2 to 3 minutes or till crisp-tender. Remove from heat.

In a mixing bowl combine one 6-ounce can *crabmeat,* drained, flaked, and cartilage removed; 2 tablespoons *soy sauce;* 2 tablespoons *dry sherry;* ⅛ teaspoon *pepper;* and the cooked vegetable mixture. Toss to mix. Makes about 2 cups (enough for 8 egg rolls or 40 wontons).

Pork and Shrimp Filling

Thaw one 6-ounce package frozen, peeled, cooked *shrimp.* Cut up shrimp. In a mixing bowl combine shrimp, ½ cup finely chopped cooked *pork,* ½ cup finely chopped *bean sprouts,* ½ cup finely chopped fresh *mushrooms,* ¼ cup sliced *green onion,* 2 tablespoons *soy sauce,* and 1 teaspoon grated *gingerroot.* Mix well. Makes 2 cups (enough for 8 egg rolls or 40 wontons).

Ham-Orange Filling

In a bowl combine ¾ cup finely chopped fully cooked *ham,* ½ cup chopped *bamboo shoots,* ½ cup finely chopped *onion,* ½ cup finely chopped *broccoli,* ½ teaspoon finely shredded *orange peel,* 2 tablespoons *orange juice,* and ⅛ teaspoon ground *red pepper.* Mix well. Makes about 2 cups (enough for 8 egg rolls or 40 wontons).

Vegetable Filling

In a steamer basket over *boiling* water place 1 cup chopped fresh *spinach,* 1 cup shredded *carrot,* 1 cup chopped fresh *mushrooms,* ½ cup shredded *zucchini,* and ¼ cup finely chopped *onion.* Cover; steam for 4 minutes. Drain well. Transfer to a mixing bowl. Stir in 2 tablespoons *soy sauce,* ½ teaspoon *dry mustard,* ¼ teaspoon *pepper,* and ⅛ teaspoon *garlic powder.* Makes 2 cups (enough for 8 egg rolls or 40 wontons).

Spinach Phyllo Triangles

> 1   **10-ounce package frozen chopped spinach**
> ½   **cup chopped onion**
> 1   **clove garlic, minced**
> 6   **ounces feta cheese, finely crumbled**
> ½   **teaspoon dried oregano, crushed**
> 12 **sheets phyllo dough (8 to 10 ounces)**
> ½   **cup margarine *or* butter, melted**   Oven 375°

For filling, cook spinach, onion, and garlic according to spinach package directions. Drain well in colander. Press the back of a spoon against mixture to force out excess moisture. Combine spinach mixture, feta cheese, and oregano.

Lightly brush *1 sheet* of phyllo with *some* of the melted margarine or butter. Place another phyllo sheet on top; brush with some margarine. Repeat with a third sheet of phyllo and margarine. (Cover the remaining phyllo with a damp cloth to prevent drying.) Cut the stack of phyllo lengthwise into 6 strips.

For *each* triangle, spoon about *1 tablespoon* of the filling about 1 inch from one end of *each* strip. Fold the end over the filling at a 45-degree angle. Continue folding to form a triangle that encloses filling. Repeat with remaining phyllo, margarine or butter, and filling.

Place triangles on a baking sheet. Brush with margarine. Bake in a 375° oven for 18 to 20 minutes or till golden. Serve warm. Makes 24.

Fold phyllo dough over filling at a 45-degree angle. Continue folding to the end of the strip.

Oysters Rockefeller

  2 cups chopped fresh spinach
  ¼ cup finely chopped onion
 24 oysters in shells
  3 tablespoons margarine *or* butter,
     melted
  2 tablespoons snipped parsley
  1 clove garlic, minced
     Several drops bottled hot pepper
     sauce
  ¼ cup fine dry seasoned bread crumbs
     Rock salt   Oven 425°

In a saucepan cook spinach and onion in a small amount of boiling water for 2 to 3 minutes or till tender. Drain; press out excess moisture.

Thoroughly wash oysters. Open shells with an oyster knife or other blunt-tipped knife. Remove oysters and dry. Discard flat top shells; wash deep bottom shells. Place each oyster in a shell.

Combine spinach mixture, *2 tablespoons* of margarine, parsley, garlic, hot sauce, and dash *pepper*. Spoon *1 teaspoon* atop *each* oyster.

Toss together crumbs and remaining margarine. Sprinkle over spinach-topped oysters.

Line a shallow baking pan with rock salt to about ½-inch depth. (*Or,* use crumpled foil to keep shells from tipping.) Arrange oysters atop. Bake in a 425° oven 10 to 12 minutes or till edges of oysters begin to curl. Makes 8 servings.

Shrimp Cocktail

  1 pound fresh *or* frozen peeled
     shrimp, cooked, deveined,
     and chilled
     Lettuce
     Cocktail Sauce (see recipe,
     page 364)
     Lemon wedges

Arrange shrimp in six lettuce-lined cocktail cups or glasses. Spoon *1 tablespoon* of the Cocktail Sauce over each. Serve with lemon. Serves 6.

Fruit Shrimp Cocktail: Prepare as above, *except* toss 1 peeled and sectioned *orange,* 1 peeled and sectioned *grapefruit,* and 1 seeded, peeled, and sliced *avocado* with the shrimp.

Crab Cocktail: Prepare as above, *except* substitute two 6-ounce packages frozen *crab-meat,* thawed, and 2 cups finely chopped *celery* for the shrimp.

Salmon Mousse

  1 6½-ounce can boneless, skinless
     salmon
  1 envelope unflavored gelatin
  ½ cup mayonnaise *or* salad dressing
  2 tablespoons chili sauce
  1 tablespoon lemon juice
  2 hard-cooked eggs, finely chopped
  ¼ cup finely chopped celery
  2 tablespoons chopped green onion
  1 tablespoon snipped chives
  ½ cup whipping cream
     Lettuce leaves
     Assorted crackers

Drain salmon, reserving liquid. Add water to liquid to make ½ *cup.* In saucepan sprinkle gelatin over reserved liquid. Let stand 5 minutes. Heat and stir till gelatin dissolves. Remove from heat.

Mix mayonnaise, chili sauce, and lemon juice. Stir into gelatin. Chill till partially set (consistency of unbeaten egg whites). Fold in salmon, eggs, celery, onion, chives, and ⅛ teaspoon *pepper.*

Beat cream till soft peaks form. Fold into gelatin mixture. Pour into a 3½- or 4-cup mold. Chill 4 to 24 hours. Unmold on lettuce-lined serving platter. Serve with crackers. Serves 24.

Codfish Balls

  4 ounces salt cod
 1½ cups chopped, peeled potatoes
  ¼ cup chopped onion
  1 egg
  2 tablespoons grated Parmesan
     cheese
  2 tablespoons snipped parsley
  1 tablespoon margarine *or* butter
     Shortening *or* cooking oil for
     deep-fat frying

Soak cod in water to cover for 4 to 24 hours; change water often. Drain; cut into small pieces.

Cook cod, potatoes, and onion in *boiling* water about 10 minutes or till tender; drain. Beat mixture till combined. Beat in egg, cheese, parsley, margarine, and ¼ teaspoon *pepper.*

In a heavy saucepan or deep-fat fryer heat 2 inches of melted shortening or oil to 375°. Drop cod mixture by heaping tablespoons, a few at a time, into hot fat. Fry about 2 minutes or till golden. Drain on paper towels. Serve with tartar or cocktail sauce, if desired. Makes 15.

Batter-Fried Vegetables

Bottled buttermilk salad dressing or sweet-and-sour sauce also make flavorful dipping sauces.

 1 **slightly beaten egg**
 1 **cup ice water, cold milk, *or* cold beer**
 1 **cup all-purpose flour**
 5 **cups of any combination of the following: fresh whole mushrooms; cauliflower *or* broccoli flowerets; green pepper strips; onion rings; green onions; fresh green beans; fresh asparagus, cut into 2-inch lengths; sweet potato, peeled and cut into ¼-inch-thick slices; eggplant, peeled and cut into 1-inch cubes**
    Shortening *or* cooking oil for deep-fat frying
    Dipping Sauce   Oven 300°

For batter, in a medium mixing bowl stir together egg and ice water, milk, *or* beer. Add flour all at once. Beat with a rotary beater or wire whisk till mixture is smooth. Set aside.

Rinse vegetables under *cold* water; drain. Pat dry with paper towels. Set aside.

In a heavy saucepan or deep-fat fryer, heat 2 inches of melted shortening or cooking oil to 375°. Dip vegetables, a few at a time, into the batter, swirling to coat. Fry for 2 to 3 minutes or till light golden brown. Drain vegetables on paper towels. Keep warm in a 300° oven. Repeat with remaining vegetables.

Serve with individual bowls of Dipping Sauce. Makes 8 servings.

Dipping Sauce: In a small saucepan stir together 1 cup *water,* ¼ cup *dry sherry,* ¼ cup *soy sauce,* and 1 teaspoon grated *gingerroot.* Bring just to boiling. Remove from heat; keep warm. Makes 1⅓ cups.

Fried Cheese

Seasoned crumbs keep the melted cheese inside.

 8 **ounces cheddar *or* Swiss cheese**
 ¾ **cup cornflake crumbs**
 ½ **teaspoon fines herbes**
 2 **beaten eggs**
    Shortening *or* cooking oil for deep-fat frying
    Taco sauce (optional)   Oven 300°

Cut the cheese into 2½x½x½-inch sticks.

Combine crumbs and fines herbes. Dip cheese sticks into eggs, then roll in crumb mixture, coating evenly. Dip cheese into egg and crumbs again. (Be sure cheese is completely coated with crumbs.) Chill 2 to 4 hours to set the coating.

In a heavy saucepan or a deep-fat fryer heat 2 inches of melted shortening or cooking oil to 375°. Fry the cheese sticks, a few at a time, for 30 to 45 seconds or till golden. Drain on paper towels. Keep warm in a 300° oven while frying the remainder. Serve warm with taco sauce, if desired. Makes about 20.

Stuffed Cherry Tomatoes

The refreshing herb-cheese filling brings out the best in these tiny tomatoes.

24 **to 26 cherry tomatoes**
 1 **8-ounce package cream cheese, softened**
 1 **tablespoon snipped fresh *or* frozen chives, *or* 1 teaspoon dried chives**
 1 **tablespoon milk**
 ¼ **teaspoon dried basil, crushed**
 ¼ **teaspoon black pepper**
 ⅛ **teaspoon garlic powder**

Slice a thin layer off top of each tomato. Using a small spoon, carefully scoop out and discard pulp. Invert tomatoes; drain on paper towels.

For filling, in a small bowl combine cream cheese, chives, milk, basil, pepper, and garlic powder. Beat till smooth. Spoon or pipe the filling into tomatoes. Serve immediately or chill up to 8 hours. Makes 24 to 26.

Chicken Liver Pâté

>   2 slices bacon
>   8 ounces chicken livers
> ½ cup chopped onion
>   1 clove garlic, minced
>   2 to 3 tablespoons milk
> ¼ teaspoon salt
> ¼ teaspoon ground nutmeg *or*
>   ⅛ teaspoon ground allspice
> ⅛ teaspoon pepper
>   Assorted crackers

In a large skillet cook bacon till crisp. Remove bacon from skillet, reserving *2 tablespoons* of drippings. Drain and crumble bacon; set aside.

Add chicken livers, onion, and garlic to reserved drippings. Cook over medium heat, stirring constantly, about 5 minutes or till livers are no longer pink. Cool slightly.

In a blender container or food processor bowl place *2 tablespoons* milk, salt, nutmeg or allspice, pepper, chicken liver mixture, and bacon. Cover and blend or process till well combined. (Add *1 tablespoon* milk if mixture appears stiff.)

Line a 1½-cup mold or small bowl with plastic wrap. Spoon mixture into mold. Cover; chill 3 to 24 hours. To serve, unmold and remove wrap. Serve with crackers. Makes 1 cup (serves 8).

Marinated Cheese And Olives

The cheese takes on a trio of Mediterranean flavors: lemon, garlic, and fennel.

>   8 ounces cheddar, Colby, Edam,
>   Gouda, *or* Monterey Jack cheese
>   2 ounces pepperoni *or* salami
> ¼ cup olive oil *or* salad oil
>   2 tablespoons lemon juice
>   1 clove garlic, minced
> ¼ teaspoon fennel seed
> ¼ teaspoon pepper
>   1 6-ounce can pitted ripe olives,
>   drained

Cut cheese and pepperoni or salami into ½-inch pieces. In a bowl combine oil, lemon juice, garlic, fennel seed, and pepper. Stir in cheese, pepperoni or salami, and olives. Cover and chill up to 3 days, stirring occasionally. Let stand 30 minutes at room temperature before serving. Serve with toothpicks. Makes about 4 cups (16 servings).

Lemon and Herb Mushrooms

Oregano and thyme add zest to these tangy mouthfuls.

> ½ pound small fresh whole
>   mushrooms (about 3 cups)
>   3 tablespoons lemon juice
>   2 tablespoons salad oil
>   1 tablespoon sugar
>   1 clove garlic, minced
> ¼ teaspoon salt
> ¼ teaspoon coarse ground black
>   pepper
> ⅛ teaspoon dried oregano, crushed
> ⅛ teaspoon dried thyme, crushed
> ½ of a small onion, sliced

Halve any large mushrooms. In a medium saucepan cook mushrooms in boiling water 1 minute. Drain and rinse with *cold* water. Set aside.

For marinade, in a small saucepan combine lemon juice, salad oil, sugar, garlic, salt, pepper, oregano, and thyme. Cook till boiling. Reduce heat and simmer, uncovered, for 5 minutes.

In a medium mixing bowl combine drained mushrooms, hot marinade, and sliced onion. Cover and chill 4 to 24 hours, stirring occasionally. Makes 1½ cups (6 servings). **Microwave directions:** In a 1-quart casserole micro-cook mushrooms and 2 tablespoons *water,* covered, on 100% power (high) for 3 to 4 minutes or till tender. Drain and set aside. In the same casserole combine lemon juice, salad oil, sugar, garlic, salt, pepper, oregano, and thyme. Cook, uncovered, on high for 1 to 2 minutes or till boiling. Assemble as above.

Melon and Prosciutto

Spicy prosciutto, a thinly sliced Italian ham, meshes perfectly with cool crisp melon.

>   1 large cantaloupe *or* honeydew
>   melon, *or* half of each melon
>   3 ounces very thinly sliced prosciutto
>   *or* fully cooked ham

Cut cantaloupe or honeydew melon in half and remove seeds. Use a melon baller to scoop out pulp, or cut pulp into bite-size cubes. Cut prosciutto or ham into 1-inch-wide strips. Wrap *one* strip of prosciutto or ham around *each* melon ball. Fasten with a toothpick. Makes about 36.

Beverages

Nutrition Analysis

	Servings Per Recipe	Calories	Protein (g)	Carbohydrate (g)	Fat (g)	Cholesterol (mg)	Sodium (mg)	Potassium (mg)	Protein	Vitamin A	Vitamin C	Thiamine	Riboflavin	Niacin	Calcium	Iron
	Per Serving								**Percent U.S. RDA Per Serving**							
Amaretto Dessert Coffee (p. 26)	1	49	0	12	0	0	2	57	0	0	0	0	0	2	0	1
Berry and Banana Daiquiris (p. 31)	8	141	0	24	0	0	1	108	1	1	15	1	2	1	1	2
Blended Margaritas (p. 31)	7	111	0	18	0	0	0	19	0	0	8	0	0	0	0	0
Bloody Marys (p. 31)	10	63	1	5	0	0	402	219	1	11	34	3	2	3	1	3
Brandy Alexanders (p. 32)	4	220	2	28	7	30	59	130	4	5	1	2	10	0	9	0
Candy Milk Shakes (p. 29)	2	407	7	40	25	64	191	377	11	14	2	22	27	1	25	1
Cappuccino (p. 26)	6	73	0	2	7	27	8	44	1	6	1	0	1	1	2	1
Chocolate-Cream Dessert Coffee (p. 26)	1	95	0	23	0	0	2	57	0	0	0	0	0	2	0	1
Chocolate-Cream Liqueur (p. 32)	9	360	6	30	15	81	84	258	9	11	3	4	17	1	19	2
Chocolate Eggnog (p. 26)	10	223	6	17	13	201	79	154	9	12	0	3	12	0	9	4
Chocolate-Mint Dessert Coffee (p. 26)	1	49	0	12	0	0	2	57	0	0	0	0	0	2	0	1
Chocolate-Orange Dessert Coffee (p. 26)	1	94	0	23	0	0	11	110	1	0	0	0	1	3	1	3
Choose-a-Flavor Float (p. 29)	1	185	2	29	7	30	58	129	4	5	1	2	10	0	9	0
Choose-a-Flavor Malts (p. 29)	2	327	7	40	16	65	162	393	11	14	2	6	26	2	26	1
Choose-a-Flavor Milk Shakes (p. 29)	2	301	7	35	16	65	147	353	11	13	2	5	25	1	25	1
Cinnamon-Apple Milk Shakes (p. 29)	2	336	7	44	16	64	148	420	11	14	8	6	26	1	26	3
Cocoa Mix (p. 27)	45	153	9	26	2	4	158	447	14	11	2	7	25	1	29	3
Coffee (p. 27)	1	3	0	1	0	0	2	81	0	0	0	0	0	4	0	1
Cookie Milk Shakes (p. 29)	2	400	8	48	20	72	244	360	12	13	2	8	27	3	26	3
Eggnog (p. 26)	10	204	6	12	13	201	75	133	9	12	0	3	12	0	9	4
Frozen Margaritas (p. 31)	7	194	0	31	0	0	1	34	0	0	15	0	0	0	0	0
Fruit Juice Float (p. 29)	1	207	3	33	7	30	60	429	5	8	103	10	11	2	10	1
Fruity Yogurt Sipper (p. 29)	4	134	6	23	3	10	83	414	10	5	8	5	18	2	21	1
Glogg (p. 28)	8	204	1	20	2	0	7	189	2	0	1	2	3	2	3	4
Golden Cadillacs (p. 32)	4	229	2	39	7	30	58	129	4	5	1	2	10	0	9	0
Grasshoppers (p. 32)	4	229	2	39	7	30	58	129	4	5	1	2	10	0	9	0
Homemade Soda Pop (p. 29)	3	138	0	36	0	0	1	50	0	0	36	1	1	1	0	1
Hot Buttered Coffee (p. 28)	10	145	0	16	9	0	114	106	0	8	0	0	1	2	2	4
Hot Buttered Rum (p. 28)	10	256	0	16	9	0	113	63	0	8	0	0	1	0	2	3
Hot Buttered Tea (p. 28)	10	146	0	17	9	0	113	92	0	8	0	0	1	0	2	3
Hot Chocolate (p. 27)	6	172	6	24	6	12	81	282	9	7	3	4	16	1	20	2
Hot Cocoa (p. 27)	6	133	6	21	4	12	107	275	9	7	3	5	17	1	20	3
Hot Mocha (p. 27)	6	172	6	24	6	12	82	296	9	7	3	4	16	2	20	2
Hot Spiced Cider (p. 28)	8	139	0	35	0	0	9	312	0	0	4	3	3	1	2	6
Ice-Cream Punch (p. 30)	32	123	1	23	4	15	30	74	2	3	7	1	5	0	4	0
Iced Tea (p. 27)	5	2	0	1	0	0	0	32	0	0	0	0	0	0	0	0
Individual Cocktails (p. 30)	12	153	0	20	0	0	4	139	0	8	24	1	1	1	1	2
Irish Dessert Coffee (p. 26)	1	56	0	4	0	0	3	73	0	0	0	0	0	2	1	2
Lemonade or Limeade (p. 31)	5	114	0	30	0	0	1	60	0	0	37	1	0	0	0	0
Lime Daiquiris (p. 31)	6	133	0	18	0	0	0	22	0	0	7	0	0	0	0	0
Malted Cocoa Mix (p. 27)	48	157	9	27	2	5	163	444	13	11	2	7	25	2	28	3
Margaritas (p. 31)	4	194	0	31	0	0	1	34	0	0	15	0	0	0	0	0
Mocha Dessert Coffee (p. 26)	1	94	0	23	0	0	11	110	1	0	0	0	1	3	1	3
Mocha Milk Shakes (p. 29)	2	302	7	35	15	64	148	379	11	13	2	5	25	2	25	1
Mocha Mix (p. 27)	45	154	9	27	2	4	158	475	14	11	2	7	25	3	29	3
Nonalcoholic Eggnog (p. 26)	10	211	6	17	13	202	82	163	9	12	1	4	13	0	10	4
Nonalcoholic Punch (p. 30)	25	38	0	10	0	0	2	66	0	4	11	1	0	1	1	1
Orange Breakfast Nog (p. 29)	2	211	7	43	2	6	199	686	11	4	126	14	19	3	24	4
Party Wine Punch (p. 30)	24	93	0	13	0	0	5	128	0	4	12	1	1	1	1	3
Peach Daiquiris (p. 31)	8	112	0	17	0	0	0	71	0	3	6	0	1	2	0	0

On the divider: Cookie Milk Shake (p. 29), Homemade Soda Pop (p. 29), and Strawberry Daiquiri (p. 31).

Nutrition Analysis

	Per Serving								Percent U.S. RDA Per Serving							
	Servings Per Recipe	Calories	Protein (g)	Carbohydrate (g)	Fat (g)	Cholesterol (mg)	Sodium (mg)	Potassium (mg)	Protein	Vitamin A	Vitamin C	Thiamine	Riboflavin	Niacin	Calcium	Iron
Peanut Butter Milk Shakes (p. 29)	2	396	11	37	24	64	222	462	18	13	2	7	26	12	26	2
Raspberry Daiquiris (p. 31)	7	145	0	23	0	0	1	56	0	0	14	1	1	1	1	2
Sangria (p. 32)	10	115	0	14	0	0	4	90	0	0	10	0	1	1	1	2
Sherbet Punch (p. 30)	32	123	1	29	1	4	22	59	1	1	8	1	2	0	3	1
Slushy Punch (p. 30)	23	76	0	19	0	0	1	149	1	1	30	3	1	1	1	1
Spiced Hot Chocolate (p. 27)	6	173	6	25	7	12	82	283	9	7	3	4	16	1	20	2
Spiked Party Punch (p. 30)	14	110	0	17	0	0	3	119	0	7	20	1	1	1	1	2
Spiked Slushy Punch (p. 30)	26	102	0	17	0	0	1	132	1	1	26	3	1	1	1	1
Strawberry Daiquiris (p. 31)	7	145	0	23	0	0	1	56	0	0	14	1	1	1	1	2
Sun Tea (p. 27)	8	1	0	0	0	0	0	20	0	0	0	0	0	0	0	0
Tea (p. 27)	5	2	0	1	0	0	0	32	0	0	0	0	0	0	0	0
Velvet Hammers (p. 32)	4	229	2	39	7	30	58	129	4	5	1	2	10	0	9	0
Virgin Marys (p. 31)	9	21	1	5	0	0	446	243	1	12	38	3	2	4	1	3
Wine Spritzer (p. 32)	1	153	0	8	0	0	9	166	0	0	0	0	1	1	2	4

Beverages

The beauty of beverages is that there are as many ways to use and serve them as there are recipes.

In this chapter you'll find basic drinks and extraordinary sippers. Looking for a drink to take the chill away? Try Hot Spiced Cider or Hot Buttered Rum. Or discover the ultimate thirst quencher by making a pitcher of homemade Lemonade or Limeade.

Party Guide

If you're planning a party, beverages are a must. Here are a few tips you should consider before the festivities begin.

● Generally expect to use 1½ ounces of liquor for each bar drink. This means you'll get about 16 drinks from a 750-milliliter bottle (fifth) of liquor.

● Chill beer to about 45° to 50°. For quick chilling, place the beer bottles or cans in a deep tub of ice cubes.

● Generally expect to use 3 ounces of wine for each drink, getting about 8 drinks from one 750-milliliter bottle. For bigger parties, consider buying wines available in larger 1.5-liter bottles.

● Remember to make a variety of nonalcoholic beverages available to your guests. Nonalcoholic Eggnog, Nonalcoholic Punch, or Homemade Soda Pop are a few of the choices in this chapter.

● Keep punches cold by floating easy-to-make ice rings in the serving bowls. To make an ice ring, fill a ring mold with water and freeze till firm. Or, for a fruit-filled ice ring, line the bottom of the ring mold with citrus slices, berries, or melon balls. Add enough water to just cover the fruit. Freeze till firm. Then fill the mold with water and freeze till firm.

● Don't buy unnecessary types of bar glasses. Ten- or 12-ounce all-purpose glasses and 9- or 10-ounce stemmed wineglasses are suitable for nearly every drink and occasion. Disposable plastic glasses, available in various sizes, are convenient to use, especially at large parties.

Coffee

¾ cup water (for each 6-ounce cup)
1 to 2 tablespoons ground coffee
(for each 6-ounce cup)

Drip Coffee: Line a coffee basket with a filter. Measure the coffee into the lined basket.

For *electric drip coffee makers,* pour *cold* water into upper compartment. Place pot on heating element; let water drip through basket.

For *nonelectric drip coffee makers,* pour *boiling* water over coffee in basket. Let water drip into pot.

When coffee is finished dripping, remove basket; discard grounds. Keep warm over low heat.

Percolator Coffee: Pour water into a percolator. Stand the stem and basket firmly in pot. Measure ground coffee into basket. Replace basket lid and cover the pot. Bring the water to boiling. Perk gently for 5 to 8 minutes. Let coffee stand for 1 to 2 minutes. Remove basket from pot. Keep coffee warm.

Dessert Coffee

⅔ cup hot strong coffee
Desired coffee flavoring
(see choices, below)
Whipped cream (optional)
Ground cinnamon *or* nutmeg
(optional)

Stir together hot coffee and desired flavoring. Top with a dollop of whipped cream and sprinkle with cinnamon or nutmeg, if desired. Makes 1 (about 6-ounce) serving.

Chocolate-Orange Dessert Coffee: Stir 1 tablespoon *chocolate-flavored syrup* and 1 tablespoon *orange liqueur* into hot coffee.

Mocha Dessert Coffee: Stir 1 tablespoon *chocolate-flavored syrup* and 1 tablespoon *coffee liqueur* into the hot coffee.

Irish Dessert Coffee: Stir 1 tablespoon *Irish whiskey* and 1 teaspoon *brown sugar* into coffee.

Amaretto Dessert Coffee: Stir 1 tablespoon *amaretto or hazelnut liqueur* into coffee.

Chocolate-Mint Dessert Coffee: Stir 1 tablespoon *chocolate-mint liqueur* into hot coffee.

Chocolate-Cream Dessert Coffee: Stir 2 tablespoons *chocolate-cream liqueur* into coffee.

Cappuccino

Brew finely ground espresso in an ordinary coffeepot. Or prepare instant espresso according to package directions.

In a small mixing bowl beat ½ cup *whipping cream* and 1 tablespoon *powdered sugar* till soft peaks form (tips curl).

Pour 2 cups hot *espresso* into six 4-ounce cups. Add a large spoonful of whipped cream mixture to each cup. Sprinkle with finely shredded *orange peel*. Gently stir to combine. Serve with cinnamon-stick stirrers, if desired. Makes 6 (about 3-ounce) servings.

Eggnog

Always a hit at our annual staff Christmas party.

6 beaten eggs
2 cups milk
⅓ cup sugar
2 to 4 tablespoons light rum
2 to 4 tablespoons bourbon
1 teaspoon vanilla
1 cup whipping cream
2 tablespoons sugar
Ground nutmeg

In a large heavy saucepan mix eggs, milk, and ⅓ cup sugar. Cook and stir over medium heat till mixture coats a metal spoon. Remove from heat. Cool quickly by placing pan in a sink or bowl of *ice* water and stirring 1 to 2 minutes. Stir in rum, bourbon, and vanilla. Chill 4 to 24 hours.

At serving time, in a bowl whip cream and 2 tablespoons sugar till soft peaks form. Transfer chilled egg mixture to a punch bowl. Fold in whipped cream mixture. Serve at once. Sprinkle each serving with nutmeg. Makes about 10 (4-ounce) servings.

Chocolate Eggnog: Prepare as above, except stir ¼ to ⅓ cup *chocolate-flavored syrup* into egg mixture before chilling.

Nonalcoholic Eggnog: Prepare as above, except omit rum and bourbon. Increase milk to 2¼ to 2½ cups.

Tea

If your Iced Tea turns cloudy, stir in a small amount of boiling water.

> **Boiling water**
> **3 to 6 teaspoons loose tea *or* 3 to 6 tea bags**
> **4 cups boiling water**

Warm a teapot by filling it with boiling water. If using loose tea, measure tea into a tea ball. Empty teapot; add tea ball or tea bags to pot. Immediately add 4 cups boiling water to teapot. Cover; let steep for 3 to 5 minutes. Remove tea ball or tea bags; serve tea at once. Makes 5 (about 6-ounce) servings.

Iced Tea: Prepare as above, *except* use *4 to 8 teaspoons* loose tea or *4 to 8* tea bags. After mixture steeps, let cool at room temperature for about 2 hours. Serve over ice. Pass sugar and lemon, if desired. Store in refrigerator.

Sun Tea: Place *6 to 8* tea bags in a 2-quart clear glass container. Add 1½ quarts *cold* water; cover. Let stand in full sun or at room temperature for 2 to 3 hours or till tea reaches desired strength. Remove tea bags. Serve over ice. Pass sugar and lemon, if desired. Store in refrigerator. Makes 8 (about 6-ounce) servings.

Hot Chocolate

A delicious way to warm up.

> **2 squares (2 ounces) unsweetened *or* semisweet chocolate, coarsely chopped, *or* ⅓ cup semisweet chocolate pieces**
> **⅓ cup sugar**
> **4 cups milk**
> **Whipped cream *or* marshmallows (optional)**

In a medium saucepan combine unsweetened or semisweet chocolate, sugar, and ½ *cup* of the milk. Cook and stir over medium heat till mixture just comes to boiling. Stir in remaining milk; heat through. *Do not boil.*

Remove from heat. If desired, beat milk mixture with a rotary beater till frothy. Serve hot in cups or mugs. Top each serving with a dollop of whipped cream or a few marshmallows, if desired. Makes 6 (about 6-ounce) servings.

Microwave directions: In an 8-cup measure or 1½-quart casserole combine chocolate, sugar, and ½ cup milk. Micro-cook, uncovered, on 100% power (high) for 2½ to 3 minutes or till mixture just comes to boiling, stirring once. Stir in remaining milk. Cook on high for 6 to 8 minutes more or till heated through, stirring once. Serve with whipped cream or marshmallows, if desired.

Hot Mocha: Prepare as above, *except* stir 1 tablespoon *instant coffee crystals* into chocolate mixture with remaining milk.

Spiced Hot Chocolate: Prepare as above, *except* stir ½ teaspoon ground *cinnamon* and ¼ teaspoon ground *nutmeg* into chocolate mixture with remaining milk.

Hot Cocoa: Prepare as above, *except* substitute ¼ cup *unsweetened cocoa powder* for the chocolate.

Cocoa Mix

> **1 8-quart package (about 10 cups) nonfat dry milk powder**
> **1 16-ounce package (about 4¾ cups) sifted powdered sugar**
> **1¾ cups unsweetened cocoa powder**
> **1 6-ounce jar (1¾ cups) powdered nondairy creamer**
> **Whipped cream *or* marshmallows (optional)**

In a large mixing bowl combine nonfat dry milk powder, powdered sugar, unsweetened cocoa powder, and nondairy creamer. Stir till thoroughly combined. Store cocoa mixture in an airtight container. Makes about 15 cups or enough for about 45 (8-ounce) servings.

For 1 serving, place ⅓ *cup* cocoa mixture in a coffee cup or mug; add ¾ cup *boiling* water. Stir to dissolve. Top with a dollop of whipped cream or a few marshmallows, if desired.

Malted Cocoa Mix: Prepare as above, *except* stir 1½ cups *instant malted milk powder* into dry ingredients. Makes about 16 cups or enough for about 48 (8-ounce) servings.

Mocha Mix: Prepare as above, *except* stir ½ cup *instant coffee crystals* into dry ingredients.

Hot Spiced Cider

8 cups apple cider *or* apple juice
¼ to ½ cup packed brown sugar
6 inches stick cinnamon
1 teaspoon whole allspice
1 teaspoon whole cloves
8 thin orange wedges *or* slices
**   (optional)**
8 whole cloves (optional)

In a large saucepan combine apple cider or juice and brown sugar. For spice bag, place cinnamon, allspice, and the 1 teaspoon whole cloves in a double thickness of cheesecloth. Bring up corners of cheesecloth and tie with string. Add spice bag to cider mixture.

Bring to boiling; reduce heat. Cover and simmer at least 10 minutes. Meanwhile, stud orange wedges or slices with cloves, if desired. Remove and discard spice bag. Serve cider in mugs with studded orange wedges or slices, if desired. Makes 8 (about 8-ounce) servings.

Hot Buttered Rum

Usually served at Christmas, this hot sipper tastes great all winter long.

¾ cup packed brown sugar
½ cup margarine *or* butter, softened
¼ teaspoon finely shredded
**   lemon peel**
¼ teaspoon ground cinnamon
¼ teaspoon ground allspice
**   Rum**
**   Boiling water**

In a small mixing bowl combine brown sugar, margarine or butter, lemon peel, cinnamon, and allspice. Beat till well combined. Use immediately or cover and chill up to 1 month. Makes about 1 cup or enough for 10 (about 6-ounce) servings.

For 1 serving, place *1 rounded tablespoon* of the butter mixture in a mug. Add *3 tablespoons* rum and *½ cup* boiling water. Stir well.

Hot Buttered Coffee or Tea: Prepare as above, *except* substitute ½ cup hot *strong coffee or tea* for the rum and boiling water.

Glogg

Before sipping this potent Swedish punch, toast everyone's good health. It's tradition.

1 750-milliliter bottle dry red wine
½ cup raisins
½ cup gin, vodka, *or* aquavit
⅓ cup sugar
**   Peel from 1 orange**
**   8 inches stick cinnamon, broken**
6 whole cloves
2 cardamom pods, opened
¼ cup blanched whole almonds

In a large saucepan stir together wine; raisins; gin, vodka, or aquavit; and sugar. For the spice bag, cut a double thickness of cheesecloth into a 6- or 8-inch square. Place orange peel, cinnamon, cloves, and cardamom in the center of the cheesecloth. Bring up the corners of the cheesecloth and tie them with a clean string. Add to saucepan with wine mixture.

Heat mixture to simmering. Simmer, uncovered, for 10 minutes. *Do not boil.* Remove and discard the spice bag. Stir in almonds just before serving. Makes 8 (about 4-ounce) servings.

Crockery-cooker directions: In a 3½- or 4-quart electric crockery cooker combine ingredients as above. Cover and cook on low-heat setting for 3 hours. Remove and discard the spice bag. Stir in almonds just before serving.

For spice bag, place peel and spices in cheesecloth. Bring up corners and tie with a string.

Choose-a-Flavor Milk Shakes

A Cookie Milk Shake is pictured on page 23.

> 1 **pint vanilla, chocolate,**
> **strawberry, butter brickle,**
> **cinnamon, *or* coffee ice cream**
> ½ **to ¾ cup milk**

Place ice cream and milk in a blender container. Cover and blend till smooth. Serve immediately. Makes 2 (about 8-ounce) servings.

    Choose-a-Flavor Malts: Prepare as above, *except* add 2 tablespoons *instant malted milk powder* to blender container with milk.

    Peanut Butter Milk Shakes: Prepare as above, *except* use vanilla or chocolate ice cream. Add 2 tablespoons *peanut butter* to blender container with milk.

    Mocha Milk Shakes: Prepare as above, *except* use chocolate ice cream. Add 2 teaspoons *instant coffee crystals* with the milk.

    Cinnamon-Apple Milk Shakes: Prepare as above, *except* use vanilla ice cream. Add 1 small cut-up *apple* and ½ teaspoon ground *cinnamon* to blender container with milk.

    Candy Milk Shakes: Prepare as above, *except* use vanilla or chocolate ice cream. Add 6 *bite-size chocolate-covered peanut butter cups* or one broken-up 1⅛-ounce bar *chocolate-covered English toffee* to blended mixture. Cover and blend just till candy is coarsely chopped.

    Cookie Milk Shakes: Prepare as above, *except* use vanilla or chocolate ice cream. Add 4 *chocolate sandwich cookies* or 4 *chocolate-covered graham crackers* to blended mixture. Cover and blend just till cookies are coarsely chopped.

Choose-a-Flavor Float

Choose your favorite ice cream and beverage.

> ½ **cup desired ice cream *or* sherbet**
> ⅔ **to ¾ cup desired carbonated**
> **beverage, chilled**

Add *half* of the ice cream to a chilled 12-ounce glass. Add enough carbonated beverage to half-fill the glass; stir gently to mix. Add remaining ice cream. Fill the glass with remaining carbonated beverage. Makes 1 (about 12-ounce) serving.

    Fruit Juice Float: Prepare as above, *except* substitute *orange, apple,* or *pineapple juice* for the carbonated beverage.

Orange Breakfast Nog

> 1½ **cups buttermilk**
> ½ **of a 6-ounce can (⅓ cup) frozen**
> **orange juice concentrate**
> 2 **tablespoons brown sugar**
> 1 **teaspoon vanilla**
> 2 *or* **3 large ice cubes**

In a blender container combine buttermilk, orange juice concentrate, brown sugar, and vanilla. Cover and blend till smooth. With blender running, add ice cubes, one at a time, through opening in lid. Blend till smooth and frothy. Makes 2 (about 10-ounce) servings.

Fruity Yogurt Sipper

> 1 **ripe large banana, 2 medium**
> **peaches, *or* 1 cup sliced**
> **strawberries**
> 1½ **cups milk**
> 1 **8-ounce carton vanilla yogurt**
> 1 **to 2 tablespoons powdered sugar**
> 3 **or 4 large ice cubes**

If using banana or peaches, cut into chunks. In a blender container combine fruit, milk, yogurt, and sugar. Cover and blend till smooth. With blender running, add ice cubes, one at a time, through opening in lid. Blend till smooth. Makes 4 (about 8-ounce) servings.

Homemade Soda Pop

A glass of orange-flavored Homemade Soda Pop is pictured on page 23.

> 1 **6-ounce can frozen lemonade**
> **concentrate *or* frozen orange,**
> **apple, grape, *or* pineapple**
> **juice concentrate**
> 18 **to 24 ounces carbonated water**

Stir together lemonade and *four* juice cans filled with carbonated water (*three* cans if using juice concentrate). Gently stir till combined.

    Using a funnel, pour mixture into a 4-cup bottle or jar; seal. Chill for up to 6 hours. Makes 3 (about 8-ounce) servings.

Party-Punch Base

  ½ **cup water**
  ⅓ **cup sugar**
 12 **inches stick cinnamon, broken**
  ½ **teaspoon whole cloves**
  4 **cups apple juice, chilled**
  1 **12-ounce can apricot nectar, chilled**
  ¼ **cup lemon juice**

In a small saucepan combine water, sugar, cinnamon, and cloves. Bring to boiling; reduce heat. Cover and simmer for 10 minutes. Chill. Strain and discard spices. Combine with apple juice, apricot nectar, and lemon juice. To serve, combine base with ingredients suggested below. Makes 6 cups.

Party Wine Punch: In punch bowl combine base and two 750-milliliter bottles of chilled *dry white wine.* Makes 24 (about 4-ounce) servings.

Spiked Party Punch: In a punch bowl combine base and 1 cup *vodka, bourbon, brandy, or rum.* Makes 14 (about 4-ounce) servings.

Nonalcoholic Punch: In a punch bowl combine base and two 1-liter bottles of chilled *club soda or carbonated water.* Makes 25 (about 4-ounce) servings.

Individual Cocktails: For each serving, place crushed ice in a glass. Add 2 to 3 tablespoons *vodka, bourbon, brandy, or rum.* Add ½ cup base; stir. Makes 12 (about 5-ounce) servings.

Ice-Cream Punch

This creamy, frothy punch is a popular choice for wedding receptions.

  2 **quarts vanilla ice cream**
1½ **cups cold water**
  1 **12-ounce can frozen lemonade**
      concentrate, thawed
  2 **1-liter bottles lemon-lime**
      carbonated beverage, chilled

Spoon ice cream by tablespoonfuls into a large punch bowl. Add water and lemonade concentrate; stir just till combined. Slowly pour carbonated beverage down the side of bowl. Stir gently to mix. Makes 32 (about 4-ounce) servings.

Sherbet Punch: Prepare as above, *except* substitute *lime, orange, lemon, or raspberry sherbet* for the ice cream.

Slushy Punch

Keep this slush in the freezer for spur-of-the-moment guests. For each serving, combine equal amounts of slush and carbonated water.

  1 **cup sugar**
  2 **ripe medium bananas, cut up**
  3 **cups unsweetened pineapple juice**
  1 **6-ounce can frozen orange juice**
      concentrate
  2 **tablespoons lemon juice**
  1 **1-liter bottle carbonated water**
      or lemon-lime carbonated
      beverage, chilled

Stir together sugar and 2¾ cups *water* till sugar dissolves. In a blender container combine bananas, *half* of the pineapple juice, and the orange juice concentrate. Cover; blend till smooth. Add to sugar mixture. Stir in remaining pineapple juice and lemon juice. Transfer to a 13x9x2-inch baking pan. Freeze for several hours or till firm.

To serve, let mixture stand at room temperature for 20 to 30 minutes. To form a slush, scrape a large spoon across the frozen mixture. Spoon into a punch bowl. Slowly pour carbonated water down the side of the bowl. Stir gently to mix. Makes 23 (about 4-ounce) servings.

Spiked Slushy Punch: Prepare as above, *except* add 1½ cups *rum or vodka* with the lemon juice. Let frozen mixture stand at room temperature for *5 to 10* minutes before scraping with a spoon. Makes 26 (about 4-ounce) servings.

To form a slush, scrape a large spoon across the surface of the frozen mixture.

Lemonade or Limeade

For fresh juice, use 4 to 5 medium lemons or 7 to 10 medium limes.

**4 cups water
1 cup lemon juice *or* lime juice
⅔ cup sugar
Ice cubes**

In a pitcher combine water, lemon or lime juice, and sugar. Stir till sugar dissolves. Serve immediately over ice or chill till serving time. Makes 5 (about 8-ounce) servings.

Lime Daiquiris

Use the empty can to measure the rum. (A Strawberry Daiquiri is pictured on page 23.)

**1 6-ounce can frozen limeade *or* lemonade concentrate
⅔ cup rum (one 6-ounce can)
20 to 24 ice cubes (about 2 cups)**

In a blender container combine limeade or lemonade concentrate and rum. Cover and blend till smooth. With blender running, add ice cubes, one at a time, through opening in lid. Blend till slushy. Makes 6 (about 4-ounce) servings.

Berry and Banana Daiquiris: Prepare as above, *except* use *half* of a 6-ounce can (⅓ cup) frozen limeade or lemonade concentrate. Then add one 10-ounce package frozen *red raspberries or sliced strawberries;* 1 ripe medium *banana,* cut up; and, if desired, ⅓ cup sifted powdered sugar. Makes 8 (about 4-ounce) servings.

Raspberry or Strawberry Daiquiris: Prepare as above, *except* use *half* of a 6-ounce can (⅓ cup) frozen limeade or lemonade concentrate. Then add one 10-ounce package frozen *red raspberries or sliced strawberries* and, if desired, ⅓ cup sifted powdered sugar. Makes 7 (about 4-ounce) servings.

Peach Daiquiris: Prepare as above, *except* use *half* of a 6-ounce can (⅓ cup) frozen limeade or lemonade concentrate. Then add 3 ripe medium *peaches,* peeled, pitted, and cut up (1½ cups), or 1½ cups frozen unsweetened *peach* slices. If desired, add ½ cup sifted powdered sugar. Makes 8 (about 4-ounce) servings.

Margaritas

Our favorite blend for this popular drink.

**½ cup lime *or* lemon juice
½ cup tequila
⅓ cup sugar
¼ cup orange liqueur
Ice cubes**

Stir together lime or lemon juice, tequila, sugar, orange liqueur, and 1 cup *cold* water till sugar dissolves. Serve over ice. Makes 4 (about 4-ounce) servings.

Blended Margaritas: Prepare as above, *except* place lime or lemon juice, tequila, sugar, and orange liqueur in a blender container. Cover; blend till sugar dissolves. With blender running, add *3 cups* ice cubes, one at a time, through opening in lid. Blend till slushy. Makes 7 (about 4-ounce) servings.

Frozen Margaritas: Prepare as above, *except* use *2 cups* cold water. Transfer mixture to an 8x4x2-inch or 9x5x3-inch pan. Freeze several hours or till firm. To serve, scrape a large spoon across surface of frozen mixture. Spoon into glasses. Makes 7 (about 4-ounce) servings.

Bloody Marys

**1 32-ounce jar tomato juice
¾ cup vodka
¼ cup lemon juice
2 teaspoons Worcestershire sauce
¼ teaspoon celery salt
Several dashes bottled hot pepper sauce
Ice cubes
Celery stalks *or* dill pickle spears (optional)**

In a pitcher stir together tomato juice, vodka, lemon juice, Worcestershire sauce, celery salt, and hot pepper sauce. Serve over ice. Garnish each glass with a celery stalk or pickle spear, if desired. Makes 10 (about 4-ounce) servings.

Virgin Marys: Prepare as above, *except* omit vodka. Makes 9 (about 4-ounce) servings.

Sangria

1 lemon
1 orange
½ cup sugar
½ cup water
1 750-milliliter bottle dry red *or* white wine, chilled
1 to 2 cups carbonated water, chilled
2 tablespoons brandy
  Ice cubes

Cut lemon and orange into ¼-inch-thick slices. Place the 4 end slices from the lemon and orange in a saucepan; set aside remaining slices. For syrup, add sugar and water to the saucepan. Bring to boiling, stirring till sugar dissolves.

Remove from heat; cool. Squeeze juice from cooked fruit into the syrup. Discard cooked fruit.

In a pitcher combine remaining fruit slices, syrup, wine, carbonated water, and brandy. Serve over ice. Makes 10 (about 4-ounce) servings.

Microwave directions: Cut fruit as above. In a 2-cup measure micro-cook fruit end slices, sugar, and water, uncovered, on 100% power (high) for 2 to 3 minutes or till boiling, stirring once. Continue as above.

Wine Spritzer

¾ cup dry white, red, *or* rosé wine, chilled
¼ cup club soda *or* lemon-lime carbonated beverage, chilled
  Ice cubes

Combine wine and soda or carbonated beverage. Serve over ice. Makes 1 (about 8-ounce) serving.

Serving Wine

Absolute rules no longer dictate which wine to serve with what food. Just follow your personal tastes. If you're unsure, ask an informed store employee to help you make a choice.

Chocolate-Cream Liqueur

Pour this luscious liqueur into decorative bottles for holiday gift giving.

2 cups light cream
1 14-ounce can (1¼ cups) *sweetened condensed* milk
2 teaspoons instant coffee crystals
1 beaten egg yolk
1 cup Irish whiskey
⅓ cup rum
2 tablespoons chocolate-flavored syrup
1 tablespoon vanilla

In a large heavy saucepan combine light cream, sweetened condensed milk, and instant coffee crystals. Cook and stir over medium heat till coffee crystals dissolve.

Gradually stir about *half* of the hot milk mixture into the beaten egg yolk; return all to the saucepan. Bring mixture to a boil. Cook and stir over medium heat for 2 minutes. Remove saucepan from heat.

Add Irish whiskey, rum, chocolate syrup, and vanilla to mixture in saucepan. Stir till well combined. Let mixture cool at room temperature.

Transfer mixture to a container with a tight-fitting lid. Chill at least 4 hours before serving. Shake well before serving. Store in the refrigerator for up to 2 months. Makes about 4½ cups or enough for 9 (about 4-ounce) servings.

Grasshoppers

Smooth and refreshing, these drinks are perfect for after dinner or dessert.

1 pint vanilla ice cream
¼ cup white crème de cacao
¼ cup green crème de menthe

In a blender container combine ice cream, crème de cacao, and crème de menthe. Cover and blend till smooth. Makes 4 (about 4-ounce) servings.

Golden Cadillacs: Prepare as above, *except* substitute *Galliano* for the crème de menthe.

Velvet Hammers: Prepare as above, *except* substitute *orange liqueur* for crème de menthe.

Brandy Alexanders: Prepare as above, *except* substitute *brandy* for the crème de menthe.

Breads

Nutrition Analysis

	Per Serving								Percent U.S. RDA Per Serving							
	Servings Per Recipe	Calories	Protein (g)	Carbohydrate (g)	Fat (g)	Cholesterol (mg)	Sodium (mg)	Potassium (mg)	Protein	Vitamin A	Vitamin C	Thiamine	Riboflavin	Niacin	Calcium	Iron
Any-Fruit Coffee Cake (p. 62)	9	275	4	46	9	31	159	80	6	7	2	11	8	7	4	7
Apple-and-Raisin Refrigerator Bran Muffins (p. 61)	14	172	4	27	7	21	157	170	5	5	5	11	10	8	8	10
Apple Bread (p. 56)	16	155	2	23	6	17	77	44	3	1	1	6	4	3	1	4
Apple-Cheese Biscuits (p. 67)	18	123	2	13	76	5	206	35	4	3	1	5	3	2	4	3
Apple Coffee Cake (p. 64)	12	302	4	39	15	24	160	129	6	3	1	11	8	6	8	9
Apple Fritters (p. 69)	24	81	2	13	3	12	78	36	2	1	1	4	3	2	3	3
Applesauce Coffee Cake (p. 63)	9	297	5	40	14	61	248	142	7	10	10	13	9	7	6	9
Apple-Streusel Ladder Loaf (p. 46)	16	129	2	22	4	1	163	56	4	2	1	8	5	5	2	5
Apricot Nut Bread (p. 57)	18	211	4	34	7	17	141	184	7	12	1	11	9	7	7	8
Bacon Sourdough Muffins (p. 43)	12	181	4	21	9	28	163	55	7	1	11	8	7	8	6	1
Bagels (p. 52)	12	179	5	38	0	0	179	53	7	0	0	20	12	13	1	11
Banana Bread (p. 56)	16	155	3	23	6	35	115	90	4	1	2	7	5	4	3	5
Banana Muffins (p. 60)	10	222	4	29	10	28	128	144	7	1	3	12	9	7	7	7
Banana-Wheat Waffles (p. 71)	3	735	17	72	44	191	580	581	26	10	9	35	33	19	38	20
Batter Dinner Rolls (p. 50)	18	146	4	22	5	32	75	59	6	1	0	11	9	7	2	7
Berry-Banana-Walnut Bread (p. 58)	18	169	3	23	8	30	69	97	4	1	10	7	5	3	1	5
Berry Coffee Cake (p. 65)	12	210	2	31	9	8	321	46	4	5	1	7	5	4	2	5
Biscuits (p. 66)	10	191	3	21	11	1	152	50	5	0	0	11	7	7	8	6
Blueberry-Banana-Walnut Bread (p. 58)	18	170	3	23	8	31	69	84	4	1	2	7	5	3	1	5
Blueberry Muffins (p. 60)	10	177	4	26	7	29	131	67	6	1	2	10	8	6	7	6
Boston Brown Bread (p. 58)	15	71	2	14	1	19	80	121	3	1	0	4	3	2	4	4
Bran Bread (p. 40)	32	83	2	16	1	0	68	55	3	0	0	8	4	6	1	5
Brioche (p. 52)	24	137	4	19	5	46	126	46	5	4	0	10	8	6	2	6
Brown Irish Soda Bread (p. 67)	16	87	3	12	3	35	133	62	5	2	0	7	5	4	3	4
Buckwheat Bread (p. 40)	32	85	2	16	1	0	68	50	3	0	0	8	4	5	1	5
Buckwheat Pancakes (p. 72)	8	108	3	13	5	37	167	114	5	2	0	6	5	3	10	3
Buttermilk Biscuits (p. 66)	10	190	3	21	10	1	188	50	5	0	0	11	7	7	8	6
Buttermilk Coffee Cake (p. 63)	9	235	4	33	10	31	156	132	6	1	1	9	7	5	7	9
Buttermilk Doughnuts (p. 68)	13	306	5	42	13	43	202	62	7	4	0	14	10	8	3	9
Buttermilk Pancakes (p. 72)	8	116	3	15	5	35	214	70	5	1	1	8	8	4	7	5
Buttermilk Waffles (p. 71)	3	709	17	64	42	187	690	361	26	5	3	37	38	20	41	22
Cajun-Style Biscuits (p. 66)	10	192	3	21	11	1	152	50	5	1	0	11	7	7	8	6
Cake Doughnuts (p. 68)	13	307	5	42	13	43	145	62	7	4	0	14	10	8	6	9
Caramel-Nut Pinwheels (p. 71)	8	206	4	26	10	0	273	90	6	2	2	104	7	7	1	8
Caramel-Pecan Rolls (p. 53)	24	206	3	31	8	24	129	78	5	6	0	11	8	6	3	8
Carrot and Pineapple Bread (p. 56)	16	158	2	24	6	17	79	68	3	20	3	7	4	4	2	5
Cheese Biscuits (p. 66)	10	214	5	21	12	7	187	56	7	2	0	11	9	7	12	6
Cheese Bread (p. 39)	32	87	3	14	2	14	69	27	5	1	0	7	6	5	4	4
Cheese Nut Bread (p. 57)	18	207	6	27	9	23	157	92	9	2	0	11	9	6	13	6
Cheese Muffins (p. 60)	10	194	5	24	8	35	165	62	8	2	0	10	9	6	11	6
Cheesy Corn Spoon Bread (p. 59)	4	234	11	23	12	90	527	292	16	24	8	7	17	4	25	6
Cherry Sourdough Coffee Cake (p. 43)	9	409	5	57	19	31	327	133	8	18	3	16	9	8	4	11
Chocolate Chip and Nut Ring (p. 64)	20	271	4	33	14	41	124	73	6	1	0	10	6	5	4	7
Chocolate Doughnuts (p. 68)	13	332	5	49	14	43	123	93	8	3	0	14	10	9	5	10
Chocolate Peanut Butter Coffee Cake (p. 63)	16	323	7	42	15	36	244	233	11	5	0	11	9	14	7	12
Chocolate Sticky Rolls (p. 65)	12	264	3	40	11	1	114	97	5	1	0	11	7	6	7	11

On the divider: Whole Wheat Dinner Rolls (p. 50), Refrigerator Bran Muffin (p. 61), Honey-Nut Wheat Muffin (p. 61), Fruit Wheat Muffin (p. 61), Biscuits (p. 66), and Blueberry Muffins (p. 60).

Nutrition Analysis

	Per Serving							Percent U.S. RDA Per Serving							
	Servings Per Recipe	Calories	Protein (g)	Carbohydrate (g)	Fat (g)	Cholesterol (mg)	Sodium (mg)	Potassium (mg)	Protein	Vitamin A	Vitamin C	Thiamine	Riboflavin	Niacin	Calcium	Iron
Chocolate Swirl Bread (p. 45)	12	478	9	67	21	50	252	190	13	10	1	25	21	16	6	17
Chocolate Waffles (p. 71)	3	786	17	82	45	192	658	387	26	10	2	33	38	9	41	25
Cinnamon Crisps (p. 55)	24	224	3	35	8	12	101	75	5	4	0	11	7	6	3	7
Cinnamon-Nut Waffles (p. 71)	3	811	19	66	53	192	591	411	29	10	3	41	39	21	41	25
Cinnamon Popovers (p. 70)	6	161	6	18	7	95	133	104	9	3	1	11	12	6	6	7
Cinnamon Rolls (p. 53)	24	181	3	31	5	24	104	86	5	4	1	10	8	6	3	7
Cinnamon-Swirl Egg Bread (p. 44)	32	105	3	19	2	18	56	43	4	2	0	9	7	5	2	5
Cocoa Ripple Ring (p. 65)	16	150	3	20	7	35	44	73	4	1	0	5	3	2	4	3
Coconut-Cherry-Carrot Bread (p. 59)	16	239	4	33	10	52	144	50	6	79	2	10	8	6	3	7
Confetti Corn Bread (p. 59)	8	251	7	29	12	78	324	143	11	25	1	12	11	6	17	7
Confetti Hush Puppies (p. 69)	14	87	2	10	5	20	89	53	3	3	2	3	2	2	3	2
Corn Bread (p. 59)	8	220	6	28	9	71	279	118	9	4	0	11	10	6	12	7
Corn Bread Miniloaf (p. 59)	4	220	6	28	9	71	279	118	9	4	0	11	10	6	12	7
Corn Fritters (p. 69)	24	65	2	9	3	12	99	36	2	1	1	4	3	3	3	2
Cornmeal Biscuits (p. 66)	10	191	3	21	11	1	152	59	5	1	0	10	6	6	8	5
Cornmeal Bubble Ring (p. 45)	32	115	3	18	3	1	142	54	4	3	0	9	7	6	2	5
Cornmeal-Cheese Bubble Ring (p. 45)	32	129	4	18	5	5	164	58	6	4	0	9	8	6	5	5
Corn Muffins (p. 60)	10	170	3	24	7	29	130	71	5	2	0	8	6	4	7	5
Corn Sticks (p. 59)	24	73	2	9	3	24	93	39	2	1	0	4	3	2	4	2
Corn Waffles (p. 71)	5	461	11	46	27	115	491	283	16	8	5	20	22	12	24	12
Corny Corn Bread (p. 59)	8	252	7	36	10	71	426	183	10	6	5	12	12	8	12	9
Cranberry Muffins (p. 60)	10	185	4	28	7	29	130	64	5	1	2	10	8	6	7	6
Cranberry Nut Bread (p. 57)	18	196	4	30	7	17	141	89	6	1	2	11	8	6	7	6
Crepes (p. 72)	18	51	2	6	2	32	48	45	3	1	0	4	5	2	3	2
Croissants (p. 54)	16	321	6	33	19	82	262	87	9	14	0	17	13	11	4	10
Crunchy Corn Bread (p. 59)	8	306	7	37	15	71	279	179	11	4	1	19	11	7	13	10
Dark Rye Bread (p. 41)	24	85	2	16	2	0	148	73	4	1	0	7	4	5	2	5
Date-Nut Muffins (p. 60)	10	229	4	34	9	29	131	153	7	1	1	12	9	7	7	7
Date-Nut Ring (p. 64)	20	274	4	37	13	41	124	117	6	1	0	10	7	6	4	7
Date-Orange Coffee Cake (p. 64)	12	314	4	42	15	24	157	170	6	3	8	12	8	7	8	9
Dessert Crepes (p. 72)	18	56	2	8	2	32	18	45	3	1	0	4	5	2	3	2
Dill Batter Bread (p. 43)	8	182	8	30	3	36	218	132	12	2	0	24	15	11	4	13
Dinner Rolls (p. 50)	24	128	3	20	4	24	56	48	5	1	0	10	8	6	2	6
Drop Biscuits (p. 66)	10	196	3	21	11	2	156	63	5	1	0	11	8	7	9	6
Easy Berry-Banana-Walnut Bread (p. 58)	18	169	3	23	8	30	69	97	4	1	10	7	5	3	1	5
Easy Beer-Cheese Triangles (p. 66)	8	104	2	11	5	4	116	18	3	1	0	6	4	4	6	3
Easy Biscuits (p. 66)	4	181	3	22	9	1	195	50	5	1	0	11	8	7	9	6
Easy Muffins (p. 66)	6	142	3	17	7	47	142	44	5	1	0	8	7	5	6	5
Easy Pancakes (p. 66)	6	144	4	16	7	48	152	75	6	2	0	9	8	5	9	5
Egg Bread (p. 44)	32	92	3	16	2	18	56	42	4	2	0	9	7	5	2	5
English-Muffin Loaves (p. 48)	32	98	3	17	2	1	75	51	4	0	0	9	7	6	2	5
English Muffins (p. 48)	12	270	8	47	6	3	200	140	12	2	1	26	20	17	6	15
Filled Croissants (p. 54)	16	382	7	36	24	98	304	105	10	19	1	18	15	11	5	11
Frankfurter Buns (p. 50)	12	257	7	41	7	47	112	96	10	2	0	21	16	13	4	12
French Bread (p. 39)	30	86	3	18	0	0	109	33	4	0	0	11	7	7	0	6
French Breakfast Puffs (p. 60)	12	186	3	25	8	24	161	42	4	7	0	7	6	4	5	5
French Toast (p. 70)	5	186	6	21	8	113	297	98	10	7	0	11	11	6	6	8
Fruit-Studded Bread (p. 47)	24	210	3	38	5	24	111	116	6	4	1	12	10	8	3	8
Fruit Wheat Muffins (p. 61)	12	153	3	25	5	24	107	63	4	1	2	7	5	4	5	4
Garden Biscuits (p. 66)	10	193	3	21	11	1	153	58	5	9	1	11	7	7	8	6
Green Chili Corn Bread (p. 59)	8	280	9	29	14	85	524	146	14	11	3	12	13	6	23	9

Nutrition Analysis

		Per Serving							Percent U.S. RDA Per Serving							
	Servings Per Recipe	Calories	Protein (g)	Carbohydrate (g)	Fat (g)	Cholesterol (mg)	Sodium (mg)	Potassium (mg)	Protein	Vitamin A	Vitamin C	Thiamine	Riboflavin	Niacin	Calcium	Iron
Hamburger Buns (p. 50)	12	257	7	41	7	47	112	96	10	2	0	21	16	13	4	12
Herb Bagels (p. 52)	12	179	5	38	0	0	179	53	7	0	0	20	12	13	1	11
Herb-Onion Dinner Rolls (p. 50)	24	128	3	20	4	24	56	48	5	1	0	10	8	6	2	6
Honey and Whole Wheat Bread (p. 40)	32	89	2	17	1	0	67	45	4	0	0	8	4	5	1	5
Honey-Nut Wheat Muffins (p. 61)	12	182	3	25	9	24	107	83	5	1	1	8	5	4	6	5
Honey Wheat Muffins (p. 61)	12	150	3	24	5	24	107	58	4	1	1	7	5	4	5	4
Hot Cross Buns (p. 55)	20	181	4	26	7	42	70	68	6	1	13	11	9	7	2	7
Hush Puppies (p. 69)	14	87	2	10	5	20	88	47	3	1	1	3	2	1	3	2
Irish Soda Bread (p. 67)	16	91	3	13	3	35	133	42	4	2	0	7	6	4	3	5
Jelly Muffins (p. 60)	10	187	4	29	7	29	131	62	5	1	0	10	8	6	7	6
Kuchen (p. 47)	18	196	4	34	5	48	117	76	6	5	1	10	9	6	3	7
Light Rye Bagels (p. 52)	12	161	5	35	1	0	179	64	7	0	0	15	9	10	1	9
Mexican Doughnut Strips (p. 69)	12	94	1	7	7	23	28	11	2	2	0	2	2	1	0	2
Mini-French-Bread Loaves (p. 39)	16	162	5	33	0	0	204	62	8	0	0	20	13	13	1	11
Molasses Rye Bread (p. 41)	24	122	3	24	1	0	92	121	5	0	0	11	7	7	3	9
Muffins (p. 60)	10	171	4	24	7	29	130	57	5	1	0	10	8	6	7	6
Nut Bread (p. 57)	18	194	4	29	7	17	141	84	6	1	1	11	8	6	7	6
Nutty Orange Pancakes (p. 72)	8	166	4	19	9	34	220	122	6	1	21	11	6	5	7	6
Nutty Sticky Rolls (p. 65)	12	245	3	36	10	1	136	75	5	2	0	11	7	6	7	10
Oatmeal Bread (p. 40)	32	99	3	18	2	0	68	45	4	0	0	10	5	5	1	6
Oatmeal Muffins (p. 60)	10	175	4	24	7	29	130	73	6	1	0	11	7	5	7	6
Oatmeal-Raisin Scones (p. 67)	12	150	3	21	6	23	108	107	5	5	0	9	5	3	5	6
Onion and Garlic Popovers (p. 70)	6	161	6	18	7	95	133	104	9	3	1	11	12	6	6	7
Onion Bagels (p. 52)	12	186	5	39	1	1	190	68	8	0	1	20	12	13	1	12
Orange Rye Bread (p. 41)	24	122	3	24	1	0	91	61	5	0	1	10	7	7	1	7
Orange Sticky Rolls (p. 65)	12	247	3	37	10	1	136	84	5	2	4	11	7	6	7	10
Pancakes (p. 72)	8	119	3	15	5	37	166	71	5	2	0	8	8	4	9	5
Parmesan-Basil Popovers (p. 70)	6	171	6	18	8	96	172	113	10	4	1	11	12	6	10	8
Parmesan Spoon Bread (p. 59)	4	175	9	16	8	80	248	203	13	10	1	6	14	2	23	3
Peanut Butter Coffee Cake (p. 63)	16	282	7	38	12	36	243	207	10	5	0	10	8	14	7	11
Peasant Rye Bread (p. 41)	24	113	3	22	2	0	103	66	5	1	1	11	8	8	1	7
Pecan Biscuit Spirals (p. 67)	15	162	3	18	9	19	186	54	4	6	0	9	6	5	6	5
Pita Bread (p. 48)	12	143	4	26	2	0	133	44	6	0	0	15	10	10	1	9
Popovers (p. 70)	6	161	6	18	7	95	133	104	9	3	1	11	12	6	6	7
Pretzels (p. 49)	20	124	4	23	2	1	119	61	5	1	0	12	9	7	3	6
Prune Kuchen (p. 47)	18	220	4	40	5	48	118	161	6	10	1	11	10	8	3	9
Puffed Oven Pancake (p. 72)	6	218	5	33	8	139	188	225	8	8	25	8	10	3	5	7
Pumpkin Bread (p. 57)	18	180	3	28	7	31	112	150	5	6	2	8	6	4	7	9
Pumpkin Muffins (p. 60)	10	196	4	26	9	29	131	99	6	55	1	11	8	6	8	8
Raisin Egg-Bread Braid (p. 44)	32	119	3	23	2	18	57	110	5	2	1	10	7	6	2	6
Raisin Sourdough Bread (p. 42)	24	264	7	55	2	0	131	132	10	1	1	26	15	17	2	16
Refrigerator Bran Muffins (p. 61)	12	182	4	26	8	24	179	160	6	5	5	12	11	9	9	11
Rhubarb-Strawberry Coffee Cake (p. 62)	9	270	4	44	9	31	160	106	6	7	9	11	9	7	5	7
Rye Bread (p. 41)	24	114	3	22	1	0	90	56	5	0	0	10	7	7	1	7
Sopaipillas (p. 69)	20	62	1	7	3	0	29	6	1	0	0	3	1	2	2	2
Sour Cream Biscuits (p. 66)	10	212	4	21	13	6	153	52	5	2	0	11	7	7	8	6
Sour Cream Coffee Cake (p. 63)	9	264	4	33	13	37	163	151	6	3	1	9	8	5	8	9
Sourdough Bread (p. 42)	24	136	3	26	2	0	130	38	5	1	0	14	9	9	1	8
Sourdough Pancakes (p. 72)	8	143	4	22	4	34	182	71	6	1	0	12	7	7	3	7
Spoon Bread (p. 59)	4	146	6	16	7	75	265	196	9	9	1	6	12	2	15	3
Stollen (p. 46)	48	87	2	15	3	6	51	60	3	2	1	5	4	3	2	3

Nutrition Analysis	Per Serving							Percent U.S. RDA Per Serving							
	Servings Per Recipe	Calories	Protein (g)	Carbohydrate (g)	Fat (g)	Cholesterol (mg)	Sodium (mg)	Potassium (mg)	Protein	Vitamin A	Vitamin C	Thiamine	Riboflavin	Niacin	Calcium	Iron
Streusel Coffee Cake (p. 64)	9	316	5	48	13	32	159	187	7	2	1	13	9	7	8	10
Stuffed French Toast (p. 70)	5	353	10	33	20	113	456	169	16	16	1	18	16	9	10	12
Sunflower-Nut Wheat Muffins (p. 61)	12	171	3	25	7	24	107	88	5	1	1	7	5	5	5	5
Sweet-Raisin Irish Soda Bread (p. 67)	16	106	3	17	3	35	134	70	5	2	0	8	6	4	4	5
Waffles (p. 71)	3	713	16	63	44	192	590	334	25	10	2	37	37	20	40	22
Wheat and Cottage Cheese Rolls (p. 50)	24	129	5	19	4	25	141	121	8	3	0	9	5	5	3	5
Wheat Germ Bread (p. 40)	32	83	2	16	1	0	68	55	3	0	0	8	4	6	1	5
White Bread (p. 38)	32	97	3	19	1	1	76	52	5	1	0	10	8	6	3	6
Whole Wheat Bagels (p. 52)	12	199	6	44	1	0	180	163	8	0	1	20	10	12	2	11
Whole Wheat Bread (p. 40)	32	87	2	17	1	0	68	51	4	0	0	8	4	5	1	5
Whole Wheat Dinner Rolls (p. 50)	24	125	3	20	4	24	56	65	5	1	0	10	7	6	2	6
Whole Wheat English Muffins (p. 48)	12	260	8	45	6	3	200	194	12	2	0	25	17	16	6	13
Whole Wheat Pita Bread (p. 48)	12	134	4	24	3	0	134	98	7	0	0	14	6	9	1	7
Whole Wheat Popovers (p. 70)	6	159	6	18	7	95	133	118	9	3	1	11	11	5	6	7
Whole Wheat Pretzels (p. 49)	20	121	4	22	2	1	119	89	6	1	0	13	8	7	3	7
Yeast Doughnuts (p. 55)	16	246	4	29	13	35	83	68	6	1	0	12	11	8	2	7
Zucchini Bread (p. 56)	16	151	2	22	6	17	78	50	3	1	1	6	4	3	1	4

Yeast Breads

Few foods are as appealing as freshly baked yeast breads. From a loaf of coarse rye to a delicate croissant, there are breads to suit every baker.

Yeast-Bread Tips
To guarantee good-looking, great-tasting breads every time, follow this list of helpful hints.
● When a recipe gives a range for the flour amount, use the minimum as a guide and knead in as much of the remaining flour as you can.
● Knead the dough to the stiffness called for in the recipe. Kneading develops the gluten of the flour, which determines the final structure of the bread loaf. To knead, fold the dough over and push down with the heel of your hand, curving your fingers over the dough. Give the dough a quarter-turn, then fold over and push down again. Continue this fold-push-turn procedure until the dough is smooth and elastic.
● Don't raise dough in a hot area because excessive heat will kill the yeast. Too much cold, on the other hand, will stunt the yeast's growth. The optimum temperature for raising dough is 80° to 85°. For best results, our Test Kitchen home economists place the bowl of dough in an unheated oven, then set a large pan of hot water under the bowl on the oven's lower rack.
● Let dough rise till it's nearly doubled in size. Don't let loaves rise to the top of the pan because the dough needs room to rise as it bakes.
● For a soft and shiny crust, brush loaves with margarine or butter after baking. For a glossy, crispy crust, brush before baking with milk, water, or beaten egg.
● Test for doneness by tapping the top of the loaf with your finger. A hollow sound means the loaf is properly baked.
● If you live at a high altitude, expect yeast doughs to rise faster than at sea level. The higher you live, the faster the doughs will rise.

Dough Stiffness
Here's how to identify the stiffness of dough specified in our bread recipes. *Soft dough* is too sticky to knead and is often used for batter breads. *Moderately soft dough* is slightly sticky, may be kneaded on a floured surface, and is used for most sweet breads. *Moderately stiff dough* is somewhat firm to the touch, kneads easily on a floured surface, and is used for most unsweet breads. *Stiff dough* is firm to the touch and is easily rolled on a floured surface. French bread is made from this type of dough.

White Bread

5¾ to 6¼ cups all-purpose flour
  1 package active dry yeast
2¼ cups milk
  2 tablespoons sugar
  1 tablespoon shortening, margarine,
     or butter
  1 teaspoon salt   Oven 375°

In a large mixing bowl combine *2½ cups* of the flour and the yeast. In a saucepan heat and stir milk; sugar; shortening, margarine, or butter; and salt till warm (120° to 130°) and shortening almost melts. Add to flour mixture. Beat with an electric mixer on low speed for 30 seconds, scraping bowl constantly. Beat on high speed for 3 minutes. Using a spoon, stir in as much remaining flour as you can.

Turn out onto a lightly floured surface. Knead in enough of the remaining flour to make a moderately stiff dough that is smooth and elastic (6 to 8 minutes total). Shape into a ball. Place in a lightly greased bowl; turn once to grease surface. Cover and let rise in a warm place till double (about 45 minutes).

Punch dough down. Turn out onto a lightly floured surface. Divide dough in half. Cover and let rest for 10 minutes. Lightly grease two 8x4x2-inch loaf pans. Shape each half of dough into a loaf by patting or rolling. To pat dough, gently pull dough into a loaf shape, tucking edges beneath. To shape dough by rolling, on a lightly floured surface, roll each half into a 12x8-inch rectangle. Roll up tightly, starting at a narrow edge. Seal with fingertips as you roll.

Place shaped dough in prepared loaf pans. Cover and let rise in a warm place till nearly double (30 to 40 minutes).

Bake in a 375° oven about 40 minutes or till bread tests done. Cover loosely with foil the last 10 minutes of baking to prevent overbrowning, if necessary. Remove from pans *immediately*. Cool on wire racks. Makes 2 loaves (32 servings).

Hand-mixed method: Prepare as above, *except* soften yeast in ¼ cup *warm* water (105° to 115°). Reduce milk to *2 cups*. After heating milk mixture in saucepan, transfer to a large mixing bowl. Stir in *2 cups* of the flour; beat well by hand. Add softened yeast; stir till smooth. Using a spoon, stir in as much remaining flour as you can. Increase kneading time to 8 to 10 minutes.

To knead, fold dough over; push down with heel of your hand. Turn, fold, and push down again.

Shape each half of dough by gently pulling the dough into a loaf shape, tucking the edges under.

Or, roll each half of dough into a rectangle. Roll up tightly, starting at one of the narrow edges.

French Bread

If you're a lover of Italian bread, try our French Bread. The loaves are just a little longer and narrower than the Italian ones.

5½ to 6 cups all-purpose flour
2 packages active dry yeast
2 cups warm water (120° to 130°)
   Cornmeal
1 slightly beaten egg white
1 tablespoon water   Oven 375°

In a large mixing bowl combine *2 cups* of the flour, the yeast, and 1½ teaspoons *salt.* Add warm water. Beat with an electric mixer on low speed for 30 seconds, scraping bowl constantly. Beat on high speed for 3 minutes. Using a spoon, stir in as much remaining flour as you can.

Turn out onto a lightly floured surface. Knead in enough remaining flour to make a stiff dough that is smooth and elastic (8 to 10 minutes total). Shape into a ball. Place in a greased bowl; turn once to grease surface. Cover; let rise in a warm place till double (about 1 hour).

Punch dough down. Turn out onto a lightly floured surface. Divide in half. Cover; let rest 10 minutes. Roll each half into a 15x10-inch rectangle. Roll up from long sides; seal well. Taper ends. Place, seam side down, on a greased baking sheet sprinkled with cornmeal. Combine egg white and water; brush over loaves. Cover; let rise till nearly double (35 to 45 minutes). With a very sharp knife, make 3 or 4 diagonal cuts about ¼ inch deep across top of each loaf.

Bake in a 375° oven for 20 minutes. Brush again with egg white and water mixture. Continue baking for 15 to 20 minutes more or till bread tests done. Remove from baking sheet; cool. Makes 2 loaves (30 servings).

Mini-French-Bread Loaves: Prepare as above, *except* cut each half of dough into quarters, making 8 pieces total. Shape into balls. Cover; let rest 10 minutes. Shape each ball into a 6-inch loaf; taper ends. Place 2½ inches apart on a greased baking sheet sprinkled with cornmeal. Brush with egg white and water mixture. Cover; let rise till nearly double (35 to 45 minutes). With a very sharp knife, make 3 shallow diagonal cuts across top of each loaf.

Bake in a 375° oven for 15 minutes. Brush again with egg white and water mixture. Continue baking for 10 to 15 minutes more or till bread tests done. Remove from baking sheet; cool. Makes 8 loaves (16 to 24 servings).

Cheese Bread

Oven 350°

Combine 1½ cups *all-purpose flour* and 1 package *active dry yeast.* Add 1 *egg;* 1½ cups shredded *cheddar cheese, Swiss cheese, or Monterey Jack cheese with jalapeño peppers;* 1¼ cups *warm water* (120° to 130°); ¼ cup *sugar;* and ½ teaspoon *salt.* Beat with an electric mixer on low speed for 30 seconds, scraping bowl. Beat on high speed for 3 minutes. Using 2½ to 3 cups *all-purpose flour,* stir in as much flour as you can.

Turn out onto a lightly floured surface. Knead in enough remaining flour to make a moderately stiff dough that is smooth and elastic (6 to 8 minutes total). Shape into a ball. Place in a greased bowl; turn once. Cover; let rise in a warm place till double (1 to 1¼ hours).

Punch dough down. Turn out onto a lightly floured surface. Divide in half. Cover; let rest 10 minutes. Lightly grease two 8x4x2-inch loaf pans. Shape each half of dough into a loaf. Place in pans. Cover; let rise in a warm place till nearly double (about 45 minutes). Bake in a 350° oven for 40 to 45 minutes or till done. Cover loosely the last 20 minutes, if necessary. Remove from pans; cool. Makes 2 loaves (32 servings).

Don't Crowd the Oven

When baking several long, individual, or round loaves of bread at the same time, you'll need an extra large (17x14-inch) baking sheet. If you don't have this size baking sheet, go ahead and shape the loaves on two smaller baking sheets and let them rise as directed. Then, while you're baking one sheet, place the other one in the refrigerator. Don't bake the two smaller sheets at the same time because too little air would circulate in the oven.

Whole Wheat Bread

Enrich this fiber-filled bread with one of the four whole grains listed below.

3 to 3½ cups all-purpose flour
1 package active dry yeast
⅓ cup packed brown sugar
3 tablespoons shortening, margarine, or butter
2 cups whole wheat flour   Oven 375°

Combine *2 cups* of all-purpose flour and the yeast. Heat and stir brown sugar, shortening, 1¾ cups *water,* and 1 teaspoon *salt* till warm (120° to 130°) and shortening almost melts. Add to flour mixture. Beat with an electric mixer on low speed for 30 seconds, scraping bowl constantly. Beat on high speed for 3 minutes. Using a spoon, stir in whole wheat flour and as much remaining all-purpose flour as you can.

Turn out onto a lightly floured surface. Knead in enough remaining all-purpose flour to make a moderately stiff dough that is smooth and elastic (6 to 8 minutes total). Shape into a ball. Place in a lightly greased bowl; turn once. Cover; let rise in a warm place till double (1 to 1½ hours).

Punch dough down. Turn out onto a lightly floured surface. Divide in half. Cover and let rest 10 minutes. Lightly grease two 8x4x2-inch loaf pans. Shape each half of dough into a loaf. Place in pans. Cover; let rise in a warm place till nearly double (45 to 60 minutes).

Bake in a 375° oven for 40 to 45 minutes or till done. Cover loosely with foil the last 10 to 20 minutes, if necessary. Remove from pans; cool. Makes 2 loaves (32 servings).

Wheat Germ Bread: Prepare as above, *except* reduce whole wheat flour to *1½ cups* and add ½ cup toasted *wheat germ.*

Bran Bread: Prepare as above, *except* reduce whole wheat flour to *1½ cups* and add ½ cup *unprocessed wheat bran (miller's bran).*

Oatmeal Bread: Prepare as above, *except* substitute *quick-cooking or regular rolled oats* for the whole wheat flour. Increase the all-purpose flour to *4¼ to 4¾ cups* total.

Buckwheat Bread: Prepare as above, *except* reduce whole wheat flour to *1¼ cups* and add ¾ cup *buckwheat flour.*

Honey and Whole Wheat Bread: Prepare as above, *except* reduce water to *1½ cups* and omit brown sugar. Add ⅓ cup *honey or molasses* to saucepan.

Proofing Yeast Dough in Your Microwave Oven

With a little help from your microwave oven, you may be able to significantly shorten the time it takes to proof (raise) your yeast breads.

Before you begin, check your owner's manual to see if proofing is recommended. Or use the following test to check your oven:

Place 2 tablespoons cold stick margarine *(do not use corn oil margarine)* in a custard cup in the center of your oven. Micro-cook, uncovered, on 10% power (low) for 4 minutes. If the margarine doesn't completely melt, your microwave can proof yeast dough. But if the margarine does completely melt, your microwave will kill the yeast before the bread has a chance to rise. If so, you'll have to raise your yeast breads conventionally.

If your oven passed the test, here's how to proceed. While kneading your dough, place 3 cups water in a 4-cup measure. Cook on 100% power (high) for 6½ to 8½ minutes or till boiling. Move measure to back of oven. Place kneaded dough in a greased bowl, turning once. Cover with waxed paper and place in microwave oven with hot water. Heat dough and water on 10% power (low) for 13 to 15 minutes or till dough has almost doubled. Punch dough down; shape as directed.

Then place shaped dough in 8x4x2-inch loaf dishes. Return to microwave oven with hot water. Cover with waxed paper. Heat on low for 6 to 8 minutes or till nearly doubled. (For round or long loaves that are shaped on baking sheets, or rolls that are shaped in muffin cups, you'll have to do the second proofing step conventionally.)

For rich yeast breads (those with eggs and a slightly higher proportion of sugar), proofing times will be slightly longer. Allow 15 to 20 minutes for the first proofing time, and 10 to 14 minutes for the second proofing time.

Rye Bread

The Orange Rye Bread variation is reminiscent of Swedish limpa.

3½ to 4 cups all-purpose flour
  2 packages active dry yeast
  2 cups warm water (120° to 130°)
¼ cup packed brown sugar
  2 tablespoons cooking oil
  1 teaspoon salt
  2 cups rye flour
  1 tablespoon caraway seed
    Cornmeal   Oven 375°

In a large mixing bowl combine *2¾ cups* all-purpose flour, the yeast, water, brown sugar, oil, and salt. Beat with an electric mixer on low speed for 30 seconds, scraping sides of bowl constantly. Beat on high speed for 3 minutes. Using a spoon, stir in rye flour, caraway seed, and as much of the remaining all-purpose flour as you can.

Turn out onto a lightly floured surface. Knead in enough of the remaining all-purpose flour to make a moderately stiff dough that is smooth and elastic (6 to 8 minutes total). Shape into a ball. Place in a lightly greased bowl; turn once to grease surface. Cover and let rise in a warm place till double (about 1 hour).

Punch dough down. Turn out onto a lightly floured surface. Divide dough in half. Cover and let rest for 10 minutes. Shape into 2 round loaves. Place on a greased baking sheet sprinkled with cornmeal. Flatten each slightly to a 6-inch diameter. (*Or,* shape each half of dough into a loaf. Place in two greased 8x4x2-inch loaf pans.) Cover and let rise in a warm place till nearly double (30 to 45 minutes).

Bake in a 375° oven for 35 to 40 minutes or till bread tests done. Remove from baking sheet or pans; cool. Makes 2 loaves (24 servings).

Orange Rye Bread: Prepare as above, *except* increase brown sugar to *½ cup,* omit the caraway seed, and add 4 teaspoons *finely shredded orange peel* to the flour mixture.

Molasses Rye Bread: Prepare as above, *except* reduce water to *1½ cups* and substitute *½ cup light molasses* for the brown sugar.

Peasant Rye Bread: Prepare as above, *except* reduce rye flour to *1 cup.* Stir in *½ cup whole bran cereal* and *½ cup yellow cornmeal* with rye flour.

Dark Rye Bread

This heavy, dark, robust bread will appeal to you if you like Russian black bread or pumpernickel.

  2 to 2½ cups all-purpose flour
  1 package active dry yeast
  1 tablespoon instant coffee crystals
  1 tablespoon caraway seed
½ teaspoon fennel seed, crushed
1¼ cups water
  3 tablespoons molasses
  2 tablespoons margarine *or* butter
½ square (½ ounce) unsweetened chocolate, cut up
  1 tablespoon vinegar
1½ teaspoons sugar
1½ teaspoons salt
  2 cups rye flour
  1 slightly beaten egg white Oven 375°

In a large mixing bowl combine *1½ cups* of the all-purpose flour, the yeast, coffee crystals, caraway seed, and fennel seed. In a saucepan heat and stir the water, molasses, margarine or butter, unsweetened chocolate, vinegar, sugar, and salt till warm (120° to 130°), and till margarine or butter and chocolate almost melt. Add to flour mixture. Beat with an electric mixer on low speed for 30 seconds, scraping bowl constantly. Beat on high speed for 3 minutes. Using a spoon, stir in rye flour and as much of the remaining all-purpose flour as you can.

Turn out onto a lightly floured surface. Knead in enough remaining all-purpose flour to make a moderately stiff dough that is smooth and elastic (6 to 8 minutes total). (Dough may be slightly sticky because of the rye flour.) Shape into a ball. Place in a greased bowl; turn once to grease surface. Cover; let rise in a warm place till double (1¼ to 1½ hours).

Punch dough down. Turn out onto a lightly floured surface. Divide in half. Cover and let rest for 10 minutes. Shape into 2 round loaves. Place on a greased baking sheet. Flatten each slightly to a 5-inch diameter. Cover and let rise in a warm place till nearly double (30 to 45 minutes). Combine the egg white and 1 tablespoon *water;* brush over loaves.

Bake in a 375° oven for 35 to 40 minutes or till bread tests done. If desired, brush again with egg white and water mixture about 5 minutes before removing from oven. Remove from baking sheet immediately; cool on wire racks. Makes 2 loaves (24 servings).

Sourdough Starter

When making starter, don't use quick-rising yeast.

In a large bowl dissolve 1 package *active dry yeast* in ½ cup *warm water* (105° to 115°). Stir in 2 cups *warm water*, 2 cups *all-purpose flour*, and 1 tablespoon *sugar or honey*. Beat till smooth. Cover bowl with cheesecloth. Let stand at room temperature for 5 to 10 days or till mixture has a fermented aroma, stirring 2 or 3 times a day. (Fermentation time depends on room temperature: a warmer room hastens fermentation.)

To store, transfer Sourdough Starter to a jar. Cover with cheesecloth and refrigerate. *Do not cover jar tightly with a metal lid.*

To use starter, bring desired amount to room temperature. Replenish starter after each use by stirring ¾ cup *all-purpose flour*, ¾ cup *water*, and 1 teaspoon *sugar or honey* into remaining starter. Cover; let stand at room temperature at least 1 day or till bubbly. Refrigerate for later use.

If starter isn't used within 10 days, stir in 1 teaspoon *sugar or honey*. Repeat every 10 days unless replenished.

Sourdough Bread

A chewy texture and slightly tangy flavor are the hallmarks of Sourdough Bread.

  1 **cup Sourdough Starter**
5½ **to 6 cups all-purpose flour**
  1 **package active dry yeast**
1½ **cups water**
  3 **tablespoons sugar**
  3 **tablespoons margarine *or* butter**
  ½ **teaspoon baking soda**   Oven 375°

Bring Sourdough Starter to room temperature. Combine *2½ cups* of the flour and the yeast. Heat and stir water, sugar, margarine, and 1 teaspoon *salt* just till warm (120° to 130°) and margarine almost melts. Add to flour mixture. Add Sourdough Starter. Beat with an electic mixer on low speed for 30 seconds, scraping bowl constantly. Beat on high speed for 3 minutes.

Combine *2½ cups* of flour and the soda. Add to yeast mixture. Stir till combined. Using a spoon, stir in as much remaining flour as you can. Turn out onto a floured surface. Knead in enough remaining flour to make a moderately stiff dough (6 to 8 minutes total). Shape into a ball. Place in a greased bowl; turn once. Cover; let rise in warm place till double (45 to 60 minutes).

Punch dough down. Turn out onto a lightly floured surface. Divide in half. Cover; let rest 10 minutes. Shape into 2 round loaves. Place on a greased baking sheet. Flatten each slightly to a 6-inch diameter. (*Or*, shape into two 9x4-inch oblong loaves. Place on a greased baking sheet.) With a sharp knife, make crisscross slashes across tops of loaves. Cover; let rise till nearly double (about 30 minutes). Bake in a 375° oven for 30 to 35 minutes or till done. Cover the last 10 minutes, if necessary. Remove from baking sheet; cool. Makes 2 loaves (24 to 36 servings).

Raisin Sourdough Bread: Prepare as above, *except* stir 1½ cups *raisins* into yeast mixture along with the flour-soda mixture. Before baking, brush loaves with *milk*. Combine 2 tablespoons *sugar* and ¼ teaspoon ground *cinnamon*. Sprinkle over loaves.

For Sourdough Bread, bring Sourdough Starter to room temperature. Add to flour mixture.

Using a sharp knife, make crisscross slashes across the tops of the round sourdough loaves.

Cherry Sourdough Coffee Cake

1½ **cups all-purpose flour**
½ **cup sugar**
½ **teaspoon baking powder**
½ **teaspoon baking soda**
¾ **cup margarine *or* butter**
½ **cup Sourdough Starter (see recipe,**
    opposite)
1 **egg**
1 **teaspoon vanilla**
  Cherry Filling
½ **cup quick-cooking rolled oats**
¼ **cup packed brown sugar**
¼ **cup chopped nuts**
3 **tablespoons all-purpose**
    flour   Oven 350°

Mix the 1½ cups flour, the sugar, baking powder, baking soda, and ¼ teaspoon *salt.* Cut in ½ *cup* margarine till mixture resembles fine crumbs. Mix Sourdough Starter, egg, and vanilla; add to flour mixture. Stir just till moistened. Spread *half* of the batter in a greased 9x9x2-inch baking pan. Spread Cherry Filling atop. Drop remaining batter in small mounds over filling. Mix oats, brown sugar, nuts, and the 3 tablespoons flour. Cut in ¼ *cup* margarine till mixture resembles coarse crumbs; sprinkle over batter. Bake in a 350° oven for 35 to 40 minutes or till golden. Serves 9.

Cherry Filling: Bring 1½ cups fresh *or* frozen unsweetened pitted tart *red cherries* to boiling; reduce heat. Cover and simmer for 5 minutes. Stir in 1 tablespoon *lemon juice.* Combine ½ cup *sugar* and 2 tablespoons *cornstarch;* add to cherry mixture. Cook and stir till bubbly. Cook and stir 2 minutes more. Cool completely.

Bacon Sourdough Muffins

                                       Oven 400°

Cook 3 slices *bacon* till crisp; drain and crumble. Set bacon aside. Stir together 1¾ cups *all-purpose flour,* ¼ cup *sugar,* 2½ teaspoons *baking powder,* and ¼ teaspoon *salt.* Make a well in the center. Combine 1 beaten *egg,* ½ cup *milk,* ½ cup *Sourdough Starter* (see recipe, opposite), and ⅓ cup *cooking oil;* add to dry mixture all at once. Stir just till moistened. Stir in bacon and ¼ cup shredded *cheddar cheese.* Grease muffin cups or line with paper bake cups; fill about ¾ full. Bake in a 400° oven for 20 to 25 minutes. Makes 12 muffins.

Dill Batter Bread

A no-knead yeast bread with a somewhat coarse texture.

2 **cups all-purpose flour**
1 **package active dry yeast**
½ **cup cream-style cottage cheese**
1 **tablespoon sugar**
1 **tablespoon dillseed *or* caraway seed**
1 **tablespoon margarine *or* butter**
1 **teaspoon dried minced onion**
1 **egg**
½ **cup toasted wheat germ**   Oven 375°

Combine *1 cup* flour and the yeast. Heat and stir cottage cheese, sugar, dillseed, margarine, onion, ½ cup *water,* and ½ teaspoon *salt* till warm (120° to 130°) and margarine almost melts. Add to flour mixture along with egg. Beat with an electric mixer on low speed 30 seconds, scraping bowl constantly. Beat on high speed 3 minutes.

Using a spoon, stir in wheat germ and remaining flour (batter will be stiff). Spoon into a well-greased 9x1½-inch round baking pan or a 1-quart casserole. Cover; let rise in a warm place till nearly double (50 to 60 minutes).

Bake in a 375° oven for 25 to 30 minutes or till golden brown. Remove from pan or casserole. Serve warm or cool. Makes 1 loaf (8 servings).

Saving Time with Quick-Rising Yeast

The bread recipes in this chapter were tested with active dry yeast. You can, however, prepare these recipes (except Sourdough Starter) using quick-rising active dry yeast. Just follow the same directions. The dough should rise in about a third less time, especially during the second rising step.

Egg Bread

The cinnamon-and-sugar-filled Cinnamon-Swirl Bread is great toasted and buttered for breakfast.

4¾ to 5¼ cups all-purpose flour
1 package active dry yeast
1⅓ cups milk
3 tablespoons sugar
3 tablespoons margarine or butter
½ teaspoon salt
2 eggs   Oven 375°

Combine *2 cups* of the flour and the yeast. In a saucepan heat and stir milk, sugar, margarine or butter, and salt till warm (120° to 130°) and margarine almost melts. Add to flour mixture along with eggs. Beat with an electric mixer on low speed for 30 seconds, scraping bowl constantly. Beat on high speed for 3 minutes. Using a spoon, stir in as much remaining flour as you can.

Turn out onto a lightly floured surface. Knead in enough of the remaining flour to make a moderately stiff dough that is smooth and elastic (6 to 8 minutes total). Shape into a ball. Place in a lightly greased bowl; turn once to grease surface. Cover and let rise in a warm place till double (about 60 minutes).

Punch dough down. Turn out onto a lightly floured surface. Divide in half. Cover and let rest 10 minutes. Lightly grease two 8x4x2-inch loaf pans. Shape each half of dough into a loaf. Place in pans. Cover and let rise till almost double (about 30 minutes). Bake in a 375° oven for 25 to 30 minutes or till done. Cover loosely the last 10 to 15 minutes of baking, if necessary. Remove from pans; cool. Makes 2 loaves (32 servings).

Raisin Egg-Bread Braid: Prepare as above, *except* add 2 cups *raisins* when stirring in flour with a spoon. (If desired, first plump the raisins by covering them with water in a saucepan. Bring to boiling. Remove from heat and let stand for 4 minutes. Drain.) When dough is punched down after first rising, turn out onto a lightly floured surface and divide into six portions. Cover; let rest 10 minutes. Roll each portion into a ball. Roll each ball into an evenly thick rope about 16 inches long. Line up *three* of the ropes, 1 inch apart, on a greased baking sheet. Starting in the middle, braid by bringing left rope *underneath* center rope; lay it down. Then bring right rope under new center rope; lay it down. Repeat to end. On the other end, braid by bringing outside ropes alternately *over* center rope to center. (Braid the ropes loosely so the bread has room to expand.) Press rope ends together to seal. Repeat braiding with remaining three ropes. Let rise and bake as at left. If desired, drizzle warm braids with Powdered Sugar Icing (see recipe, page 88). Makes 2 braids (32 servings).

Cinnamon-Swirl Egg Bread: Prepare Egg Bread as above, *except,* instead of shaping into loaves, on a lightly floured surface, roll each half of dough into a 12x7-inch rectangle. Brush lightly with water. Combine ½ cup *sugar* and 2 teaspoons ground *cinnamon*. Sprinkle *half* of the sugar-cinnamon mixture over *each* rectangle. Roll up from one of the short sides. Seal edge and ends. Place, seam side down, in greased loaf pans. Let rise and bake as at left. If desired, drizzle warm loaves with Powdered Sugar Icing (see recipe, page 88). Makes 2 loaves (32 servings).

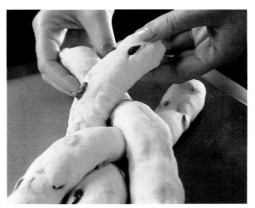

Braid the ropes of dough loosely, working from the center of each to the end.

Cornmeal Bubble Ring

Oven 375°

Combine 2½ cups *all-purpose flour* and 1 package *active dry yeast*. Heat and stir 2 cups *milk*, ¼ cup *margarine or butter*, 2 tablespoons *sugar*, and 1½ teaspoons *salt* till warm (120° to 130°) and margarine almost melts. Add to flour mixture. Beat with an electric mixer on low speed for 30 seconds, scraping bowl. Beat on high speed for 3 minutes. Using a spoon, stir in ¾ cup yellow *cornmeal*. Using 2¼ to 2¾ cups *all-purpose flour*, stir in as much flour as you can.

Turn out onto a floured surface. Knead in enough remaining flour to make a moderately stiff dough (6 to 8 minutes total). Shape into a ball in a greased bowl; turn once. Cover; let rise in a warm place till double (about 1 hour). Punch down. Turn out onto a floured surface. Divide into 4 portions. Divide each portion into 8 pieces (32 pieces total). Roll each piece into a ball. Dip balls into ¼ cup melted *margarine or butter*. Arrange balls in a greased 10-inch tube pan. Cover; let rise in a warm place till nearly double (35 to 45 minutes). Bake in a 375° oven for 40 to 45 minutes or till golden brown. Cover loosely with foil the last 10 to 15 minutes of baking, if necessary. Remove from pan immediately. Cool on a wire rack. Makes 1 ring (32 servings).

Cornmeal-Cheese Bubble Ring: Prepare as above, *except* add 1 cup shredded *cheddar or American cheese* to saucepan with milk mixture.

When to Use the Hand-Mixed Method

Most of our yeast breads use the electric-mixer method, which calls for the dry yeast to be combined directly with the flour. But if you don't have an electric mixer, or if you live in Canada, where the available yeast doesn't work well using this method, use the hand-mixed method described on page 38.

Here's how to convert recipes to this method. Change ¼ *cup* of the liquid to *warm* water; add yeast to dissolve. Heat remaining liquid and continue as directed in the instructions on page 38.

Chocolate Swirl Bread

Start the dough for this coffee bread a day ahead and let it rise in the refrigerator up to 24 hours. Then shape, let rise about 45 minutes, and bake.

  4½ **to 5 cups all-purpose flour**
  2   **packages active dry yeast**
  ¾   **cup sugar**
  ⅔   **cup water**
  ½   **cup margarine or butter**
  1   **5-ounce can (⅔ cup) evaporated milk**
  2   **eggs**
  1   **6-ounce package (1 cup) semisweet chocolate pieces**
  2   **tablespoons sugar**
  ¼   **to ½ teaspoon ground cinnamon**
      Streusel Topping   Oven 350°

Combine *2 cups* flour and the yeast. Heat and stir the ¾ cup sugar, the water, margarine, ⅓ *cup* evaporated milk, and ½ teaspoon *salt* till warm (120° to 130°) and margarine almost melts. Add to flour mixture along with eggs. Beat with an electric mixer on low speed for 30 seconds. Beat on high speed for 3 minutes. Using a spoon, stir in as much of the remaining flour as you can.

Turn out onto a lightly floured surface. Knead in enough remaining flour to make a moderately soft dough (3 to 5 minutes total). Shape into a ball in a greased bowl; turn once. Cover; let rise in a warm place till double (1¼ to 1½ hours).

Punch dough down. Turn out onto a lightly floured surface. Cover; let rest 10 minutes. Meanwhile, combine ¾ cup chocolate pieces (set aside remaining ¼ cup for Streusel Topping), remaining evaporated milk, the 2 tablespoons sugar, and the cinnamon. Cook and stir over low heat till chocolate melts; cool.

Roll dough into an 18x10-inch rectangle. Spread chocolate mixture to within ½ inch of edges. Roll up from one of the long sides. Pinch to seal. Bring ends together to form a ring; seal ends. Place, seam side down, in a greased 10-inch tube pan. Sprinkle Streusel Topping over dough. Cover; let rise till nearly double (about 45 minutes). Bake on lower rack in a 350° oven for 45 to 50 minutes. Cool 15 minutes; remove from pan. Makes 1 coffee cake (12 servings).

Streusel Topping: Stir together ¼ cup *all-purpose flour*, ¼ cup *sugar*, and 1 teaspoon ground *cinnamon*. Cut in ¼ cup *margarine or butter*. Stir in ¼ cup chopped *nuts* and the remaining *chocolate pieces*.

Stollen

This sweet German favorite is packed with fruits and nuts.

    4   to 4½ cups all-purpose flour
    1   package active dry yeast
    ¼   teaspoon ground cardamom
    1¼ cups milk
    ½   cup margarine *or* butter
    ¼   cup sugar
    1   egg
    1   cup raisins *or* currants
    ¼   cup diced mixed candied fruits and
        peels
    ¼   cup chopped blanched almonds
    1   tablespoon finely shredded orange
        peel
    1   tablespoon finely shredded lemon
        peel
    1   cup sifted powdered sugar
    2   tablespoons hot water
    ½   teaspoon margarine
        or butter   Oven 375°

In a large mixing bowl combine *2 cups* flour, the yeast, and cardamom. In a saucepan heat and stir milk, the ½ cup margarine or butter, the sugar, and ½ teaspoon *salt* till warm (120° to 130°) and margarine almost melts. Add to flour mixture along with egg. Beat with an electric mixer on low speed for 30 seconds, scraping bowl constantly. Beat on high speed for 3 minutes. Using a spoon, stir in as much of the remaining flour as you can. Stir in raisins or currants, candied fruits and peels, almonds, and orange and lemon peels.

Turn out onto a lightly floured surface. Knead in enough remaining flour to make a moderately soft dough that is smooth and elastic (3 to 5 minutes total). Shape into a ball. Place in a greased bowl; turn once. Cover; let rise in a warm place till double (about 1¾ hours).

Punch dough down. Turn out onto a lightly floured surface. Divide into thirds. Cover; let rest 10 minutes. Roll one portion of the dough into a 10x6-inch oval. Without stretching, fold one of the long sides over to within 1 inch of the opposite side; press edges lightly to seal. Place on a greased baking sheet; repeat with remaining dough. Cover; let rise till nearly double (about 1 hour). Bake in a 375° oven for 18 to 20 minutes or till golden. Remove from baking sheet; cool 30 minutes. Combine powdered sugar, hot water, and the ½ teaspoon margarine or butter; brush over warm bread. Makes 3 loaves (48 servings).

Apple-Streusel Ladder Loaf

Use tart apples like Jonathans, Granny Smiths, or Winesaps for this blue-ribbon bread.

    1   16-ounce loaf frozen sweet bread
        dough *or* frozen bread dough,
        thawed
    2   tablespoons margarine *or* butter,
        softened
    ¼   cup packed brown sugar
    1   tablespoon all-purpose flour
    1   teaspoon ground cinnamon
    2   cups finely chopped peeled apples
        Milk
    2   tablespoons all-purpose flour
    2   tablespoons sugar
    1   tablespoon margarine *or* butter
    ¼   cup slivered almonds
        (optional)   Oven 350°

Divide bread dough in half. On a lightly floured surface, roll each half into an 8-inch square. (For easier rolling, let dough rest a few minutes.) Spread *each* square with *1 tablespoon* softened margarine or butter. For filling, combine brown sugar, the 1 tablespoon flour, and the cinnamon. Add apples; toss to coat.

Spoon *half* of the filling down the center of *each* square. Cutting from the right edge toward the filling, make 2½-inch-long cuts in dough at 1-inch intervals. Repeat from the left edge. Fold strips alternately over filling; fold under ends.

Place loaves on a greased 15x10x1-inch baking pan. Brush with milk. Combine the 2 tablespoons flour and the sugar. Cut in the 1 tablespoon margarine till mixture resembles coarse crumbs. Sprinkle *half* of the crumb mixture over *each* loaf. Top with almonds, if desired. Cover and let loaves rise till nearly double (45 to 60 minutes).

Bake in a 350° oven 30 minutes or till golden. Serve warm. Makes 2 loaves (32 servings).

Fruit-Studded Bread

Maybe you know this rich yeast bread by its Scandinavian name, julekage.

4¾   **to 5¼ cups all-purpose flour**
  2   **packages active dry yeast**
  ¾   **teaspoon ground cardamom**
1¼   **cups milk**
  ½   **cup sugar**
  ½   **cup margarine *or* butter**
  1   **egg**
  1   **cup diced mixed candied fruits
        and peels**
  1   **cup light raisins**
  1   **slightly beaten egg yolk**
  2   **tablespoons water**
  1   **cup sifted powdered sugar**
  ¼   **teaspoon vanilla**
        Milk
        Almonds (optional)
        **Candied cherries
        (optional)**   Oven 375°

Combine *2 cups* of the flour, the yeast, and cardamom. Heat and stir the 1¼ cups milk, the sugar, margarine, and ½ teaspoon *salt* till warm (120° to 130°) and margarine almost melts. Add to flour mixture along with egg. Beat with an electric mixer on low speed for 30 seconds, scraping bowl. Beat on high speed for 3 minutes. Using a spoon, stir in candied fruits and peels, raisins, and as much of the remaining flour as you can.

Turn out onto a lightly floured surface. Knead in enough of the remaining flour to make a moderately stiff dough that is smooth and elastic (6 to 8 minutes total). Shape into a ball. Place dough in a greased bowl; turn once. Cover; let rise in a warm place till double (about 1½ hours).

Punch dough down. Turn out onto a lightly floured surface. Divide in half. Cover; let rest 10 minutes. Shape into 2 round loaves. Place on a greased baking sheet. Flatten each slightly to a 6-inch diameter. Cover; let rise in a warm place till nearly double (45 to 60 minutes). Combine egg yolk and water; brush over loaves.

Bake in a 375° oven for 30 to 35 minutes or till golden. Cover loosely with foil the last 10 to 15 minutes, if necessary. Remove from baking sheet. Cool completely on a wire rack.

Meanwhile, for glaze, combine powdered sugar, vanilla, and enough milk to make of drizzling consistency. Drizzle glaze over cooled loaves. Garnish with almonds and candied cherries, if desired. Makes 2 loaves (24 servings).

Kuchen

Brunch guests will gobble up this warm-from-the-oven fruit-filled coffee cake.

  3   **cups all-purpose flour**
  1   **package active dry yeast**
  ¾   **cup milk**
  ⅓   **cup margarine *or* butter**
  ⅓   **cup sugar**
  ½   **teaspoon salt**
  2   **eggs**
  1   **beaten egg**
  3   **tablespoons light cream *or* milk**
  1   **cup sugar**
1½   **teaspoons ground cinnamon**
  2   **cups thinly sliced peeled apples***
        **or peaches, sliced plums,
        or cottage cheese**   Oven 375°

In a mixing bowl combine *1½ cups* of the flour and the yeast. In a saucepan heat and stir milk, margarine or butter, the ⅓ cup sugar, and the salt till warm (120° to 130°) and margarine or butter almost melts. Add to flour mixture along with the 2 eggs. Beat with an electric mixer on low speed for 30 seconds, scraping bowl constantly. Beat on high speed for 3 minutes. Using a spoon, stir in remaining flour.

Divide dough mixture in half. With lightly greased fingers, pat evenly into two greased 9x9x2-inch or 11x7x1½-inch baking pans, pressing dough up the sides of each pan slightly to form a rim. Cover and let rise in a warm place till double (45 to 50 minutes).

Combine the beaten egg and light cream. Stir in the 1 cup sugar and the cinnamon. If using fruit, arrange atop raised dough. Carefully spoon cream-sugar mixture over fruit. (If using cottage cheese, stir into cream-sugar mixture. Spoon atop raised dough.) Bake in a 375° oven for 18 to 20 minutes. Cool slightly. Cut into squares; serve warm. Makes 2 coffee cakes (18 servings).

Prune Kuchen: Prepare as above, *except* omit apples, peaches, plums, or cottage cheese. While dough is rising, make prune filling. In a saucepan combine 1½ cups coarsely snipped pitted *prunes* and enough water to come 1 inch above prunes. Bring to boiling. Reduce heat and simmer, covered, for 10 minutes; drain. Spoon cooked prunes atop raised dough. Carefully spoon cream-sugar mixture over fruit.

***Note:** If using apples, simmer the sliced fruit, covered, in water about 2 minutes or just till tender. Drain well; place atop dough.

English Muffins

5¼ to 5¾ cups all-purpose flour
2 packages active dry yeast
2 cups milk
¼ cup shortening, margarine, *or* butter
2 tablespoons sugar
1 teaspoon salt
Cornmeal   Oven 375°

In a mixing bowl combine *2 cups* of the flour and the yeast. In a saucepan heat and stir milk, shortening, sugar, and salt till warm (120° to 130°) and shortening almost melts. Add to flour mixture. Beat with an electric mixer on low speed for 30 seconds, scraping bowl constantly. Beat on high speed for 3 minutes. Using a spoon, stir in as much of the remaining flour as you can.

Turn out onto a lightly floured surface. Knead in enough remaining flour to make a moderately stiff dough that is smooth and elastic (6 to 8 minutes total). Shape into a ball. Place in greased bowl; turn once to grease surface. Cover; let rise in a warm place till double (about 1 hour).

Punch dough down. Turn out onto a lightly floured surface. Cover; let rest for 10 minutes. Roll dough to slightly less than ½ inch thick. Cut with a 4-inch-round cutter, rerolling scraps. Dip both sides of each muffin into cornmeal. (If necessary, to make cornmeal adhere, lightly brush muffins with water.) Cover; let rise in a warm place till very light (about 30 minutes).

Cook muffins, four at a time, in an ungreased electric skillet at 325° for 25 to 30 minutes or till done, turning every 5 minutes. (Keep any remaining muffins in the refrigerator for up to 8 hours.) *Or,* cook over low heat on an ungreased large griddle or several skillets for 25 to 30 minutes, turning frequently. Cool thoroughly. Split muffins horizontally. Toast or broil muffin halves before serving. Makes about 12 muffins.

Whole Wheat English Muffins: Prepare as above, *except* substitute 1½ cups *whole wheat flour* and ½ cup *cracked wheat* for 2 cups of the stirred-in all-purpose flour.

English-Muffin Loaves: Prepare as above, *except* reduce flour to *5 cups. Do not knead.* Batter will be stiff. Grease two 8x4x2-inch loaf pans. Sprinkle lightly with *cornmeal.* Spoon batter into pans. Sprinkle tops lightly with *cornmeal.* Cover; let rise till nearly double (about 45 minutes). Bake in a 375° oven about 35 minutes or till done. Remove from pans immediately. Cool on wire racks. Makes 2 loaves (32 servings).

Pita Bread

Follow the rolling directions carefully. If you overwork the dough, it won't puff during baking.

3¼ to 3¾ cups all-purpose flour
1 package active dry yeast
1¼ cups water
2 tablespoons shortening,
    margarine, *or* butter
¾ teaspoon salt   Oven 450°

In a mixing bowl combine *1¼ cups* of the flour and the yeast. In a saucepan heat and stir water, shortening, and salt till warm (120° to 130°) and shortening almost melts. Add to flour mixture. Beat with an electric mixer on low speed for 30 seconds, scraping bowl constantly. Beat on high speed for 3 minutes. Using a spoon, stir in as much of the remaining flour as you can.

Turn out onto a lightly floured surface. Knead in enough remaining flour to make a moderately soft dough that is smooth and elastic (3 to 5 minutes total). Cover; let rest in a warm place for 15 minutes. Divide dough into 12 equal portions.

Roll each dough portion between well-floured hands into a *very* smooth ball. Cover the dough balls with plastic wrap or a damp cloth and let rest for 10 minutes. Gently flatten balls with your fingers, making sure not to crease dough. Cover; let rest for 10 minutes. (Keep the dough balls covered till ready to use.)

On a well-floured surface, lightly roll *one* dough ball into a 7-inch round, *turning dough over once* while rolling. Roll dough from center to edge. *Do not stretch, puncture, or crease dough.* Repeat rolling with another ball of dough. (Work with enough flour on the surface so that the dough does not stick.)

Place *two* dough rounds on a preheated ungreased baking sheet. Bake in a 450° oven about 3 minutes or till bread is puffed and softly set. Turn over with a wide spatula. Bake about 2 minutes more or till bread begins to lightly brown. Cool slightly on a wire rack. While still warm, place bread in a paper sack or plastic bag to keep it soft and prevent it from drying out.

Repeat with remaining dough, baking one batch before rolling and baking the next batch. To serve, halve each pita crosswise. Fill as desired. Makes 12.

Whole Wheat Pita Bread: Prepare as above, *except* substitute 2 cups *whole wheat flour* for 2 cups of the stirred-in all-purpose flour.

Pretzels

Shaping a pretzel isn't hard, but you may need a couple of practice twists to get the knack.

  4 to 4½ cups all-purpose flour
  1 package active dry yeast
1½ cups milk
  ¼ cup sugar
  2 tablespoons cooking oil
  1 teaspoon salt
  2 tablespoons salt
  3 quarts boiling water
  1 slightly beaten egg white
  1 tablespoon water
    Sesame seed, poppy seed, or
      coarse salt   Oven 475°

In a mixing bowl stir together *1½ cups* of the flour and the yeast. In a saucepan heat and stir milk, sugar, oil, and the 1 teaspoon salt till warm (120° to 130°). Add to flour mixture. Beat with an electric mixer on low speed for 30 seconds, scraping bowl constantly. Beat on high speed for 3 minutes. Using a spoon, stir in as much of the remaining flour as you can.

Turn out onto a lightly floured surface. Knead in enough of the remaining flour to make a moderately stiff dough that is smooth and elastic (6 to 8 minutes total). Shape dough into a ball. Place dough in a greased bowl; turn once to grease surface. Cover and let rise in a warm place till double (about 1¼ hours).

Punch dough down. Turn out onto a lightly floured surface. Cover; let rest 10 minutes. Roll dough into a 12x10-inch rectangle. Cut into twenty 12x½-inch strips. Gently pull each strip into a rope about 16 inches long.

Shape each pretzel by crossing one end over the other to form a circle, overlapping about 4 inches from each end. Take one end of dough in each hand and twist once at the point where the dough overlaps. Carefully lift each end across to the edge of the circle opposite it. Tuck ends under edges to make a pretzel shape. Moisten ends; press to seal.

Place pretzels on greased baking sheets. Bake in a 475° oven for 4 minutes. Remove from oven. Lower oven temperature to 350°.

Dissolve the 2 tablespoons salt in the boiling water. Lower pretzels, three or four at a time, into boiling water. Boil for 2 minutes, turning once. Remove with a slotted spoon; drain on paper towels. Let stand a few seconds, then place about ½ inch apart on well-greased baking sheets.

Combine egg white and the 1 tablespoon water. Brush pretzels with a little of the egg white and water mixture. Sprinkle pretzels lightly with sesame seed, poppy seed, or coarse salt. Bake in a 350° oven for 20 to 25 minutes or till golden brown. Remove from baking sheets. Cool on wire racks. Makes 20 pretzels.

Whole Wheat Pretzels: Prepare as above, *except* reduce all-purpose flour to *2¾ to 3¼ cups.* Combine 1 cup *whole wheat flour* and ⅓ cup toasted *wheat germ* with the stirred-in all-purpose flour.

Twist once where the dough overlaps. Lift ends across to opposite edges; tuck ends under.

Dinner Rolls

Whole Wheat Dinner Rolls in rosette, cloverleaf, and butterhorn shapes are pictured on page 33.

4¼ to 4¾ **cups all-purpose flour**
 1 **package active dry yeast**
 1 **cup milk**
 ⅓ **cup sugar**
 ⅓ **cup shortening, margarine, or butter**
 ½ **teaspoon salt**
 2 **eggs**   Oven 375°

Combine *2 cups* of the flour and the yeast. Heat and stir milk, sugar, shortening, and salt just till warm (120° to 130°) and shortening almost melts. Add to flour mixture along with eggs. Beat with an electric mixer on low speed for 30 seconds, scraping bowl constantly. Beat on high speed for 3 minutes. Using a spoon, stir in as much of the remaining flour as you can.

Turn dough out onto a lightly floured surface. Knead in enough remaining flour to make a moderately stiff dough that is smooth and elastic (6 to 8 minutes total). Shape dough into a ball. Place dough in a greased bowl; turn once to grease surface. Cover and let rise in a warm place till double (about 1 hour).

Punch dough down. Turn out onto a lightly floured surface. Divide dough in half. Cover and let rest for 10 minutes. Shape the dough into desired rolls (see directions, opposite). Cover and let rise in a warm place till nearly double (about 30 minutes).

Bake in a 375° oven for 12 to 15 minutes or till golden brown. Makes 24 to 32 rolls.

Brown-and-Serve Dinner Rolls: Prepare as above, *except* bake in a 325° oven for 10 minutes; *do not brown.* Remove rolls from baking sheets or pans; cool. Wrap in moisture- and vaporproof material. Seal, label, and *freeze.* To serve, thaw frozen rolls in open packages at room temperature for 10 to 15 minutes. Unwrap completely. Place on ungreased baking sheets. Bake in a 375° oven about 10 minutes or till golden.

Batter Dinner Rolls: Prepare as above, *except* reduce stirred-in flour to *1¼ cups.* (Use a total of 3¼ cups all-purpose flour.) Spoon batter into greased muffin cups, filling half full. Cover and let rise in a warm place till nearly double (about 45 minutes). Brush roll tops with *milk,* and, if desired, sprinkle with poppy seed or sesame seed. Bake in a 375° oven for 15 to 18 minutes or till done. Makes 18 rolls.

Herb-Onion Dinner Rolls: Prepare as above, *except* add 1 tablespoon *dried minced onion* and ½ teaspoon dried *basil, oregano, or Italian seasoning,* crushed, to milk mixture.

Whole Wheat Dinner Rolls: Prepare as above, *except* substitute 1¼ cups *whole wheat flour* for 1¼ cups of the stirred-in all-purpose flour.

Hamburger or Frankfurter Buns: Prepare as above, *except* divide dough into 12 portions. Cover and let rest for 10 minutes. For *hamburger buns,* shape each portion into an even circle, folding edges under. Press flat between your hands. Place on a greased baking sheet. Press into a 4-inch circle. For *frankfurter buns,* shape each portion into a roll about 5½ inches long, tapering ends. Place on a greased baking sheet. Let buns rise. Makes 12 buns.

Wheat and Cottage Cheese Rolls

1½ **cups cream-style cottage cheese**
   Milk
4¼ to 4¾ **cups whole wheat flour**
 1 **package active dry yeast**
 ⅓ **cup packed brown sugar**
 ⅓ **cup margarine *or* butter**
 2 **eggs**   Oven 375°

Drain cottage cheese, reserving liquid. Add milk to reserved liquid to measure ¾ cup. Set aside.

Combine *1½ cups* flour and the yeast. Heat and stir cottage cheese, reserved milk mixture, brown sugar, margarine, and ½ teaspoon *salt* till warm (120° to 130°) and margarine almost melts. Add to flour mixture along with eggs. Beat with an electric mixer on low speed for 30 seconds, scraping bowl constantly. Beat on high speed for 3 minutes. Using a spoon, stir in as much of the remaining flour as you can.

Turn out onto a lightly floured surface. Knead in enough remaining flour to make a moderately stiff dough that is smooth and elastic (8 to 10 minutes total). Shape into a ball. Place in a greased bowl; turn once. Cover; let rise in a warm place till double (30 to 45 minutes).

Punch dough down. Turn out onto a lightly floured surface. Cover; let rest 10 minutes. Shape into 24 smooth balls. Place in greased muffin pans. Cover; let rise in a warm place till nearly double (about 20 minutes). Bake in a 375° oven for 12 to 15 minutes or till done. Makes 24 rolls.

To make Butterhorns, lightly grease baking sheets. On a lightly floured surface, roll each *half* of dough into a 12-inch circle. Brush with melted *margarine or butter.* Cut *each* circle into *12* wedges. To shape, begin at wide end of wedge and roll toward point. Place, point side down, 2 to 3 inches apart on baking sheets. Let rise and bake as directed opposite. Makes 24 rolls.

To make Rosettes, lightly grease baking sheets. Divide each *half* of dough into 16 pieces. On a lightly floured surface, roll each piece into a 12-inch rope. Tie in a loose knot, leaving 2 long ends. Tuck top end under roll. Bring bottom end up and tuck into center of roll. Place 2 to 3 inches apart on baking sheet. Let rise and bake as directed opposite. Makes 32 rolls.

To make Parker House Rolls, lightly grease baking sheets. On a lightly floured surface, roll each *half* of dough to ¼-inch thickness. Cut with a floured 2½-inch-round cutter. Brush with melted *margarine or butter.* Use the dull edge of a table knife to make an off-center crease in each round. Fold each round along the crease so the large half is on top. Press folded edge firmly. (Dough will recede during baking, making the top half shorter than the bottom one.) Place rolls 2 to 3 inches apart on baking sheets. Let rise and bake as directed opposite. Makes 30 rolls.

To make Cloverleaves, lightly grease 24 muffin cups. Divide each *half* of dough into 36 pieces. Shape each piece into a ball, pulling edges under to make a smooth top. Place *three* balls in *each* greased muffin cup, smooth side up. Let rise; bake as directed opposite. Makes 24.
To make Shortcut Cloverleaves, lightly grease 24 muffin cups. Divide each *half* of dough into 12 pieces. Shape each piece into a ball. Place *one* ball in *each* muffin cup. With floured scissors, snip top in half, then snip again to make 4 points. Let rise; bake as directed opposite. Makes 24.

Bagels

Three steps—broiling, boiling, and baking—give bagels their crusty, glazed appearance and typically chewy texture.

   4¼ to 4¾ cups all-purpose flour
   1 package active dry yeast
   1½ cups warm water (120° to 130°)
   ¼ cup sugar   Oven 375°

Combine 2 *cups* of the flour and the yeast. Add warm water, *3 tablespoons* of the sugar, and 1 teaspoon *salt.* Beat with an electric mixer on low speed for 30 seconds, scraping bowl constantly. Beat on high speed for 3 minutes. Using a spoon, stir in as much remaining flour as you can.

   Turn out onto a lightly floured surface. Knead in enough remaining flour to make a moderately stiff dough that is smooth and elastic (6 to 8 minutes total). Cover; let rest 10 minutes. Working quickly, divide dough into 12 portions. Shape each portion into a smooth ball. Punch a hole in the center of each ball with a floured finger. Pull dough gently to make about a 2-inch hole, keeping bagel uniformly shaped. Place on a greased baking sheet. Cover; let rise for 20 minutes. (Start timing after first bagel is shaped.)

   Broil raised bagels about 5 inches from heat for 3 to 4 minutes, turning once (tops should not brown). Meanwhile, in a 12-inch skillet or 4½-quart Dutch oven bring 6 cups *water* and remaining 1 tablespoon sugar to boiling. Reduce heat and simmer bagels, four or five at a time, for 7 minutes, turning once. Drain on paper towels. Place drained bagels on a well-greased baking sheet. Bake in a 375° oven for 25 to 30 minutes or till tops are golden brown. Makes 12 bagels.

   Light Rye Bagels: Prepare as above, *except* stir 1 teaspoon caraway seed, if desired, in with the yeast. Substitute 1½ cups *rye flour* for 1½ cups of the stirred-in all-purpose flour.

   Herb Bagels: Prepare as above, *except* stir 1½ teaspoons dried *basil,* crushed; 1½ teaspoons dried *dillweed; or* 1 to 1½ teaspoons *garlic powder* in with the yeast.

   Onion Bagels: Prepare as above, *except* stir 2 tablespoons *dried minced onion* and, if desired, 2 tablespoons cooked bacon pieces into the flour with the yeast.

   Whole Wheat Bagels: Prepare as above, *except* substitute 1½ cups *whole wheat flour* for 1½ cups of the stirred-in all-purpose flour. Stir ¾ cup raisins, if desired, in with whole wheat flour.

Brioche

These egg- and butter-rich rolls are shaped like fat buns with topknots.

   1 package active dry yeast
   ¼ cup warm water (105° to 115°)
   ½ cup margarine or butter
   ⅓ cup sugar
   ¾ teaspoon salt
   4 cups all-purpose flour
   ½ cup milk
   4 eggs
   1 tablespoon water   Oven 375°

Soften yeast in the ¼ cup warm water. In a mixing bowl beat margarine or butter, sugar, and salt till fluffy. Add *1 cup* of the flour and the milk to beaten mixture. Separate *one* of the eggs. Add yolk and remaining 3 eggs to beaten mixture (refrigerate the egg white in a covered container). Add softened yeast and beat well. Using a spoon, stir in the remaining flour till smooth. Place in a greased bowl. Cover; let rise in a warm place till double (about 2 hours), then refrigerate dough for 6 hours. (*Or,* omit the 2-hour rising time and refrigerate the dough up to 24 hours.)

   Stir dough down. Turn out onto a lightly floured surface. Divide dough into 4 portions; set 1 portion aside. Divide each of the remaining 3 portions into 8 pieces, making a total of 24.

   With floured hands, form each piece into a ball, tucking under edges. Place in greased muffin cups. Divide reserved dough portion into 24 pieces; shape into balls. With a floured finger, make an indentation in each large ball. Press a small ball into each indentation.

   Combine reserved egg white and the 1 tablespoon water; brush over rolls. Cover; let rise in a warm place till nearly double (45 to 55 minutes).

   Bake in a 375° oven about 15 minutes or till golden brown, brushing again with egg white and water mixture after 7 minutes. Remove from pans. Cool on wire racks. Makes 24 rolls.

   Individual-brioche-pan directions: Prepare dough as above. After dividing dough into 4 portions and setting 1 portion aside, divide each of the remaining 3 portions into 6 pieces, making a total of 18. Form each piece into a ball. Place in 18 greased individual brioche pans. Divide reserved dough portion into 18 pieces; shape into balls. Place *one* small ball atop *each* larger ball. Makes 18 rolls.

Sweet Rolls

Oven 375°

Combine 2 cups *all-purpose flour* and 1 package *active dry yeast.* Heat and stir 1 cup *milk,* ⅓ cup *sugar,* ⅓ cup *margarine or butter,* and ½ teaspoon *salt* till warm (120° to 130°) and margarine almost melts. Add to flour mixture along with 2 *eggs.* Beat with an electric mixer on low speed 30 seconds, scraping bowl. Beat on high speed 3 minutes. Using a spoon, stir in as much of 2 to 2½ cups *all-purpose flour* as you can.

Turn out onto a lightly floured surface. Knead in enough of the remaining flour to make a moderately stiff dough that is smooth and elastic (6 to 8 minutes total). Shape into a ball. Place in a lightly greased bowl; turn once. Cover; let rise in a warm place till double (about 1 hour).

Punch dough down. Divide in half. Cover; let rest 10 minutes. Shape and bake as directed below. Serve warm, if desired. Makes 24 rolls.

Caramel-Pecan Rolls: While dough is rising, combine ⅔ cup packed *brown sugar,* ¼ cup *margarine or butter,* and 2 tablespoons *light corn syrup.* Cook and stir till combined. Divide between two 9x1½-inch round baking pans. Sprinkle *each* pan with ⅓ cup chopped *pecans.* Set the pans aside.

Roll *half* of the dough into a 12x8-inch rectangle. Melt 3 tablespoons *margarine or butter;* brush *half* of margarine over dough. Combine ½ cup *sugar* and 1 teaspoon ground *cinnamon;* sprinkle *half* of mixture over dough. Roll up from one of the long sides. Seal seams. Slice dough into 12 pieces. Repeat with remaining dough, margarine, and sugar mixture. Place rolls in pans. Cover; let rise till nearly double (about 30 minutes). Bake in a 375° oven for 20 to 25 minutes. Invert onto a serving plate.

Cinnamon Rolls: Roll *half* of the dough into a 12x8-inch rectangle. Melt 3 tablespoons *margarine or butter;* brush *half* of margarine over dough. Combine ½ cup *sugar* and 2 teaspoons ground *cinnamon;* sprinkle *half* of mixture over dough. If desired, measure ¾ cup raisins; sprinkle *half* of raisins over dough. Roll up from one of the long sides. Seal seams. Slice dough into 12 pieces. Repeat with remaining dough, margarine, sugar mixture, and raisins. Place rolls in two greased 9x1½-inch round baking pans. Cover; let rise till nearly double (about 30 minutes). Bake in a 375° oven for 20 to 25 minutes. Cool slightly; remove from pans. Drizzle with *Powdered Sugar Icing* (see recipe, page 88).

Brush dough rectangle with margarine; sprinkle with sugar mixture. Roll up from a long side.

Place a piece of heavy-duty thread under dough. Crisscross thread over dough, pulling quickly.

Croissants

You don't have to be a pro to make croissants with our easy method.

1½ **cups cold butter**
3 **cups all-purpose flour**
1½ **cups all-purpose flour**
1 **package active dry yeast**
1¼ **cups milk**
¼ **cup sugar**
½ **teaspoon salt**
1 **egg**
¼ **to ½ cup all-purpose flour**
1 **egg**
1 **tablespoon water *or* milk**   Oven 375°

Cut butter into ½-inch slices. Stir butter slices into the 3 cups flour till coated and separated; chill. Combine the 1½ cups of flour and the yeast. Heat and stir milk, sugar, and salt till warm (120° to 130°). Add to flour-yeast mixture along with 1 egg. Beat with an electric mixer on low speed for 30 seconds, scraping bowl constantly. Beat on high speed for 3 minutes. Using a spoon, stir in the chilled butter-flour mixture till flour is well moistened (butter will stay in large pieces).

Sprinkle a pastry cloth or surface with the ¼ cup flour. Turn dough out onto floured surface. With floured hands, knead dough very gently *about eight times.* With a well-floured rolling pin, roll dough into a 21x12-inch rectangle (sprinkle surface with enough remaining flour to prevent sticking, if necessary). Fold dough crosswise into thirds to form a 12x7-inch rectangle. Wrap loosely; place in freezer for 20 to 30 minutes (or in re-frigerator for 1½ hours) or till dough is firm but not excessively stiff.

On a floured surface, roll again into a 21x12-inch rectangle. Fold into thirds again and give dough a quarter-turn; roll, fold, and turn twice more, flouring surface as needed (it's not neces-sary to chill dough between rolling times). Place dough in a plastic bag; seal, leaving room for expansion. Chill dough for 4 to 24 hours.

Cut dough crosswise into fourths. Return 3 pieces to refrigerator till ready to use. On a lightly floured surface, roll dough into a 16x8-inch rect-angle. Cut rectangle in half crosswise, forming 2 squares. Cut each square in half diagonally, for a total of 4 triangles. Roll up each triangle *loosely,* starting from an 8-inch side and rolling toward the opposite point. Repeat rolling, cutting, and shaping with remaining 3 portions of dough. Place rolls on ungreased baking sheets, points

down; curve ends. Cover; let rise till almost dou-ble (about 1 hour). Beat 1 egg with water or milk; brush lightly over rolls. Bake in a 375° oven about 15 minutes or till golden. Remove from baking sheets; cool. Makes 16.

Filled Croissants: Prepare as above, *except* cut each 16x8-inch rectangle into four 8x4-inch rectangles. Combine one 8-ounce package *cream cheese,* softened; ¼ cup *sugar;* and 2 teaspoons *finely shredded orange peel.* Fill center of *each* rectangle with *1 tablespoon* cream cheese mix-ture. (*Or,* fill center of *each* rectangle with 1 table-spoon *semisweet chocolate pieces or fruit preserves.*) Brush edges with egg mixture. Fold short sides in over filling to overlap in center (you'll have approximately 3½x4-inch bundles). Pinch edges to seal. Place on ungreased baking sheets, seam side down.

Stir the chilled butter-flour mixture into the yeast mixture. The butter will remain in large pieces.

Roll up triangles *loosely,* starting from an 8-inch side and rolling toward the opposite point.

Hot Cross Buns

Oven 375°

Combine 1½ cups *all-purpose flour,* 1 package *active dry yeast,* and 1 teaspoon ground *cinnamon.* Heat and stir ¾ cup *milk,* ½ cup *cooking oil,* ⅓ cup *sugar,* and ½ teaspoon *salt* till warm (120° to 130°). Add to flour mixture along with 3 *eggs.* Beat with an electric mixer on low speed for 30 seconds, scraping bowl. Beat on high speed for 3 minutes. Using a spoon, stir in ⅔ cup *currants or raisins* and as much of 2 to 2¾ cups *all-purpose flour* as you can. Turn out onto a floured surface. Knead in enough remaining flour to make a moderately soft dough (3 to 5 minutes total). Shape into a ball in a greased bowl; turn once. Cover; let rise till double (about 1½ hours).

Punch down. Turn out onto floured surface. Cover; let rest 10 minutes. Divide into 20 portions; shape into smooth balls. Place 1½ inches apart on a greased baking sheet. Cover; let rise till nearly double (30 to 45 minutes). Make a crisscross slash across each. Brush with 1 slightly beaten *egg white.* Bake in a 375° oven for 12 to 15 minutes or till golden brown. Cool slightly. Drizzle buns with *Powdered Sugar Icing* (see recipe, page 88). Serve warm. Makes 20.

Yeast Doughnuts

Combine 1½ cups *all-purpose flour* and 2 packages *active dry yeast.* Heat and stir ¾ cup *milk;* ⅓ cup *sugar;* ¼ cup *shortening, margarine, or butter;* and ½ teaspoon *salt* till warm (120° to 130°) and shortening almost melts. Add to flour; add 2 *eggs.* Beat with an electric mixer on low speed for 30 seconds, scraping bowl. Beat on high for 3 minutes. Using a spoon, stir in as much of 1½ to 2 cups *all-purpose flour* as you can. Turn out onto a floured surface. Knead in enough remaining flour to make a moderately soft dough (3 to 5 minutes total). Shape into a ball in a greased bowl; turn once. Cover; let rise in a warm place till double (45 to 60 minutes).

Punch down. Turn out onto a floured surface. Divide in half. Cover; let rest 10 minutes. Roll each half to ½-inch thickness. Cut with a floured doughnut cutter. Reroll and cut trimmings. Cover; let rise till *very light* (45 to 60 minutes). Heat *cooking oil for deep-fat frying* to 365°. Carefully fry doughnuts, 2 or 3 at a time, about 2 minutes, turning once; drain. Glaze with *Powdered Sugar Icing* (see recipe, page 88). Makes 16 to 18.

Cinnamon Crisps

These buttery, cinnamon-sugar-filled rounds are the homemade version of what bakeries call elephant ears or crispies.

3¾ to 4¼ cups all-purpose flour
** 1 package active dry yeast**
1¼ cups milk
** ¼ cup sugar**
** ¼ cup shortening, margarine, or**
**   butter**
** 1 egg**
** ½ cup sugar**
** ½ cup packed brown sugar**
** ½ cup margarine or butter, melted**
1½ teaspoons ground cinnamon
** 1 cup sugar**
** ½ cup chopped pecans**   Oven 400°

Combine *2 cups* of the flour and the yeast. Heat and stir milk, the ¼ cup sugar, shortening, and ½ teaspoon *salt* till warm (120° to 130°) and shortening almost melts. Add to flour mixture along with egg. Beat with an electric mixer on low speed for 30 seconds, scraping bowl. Beat on high speed for 3 minutes. Using a spoon, stir in as much of the remaining flour as you can.

Turn out onto a lightly floured surface. Knead in enough remaining flour to make a moderately soft dough (3 to 5 minutes total). Shape into a ball. Place in a greased bowl; turn once. Cover; let rise in a warm place till double (1 to 1½ hours).

Punch dough down. Turn out onto a lightly floured surface. Divide in half. Cover; let rest for 10 minutes. Roll *half* of the dough into a 12-inch square. Combine the ½ cup sugar, brown sugar, *¼ cup* melted margarine or butter, and *½ teaspoon* ground cinnamon; crumble *half* of mixture over dough. Roll up from one of the long sides. Seal seams. Cut into 12 pieces. Place on a floured surface 3 to 4 inches apart. Flatten rolls to about 3 inches in diameter. Repeat with remaining dough. Cover; let rise in a warm place till nearly double (about 30 minutes). Place on baking sheets 7 to 8 inches apart. Cover with waxed paper or plastic wrap. Use a rolling pin to flatten rolls to about 6 inches in diameter; remove paper.

Brush rolls with remaining melted margarine or butter. Combine the 1 cup sugar, pecans, and remaining ground cinnamon. Sprinkle over rolls. Cover with waxed paper or plastic wrap; roll flat again. Remove paper. Bake in a 400° oven for 8 to 10 minutes. Remove from baking sheets immediately; cool. Makes 24.

Quick Breads

For mouth-watering breads that don't require a lot of time, turn to quick breads. By using baking powder, baking soda, steam, or air instead of yeast to leaven dough, you can have hot breads to serve in a flash.

In this section, you'll find everything from tender Corn Bread and Refrigerator Bran Muffins to featherlight Waffles and Pancakes.

Banana Bread

> 1¾ **cups all-purpose flour**
> ⅔ **cup sugar**
> 2 **teaspoons baking powder**
> ½ **teaspoon baking soda**
> ¼ **teaspoon salt**
> 1 **cup mashed ripe banana (2 to 3 medium bananas)**
> ⅓ **cup shortening, margarine, _or_ butter**
> 2 **tablespoons milk**
> 2 **eggs**
> ¼ **cup chopped nuts**   Oven 350°

In a large mixer bowl combine *1 cup* of the flour, the sugar, baking powder, baking soda, and salt. Add mashed banana; shortening, margarine or butter; and milk. Beat with an electric mixer on low speed till blended, then on high speed for 2 minutes. Add eggs and remaining flour; beat till blended. Stir in nuts.

Pour batter into a greased 8x4x2-inch loaf pan. Bake in a 350° oven for 55 to 60 minutes or till a toothpick inserted near the center comes out clean. Cool for 10 minutes on a wire rack. Remove from the pan; cool thoroughly on a wire rack. Wrap and store overnight before slicing. Makes 1 loaf (16 servings).

Zucchini Bread

Lemon and nutmeg accent the zucchini flavor.

> 1½ **cups all-purpose flour**
> 1 **teaspoon ground cinnamon**
> ½ **teaspoon baking soda**
> ¼ **teaspoon salt**
> ¼ **teaspoon baking powder**
> ¼ **teaspoon ground nutmeg**
> 1 **cup sugar**
> 1 **cup finely shredded unpeeled zucchini**
> ¼ **cup cooking oil**
> 1 **egg**
> ¼ **teaspoon finely shredded lemon peel**
> ½ **cup chopped walnuts**   Oven 350°

In a mixing bowl combine flour, cinnamon, baking soda, salt, baking powder, and nutmeg. In another mixing bowl combine sugar, shredded zucchini, cooking oil, egg, and lemon peel; mix well. Add flour mixture; stir just till combined. Stir in chopped walnuts.

Pour batter into a greased 8x4x2-inch loaf pan. Bake in a 350° oven for 55 to 60 minutes or till a toothpick inserted near the center comes out clean. Cool for 10 minutes on a wire rack.

Remove bread from the pan; cool thoroughly on a wire rack. Wrap and store overnight before slicing. Makes 1 loaf (16 servings).

Apple Bread: Prepare as above, *except* substitute 1 cup finely shredded peeled *apple* for the shredded zucchini.

Carrot and Pineapple Bread: Prepare as above, *except* omit zucchini. Drain one 8¼-ounce can crushed *pineapple,* reserving *2 tablespoons* juice. Stir drained pineapple, reserved pineapple juice, and ½ cup finely shredded *carrot* into the sugar mixture.

Nut Bread

Choose your favorite nut—pecans, almonds, walnuts, peanuts, or hazelnuts (filberts)—to flavor this bread.

> 3 **cups all-purpose flour**
> 1 **cup sugar**
> 1 **tablespoon baking powder**
> ½ **teaspoon salt**
> ¼ **teaspoon baking soda**
> 1 **beaten egg**
> 1⅔ **cups milk**
> ¼ **cup cooking oil**
> ¾ **cup chopped nuts**   Oven 350°

In a mixing bowl stir together flour, sugar, baking powder, salt, and baking soda. In another mixing bowl combine beaten egg, milk, and cooking oil. Add to flour mixture, stirring just till combined. Stir nuts into batter.

Pour nut-bread batter into a greased 9x5x3-inch loaf pan, two 7½x3½x2-inch loaf pans, *or* six 4½x2½x1½-inch loaf pans. Bake in a 350° oven for 1 to 1¼ hours for the 9x5x3-inch loaf (for 40 to 45 minutes for the 7½x3½x2-inch loaves; for 30 to 35 minutes for 4½x2½x1½-inch loaves) or till a toothpick inserted near the loaf center or centers comes out clean.

Cool in the pan or pans for 10 minutes. Remove; cool thoroughly on wire racks. Wrap and store overnight before slicing. Makes 1 large loaf, 2 small loaves, or 6 miniloaves (18 servings).

Cheese Nut Bread: Prepare as above, *except* reduce sugar to ¾ *cup* and add ½ teaspoon dried *oregano*, crushed, *or* dried *basil*, crushed, to the flour mixture. Add 1 cup shredded *Swiss cheese or* shredded *cheddar cheese* (4 ounces) to batter with the nuts.

Cranberry Nut Bread: Prepare as above, *except* add 2 teaspoons finely shredded *orange peel* to the flour mixture. Add 1 cup coarsely chopped *cranberries* to batter with the nuts.

Apricot Nut Bread: Prepare as above, *except* add 2 teaspoons finely shredded *orange peel or* finely shredded *lemon peel* to the flour mixture. Place 1 cup snipped dried *apricots* in a small bowl; pour *boiling* water over apricots. Let stand 5 minutes; drain well. Stir apricots into batter with the nuts.

Pumpkin Bread

> 2 **cups all-purpose flour**
> 1 **cup packed brown sugar**
> 1 **tablespoon baking powder**
> 1 **teaspoon ground cinnamon**
> ¼ **teaspoon salt**
> ¼ **teaspoon baking soda**
> ¼ **teaspoon ground nutmeg**
> ⅛ **teaspoon ground ginger**
>   **or ground cloves**
> 1 **cup canned pumpkin**
> ½ **cup milk**
> 2 **eggs**
> ⅓ **cup shortening**
> ½ **cup chopped walnuts**
> ½ **cup raisins**   Oven 350°

In a large mixer bowl combine *1 cup* of the flour, the brown sugar, baking powder, cinnamon, salt, baking soda, nutmeg, and ginger or cloves. Add pumpkin, milk, eggs, and shortening.

Beat with an electric mixer on low speed till blended, then on high speed for 2 minutes. Add remaining flour; beat well. Stir in nuts and raisins.

Pour batter into a greased 9x5x3-inch loaf pan. Bake in a 350° oven for 60 to 65 minutes or till a toothpick inserted near the center comes out clean. Cool for 10 minutes on a wire rack. Remove from the pan; cool thoroughly on a wire rack. Wrap and store overnight before slicing. Makes 1 loaf (18 servings).

No Ledges on the Edges

Have you noticed rims around the edges of your nut breads and muffins instead of evenly rounded tops?

There's a simple remedy to this problem: grease the baking pans or muffin cups on the bottom and only ½ inch up the sides. Do this and your batter will cling to the sides of the pan instead of sliding back down during baking. (Don't use nonstick spray coating in muffin cups because it will coat too high up on the sides.)

Berry-Banana-Walnut Bread

1½ cups all-purpose flour
¾ teaspoon ground cinnamon
½ teaspoon baking soda
¼ teaspoon ground nutmeg
2 beaten eggs
1 cup sugar
¾ cup mashed strawberries *or*
    raspberries (about 1½ cups
    whole berries)
½ cup mashed ripe banana
¼ cup cooking oil
1½ teaspoons finely shredded orange
    peel
1 cup chopped walnuts   Oven 350°

In a bowl combine flour, cinnamon, baking soda, nutmeg, and ¼ teaspoon *salt.* In another bowl stir together eggs, sugar, mashed berries, banana, oil, and orange peel. Add to flour mixture, stirring just till combined. Stir in nuts. Pour into a greased 9x5x3-inch loaf pan. Bake in a 350° oven for 60 to 70 minutes or till a toothpick inserted near the center comes out clean. Cool 10 minutes. Remove from pan; cool on a rack. Wrap and store overnight. Makes 1 loaf (18 servings).

Blueberry-Banana-Walnut Bread: Prepare as above, *except* omit strawberries or raspberries and stir in 1 cup fresh *or* frozen *whole blueberries* with the nuts.

Making Better Nut Breads

Nut breads are best if stored overnight before slicing. The flavors mellow and the loaves are easier to slice. Just follow these steps: After baking, let the loaves cool completely on a wire rack, then wrap them in foil or clear plastic wrap and store them at room temperature. Use these other tips, too, when making nut breads.

● Check the bread 10 to 15 minutes before the baking time is completed. Cover with foil if it's browning too fast.

● Don't be concerned about the crack down the top of the loaf. This is typical of nut breads.

Boston Brown Bread

Traditionally, this sweet steamed bread is served with baked beans. It's also good when used for sandwiches or spread with cream cheese.

½ cup whole wheat flour
¼ cup all-purpose flour
¼ cup cornmeal
½ teaspoon baking powder
¼ teaspoon salt
¼ teaspoon baking soda
1 egg
½ cup buttermilk *or* sour milk
¼ cup molasses
2 tablespoons sugar
2 teaspoons cooking oil
⅓ cup raisins

In a mixing bowl stir together whole wheat flour, all-purpose flour, cornmeal, baking powder, salt, and baking soda. In another mixing bowl combine egg, buttermilk or sour milk, molasses, sugar, and oil. Add to flour mixture, stirring till well combined. Stir in raisins.

Pour batter into a well-greased 4- to 4½-cup heatproof mold or bowl, or a 7½x3½x2-inch loaf pan. Cover tightly with greased foil, greased side down. Place on a rack set in a Dutch oven.

Pour *hot* water into the Dutch oven around the mold or pan till water covers 1 inch of the mold or pan. Bring to boiling; reduce heat. Cover; simmer for 2 to 2½ hours or till a toothpick inserted near the center of the bread comes out clean. Add additional *boiling* water as needed.

Remove mold, bowl, or pan from the Dutch oven; let stand 10 minutes. Remove bread from the mold, bowl, or pan. Serve warm. *Or,* for later use, cool thoroughly on a wire rack, wrap, and chill. Makes 1 loaf (15 servings).

To reheat: Unwrap the chilled bread and return it to the mold, bowl, or loaf pan. Cover tightly with foil and place on a rack in a Dutch oven. Add *hot* water and steam as above for 15 minutes. Unmold and serve warm.

To reheat in the *microwave oven,* unwrap bread and place on a plate. Cover with waxed paper. Micro-cook on 50% power (medium) for 6 to 8 minutes or till heated through. Let stand 5 minutes before slicing.

Coconut-Cherry-Carrot Bread

Oven 350°

In a bowl combine 2½ cups *all-purpose flour,* 1 cup *sugar,* 1 teaspoon *baking powder,* 1 teaspoon *baking soda,* ½ teaspoon ground *nutmeg or mace,* and ¼ teaspoon *salt.* In another bowl combine 3 beaten *eggs,* ½ cup *cooking oil,* and ½ cup *milk.* Add to flour mixture; mix well. Stir in 2 cups finely shredded *carrot,* one 3½-ounce can (1⅓ cups) flaked *coconut,* and ½ cup chopped, well-drained *maraschino cherries.*

Grease two 7½x3½x2-inch, four 5½x3x2-inch, or six 4½x2½x1½-inch loaf pans; pour batter into pans. Bake in a 350° oven for 40 to 50 minutes or till a toothpick inserted near center comes out clean. Cool in pans 10 minutes. Remove from pans; cool thoroughly on wire racks. Wrap; store overnight before slicing. Serves 16.

Spoon Bread

So light and fluffy, you'll need a spoon to serve it.

1½ cups milk
½ cup cornmeal
1 tablespoon margarine or butter
½ teaspoon baking powder
1 beaten egg yolk
1 stiffly beaten egg white
Margarine or butter   Oven 325°

In a medium saucepan stir *1 cup* of the milk into cornmeal. Cook, stirring constantly, till mixture is very thick and pulls away from the sides of pan. Remove from the heat. Stir in remaining milk, 1 tablespoon margarine, the baking powder, and ¼ teaspoon *salt.* Stir *1 cup* of hot mixture into egg yolk; return all to saucepan. Gently fold in beaten egg white. Pour into a greased 1-quart casserole. Bake in a 325° oven for 35 to 40 minutes or till a knife inserted near the center comes out clean. Serve immediately with margarine or butter. Makes 4 servings.

Parmesan Spoon Bread: Prepare as above, *except* omit salt and stir ¼ cup grated *Parmesan cheese* into cooked cornmeal mixture.

Cheesy Corn Spoon Bread: Prepare as above, *except* add one 8-ounce can whole kernel *corn,* drained; ½ cup shredded *cheddar cheese* (2 ounces); and 2 tablespoons diced *green chili peppers,* drained, to the cooked cornmeal mixture. Bake for 40 to 45 minutes.

Corn Bread

Freeze any extra to have on hand for busy days.

1 cup all-purpose flour
1 cup yellow, white, or blue cornmeal
2 to 4 tablespoons sugar
1 tablespoon baking powder
½ teaspoon salt
2 eggs
1 cup milk
¼ cup cooking oil or shortening, melted   Oven 425°

In a mixing bowl stir together flour, cornmeal, sugar, baking powder, and salt. In another bowl beat together eggs, milk, and oil or melted shortening. Add to flour mixture and stir just till batter is smooth (*do not overbeat*).

Pour into a greased 9x9x2-inch baking pan. Bake in a 425° oven for 20 to 25 minutes or till golden brown. Makes 8 or 9 servings.

Corn Sticks or Corn Muffins: Prepare as above, *except* spoon batter into greased corn stick pans or muffin pans, filling pans ⅔ full. Bake in a 425° oven for 12 to 15 minutes or till brown. Makes 24 to 26 sticks or 12 muffins.

Corny Corn Bread: Prepare as above, *except* stir one 12-ounce can *whole kernel corn with sweet peppers,* drained, into the batter.

Crunchy Corn Bread: Prepare as above, *except* pour 1 cup *boiling water* over ¼ cup *cracked wheat or bulgur.* Let stand 5 minutes; drain. Add ½ cup *quick-cooking rolled oats* to flour mixture. Add cracked wheat or bulgur mixture and egg mixture to the flour mixture. Stir just till smooth. Fold in ½ cup chopped *pecans.*

Confetti Corn Bread: Prepare as above, *except* stir ½ cup shredded *cheddar cheese,* ¼ cup finely shredded *carrot,* and ¼ cup finely shredded *zucchini* into batter.

Green Chili Corn Bread: Prepare as above, *except* fold 1 cup shredded *cheddar cheese or Monterey Jack cheese* and one 4-ounce can diced *green chili peppers,* drained, into batter.

Corn Bread Miniloaf: Prepare as above, *except* use ½ cup all-purpose flour, ½ cup cornmeal, *1 to 2 tablespoons* sugar, *1½ teaspoons* baking powder, *¼ teaspoon* salt, *1 egg,* *½ cup* milk, and *2 tablespoons* cooking oil or shortening, melted. Pour into a greased 9x5x3-inch loaf pan. Bake in a 425° oven for 20 to 25 minutes or till golden brown. Makes 4 servings.

Muffins

Blueberry Muffins are pictured on page 33.

1¾ **cups all-purpose flour**
⅓ **cup sugar**
2 **teaspoons baking powder**
1 **beaten egg**
¾ **cup milk**
¼ **cup cooking oil**   Oven 400°

In a mixing bowl combine flour, sugar, baking powder, and ¼ teaspoon *salt.* Make a well in the center. Combine egg, milk, and oil; add all at once to flour mixture. Stir just till moistened (batter should be lumpy). Lightly grease muffin cups or line with paper bake cups; fill ⅔ full. Bake in a 400° oven about 20 minutes or till golden. Remove from pans; serve warm. Makes 10 to 12.

Blueberry Muffins: Prepare as above, *except* fold ¾ cup fresh or frozen *blueberries* and, if desired, 1 teaspoon finely shredded lemon peel into muffin batter.

Cranberry Muffins: Prepare as above, *except* combine 1 cup coarsely chopped *cranberries* and 2 tablespoons additional *sugar.* Fold into muffin batter.

Jelly Muffins: Prepare as above, *except* do not use paper bake cups. Fill muffin cups ⅓ full with batter, top *each* with 1 teaspoon *jelly, jam, or preserves,* then top with enough batter to fill each muffin cup ⅔ full.

Date-Nut Muffins: Prepare as above, *except* fold ⅔ cup snipped pitted whole *dates* and ⅓ cup chopped *nuts* into muffin batter.

Cheese Muffins: Prepare as above, *except* stir ½ cup shredded *cheddar or Monterey Jack cheese* (2 ounces) into flour mixture.

Banana Muffins: Prepare as above, *except* reduce milk to ½ *cup.* Add ¾ cup mashed *banana* and ½ cup chopped *nuts* to flour mixture with egg mixture. Do not use paper bake cups.

Pumpkin Muffins: Prepare as above, *except* add 1 teaspoon ground *cinnamon,* ½ teaspoon ground *nutmeg,* and ⅛ teaspoon ground *cloves* to flour mixture. Add ½ cup canned *pumpkin* to egg mixture. Stir ¼ cup chopped *nuts* into batter. Do not use paper bake cups.

Corn Muffins: Prepare as above, *except* reduce flour to *1 cup* and add ¾ cup *cornmeal* to flour mixture. Do not use paper bake cups.

Oatmeal Muffins: Prepare as above, *except* reduce flour to *1⅓ cups* and add ¾ cup *rolled oats* to flour mixture.

French Breakfast Puffs

Oven 350°

Combine ¼ cup *sugar* and ½ teaspoon ground *cinnamon;* set aside. In a bowl stir together 1½ cups *all-purpose flour,* ½ cup *sugar,* 1½ teaspoons *baking powder,* ¼ teaspoon ground *nutmeg,* and ⅛ teaspoon *salt.* In another bowl combine 1 beaten *egg,* ½ cup *milk,* and ⅓ cup melted *margarine or butter;* add to flour mixture, stirring just till moistened.

Lightly grease muffin cups or line with paper bake cups; fill ⅔ full. Bake in a 350° oven for 20 to 25 minutes or till golden. Immediately dip tops into 3 tablespoons melted *margarine,* then into sugar-cinnamon mixture. Serve warm. Makes 12.

Resist the temptation to beat the muffin batter. A few lumps should remain.

Fill the muffin cups only two-thirds full. Use a rubber scraper to keep your fingers clean.

Refrigerator Bran Muffins

Serving tasty, warm muffins is a snap when the batter is ready and waiting. (A plain Refrigerator Bran Muffin is pictured on page 33.)

1½ cups all-purpose flour
  1 cup whole bran cereal *or* ½ cup
      toasted wheat bran
2½ teaspoons baking powder
  1 teaspoon ground cinnamon
  ¼ teaspoon salt
  ¼ teaspoon ground nutmeg
  1 beaten egg
  1 cup milk
  ½ cup packed brown sugar
  ¼ cup cooking oil
  1 teaspoon finely shredded lemon
      peel *or* orange peel
  ⅓ cup chopped nuts   Oven 400°

In a bowl stir together flour, whole bran cereal or toasted wheat bran, baking powder, cinnamon, salt, and nutmeg. Make a well in the center.

In another bowl stir together egg, milk, sugar, oil, and lemon or orange peel. Add egg mixture all at once to flour mixture. Stir just till moistened (batter will be lumpy). Fold in nuts. Store in a covered container in the refrigerator up to 7 days.

To bake, gently stir batter. Grease desired number of muffin cups or line with paper bake cups; fill cups ⅔ full. Bake in a 400° oven for 15 to 20 minutes or till golden. Remove from pans; serve warm. Makes 12.

Microwave directions: Prepare batter as above. Line one or two 6-ounce custard cups with paper bake cups. Spoon *2 slightly rounded tablespoons* of batter into *each* cup. For one muffin, micro-cook, uncovered, on 100% power (high) for 30 to 60 seconds or till done. (Scratch the slightly wet surface with a wooden toothpick. The muffin should be cooked underneath.) For two muffins, cook on high for 1 to 1½ minutes or till done. Remove from cups and let stand on a wire rack for 5 minutes.

Apple-and-Raisin Refrigerator Bran Muffins: Prepare as above, *except* combine ½ cup snipped dried *apple* and ¼ cup *raisins* in a small bowl; pour enough *boiling* water over fruit to cover. Let stand 5 minutes; drain well. Fold mixture into batter with nuts. Makes 14 to 16.

Honey Wheat Muffins

The lemon adds a just-right touch to the honey flavor. (A Honey-Nut Wheat Muffin and a Fruit Wheat Muffin are pictured on page 33.)

  1 cup all-purpose flour
  ½ cup whole wheat flour
  2 teaspoons baking powder
  ¼ teaspoon salt
  1 beaten egg
  ½ cup milk
  ½ cup honey
  ¼ cup cooking oil
  ½ teaspoon finely shredded
      lemon peel   Oven 400°

In a mixing bowl stir together all-purpose flour, whole wheat flour, baking powder, and salt. Make a well in the center.

In another bowl combine beaten egg, milk, honey, cooking oil, and lemon peel. Add egg mixture all at once to dry mixture. Stir just till moistened (batter should be lumpy). Grease muffin cups or line with paper bake cups; fill ⅔ full.

Bake in a 400° oven for 18 to 20 minutes or till golden. Remove muffins from pans; serve warm. Makes 12.

Microwave directions: Prepare batter as above. Line *six* custard cups or a microwave-safe muffin pan with paper bake cups. Spoon *2 slightly rounded tablespoons* of batter into *each* cup. For custard cups, arrange in a ring on a plate. Micro-cook, uncovered, on 100% power (high) for 1¾ to 2¼ minutes or till done, giving plate or pan a half-turn every minute. (Scratch the slightly wet surfaces with a toothpick. The muffins should be cooked underneath.) Repeat, making 6 more muffins. Cook remaining 1 or 2 muffins for 30 to 60 seconds. Serve warm. Makes 13 or 14.

Sunflower-Nut Wheat Muffins: Prepare as above, *except* stir ½ cup *sunflower nuts* into the flour mixture. (If using salted nuts, reduce salt to ⅛ *teaspoon.*)

Fruit Wheat Muffins: Prepare as above, *except* fold ½ cup fresh or frozen *blueberries, raisins,* snipped pitted whole *dates, or* chopped *apple* into the batter. Do not use the microwave directions.

Honey-Nut Wheat Muffins: Prepare as above, *except* fold ½ cup chopped *walnuts, pecans, peanuts, or* toasted *almonds* into the batter.

Any-Fruit Coffee Cake

When serving a crowd, double the recipe and bake the coffee cake in a 13x9x2-inch baking pan for 45 to 50 minutes.

1½ **cups chopped, peeled apples, apricots, peaches, *or* pineapple; *or* 1½ cups blueberries *or* raspberries**
1 **cup sugar**
2 **tablespoons cornstarch**
1½ **cups all-purpose flour**
½ **teaspoon baking powder**
¼ **teaspoon baking soda**
6 **tablespoons margarine *or* butter**
1 **beaten egg**
½ **cup buttermilk *or* sour milk**
½ **teaspoon vanilla**
¼ **cup all-purpose flour**   Oven 350°

In a saucepan combine choice of fruit and ¼ cup *water*. Bring to boiling; reduce heat. Cover and simmer* about 5 minutes or till tender. Combine ¼ *cup* of the sugar and the cornstarch. Stir into fruit mixture. Cook and stir till thickened and bubbly. Cook and stir 2 minutes more. Set aside.

In a mixing bowl stir together ½ *cup* of the sugar, the 1½ cups flour, the baking powder, and baking soda. Cut in 4 *tablespoons* margarine or butter till mixture resembles fine crumbs. Combine egg, buttermilk or sour milk, and vanilla. Add to flour mixture. Stir just till moistened.

Spread *half* of the batter into an 8x8x2-inch baking pan. Spread fruit mixture over batter. Drop remaining batter in small mounds atop filling.

Combine the remaining ¼ cup sugar and the ¼ cup flour. Cut in remaining 2 tablespoons margarine or butter till mixture resembles fine crumbs. Sprinkle over batter. Bake in a 350° oven for 40 to 45 minutes or till golden brown. Serve warm. Makes 9 servings.

Rhubarb-Strawberry Coffee Cake: Prepare as above, *except* substitute ¾ cup fresh or frozen cut-up *rhubarb* and ¾ cup frozen unsweetened whole *strawberries* for the fruit.

*Note: Do not simmer raspberries.

Using two tablespoons, drop the remaining half of the batter atop the fruit filling in small mounds.

Buttermilk Coffee Cake

1¼ cups all-purpose flour
 ¾ cup packed brown sugar
 ¼ teaspoon salt
 ⅓ cup shortening, margarine, or butter
  1 teaspoon baking powder
 ¼ teaspoon baking soda
 ¼ teaspoon ground cinnamon
 ¼ teaspoon ground nutmeg
 ⅔ cup buttermilk or sour milk
  1 beaten egg
 ¼ cup chopped nuts   Oven 350°

Combine flour, brown sugar, and salt. Cut in shortening till crumbly; set aside ¼ cup crumb mixture. To remaining crumb mixture add baking powder, baking soda, cinnamon, and nutmeg. Mix well. Add buttermilk and egg; mix well.

Spread batter into a greased 8x8x2-inch baking pan. Stir together reserved crumbs and nuts; sprinkle atop batter. Bake in a 350° oven for 30 to 35 minutes or till a toothpick inserted near the center comes out clean. Serve warm. Serves 9.

Sour Cream Coffee Cake: Prepare as above, *except* substitute ½ cup dairy *sour cream* for the buttermilk.

Applesauce Coffee Cake

1¾ cups all-purpose flour
 ½ cup sugar
 ½ cup margarine or butter
 ¼ cup chopped nuts
 ½ teaspoon ground cinnamon
1½ teaspoons baking powder
 ½ teaspoon baking soda
  2 beaten eggs
  1 cup applesauce or apple butter
  1 teaspoon vanilla
 ½ cup raisins (optional)   Oven 375°

In a bowl combine ¾ cup flour and the sugar; cut in margarine. For topping, remove ½ cup crumb mixture; stir in nuts and cinnamon. Set aside.

To remaining crumb mixture add remaining flour, baking powder, and baking soda. Add eggs, applesauce or apple butter, and vanilla; beat till well blended. If desired, stir in raisins. Pour into a greased 9x9x2-inch baking pan. Sprinkle topping on batter. Bake in a 375° oven for 30 to 35 minutes or till a toothpick inserted near the center comes out clean. Serve warm. Serves 9.

Peanut Butter Coffee Cake

Share this easy-to-carry coffee cake with your coworkers at break time.

 ½ cup packed brown sugar
 ½ cup all-purpose flour
 ¼ cup peanut butter
  3 tablespoons margarine or butter
  2 cups all-purpose flour
  1 cup packed brown sugar
  2 teaspoons baking powder
 ½ teaspoon baking soda
 ¼ teaspoon salt
  1 cup milk
 ½ cup peanut butter
  2 eggs
 ¼ cup margarine or butter   Oven 375°

For topping, in a bowl stir together ½ cup brown sugar and ½ cup all-purpose flour; cut in ¼ cup peanut butter and 3 tablespoons margarine or butter till crumbly. Set aside.

In a bowl stir together 2 cups flour, 1 cup brown sugar, the baking powder, baking soda, and salt. Add milk, ½ cup peanut butter, the eggs, and ¼ cup margarine or butter. Beat with an electric mixer on low speed till blended. Beat at high speed for 3 minutes, scraping the sides of the bowl frequently.

Pour batter into a greased 13x9x2-inch baking pan, spreading evenly. Sprinkle with topping mixture. Bake in a 375° oven about 30 minutes or till a toothpick inserted near the center comes out clean. Serve warm or cool. Serves 16.

Chocolate Peanut Butter Coffee Cake: Prepare as above, *except* add ¼ cup miniature *semisweet chocolate pieces* to topping and stir ½ cup miniature *semisweet chocolate pieces* into batter after beating.

Making Sour Milk

Here's how to make the sour milk called for in some of our recipes. For each cup of sour milk, place 1 tablespoon lemon juice or vinegar in a glass measuring cup. Add enough milk to make 1 cup total liquid; stir. Let the mixture stand 5 minutes before using.

Date-Orange Coffee Cake

   2 **cups all-purpose flour**
   ½ **cup sugar**
   1 **tablespoon baking powder**
   1 **beaten egg**
   ½ **cup milk**
   ½ **cup cooking oil**
   ½ **cup snipped pitted whole dates**
   2 **teaspoons finely shredded orange peel**
   ½ **cup orange juice**
   ½ **cup packed brown sugar**
   2 **tablespoons all-purpose flour**
   1 **teaspoon ground cinnamon**
   2 **tablespoons margarine or butter**
   ½ **cup chopped walnuts**   Oven 375°

In a bowl combine the 2 cups flour, the sugar, baking powder, and ¼ teaspoon *salt.* Make a well in the center. In another bowl combine egg, milk, oil, dates, orange peel, and orange juice; add all at once to flour mixture. Stir just till mixed. Spread evenly into a greased 11x7x1½-inch baking pan.

In a bowl combine brown sugar, 2 tablespoons flour, and the cinnamon; cut in margarine or butter till crumbly. Stir in nuts. Sprinkle over batter in the pan. Bake in a 375° oven about 30 minutes or till a toothpick inserted near the center comes out clean. Serve warm. Serves 12.

Apple Coffee Cake: Prepare as above, *except* substitute ½ cup snipped *dried apple* for dates, omit orange peel, and substitute ½ cup *apple juice* for orange juice.

Streusel Coffee Cake

Oven 375°

In a bowl stir together 1½ cups *all-purpose flour,* ¾ cup *sugar,* 2 teaspoons *baking powder,* and ¼ teaspoon *salt.* In another bowl stir together 1 beaten *egg,* ½ cup *milk,* and ¼ cup *cooking oil;* add to flour mixture. Mix well. Stir in ¾ cup *raisins or semisweet chocolate pieces.* Pour into a greased 9x9x2-inch baking pan.

Combine 2 tablespoons *brown sugar,* 1 tablespoon *all-purpose flour,* and 1 teaspoon ground *cinnamon;* cut in 1 tablespoon *margarine or butter* till crumbly. Stir in ½ cup chopped *nuts.* Sprinkle over batter. Bake in a 375° oven about 30 minutes or till a toothpick inserted near the center comes out clean. Serve warm. Serves 9.

Date-Nut Ring

Serve some warm today and freeze the extra slices for easy treats.

 1½ **cups water**
   1 **cup snipped pitted whole dates, snipped dried figs, *or* raisins**
   ¾ **cup cooking oil**
   1 **teaspoon vanilla**
   3 **eggs**
   3 **cups all-purpose flour**
 1½ **cups sugar**
   1 **tablespoon baking powder**
   ½ **teaspoon salt**
   ¼ **teaspoon baking soda**
   1 **cup chopped walnuts**   Oven 350°

In a medium saucepan bring water to boiling. Remove from the heat. Stir in snipped dates, snipped figs, or raisins. Let stand for 15 minutes. *Do not drain.*

Add cooking oil and vanilla to date mixture; stir together. Add eggs, one at a time, beating with a fork till well combined after each addition.

In a large mixing bowl stir together flour, sugar, baking powder, salt, and baking soda. Add date mixture to flour mixture. Stir to mix well. Stir in chopped nuts.

Pour batter into a greased 10-inch tube pan, two 9x5x3-inch loaf pans, or two 8x4x2-inch loaf pans. Bake in a 350° oven for 50 to 60 minutes for the tube pan (for 45 to 50 minutes for the loaf pan or pans) or till a toothpick inserted near the center or centers comes out clean.

Cool in the pan or pans on a wire rack for 15 minutes. Remove from the pan or pans. Cool on a wire rack. Serve warm, or cool completely, wrap, and store overnight. Makes 1 large ring or 2 loaves (20 servings).

Chocolate Chip and Nut Ring: Prepare as above, *except* omit the 1½ cups boiling water and snipped dates, figs, or raisins. In a mixing bowl beat the eggs. Add 1¼ cups *water.* Stir in cooking oil and vanilla. In another mixing bowl stir together flour, sugar, baking powder, salt, and baking soda. Add egg mixture to flour mixture. Stir to mix well. Stir in chopped nuts and ½ cup miniature *semisweet chocolate pieces.*

Cocoa Ripple Ring

1¼ cups all-purpose flour
⅔ cup sugar
1½ teaspoons baking powder
⅓ cup milk
⅓ cup cooking oil
2 eggs
¼ cup presweetened cocoa powder
(*not* low calorie)
⅓ cup chopped walnuts
Powdered Sugar Glaze (see
recipe, below)   Oven 350°

In a bowl combine first 3 ingredients. Add milk
and oil; beat with an electric mixer on low speed
till blended. Beat on high for 2 minutes. Add
eggs; beat 2 minutes. Pour *¾ cup* batter into a
greased and floured 6-cup fluted tube pan or
6½-cup ring mold. Mix cocoa powder and nuts;
sprinkle *half* of mixture over batter in pan. Repeat
layers. Bake in a 350° oven for 30 to 35 minutes
or till a toothpick inserted near the center comes
out clean. Cool 5 minutes. Remove from pan.
Drizzle with Powdered Sugar Glaze. Serves 16.

Berry Coffee Cake   EASY

1 3-ounce package cream cheese
¼ cup margarine *or* butter
2 cups packaged biscuit mix *or*
Easy Biscuit Mix (see recipe,
page 66)
¼ cup milk
½ cup raspberry, strawberry, *or* peach
preserves
Powdered Sugar Glaze   Oven 375°

Cut cream cheese and margarine into biscuit mix
till crumbly. Add milk; stir till mixed. On lightly
floured surface, knead dough 10 to 12 strokes.
On waxed paper, roll or pat dough into a 12x8-
inch rectangle. Invert onto a greased baking
sheet; remove paper. Spread preserves down
center of dough. Make 2½-inch cuts from long
sides toward the center at 1-inch intervals. Fold
strips alternately over filling. Bake in a 375° oven
for 20 to 25 minutes or till golden. Drizzle with
Powdered Sugar Glaze. Serve warm. Serves 12.

Powdered Sugar Glaze: In a bowl stir together ½ cup sifted *powdered sugar,* ¼ teaspoon *vanilla,* and enough *milk* to make of
drizzling consistency (1 to 2 teaspoons).

Nutty Sticky Rolls

*Eat these rolls with a fork so you won't miss a bite
of the maple, orange, or chocolate topping.*

½ cup light corn syrup *or* maple-
flavored syrup
¼ cup packed brown sugar
2 tablespoons margarine *or* butter
1 tablespoon water
⅓ cup coarsely chopped pecans *or*
walnuts
2 cups all-purpose flour
2 teaspoons baking powder
¼ teaspoon salt
⅓ cup shortening, margarine, *or* butter
¾ cup milk
¼ cup sugar
½ teaspoon ground
cinnamon   Oven 425°

In a small saucepan combine syrup, brown sugar,
the 2 tablespoons margarine, and the water.
Cook and stir over low heat just till margarine or
butter melts; *do not boil.* Spread onto the bottom
of a 9x9x2-inch baking pan. Sprinkle nuts over
syrup mixture.

In a mixing bowl stir together flour, baking
powder, and salt. Cut in ⅓ cup shortening, margarine, or butter till mixture resembles coarse
crumbs. Make a well in center. Add milk all at
once, stirring just till dough clings together.

On a lightly floured surface, knead dough
gently for 15 to 20 strokes. Roll dough into a
12x10-inch rectangle. Combine ¼ cup sugar and
the cinnamon; sprinkle over dough. Roll up from
one of the long sides. Slice into 1-inch pieces.
Place, cut side down, atop nuts in the baking pan.

Bake in a 425° oven about 25 minutes or till
golden. *Immediately* loosen sides and invert onto
a serving plate. Spoon any topping in pan over
rolls. Serve warm. Makes 12.

Orange Sticky Rolls: Prepare as above, *except,* in the syrup mixture, substitute 1 tablespoon *orange juice* for the water and add 1
teaspoon finely shredded *orange peel.* Add 1 teaspoon additional finely shredded *orange peel* to
dough with the milk.

Chocolate Sticky Rolls: Prepare as above,
except, in the syrup mixture, omit the 2 tablespoons margarine or butter and add ¼ cup miniature *semisweet chocolate pieces;* cook and stir
till melted. After sprinkling rolled dough with cin-
namon-sugar mixture, sprinkle with ¼ cup additional miniature *semisweet chocolate pieces.*

Biscuits

For different shapes, use a sharp knife to cut the rolled dough into squares, triangles, or strips. (Plain Biscuits are pictured on page 33.)

 2 **cups all-purpose flour**
 1 **tablespoon baking powder**
 2 **teaspoons sugar**
 ½ **teaspoon cream of tartar**
 ¼ **teaspoon salt**
 ½ **cup shortening, margarine, *or* butter**
 ⅔ **cup milk**   Oven 450°

In a bowl stir together flour, baking powder, sugar, cream of tartar, and salt. Cut in shortening, margarine, or butter till mixture resembles coarse crumbs. Make a well in the center; add milk all at once. Stir just till dough clings together.

On a lightly floured surface, knead dough gently for 10 to 12 strokes. Roll or pat dough to ½-inch thickness. Cut with a 2½-inch biscuit cutter, dipping cutter into flour between cuts. Transfer biscuits to a baking sheet. Bake in a 450° oven for 10 to 12 minutes or till golden. Serve warm. Makes 10.

Buttermilk Biscuits: Prepare as above, *except* stir ¼ teaspoon *baking soda* into flour mixture and substitute ¾ cup *buttermilk* for the milk.

Cornmeal Biscuits: Prepare as above, *except* reduce flour to *1½ cups* and add ½ cup *cornmeal* to flour mixture.

Garden Biscuits: Prepare as above, *except* add 2 tablespoons finely shredded *carrot,* 1 tablespoon finely snipped *parsley,* and 1 tablespoon finely chopped *green onion* to flour mixture with the milk.

Sour Cream Biscuits: Prepare as above, *except* reduce milk to *¼ cup* and add ½ cup dairy *sour cream* to flour mixture with the milk.

Cheese Biscuits: Prepare as above, *except* add ½ cup shredded *cheddar cheese* to the flour mixture with the milk.

Cajun-Style Biscuits: Prepare as above, *except* stir ¼ teaspoon ground *red pepper* and ¼ teaspoon *black pepper* into flour mixture.

Drop Biscuits: Prepare as above, *except* increase milk to *1 cup. Do not knead, roll, or cut dough.* Drop dough from a tablespoon onto a greased baking sheet. Makes 10 to 12.

Easy Biscuit Mix

Use shortening that does not require refrigeration for this handy mix.

 10 **cups all-purpose flour, *or* 6 cups all-purpose flour and 4 cups whole wheat flour**
 ⅓ **cup baking powder**
 ¼ **cup sugar**
 2 **cups shortening** Oven 450° or 400°

In a bowl stir together flour, baking powder, sugar, and 2 teaspoons *salt.* Cut in shortening till mixture resembles coarse crumbs. Store in an airtight container for up to 6 weeks at room temperature or for up to 6 months in the freezer. Use to make Easy Biscuits, Easy Muffins, Easy Pancakes, or Easy Beer-Cheese Triangles. To use, spoon mixture lightly into a measuring cup; level off with a straight-edged spatula. (If frozen, bring mix to room temperature.) Makes about 12 cups.

Easy Biscuits: Place 1 cup *Easy Biscuit Mix* in a bowl; make a well in the center. Add ¼ cup *milk.* Stir with a fork just till dough clings together. On a lightly floured surface, knead dough gently for 10 to 12 strokes. Roll or pat to ½-inch thickness. Cut with a 2½-inch biscuit cutter, dipping cutter into flour between cuts. Place on a baking sheet. Bake in a 450° oven for 8 to 10 minutes or till golden. Serve warm. Makes 4.

Easy Muffins: In a mixing bowl combine 1 cup *Easy Biscuit Mix* and 1 to 3 tablespoons *sugar.* Combine 1 beaten *egg* and ¼ cup *milk;* add all at once to biscuit mixture. Stir just till moistened (should be lumpy). Fill greased muffin cups ⅔ full. Bake in a 400° oven for 15 to 20 minutes or till golden. Serve warm. Makes 6.

Easy Pancakes: Place 1 cup *Easy Biscuit Mix* in a bowl. Add 1 beaten *egg* and ¾ cup *milk* all at once to biscuit mix, stirring with a whisk till well blended. For each pancake, pour about ¼ *cup* batter onto a hot, lightly greased griddle or heavy skillet. Cook till golden brown, turning to cook second side when pancake has a bubbly surface and slightly dry edges. Makes 6.

Easy Beer-Cheese Triangles: In a bowl combine 1 cup *Easy Biscuit Mix* and ¼ cup shredded *cheddar cheese.* Make a well in the center. Add ¼ cup *beer or milk.* Stir just till dough clings together. On a lightly floured surface, knead gently for 12 strokes. Pat dough into a 6-inch circle. Cut into 8 wedges. Place on a baking sheet. Bake in a 450° oven for 8 to 10 minutes or till golden. Serve warm. Makes 8.

Pecan Biscuit Spirals

  2 cups all-purpose flour
  2 tablespoons sugar
  1 tablespoon baking powder
  ½ cup margarine *or* butter
  1 beaten egg
  ½ cup milk
  1 tablespoon margarine *or* butter
  ¼ cup finely chopped pecans
  3 tablespoons brown sugar Oven 450°

In a mixing bowl combine flour, 2 tablespoons sugar, the baking powder, and ¼ teaspoon *salt.* Cut in ½ cup margarine or butter till mixture resembles coarse crumbs. Make a well in the center. Combine egg and milk; add all at once to flour mixture. Stir just till dough clings together. On a floured surface, knead gently for 15 strokes.

Roll dough into a 15x8-inch rectangle. Melt 1 tablespoon margarine; brush on dough. Combine nuts and brown sugar; sprinkle over dough. Fold dough in half *lengthwise.* Cut into fifteen 1-inch-wide strips. Holding a strip at both ends, carefully twist in opposite directions twice. Place on a lightly greased baking sheet, pressing both ends down. Repeat. Bake in a 450° oven for 8 to 10 minutes or till golden. Serve warm. Makes 15.

Apple-Cheese Biscuits

  ⅓ cup sugar
  ⅓ cup finely chopped walnuts
  ½ teaspoon ground cinnamon
1¾ cups packaged biscuit mix *or*
      Easy Biscuit Mix (see recipe,
      opposite)
  ¾ cup shredded cheddar cheese
  1 medium apple, peeled, cored, and
      finely chopped (about ¾ cup)
  ¼ cup margarine *or* butter,
      melted Oven 400°

Combine sugar, nuts, and cinnamon. Set aside. In a bowl combine biscuit mix, cheese, and apple. Make a well in the center. Add ⅓ cup *water* all at once. Stir just till mixture forms a ball. Divide into 18 pieces. Shape each piece into a ball. Roll balls in melted margarine, then in the sugar mixture. Arrange in a single layer in a greased 9x1½-inch round baking pan. Bake in a 400° oven for 25 to 30 minutes or till golden. Cool for 5 minutes. Remove from the pan; serve warm. Makes 18.

Irish Soda Bread

  2 cups all-purpose flour
  1 teaspoon baking powder
  ½ teaspoon baking soda
  3 tablespoons margarine *or* butter
  1 beaten egg
  ¾ cup buttermilk *or* sour milk
  1 beaten egg Oven 375°

In a bowl combine flour, baking powder, baking soda, and ¼ teaspoon *salt.* Cut in margarine till mixture resembles coarse crumbs. Combine 1 egg and buttermilk; add to flour mixture. Stir just till moistened. On a lightly floured surface, knead gently for 12 strokes. On a greased baking sheet, shape dough into a 6-inch-round loaf. Cut a 4-inch cross, ¼ inch deep, on the top. Brush with 1 beaten egg. Bake in a 375° oven about 35 minutes or till golden. Cool on a rack. Serves 16.

Brown Irish Soda Bread: Prepare as above, *except* reduce all-purpose flour to *1 cup* and add 1 cup *whole wheat flour.*

Sweet-Raisin Irish Soda Bread: Prepare as above, *except* add 2 tablespoons *brown sugar* to the flour mixture and ⅓ cup *raisins or currants* to the buttermilk mixture.

Oatmeal-Raisin Scones

  1 cup all-purpose flour
  3 tablespoons brown sugar
1½ teaspoons baking powder
  ½ teaspoon ground cinnamon
  ⅓ cup margarine *or* butter
  1 cup quick-cooking rolled oats
  ½ cup raisins, coarsely chopped;
      currants; *or* miniature
      semisweet chocolate pieces
  1 beaten egg
  ¼ cup milk
      Milk Oven 400°

In a bowl combine flour, sugar, baking powder, and cinnamon. Cut in margarine till mixture resembles coarse crumbs. Stir in oats and raisins, currants, or chocolate pieces. Combine egg and ¼ cup milk; add to flour mixture. Stir just till moistened (will be sticky). On a lightly floured surface, pat dough into a 7-inch circle. Cut into 12 wedges; place on a baking sheet. Brush with milk. Bake in a 400° oven for 10 to 12 minutes or till light brown. Serve warm. Makes 12.

Cake Doughnuts

Mix, cut, and fry. That's all there is to making these doughnuts.

3¼ cups all-purpose flour
2 teaspoons baking powder
½ teaspoon ground cinnamon
¼ teaspoon salt
¼ teaspoon ground nutmeg
2 beaten eggs
⅔ cup sugar
1 teaspoon vanilla
⅔ cup milk
¼ cup margarine *or* butter, melted
  Shortening *or* cooking oil for
    deep-fat frying
  Chocolate Glaze (see recipe,
    page 89) *or* sugar (optional)

Cut the doughnuts by pressing straight down with a floured cutter; avoid twisting the cutter.

In a mixing bowl stir together *2¼ cups* of the flour, the baking powder, cinnamon, salt, and nutmeg. In a large mixing bowl combine eggs, sugar, and vanilla; beat with an electric mixer till thick. Combine milk and melted margarine or butter. Add flour mixture and milk mixture alternately to egg mixture, beating just till blended after each addition. Stir in remaining 1 cup flour. Cover dough; chill about 2 hours.

On a lightly floured surface, roll dough to ½-inch thickness. Cut with a floured 2½-inch doughnut cutter. Reroll as necessary.

Fry two or three doughnuts at a time in deep hot fat (375°) about 1 minute on each side or till golden, turning once with a slotted spoon. Drain on paper towels. Repeat with remaining doughnuts and doughnut holes.

If desired, drizzle warm doughnuts with Chocolate Glaze, dip tops into glaze, or shake warm doughnuts in a bag with sugar. Cool. Makes 13 to 15 doughnuts and doughnut holes.

Chocolate Doughnuts: Prepare as above, *except* omit cinnamon and nutmeg, increase sugar to *1 cup*, reduce milk to *½ cup*, reduce margarine or butter to *2 tablespoons*, and melt 2 squares (2 ounces) *unsweetened chocolate* with margarine or butter.

Buttermilk Doughnuts: Prepare as above, *except* reduce baking powder to *½ teaspoon*, add 1 teaspoon *baking soda* to flour mixture, and substitute *buttermilk or sour milk* for the milk.

Use a slotted spoon to carefully lower the doughnuts into the oil and to turn them.

Corn Fritters

Delicious with warm maple-flavored syrup or served plain as a snack or meal accompaniment.

   1 **8¾-ounce can whole kernel corn**
      Milk
1½ **cups all-purpose flour**
   ¼ **cup cornmeal**
   2 **teaspoons baking powder**
   1 **beaten egg**
      Shortening *or* cooking oil for
         deep-fat frying

Drain corn, reserving liquid. Add enough milk to reserved corn liquid to make *1 cup.* In a mixing bowl stir together flour, cornmeal, baking powder, and ½ teaspoon *salt.* Add corn, milk mixture, and beaten egg. Stir just till moistened.

Drop batter by tablespoons, four or five at a time, into deep hot fat (375°). Cook for 3 to 4 minutes or till golden brown, turning once. Drain on paper towels. Repeat. Serve warm. Makes 24.

Apple Fritters: Prepare as above, *except* substitute 1 cup chopped *apple* for the corn and use *1 cup* milk. Stir 2 tablespoons *sugar* into flour mixture. Roll hot fritters in a mixture of *sugar* and ground *cinnamon.*

Hush Puppies

   1 **beaten egg**
   ½ **cup buttermilk *or* sour milk**
   ¼ **cup sliced green onion**
   1 **cup cornmeal**
   ¼ **cup all-purpose flour**
   2 **teaspoons sugar**
   ¾ **teaspoon baking powder**
   ¼ **teaspoon baking soda**
      Shortening *or* cooking oil for
         deep-fat frying

In a bowl stir together egg, buttermilk or sour milk, and onion. In another bowl combine cornmeal, flour, sugar, baking powder, baking soda, and ¼ teaspoon *salt.* Add egg mixture to cornmeal mixture; stir just till moistened.

Drop batter by tablespoons into deep hot fat (375°). Fry about 1 minute or till golden, turning once. Drain on paper towels. Makes 14 to 18.

Confetti Hush Puppies: Prepare as above, *except* add 2 tablespoons diced *pimiento* and 2 tablespoons snipped *parsley* to egg mixture. Add ⅛ teaspoon *garlic powder* to cornmeal mixture.

Sopaipillas

The secret to puffy sopaipillas (soh-pie-PEEL-yahs) is heating the oil to the right temperature.

   1 **cup all-purpose flour**
1½ **teaspoons baking powder**
   1 **tablespoon shortening, margarine,**
         or butter
      Shortening *or* cooking oil for
         deep-fat frying
      Sifted powdered sugar
      Honey   Oven 300°

In a bowl combine flour, baking powder, and dash *salt.* Cut in shortening till mixture resembles fine crumbs. Gradually add ⅓ cup *warm water* (110° to 115°), stirring with a fork (dough will be crumbly). On a lightly floured surface, knead dough for 3 to 5 minutes or till smooth. Cover; let rest 10 minutes. Roll dough into a 12½ × 10-inch rectangle. Using a fluted pastry wheel or knife, cut into 2½-inch squares (*do not reroll or patch*).

Fry squares, two or three at a time, in deep hot fat (425°) about 30 seconds on each side or till golden. Drain on paper towels. Keep warm in a 300° oven while frying remaining squares. Sprinkle with sugar. Serve with honey. Makes 20.

Mexican Doughnut Strips

Traditionally served with hot chocolate.

   2 **tablespoons margarine *or* butter**
1½ **teaspoons sugar**
   ½ **cup all-purpose flour**
   1 **egg**
      Shortening *or* cooking oil for
         deep-fat frying
      Sugar

In a small saucepan bring margarine or butter, 1½ teaspoons sugar, and ½ cup *water* to boiling. Add flour all at once, stirring vigorously with a wooden spoon. Cook and stir till mixture forms a ball that doesn't separate. Remove from heat and cool 10 minutes. Add egg; beat till smooth.

Spoon dough into a pastry bag fitted with a large star tip. Pipe dough into 3x¾-inch strips onto a baking sheet lined with waxed paper. Freeze 10 to 20 minutes or till paper can be peeled off. (*Do not freeze firm.*) Fry, a few at a time, in deep hot fat (375°) for 4 to 5 minutes or till golden, turning occasionally. Drain on paper towels. Roll in sugar. Serve warm. Makes 12.

Popovers

These crispy, hollow puffs will be the hit of the meal whether you serve them with the appetizer, salad, or main course.

  1 tablespoon shortening *or* nonstick spray coating
  2 beaten eggs
  1 cup milk
  1 tablespoon cooking oil
  1 cup all-purpose flour
  ¼ teaspoon salt   Oven 400°

Using ½ *teaspoon* shortening for *each* cup, grease the bottom and sides of six 6-ounce custard cups or the cups of a popover pan. Or, spray cups with nonstick coating. Place the custard cups on a 15x10x1-inch baking pan; set aside.

In a mixing bowl combine beaten eggs, milk, and cooking oil. Add flour and salt. Beat with a rotary beater or wire whisk till mixture is smooth. Fill the greased cups *half* full. Bake in a 400° oven about 40 minutes or till very firm.

Immediately after removal from the oven, prick each popover with a fork to let steam escape. Then, if crisper popovers are desired, return the popovers to the oven for 5 to 10 minutes more or till desired crispness (be sure the oven is turned off). Serve hot. Makes 6 popovers.

Blender Popovers: Prepare as above, *except* combine eggs, milk, cooking oil, flour, and salt in a *blender container or food processor bowl.* Cover and blend or process about 30 seconds or till smooth. Scrape sides of blender or bowl, if necessary.

Whole Wheat Popovers: Prepare as above, *except* reduce all-purpose flour to ¾ *cup* and add ¼ cup *whole wheat flour.*

Parmesan-Basil Popovers: Prepare as above, *except* add 2 tablespoons grated *Parmesan cheese* and ¾ teaspoon dried *basil,* crushed, with the flour.

Onion and Garlic Popovers: Prepare as above, *except* add ¼ teaspoon *onion powder* and ¼ teaspoon *garlic powder* with the flour.

Cinnamon Popovers: Prepare as above, *except* add ½ teaspoon ground *cinnamon* with the flour. Serve with honey and margarine or butter, if desired.

◀ Prick the popovers as soon as you remove them from the oven to let steam escape.

French Toast

Use French bread if you like a custardlike center; use sliced white bread if you prefer a toasty, crisp French Toast.

  2 beaten eggs
  ½ cup milk
  ¼ teaspoon vanilla
  ⅛ teaspoon ground cinnamon
  5 1-inch-thick slices French bread *or* 6 slices dry white bread
    Margarine, butter, *or* cooking oil
    Maple-flavored syrup (optional)

In a shallow bowl beat together eggs, milk, vanilla, and cinnamon. Dip bread into egg mixture, coating both sides (if using French bread, let soak in egg mixture about 30 seconds on each side).

In a skillet or on a griddle cook bread on both sides in a small amount of hot margarine, butter, or oil over medium heat for 2 to 3 minutes on each side or till golden brown. Add more margarine as needed. Serve with maple-flavored syrup, if desired. Makes 5 or 6 slices.

Stuffed French Toast: Prepare as above, *except* use five *1½-inch-thick* slices French bread. Cut a pocket horizontally into each slice of French bread. In a bowl beat together *half* of an 8-ounce container soft-style *cream cheese with strawberry or pineapple* and ½ teaspoon *vanilla.* Stir in ¼ cup chopped *walnuts.* Spoon *1 rounded tablespoon* cream cheese mixture into *each* bread pocket. To serve, sprinkle cooked Stuffed French Toast with *powdered sugar.*

Caramel-Nut Pinwheels

Always keep a supply of these easy ingredients on hand for great short-notice sweet rolls.

⅓ **cup caramel topping, butterscotch topping, *or* chocolate-flavored syrup**
2 **tablespoons margarine *or* butter, melted**
½ **cup chopped pecans *or* walnuts**
1 **package (8) refrigerated breadsticks**   Oven 350°

In a 9x1½-inch round baking pan stir together topping or syrup and melted margarine or butter. Sprinkle with pecans or walnuts. Separate, but *do not uncoil,* breadsticks. Arrange dough coils in pan atop nuts.

Bake, uncovered, in a 350° oven for 20 to 25 minutes or till golden. Let stand 2 to 3 minutes. Loosen sides and invert onto a serving platter. Spread any remaining topping onto rolls. Serve warm. Makes 8.

Keeping Them Warm

When frying or cooking foods a few at a time, here's how to keep the early batches warm until serving time. Arrange fried foods and waffles in a single layer on a wire rack. Set the rack atop a baking sheet and place it in a 300° oven. To keep pancakes or French toast warm, put them on a ovenproof plate and place them in a 300° oven.

Waffles

1¾ **cups all-purpose flour**
1 **tablespoon baking powder**
¼ **teaspoon salt**
2 **egg yolks**
1¾ **cups milk**
½ **cup cooking oil**
2 **egg whites**

In a mixing bowl combine flour, baking powder, and salt. In another bowl beat egg yolks slightly. Beat in milk and oil. Add egg yolk mixture to flour mixture all at once. Stir just till combined but still slightly lumpy.

In a small bowl beat egg whites till stiff peaks form (tips stand straight). Gently fold beaten egg whites into flour and egg yolk mixture, leaving a few fluffs of egg white. *Do not overmix.*

Pour 1 to 1¼ cups batter onto grids of a preheated, lightly greased waffle baker. Close lid quickly; do not open during baking. Bake according to manufacturer's directions. When done, use a fork to lift waffle off grid. Repeat with remaining batter. Makes 3 or 4 waffles.

Easy Waffles: Prepare as above, *except* do not separate eggs. In a mixing bowl beat *whole eggs* slightly. Beat in milk and oil. Add to flour mixture all at once. Beat just till combined but still slightly lumpy.

Chocolate Waffles: Prepare as above, *except* reduce flour to *1½ cups.* Add ⅓ cup sifted *unsweetened cocoa powder* and ⅓ cup *sugar* to the flour mixture. Add 1 teaspoon *vanilla* to the egg yolk mixture.

Cinnamon-Nut Waffles: Prepare as above, *except* add ½ teaspoon ground *cinnamon* to flour mixture and sprinkle about 2 tablespoons chopped *walnuts or pecans* over *each* waffle before closing lid to bake.

Banana-Wheat Waffles: Prepare as above, *except* reduce all-purpose flour to *1 cup* and add ¾ cup *whole wheat flour.* Add ⅛ teaspoon ground *nutmeg* to flour mixture, reduce milk to *1½ cups,* and add ⅔ cup mashed ripe *banana* to egg yolk mixture.

Buttermilk Waffles: Prepare as above, *except* substitute 2 cups *buttermilk* for milk.

Corn Waffles: Prepare as above, *except* reduce flour to *1¼ cups* and add ½ cup *cornmeal.* Add one 8¾-ounce can *cream-style corn* to egg yolk mixture. Makes 5 or 6.

Pancakes

Turn your kitchen into a pancake house with these five delicious flavors.

> 1 **cup all-purpose flour**
> 1 **tablespoon sugar**
> 2 **teaspoons baking powder**
> ¼ **teaspoon salt**
> 1 **beaten egg**
> 1 **cup milk**
> 2 **tablespoons cooking oil**

In a mixing bowl stir together flour, sugar, baking powder, and salt. In another mixing bowl combine egg, milk, and cooking oil. Add to flour mixture all at once. Stir mixture just till blended but still slightly lumpy.

Pour about ¼ *cup* batter onto a hot, lightly greased griddle or heavy skillet for each standard-size pancake or about *1 tablespoon* batter for each dollar-size pancake.

Cook till pancakes are golden brown, turning to cook second sides when pancakes have bubbly surfaces and slightly dry edges. Makes 8 to 10 standard-size or 36 dollar-size pancakes.

Buttermilk Pancakes: Prepare as above, *except* reduce baking powder to *1 teaspoon* and add ½ teaspoon *baking soda* to flour mixture; substitute *buttermilk or sour milk* for milk. Add additional *buttermilk* to thin batter, if necessary.

Buckwheat Pancakes: Prepare as above, *except* substitute ½ cup *whole wheat flour* and ½ cup *buckwheat flour* for the all-purpose flour; substitute *brown sugar* for the sugar.

Nutty Orange Pancakes: Prepare as above, *except* add ½ teaspoon *baking soda* and ½ teaspoon ground *cinnamon* to the flour mixture; substitute *orange juice* for the milk. Fold ½ cup finely chopped *nuts* into the batter.

Sourdough Pancakes: Prepare as above, *except* bring 1¼ cups *Sourdough Starter* (see recipe, page 42) to room temperature. Reduce baking powder to *1 teaspoon* and add ½ teaspoon *baking soda* to the flour mixture. Substitute the 1¼ cups room-temperature Sourdough Starter for the 1 cup milk.

Crepes

Place two layers of waxed paper between any extra crepes and freeze them. Let crepes thaw at room temperature for one hour before using.

> 1½ **cups milk**
> 1 **cup all-purpose flour**
> 2 **eggs**
> 1 **tablespoon cooking oil**

In a bowl combine milk, flour, eggs, oil, and ¼ teaspoon *salt*. Beat with a rotary beater till well mixed. Heat a lightly greased 6-inch skillet. Remove from the heat. Spoon in *2 tablespoons* of the batter; lift and tilt the skillet to spread batter. Return to heat; brown on one side only. (Or, cook on an inverted crepe maker according to manufacturer's directions.) Invert pan over paper towels; remove crepe. Repeat with remaining batter, greasing skillet occasionally. Makes 18.

Dessert Crepes: Prepare as above, *except* omit salt and add 2 tablespoons *sugar*.

Puffed Oven Pancake

> 2 **tablespoons margarine *or* butter**
> 3 **eggs**
> ½ **cup all-purpose flour**
> ½ **cup milk**
> ¼ **teaspoon salt**
> **Apple-Raisin Sauce**
> **Powdered sugar**   Oven 400°

Place margarine or butter in a 10-inch ovenproof skillet. Place in a 400° oven for 3 to 5 minutes or till margarine or butter melts. In a bowl beat eggs with a rotary beater till combined. Add flour, milk, and salt. Beat till smooth. Immediately pour into the hot skillet. Bake about 25 minutes or till puffed and well browned.

Meanwhile, prepare the Apple-Raisin Sauce. Sprinkle pancake with powdered sugar and cut into wedges. Serve with sauce. Serves 6.

Apple-Raisin Sauce: In a skillet combine 2 large cooking *apples,* peeled, cored, and thinly sliced; ¾ cup *apple juice or water;* ⅓ cup *raisins;* 2 tablespoons *sugar;* and ¼ teaspoon ground *cinnamon.* Simmer, covered, till apples are just tender. Stir together 2 tablespoons *cornstarch* and 2 tablespoons *cold water.* Add to apple mixture. Cook and stir till thickened and bubbly. Cook and stir 2 minutes more. Stir in 1 teaspoon *margarine or butter.* Keep warm. Makes 2 cups.

Nutrition Analysis

	Per Serving								Percent U.S. RDA Per Serving							
	Servings Per Recipe	Calories	Protein (g)	Carbohydrate (g)	Fat (g)	Cholesterol (mg)	Sodium (mg)	Potassium (mg)	Protein	Vitamin A	Vitamin C	Thiamine	Riboflavin	Niacin	Calcium	Iron
Almond Sponge Cake (p. 84)	12	188	5	36	3	136	30	64	7	3	6	7	8	4	2	6
Angel Cake (p. 85)	12	161	4	37	0	0	49	53	6	0	0	0	6	0	1	0
Applesauce Spice Cake (p. 78)	12	282	4	46	10	69	190	61	6	5	1	10	8	6	4	8
Apricot Upside-Down Cake (p. 76)	8	283	4	45	10	36	201	148	6	20	1	10	9	6	9	9
Banana Cake (p. 81)	12	281	4	46	10	46	220	122	6	1	3	10	8	6	5	7
Black Forest Cake (p. 82)	12	532	5	90	20	62	239	171	8	6	2	10	9	7	5	12
Blueberry Sour Cream Pound Cake (p. 83)	10	281	4	36	14	113	144	65	7	11	2	9	9	5	3	7
Broiled Coconut Topping (p. 90)	9	66	0	8	4	0	33	39	0	2	0	0	0	0	1	2
Busy-Day Cake (p. 77)	8	211	4	34	7	36	162	64	6	6	0	10	8	6	8	6
Butter Frosting (p. 89)	12	198	0	38	6	16	62	11	0	5	0	0	1	0	1	0
Carrot Cake (p. 79)	12	404	5	52	20	92	150	133	7	157	4	12	9	7	4	8
Chiffon Cake (p. 85)	12	298	5	42	13	159	154	58	8	4	1	2	6	1	7	4
Chocolate Butter Frosting (p. 89)	12	191	1	35	7	16	87	34	1	5	0	0	2	0	1	2
Chocolate Cake Roll (p. 86)	10	274	4	33	15	142	96	80	6	11	0	4	7	2	3	5
Chocolate Cream Cheese Frosting (p. 88)	12	259	1	37	13	16	145	34	2	10	0	0	2	0	2	2
Chocolate Glaze (p. 89)	12	121	0	18	6	0	34	32	1	2	0	0	1	0	0	1
Chocolate Marble Pound Cake (p. 83)	12	318	5	37	18	133	208	65	7	13	0	10	8	6	3	8
Chocolate Powdered Sugar Icing (p. 88)	12	35	0	9	0	0	8	9	0	0	0	0	0	0	0	1
Chocolate-Sour-Cream Frosting (p. 89)	12	208	1	29	11	4	51	63	1	5	0	0	2	0	2	2
Chocolate Sponge Cake (p. 84)	12	185	5	35	3	136	47	77	7	3	5	7	8	3	2	7
Choose-a-Fruit Filling (p. 90)	12	29	0	7	0	0	1	46	1	1	2	0	1	1	1	1
Citrus Yellow Cake (p. 77)	12	340	5	59	9	48	192	94	8	8	1	15	12	8	10	9
Coconut-Pecan Frosting (p. 90)	12	174	2	17	11	27	67	98	3	4	1	4	4	1	4	2
Cream Cheese Frosting (p. 88)	12	262	1	38	13	16	132	22	2	10	0	0	2	0	1	1
Creamy White Frosting (p. 88)	12	294	0	37	17	0	2	7	0	0	0	0	0	0	0	0
Date Cake (p. 80)	12	261	3	43	10	46	153	150	5	1	0	8	6	6	5	6
Devil's Food Cake (p. 83)	12	316	5	52	11	48	235	102	7	2	0	10	10	6	5	8
Fluffy White Frosting (p. 88)	12	67	1	17	0	0	9	8	1	0	0	0	1	0	0	0
Fruitcake (p. 87)	16	202	3	33	7	34	92	179	4	4	7	10	5	4	4	8
Fudge Cake (p. 82)	12	311	4	47	13	46	151	91	6	10	0	10	7	6	3	9
German Chocolate Cake (p. 81)	12	292	4	42	13	69	216	83	7	8	0	9	8	5	4	7
Gingerbread (p. 80)	9	280	3	37	13	34	106	276	5	1	0	12	8	8	9	15
Hot-Milk Sponge Cake (p. 85)	9	183	3	34	4	62	86	51	5	4	0	7	7	4	5	5
Jelly Roll (p. 86)	10	162	3	33	2	109	56	44	5	3	1	4	6	2	3	5
Lady Baltimore Cake (p. 78)	12	388	5	66	12	1	139	161	8	1	2	15	11	8	6	8
Lemon Butter Frosting (p. 89)	12	197	0	38	6	16	59	9	0	4	4	0	0	0	0	0
Lemon Filling (p. 90)	12	73	0	14	2	45	13	8	1	2	3	1	1	0	1	1
Lemon-Poppy-Seed Pound Cake (p. 83)	10	273	5	37	12	108	144	79	7	9	2	7	9	5	6	7
Lemon Sponge Cake (p. 84)	12	184	4	35	3	136	30	50	7	3	3	7	8	4	2	6
Light Fruitcake (p. 87)	16	206	3	34	7	34	97	170	5	4	12	8	7	5	4	8
Lime Sponge Cake (p. 84)	12	184	4	35	3	136	30	50	7	3	3	7	8	4	2	6
Liqueur Powdered Sugar Icing (p. 88)	12	36	0	9	0	0	0	2	0	0	0	0	0	0	0	0
Mocha Butter Frosting (p. 89)	12	198	0	38	6	16	62	11	0	5	0	0	1	0	1	0
No-Cook Fudge Frosting (p. 89)	12	230	1	41	9	0	115	29	1	6	0	0	1	0	1	2
Nutmeg Cake (p. 78)	12	272	4	42	10	69	201	72	7	5	1	10	9	6	5	7
Nut Torte (p. 87)	12	240	6	18	17	92	51	150	9	2	2	8	5	2	5	6
One-Layer Chocolate Cake (p. 81)	8	237	4	39	8	36	179	77	6	2	0	8	8	5	6	6
One-Layer Mocha Cake (p. 81)	8	237	4	39	8	36	179	77	6	2	0	8	8	5	6	6
One-Layer Peanut Butter and Chocolate Cake (p. 81)	8	257	6	41	9	36	216	132	9	2	0	9	8	10	6	7
Orange Butter Frosting (p. 89)	12	197	0	38	6	16	59	9	0	4	4	0	0	0	0	0
Peanut-Butter Frosting (p. 89)	12	189	2	39	4	0	37	58	3	0	0	1	1	5	1	1

On the divider: Carrot Cake (p. 79) with Cream Cheese Frosting (p. 88).

Nutrition Analysis

	Per Serving								Percent U.S. RDA Per Serving							
	Servings Per Recipe	Calories	Protein (g)	Carbohydrate (g)	Fat (g)	Cholesterol (mg)	Sodium (mg)	Potassium (mg)	Protein	Vitamin A	Vitamin C	Thiamine	Riboflavin	Niacin	Calcium	Iron
Pear-Raisin Upside-Down Cake (p. 76)	8	286	4	46	10	36	199	129	6	9	1	10	9	6	9	8
Penuche Frosting (p. 90)	12	253	0	47	8	1	100	82	1	7	0	0	1	0	3	4
Peppermint Frosting (p. 87)	12	99	1	25	0	9	0	8	1	0	0	0	1	0	0	0
Petits Fours (p. 78)	36	104	2	18	3	0	46	27	2	0	0	4	3	2	2	2
Petits Fours Icing (p. 88)	36	107	0	28	0	0	0	1	0	0	0	0	0	0	0	0
Pineapple Carrot Cake (p. 79)	12	430	5	56	21	92	151	167	7	157	7	13	9	7	4	10
Pineapple Upside-Down Cake (p. 76)	8	282	4	45	10	36	198	133	6	9	3	12	9	6	9	8
Pound Cake (p. 83)	12	302	4	32	17	133	205	47	7	13	0	10	8	6	3	7
Pound Cake Ring (p. 83)	18	303	4	33	17	133	205	48	7	13	0	10	8	6	3	7
Powdered Sugar Icing (p. 88)	12	33	0	8	0	0	1	3	0	0	0	0	0	0	0	0
Pumpkin Cake Roll (p. 86)	10	446	5	70	17	128	213	85	7	69	1	4	8	2	5	6
Pumpkin-Molasses Cake (p. 79)	12	311	4	52	10	46	133	249	7	46	1	13	10	8	9	16
Raisin-Nut Carrot Cake (p. 79)	12	454	5	58	23	92	151	203	8	157	5	14	10	7	5	10
Rocky Road Frosting (p. 89)	8	146	1	22	7	0	36	51	2	2	0	1	1	0	1	2
Seven-Minute Frosting (p. 87)	12	99	1	25	0	9	0	8	1	0	0	0	1	0	0	0
Sour Cream Devil's Food Cake (p. 83)	12	334	5	53	13	52	238	109	8	4	1	11	11	6	6	8
Sour Cream Pound Cake (p. 83)	10	277	4	35	14	113	143	58	7	10	0	9	8	5	3	7
Spice Cake (p. 78)	12	272	4	42	10	69	201	72	7	5	1	10	9	6	5	7
Spiced Pecan Busy-Day Cake (p. 77)	8	260	4	35	12	36	162	93	7	6	1	14	9	6	8	7
Sponge Cake (p. 84)	12	188	5	36	3	136	30	64	7	3	6	7	8	4	2	6
Wheat and Raisin Busy-Day Cake (p. 77)	8	221	4	36	7	36	162	118	6	6	1	10	7	5	8	6
White Cake (p. 78)	12	313	5	54	9	1	138	81	7	0	0	12	10	7	5	7
Yellow Cake (p. 77)	12	340	5	59	9	48	192	94	8	8	1	15	12	8	10	9

Cakes

Great news! Baking a cake is now as easy as dumping all the ingredients into a bowl and beating them together. Our new method saves you time yet keeps the texture and flavor of old-fashioned cakes.

Follow these tips when baking cakes.
● Use the exact ingredients listed in a recipe. Substitutions, such as shortening for margarine or butter, will alter the cake's texture and flavor.
● Turn your oven on to preheat, then start mixing your cake. Your oven should be preheated (allow 10 to 15 minutes) at about the same time you're done mixing the cake.
● Cool layer cakes in their pans on wire racks for 10 minutes (loaf cakes, 15 minutes), then loosen the edges. Place an inverted rack on each cake and turn over; lift off the pan. Place a second rack over the cake and invert again.

Invert angel, sponge, and chiffon cakes in their pans as soon as they are removed from the oven to prevent them from shrinking or falling. Then cool completely.

Using the Nutrition Chart

The chart opposite and above lists each cake, frosting, and filling separately. To determine the nutritional amounts for a cake made with a filling or frosting from elsewhere in the chapter, add the numbers for the cake and filling or frosting. If a cake recipe lists the ingredients for its filling or frosting, the analysis for these ingredients is included with the cake analysis.

Pineapple Upside-Down Cake

>   **2 tablespoons margarine *or* butter**
> **⅓ cup packed brown sugar**
>   **1 8-ounce can pineapple slices,**
>   **drained and halved**
>   **4 maraschino cherries, halved**
>   **Batter for Busy-Day Cake (see**
>   **recipe, opposite)**   Oven 350°

Melt margarine in a 9x1½-inch round baking pan. Stir in sugar and 1 tablespoon *water*. Arrange pineapple and cherries in the pan. Prepare batter for Busy-Day Cake; spoon into the pan. Bake in a 350° oven for 30 to 35 minutes or till a toothpick inserted near the center comes out clean. Cool on a wire rack for 5 minutes. Loosen sides; invert onto a plate. Serve warm. Serves 8.

Apricot Upside-Down Cake: Prepare as above, *except* substitute one 8¾-ounce can *apricot halves,* drained and halved, *or peach slices,* drained, and 2 tablespoons toasted *coconut* for the pineapple and cherries.

Pear-Raisin Upside-Down Cake: Prepare as above, *except* substitute one 8½-ounce can *pear slices,* drained, and 2 tablespoons *raisins* for the pineapple and cherries.

Slowly pour the cake batter into the pan to avoid disturbing the pineapple-cherry arrangement.

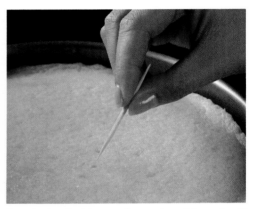

Insert a toothpick near the center of the cake. If no batter clings to the pick, the cake is done.

Busy-Day Cake

Stir up this one-layer cake in only minutes with easy-to-keep-on-hand ingredients.

- 1⅓ **cups all-purpose flour**
- ⅔ **cup sugar**
- 2 **teaspoons baking powder**
- ⅔ **cup milk**
- ¼ **cup margarine *or* butter, softened**
- 1 **egg**
- 1 **teaspoon vanilla**
  Broiled Coconut Topping (see recipe, page 90) *or* whipped cream and fresh fruit (optional)   Oven 350°

In a bowl combine flour, sugar, and baking powder. Add milk, margarine or butter, egg, and vanilla. Beat with an electric mixer on low speed till combined. Beat on medium speed for 1 minute. Pour batter into a greased and floured 8x1½-inch round baking pan.

Bake in a 350° oven for 25 to 30 minutes or till a toothpick inserted near the center comes out clean. Frost warm cake with Broiled Coconut Topping, if desired. *Or,* cool in the pan on a wire rack for 5 minutes. Remove cake from pan. Cool thoroughly. Serve with whipped cream and fresh fruit, if desired. Makes 8 servings.

Microwave directions: Prepare batter as above, *except* increase margarine or butter to ⅓ *cup.* Grease an 8x1½-inch round baking dish; line bottom of dish with waxed paper. Pour batter into dish. Micro-cook, uncovered, on 50% power (medium) for 10 minutes, giving the dish a quarter-turn *every* 3 minutes. If not done, cook on 100% power (high) for 30 seconds to 2 minutes more or till surface is nearly dry. Cool on a wire rack for 5 minutes. Loosen, then invert onto a wire rack; remove waxed paper. If desired, place cake on a baking sheet and frost with Broiled Coconut Topping (do not put baking dish under broiler). *Or,* cool cake thoroughly. Serve with whipped cream and fruit, if desired.

Spiced Pecan Busy-Day Cake: Prepare as above, *except* add ⅛ teaspoon ground *nutmeg or allspice* with the flour. Stir in ½ cup chopped *pecans, walnuts, or peanuts* after beating.

Wheat and Raisin Busy-Day Cake: Prepare as above, *except* reduce all-purpose flour to *1 cup* and add ⅓ cup *whole wheat flour* to flour mixture. Sprinkle ¼ cup *raisins or* snipped pitted whole *dates* atop batter in the baking pan.

Yellow Cake

Delicious with just a dusting of powdered sugar.

- 3 **cups all-purpose flour**
- 2 **cups sugar**
- 1 **tablepoon baking powder**
- 1½ **cups milk**
- ½ **cup margarine *or* butter, softened**
- 1½ **teaspoons vanilla**
- 2 **eggs**   Oven 375°

In a bowl combine flour, sugar, and baking powder. Add milk, margarine, and vanilla. Beat with an electric mixer on low speed till combined. Beat on high speed for 2 minutes. Add eggs and beat 2 minutes more. Pour into 2 greased and floured 9x1½-inch round baking pans. Bake in a 375° oven for 25 to 30 minutes or till a toothpick inserted near the centers comes out clean. Cool on wire racks for 10 minutes. Remove from pans. Cool thoroughly on racks. Serves 12.

Citrus Yellow Cake: Prepare as above, *except* add 2 teaspoons finely shredded *orange peel or* 1 teaspoon finely shredded *lemon peel* to the flour mixture. Fill with Lemon Filling (see recipe, page 90) and frost with Lemon or Orange Butter Frosting (see recipe, page 89), if desired.

Greasing Cake Pans

Use the following guidelines for greasing and flouring cake pans:
- Use a paper towel to evenly spread the shortening.
- If the cake will be removed from the pan, grease the bottom and the sides. Use 2 to 3 teaspoons shortening for an 8- or 9-inch pan and 1½ to 2 tablespoons shortening for a 13x9x2- or 15x10x1-inch pan. Sprinkle a little flour into the pan. Tilt and tap the pan so the flour covers all the greased surfaces. Tap out the excess flour.
- If the cake will be left in the pan, grease only the bottom of the pan and do not flour it.

White Cake

Buttermilk flavors this light, tender cake.

2½ cups all-purpose flour
2 cups sugar
1 teaspoon baking powder
½ teaspoon baking soda
1⅓ cups buttermilk *or* sour milk
½ cup shortening, margarine, *or* butter
1 teaspoon vanilla
4 egg whites   Oven 350°

In a bowl combine flour, sugar, baking powder, baking soda, and ⅛ teaspoon *salt.* Add buttermilk, shortening, and vanilla. Beat with an electric mixer on low speed for 30 seconds, scraping bowl. Beat on medium to high speed for 2 minutes, scraping bowl occasionally. Add egg whites and beat for 2 minutes more, scraping bowl.

Pour into 2 greased and floured 9x1½-inch round baking pans. Bake in a 350° oven for 30 to 35 minutes or till a toothpick inserted near the centers comes out clean. Cool on wire racks for 10 minutes. Loosen sides. Remove from pans. Cool thoroughly on wire racks. Serves 12.

Lady Baltimore Cake: Prepare as above. Prepare *Seven-Minute Frosting* (see recipe, page 87). For filling, combine *one-fourth* of the frosting, ½ cup chopped *candied cherries,* ½ cup chopped *pecans,* and ½ cup snipped pitted whole *dates,* chopped *figs, or raisins.* Spread filling between layers. Frost with remaining frosting.

Petits Fours: Prepare as above, *except* pour batter into a greased and floured 13x9x2-inch baking pan. Bake in a 350° oven for 40 to 45 minutes or till a toothpick inserted near the center comes out clean. Cool on a wire rack for 10 minutes; remove from pan. Cool thoroughly. Prepare *Petits Fours Icing* (see recipe, page 88).

Trim sides of cake to make smooth, straight edges. Cut cake into 1½-inch squares, diamonds, or circles. With fingertips, brush off crumbs. Place cake pieces on wire racks over waxed paper.

Insert a 2- or 3-prong long-handled fork into the side of *one* cake piece. Holding cake over icing, spoon on enough icing to cover sides and top. Place on a wire rack. Repeat with remaining cake pieces. (Sides of pieces should not touch.) Let dry 15 minutes.

Repeat for a second coat of icing, except place cake pieces *atop* prongs of the fork (do not spear). Repeat for a third layer of icing, if desired. Reuse the icing from the waxed paper, straining crumbs, if necessary. Makes 36 to 40.

◄ Add egg whites and beat on medium speed. If the mixer seems to strain, shift to high speed.

Spice Cake

One of our taste testers exclaimed, "It's perfect!"

2 cups all-purpose flour
1½ cups sugar
1 teaspoon baking powder
1 teaspoon baking soda
1 teaspoon ground cinnamon
¼ teaspoon ground nutmeg
¼ teaspoon ground cloves
¼ teaspoon ground ginger
1 cup buttermilk *or* sour milk
¼ cup margarine *or* butter, softened
¼ cup shortening
½ teaspoon vanilla
3 eggs   Oven 350°

In a bowl combine flour, sugar, baking powder, baking soda, cinnamon, nutmeg, cloves, and ginger. Add buttermilk or sour milk, margarine or butter, shortening, and vanilla. Beat with an electric mixer on low to medium speed till combined. Beat 2 minutes on high speed. Add eggs and beat 2 minutes more.

Pour batter into a greased 13x9x2-inch baking pan. Bake in a 350° oven for 30 to 35 minutes or till a toothpick inserted near the center comes out clean. Cool on a wire rack. Makes 12 servings.

Nutmeg Cake: Prepare as above, *except* omit cinnamon, cloves, and ginger. Increase nutmeg to *1½ teaspoons.*

Applesauce Spice Cake: Prepare as above, *except* reduce buttermilk or sour milk to *¼ cup* and add 1 cup *applesauce.*

Pumpkin-Molasses Cake

Complement the flavor of this moist cake with Lemon Butter Frosting (see recipe, page 89).

2½ **cups all-purpose flour**
1½ **cups packed brown sugar**
  1 **teaspoon baking powder**
  ¾ **teaspoon baking soda**
  ½ **teaspoon ground cinnamon**
  ½ **teaspoon ground ginger**
  ¾ **cup buttermilk *or* sour milk**
  ½ **cup shortening, margarine, *or* butter, softened**
  ½ **cup canned pumpkin *or* mashed cooked sweet potato**
  ¼ **cup light molasses**
  1 **teaspoon finely shredded orange peel**
  2 **eggs**   Oven 350°

In a bowl combine flour, brown sugar, baking powder, baking soda, cinnamon, and ginger. Add buttermilk, shortening, pumpkin or sweet potato, molasses, and orange peel. Beat with an electric mixer on low to medium speed till combined. Beat on high speed for 2 minutes. Add eggs and beat 2 minutes more. Pour into a greased 13x9x2-inch baking pan.

Bake in a 350° oven for 30 to 35 minutes or till a toothpick inserted near the center comes out clean. Cool on a wire rack. Serves 12.

Carrot Cake

To match the picture on page 73, frost with Cream Cheese Frosting (see recipe, page 88) and top with walnut halves and strips of orange peel.

  2 **cups all-purpose flour**
  2 **cups sugar**
  1 **teaspoon baking powder**
  1 **teaspoon baking soda**
  1 **teaspoon ground cinnamon**
  3 **cups finely shredded carrot**
  1 **cup cooking oil**
  4 **eggs**   Oven 350°

In a bowl combine flour, sugar, baking powder, baking soda, and cinnamon. Add carrot, oil, and eggs. Beat with an electric mixer till combined.

Pour into 2 greased and floured 9x1½-inch round baking pans. Bake in a 350° oven for 30 to 35 minutes or till a toothpick inserted near the centers comes out clean. Cool on wire racks for 10 minutes. Remove cakes from pans. Cool thoroughly on racks. Makes 12 to 15 servings.

Pineapple Carrot Cake: Prepare as above, *except* add one 8¼-ounce can *undrained* crushed *pineapple* and ½ cup *coconut* with carrot. Bake about 40 minutes.

Raisin-Nut Carrot Cake: Prepare as above, *except* stir ½ cup *raisins or currants* and ½ cup chopped *nuts* into batter.

Choose-a-Pan Cakes

Two-layer cakes suit some occasions, and carry-in-the-pan cakes are handy for picnics and potlucks. For the cake batters on pages 77 to 83, choose the size pan that best fits your needs.

Fill the baking pans no more than half full. Use any remaining batter to make some cupcakes. Baking times given are approximate and may vary from cake to cake.

Pan Size	Estimated Baking Time in a 350° Oven
Two 8x1½-inch round baking pans	35 to 40 minutes
Two 9x1½-inch round baking pans	30 to 35 minutes
Two 8x8x2-inch baking pans	25 to 35 minutes
Two 9x9x2-inch baking pans	25 to 35 minutes
One 13x9x2-inch baking pan	30 to 35 minutes
One 15x10x1-inch baking pan	25 to 30 minutes
Cupcakes (half full of batter)	18 to 23 minutes

Date Cake

Don't worry about letting this light cake cool thoroughly. It's delicious served warm.

Oven 350°

In a bowl combine one 8-ounce package (1⅓ cups) pitted whole *dates,* snipped, and 1 cup *boiling water;* cool to room temperature (about 1 hour). *Do not drain.*

In a bowl combine 1½ cups *all-purpose flour,* 1 cup *sugar,* 2 teaspoons *baking powder,* ½ teaspoon *baking soda,* and ¼ teaspoon *salt.* Add date mixture, ½ cup *shortening,* 2 *eggs,* and 1 teaspoon *vanilla.* Beat with an electric mixer on low to medium speed till combined. Beat on high speed for 3 minutes. Stir in 1 cup chopped *nuts.*

Pour into a greased 13x9x2-inch baking pan. Bake in a 350° oven for 35 to 40 minutes or till a toothpick inserted near the center comes out clean. Cool on a wire rack. Serve with whipped cream, if desired. Serves 12.

Gingerbread

1½	cups all-purpose flour
¼	cup packed brown sugar
¾	teaspoon ground cinnamon
¾	teaspoon ground ginger
½	teaspoon baking powder
½	teaspoon baking soda
½	cup shortening
½	cup light molasses
1	egg

Oven 350°

In a bowl combine flour, brown sugar, cinnamon, ginger, baking powder, and baking soda. Add shortening, molasses, egg, and ½ cup *water.* Beat with an electric mixer on low to medium speed till combined. Beat on high speed for 2 minutes. Pour into a greased and floured 8x8x2-inch baking pan. Bake in a 350° oven for 35 to 40 minutes or till a toothpick inserted near the center comes out clean. Cool on a rack 10 minutes. Remove from pan; serve warm. Serves 9.

Microwave directions: Prepare batter as above, *except* substitute *cooking oil* for shortening. Grease a 2-quart ring mold. Coat with 2 tablespoons toasted *wheat germ.* Pour batter into mold. Micro-cook, uncovered, on 50% power (medium) for 10 minutes, giving dish a quarter-turn every 3 minutes. If not done, cook on 100% power (high) for 30 seconds to 2 minutes more or till surface is nearly dry. Cool for 5 minutes.

Fixing Up Cake Mixes

Create a special cake by using one of the following suggestions with a yellow, white, or chocolate two-layer cake mix.

Add one of these to the dry cake mix:
   ¾ teaspoon ground cinnamon
   ¾ teaspoon ground ginger
   ½ teaspoon ground allspice
   ¼ teaspoon ground nutmeg

Add one of these with the eggs:
   ½ cup applesauce
   1 tablespoon instant coffee crystals
      (dissolved in the water called for
      in the mix directions)
   1 tablespoon finely shredded orange
      peel
   1 teaspoon maple flavoring
   ½ teaspoon almond extract

Substitute an equal amount of unsweetened pineapple juice for the water in a white or yellow cake mix.

Stir one of these into the mixed cake batter:
   1 cup coconut
   ½ cup finely chopped nuts
   ½ cup miniature semisweet
      chocolate pieces
   ½ cup well-drained, chopped
      maraschino cherries

To *one-third* of the white or yellow cake batter, add a half cup chocolate-flavored syrup. Pour the plain batter into the baking pans; pour chocolate batter on top of the plain batter. Swirl gently with a spatula.

Banana Cake

> 2 cups all-purpose flour
> 1½ cups sugar
> 1½ teaspoons baking powder
> ¾ teaspoon baking soda
> 1 cup mashed ripe banana
> ½ cup buttermilk *or* sour milk
> ½ cup shortening
> 2 eggs
> 1 teaspoon vanilla   Oven 350°

In a bowl combine flour, sugar, baking powder, baking soda, and ½ teaspoon *salt*. Add banana, buttermilk, shortening, eggs, and vanilla. Beat with an electric mixer on low speed till combined. Beat on medium speed for 3 minutes.

Pour batter into 2 greased and floured 8x1½- or 9x1½-inch round baking pans. Bake in a 350° oven for 30 to 35 minutes or till a toothpick comes out clean. Cool on racks for 10 minutes. Remove from pans; cool on racks. Serves 12.

German Chocolate Cake

> 1 4-ounce package German sweet cooking chocolate
> 1⅔ cups all-purpose flour
> 1⅓ cups sugar
> 1 teaspoon baking powder
> ½ teaspoon baking soda
> ⅔ cup buttermilk *or* sour milk
> ½ cup margarine *or* butter, softened, *or* shortening
> 1 teaspoon vanilla
> 3 eggs
>   Coconut-Pecan Frosting
>   (see recipe, page 90)   Oven 350°

In a saucepan combine chocolate and ⅓ cup *water;* cook and stir over low heat till melted. Cool. In a bowl combine flour, sugar, baking powder, soda, and ⅛ teaspoon *salt*. Add chocolate mixture, milk, margarine, and vanilla. Beat with an electric mixer on low to medium speed till combined. Beat on high speed for 2 minutes.

Add eggs and beat 2 minutes more. Pour into 2 greased and floured 8x1½- or 9x1½-inch round baking pans. Bake in a 350° oven for 30 to 40 minutes or till a toothpick comes out clean. Cool on racks 10 minutes. Remove from pans. Cool on racks. Frost with Coconut-Pecan Frosting. Makes 12 servings.

One-Layer Chocolate Cake

Just the right size for one meal and a few snacks.

> 1 cup all-purpose flour
> 1 cup sugar
> ¼ cup unsweetened cocoa powder
> 1 teaspoon baking powder
> ¼ teaspoon baking soda
> ¾ cup milk
> ¼ cup shortening
> ½ teaspoon vanilla
> 1 egg   Oven 350°

In a bowl combine flour, sugar, cocoa powder, baking powder, baking soda, and ¼ teaspoon *salt*. Add milk, shortening, and vanilla. Beat with an electric mixer on low speed till combined. Beat on medium speed for 2 minutes. Add egg and beat 2 minutes more. Pour into a greased and floured 9x1½-inch round baking pan.

Bake in a 350° oven for 30 to 35 minutes or till a toothpick inserted near the center comes out clean. Cool on a rack for 10 minutes. Remove from pan. Cool thoroughly on a rack. Serves 8.

Microwave directions: Prepare batter as above, *except* substitute *softened margarine or butter* for shortening. Grease the bottom of a 2-quart ring mold; line with waxed paper. Pour batter into the mold. Micro-cook, uncovered, on 50% power (medium) for 10 minutes, giving dish a quarter-turn every 3 minutes. If not done, cook on 100% power (high) for 30 seconds to 2 minutes more or till surface is nearly dry. Cool on a wire rack for 5 minutes. Invert onto a plate; remove waxed paper. Cool.

One-Layer Mocha Cake: Prepare as above, *except* add 1 to 2 tablespoons instant *coffee crystals* to the milk; stir to dissolve.

One-Layer Peanut Butter and Chocolate Cake: Prepare as above, *except* reduce the shortening to *2 tablespoons* and add ¼ cup *peanut butter* to the flour mixture.

Moist Microwave Cakes

To keep a cake baked in the microwave oven moist, cover the cooled cake with plastic wrap. Better yet, frost it.

Fudge Cake

Satisfy those chocolate cravings with this luscious layer cake.

      2   **cups all-purpose flour**
   1¾   **cups sugar**
      1   **teaspoon baking powder**
      ¾   **teaspoon baking soda**
      ¼   **teaspoon salt**
   1⅓   **cups water**
      ½   **cup shortening**
      1   **teaspoon vanilla**
      2   **eggs**
      3   **squares (3 ounces) unsweetened**
          chocolate, melted
          and cooled   Oven 350°

In a bowl combine flour, sugar, baking powder, baking soda, and salt. Add water, shortening, and vanilla. Beat with an electric mixer on low to medium speed till combined. Beat on high speed for 2 minutes. Add eggs and melted chocolate; beat 2 minutes more.

Pour batter into 2 greased and floured 8x1½- or 9x1½-inch round baking pans. Bake in a 350° oven for 30 to 35 minutes or till a toothpick inserted near the centers comes out clean.

Cool on wire racks for 10 minutes. Remove cakes from the pans. Cool thoroughly on wire racks. Makes 12 servings.

Black Forest Cake

Black Forest Cake

This traditional German dessert is a wonderful combination of chocolate and cherries.

      Fudge Cake (see recipe, left)
      Choose-a-Fruit Filling (cherry
          option) (see recipe, page 90)
      Chocolate Butter Frosting (see
          recipe, page 89)
      Whipped cream (optional)
      Chocolate shavings (optional)

Prepare Fudge Cake; cool thoroughly. Prepare Choose-a-Fruit Filling using cherries; chill well. Prepare Chocolate Butter Frosting.

Place *one* cake layer on a serving plate. Using *1 cup* of the frosting, make a border around the edge of the layer ½ inch wide and 1 inch high. Using *½ cup* more of the frosting, make a solid circle in the center of cake layer about 2½ inches in diameter and 1 inch high. Spread the chilled filling between the frosting border and the circle.

Place second cake layer on top. Frost with remaining frosting. If desired, garnish with dollops of whipped cream and chocolate shavings. Chill. Let stand at room temperature 20 minutes before serving. Makes 12 servings.

Devil's Food Cake

2 cups all-purpose flour
2 cups sugar
½ cup unsweetened cocoa powder
1½ teaspoons baking soda
1½ cups milk
½ cup shortening
1 teaspoon vanilla
2 eggs   Oven 350°

In a bowl combine flour, sugar, cocoa powder, baking soda, and ¼ teaspoon *salt*. Add milk, shortening, and vanilla. Beat with an electric mixer on low speed till combined. Beat on high speed for 2 minutes. Add eggs and beat 2 minutes more. Pour into 2 greased and floured 9x1½-inch round baking pans. Bake in a 350° oven for 30 to 35 minutes or till a toothpick comes out clean. Cool on racks 10 minutes. Remove from pans. Cool on racks. Serves 12.

Sour Cream Devil's Food Cake: Prepare as above, *except* reduce milk to *1¼ cups* and add ½ cup dairy *sour cream* with the milk.

Sour Cream Pound Cake

Oven 325°

Bring ½ cup *butter*, 3 *eggs,* and ½ cup dairy *sour cream* to room temperature. Combine 1½ cups *all-purpose flour*, ¼ teaspoon *baking powder,* and ⅛ teaspoon *baking soda.*

In a bowl beat butter with an electric mixer on medium to high speed for 30 seconds. Gradually add 1 cup *sugar,* beating about 10 minutes or till very light and fluffy. Add ½ teaspoon *vanilla.* Add eggs, one at a time, beating 1 minute after each addition and scraping bowl often.

Add flour mixture and sour cream to egg mixture alternately, beating on low to medium speed after each addition just till combined. Pour into a greased and floured 8x4x2- or 9x5x3-inch loaf pan. Bake in a 325° oven for 60 to 75 minutes or till a toothpick comes out clean. Cool on a rack 10 minutes. Remove from pan. Cool. Serves 10.

Lemon-Poppy-Seed Pound Cake: Prepare as above, *except* substitute ½ cup *lemon yogurt* for sour cream. Add 1 teaspoon finely shredded *lemon peel,* 2 tablespoons *lemon juice,* and 2 tablespoons *poppy seed* to batter.

Blueberry Sour Cream Pound Cake: Prepare as above, *except* gently fold ½ cup fresh or frozen *blueberries* into the batter.

Pound Cake

Pound cake originally was made with a pound each of butter, sugar, eggs, and flour. We cut the recipe but kept the rich flavor.

1 cup butter
4 eggs
2 cups all-purpose flour
1 teaspoon baking powder
¼ teaspoon ground nutmeg (optional)
1 cup sugar
1 teaspoon vanilla
Powdered Sugar Icing (see recipe, page 88) (optional)   Oven 325°

Bring butter and eggs to room temperature. In a mixing bowl stir together flour, baking powder, and, if desired, nutmeg. In another bowl beat butter with an electric mixer on medium speed for 30 seconds.

Gradually add sugar to butter, *2 tablespoons* at a time, beating on medium to high speed about 6 minutes total or till very light and fluffy. Add vanilla. Add eggs, one at a time, beating 1 minute after each addition, scraping bowl often. Gradually add flour mixture to butter mixture, beating on low to medium speed just till combined.

Pour batter into a greased and floured 9x5x3-inch loaf pan. Bake in a 325° oven for 55 to 65 minutes or till a toothpick inserted near the center comes out clean. Cool on a wire rack for 10 minutes. Remove cake from pan. Cool thoroughly on a wire rack. Drizzle Powdered Sugar Icing over cake, if desired. Makes 12 servings.

Chocolate Marble Pound Cake: Prepare as above, *except,* to *one-third* of the batter (about 1½ cups), add ¼ cup *chocolate-flavored syrup.* Stir till combined. Spoon *half* of the light batter into the baking pan. Top with the chocolate batter, then the remaining light batter. Use a knife to cut a zigzag pattern through the batter.

Pound Cake Ring: Prepare as above, *except* use *1½ cups* butter; *6* eggs; *3 cups* all-purpose flour; *1½ teaspoons* baking powder; if desired, *½ teaspoon* ground nutmeg; *1½ cups* sugar; and *1½ teaspoons* vanilla. Pour into a greased and floured *10-inch fluted tube pan.* Bake in a 325° oven about 65 minutes or till a toothpick inserted near the center comes out clean. Cool on a wire rack for 10 minutes. Remove from pan. Cool thoroughly on a rack. Serves 18.

Sponge Cake

A hint of orange accents this moist, tender cake.

  6 **egg yolks**
  1 **tablespoon finely shredded orange
      peel**
 ½ **cup orange juice** *or* **pineapple juice**
  1 **teaspoon vanilla**
  1 **cup sugar**
1¼ **cups all-purpose flour**
  6 **egg whites**
 ½ **teaspoon cream of tartar**
 ½ **cup sugar**   Oven 325°

In a bowl beat yolks with an electric mixer on high speed about 5 minutes or till thick and lemon colored. Add orange peel, juice, and vanilla. Beat at low speed till combined. Gradually beat in the 1 cup sugar at low speed. Increase to medium speed; beat till mixture thickens slightly and doubles in volume (about 5 minutes total).

Sprinkle *¼ cup* flour over yolk mixture; fold in till combined. Repeat with remaining flour, ¼ cup at a time. Set yolk mixture aside.

Thoroughly wash beaters. In a large bowl beat egg whites and cream of tartar at medium speed till soft peaks form (tips curl). Gradually add the ½ cup sugar, beating at high speed till stiff peaks form (tips stand straight).

Fold *1 cup* of the beaten egg white mixture into the yolk mixture; fold yolk mixture into remaining white mixture. Pour into an *ungreased* 10-inch tube pan.

Bake in a 325° oven for 55 to 60 minutes or till cake springs back when lightly touched near center. *Immediately* invert cake (leave in pan); cool thoroughly. Loosen sides of cake from pan; remove cake from pan. Makes 12 servings.

Lemon or Lime Sponge Cake: Prepare as above, *except* substitute 2 teaspoons finely shredded *lemon peel or lime peel* for the orange peel and ¼ cup *lemon juice or lime juice* plus ¼ cup *water* for the orange juice or pineapple juice.

Chocolate Sponge Cake: Prepare cake as above, *except* omit orange peel. Reduce flour to *1 cup.* Stir ⅓ cup *unsweetened cocoa powder* into the flour.

Almond Sponge Cake: Prepare as above, *except* omit shredded orange peel and add ½ teaspoon *almond extract* with the orange juice or pineapple juice.

To fold in flour, cut down through the mixture, then across the bottom and up and over the top.

Using the same folding motion as above, fold some of the beaten whites into the yolk mixture.

Turn cake upside down after you remove it from the oven. Let it cool completely in that position.

Hot-Milk Sponge Cake

Great with Broiled Coconut Topping (see recipe, page 90).

1 cup all-purpose flour
1 teaspoon baking powder
2 eggs
1 cup sugar
½ cup milk
2 tablespoons margarine
     or butter   Oven 350°

Combine flour and baking powder. In a bowl beat eggs with an electric mixer on high speed about 4 minutes or till thick. Gradually add sugar; beat at medium speed for 4 to 5 minutes or till light and fluffy. Add flour mixture; beat at low to medium speed just till combined. In a saucepan heat and stir milk and margarine till margarine melts; add to batter, beating till combined. Pour into a greased 9x9x2-inch baking pan. Bake in a 350° oven for 20 to 25 minutes or till a toothpick comes out clean. Serve warm or cool. Serves 9.

Angel Cake

Eat your cake and diet, too. Angel Cake is low in calories and has no fat.

1½ cups egg whites (10 to 12 large)
1½ cups sifted powdered sugar
1 cup sifted cake flour *or* sifted
     all-purpose flour
1½ teaspoons cream of tartar
1 teaspoon vanilla
1 cup sugar   Oven 350°

Bring egg whites to room temperature. Sift powdered sugar and flour together 3 times. In a large bowl beat egg whites, cream of tartar, and vanilla with an electric mixer on medium speed till soft peaks form (tips curl). Gradually add sugar, about *2 tablespoons* at a time, beating till stiff peaks form (tips stand straight).

Sift about *one-fourth* of the flour mixture over beaten egg whites; fold in gently. (If bowl is too full, transfer to a larger bowl.) Repeat, folding in remaining flour mixture by fourths.

Pour into an *ungreased* 10-inch tube pan. Bake on the lowest rack in a 350° oven for 40 to 45 minutes or till top springs back when lightly touched. *Immediately* invert cake (leave in pan); cool thoroughly. Loosen sides of cake from pan; remove cake. Makes 12 servings.

Chiffon Cake

2¼ cups sifted cake flour *or* 2 cups
     sifted all-purpose flour
1½ cups sugar
1 tablespoon baking powder
½ cup cooking oil
7 egg yolks
2 teaspoons finely shredded orange
     peel
1 teaspoon finely shredded lemon
     peel
1 teaspoon vanilla
7 egg whites
½ teaspoon cream of tartar   Oven 325°

In a bowl combine flour, sugar, baking powder, and ¼ teaspoon *salt*. Add oil, yolks, orange and lemon peels, vanilla, and ¾ cup *cold water*. Beat with an electric mixer on low speed till combined. Beat on high speed 5 minutes or till satin smooth.

Thoroughly wash beaters. In a bowl combine egg whites and cream of tartar. Beat till stiff peaks form (tips stand straight). Pour batter in a thin stream over beaten egg whites; fold in gently. Pour into an *ungreased* 10-inch tube pan. Bake in a 325° oven for 65 to 70 minutes or till top springs back when lightly touched. *Immediately* invert cake (leave in pan); cool. Serves 12.

High-Altitude Adjustments

If you live more than 3,000 feet above sea level, use this chart to adjust the cake ingredients listed. Try the smaller amounts first, then make any necessary adjustments next time around.

Ingredient	3,000 Feet	5,000 Feet	7,000 Feet
Liquid: Add for each cup	1 to 2 table-spoons	2 to 4 table-spoons	3 to 4 table-spoons
Baking powder: Decrease for each teaspoon	⅛ tea-spoon	⅛ to ¼ tea-spoon	¼ tea-spoon
Sugar: Decrease for each cup	0 to 1 table-spoon	0 to 2 table-spoons	1 to 3 table-spoons

Jelly Roll

Make a yule log by using apricot jam. Frost with chocolate frosting and draw bark lines with a fork. (Pumpkin Cake Roll is pictured below right.)

  ½　**cup all-purpose flour**
  1　**teaspoon baking powder**
  4　**egg yolks**
  ½　**teaspoon vanilla**
  ⅓　**cup sugar**
  4　**egg whites**
  ½　**cup sugar**
　　Sifted powdered sugar
  ½　**cup jelly *or* jam***   Oven 375°

Starting at a short end of the cake, roll the warm cake and powdered-sugar-coated towel together.

Combine flour and baking powder; set aside. In a mixing bowl beat egg yolks and vanilla with an electric mixer on high speed for 5 minutes or till thick and lemon colored. Gradually add the ⅓ cup sugar, beating on high speed till sugar is nearly dissolved. Thoroughly wash beaters.

In another bowl beat egg whites on medium speed till soft peaks form (tips curl). Gradually add the ½ cup sugar, beating till stiff peaks form (tips stand straight). Fold yolk mixture into beaten egg whites. Sprinkle flour mixture over egg mixture; fold in gently just till combined.

Spread batter evenly into a greased and floured 15x10x1-inch jelly-roll pan. Bake in a 375° oven for 12 to 15 minutes or till cake springs back when lightly touched near center.

Immediately loosen edges of cake from pan and turn cake out onto a towel sprinkled with powdered sugar. Roll up towel and cake, jelly roll style, starting from one of the cake's short sides. Cool on a rack. Unroll cake; remove towel. Spread cake with jelly or jam to within 1 inch of edges. Roll up cake. Serves 10.

Chocolate Cake Roll: Prepare as above, *except* reduce flour to ⅓ *cup* and omit baking powder. Add ¼ cup *unsweetened cocoa powder* and ¼ teaspoon *baking soda* to flour. Fill with 2 cups *whipped cream or* cooled *chocolate pudding.* Roll up cake. Drizzle *half* of *Chocolate Glaze* (see recipe, page 89) over cake. Chill.

Pumpkin Cake Roll: Prepare as above, *except* add 2 teaspoons *pumpkin pie spice* to flour mixture and stir ½ cup canned *pumpkin* into egg yolk and sugar mixture. Fill with *Cream Cheese Frosting* (see recipe, page 88). Roll up cake. Sprinkle with sifted *powdered sugar.*

***Note:** For another filling, try 2 cups softened *ice cream.* Freeze ice-cream-filled roll.

Unroll the cake and spread frosting, jelly, or filling over it to within ½ to 1 inch of the edges.

Fruitcake

1½ cups all-purpose flour
1 teaspoon ground cinnamon
½ teaspoon baking powder
¼ teaspoon baking soda
¼ teaspoon ground nutmeg
¼ teaspoon ground allspice
¼ teaspoon ground cloves
¾ cup diced mixed candied fruits and peels, *or* snipped mixed dried fruit
½ cup raisins *or* snipped pitted dates
½ cup candied red *or* green cherries, quartered
½ cup chopped pecans, walnuts, or toasted slivered almonds
2 eggs
½ cup packed brown sugar
½ cup orange juice *or* apple juice
⅓ cup margarine *or* butter, melted
2 tablespoons light molasses
  Brandy *or* fruit juice   Oven 300°

Grease an 8x4x2-inch loaf pan. Line bottom and sides of pan with brown paper to prevent over-browning; grease paper. In a bowl combine flour, cinnamon, baking powder, baking soda, nutmeg, allspice, and cloves. Add fruits and peels, raisins, cherries, and nuts; mix well. Beat eggs; stir in sugar, juice, margarine, and molasses till combined. Stir into fruit mixture. Pour batter into pan.

Bake in a 300° oven for 1¼ to 1½ hours or till a toothpick inserted near the center comes out clean. (Cover pan loosely with foil after 1 hour of baking to prevent overbrowning.) Cool in pan on rack. Remove from pan. Wrap cake in brandy- or fruit-juice-moistened cheesecloth. Overwrap with foil. Store in the refrigerator for 2 to 8 weeks to mellow flavors. Remoisten cheesecloth about once a week, or as needed. Serves 16.

Microwave directions: Grease a 10-inch fluted tube dish or 2-quart ring mold. Coat with 2 tablespoons crushed *graham crackers.* Prepare batter as above. Pour batter into dish or mold. Micro-cook, uncovered, on 50% power (medium) for 15 minutes, giving dish a quarter-turn every 5 minutes. If not done, cook on 100% power (high) for 30 seconds to 2 minutes more or till surface is nearly dry.

Light Fruitcake: Prepare as above, *except* omit nutmeg, allspice, and cloves. Substitute *light corn syrup* for the molasses. Add 1 teaspoon finely shredded *lemon peel* and 1 tablespoon *lemon juice* with the corn syrup.

Nut Torte

A blender or a food processor makes for fast mixing of this rich cake.

2 tablespoons all-purpose flour
1 teaspoon baking powder
1 teaspoon finely shredded orange peel
4 eggs
¾ cup sugar
2½ cups walnuts, pecans, *or* hazelnuts
  Chocolate Butter Frosting
  (see recipe, page 89)   Oven 350°

Stir together flour, baking powder, and orange peel; set aside. In a blender container or food processor bowl place eggs and sugar. Cover and blend or process till smooth. Add nuts. Blend or process about 1 minute or till nearly smooth. Add flour mixture; blend or process just till combined.

Spread batter evenly into 2 greased and floured 8x1½-inch round baking pans. Bake in a 350° oven about 20 minutes or till lightly browned. Cool on wire racks for 10 minutes. Remove from pans; cool thoroughly on racks. Frost with Chocolate Butter Frosting. Serves 12.

Seven-Minute Frosting

This glossy, divinitylike frosting requires a sturdy portable electric mixer.

1½ cups sugar
⅓ cup cold water
2 egg whites
¼ teaspoon cream of tartar *or* 2 teaspoons light corn syrup
1 teaspoon vanilla

In the top of a double boiler combine sugar, water, egg whites, and cream of tartar. Beat with an electric mixer on low speed for 30 seconds.

Place over *boiling* water (upper pan should not touch water). Cook, beating constantly with the electic mixer on high speed, about 7 minutes or till frosting forms stiff peaks. Remove from the heat; add vanilla. Beat 2 to 3 minutes more or till of spreading consistency. Frosts tops and sides of two 8- or 9-inch cake layers or top and sides of one 10-inch tube cake.

Peppermint Frosting: Prepare as above, *except* substitute a few drops of *peppermint extract* for the vanilla. Garnish cake with crushed *peppermint candies.*

Fluffy White Frosting

  1 cup sugar
  ⅓ cup water
  ¼ teaspoon cream of tartar
  2 egg whites
  1 teaspoon vanilla

In a saucepan combine sugar, water, and cream of tartar. Cook and stir till bubbly and sugar dissolves. In a small mixer bowl combine egg whites and vanilla. Add sugar mixture very slowly to egg whites, beating constantly with an electric mixer on high speed about 7 minutes or till stiff peaks form (tips stand up). Frosts tops and sides of two 8- or 9-inch cake layers or one 10-inch tube cake.

Creamy White Frosting

Firm enough to use for piping decorations.

  1 cup shortening
1½ teaspoons vanilla
  ½ teaspoon lemon extract, orange
      extract, *or* almond extract
4½ cups sifted powdered sugar
  3 to 4 tablespoons milk

Beat shortening, vanilla, and extract with an electric mixer on medium speed for 30 seconds. Slowly add *half* of the powdered sugar, beating well. Add *2 tablespoons* milk. Gradually beat in remaining powdered sugar and enough remaining milk to make of spreading consistency. Frosts tops and sides of two 8- or 9-inch cake layers.

Powdered Sugar Icing

  1 cup sifted powdered sugar
  ¼ teaspoon vanilla
      Milk *or* orange juice

Mix powdered sugar, vanilla, and *1 tablespoon* milk or juice. Stir in milk or juice, *1 teaspoon* at a time, till of drizzling consistency. Makes ½ cup or enough to drizzle over one 10-inch tube cake. (Let cake stand 2 hours before slicing.)
  Chocolate Powdered Sugar Icing: Prepare as above, *except* add 2 tablespoons *unsweetened cocoa powder* to the powdered sugar.
  Liqueur Powdered Sugar Icing: Prepare as above, *except* substitute 1 tablespoon desired *liqueur* for the first 1 tablespoon milk or juice.

Cream Cheese Frosting

The tangy flavor of the cream cheese provides a nice accent to both cakes and cookies.

  2 3-ounce packages cream cheese
  ½ cup softened margarine *or* butter
  2 teaspoons vanilla
4½ to 4¾ cups sifted powdered sugar

In a bowl beat together cream cheese, margarine or butter, and vanilla till light and fluffy. Gradually add *2 cups* powdered sugar, beating well.
  Gradually beat in enough remaining powdered sugar to make frosting of spreading consistency. Frosts tops and sides of two 8- or 9-inch cake layers. Cover cake; store in refrigerator.
  Chocolate Cream Cheese Frosting: Prepare as above, *except* substitute ¼ cup *unsweetened cocoa powder* for ¼ cup powdered sugar.

Petits Fours Icing

This glossy icing coats cake cutouts beautifully. Use it with Petits Fours (see recipe, page 78) or Hot-Milk Sponge Cake (see recipe, page 85).

  3 cups sugar
1½ cups hot water
  ¼ teaspoon cream of tartar
  1 teaspoon clear vanilla
      flavoring *or* vanilla
      Sifted powdered sugar
      Food coloring (optional)

In a medium saucepan combine sugar, water, and cream of tartar. Bring mixture to boiling over medium-high heat, stirring constantly till sugar dissolves (allow 5 to 9 minutes).
  Reduce heat to medium-low. Clip a candy thermometer to the side of the saucepan. Cook till thermometer registers 226°, stirring only as necessary to prevent sticking. Remove saucepan from the heat. Cool at room temperature, without stirring, to 110° (allow about 1 hour).
  Add vanilla. Stir in enough powdered sugar (about 4 cups) to make of drizzling consistency. If necessary, beat icing with a rotary beater or wire whisk to remove any lumps. If desired, stir in a few drops of food coloring. Makes about 3½ cups or enough for 36 to 40 petits fours.
  Note: If icing becomes too thick, beat in a few drops of *warm* water.

Butter Frosting

An easy-to-spread frosting in six flavors.

⅓ **cup butter *or* margarine**
4½ **cups sifted powdered sugar**
¼ **cup milk**
1½ **teaspoons vanilla**
    Milk

In a bowl beat butter or margarine till fluffy. Gradually add *2 cups* of the powdered sugar, beating well. Slowly beat in the ¼ cup milk and vanilla.

Slowly beat in remaining sugar. Beat in additional milk, if needed, to make of spreading consistency. Tint with food coloring, if desired. Frosts tops and sides of two 8- or 9-inch cake layers.

Chocolate Butter Frosting: Prepare as above, *except* beat ½ cup *unsweetened cocoa powder* into butter; reduce sugar to *4 cups.*

Mocha Butter Frosting: Prepare as above, *except* beat ½ cup *unsweetened cocoa powder* into butter or margarine. Add 1 tablespoon instant *coffee crystals* to the ¼ cup milk. Let stand 3 minutes; stir well.

Lemon or Orange Butter Frosting: Prepare as above, *except* substitute fresh *lemon juice or orange juice* for the milk and add ½ teaspoon finely shredded *lemon peel or* 1 teaspoon finely shredded *orange peel* with the juice.

Peanut-Butter Frosting: Prepare as above, *except* substitute creamy *peanut butter* for the butter or margarine.

Chocolate Glaze

4 **squares (4 ounces) semisweet**
    chocolate, cut up
3 **tablespoons margarine *or* butter**
1½ **cups sifted powdered sugar**

In a small saucepan melt chocolate and margarine or butter over low heat, stirring frequently. Remove from heat; stir in powdered sugar and 3 tablespoons *hot water.* Stir in additional hot water, if needed, to make of drizzling consistency.

Spoon over cake, allowing excess to drip down sides. Glazes top of a 10-inch tube cake or tops of two 8- or 9-inch cake layers.

Microwave directions: In a 1-quart casserole micro-cook chocolate and margarine or butter, uncovered, on 100% power (high) for 1 to 1½ minutes or till softened, stirring once. Stir till smooth. Continue as above.

No-Cook Fudge Frosting

4¾ **cups sifted powdered sugar**
½ **cup unsweetened cocoa powder**
½ **cup margarine *or* butter, softened**
⅓ **cup boiling water**
1 **teaspoon vanilla**

Mix powdered sugar and cocoa. Add margarine, boiling water, and vanilla. Beat with an electric mixer on low speed till combined. Beat for 1 minute on medium speed. Cool for 20 to 30 minutes or till of spreading consistency. Frosts tops and sides of two 8- or 9-inch cake layers.

Chocolate-Sour-Cream Frosting

1 **cup semisweet chocolate pieces**
¼ **cup margarine *or* butter**
½ **cup dairy sour cream**
2½ **cups sifted powdered sugar**

In a saucepan melt chocolate and margarine over low heat, stirring frequently. Cool about 5 minutes. Stir in sour cream. Gradually add powdered sugar, beating till smooth and of spreading consistency. Frosts tops and sides of two 8- or 9-inch cake layers. Store cake in the refrigerator.

Microwave directions: In a 1½-quart casserole micro-cook chocolate pieces and margarine, uncovered, on 100% power (high) for 1 to 2 minutes or till softened, stirring once. Stir till smooth. Cool 5 minutes. Continue as above.

Rocky Road Frosting

½ **cup tiny marshmallows**
1 **square (1 ounce) unsweetened**
    chocolate, cut up
2 **tablespoons margarine *or* butter**
1¼ **cups sifted powdered sugar**
1 **teaspoon vanilla**
½ **cup tiny marshmallows**
¼ **cup coarsely chopped walnuts**

In a medium saucepan combine ½ cup marshmallows, the chocolate, margarine, and 2 tablespoons *water.* Cook and stir over low heat till marshmallows and chocolate melt. Cool 5 minutes. Add powdered sugar and vanilla; beat till smooth. Stir in ½ cup marshmallows and the walnuts. Frosts top of one 8- or 9-inch cake layer.

Coconut-Pecan Frosting

  1 **egg**
  1 **5-ounce can (⅔ cup) evaporated milk**
  ⅔ **cup sugar**
  ¼ **cup margarine *or* butter**
 1⅓ **cups flaked coconut**
  ½ **cup chopped pecans**

In a saucepan beat egg slightly. Stir in milk, sugar, and margarine. Cook and stir over medium heat about 12 minutes or till thickened and bubbly. Stir in coconut and pecans. Cool thoroughly. Spread on cake. Frosts top of one 13x9-inch cake or tops of two 8- or 9-inch cake layers.

Broiled Coconut Topping

Bake the cake in a metal pan so it's broiler-ready.

  ¼ **cup packed brown sugar**
  2 **tablespoons margarine *or* butter, softened**
  1 **tablespoon milk**
  ½ **cup flaked coconut**
  ¼ **cup chopped nuts (optional)**

In a bowl beat sugar and margarine till combined. Stir in milk. Stir in coconut and, if desired, nuts. Spread over *warm* cake in pan. Broil about 4 inches from heat for 3 to 4 minutes or till golden. Serve warm. Frosts one 8- or 9-inch cake layer.

Penuche Frosting

  ½ **cup margarine *or* butter**
  1 **cup packed brown sugar**
  ¼ **cup milk**
 3½ **cups sifted powdered sugar**

In saucepan melt margarine; stir in brown sugar. Cook and stir till bubbly. Remove from the heat. Add milk; beat vigorously till smooth. Add powdered sugar; beat by hand till of spreading consistency. *Immediately* frost tops of two 8- or 9-inch cake layers or top of one 13x9-inch cake.

  Microwave directions: In a 1-quart casserole micro-cook margarine on 100% power (high) for 1 to 1½ minutes or till melted. Stir in brown sugar. Cook on high for 1 to 2 minutes or till bubbly over entire surface, stirring *every minute.* Add *3 tablespoons* milk; continue as above.

Choose-a-Fruit Filling

No liqueur on hand? Substitute two tablespoons orange juice for the liqueur.

  1 **15- to 17-ounce can pitted dark sweet cherries, peach slices, blueberries, *or* crushed pineapple**
  1 **tablespoon cornstarch**
  2 **tablespoons cherry liqueur *or* orange liqueur**

Drain fruit, reserving ⅔ *cup* liquid. Cut up any large pieces of fruit. In a medium saucepan combine reserved liquid and cornstarch; add fruit.

  Cook and stir till thickened and bubbly. Cook and stir 2 minutes more. Stir in liqueur. Cool. Cover; chill thoroughly without stirring. Makes enough to spread between two 8- or 9-inch cake layers (about 1¼ cups).

  Microwave directions: Drain and cut up fruit as above. In a 4-cup measure stir together reserved fruit liquid and cornstarch; add fruit. Micro-cook, uncovered, on 100% power (high) for 3 to 4 minutes or till mixture is thickened and bubbly, stirring every minute. Cook on high for 30 seconds more. Stir in liqueur. Cool. Cover; chill.

Lemon Filling

Transforms a simple cake into a luscious dessert.

  ¾ **cup sugar**
  2 **tablespoons cornstarch**
  ½ **cup water**
  2 **beaten egg yolks**
  1 **teaspoon finely shredded lemon peel**
  3 **tablespoons lemon juice**
  1 **tablespoon margarine *or* butter**

In a small saucepan combine sugar and cornstarch. Stir in water. Stir in egg yolks, lemon peel, and juice. Cook and stir over medium heat till bubbly. Cook for 2 minutes more. Stir in margarine or butter till melted. Cover surface with clear plastic wrap; cool. Makes enough to spread between two 8- or 9-inch cake layers (about 1 cup).

  Microwave directions: In a 1-quart casserole combine sugar and cornstarch. Stir in water. Stir in egg yolks, lemon peel, and lemon juice. Micro-cook, uncovered, on 100% power (high) for 3 to 4 minutes or till thickened and bubbly, stirring every minute. Cook 30 seconds more. Stir in margarine till melted. Cover; cool.

Candy

Nutrition Analysis

	Servings Per Recipe	Calories	Protein (g)	Carbohydrate (g)	Fat (g)	Cholesterol (mg)	Sodium (mg)	Potassium (mg)	Protein	Vitamin A	Vitamin C	Thiamine	Riboflavin	Niacin	Calcium	Iron
	Per Serving								**Percent U.S. RDA Per Serving**							
Caramel Apples (p. 95)	14	439	1	68	20	23	192	292	2	17	11	2	5	1	8	13
Caramel Corn (p. 97)	9	169	1	27	7	0	120	81	1	6	0	2	1	1	2	6
Caramels (p. 95)	64	81	0	11	4	5	42	35	0	3	0	0	1	0	2	3
Caramel Snappers (p. 100)	30	85	1	8	6	0	19	45	1	0	0	3	1	0	1	2
Chocolate-Covered Cherries (p. 98)	60	66	0	10	3	1	14	24	1	1	0	0	1	0	2	0
Chocolate-Dipped Fruit (p. 98)	50	29	0	4	1	1	4	39	1	0	14	0	1	0	1	0
Chocolate Pralines (p. 96)	36	139	1	19	8	4	17	79	1	2	0	4	1	1	2	3
Cream Cheese Mints (p. 100)	48	34	0	7	1	2	5	3	0	1	0	0	0	0	0	0
Divinity (p. 96)	40	67	0	17	0	0	5	6	0	0	0	0	0	0	0	1
Fondant (p. 98)	24	69	0	18	0	0	1	1	0	0	0	0	0	0	0	0
Glazed Nuts (p. 97)	12	150	3	14	10	0	25	100	4	2	0	2	2	1	1	6
Mint Patties (p. 98)	30	59	0	14	0	0	6	1	0	0	0	0	0	0	0	0
Mocha Caramels (p. 95)	64	80	0	11	4	5	34	43	0	3	0	0	1	0	2	3
Nut Brittle (p. 97)	72	72	1	10	3	1	37	36	2	1	0	1	0	4	1	2
Nutty Caramel Corn (p. 97)	10	278	6	28	17	0	111	224	10	5	0	6	2	17	4	8
Old-Time Fudge (p. 94)	32	67	0	13	2	0	12	24	1	1	0	0	1	0	1	1
Opera Fudge (p. 94)	32	60	0	13	1	3	8	11	0	0	0	0	0	0	0	0
Peanut Butter Balls (p. 99)	30	90	2	9	6	1	40	53	3	1	0	1	2	3	2	1
Peanut Clusters (p. 100)	36	105	3	8	8	1	7	91	4	0	0	2	2	6	2	2
Penuche (p. 95)	32	87	0	17	2	2	13	39	0	1	0	1	1	0	1	2
Pralines (p. 96)	36	132	1	19	7	4	17	66	1	2	0	4	1	0	2	3
Remarkable Fudge (p. 95)	96	86	1	13	4	1	27	30	0	2	0	0	0	0	1	0
Rocky Road (p. 100)	36	97	2	10	6	3	13	65	2	1	0	1	3	0	3	2
Saltwater Taffy (p. 96)	48	56	0	13	0	0	10	1	0	0	0	0	0	0	0	0
Shortcut Caramels (p. 95)	64	86	1	14	3	2	47	48	1	3	0	0	2	0	3	3
Toffee Butter Crunch (p. 97)	48	83	1	7	6	11	42	30	1	3	0	0	1	1	1	1
Truffles (p. 99)	32	108	1	10	7	12	27	52	2	2	0	1	2	0	3	1
Walnut Caramels (p. 95)	64	94	1	11	5	5	42	45	1	3	0	1	1	0	2	3

On the divider: Penuche (p. 95), Caramel Snappers (p. 100), Chocolate-Dipped Fruit (p. 98), and Truffles (p. 99).

Candy

Nothing satisfies a sweet tooth like candy. From classic Old-Time Fudge, to rich Truffles, to easy Rocky Road, you'll find them all here.

Before you begin making any of this chapter's delights, read these important pointers.

Consider the Humidity
Humidity affects the preparation of all candies, so avoid making candy on wet or very humid days. The amount of water in the air is especially critical for divinity. Plan to make it only on dry days. If the air is too damp, no amount of beating will make divinity set up.

Testing Candy Mixtures
The easiest way to make sure your candy comes out right is with a candy thermometer. Always begin each candy-making session by checking

your thermometer's accuracy. First, place the thermometer in boiling water for a few minutes, then read it. If the thermometer registers above or below 212°, add or subtract the same difference in degrees from the recipe temperature.

For an accurate reading, make sure the bulb of the thermometer is completely covered with liquid, not just foam, and that it doesn't touch the bottom of the pan.

If you don't own a candy thermometer, use the following test. For best results, test your candy shortly before it reaches the minimum cooking time. Working quickly, drop a few drops of the hot mixture from a spoon into a cup of very cold (but not icy) water. With your fingers, form the drops into a ball. Remove the ball from the water. The firmness of the ball will indicate the temperature of the mixture (see descriptions, right).

If the mixture has not reached the correct stage, continue cooking it for another two to three minutes. Quickly retest the candy, using fresh water and a clean spoon. Continue cooking and retesting until your candy reaches the desired stage. Even if candies are similar and are cooked to the same stage, the cooking times and final temperatures may vary. Follow the recipes carefully, and cook to the stages recommended.

Storing Candies

Most candies will stay fresh for two to three weeks if kept tightly covered in a cool, dry place. Store different types of candies separately. Layer brittles and toffees between sheets of waxed paper in airtight containers. Wrap fudge and fondant in foil or clear plastic wrap and place in airtight containers. Store divinity in airtight containers lined with waxed paper.

Boiling Candy Mixtures

Candy mixtures should boil at a moderate, steady rate over their entire surface. To guide you, our recipes list suggested range-top temperatures for cooking the candy mixtures. Depending on your range, though, you may have to use slightly higher or lower temperatures to cook the candy mixtures within the recommended times. Cooking too fast or slow will make candies too hard or soft.

1. Thread stage (230° to 233°):
When a teaspoon is dipped into the hot mixture, then removed, the candy falls off the spoon in a fine, thin thread.

2. Soft-ball stage (234° to 240°):
When the ball of candy is removed from the cold water, the candy *instantly* flattens and runs between your fingers.

3. Firm-ball stage (244° to 248°):
When the ball of candy is removed from the water, it is firm enough to hold its shape, but quickly flattens at room temperature.

4. Hard-ball stage (250° to 266°):
When the ball of candy is removed from the water, it doesn't flatten until pressed.

5. Soft-crack stage (270° to 290°):
When dropped into water, the candy separates into hard, but pliable and elastic, threads.

6. Hard-crack stage (295° to 310°):
When dropped into water, the candy separates into hard, brittle threads that snap easily.

Opera Fudge

    2 cups sugar
    ½ cup milk
    ½ cup light cream
    1 tablespoon light corn syrup
    1 tablespoon margarine *or* butter
    1 teaspoon vanilla

Line an 8x4x2-inch loaf pan with foil, extending foil over edges of pan. Butter foil; set aside.

Butter the sides of a heavy 2-quart saucepan. In saucepan combine sugar, milk, cream, and corn syrup. Cook and stir over medium-high heat to boiling. Carefully clip a candy thermometer to side of pan. Cook and stir over medium-low heat to 238°, soft-ball stage (25 to 35 minutes).

Remove saucepan from heat. Add margarine and vanilla, but *do not stir.* Cool, without stirring, to 110°, lukewarm (about 55 minutes). Remove candy thermometer from saucepan. Beat mixture vigorously with a wooden spoon till fudge becomes very thick and just starts to lose its gloss (about 10 minutes total).

Immediately spread fudge into prepared pan. Score into squares while warm. When candy is firm, use the foil to lift it out of the pan; cut into squares. Store tightly covered. Makes about 1 pound (32 servings).

Old-Time Fudge

So rich and creamy, it melts in your mouth.

    2 cups sugar
    ¾ cup milk
    2 squares (2 ounces) unsweetened
          chocolate, cut up
    1 teaspoon light corn syrup
    2 tablespoons margarine *or* butter
    1 teaspoon vanilla
    ½ cup chopped nuts (optional)

Line a 9x5x3-inch loaf pan with foil, extending foil over edges of pan. Butter the foil; set aside.

Butter the sides of a heavy 2-quart saucepan. In saucepan combine sugar, milk, chocolate, and corn syrup. Cook and stir over medium-high heat to boiling. Carefully clip a candy thermometer to side of pan. Cook and stir over medium-low heat to 234°, soft-ball stage (20 to 25 minutes).

Remove saucepan from heat. Add margarine and vanilla, but *do not stir.* Cool, without stirring, to 110°, lukewarm (about 55 minutes).

Remove candy thermometer from saucepan. Beat mixture vigorously with a wooden spoon till fudge just begins to thicken. Add chopped nuts, if desired. Continue beating till fudge becomes very thick and just starts to lose its gloss (about 10 minutes total).

Immediately spread fudge into prepared pan. Score into squares while warm. When candy is firm, use foil to lift it out of pan; cut candy into squares. Store tightly covered. Makes about 1¼ pounds (32 servings).

Beat vigorously with a wooden spoon till fudge just begins to thicken.

Continue beating till fudge becomes very thick and just starts to lose its gloss.

Remarkable Fudge

4 cups sugar
2 5-ounce cans (1⅓ cups total)
   evaporated milk
1 cup margarine *or* butter
1 12-ounce package (2 cups)
   semisweet chocolate pieces
1 7-ounce jar marshmallow creme
1 cup chopped walnuts
1 teaspoon vanilla

Line a 13x9x2-inch baking pan with foil; extend foil over edges. Butter foil; set aside. Butter sides of a heavy 3-quart saucepan. In it, combine sugar, milk, and margarine. Cook and stir over medium-high heat to boiling. Clip candy thermometer to side of pan. Cook and stir over medium heat to 236°, soft-ball stage (about 12 minutes).

Remove saucepan from heat; remove thermometer. Add chocolate pieces, marshmallow creme, nuts, and vanilla; stir till chocolate melts. Spread into pan. Score into squares while warm. When firm, cut into squares. Store in the refrigerator. Makes about 3½ pounds (96 servings).

Penuche

This brown sugar fudge is pictured on page 91.

1½ cups sugar
 1 cup packed brown sugar
 ⅓ cup light cream
 ⅓ cup milk
 2 tablespoons margarine *or* butter
 1 teaspoon vanilla
 ½ cup chopped pecans *or* walnuts

Line an 8x4x2- or a 9x5x3-inch loaf pan with foil; extend foil over edges. Butter foil; set aside. Butter the sides of a heavy 2-quart saucepan. Combine sugars, cream, and milk. Cook and stir over medium-high heat to boiling. Clip candy thermometer to side of pan. Cook and stir over medium-low heat to 236°, soft-ball stage (15 to 20 minutes). Remove from heat. Add margarine and vanilla, but *do not stir.* Cool, without stirring, to 110°, lukewarm (about 50 minutes). Remove thermometer. Beat mixture vigorously till penuche just begins to thicken; add nuts. Continue beating till penuche becomes very thick and just starts to lose its gloss (about 10 minutes total). Spread into pan. Score into squares. Cut when firm. Makes about 1¼ pounds (32 servings).

Caramels

Don't use corn-oil margarine. It will make your caramels too soft.

1 cup margarine *or* butter
1 16-ounce package (2¼ cups)
   packed brown sugar
2 cups light cream
1 cup light corn syrup
1 teaspoon vanilla

Line an 8x8x2- or 9x9x2-inch baking pan with foil, extending foil over edges of pan. Butter foil; set aside.

In a heavy 3-quart saucepan melt margarine or butter over low heat. Add brown sugar, cream, and corn syrup; mix well. Cook and stir over medium-high heat to boiling. Carefully clip a candy thermometer to the side of the pan. Cook and stir mixture over medium heat to 248°, firm-ball stage (45 to 60 minutes).

Remove the saucepan from heat; remove thermometer. Stir in vanilla. *Immediately* pour caramel mixture into the prepared pan. When caramel mixture is firm, use foil to lift it out of pan. Use a buttered knife to cut into 1-inch squares. Wrap each caramel in clear plastic wrap. Makes about 2 pounds (64 servings).

Walnut Caramels: Prepare as above, *except* sprinkle 1 cup chopped *walnuts* onto the bottom of the buttered, foil-lined pan. Pour hot caramel mixture over nuts in prepared pan.

Mocha Caramels: Prepare as above, *except* reduce margarine or butter to ¾ cup and melt 2 squares (2 ounces) *unsweetened chocolate* with the margarine. Add 1 tablespoon *instant coffee crystals* to margarine mixture with sugar, cream, and corn syrup.

Shortcut Caramels: Prepare as above, *except* substitute one 14-ounce can (1¼ cups) *sweetened condensed milk* for the cream. This mixture will take less time to reach 248° (about 15 to 20 minutes instead of 45 to 60 minutes).

Caramel Apples: Wash and dry 14 to 16 small tart *apples;* remove stems. Insert a wooden skewer into the stem end of each apple.

Prepare as above, *except* do not pour caramel mixture into prepared pan. Working quickly, dip each apple into hot caramel mixture; turn to coat. If desired, dip bottoms of apples into 1 cup chopped peanuts. Set on a buttered baking sheet; chill, if desired. Makes 14 to 16 caramel apples.

Saltwater Taffy

Be sure to recruit some help when it's time to pull this tasty taffy.

     2 **cups sugar**
     1 **cup light corn syrup**
     2 **tablespoons margarine *or* butter**
    ¼ **teaspoon peppermint extract, rum flavoring, *or* few drops oil of cinnamon (optional)**
        Few drops food coloring (optional)

Butter a 15x10x1-inch baking pan; set aside. Butter the sides of a heavy 2-quart saucepan. In saucepan combine sugar, corn syrup, 1 cup *water,* and 1½ teaspoons *salt.* Cook and stir over medium-high heat to boiling. Clip candy thermometer to side of pan. Cook over medium heat, without stirring, to 265°, hard-ball stage (about 40 minutes). Remove saucepan from heat. Stir in margarine. Stir in flavoring and coloring, if desired. Pour into prepared pan. Cool for 15 to 20 minutes or till easy to handle.

Butter hands; divide candy into four pieces. Twist and pull each piece till it turns a creamy color (about 10 minutes). Candy is ready if it cracks when tapped on counter. With buttered scissors, snip taffy into bite-size pieces. Wrap in clear plastic wrap. Makes about 1½ pounds (48 servings).

Pralines

    1½ **cups sugar**
    1½ **cups packed brown sugar**
     1 **cup light cream**
     3 **tablespoons margarine *or* butter**
     2 **cups pecan halves**

Butter sides of a heavy 2-quart saucepan. In it, combine sugars and cream. Cook and stir over medium-high heat to boiling. Clip candy thermometer to side of pan. Cook and stir over medium-low heat to 234°, soft-ball stage (16 to 18 minutes). Remove from heat. Add margarine, but *do not stir.* Cool, without stirring, to 150° (about 30 minutes). Stir in nuts. Beat till candy just begins to thicken but is still glossy (about 3 minutes). Drop by spoonfuls onto waxed paper. If candy becomes too stiff, stir in a few drops *hot* water. Store tightly covered. Makes about 36.

Chocolate Pralines: Prepare as above, *except* add 2 squares (2 ounces) finely chopped *unsweetened chocolate* with the margarine.

Divinity

    2½ **cups sugar**
     ½ **cup light corn syrup**
     2 **egg whites**
     1 **teaspoon vanilla**
     1 ***or* 2 drops food coloring (optional)**
     ½ **cup chopped candied fruit *or* nuts**

In a heavy 2-quart saucepan mix sugar, corn syrup, and ½ cup *water.* Cook and stir over medium-high heat to boiling. Clip candy thermometer to pan. Cook over medium heat, without stirring, to 260°, hard-ball stage (10 to 15 minutes). Remove from heat. Remove candy thermometer.

In a large mixing bowl, beat egg whites with a sturdy, freestanding electric mixer on medium speed till stiff peaks form (tips stand straight). *Gradually* pour hot mixture in a thin stream over whites, beating on high about 3 minutes; scrape bowl. Add vanilla and, if desired, food coloring. Continue beating on high just till candy starts to lose its gloss. When beaters are lifted, mixture should fall in a ribbon that mounds on itself. This final beating should take 5 to 6 minutes.

Drop a spoonful of candy mixture onto waxed paper. If it stays mounded, the mixture has been beaten sufficiently. *Immediately* stir in fruit or nuts. *Quickly* drop remaining mixture from a teaspoon onto waxed paper. If mixture flattens out, beat ½ to 1 minute more; check again. If mixture is too stiff to spoon, beat in a few drops *hot* water till candy is a softer consistency. Store tightly covered. Makes about 40 pieces.

When the candy just starts to lose its gloss, lift the beaters. The candy should fall in a mound.

Nut Brittle

2 **cups sugar**
1 **cup light corn syrup**
¼ **cup margarine or butter**
2½ **cups raw peanuts or other coarsely chopped nuts**
1½ **teaspoons baking soda, sifted**

Butter 2 large baking sheets; set aside. Butter sides of a heavy 3-quart saucepan. In saucepan combine sugar, corn syrup, margarine, and ½ cup *water*. Cook and stir over medium-high heat to boiling. Clip candy thermometer to side of pan. Cook and stir over medium-low heat to 275°, soft-crack stage (about 30 minutes). Add nuts; cook and stir to 295°, hard-crack stage (15 to 20 minutes more). Remove saucepan from heat; remove thermometer.

Quickly sprinkle soda over mixture, stirring constantly. *Immediately* pour onto prepared baking sheets. Cool; break into pieces. Store tightly covered. Makes about 2¼ pounds (72 servings).

Toffee Butter Crunch

Butter is a must for top-notch toffee flavor.

½ **cup coarsely chopped toasted almonds or pecans**
1 **cup butter**
1 **cup sugar**
1 **tablespoon light corn syrup**
¾ **cup semisweet chocolate pieces**
½ **cup finely chopped toasted almonds or pecans**

Line a 13x9x2-inch baking pan with foil, extending foil over edges. Sprinkle the ½ cup coarsely chopped nuts in pan. Butter sides of a heavy 2-quart saucepan. In saucepan melt butter. Add sugar, corn syrup, and 3 tablespoons *water*. Cook and stir over medium-high heat to boiling.

Clip candy thermometer to pan. Cook and stir over medium heat to 290°, soft-crack stage (about 15 minutes). Watch carefully after 280° to prevent scorching. Remove saucepan from heat; remove thermometer. Pour mixture into prepared pan. Let stand 5 minutes or till firm; sprinkle with chocolate pieces. Let stand 1 to 2 minutes. When softened, spread chocolate over mixture. Sprinkle with nuts. Chill till firm. Lift candy out of pan; break into pieces. Store tightly covered. Makes about 1½ pounds (48 servings).

Glazed Nuts

Cashews, peanuts, whole almonds, or pecan halves all taste great in this crunchy candy.

1½ **cups raw or roasted nuts**
½ **cup sugar**
2 **tablespoons margarine or butter**
½ **teaspoon vanilla**

Line a baking sheet with foil. Butter the foil; set aside. In a heavy 10-inch skillet combine nuts, sugar, margarine or butter, and vanilla. Cook over medium-high heat, shaking skillet occasionally, till sugar begins to melt. *Do not stir.* Reduce heat to low and cook till sugar is golden brown, stirring occasionally. Remove skillet from heat. Pour onto prepared baking sheet. Cool completely. Break candy into clusters. Store tightly covered. Makes about 10 ounces (12 servings).

Caramel Corn

This sweet snack is oven-baked for extra crunch.

8 **cups popped popcorn (about ⅓ to ½ cup unpopped)**
¾ **cup packed brown sugar**
⅓ **cup margarine or butter**
3 **tablespoons light corn syrup**
¼ **teaspoon baking soda**
¼ **teaspoon vanilla**   Oven 300°

Remove all unpopped kernels from popped corn. Place popcorn in a greased 17x12x2-inch baking pan. Keep popcorn warm in a 300° oven while making caramel mixture.

Butter the sides of a heavy 1½-quart saucepan. In saucepan combine brown sugar, margarine or butter, and corn syrup. Cook and stir over medium heat to boiling. Clip candy thermometer to side of pan. Cook and stir over medium heat to 255°, hard-ball stage (about 4 minutes).

Remove saucepan from heat. Stir in baking soda and vanilla; pour over popcorn. Stir gently to coat. Bake in a 300° oven for 15 minutes; stir. Bake 5 minutes more. Transfer popcorn mixture to a large piece of foil; cool completely. Break into clusters. Store tightly covered. Makes about 9 cups (9 servings).

Nutty Caramel Corn: Prepare as above, *except* add 1½ cups *peanuts, walnut halves, cashews, or pecan halves* to caramel-coated corn before baking. Toss gently. Makes about 10½ cups (10 servings).

Chocolate-Covered Cherries

**60 maraschino cherries with stems
(about three 10-ounce jars)
3 tablespoons margarine *or* butter,
softened
3 tablespoons light corn syrup
2 cups sifted powdered sugar
1 pound chocolate-flavored
confectioners' coating**

Drain cherries thoroughly on paper towels for several hours. Combine margarine and corn syrup. Stir in powdered sugar; knead mixture till smooth (chill if too soft to handle).

Shape about *½ teaspoon* powdered sugar mixture around *each* cherry. Place coated cherries upright on a baking sheet lined with waxed paper; chill about 1 hour or till firm (do not chill too long or sugar mixture will begin to dissolve). Melt confectioners' coating (see tip, opposite). Holding cherries by stems, dip into coating. (Be sure to completely seal cherries in coating to prevent cherry juice from leaking.) Let excess coating drip off cherries. Place cherries, stem side up, on a baking sheet lined with waxed paper. Chill till coating is firm. Store in refrigerator in a tightly covered container. Let candies ripen in refrigerator for 1 to 2 weeks before serving. (Ripening allows powdered sugar mixture around cherries to soften and liquefy.) Makes 60 pieces.

Chocolate-Dipped Fruit

Chocolate-dipped strawberries are pictured on page 91.

**2½ cups fresh strawberries, maraschino
cherries, canned pineapple
chunks *or* mandarin orange
sections, or a combination
8 ounces chocolate- *or* vanilla-
flavored confectioners' coating**

Drain fruit on paper towels for several hours. Melt confectioners' coating (see tip, opposite). Holding fruit by one end, dip a portion into melted coating. (*Or,* to completely cover the fruit, drop one piece at a time into melted coating. Use a fork to lift fruit out of coating.) Let excess coating drip off fruit; place on a baking sheet lined with waxed paper. Let dry. If desired, drizzle with additional melted coating. Serve fruit the same day it is dipped. Makes about 50 pieces.

Fondant

**2 cups sugar
2 tablespoons light corn syrup**

Butter sides of a heavy 1½-quart saucepan. In saucepan combine sugar, corn syrup, and 1½ cups *water.* Cook and stir over medium-high heat to boiling. Cover and cook 45 seconds more. Uncover; clip candy thermometer to pan. Cook over medium-low heat, without stirring, to 240°, soft-ball stage (35 to 45 minutes). Pour mixture onto a 12-inch platter. *Do not scrape pan.* Cool, without stirring, till slightly warm to the touch (about 50 minutes).

Using a wooden spoon or a heavy-duty rubber spatula, beat vigorously till candy is white and firm (about 10 minutes). Knead till smooth, about 5 minutes. Form into a ball. Wrap in clear plastic wrap; let ripen at room temperature for 24 hours. (Ripening is necessary for smooth and creamy fondant.) If desired, use fondant to stuff whole pitted dates, prunes, or dried figs. *Or,* shape into ¾-inch balls and dip into melted confectioners' coating (see tip, opposite). Makes about ¾ pound (24 servings).

Mint Patties: Prepare as above, *except* heat and stir ripened fondant in top of a double boiler over hot, not boiling, water till melted. Remove pan from heat, but leave fondant over hot water. Stir in 1 tablespoon softened *margarine,* 2 to 3 drops *oil of peppermint or oil of cinnamon,* and a few drops *food coloring.* Drop from a teaspoon onto waxed paper, swirling tops. Let stand till set. Cover to store. Makes 30 to 36 (1½-inch) patties.

Knead fondant by turning and folding the candy mixture continuously in your hands.

Truffles

Instead of dipping them into coating, roll these nuggets in cocoa powder, chocolate sprinkles, or chopped nuts. (Pictured on page 91.)

> **6 squares (6 ounces) semisweet chocolate, coarsely chopped**
> **¼ cup margarine *or* butter**
> **3 tablespoons whipping cream**
> **1 beaten egg yolk**
> **3 tablespoons rum, Irish whiskey, brandy, coffee liqueur, *or* orange liqueur**
> **12 ounces chocolate-flavored confectioners' coating**

In a heavy 2-quart saucepan combine semisweet chocolate, margarine or butter, and whipping cream. Cook and stir over low heat till chocolate melts (about 10 minutes). Remove saucepan from heat.

Gradually stir about *half* of the hot mixture into the beaten egg yolk. Return the mixture to the saucepan. Cook and stir over medium heat till the mixture is slightly thickened. Remove saucepan from heat.

Stir in rum, whiskey, brandy, or coffee or orange liqueur. Transfer mixture to a small mixing bowl. Cover and chill till completely cool and smooth, stirring occasionally (about 1½ hours).

Beat chilled mixture with an electric mixer on medium speed till slightly fluffy (about 2 minutes). Chill till mixture holds its shape (10 to 15 minutes). Drop mixture by well-rounded teaspoons onto a baking sheet lined with waxed paper. Chill till firm (about 30 minutes). If desired, gently shape into balls.

Melt chocolate-flavored confectioners' coating (see tip, right). Dip candy into melted confectioners' coating; let excess coating drip off candy. Place dipped candy on a baking sheet lined with waxed paper; let stand till coating is dry. Store tightly covered in a cool, dry place up to 2 weeks. Makes about 32 pieces.

Peanut Butter Balls

Fun for kids to make and eat.

> **½ cup peanut butter**
> **3 tablespoons margarine *or* butter, softened**
> **1 cup sifted powdered sugar**
> **8 ounces chocolate-flavored confectioners' coating**

Stir together peanut butter and margarine. Gradually add sugar, stirring till combined. Shape into 1-inch balls; place on waxed paper. Let stand till dry (about 20 minutes). Melt confectioners' coating (see tip, below). Cool slightly. Dip balls into melted coating; let excess drip off. Place on waxed paper; let stand till coating is dry. Makes about 30 pieces.

Dipping Candy

The easiest way to coat candy is to dip it into confectioners' coating. Confectioners' coating is a chocolatelike product that also is called white chocolate, almond bark, or summer coating. It usually comes in chocolate and vanilla flavors. What makes confectioners' coating so easy is that it doesn't speckle as it hardens and that it easily heats without scorching. Before dipping candy, chop the coating and melt it in a heavy saucepan over low heat.

Semisweet chocolate and milk chocolate also can be used for dipping. But these products usually need to be tempered (melted and then cooled to the correct dipping temperature). Without tempering, the chocolate often speckles or develops gray streaks as it hardens. This speckling is called blooming and affects only the appearance, not the quality or flavor, of the candy. If a small amount of speckling doesn't bother you, go ahead and use untempered chocolate for dipping. To learn more about tempering, see a candy-making cook book.

Peanut Clusters

To keep the chocolate firm, remove only a few clusters at a time from the refrigerator.

- ½ **pound vanilla-flavored confectioners' coating, cut up**
- 1 **6-ounce package (1 cup) semisweet chocolate pieces**
- 2 **cups peanuts *or* cashews**

In a heavy medium saucepan melt confectioners' coating and chocolate pieces over low heat, stirring constantly. Stir in peanuts or cashews. Drop mixture from a teaspoon onto a baking sheet lined with waxed paper. Chill till firm (about 30 minutes). Store tightly covered in the refrigerator. Makes about 36 pieces.

Microwave directions: In a medium bowl micro-cook confectioners' coating and chocolate pieces, uncovered, on 100% power (high) for 2½ to 3 minutes or till mixture becomes smooth when stirred. Stir in nuts. Continue as above.

Caramel Snappers

Layers of toasted pecans, chewy caramel, and creamy chocolate make an irresistible candy. (Pictured on page 91.)

- 90 **pecan halves (about 1½ cups)**
- ½ **of a 14-ounce package (about 25) vanilla caramels**
- 1 **tablespoon margarine *or* butter**
- ½ **cup semisweet chocolate pieces**
- 1 **teaspoon shortening**   Oven 350°

Spread pecans into a single layer in a shallow baking pan. Bake in a 350° oven about 10 minutes or till toasted, stirring occasionally. Line a baking sheet with foil. Butter the foil. On foil, arrange pecans in groups of 3, flat side down.

In a heavy saucepan combine caramels and margarine. Cook and stir over low heat till melted and smooth. Remove from heat. Drop about *1 teaspoon* melted caramel mixture onto *each* group of pecans. Let caramel pieces stand till firm (about 20 minutes).

In a small saucepan heat chocolate pieces and shortening over low heat, stirring constantly, till melted and smooth. Remove from heat. With a narrow spatula, spread a small amount of melted chocolate mixture over the top of each caramel piece. Let stand till firm. Remove from baking sheet. Store tightly covered. Makes 30 pieces.

Rocky Road

Marshmallows and chopped nuts are the rocks in this delicious chocolate road.

- 2 **8-ounce bars milk chocolate, broken up**
- 2½ **cups tiny marshmallows**
- 1 **cup coarsely chopped nuts**

Line an 8x8x2-inch baking pan with foil, extending foil over edges of pan. Butter foil; set aside. In a medium saucepan slowly melt chocolate over low heat, stirring constantly. Remove from heat. Stir in marshmallows and nuts. Spread into prepared pan. Chill till firm (at least 1 hour). Use foil to lift candy out of pan; cut into squares. Store in the refrigerator. Makes about 36 pieces.

Microwave directions: Line pan and butter foil as above. In a medium bowl micro-cook chocolate, uncovered, on 100% power (high) for 1½ to 2½ minutes or till chocolate becomes smooth when stirred. Stir in marshmallows and nuts. Spread into prepared pan. Chill till firm. Lift candy from the pan and cut into squares. Store in the refrigerator.

Cream Cheese Mints

Make these rich-tasting mints ahead, then store them in the freezer for up to 1 month.

- 1 **3-ounce package cream cheese, softened**
- ½ **teaspoon peppermint extract**
- 3 **cups sifted powdered sugar**
  Few drops food coloring
  Sugar

In a small mixing bowl stir together softened cream cheese and peppermint extract. Gradually add powdered sugar, stirring till mixture is smooth. (Knead in the last of the powdered sugar with your hands.) Add food coloring. Knead till food coloring is evenly distributed.

Form cream cheese mixture into ¾-inch balls. Roll each ball in sugar; place on waxed paper. Flatten each ball with the bottom of a juice glass or with the tines of a fork. (*Or*, sprinkle small candy molds lightly with sugar. Press about ¾ to *1 teaspoon* cream cheese mixture into *each* mold. Remove from molds.)

Cover mints with paper towels; let dry overnight. Store tightly covered in the refrigerator. Makes 48 to 60 mints.

Cookies

Nutrition Analysis

	Servings Per Recipe	Calories	Protein (g)	Carbohydrate (g)	Fat (g)	Cholesterol (mg)	Sodium (mg)	Potassium (mg)	Protein	Vitamin A	Vitamin C	Thiamine	Riboflavin	Niacin	Calcium	Iron
	Per Serving								**Percent U.S. RDA Per Serving**							
Almond Strips (p. 118)	48	58	1	8	3	6	37	15	1	2	0	2	2	1	1	1
Applesauce Bars (p. 106)	48	97	1	12	5	23	55	17	2	0	0	3	2	1	1	2
Banana-Spice Cookies (p. 112)	60	58	1	9	2	9	30	36	1	2	1	3	2	1	1	2
Brandy Snaps (p. 119)	54	28	0	4	1	0	14	26	0	1	0	1	1	1	1	1
Buttermilk Brownies (p. 108)	36	158	2	23	7	15	138	29	2	6	0	3	3	2	1	3
Butter-Pecan Shortbread (p. 120)	16	102	1	10	6	16	60	24	2	4	0	5	3	3	1	3
Cake Brownies (p. 107)	36	112	2	12	7	16	77	46	3	4	0	4	3	2	2	3
Candy-Window Sugar-Cookie Cutouts (p. 113)	36	85	1	12	4	8	39	10	1	2	0	3	2	1	1	2
Cashew-Nutmeg Drops (p. 112)	48	77	1	10	4	7	41	44	2	2	0	3	2	2	1	3
Chocolate-Candy Cookies (p. 109)	60	103	1	14	5	9	31	21	2	1	0	2	2	1	2	3
Chocolate Chip Cookies (p. 109)	60	99	1	12	5	9	31	39	2	1	0	2	2	2	1	3
Chocolate-Coconut Pinwheels (p. 116)	72	48	1	6	2	5	25	15	1	1	0	1	1	1	0	1
Chocolate Cream Cheese Cutouts (p. 114)	60	53	1	7	2	6	26	11	1	2	0	2	1	1	0	1
Chocolate Crinkles (p. 120)	48	76	1	10	4	17	17	29	2	0	0	2	2	2	1	3
Chocolate-Kiss Peanut Butter Cookies (p. 117)	36	116	2	14	6	9	73	62	3	2	0	3	3	4	2	3
Chocolate-Peanut Drop Cookies (p. 110)	30	83	2	9	5	9	43	39	2	2	0	2	2	3	1	2
Chocolate Revel Bars (p. 107)	60	145	2	20	7	12	72	93	4	4	0	5	4	2	3	5
Chocolate Spritz (p. 118)	84	58	1	6	3	3	45	9	1	3	0	2	1	1	0	1
Choose-a-Chip Oatmeal Cookies (p. 110)	54	96	1	13	5	5	43	47	2	2	0	4	2	1	1	3
Cinnamon Snaps (p. 119)	54	30	0	5	1	0	14	10	0	1	0	1	1	1	0	1
Citrus Cream Cheese Cutouts (p. 114)	60	48	1	7	2	6	26	8	1	2	0	2	1	1	0	1
Coconut Macaroons (p. 111)	30	34	0	6	1	0	4	15	1	0	0	0	0	0	0	0
Coconut-Pecan Drop Cookies (p. 110)	36	87	1	8	6	7	22	31	1	1	0	3	1	1	0	2
Cranberry-Pecan Bars (p. 106)	24	77	1	10	4	11	45	46	2	2	4	4	2	2	1	3
Cream Cheese Cutouts (p. 114)	60	48	1	7	2	6	26	8	1	2	0	2	1	1	0	1
Crispy Cereal Squares (p. 104)	25	112	3	14	5	0	109	83	5	4	4	5	5	11	1	5
Date-Filled Rounds (p. 116)	36	135	1	20	6	8	64	68	2	2	1	5	3	4	1	4
Date Pinwheel Cookies (p. 116)	72	62	1	9	3	4	32	33	1	1	0	2	1	1	0	2
Drop Cookies (p. 110)	24	82	1	10	4	11	32	17	1	2	0	2	2	1	0	2
Filled Sugar-Cookie Cutouts (p. 113)	24	212	2	33	9	19	88	21	2	5	0	5	3	3	2	3
Florentines (p. 111)	24	124	2	12	8	0	44	109	3	3	6	3	4	2	3	3
Fruit-Filled Oatmeal Bars with Apple-Cinnamon Filling (p. 105)	25	96	1	14	4	0	56	52	2	3	2	4	2	2	1	3
Fruit-Filled Oatmeal Bars with Apricot-Coconut Filling (p. 105)	25	113	1	18	4	0	57	115	2	11	0	4	2	2	1	5
Fruit-Filled Oatmeal Bars with Raisin Filling (p. 105)	25	107	1	17	4	0	57	82	2	3	0	4	2	2	1	4
Fruit-Topped Oatmeal Cookies (p. 110)	48	100	1	16	4	6	49	50	2	3	0	4	2	1	1	3
Fudge Brownies (p. 107)	24	115	2	13	7	23	51	44	2	4	0	3	2	1	1	3
Fudge Ecstasies (p. 109)	36	105	1	11	7	15	14	65	2	1	0	2	2	1	1	3
Giant Chocolate Chip Cookies (p. 109)	20	297	3	37	16	27	92	117	5	4	0	7	6	5	2	9
Gingerbread Cutouts (p. 114)	36	80	1	12	3	8	27	60	2	0	0	4	3	3	2	4
Gingerbread People Cutouts (p. 114)	12	240	3	37	9	23	82	181	5	0	0	12	8	8	6	12
Gingersnaps (p. 117)	48	76	1	11	3	6	26	42	1	0	1	3	2	2	1	3

On the divider: Orange-Date Bars (p. 106), Spiced Raisin Drop Cookies (p. 110), Chocolate-Peanut Drop Cookies (p. 110), Santa's Whiskers (p. 115), and Jam Thumbprints (p. 120).

Nutrition Analysis	Servings Per Recipe	Calories	Protein (g)	Carbohydrate (g)	Fat (g)	Cholesterol (mg)	Sodium (mg)	Potassium (mg)	Protein	Vitamin A	Vitamin C	Thiamine	Riboflavin	Niacin	Calcium	Iron
	Per Serving								**Percent U.S. RDA Per Serving**							
Granola Bars (p. 104)	24	139	2	16	8	11	5	99	4	0	1	6	3	2	1	4
Gumdrop Drop Cookies (p. 110)	30	87	1	14	3	9	28	14	1	1	0	2	1	1	0	2
Hermits (p. 112)	36	84	1	12	4	8	42	64	2	2	0	3	2	2	1	3
Jam Thumbprints (p. 120)	42	80	1	8	5	13	37	25	2	3	0	3	2	1	1	2
Lemon and Poppy Seed Shortbread (p. 120)	16	98	1	10	6	16	59	15	2	4	0	4	2	3	1	3
Lemon Bars (p. 104)	20	100	1	16	4	27	47	18	2	3	2	3	3	2	1	2
Lemon Macaroons (p. 111)	30	34	0	6	1	0	4	15	1	0	0	0	0	0	0	0
Lemon Tea Cookies (p. 111)	48	52	1	8	2	6	31	11	1	2	1	2	1	1	1	1
Macadamia Nut and White Chocolate Chunk Cookies (p. 109)	60	112	1	13	6	10	36	44	2	1	0	3	3	2	2	2
Nutty Macaroons (p. 111)	30	47	1	6	2	0	4	31	1	0	0	0	1	0	1	1
Nutty Spritz (p. 118)	84	61	1	6	4	3	43	14	1	3	0	2	2	1	1	1
Oatmeal Cookies (p. 110)	48	82	1	12	3	6	48	35	2	3	0	4	2	1	1	3
Oatmeal Shortbread (p. 120)	16	95	1	9	6	16	59	15	2	4	0	4	2	2	0	2
Oat Spiced Slices (p. 115)	60	60	1	6	4	5	29	22	1	1	0	2	2	1	1	2
Orange-Chocolate Slices (p. 115)	60	68	1	9	4	5	24	17	1	1	1	3	2	2	0	2
Orange-Date Bars (p. 106)	24	86	1	12	4	11	45	71	2	2	3	4	2	2	1	3
Peanut Butter Bars (p. 106)	20	85	2	10	5	14	36	53	3	0	0	3	2	3	1	3
Peanut Butter Cookies (p. 117)	36	91	2	12	5	8	69	44	3	2	0	2	2	4	1	2
Pecan Snaps (p. 119)	54	36	0	4	2	0	15	31	0	1	0	1	1	0	1	1
Pineapple-Coconut Drop Cookies (p. 110)	30	79	1	10	4	9	26	27	1	1	1	2	1	1	0	2
Pumpkin Bars (p. 106)	48	93	1	11	5	23	52	31	2	42	1	3	2	2	1	3
Raisin Oatmeal Cookies (p. 110)	54	81	1	13	3	5	43	51	2	2	0	4	2	1	1	3
Ranger Cookies (p. 112)	54	63	1	10	2	5	43	40	1	2	1	2	2	2	1	2
Sandies (p. 118)	36	113	1	11	7	0	60	23	2	4	0	5	2	2	0	2
Santa's Whiskers (p. 115)	60	60	1	8	3	0	27	15	1	2	0	2	1	1	0	1
Shortbread (p. 120)	16	95	1	10	6	16	59	11	2	4	0	4	2	3	0	2
Snickerdoodles (p. 117)	36	68	1	10	3	8	40	9	1	2	0	2	2	1	0	2
Spiced Raisin Drop Cookies (p. 110)	30	81	1	12	3	9	26	50	1	1	0	2	2	1	1	2
Spiced Shortbread (p. 120)	16	96	1	10	6	16	60	21	2	4	0	4	2	3	1	3
Spiced Slices (p. 115)	60	65	1	7	4	5	29	19	1	1	0	2	2	1	1	2
Spicy Prune Bars (p. 106)	24	84	1	12	4	11	45	72	2	3	3	3	2	2	2	3
Spritz (p. 118)	84	58	1	6	3	3	43	8	1	3	0	2	1	1	0	1
Sugar-Cookie Cutouts (p. 113)	36	75	1	10	4	8	38	10	1	2	0	3	2	2	1	2
Tiny Tarts with Lemon-Coconut Filling (p. 119)	24	100	1	9	7	27	72	21	2	5	1	3	3	1	1	2
Tiny Tarts with Pecan Filling (p. 119)	24	115	1	11	7	15	66	47	2	5	0	4	2	2	1	3
Tiny Tarts with Pumpkin Filling (p. 119)	24	80	1	7	5	16	59	29	2	27	0	3	3	2	1	2
Tiny Tarts with Spiced Fruit Filling (p. 119)	24	102	1	14	5	4	58	106	2	6	1	3	2	1	1	3
Toffee Bars (p. 108)	36	115	1	16	5	4	74	55	2	4	1	2	4	1	4	1
Whole Wheat Chocolate Revel Bars (p. 107)	60	144	2	20	7	12	72	98	4	4	0	5	4	2	3	4
Whole Wheat Spiced Slices (p. 115)	60	65	1	7	4	5	29	25	1	1	0	2	2	1	1	2
Whole Wheat Spritz (p. 118)	84	58	1	6	3	3	43	11	1	3	0	2	1	1	1	1

Cookies

You'll find cookies here for any occasion, from after-school snacks to holiday-dinner desserts.

For maximum taste and minimum effort, follow these hints when making cookies.
● Save time by skipping the traditional step of beating the sugar and margarine, butter, or shortening together separately. Our cookie recipes now allow you to add all of the ingredients to a bowl and mix. We think this new method gives you the same great taste with less work.
● If you use 100-percent-corn-oil margarine in your cookies, keep in mind that your dough will be softer than doughs made with regular margarine or butter. (Do not use spread, diet, or soft-style margarine products in cookie doughs. Your cookies will not turn out satisfactorily.) When using corn-oil margarine, make the following adjustments so your dough will be easier to handle:
　　For sliced cookies, chill the rolls of dough in the freezer instead of the refrigerator.
　　For rolled cookies, chill the dough before rolling it, or freeze it just until it's firm enough to roll.
● With a standard mixer, start mixing on low speed so you don't sling the flour out of the bowl.
● If you use a portable mixer when making cookies and notice that it strains or becomes hot, stir in any remaining ingredients by hand. Many cookie doughs are so stiff that beating them with a portable mixer may not be possible, especially when you're adding the last of the flour.

Crispy Cereal Squares

Make these in the microwave, too.

In a medium saucepan combine ⅔ cup *light corn syrup* and ¼ cup packed *brown sugar*. Cook and stir till mixture comes to a full rolling boil.
　　Remove saucepan from heat and stir in 1 cup *peanut butter* and ½ teaspoon *vanilla*. Stir in 4 cups *crisp rice cereal*.
　　Press into an ungreased 9x9x2-inch pan. Chill about 1 hour or till firm. Cut into bars. Makes 25.
　　Microwave directions: In a 2-quart casserole micro-cook corn syrup, brown sugar, peanut butter, and vanilla on 100% power (high) for 2 to 3 minutes or till bubbly over entire surface, stirring twice. Stir in cereal. Continue as above.

Lemon Bars

　⅓　**cup margarine *or* butter**
　1　**cup sugar**
　1　**cup all-purpose flour**
　2　**eggs**
　2　**tablespoons all-purpose flour**
　2　**teaspoons finely shredded lemon peel**
　3　**tablespoons lemon juice**
　¼　**teaspoon baking powder**
　　　Powdered sugar (optional)　　　Oven 350°

Beat margarine with an electric mixer on medium to high speed for 30 seconds. Add ¼ cup of the sugar. Beat till combined. Beat in the 1 cup flour till crumbly. Press into the bottom of an ungreased 8x8x2-inch baking pan. Bake in a 350° oven for 15 to 18 minutes or just till golden.
　　Meanwhile, combine eggs, the remaining sugar, the 2 tablespoons flour, lemon peel, juice, and baking powder. Beat for 2 minutes or till thoroughly combined. Pour over hot baked layer.
　　Bake in a 350° oven about 20 minutes more or till lightly browned around the edges and center is set. Cool on a wire rack. If desired, sift powdered sugar over top. Cut into bars. Makes 20.

Granola Bars

This soft, moist, and chewy bar cookie is loaded with granola and oats.

　1　**cup granola**
　1　**cup quick-cooking rolled oats**
　1　**cup chopped nuts**
　½　**cup all-purpose flour**
　½　**cup raisins *or* mixed dried fruit bits**
　1　**beaten egg**
　⅓　**cup honey**
　⅓　**cup cooking oil**
　¼　**cup packed brown sugar**
　½　**teaspoon ground cinnamon (optional)**　　　Oven 325°

Line an 8x8x2-inch baking pan with foil. Grease the foil; set pan aside. In a mixing bowl combine granola, oats, nuts, flour, and raisins. Stir in egg, honey, oil, brown sugar, and, if desired, cinnamon. Press evenly into the prepared pan.
　　Bake in a 325° oven for 30 to 35 minutes or till lightly browned around the edges. Cool. Use foil to remove from pan. Cut into bars. Makes 24.

Fruit-Filled Oatmeal Bars

Need a shortcut? Substitute a 10-ounce jar of preserves for the homemade filling.

1 cup all-purpose flour
1 cup quick-cooking rolled oats
⅔ cup packed brown sugar
¼ teaspoon baking soda
½ cup margarine *or* butter
    Raisin Filling, Apple-Cinnamon
      Filling, *or* Apricot-Coconut
      Filling   Oven 350°

In a mixing bowl combine flour, oats, brown sugar, and baking soda. Cut in margarine or butter till mixture resembles coarse crumbs. Reserve ½ *cup* of the flour mixture. Press remaining flour mixture into the bottom of an ungreased 9x9x2-inch baking pan. Spread with desired filling. Sprinkle with reserved flour mixture.

Bake in a 350° oven for 30 to 35 minutes or till the top is golden. Cool in the pan on a wire rack. Cut into bars. Makes 25.

Raisin Filling: In a medium saucepan combine ½ cup *water,* 2 tablespoons *sugar,* and 2 teaspoons *cornstarch.* Add 1 cup *raisins.* Cook and stir till thickened and bubbly.

Apple-Cinnamon Filling: Peel, core, and chop 2 medium *apples* (about 10 ounces). In a medium saucepan combine apples, 2 table-spoons *sugar,* 2 tablespoons *water,* 1 tablespoon *lemon juice,* ½ teaspoon ground *cinnamon,* and a dash ground *cloves.* Bring apple mixture to boiling; reduce heat. Simmer for 8 to 10 minutes or till apples are very tender.

Apricot-Coconut Filling: In a medium saucepan combine 1 cup snipped *dried apricots* and ¾ cup *water.* Bring apricot mixture to boiling; reduce heat. Cover and simmer for 5 minutes. Meanwhile, combine ¼ cup *sugar* and 1 tablespoon *all-purpose flour.* Stir into apricot mixture. Cook and stir about 1 minute more or till very thick. Stir in ½ cup *coconut.*

Using your hands, press the flour mixture *evenly* into the bottom of the baking pan.

Orange-Date Bars

Orange-Date Bars are pictured on page 101.

¼ **cup margarine** *or* **butter**
1 **cup all-purpose flour**
½ **cup packed brown sugar**
1 **teaspoon finely shredded**
      orange peel
½ **cup orange juice**
1 **egg**
½ **teaspoon baking powder**
¼ **teaspoon baking soda**
½ **cup chopped walnuts**
½ **cup chopped pitted dates**
      Powdered sugar   Oven 350°

For batter, in a mixing bowl beat margarine or butter with an electric mixer on medium to high speed for 30 seconds. Add about *half* of the flour, the brown sugar, orange peel, *half* of the orange juice, the egg, baking powder, and baking soda. Beat till thoroughly combined. Beat in remaining flour and orange juice. Stir in walnuts and dates.

Spread batter into an ungreased 11x7x1½-inch baking pan. Bake in a 350° oven about 25 minutes or till a toothpick inserted near the center comes out clean. Cool in the pan on a wire rack. Sift powdered sugar over the top. Cut into bars. Makes 24.

Microwave directions: Prepare batter as above. Spread batter into an ungreased 8x8x2-inch baking dish. Micro-cook, uncovered, on 50% power (medium) for 11 minutes, giving the dish a quarter-turn every 3 minutes. If not done, cook on 100% power (high) for 30 seconds to 2 minutes more or till the surface is nearly dry. Cool; sprinkle with the powdered sugar. Cut into bars.

Spicy Prune Bars: Prepare as above, *except* add ½ teaspoon ground *cinnamon* and dash ground *cloves* with the first half of flour, and substitute snipped dried pitted *prunes* for dates.

Cranberry-Pecan Bars: Prepare as above, *except* substitute chopped *pecans* for the walnuts and chopped *cranberries* for the dates.

Pumpkin Bars

2 **cups all-purpose flour**
1½ **cups sugar**
2 **teaspoons baking powder**
2 **teaspoons ground cinnamon**
1 **teaspoon baking soda**
¼ **teaspoon salt**
¼ **teaspoon ground cloves**
4 **beaten eggs**
1 **16-ounce can pumpkin**
1 **cup cooking oil**
½ **recipe Cream Cheese Frosting**
      (see recipe, page 88)   Oven 350°

Combine flour, sugar, baking powder, cinnamon, soda, salt, and cloves. Stir in eggs, pumpkin, and cooking oil till thoroughly combined. Spread batter into an ungreased 15x10x1-inch baking pan.

Bake in a 350° oven for 25 to 30 minutes or till a toothpick inserted near the center comes out clean. Cool on a wire rack. Frost with Cream Cheese Frosting. Cut into bars. Makes 48.

Applesauce Bars: Prepare as above, *except* substitute *applesauce* for the pumpkin.

Peanut Butter Bars

⅔ **cup all-purpose flour**
½ **cup packed brown sugar**
¼ **cup peanut butter**
¼ **cup shortening**
1 **egg**
1 **tablespoon milk**
½ **teaspoon vanilla**
¼ **teaspoon baking soda**
¼ **cup quick-cooking rolled oats**
½ **recipe Peanut-Butter Frosting**
      (see recipe, page 89)   Oven 375°

Combine about *half* of the flour, the brown sugar, peanut butter, shortening, egg, milk, vanilla, and soda. Beat with an electric mixer on medium to high speed till thoroughly combined. Beat in remaining flour. Stir in oats. Spread batter into an ungreased 8x8x2-inch baking pan.

Bake in a 375° oven for 15 to 18 minutes or till a toothpick inserted near the center comes out clean. Cool in pan on a wire rack. Frost with Peanut-Butter Frosting. Cut into bars. Makes 20.

Chocolate Revel Bars

Our staff has loved these tempting bars for years.

- 1 cup margarine *or* butter
- 2½ cups all-purpose flour
- 2 cups packed brown sugar
- 2 eggs
- 4 teaspoons vanilla
- 1 teaspoon baking soda
- 3 cups quick-cooking rolled oats
- 1½ cups semisweet chocolate pieces
- 1 14-ounce can (1¼ cups) *sweetened condensed* milk
- 2 tablespoons margarine *or* butter
- ½ cup chopped walnuts *or pecans*   Oven 350°

In a mixing bowl beat the 1 cup margarine or butter with an electric mixer on medium to high speed for 30 seconds. Add about *half* of the flour, the brown sugar, eggs, *2 teaspoons* of the vanilla, and the baking soda. Beat till thoroughly combined. Beat in remaining flour. Stir in oats.

In a medium saucepan combine chocolate pieces, sweetened condensed milk, and the 2 tablespoons margarine or butter. Cook over low heat till chocolate melts, stirring occasionally. Remove from heat. Stir in walnuts and remaining 2 teaspoons vanilla.

Press *two-thirds* (about 3⅓ cups) of the rolled-oats mixture into the bottom of an ungreased 15x10x1-inch baking pan. Spread chocolate mixture over the oat mixture. Using your fingers, dot remaining oat mixture over chocolate.

Bake in a 350° oven about 25 minutes or till top is lightly browned (chocolate mixture will still look moist). Cool on a wire rack. Makes 60.

Whole Wheat Chocolate Revel Bars: Prepare as above, *except* reduce all-purpose flour to *1½ cups* and add 1 cup *whole wheat flour.*

Fudge Brownies

A chocolaty delight even without the frosting.

- ½ cup margarine *or* butter
- 2 squares (2 ounces) unsweetened chocolate
- 1 cup sugar
- 2 eggs
- 1 teaspoon vanilla
- ¾ cup all-purpose flour
- ½ cup chopped nuts
- ½ recipe No-Cook Fudge Frosting *or* ½ recipe Chocolate Glaze (see recipes, page 89)
- Chopped nuts (optional)   Oven 350°

In a medium saucepan melt margarine and chocolate over low heat. Remove from heat. Stir in sugar, eggs, and vanilla. Beat *lightly* by hand just till combined. Stir in flour and ½ cup nuts. Spread batter into an 8x8x2-inch baking pan. Bake in a 350° oven for 30 minutes. Cool on a wire rack. Frost or glaze top. If desired, sprinkle with chopped nuts. Cut into bars. Makes 24.

Cake Brownies

- 1¼ cups sugar
- ¾ cup margarine *or* butter
- ½ cup unsweetened cocoa powder
- 2 eggs
- 1 teaspoon vanilla
- 1½ cups all-purpose flour
- 1 teaspoon baking powder
- ¼ teaspoon baking soda
- 1 cup milk
- 1 cup chopped walnuts *or* pecans
- No-Cook Fudge Frosting (see recipe, page 89)   Oven 350°

In a large saucepan heat sugar, margarine or butter, and cocoa powder over medium heat till margarine melts, stirring constantly. Remove from heat. Add eggs and vanilla. Beat lightly just till combined. Combine flour, baking powder, and soda. Add dry ingredients and milk alternately to the chocolate mixture, beating after each addition. Stir in nuts. Pour batter into a greased 15x10x1-inch baking pan.

Bake in a 350° oven about 20 minutes or till a toothpick inserted near the center comes out clean. Cool in pan on a wire rack. Frost with No-Cook Fudge Frosting. Cut into bars. Makes 36.

Buttermilk Brownies

The buttermilk adds a delightful tang to these moist, fine-textured brownies.

    2   cups all-purpose flour
    2   cups sugar
    1   teaspoon baking soda
    ¼   teaspoon salt
    1   cup margarine *or* butter
    1   cup water
    ⅓   cup unsweetened cocoa powder
    2   eggs
    ½   cup buttermilk
    1½ teaspoons vanilla
    ¼   cup margarine *or* butter
    3   tablespoons unsweetened cocoa
        powder
    3   tablespoons buttermilk
    2¼ cups sifted powdered sugar
    ½   teaspoon vanilla
    ¾   cup coarsely chopped pecans
        (optional)   Oven 350°

In a mixing bowl combine flour, sugar, baking soda, and salt. Set aside.

In a medium saucepan combine the 1 cup margarine or butter, the water, and the ⅓ cup unsweetened cocoa powder. Bring mixture just to boiling, stirring constantly. Remove from heat. Add the chocolate mixture to dry ingredients and beat with an electric mixer on medium to high speed till thoroughly combined. Add eggs, the ½ cup buttermilk, and the 1½ teaspoons vanilla. Beat for 1 minute (batter will be thin).

Pour the batter into a greased and floured 15x10x1-inch baking pan. Bake in a 350° oven about 25 minutes or till a toothpick inserted near the center comes out clean.

Meanwhile, for frosting, in a medium saucepan combine the ¼ cup margarine or butter, the 3 tablespoons unsweetened cocoa powder, and the 3 tablespoons buttermilk. Bring to boiling. Remove from heat. Add powdered sugar and the ½ teaspoon vanilla. Beat till smooth. Stir in chopped pecans, if desired. Pour warm frosting over the warm brownies, spreading evenly. Cool in pan on a wire rack. Cut into bars. Makes 36.

Toffee Bars

For an easy topping, sprinkle chocolate pieces over the hot bars. See the note below for details.

    ½   cup margarine *or* butter
    ½   cup sugar
    ¼   teaspoon salt
    1   cup all-purpose flour
    1   14-ounce can (1¼ cups) *sweetened
        condensed* milk
    2   tablespoons margarine *or* butter
    2   teaspoons vanilla
    1   square (1 ounce) unsweetened
        chocolate
    2   tablespoons margarine *or* butter
    1½ cups sifted powdered sugar
    1   teaspoon vanilla   Oven 350°

In a mixing bowl beat the ½ cup margarine or butter, the sugar, and salt with an electric mixer on medium to high speed till thoroughly combined. Stir in flour. Press into the bottom of an ungreased 13x9x2-inch baking pan. Bake in a 350° oven about 15 minutes or till edges are lightly browned.

In a heavy medium saucepan heat condensed milk and the 2 tablespoons margarine or butter over medium heat till bubbly, stirring constantly. Cook and stir for 5 minutes more. (Mixture will thicken and become smooth.) Stir in the 2 teaspoons vanilla. Spread over baked layer. Bake for 12 to 15 minutes or till golden.

For fudge icing,* in a small saucepan heat chocolate and the 2 tablespoons margarine or butter over low heat till melted, stirring occasionally. Remove from heat; stir in powdered sugar and the 1 teaspoon vanilla. Stir in enough *hot* water (1 to 2 tablespoons) to make an icing of pouring consistency. Spread over warm cookie and immediately cut into bars. Cool. Makes 36.

*__Note:__ To save effort when frosting the cookie, substitute one 6-ounce package *semisweet chocolate pieces* for the fudge icing. Sprinkle pieces over the cookie *immediately* after removing from the oven. Let stand for 2 to 3 minutes or till softened. Spread evenly over top. Cool; chill 5 to 10 minutes or till chocolate layer is set. Cut into bars.

Chocolate Chip Cookies

½ cup shortening
½ cup margarine *or* butter
2½ cups all-purpose flour
1 cup packed brown sugar
½ cup sugar
2 eggs
1 teaspoon vanilla
½ teaspoon baking soda
1 12-ounce package (2 cups)
    semisweet chocolate pieces
1 cup chopped walnuts, pecans,
    or hazelnuts (filberts)
    (optional)   Oven 375°

In a mixing bowl beat the shortening and margarine or butter with an electric mixer on medium to high speed for 30 seconds. Add about *half* of the flour, the brown sugar, sugar, eggs, vanilla, and baking soda. Beat mixture till thoroughly combined. Beat in the remaining flour. Stir in chocolate pieces and, if desired, nuts.

Drop dough by rounded teaspoons 2 inches apart onto an ungreased cookie sheet. Bake in a 375° oven for 8 to 10 minutes or till edges are lightly browned. Cool cookies on a wire rack. Makes about 60.

Chocolate-Candy Cookies: Prepare as above, *except* substitute *candy-coated milk chocolate pieces* for the semisweet chocolate pieces.

Giant Chocolate Chip Cookies: Prepare as above, *except* drop dough from a ¼-cup measure or scoop about 4 inches apart onto cookie sheet. Bake for 11 to 13 minutes or till edges are lightly browned. Makes about 20.

Macadamia Nut and White Chocolate Chunk Cookies: Prepare as above, *except* substitute chopped *white baking bars (or pieces) with cocoa butter or vanilla-flavored confectioners' coating* for the semisweet chocolate pieces. Stir in one 3½-ounce jar *macadamia nuts,* chopped, with the white chocolate.

Fudge Ecstasies

If ever a cookie deserved its name, it's this one.

1 12-ounce package (2 cups)
    semisweet chocolate pieces
2 squares (2 ounces) unsweetened
    chocolate
2 tablespoons margarine *or* butter
2 eggs
⅔ cup sugar
¼ cup all-purpose flour
1 teaspoon vanilla
¼ teaspoon baking powder
1 cup chopped nuts   Oven 350°

In a heavy medium saucepan heat *half* of the chocolate pieces, the unsweetened chocolate, and margarine or butter till melted, stirring occasionally. Add eggs, sugar, flour, vanilla, and baking powder. Beat till thoroughly combined. Stir in remaining chocolate pieces and nuts.

Drop by rounded teaspoons 2 inches apart onto a greased cookie sheet. Bake in a 350° oven for 8 to 10 minutes or till edges are firm and surfaces are dull and cracked. Cool cookies on a wire rack. Makes about 36.

How to Use the Nutrition Analysis Charts

The nutrition analysis for each cookie recipe in this chapter is listed in the charts on pages 102 and 103. For cookie recipes that include their own frosting directions, the nutritional values of the frosting are included in the numbers listed for the cookie. To determine the total nutrition analysis for a cookie made with a frosting from the "Cakes" chapter (see pages 87 to 90), add the separate analyses for the cookie and the frosting.

Drop Cookies

For a peek at the Chocolate-Peanut and Spiced Raisin drop cookies, turn to page 101.

¼ **cup shortening**
¼ **cup margarine *or* butter**
1 **cup all-purpose flour**
½ **cup sugar**
¼ **cup packed brown sugar**
1 **egg**
1 **teaspoon vanilla**
⅛ **teaspoon baking soda**   Oven 375°

In a mixing bowl beat shortening and margarine or butter with an electric mixer on medium to high speed for 30 seconds. Add about *half* of the flour, the sugar, brown sugar, egg, vanilla, and baking soda. Beat till thoroughly combined. Beat in remaining flour.

Drop by rounded teaspoons 2 inches apart onto an ungreased cookie sheet. Bake in a 375° oven for 8 to 10 minutes or till edges are golden. Cool cookies on the cookie sheet for 1 minute, then remove cookies and cool on a wire rack. Makes about 24.

Chocolate-Peanut Drop Cookies: Prepare as above, *except* add ⅓ cup *unsweetened cocoa powder* and 3 tablespoons *milk* with the sugar. After beating in all the flour, stir in ½ cup chopped *peanuts*. Makes about 30.

Pineapple-Coconut Drop Cookies: Prepare as above, *except* add ½ cup well-drained crushed *pineapple* and ¼ teaspoon ground *ginger* with the sugar. After beating in all the flour, stir in 1 cup *coconut*. Makes about 30.

Spiced Raisin Drop Cookies: Prepare as above, *except* add ½ teaspoon ground *cinnamon* and ½ teaspoon ground *nutmeg* with the sugar. After beating in all the flour, stir in 1 cup *raisins or mixed dried fruit bits*. Makes about 30.

Coconut-Pecan Drop Cookies: Prepare as above, *except,* after beating in all the flour, stir in 1 cup *coconut* and 1 cup chopped *pecans*. Makes about 36.

Gumdrop Drop Cookies: Prepare as above, *except,* after beating in all the flour, stir in 1 cup snipped *gumdrops*. Makes about 30.

Oatmeal Cookies

¾ **cup margarine *or* butter**
1¾ **cups all-purpose flour**
1 **cup packed brown sugar**
½ **cup sugar**
1 **egg**
1 **teaspoon baking powder**
1 **teaspoon vanilla**
¼ **teaspoon baking soda**
½ **teaspoon ground cinnamon (optional)**
¼ **teaspoon ground cloves (optional)**
2 **cups rolled oats**   Oven 375°

In a mixing bowl beat margarine or butter with an electric mixer on medium to high speed for 30 seconds. Add about *half* of the flour, the brown sugar, sugar, egg, baking powder, vanilla, and baking soda. If desired, stir in cinnamon and cloves. Beat till thoroughly combined. Beat in remaining flour. Stir in oats.

Drop by rounded teaspoons 2 inches apart onto an ungreased cookie sheet. Bake in a 375° oven for 10 to 12 minutes or till edges are golden. Cool cookies on a wire rack. Makes about 48.

Fruit-Topped Oatmeal Cookies: Prepare as above, *except,* for topping, in a medium saucepan combine 1½ cups finely chopped peeled *apples, pears, or peaches;* ½ cup *sugar;* ⅓ cup *raisins;* ⅓ cup chopped *pecans;* and 2 tablespoons *water.* Bring to boiling, stirring constantly. Reduce heat. Simmer till fruit is tender and most of the liquid has evaporated, stirring occasionally. After dropping dough onto cookie sheet, press centers with your thumb. Fill each indentation with a level teaspoon of topping.

Raisin Oatmeal Cookies: Prepare as above, *except,* after stirring in oats, stir in 1 cup *raisins or currants*. Makes about 54.

Choose-a-Chip Oatmeal Cookies: Prepare as above, *except,* after stirring in oats, stir in 1 cup *semisweet chocolate, butterscotch-flavored, or peanut-butter-flavored pieces* and ½ cup chopped *walnuts or pecans*. Makes about 54.

Lemon Tea Cookies

 1 **teaspoon finely shredded lemon peel (set aside)**
 2 **teaspoons lemon juice**
 ⅓ **cup milk**
 ½ **cup margarine *or* butter**
 1¾ **cups all-purpose flour**
 1 **cup sugar**
 1 **egg**
 1 **teaspoon baking powder**
 ¼ **teaspoon baking soda**
 2 **tablespoons lemon juice**   Oven 350°

Stir the 2 teaspoons lemon juice into milk. Let stand 5 minutes. Beat margarine or butter with an electric mixer on medium to high speed for 30 seconds. Add about *half* of the flour, ¾ *cup* of the sugar, the egg, baking powder, soda, lemon peel, and milk mixture. Beat till thoroughly combined. Beat in remaining flour.

Drop by rounded teaspoons 2 inches apart onto an ungreased cookie sheet. Bake in a 350° oven for 10 to 12 minutes or till edges are lightly browned. Cool cookies on a wire rack. Stir together remaining sugar and the 2 tablespoons lemon juice; brush on cookies. Makes about 48.

Coconut Macaroons

A light and airy cookie that's crispy on the outside and chewy on the inside.

 2 **egg whites**
 ½ **teaspoon vanilla**
 ⅔ **cup sugar**
 1 **3½-ounce can (1⅓ cups) flaked coconut**   Oven 325°

In a mixing bowl beat egg whites and vanilla till soft peaks form (tips curl). Gradually add sugar, beating till stiff peaks form (tips stand straight). Fold in coconut. Drop by rounded teaspoons 2 inches apart onto a greased cookie sheet. Bake in a 325° oven about 20 minutes or till edges are lightly browned. Cool cookies on a wire rack. Makes about 30.

Nutty Macaroons: Prepare as above, *except* add ½ cup chopped toasted *almonds, pecans, or hazelnuts (filberts)* with the coconut.

Lemon Macaroons: Prepare as above, *except* substitute 1 tablespoon *lemon juice* for the vanilla and add 1 teaspoon finely shredded *lemon peel* with the coconut.

Florentines

The thin layer of chocolate makes this fruit-filled crispy cookie, oh, so elegant.

 ⅓ **cup margarine *or* butter**
 ⅓ **cup milk**
 ¼ **cup sugar**
 1 **cup toasted almonds, chopped**
 ¾ **cup diced mixed candied fruits and peels, finely chopped**
 1 **teaspoon finely shredded orange peel**
 ¼ **cup all-purpose flour**
 ¾ **cup semisweet chocolate pieces**
 2 **tablespooons margarine *or* butter**   Oven 350°

In a medium saucepan combine the ⅓ cup margarine or butter, the milk, and sugar. Bring to a full rolling boil, stirring occasionally. Remove from heat. Stir in almonds, candied fruits and peels, and orange peel. Stir in flour.

Drop by level tablespoons at least 3 inches apart onto a *greased and floured* cookie sheet. (Grease and flour cookie sheet for each batch.) Using the back of a spoon, spread the batter into 3-inch circles. Bake in a 350° oven for 8 to 10 minutes or till edges are lightly browned. Cool on the cookie sheet for 1 minute, then carefully transfer to waxed paper. Cool thoroughly.

In a small heavy saucepan heat chocolate pieces and the 2 tablespoons margarine over low heat till melted, stirring occasionally. Spread a scant *teaspoon* of the chocolate mixture evenly over the *bottom* of each cookie. When chocolate is almost set, draw wavy lines through it with the tines of a fork. Cover and store cookies in the refrigerator. Makes about 24.

Dropping the Drops

Drop-cookie doughs tend to spread more than other cookie doughs do. So, to keep them from spreading too much, drop them onto *cool* cookie sheets. Be sure, too, to let cookie sheets that are straight from the oven cool for several minutes before reusing.

Cashew-Nutmeg Drops

½ cup margarine *or* butter
2 cups all-purpose flour
1 cup packed brown sugar
½ cup dairy sour cream *or* buttermilk
1 egg
1 teaspoon vanilla
½ teaspoon baking powder
½ teaspoon baking soda
½ teaspoon ground nutmeg
1 cup chopped cashews *or* pecans
2 recipes Powdered Sugar Icing
  (see recipe, page 88) Oven 375°

In a mixing bowl beat margarine or butter with an electric mixer on medium to high speed for 30 seconds. Add about *half* of the flour, the brown sugar, sour cream, egg, vanilla, baking powder, baking soda, and nutmeg. Beat till thoroughly combined. Beat in remaining flour. Stir in nuts.

Drop by rounded teaspoons 2 inches apart onto an ungreased cookie sheet. Bake in a 375° oven for 8 to 10 minutes or till lightly browned. Cool cookies on a wire rack. Frost with Powdered Sugar Icing. Makes about 48.

Banana-Spice Cookies

½ cup margarine *or* butter
2¼ cups all-purpose flour
1 cup sugar
2 eggs
1 teaspoon baking powder
1 teaspoon vanilla
½ teaspoon ground cinnamon
¼ teaspoon baking soda
⅛ teaspoon ground cloves
3 bananas, mashed (1 cup)
½ cup chopped nuts
  Butter Frosting (see recipe,
  page 89) Oven 375°

Beat margarine with an electric mixer on medium to high speed for 30 seconds. Add about *half* of the flour, the sugar, eggs, baking powder, vanilla, cinnamon, soda, and cloves. Beat till thoroughly combined. Beat in remaining flour. Beat in bananas. Stir in nuts. Drop by rounded teaspoons 2 inches apart onto a greased cookie sheet. Bake in a 375° oven for 8 to 10 minutes or till edges are lightly browned. Cool cookies on a rack. Frost with Butter Frosting. Makes 60.

Hermits

½ cup margarine *or* butter
1½ cups all-purpose flour
¾ cup packed brown sugar
1 egg
2 tablespoons milk
1 teaspoon vanilla
½ teaspoon baking soda
½ teaspoon ground cinnamon
¼ teaspoon ground nutmeg
⅛ teaspoon ground cloves
1 cup raisins, currants, *or* diced
  mixed candied fruits and peels
½ cup chopped nuts Oven 375°

In a mixing bowl beat margarine or butter with an electric mixer on medium to high speed for 30 seconds. Add about *half* of the flour, the brown sugar, egg, milk, vanilla, soda, cinnamon, nutmeg, and cloves. Beat till thoroughly combined. Beat in remaining flour. Stir in raisins and nuts. Drop by rounded teaspoons 2 inches apart onto a greased cookie sheet. Bake in a 375° oven about 10 minutes or till edges are lightly browned. Cool cookies on a rack. Makes 36.

Ranger Cookies

½ cup margarine *or* butter
1¼ cups all-purpose flour
½ cup sugar
½ cup packed brown sugar
1 egg
1 teaspoon vanilla
½ teaspoon baking powder
¼ teaspoon baking soda
2 cups crisp rice cereal *or* 1 cup
  rolled oats
1 3½-ounce can (1⅓ cups) flaked
  coconut
1 cup snipped pitted whole
  dates, *or* raisins Oven 375°

Beat margarine with an electric mixer on medium to high speed for 30 seconds. Add about *half* of the flour, the sugars, egg, vanilla, baking powder, and soda. Beat till thoroughly combined. Beat in remaining flour. Stir in cereal, coconut, and dates. Drop by rounded teaspoons onto an ungreased cookie sheet. Bake in a 375° oven about 8 minutes or till done. Cool on cookie sheet 1 minute. Remove; cool on rack. Makes 54.

Sugar-Cookie Cutouts

⅓ **cup margarine *or* butter**
⅓ **cup shortening**
2 **cups all-purpose flour**
1 **egg**
¾ **cup sugar**
1 **tablespoon milk**
1 **teaspoon baking powder**
1 **teaspoon vanilla**
Dash salt
Powdered Sugar Icing
(see recipe, page 88)
(optional)   Oven 375°

Beat margarine and shortening with an electric mixer on medium to high speed for 30 seconds. Add about *half* of the flour, the egg, sugar, milk, baking powder, vanilla, and salt. Beat till thoroughly combined. Beat in remaining flour. Divide dough in half. Cover; chill for 3 hours.

On a lightly floured surface, roll *half* of the dough at a time ⅛ inch thick. Cut into desired shapes with a 2½-inch cookie cutter. Place on an ungreased cookie sheet. If desired, sprinkle with sugar and cinnamon. Bake in a 375° oven for 7 to 8 minutes or till edges are firm and bottoms are very lightly browned. Cool cookies on a rack.

If desired, frost cookies with Powdered Sugar Icing, then sprinkle with decorative candies, colored sugar, or chopped nuts. Makes 36 to 48.

Candy-Window Sugar-Cookie Cutouts: Prepare as above, *except,* before baking, place cookies on a *foil-lined* cookie sheet. Cut out small shapes in cookie centers. Finely crush 3 ounces *hard candy* (about ½ cup). Spoon some candy into each center to fill hole(s). When baked, cool cookies on foil; remove. Store tightly covered.

Filled Sugar-Cookie Cutouts: Prepare as above, *except* make *Butter Frosting* (see recipe, page 89), adding a few drops food coloring, if desired. Before serving, spread *1 tablespoon* frosting on the bottoms of *half* of the cookies. Top *each* with another cookie. Makes 24.

With a floured cookie cutter, cut desired shapes out of dough as close together as possible.

Gingerbread Cutouts

Making plump gingerbread people is a snap with this spicy dough.

½ cup shortening
2½ cups all-purpose flour
½ cup sugar
½ cup molasses
1 egg
1 tablespoon vinegar
1 teaspoon baking powder
1 teaspoon ground ginger
½ teaspoon baking soda
½ teaspoon ground cinnamon
½ teaspoon ground cloves
    Powdered Sugar Icing (see recipe,
      page 88)(optional)
    Decorative candies
      (optional)   Oven 375°

In a mixing bowl beat shortening with an electric mixer on medium to high speed for 30 seconds. Add about *half* of the flour, the sugar, molasses, egg, vinegar, baking powder, ginger, baking soda, cinnamon, and cloves. Beat till thoroughly combined. Beat in remaining flour. Cover and chill for 3 hours or till easy to handle.

Divide the chilled dough in half. On a lightly floured surface, roll *half* of the dough at a time ⅛ inch thick. Cut into desired shapes with a 2½-inch cookie cutter. Place 1 inch apart on a greased cookie sheet. Bake in a 375° oven for 5 to 6 minutes or till edges are lightly browned. Cool on the cookie sheet for 1 minute. Remove and cool on a wire rack.

If desired, prepare Powdered Sugar Icing, adding a few drops food coloring. Decorate cookies with icing and decorative candies, if desired. Makes 36 to 48.

Gingerbread People Cutouts: Prepare as above, *except* roll dough ¼ *inch* thick. Cut with 4½- to 6-inch people cookie cutters. Bake in a 375° oven for 6 to 8 minutes or till edges are lightly browned. Makes 12 to 18.

Cream Cheese Cutouts

Cream cheese adds a touch of richness and tang to these cookies.

½ cup margarine *or* butter
1 3-ounce package cream cheese
2 cups all-purpose flour
1 cup sugar
1 egg
½ teaspoon baking powder
½ teaspoon vanilla   Oven 375°

In a mixing bowl beat margarine and cream cheese with an electric mixer on medium to high speed for 30 seconds. Add about *half* of the flour, the sugar, egg, baking powder, and vanilla. Beat till thoroughly combined. Beat in remaining flour. Cover; chill 1 hour or till easy to handle.

Divide the chilled dough in half. On a lightly floured surface, roll *half* of the dough at a time ⅛ inch thick. Cut into desired shapes with a 2½-inch cookie cutter. Place 1 inch apart on an ungreased cookie sheet. Bake in a 375° oven about 8 minutes or till edges are lightly browned. Cool cookies on a wire rack. Makes about 60.

Chocolate Cream Cheese Cutouts: Prepare as above, *except* add 2 squares (2 ounces) *semisweet chocolate,* melted and cooled, with the first half of the flour.

Citrus Cream Cheese Cutouts: Prepare as above, *except* add ½ teaspoon finely shredded *lemon or orange peel* and 1 tablespoon *lemon or orange juice* with the vanilla.

Perfect Rolled Cookies

● Keep any unused dough chilled until you need it. Chilled dough absorbs less flour when it is rolled, giving you tenderer cookies.
● To avoid sticking, roll *half* of the dough at a time on a lightly floured surface with a floured rolling pin. Dip your cookie cutter into flour, too.
● When cutting the dough, leave as little room as possible between cutouts. Reroll the scraps and cut more cookies. For tender cookies, reroll the dough as few times as possible.

Orange-Chocolate Slices

½ cup margarine *or* butter
½ cup shortening
3 cups all-purpose flour
½ cup sugar
½ cup packed brown sugar
1 egg
2 tablespoons finely shredded
   orange peel
2 tablespoons orange juice
¼ teaspoon baking soda
1 square (1 ounce) semisweet
   chocolate, finely
   chopped   Oven 375°

In a mixing bowl beat margarine and shortening with an electric mixer on medium to high speed for 30 seconds. Add about *half* of the flour, the sugar, brown sugar, egg, orange peel, orange juice, and soda. Beat till thoroughly combined. Beat in remaining flour. Stir in chocolate. Shape dough into two 8-inch rolls. Wrap in waxed paper or clear plastic wrap and chill 4 to 24 hours.

Cut into ¼-inch slices. Place on an ungreased cookie sheet. Bake in a 375° oven 10 to 12 minutes or till edges are lightly browned. Cool cookies on a wire rack. Makes about 60.

Santa's Whiskers

The coconut on the edges forms the whiskers. (Pictured on page 101.)

¾ cup margarine *or* butter
2 cups all-purpose flour
¾ cup sugar
1 tablespoon milk
1 teaspoon vanilla
¾ cup finely chopped candied red *or*
   green cherries
⅓ cup finely chopped pecans
¾ cup coconut   Oven 375°

Beat margarine with an electric mixer on medium to high speed for 30 seconds. Add about *half* of the flour, the sugar, milk, and vanilla. Beat till thoroughly combined. Stir in remaining flour. Stir in cherries and pecans. Shape into two 8-inch rolls. Roll in coconut. Wrap in waxed paper; chill 2 to 24 hours. Cut into ¼-inch slices. Place on an ungreased cookie sheet. Bake in a 375° oven 10 to 12 minutes or till edges are golden. Cool cookies on a wire rack. Makes about 60.

Spiced Slices

½ cup margarine *or* butter
½ cup shortening
2¼ cups all-purpose flour
½ cup sugar
½ cup packed brown sugar
1 egg
1 teaspoon ground cinnamon
½ teaspoon baking soda
½ teaspoon vanilla
¼ teaspoon ground nutmeg
¼ teaspoon ground cloves
½ cup toasted sliced almonds,
   finely chopped   Oven 375°

In a mixing bowl beat margarine and shortening with an electric mixer on medium to high speed for 30 seconds. Add about *half* of the flour, the sugars, egg, cinnamon, soda, vanilla, nutmeg, and cloves. Beat till thoroughly combined. Beat in remaining flour. Stir in nuts. Shape into two 7-inch rolls. Wrap; chill 5 to 24 hours. Cut into ¼-inch slices. Place 1 inch apart on an ungreased cookie sheet. Bake in a 375° oven about 8 minutes or till edges are golden. Cool on cookie sheet 1 minute. Remove; cool on rack. Makes 60.

Whole Wheat Spiced Slices: Prepare as above, *except* reduce all-purpose flour to *1½ cups* and add ¾ cup *whole wheat flour*. Before chilling, roll shaped dough in 2 tablespoons *toasted wheat germ*.

Oat Spiced Slices: Prepare as above, *except* reduce all-purpose flour to *1¾ cups* and add 1 cup *quick-cooking rolled oats*.

Use a sharp knife and a sawing motion to cut slices from the rolls of chilled dough.

Date Pinwheel Cookies

  1   **8-ounce package (1⅓ cups) pitted whole dates, snipped**
  ½   **cup water**
  ⅓   **cup sugar**
  2   **tablespoons lemon juice**
  ½   **teaspoon vanilla**
  ½   **cup margarine** *or* **butter**
  ½   **cup shortening**
  3   **cups all-purpose flour**
  ½   **cup sugar**
  ½   **cup packed brown sugar**
  1   **egg**
  3   **tablespoons milk**
  1   **teaspoon vanilla**
  ½   **teaspoon baking soda**
  ¼   **teaspoon salt**   Oven 375°

For filling, in a medium saucepan combine dates, water, and the ⅓ cup sugar. Bring to boiling; reduce heat. Cook and stir about 2 minutes or till thick. Stir in lemon juice and the ½ teaspoon vanilla; cool.

In a mixing bowl beat margarine or butter and shortening with an electric mixer on medium to high speed for 30 seconds. Add about *half* of the flour, the ½ cup sugar, the brown sugar, egg, milk, the 1 teaspoon vanilla, the baking soda, and salt. Beat till thoroughly combined. Beat in remaining flour. Cover and chill 1 hour or till easy to handle. Divide dough in half. Roll *half* of the dough between waxed paper into a 12x10-inch rectangle. Spread *half* of the filling over dough. Roll up from one of the long sides. Moisten and pinch edges to seal. Wrap in waxed paper or clear plastic wrap. Repeat with remaining dough and filling. Chill 2 to 24 hours.

Cut into ¼-inch slices. Place 1 inch apart on a greased cookie sheet. Bake in a 375° oven for 10 to 12 minutes or till edges are lightly browned. Cool cookies on a wire rack. Makes about 72.

Date-Filled Rounds: Prepare as above, *except,* on a *lightly floured surface,* roll *half* of dough at a time about ⅛ inch thick. Cut with a 2½-inch-round cutter. Place a rounded *teaspoon* of filling on *half* of the rounds; spread to within ½ inch of edges. Top with remaining rounds; seal edges with tines of a fork. Place on an *ungreased* cookie sheet. Bake in a 375° oven for 10 to 12 minutes or till edges are lightly browned. Makes about 36.

Chocolate-Coconut Pinwheels

The taste of these cookies will remind you of German chocolate cake.

  1   **3-ounce package cream cheese, softened**
  ⅓   **cup sugar**
  1   **teaspoon vanilla**
  1   **cup coconut**
  ½   **cup finely chopped nuts**
  ⅓   **cup margarine** *or* **butter**
 1½   **cups all-purpose flour**
  1   **cup sugar**
  ¼   **cup unsweetened cocoa powder**
  1   **egg**
  1   **tablespoon milk**
  ½   **teaspoon baking soda**   Oven 375°

For filling, in a mixing bowl beat cream cheese, the ⅓ cup sugar, and the vanilla till smooth. Stir in coconut and nuts. Set aside.

In a mixing bowl beat margarine with an electric mixer on medium to high speed for 30 seconds. Add about *half* of the flour, the 1 cup sugar, the cocoa powder, egg, milk, and soda. Beat till thoroughly combined. Beat in remaining flour.

Roll *half* of the dough between waxed paper into a 10x8-inch rectangle. Spread *half* of the filling over dough. Roll up from one of the long sides. Moisten and pinch edges to seal. Wrap in waxed paper or clear plastic wrap. Repeat with remaining dough and filling. Chill 3 to 24 hours.

Cut into ¼-inch slices. Place 1 inch apart on a greased cookie sheet. Bake in a 375° oven about 8 minutes or till edges are lightly browned. Cool cookies on a wire rack. Makes about 72.

Shapely Sliced Cookies

For nicely rounded sliced cookies, follow these hints.
● To prevent the rolls from developing a flat side, gently roll them on a flat surface several times while they chill.
● Make sure the rolls of dough are well chilled before slicing. (Chill them in the freezer if you used corn-oil margarine.)
● If the slices become misshapen, reshape them with your fingers.

Snickerdoodles

To turn these into drop cookies, skip the chilling and sprinkle the dropped dough with the sugar and cinnamon.

　½　**cup margarine *or* butter**
1½　**cups all-purpose flour**
　1　**cup sugar**
　1　**egg**
　½　**teaspoon vanilla**
　¼　**teaspoon baking soda**
　¼　**teaspoon cream of tartar**
　2　**tablespoons sugar**
　1　**teaspoon ground
　　　cinnamon**　　　　　Oven 375°

In a mixing bowl beat margarine or butter with an electric mixer on medium to high speed for 30 seconds. Add about *half* of the flour, the 1 cup sugar, the egg, vanilla, baking soda, and cream of tartar. Beat till thoroughly combined. Beat in remaining flour. Cover and chill 1 hour.

　Shape dough into 1-inch balls. Combine the 2 tablespoons sugar and the cinnamon. Roll balls in sugar-cinnamon mixture. Place 2 inches apart on an ungreased cookie sheet. Bake in a 375° oven for 10 to 11 minutes or till edges are golden. Cool cookies on a wire rack. Makes about 36.

Gingersnaps

2¼　**cups all-purpose flour**
　1　**cup packed brown sugar**
　¾　**cup shortening *or* cooking oil**
　¼　**cup molasses**
　1　**egg**
　1　**teaspoon baking soda**
　1　**teaspoon ground ginger**
　1　**teaspoon ground cinnamon**
　½　**teaspoon ground cloves**
　¼　**cup sugar**　　　　　Oven 375°

In a mixing bowl combine about *half* of the flour, the brown sugar, shortening, molasses, egg, baking soda, ginger, cinnamon, and cloves. Beat with an electric mixer on medium to high speed till thoroughly combined. Beat in remaining flour.

　Shape dough into 1-inch balls. Roll in sugar. Place 2 inches apart on an ungreased cookie sheet. Bake in a 375° oven for 8 to 10 minutes or till set and tops are crackled. Cool cookies on a wire rack. Makes about 48.

Peanut Butter Cookies

For double the peanut flavor, add ¾ cup of chopped peanuts to the dough.

　½　**cup margarine *or* butter**
　½　**cup peanut butter**
1¼　**cups all-purpose flour**
　½　**cup sugar**
　½　**cup packed brown sugar *or*
　　　¼ cup honey**
　1　**egg**
　½　**teaspoon baking soda**
　½　**teaspoon baking powder**
　½　**teaspoon vanilla**
　　　Sugar　　　　　Oven 375°

In a mixing bowl beat margarine and peanut butter with an electric mixer on medium to high speed for 30 seconds. Add ½ cup of the flour, the sugars, egg, baking soda, baking powder, and vanilla. Beat till thoroughly combined. Beat in remaining flour. If necessary, cover and chill dough till easy to handle.

　Shape dough into 1-inch balls. If desired, roll in additional sugar. Place 2 inches apart on an ungreased cookie sheet. Flatten by crisscrossing with the tines of a fork.

　Bake in a 375° oven for 7 to 9 minutes or till bottoms are lightly browned. Cool cookies on a wire rack. Makes about 36.

　Chocolate-Kiss Peanut Butter Cookies: Prepare as above, *except* do not flatten with a fork before baking. *Immediately* after baking, press 1 *milk chocolate kiss* into *each* cookie.

Use a table fork to mark the traditional crisscrosses on the balls of peanut-butter-cookie dough.

Sandies

You also might have heard these cookies called Russian tea cakes or Mexican wedding cakes.

     1 **cup butter**
  2¼ **cups all-purpose flour**
     ⅓ **cup sugar**
     1 **teaspoon vanilla**
     1 **cup chopped pecans**
     1 **cup sifted powdered
          sugar**   Oven 325°

In a mixing bowl beat butter with an electric mixer on medium to high speed for 30 seconds. Add about *half* of the flour, the sugar, vanilla and 1 tablespoon *water.* Beat till thoroughly combined. Beat in remaining flour. Stir in pecans.

Shape into 1-inch balls or 2x½-inch fingers or crescents. Place on an ungreased cookie sheet. Bake in a 325° oven about 20 minutes or till bottoms are lightly browned. Cool cookies on a wire rack. Gently shake cooled cookies in a bag with powdered sugar. Makes about 36.

Almond Strips

     ½ **cup margarine *or* butter**
  1¾ **cups all-purpose flour**
     1 **cup sugar**
     1 **egg**
     2 **teaspoons baking powder**
     ½ **teaspoon almond extract**
          Milk
     ½ **cup sliced almonds, coarsely
          chopped**
          **Powdered Sugar Icing
          (see recipe, page 88)**   Oven 325°

In a mixing bowl beat margarine or butter with an electric mixer on medium to high speed for 30 seconds. Add about *half* of the flour, the sugar, egg, baking powder, and almond extract. Beat till thoroughly combined. Beat in remaining flour.

Divide dough into 4 portions. Shape each portion into a 12-inch-long roll. Place 2 rolls, 4 to 5 inches apart, on an ungreased cookie sheet. Using your hand, flatten each to 3 inches wide. Repeat with remaining rolls. Brush flattened rolls with milk and sprinkle with almonds.

Bake in a 325° oven for 12 to 14 minutes or till edges are lightly browned. Cut *warm* cookies diagonally into 1-inch strips. Cool cookies on a wire rack. Drizzle with icing. Makes about 48.

Spritz

No cookie press? These buttery morsels are just as delicious dropped on a cookie sheet.

  1½ **cups margarine *or* butter**
  3½ **cups all-purpose flour**
     1 **cup sugar**
     1 **egg**
     1 **teaspoon baking powder**
     1 **teaspoon vanilla**
     ½ **teaspoon almond extract (optional)**
          **Powdered Sugar Icing (see
          recipe, page 88)**
          (optional)   Oven 375°

Beat margarine with an electric mixer on medium to high speed for 30 seconds. Add *1 cup* of the flour, the sugar, egg, baking powder, vanilla, and, if desired, almond extract. Beat till thoroughly combined. Beat in remaining flour.

Force *unchilled* dough through a cookie press onto an ungreased cookie sheet. Bake in a 375° oven for 8 to 10 minutes or till edges are firm but not brown. Cool cookies on a wire rack. If desired, dip tops into icing, then sprinkle with chopped nuts or colored sugar. Makes about 84.

Whole Wheat Spritz: Prepare as above, *except* reduce all-purpose flour to *2½ cups* and add 1 cup *whole wheat flour.*

Nutty Spritz: Prepare as above, *except* reduce all-purpose flour to *3 cups* and add 1 cup finely ground *almonds or pecans.*

Chocolate Spritz: Prepare as above, *except* reduce all-purpose flour to *3¼ cups.* Add ¼ cup *unsweetened cocoa powder* with the sugar.

Pack *unchilled* dough into a cookie press. Press dough portions about 1 inch apart onto sheet.

Tiny Tarts

To make pecan tassies, use the pecan filling.

½ **cup margarine *or* butter,
     softened**
1 **3-ounce package cream cheese,
     softened**
1 **cup all-purpose flour**
     **Pumpkin Filling, Pecan Filling,
     Lemon-Coconut Filling, *or*
     Spiced Fruit Filling**   Oven 325°

For pastry, in a mixing bowl beat margarine or butter and cream cheese till thoroughly combined. Stir in flour.

Press a rounded teaspoon of pastry evenly into the bottom and up the sides of each of 24 ungreased 1¾-inch muffin cups. Fill *each* pastry-lined muffin cup with about *1 heaping teaspoon* desired filling. Bake in a 325° oven about 30 minutes or till pastry is golden and filling is puffed. Cool slightly in the pan, then remove and cool completely on a wire rack. Makes 24.

Pumpkin Filling: Beat together 1 *egg,* ½ cup canned *pumpkin,* ¼ cup *sugar,* ¼ cup *milk,* and 1 teaspoon *pumpkin pie spice.*

Pecan Filling: Beat together 1 *egg,* ¾ cup packed *brown sugar,* and 1 tablespoon *margarine or butter,* melted. Stir in ½ cup coarsely chopped *pecans.*

Lemon-Coconut Filling: Divide ¼ cup *coconut* among the pastry-lined muffin cups. Combine 2 *eggs;* ½ cup *sugar;* 2 tablespoons *margarine or butter,* melted; ½ teaspoon finely shredded *lemon peel;* and 1 tablespoon *lemon juice.* Spoon mixture over coconut in pastry-lined muffin cups.

Spiced Fruit Filling: In a small saucepan combine 1½ cups chopped *mixed dried fruit* and 1½ cups *apple juice or water.* Bring to boiling; reduce heat. Cover and simmer about 8 minutes or till fruit is very tender. Drain. Stir in ¼ cup *orange marmalade,* 1 teaspoon ground *nutmeg,* and ¼ teaspoon ground *cloves.*

Brandy Snaps

Fill these delicate, lacy cookies with plain or flavored whipped cream.

½ **cup packed brown sugar**
⅓ **cup margarine *or* butter,
     melted**
¼ **cup light molasses**
1 **tablespoon brandy**
¾ **cup all-purpose flour**
½ **teaspoon ground ginger**
½ **teaspoon ground nutmeg**   Oven 350°

In a mixing bowl combine brown sugar, margarine, molasses, and brandy. Stir in flour, ginger, and nutmeg till thoroughly combined.

Line a cookie sheet with foil. Grease the foil. Drop batter by level teaspoons 5 inches apart onto foil.

Bake in a 350° oven for 5 to 6 minutes or till bubbly and deep golden brown. Let stand 2 minutes or till set. *Immediately* remove from foil. With the flat side to the inside, roll each cookie around a metal cone or the greased handle of a wooden spoon, or shape over the bottom of a muffin cup. Cool. (If the cookies harden before you can shape them, return them to the hot oven for 1 minute or till softened.) Makes 54.

Pecan Snaps: Prepare as above, *except* reduce flour to *½ cup* and add 1 cup ground *pecans, hazelnuts (filberts), or almonds.* Omit ginger and nutmeg.

Cinnamon Snaps: Prepare as above, *except* substitute *honey* for the molasses and ground *cinnamon* for the ginger. Omit the nutmeg.

Wrap the warm cookies around a metal cone. Slip the cookies off the cone and cool.

Jam Thumbprints

A great way to show off your favorite homemade jam. (Pictured on page 101.)

(Pictured on page 101.)

 ⅔ **cup margarine *or* butter**
1½ **cups all-purpose flour**
 ½ **cup sugar**
 2 **egg yolks**
 1 **teaspoon vanilla**
 2 **slightly beaten egg whites**
 1 **cup finely chopped walnuts**
 ⅓ **to ½ cup strawberry, cherry,**
   ***or* apricot jam**
   ***or* preserves**   Oven 375°

In a mixing bowl beat margarine or butter with an electric mixer on medium to high speed for 30 seconds. Add about *half* of the flour, the sugar, egg yolks, and vanilla. Beat till thoroughly combined. Beat in remaining flour. Cover and chill about 1 hour or till easy to handle.

Shape dough into 1-inch balls. Roll balls in egg whites, then in walnuts. Place 1 inch apart on a greased cookie sheet. Press centers with your thumb. Bake in a 375° oven for 10 to 12 minutes or till edges are lightly browned. Cool cookies on a wire rack. Just before serving, fill centers with jam or preserves. Makes about 42.

Chocolate Crinkles

 3 **beaten eggs**
1½ **cups sugar**
 4 **squares (4 ounces) unsweetened**
   chocolate, melted
 ½ **cup cooking oil**
 2 **teaspoons baking powder**
 2 **teaspoons vanilla**
 2 **cups all-purpose flour**
   Sifted powdered sugar   Oven 375°

In a mixing bowl combine beaten eggs, sugar, melted chocolate, cooking oil, baking powder, and vanilla. Gradually add flour to chocolate mixture, stirring till thoroughly combined. Cover and chill for 1 to 2 hours or till easy to handle.

Shape dough into 1-inch balls. Roll balls in powdered sugar to coat generously. Place 1 inch apart on an ungreased cookie sheet. Bake in a 375° oven for 8 to 10 minutes or till edges are set and tops are crackled. Cool cookies on a wire rack. If desired, sprinkle with additional powdered sugar. Makes about 48.

Shortbread

Our taste panel felt butter, not margarine, was the only choice for these rich, scrumptious cookies.

1¼ **cups all-purpose flour**
 3 **tablespoons sugar**
 ½ **cup butter**   Oven 325°

In a mixing bowl combine flour and sugar. Cut in butter till mixture resembles fine crumbs and starts to cling. Form the mixture into a ball and knead till smooth.

To make wedges,* on an ungreased cookie sheet pat or roll the dough into an 8-inch circle. Using your fingers, press to make a scalloped edge. With a knife, cut circle into 16 pie-shape wedges. Leave wedges in the circle shape. Bake in a 325° oven for 25 to 30 minutes or till bottom just starts to brown and center is set. Cut circle into wedges again while warm. Cool on the cookie sheet for 5 minutes. Remove from cookie sheet; cool on a wire rack. Makes 16.

Spiced Shortbread: Prepare as above, *except* substitute *brown sugar* for the sugar and stir ½ teaspoon ground *cinnamon*, ¼ teaspoon ground *ginger*, and ⅛ teaspoon ground *cloves* into the flour-sugar mixture.

Lemon and Poppy Seed Shortbread: Prepare as above, *except* stir 1 tablespoon *poppy seed* into flour-sugar mixture and add 1 teaspoon finely shredded *lemon peel* with the butter.

Butter-Pecan Shortbread: Prepare as above, *except* substitute *brown sugar* for the sugar. After cutting in butter, stir 2 tablespoons finely chopped *pecans* into the flour mixture. Sprinkle mixture with ½ teaspoon *vanilla*.

Oatmeal Shortbread: Prepare as above, *except* reduce all-purpose flour to *1 cup*. After cutting in butter, stir ⅓ cup *quick-cooking rolled oats* into the flour mixture.

Note: For strips or rounds, on a lightly floured surface, pat or roll dough ½ inch thick. Using a knife, cut into twenty-four 2x1-inch strips; or, using a 1½-inch-round cookie cutter, cut into 24 rounds. Place 1 inch apart on an ungreased cookie sheet. Bake in a 325° oven 20 to 25 minutes or till bottoms just start to brown. Cool cookies on a wire rack.

Desserts

Nutrition Analysis	Servings Per Recipe	Calories	Protein (g)	Carbohydrate (g)	Fat (g)	Cholesterol (mg)	Sodium (mg)	Potassium (mg)	Protein	Vitamin A	Vitamin C	Thiamine	Riboflavin	Niacin	Calcium	Iron
Amaretto Soufflé (p. 129)	6	220	7	24	11	184	100	134	10	9	0	5	13	2	7	6
Amaretto Stirred Custard (p. 135)	6	129	6	16	4	144	75	159	9	6	1	4	12	0	11	3
Apple Dumplings (p. 124)	6	619	5	92	27	0	135	162	8	4	4	21	12	13	2	13
Applesauce (p. 124)	8	120	0	31	0	0	0	176	0	1	7	1	0	0	0	0
Baked Alaska (p. 129)	8	394	7	61	15	51	344	200	11	11	0	7	19	4	13	4
Baked Apples (p. 124)	4	172	1	45	1	0	5	344	1	1	10	4	2	1	3	6
Baked Custards (p. 134)	4	170	8	21	6	214	98	191	12	8	0	5	16	0	13	5
Baked Rice Pudding (p. 134)	6	186	6	32	4	142	67	228	9	5	2	7	11	3	10	6
Bananas Foster (p. 126)	4	554	4	79	23	30	250	734	6	20	13	6	18	4	13	9
Blueberry Crisp (p. 125)	6	328	4	56	12	0	103	233	6	9	19	13	7	5	4	9
Brandied Pudding (p. 132)	6	236	6	34	8	191	89	200	9	11	2	5	15	1	17	4
Brandy Hard Sauce (p. 140)	10	83	0	10	5	0	54	3	0	4	0	0	0	0	0	0
Bread Pudding (p. 135)	6	231	9	35	6	190	220	257	14	7	2	9	18	5	15	10
Brownie Pudding Cake (p. 130)	4	266	4	45	9	1	94	104	6	0	0	9	7	5	7	7
Butter-Pecan Ice Cream (p. 136)	16	356	2	25	28	91	43	103	4	20	1	4	7	0	7	0
Caramel Flan (p. 134)	4	232	8	38	6	214	98	191	12	8	1	5	16	0	13	5
Caramel Sauce (p. 139)	8	101	0	18	3	7	28	60	0	2	0	0	1	0	2	4
Cheesecake Supreme (p. 130)	12	420	7	29	32	131	356	154	11	24	0	4	14	3	7	9
Cherries Jubilee (p. 126)	6	259	3	42	7	30	61	239	4	8	4	3	12	2	10	2
Cherry Crisp (p. 125)	6	365	4	65	12	0	101	379	7	4	25	12	7	6	5	11
Chocolate Ice Cream (p. 136)	24	339	6	23	27	135	50	203	9	16	1	3	12	2	10	5
Chocolate Mousse (p. 129)	5	258	4	25	17	142	33	98	6	10	0	2	6	0	3	5
Chocolate-Mousse Cake (p. 131)	16	372	5	35	26	123	102	181	8	9	0	7	9	3	3	9
Chocolate Pots de Crème (p. 133)	4	320	5	21	26	244	39	160	8	13	0	4	11	0	10	6
Chocolate Pudding (p. 132)	6	231	6	35	9	190	117	212	10	10	2	5	15	1	15	7
Chocolate Soufflé (p. 129)	6	228	6	23	13	184	99	140	9	9	0	5	11	2	6	7
Chocolate Swirl Cheesecake (p. 130)	12	444	7	32	33	131	356	169	11	24	0	4	14	3	7	9
Chocolaty Velvet Ice Cream (p. 138)	8	382	5	32	28	90	69	237	7	19	2	4	12	1	12	3
Choose-a-Fruit Frozen Yogurt (p. 137)	8	111	3	24	1	3	41	205	5	0	36	2	9	1	11	2
Coconut Bread Pudding (p. 135)	6	245	9	36	7	190	221	269	14	7	2	9	18	5	15	10
Cream Cheese Hearts (p. 133)	6	305	4	20	24	82	125	140	6	29	6	2	7	1	6	4
Cream Puffs (p. 133)	10	297	7	30	16	225	215	163	11	16	0	10	16	4	12	8
Crepes Suzette (p. 127)	6	412	7	44	21	96	233	184	10	17	10	13	14	6	9	7
Éclairs (p. 133)	12	369	7	43	20	187	213	168	10	16	0	8	14	3	10	8
Flavored Whipped Cream (p. 140)	8	124	1	6	11	41	21	31	1	9	0	1	2	0	2	1
Fresh-Fruit Bowl (p. 126)	4	154	1	39	0	0	9	414	2	4	144	9	5	4	4	2
Frosty Cranberry Squares (p. 138)	12	297	3	32	18	27	108	94	5	12	6	7	6	3	3	4
Frosty Strawberry Squares (p. 138)	12	304	3	34	18	27	109	150	5	1	42	7	7	4	3	5
Fruit Cobbler with Apple Filling (p. 125)	6	287	4	53	7	46	133	174	6	7	6	11	8	6	6	7
Fruit Cobbler with Blueberry Filling (p. 125)	6	278	4	51	7	46	139	133	6	8	15	13	10	7	6	7
Fruit Cobbler with Peach Filling (p. 125)	6	272	4	49	7	46	133	270	7	18	8	11	10	11	6	7
Fruit Cobbler with Pear Filling (p. 125)	6	322	4	62	8	46	133	256	6	7	9	12	11	6	7	8
Fruit Cobbler with Red Cherry Filling (p. 125)	6	368	5	73	7	46	137	244	7	0	19	12	10	8	7	8
Fruit Cobbler with Rhubarb Filling (p. 125)	6	337	5	65	7	46	138	399	7	8	16	11	9	7	16	8
Fruit Crisp (p. 125)	6	282	3	45	12	0	96	224	4	7	5	8	3	3	3	7
Fruit Ice (p. 137)	6	105	1	26	0	0	1	203	1	1	97	3	3	1	1	2
Fruit Sauce (p. 139)	6	49	0	13	0	0	2	74	0	10	9	1	0	0	0	0
Hard Sauce (p. 140)	10	79	0	10	5	0	54	3	0	4	0	0	0	0	0	0

On the divider: Strawberry Shortcake (p. 130).

Nutrition Analysis

	Per Serving							Percent U.S. RDA Per Serving							
Servings Per Recipe	Calories	Protein (g)	Carbohydrate (g)	Fat (g)	Cholesterol (mg)	Sodium (mg)	Potassium (mg)	Protein	Vitamin A	Vitamin C	Thiamine	Riboflavin	Niacin	Calcium	Iron
Hot Fudge Sauce (p. 139) 8	220	2	27	13	5	86	109	3	6	0	0	4	0	5	3
Ice-Cream Torte (p. 138) 8	396	4	47	22	104	245	110	7	15	0	9	11	3	6	5
Lemon Meringue Torte (p. 128) 8	298	3	44	13	143	50	56	5	11	4	2	6	0	3	2
Lemon Pudding Cake (p. 131) 4	241	6	34	10	141	127	149	9	10	11	6	13	2	9	4
Lemon Sauce (p. 139) 4	72	0	15	2	0	21	6	0	2	2	0	0	0	0	0
Lemon Sherbet (p. 137) 16	84	1	20	0	1	11	36	1	0	5	0	2	0	2	0
Liqueur Cheesecake (p. 130) 12	433	7	33	32	131	353	146	11	24	0	4	14	3	6	8
Meringue Shells (p. 128) 8	102	1	25	0	0	36	18	2	0	0	0	2	0	0	0
Mint-Chocolate Mousse (p. 129) 5	267	4	28	17	142	33	98	6	10	0	2	6	0	3	5
Mocha Brownie Pudding Cake (p. 130) 4	266	4	45	9	1	94	104	6	0	0	9	7	5	7	7
Mocha Mousse (p. 129) 5	258	4	25	17	142	33	98	6	10	0	2	6	0	3	5
Mocha Toffee Squares (p. 137) 9	339	4	29	24	126	226	92	7	15	0	11	8	2	3	6
No-Cook Cherry-Nut Ice Cream (p. 136) 16	354	3	24	29	91	35	133	5	20	2	3	8	0	8	1
No-Cook Chocolate-Almond Ice Cream (p. 136) 16	383	4	34	28	91	50	198	6	20	1	3	10	1	9	4
No-Cook Chocolate Chip and Mint Ice Cream (p. 136) 16	367	3	28	29	91	35	123	4	20	0	2	7	0	7	2
No-Cook Coffee Ice Cream (p. 136) 16	340	2	25	27	91	35	115	4	20	0	2	7	0	7	1
No-Cook Peach Ice Cream (p. 136) 16	331	2	26	2	91	35	172	4	24	6	2	8	2	7	0
No-Cook Strawberry Ice Cream (p. 136) 16	324	2	24	25	91	35	150	4	20	36	2	8	0	8	1
No-Cook Vanilla Ice Cream (p. 136) 16	313	2	22	25	91	35	88	3	19	0	2	7	0	7	0
Orange Hard Sauce (p. 140) 10	80	0	10	5	0	54	6	0	4	1	0	0	0	0	0
Orange Sauce (p. 139) 4	94	0	19	2	0	22	90	0	2	21	2	0	0	0	0
Orange Sherbet (p. 137) 16	107	1	26	0	1	9	135	2	2	38	3	2	0	2	0
Pavlova (p. 128) 8	275	3	44	11	41	49	264	4	19	79	3	7	3	4	2
Peach and Banana Flambé (p. 126) 4	567	4	79	25	30	251	716	6	24	13	5	17	5	13	9
Peach Melba (p. 124) 4	266	3	49	7	30	61	415	5	29	24	4	13	6	10	2
Peanut-Butter Fudge Sauce (p. 139) 8	268	4	29	17	5	125	165	7	6	0	0	5	6	6	3
Pears Hélène (p. 124) 4	677	7	96	33	40	232	528	11	17	1	5	22	2	21	8
Pineapple Crepes (p. 127) 6	404	7	43	21	96	233	230	10	17	15	15	15	7	10	8
Pineapple Sherbet (p. 137) 16	114	1	27	0	1	9	103	2	0	11	2	2	0	3	1
Plum Pudding (p. 131) 8	621	6	90	28	41	263	526	10	7	9	15	13	9	12	15
Poached Pears (p. 124) 4	160	1	39	1	0	1	191	0	0	9	2	3	0	2	2
Rhubarb Crisp (p. 125) 6	377	3	68	11	0	98	233	5	9	6	11	5	4	22	10
Rhubarb Sauce (p. 139) 8	58	0	15	0	0	2	132	0	0	4	0	0	0	4	0
Shortcut Trifle (p. 135) 8	197	4	35	5	42	91	221	6	10	8	4	10	4	12	4
Sour Cream Cheesecake (p. 130) 12	473	7	31	37	135	328	206	12	28	1	5	16	3	11	7
Stirred Custard (p. 135) 6	112	6	12	4	144	75	159	9	6	1	4	12	0	11	3
Stirred Rice Pudding (p. 135) 5	186	6	35	3	11	75	310	9	6	3	8	15	3	19	4
Strawberry Shortcake (p. 130) 8	393	6	51	19	56	236	405	10	16	181	17	19	11	12	13
Swedish Fruit Soup (p. 126) 8	112	1	28	0	0	6	240	1	4	14	3	1	1	2	4
Tangy Vanilla Pudding (p. 132) 6	294	7	36	14	208	87	254	11	15	2	6	18	0	21	4
Trifle (p. 135) 8	410	9	62	14	198	160	295	14	18	6	11	20	7	16	9
Vanilla Ice Cream (p. 136) 24	271	4	19	20	135	49	104	6	16	0	2	8	0	7	2
Vanilla Pudding (p. 132) 6	230	6	34	8	191	89	200	9	11	2	5	15	0	17	4
Vanilla Sauce (p. 140) 12	60	1	4	5	60	9	21	1	4	0	0	2	0	2	1
Whipped Cream (p. 140) 8	115	1	4	11	41	11	23	0	9	0	0	2	0	2	0
Whiskey Sauce (p. 140) 8	116	0	13	6	34	68	5	0	5	0	0	0	0	0	0

Desserts

For a grand finale to any meal, come to this chapter. You'll find an assortment of recipes for fruit desserts, puddings, custards, ice creams, and many other tempting creations.

Poached Pears

   ⅓ **cup sugar**
   ¼ **cup sweet white wine *or* orange juice**
  2½ **to 3 inches stick cinnamon**
   1 **teaspoon vanilla**
   4 **medium pears, peeled, halved, and cored; *or* medium peaches, peeled, halved, and pitted**

In a large skillet bring sugar, wine, cinnamon, vanilla, and ¾ cup *water* to boiling. Add pears or peaches. Reduce heat. Simmer, covered, for 10 to 15 minutes or till tender. Remove cinnamon. Serve warm or chilled. Serves 4.

Microwave directions: In a 2-quart casserole micro-cook sugar, wine, cinnamon, vanilla, and ¾ cup *water,* uncovered, on 100% power (high) 4 to 6 minutes or till boiling. Add fruit and cook, covered, on high for 4 to 6 minutes or till fruit is tender; stir once. Continue as above.

Pears Hélène: Prepare as above using pears. Serve drained and chilled with *vanilla ice cream* and *Hot Fudge Sauce* (see recipe, page 139).

Peach Melba: Prepare as above using peaches. Serve drained and chilled with *vanilla ice cream* and *Fruit Sauce* made with raspberries (see recipe, page 139).

Applesauce

In a Dutch oven combine 3 pounds *cooking apples* (9 medium), peeled, quartered, and cored; 1 cup *water;* ⅓ to ⅔ cup *sugar;* and, if desired, ¼ teaspoon ground cinnamon. Bring to boiling; reduce heat. Cover and simmer for 8 to 10 minutes or till tender, adding more water, if necessary.

Remove from heat. Mash with a potato masher or process in a blender or food processor to desired texture. Serve warm or chilled. Stir before serving. Makes about 4½ cups (8 servings).

Apple Dumplings

  1¼ **cups sugar**
   ½ **teaspoon ground cinnamon**
   ½ **teaspoon ground nutmeg**
   2 **tablespoons margarine *or* butter**
  2¼ **cups all-purpose flour**
   ⅔ **cup shortening**
   6 **small apples, pears, or peaches**   Oven 375°

For syrup, mix *1 cup* of the sugar, ¼ *teaspoon* cinnamon, ¼ *teaspoon* nutmeg, and 1¾ cups *water.* Bring to boiling; reduce heat. Simmer 5 minutes. Remove from heat; stir in margarine.

For pastry, mix flour and ¼ teaspoon *salt.* Cut in shortening till coarse crumbs form. Add 6 to 8 tablespoons *water,* a little at a time, mixing till moistened. Form into a ball. Roll into an 18x12-inch rectangle; cut into six 6-inch squares.

Peel and core apples or pears. (For peaches, peel, halve, and pit.) Place *one* fruit on *each* pastry square. Combine remaining sugar, cinnamon, and nutmeg. Sprinkle over fruit. Moisten edges of pastry; fold corners to center atop fruit. Pinch to seal. Place in an 11x7x1½-inch baking pan. Pour syrup over. Bake in a 375° oven about 45 minutes or till fruit is tender and pastry is brown. Serve with ice cream, if desired. Serves 6.

Baked Apples

   4 **medium cooking apples**
   ½ **cup raisins, snipped pitted whole dates, *or* mixed dried fruit bits**
   2 **tablespoons brown sugar**
   ½ **teaspoon ground cinnamon**
   ¼ **teaspoon ground nutmeg**
   ⅓ **cup apple juice *or* water**   Oven 350°

Core apples; peel a strip from the top of each. Place apples in a 2-quart casserole. Combine the raisins, brown sugar, cinnamon, and nutmeg. Spoon into centers of apples. Add apple juice to dish. Bake in a 350° oven for 40 to 45 minutes or till apples are tender, basting occasionally with the cooking liquid. Serve warm with ice cream, light cream, or yogurt, if desired. Serves 4.

Microwave directions: Reduce apple juice or water to *2 tablespoons.* Assemble as above. Micro-cook, covered, on 100% power (high) for 4 to 8 minutes or till tender, rearranging and basting apples after 3 minutes.

Fruit Crisp

Pair your favorite fruit with this crunchy topping.

  **5 cups sliced, peeled apples, pears,
      peaches, *or* apricots; *or* frozen
      unsweetened peach slices**
  2 to 4 tablespoons sugar
  ½ cup regular rolled oats
  ½ cup packed brown sugar
  ¼ cup all-purpose flour
  **¼ teaspoon ground nutmeg, ginger,
      or cinnamon**
  ¼ cup margarine *or* butter
  **¼ cup chopped nuts *or* coconut
      Vanilla ice cream *or* light
      cream (optional)**   Oven 375°

For filling, thaw fruit, if frozen. *Do not drain.* Place fruit in an 8x1½-inch round baking dish. Stir in sugar.

    For topping, in a mixing bowl combine oats, brown sugar, flour, and nutmeg, ginger, or cinnamon. Cut in margarine or butter till mixture resembles coarse crumbs. Stir in nuts or coconut. Sprinkle topping over filling.

    Bake in a 375° oven for 30 to 35 minutes (40 minutes for thawed fruit) or till fruit is tender and topping is golden. Serve warm with ice cream or light cream, if desired. Serves 6.

    Microwave directions: Assemble filling as above. Cook filling, covered with vented plastic wrap, on 100% power (high) for 5 to 7 minutes or till fruit is tender, stirring twice.

    Assemble topping as above. Sprinkle over filling. Cook, uncovered, on high about 3 minutes or till topping is heated through, giving the dish a half-turn once. Serve warm with ice cream or light cream, if desired.

    Blueberry Crisp: Prepare as above, *except,* for the filling, combine *4 tablespoons* sugar and 3 tablespoons *all-purpose flour.* Toss with 5 cups fresh *or* frozen* *blueberries.*

    Cherry Crisp: Prepare as above, *except,* for the filling, combine *½ cup* sugar and 3 tablespoons *all-purpose flour.* Toss with 5 cups fresh *or* frozen* unsweetened pitted *tart red cherries.*

    Rhubarb Crisp: Prepare as above, *except,* for filling, combine *1 cup* sugar and 3 tablespoons *all-purpose flour.* Toss with 5 cups fresh *or* frozen* unsweetened sliced *rhubarb.*

    ***Note:** If fruit is frozen, thaw, but *do not drain.*

Fruit Cobbler

    Desired filling (see below)
  1 cup all-purpose flour
  ¼ cup sugar
  1 teaspoon baking powder
  **½ teaspoon ground cinnamon
      (optional)**
  3 tablespoons margarine *or* butter
  1 beaten egg
  3 tablespoons milk   Oven 400°

Prepare filling. Keep hot. For topping, mix flour, sugar, baking powder, and, if desired, cinnamon. Cut in margarine till mixture resembles coarse crumbs. Combine egg and milk. Add to flour mixture, stirring just to moisten.

    Transfer filling to an 8x8x2-inch baking dish. Drop topping into 6 mounds atop hot filling. Bake in a 400° oven 20 to 25 minutes or till a toothpick inserted into topping comes out clean. Serve warm with ice cream, if desired. Serves 6.

    Microwave directions: In an 8x8x2-inch baking dish combine ingredients for Blueberry or Peach Filling. Micro-cook, uncovered, on 100% power (high) for 8 to 10 minutes or till thickened and bubbly, stirring every 2 minutes till slightly thickened, then every minute. Keep hot. Prepare topping as above, *except* reduce all-purpose flour to *¾* cup and add ¼ cup *whole wheat flour.* Drop topping into 6 mounds atop hot filling, leaving center open. Cook, uncovered, on 50% power (medium) for 8 to 10 minutes or till a cooked texture forms underneath surface of topping, turning dish once.

    Blueberry or Peach Filling: In a saucepan combine ⅓ to ⅔ cup *sugar* and 1 tablespoon *cornstarch.* Add ¼ cup *water.* Stir in 4 cups fresh *or* frozen *blueberries or* unsweetened *peach slices.* Cook and stir till thickened and bubbly.

    Apple or Pear Filling: Cook and stir 6 cups sliced, peeled *apples or pears,* ⅓ to ⅔ cup *sugar,* 3 tablespoons *water,* and 1 tablespoon *lemon juice* till boiling. Reduce heat. Cover and simmer for 5 minutes or till fruit is almost tender, stirring occasionally. Combine 2 tablespoons *water* and 1 tablespoon *cornstarch;* add to filling. Cook and stir till thickened and bubbly.

    Red Cherry or Rhubarb Filling: Mix 6 cups fresh *or* frozen unsweetened pitted *tart red cherries or* sliced *rhubarb,* 1 to 1¼ cups *sugar,* ¼ cup *water,* and 4 teaspoons *cornstarch.* Let stand 10 minutes (20 minutes for frozen fruit). Cook and stir till thickened and bubbly.

Cherries Jubilee

Your meal will end with pizzazz when you ladle this flaming sauce over ice cream.

   1 **16-ounce can pitted dark sweet cherries**
   ¼ **cup sugar**
   1 **tablespoon cornstarch**
   ¼ **cup brandy, cherry brandy, or kirsch**
      Vanilla ice cream

Drain cherries, reserving ½ *cup* syrup. Set cherries aside. In a medium saucepan or the blazer pan of a chafing dish combine reserved syrup, sugar, and cornstarch. Cook and stir till thickened and bubbly. Cook and stir for 2 minutes more. Stir in cherries and heat through.

   In a small saucepan heat brandy or kirsch till it almost simmers. (If desired, pour heated brandy into a large ladle.) Carefully ignite brandy and pour over cherry mixture. Serve immediately over ice cream. Makes 6 to 8 servings.

Fresh-Fruit Bowl

For a tropical flavor, choose the papaya and kiwi fruit or carambola.

   2 **medium oranges**
   ⅓ **cup sugar or honey**
   ½ **teaspoon finely shredded lemon or lime peel**
   1 **tablespoon lemon or lime juice**
   ⅛ **teaspoon ground cinnamon, ginger, or nutmeg**
   1½ **cups cubed honeydew melon, cantaloupe, or papaya**
   1 **cup halved strawberries or seedless green grapes; peeled, sliced kiwi fruit; or sliced carambola (star fruit)**
   1 **cup blueberries or raspberries**
      Fruit-flavored yogurt (optional)
      Toasted coconut or toasted slivered almonds (optional)

Over a bowl, peel and section oranges, reserving juice. Combine reserved juice, sugar or honey, lemon or lime peel, lemon or lime juice, and cinnamon, ginger, or nutmeg. In a large serving bowl place all the fruit *except* berries. Drizzle juice mixture over fruit. Cover; chill 2 to 24 hours.

   To serve, stir in berries. Top with yogurt and coconut or almonds, if desired. Makes 4 servings.

Bananas Foster

Bananas plus brown-sugar-rum sauce plus vanilla ice cream equal a truly divine dessert.

   4 **ripe medium bananas**
   ⅓ **cup margarine or butter**
   ⅔ **cup packed brown sugar**
   ¼ **cup light rum**
      Vanilla ice cream

Peel bananas; halve crosswise, then lengthwise. In a large skillet or the blazer pan of a chafing dish melt margarine or butter over medium heat. Stir in brown sugar. Add bananas. Cook and stir for 3 to 4 minutes or till heated through. In a small saucepan heat rum till it almost simmers. (If desired, pour heated rum into a large ladle.) Carefully ignite rum and pour over bananas. Serve immediately over ice cream. Serves 4.

   Peach and Banana Flambé: Prepare as above, *except* substitute 1 cup sliced, peeled *peaches* (2 medium) for 1 banana. Sprinkle *each* serving with 1 tablespoon toasted *coconut*.

Swedish Fruit Soup

Make a delicious dessert of soup with dried fruit, raisins, and orange.

   ½ **of an 8-ounce package (about ¾ cup) mixed dried fruit**
   2 **cups water**
   ¼ **cup raisins**
   2 **inches stick cinnamon**
   1 **cup unsweetened pineapple juice**
   1 **tablespoon quick-cooking tapioca**
   ¼ **cup currant jelly**
   2 **tablespoons brown sugar**
   1 **medium orange, peeled, thinly sliced, and quartered**

Pit prunes. Cut up large pieces of dried fruit. In a medium saucepan combine mixed dried fruit, water, raisins, and cinnamon. Bring to boiling; reduce heat. Cover and simmer for 10 minutes. Meanwhile, combine pineapple juice and tapioca; let stand 5 minutes. Stir into cooked fruit mixture along with jelly and brown sugar. Bring to boiling; reduce heat. Cover and simmer for 5 minutes, stirring occasionally. Remove stick cinnamon. Stir in orange. Serve warm or chilled. Makes 8 servings.

Crepes Suzette

Dazzle both family and friends with these folded crepes heated in a buttery orange sauce.

Dessert Crepes (see recipe, page 72)
½ **cup margarine *or* butter**
¼ **teaspoon finely shredded orange peel**
½ **cup orange juice**
⅓ **cup sugar**
¼ **cup orange liqueur**
¼ **cup brandy**

Prepare crepes. Fold each crepe in half, browned side out. Fold in half again, forming a triangle. Set aside.

For orange sauce, in a large skillet or the blazer pan of a chafing dish combine margarine or butter, shredded orange peel, orange juice, sugar, and orange liqueur. Cook and stir till thickened and bubbly.

Arrange folded crepes in sauce. Simmer for 3 to 5 minutes or just till heated through, spooning sauce over crepes occasionally.

In a small saucepan heat the brandy till it almost simmers. (If desired, pour heated brandy into a large ladle.) Carefully ignite brandy and pour over crepes. Makes 6 to 8 servings.

Pineapple Crepes: Prepare as above, *except* omit the orange liqueur. Drain one 8-ounce can *sliced pineapple* (juice pack), reserving juice. Cut the pineapple slices into small pieces.

Stir the pineapple pieces and reserved pineapple juice into the uncooked orange juice mixture in the skillet or blazer pan.

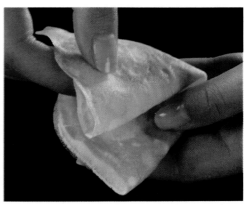

Fold each crepe in half, forming a semicircle. Fold in half again to make a triangle.

Crepes Suzette

Meringue Shells

  3 egg whites
  1 teaspoon vanilla
  ¼ teaspoon cream of tartar
  1 cup sugar
     Dash salt   Oven 300°

Let egg whites stand in a large mixing bowl about 1 hour or till they come to room temperature. Meanwhile, cover a baking sheet with plain brown paper. Draw one 9-inch circle *or* eight 3-inch circles on paper.

For meringue, add vanilla, cream of tartar, and salt to egg whites. Beat with an electric mixer on medium speed till soft peaks form (tips curl). Add sugar, a tablespoon at a time, beating on high speed till very stiff peaks form (tips stand straight) and sugar is almost dissolved (about 7 minutes).

Pipe meringue through a pastry tube onto the circle or circles on the brown paper, building the sides up to form a shell or shells. *Or,* use the back of a spoon to spread the meringue over circle or circles, building the sides up.

Bake in a 300° oven for 45 minutes for large shell (35 minutes for small shells). Turn off oven. Let shell or shells dry in oven, with door closed, for 1 hour. Remove from paper. Store in an airtight container. If desired, fill shell or shells with ice cream or pudding and top with whipped cream. Makes 8 servings.

Lemon Meringue Torte: Prepare as above, *except* spread meringue into the bottom of a well-greased 9-inch pie plate. Build up the sides to form a shell. Bake and dry as above for the large shell.

For filling, in a saucepan combine ½ cup *sugar* and 2 tablespoons *cornstarch.* Stir in 3 beaten *egg yolks,* ⅓ cup *water,* 1 teaspoon finely shredded *lemon peel,* and ¼ cup *lemon juice.* Cook and stir till thickened and bubbly. Cook and stir for 2 minutes more. Remove from heat. Cover surface with plastic wrap; cool (mixture will be very thick). To assemble, spread cooled filling in shell. Beat 1 cup *whipping cream* and 2 tablespoons *sugar* till soft peaks form. Spread over filling. Chill 5 to 24 hours. Cut with wet knife.

Pavlova: Prepare *large* Meringue Shell on paper as above. Fill with 5 cups peeled and sliced *kiwi fruit,* halved *strawberries,* peeled and sliced *peaches,* peeled and cut-up *papaya, or pineapple chunks,* or a combination. Beat 1 cup *whipping cream* and ¼ cup *sugar* till soft peaks form. Dollop whipped cream over fruit. Garnish with additional fruit, if desired. Serve *immediately.*

Pavlova

Chocolate Mousse

So luscious and creamy.

- ¼ cup sugar
- ¼ cup water
- 3 squares (3 ounces) semisweet chocolate, coarsely chopped
- 2 beaten egg yolks
- 2 egg whites
- ⅛ teaspoon cream of tartar
- 2 tablespoons sugar
- ½ cup whipping cream
  - Whipped cream (optional)
  - Chocolate curls *or* grated chocolate (optional)

In a small heavy saucepan combine the ¼ cup sugar and the water. Cook and stir over medium-low heat till sugar dissolves. Add chocolate; cook and stir over low heat till chocolate melts. Gradually stir the chocolate mixture into beaten egg yolks. Return mixture to saucepan. Bring to a gentle boil. Cook and stir for 2 minutes more. Cool to lukewarm, stirring occasionally.

In a bowl beat egg whites and cream of tartar with an electric mixer on high speed till soft peaks form (tips curl). Gradually add the 2 tablespoons sugar, beating till stiff peaks form (tips stand straight). Pour the lukewarm chocolate mixture over beaten egg whites; fold in gently.

Beat the ½ cup whipping cream till soft peaks form; fold whipped cream into the chocolate and egg white mixture. Spoon into dessert dishes. Cover and chill for 4 to 24 hours before serving. Garnish with whipped cream and chocolate curls or grated chocolate, if desired. Serves 5 or 6.

Microwave directions: In a 2-cup measure micro-cook the ¼ cup sugar and the water, uncovered, on 100% power (high) for 1 to 2 minutes or till sugar dissolves. Stir in chocolate. Cook, uncovered, on high for 1½ to 2½ minutes more or till chocolate melts. Stir; cook for 30 to 60 seconds more or till the mixture is smooth. Place beaten yolks in a small bowl. Stir in the chocolate mixture. Cook, uncovered, on high for 30 to 60 seconds or just till mixture bubbles. Cool to lukewarm. Continue as above.

Mocha Mousse: Prepare as above, *except* add 1 teaspoon *instant coffee crystals* to the sugar-water mixture before cooking.

Mint-Chocolate Mousse: Prepare as above, *except* stir 1 tablespoon *crème de menthe* or a few drops *mint extract* into the ½ cup whipping cream before whipping.

Chocolate Soufflé

- 2 tablespoons margarine *or* butter
- 3 tablespoons all-purpose flour
- ¾ cup milk
- ½ cup semisweet chocolate pieces
- 4 beaten egg yolks
- 4 egg whites
- ½ teaspoon vanilla
- ¼ cup sugar   Oven 350°

Butter the sides of a 2-quart soufflé dish. Sprinkle sides with a little sugar. Set aside.

In a small saucepan melt margarine. Stir in flour. Add milk all at once. Cook and stir till thickened and bubbly. Add chocolate; stir till melted. Remove from heat. Gradually stir chocolate mixture into beaten egg yolks. Set aside.

Beat egg whites and vanilla till soft peaks form (tips curl). Gradually add ¼ cup sugar, beating till stiff peaks form (tips stand straight). Fold about *1 cup* beaten whites into chocolate mixture. Then fold chocolate mixture into remaining beaten whites. Transfer to prepared dish. Bake in a 350° oven 35 to 40 minutes or till a knife inserted near center comes out clean. Serve *at once* with whipped cream, if desired. Serves 6.

Amaretto Soufflé: Prepare as above, *except* omit chocolate pieces. Stir ¼ cup *amaretto* and ¼ cup finely chopped toasted *almonds* into the thickened milk mixture.

Baked Alaska

- 1 quart ice cream (any flavor)
- 1 9-inch cake layer (any flavor)
- 5 egg whites
- 1 teaspoon vanilla
- ½ teaspoon cream of tartar
- ⅔ cup sugar   Oven 500°

Stir ice cream to soften. Spoon into a 1½-quart bowl lined with clear plastic wrap. Invert ice cream onto cake; remove bowl. Freeze till firm.

For meringue, beat egg whites, vanilla, and cream of tartar till soft peaks form (tips curl). Gradually add sugar, beating till stiff peaks form (tips stand straight). Transfer cake and ice cream to a baking sheet; remove plastic wrap. Spread meringue over all, sealing edge to baking sheet. Place oven rack in the lowest position. Bake in a 500° oven for 2 to 3 minutes or till golden. Serve *immediately.* Makes 8 servings.

Cheesecake Supreme

Your cheesecake is done when its center appears nearly set but jiggles slightly when gently shaken.

1¾ **cups finely crushed graham crackers**
¼ **cup finely chopped walnuts**
½ **teaspoon ground cinnamon**
½ **cup margarine *or* butter, melted**
3 **8-ounce packages cream cheese, softened**
1 **cup sugar**
2 **tablespoons all-purpose flour**
1 **teaspoon vanilla**
½ **teaspoon finely shredded lemon peel (optional)**
2 **eggs**
1 **egg yolk**
¼ **cup milk**
Fruit Sauce (see recipe, page 139) (optional)   Oven 375°

For crust, combine crushed crackers, nuts, and cinnamon. Stir in margarine or butter. Reserve ¼ *cup* of the crumb mixture for topping, if desired. Press remaining onto bottom and about 2 inches up sides of an 8- or 9-inch springform pan.

In a mixer bowl combine cream cheese, sugar, flour, vanilla, and, if desired, lemon peel. Beat with an electric mixer till fluffy. Add eggs and yolk all at once, beating on low speed just till combined. Stir in milk. Pour into crust-lined pan. Sprinkle with reserved crumbs, if any. Place on a shallow baking pan in oven. Bake in a 375° oven for 45 to 50 minutes for the 8-inch pan (35 to 40 minutes for the 9-inch pan) or till center appears nearly set when shaken. Cool 15 minutes. Loosen crust from sides of pan. Cool for 30 minutes more; remove sides of pan. Cool completely. Chill at least 4 hours. Serve with Fruit Sauce, if desired. Makes 12 to 16 servings.

Sour Cream Cheesecake: Prepare as above, *except* reduce cream cheese to *2 packages* and omit the milk. Add three 8-ounce cartons dairy *sour cream* with the eggs. Bake in 8-inch pan about 55 minutes (9-inch pan, 50 minutes).

Liqueur Cheesecake: Prepare as above, *except* substitute *white crème de menthe, crème de cacao, coffee liqueur, or amaretto* for milk.

Chocolate Swirl Cheesecake: Prepare as above, *except* omit lemon peel. Stir 2 squares (2 ounces) *semisweet chocolate*, melted and cooled, into *half* of the batter. Pour *half* of each batter mixture into crust; repeat. Use a spatula to gently swirl batters.

Strawberry Shortcake

Next time, try sliced peaches instead of berries. (Strawberry Shortcake is pictured on page 121.)

6 **cups sliced strawberries**
½ **cup sugar**
2 **cups all-purpose flour**
2 **teaspoons baking powder**
½ **cup margarine *or* butter**
1 **beaten egg**
⅔ **cup milk**
Whipped Cream (see recipe, page 140)   Oven 450°

Stir together berries and ¼ *cup* of the sugar; set aside. Stir together remaining sugar, flour, and baking powder. Cut in margarine till mixture resembles coarse crumbs. Combine egg and milk; add all at once to dry ingredients. Stir just to moisten. Spread into a greased 8x1½-inch round baking pan, building up edge slightly. Bake in a 450° oven for 15 to 18 minutes or till toothpick inserted near center comes out clean. Cool in pan 10 minutes. Remove from pan. Split into 2 layers. Spoon the fruit and Whipped Cream between layers and over top. Serve immediately. Serves 8.

Brownie Pudding Cake

½ **cup all-purpose flour**
¼ **cup sugar**
3 **tablespoons unsweetened cocoa powder**
¾ **teaspoon baking powder**
¼ **cup milk**
1 **tablespoon cooking oil**
½ **teaspoon vanilla**
¼ **cup chopped walnuts**
⅓ **cup sugar**
¾ **cup boiling water**   Oven 350°

Stir together flour, the ¼ cup sugar, *1 tablespoon* of the cocoa powder, and the baking powder. Add milk, oil, and vanilla. Stir till smooth. Stir in nuts. Transfer batter to a 1-quart casserole. Combine the ⅓ cup sugar and remaining cocoa powder. Gradually stir in boiling water. Pour evenly over batter. Bake in a 350° oven about 30 minutes or till a toothpick inserted into cake comes out clean. Serve warm. Makes 4 servings.

Mocha Brownie Pudding Cake: Prepare as above, *except* add 2 teaspoons *instant coffee crystals* with the boiling water.

Lemon Pudding Cake

Tastes like lemon meringue pie.

½ cup sugar
3 tablespoons all-purpose flour
1 teaspoon finely shredded lemon
   peel
3 tablespoons lemon juice
2 tablespoons margarine, melted
2 slightly beaten egg yolks
1 cup milk
2 egg whites   Oven 350°

Combine sugar and flour. Stir in lemon peel, juice, and melted margarine. Combine yolks and milk. Add to flour mixture; stir just till combined.

Beat egg whites till stiff peaks form (tips stand straight). Gently fold egg whites into lemon batter. Transfer batter to a 1-quart casserole. Place in a larger pan on oven rack. Add *hot* water to larger pan to a depth of 1 inch. Bake in a 350° oven about 40 minutes or till golden and top springs back. Serve warm. Serves 4.

Chocolate-Mousse Cake

1 cup toasted pecans, coarsely ground
1 cup graham cracker crumbs
¼ cup margarine *or* butter, melted
2 tablespoons sugar
2 8-ounce packages (16 squares)
   semisweet chocolate, cut up
1 cup whipping cream
6 beaten eggs
¾ cup sugar
⅓ cup all-purpose flour   Oven 325°

For crust, combine ground nuts, cracker crumbs, margarine, and the 2 tablespoons sugar. Press onto bottom and about 1½ inches up sides of a greased 9-inch springform pan. Set aside.

Cook and stir chocolate and cream over low heat till chocolate melts. Transfer to a large bowl.

Combine eggs, the ¾ cup sugar, and flour; beat 10 minutes or till thick and lemon colored. Fold *one-fourth* of the egg mixture into the chocolate mixture, then fold chocolate mixture into remaining egg mixture. Pour into crust-lined pan.

Bake in a 325° oven 55 minutes or till puffed around edge and halfway to center (center will be slightly soft). Cool 20 minutes. Remove sides of pan. Cool for 4 hours. Serve with whipped cream, if desired. Chill leftovers. Serves 16.

Plum Pudding

3 slices white bread, torn into pieces
1 5-ounce can (⅔ cup) evaporated
   milk
2 ounces beef suet, ground (⅔ cup),
   or ⅔ cup shortening
⅔ cup packed brown sugar
1 beaten egg
1 teaspoon finely shredded orange
   peel
¼ cup orange juice *or* rum
1½ cups raisins
¾ cup snipped pitted whole dates
½ cup diced mixed candied
   fruits and peels
⅓ cup chopped walnuts
¾ cup all-purpose flour
1½ teaspoons ground cinnamon
¾ teaspoon baking soda
½ teaspoon ground cloves
½ teaspoon ground mace *or* nutmeg
¼ cup rum (optional)
   Hard Sauce (see recipe, page 140)

In a bowl soak the bread in evaporated milk about 3 minutes or till softened. Beat lightly to break up. Stir in suet or shortening, brown sugar, egg, orange peel, and orange juice. Stir in raisins, dates, fruits and peels, and nuts.

Stir together flour, cinnamon, baking soda, cloves, and mace. Add to fruit mixture; stir till combined. Transfer mixture to a well-greased 6-cup tower mold. Cover with foil, pressing foil tightly against the rim of mold. Place on a rack in a deep kettle. Add *boiling* water till water reaches 1 inch above the bottom of the mold. Cover kettle. Bring to a gentle boil. Steam for 2½ to 3 hours or till a toothpick inserted near center comes out clean, adding more *boiling* water, if necessary. Cool 10 minutes; remove mold. Serve immediately. (*Or,* wrap and store in the refrigerator up to 2 weeks; reheat before serving as directed below.) If desired, heat rum till hot. Ignite with a match and pour over pudding. Serve with Hard Sauce. Makes 8 to 10 servings.

To reheat: Wrap pudding in foil and place on a baking sheet. Bake in a 350° oven for 30 to 40 minutes or till heated through.

Vanilla Pudding

Rich and creamy Chocolate Pudding spills from a Cream Puff (see recipe, opposite) in the photo below right.

- ¾ **cup sugar**
- 3 **tablespoons cornstarch *or* ⅓ cup all-purpose flour**
- 3 **cups milk**
- 4 **beaten egg yolks *or* 2 beaten eggs**
- 1 **tablespoon margarine *or* butter**
- 1½ **teaspoons vanilla**

In a heavy medium saucepan combine sugar and cornstarch or flour. Stir in milk. Cook and stir over medium heat till mixture is thickened and bubbly. Cook and stir for 2 minutes more. Remove from heat. Gradually stir about *1 cup* of the hot mixture into beaten egg yolks or eggs.

Return all of the egg mixture to the saucepan. If using egg yolks, bring to a gentle boil; if using whole eggs, cook till nearly bubbly, but *do not boil.* Reduce heat. Cook and stir for 2 minutes more. Remove from heat. Stir in margarine and vanilla. Pour pudding into a bowl. Cover the surface with clear plastic wrap. Chill. *Do not stir.* Makes 6 servings.

Microwave directions: In a 1½-quart casserole combine sugar and flour or cornstarch. Stir in milk. Micro-cook, uncovered, on 100% power (high) for 8 to 10 minutes or till thickened and bubbly, stirring every 2 minutes till slightly thickened, then every 30 seconds. Cook for 1 minute more. Gradually stir about *1 cup* of the hot mixture into beaten egg yolks or eggs. Return all the egg mixture to casserole. Cook on high for 1 to 2 minutes or till bubbly around the edges, stirring every 30 seconds. Cook for 30 seconds more. Stir in margarine and vanilla. Cover the surface with clear plastic wrap. Chill. *Do not stir.*

Chocolate Pudding: Prepare as above, *except* add ⅓ cup *unsweetened cocoa powder* to sugar. Use *2 tablespoons* cornstarch *or* ¼ cup all-purpose flour, 2⅔ *cups* milk, and egg yolks (not whole eggs).

Tangy Vanilla Pudding: Prepare as above, *except* omit margarine or butter. After chilling, stir in one 8-ounce carton dairy *sour cream or plain yogurt.*

Brandied Pudding: Prepare as above, *except* substitute 1 to 2 tablespoons *brandy, amaretto, coffee liqueur, or orange liqueur* for vanilla.

Gradually stir about *1 cup* of the hot milk mixture into the beaten egg yolks.

Cover the pudding with plastic wrap to prevent a skin from forming on its surface.

Cream Puffs

½ **cup margarine *or* butter**
1 **cup all-purpose flour**
4 **eggs**
   Pudding, whipped cream, ice cream,
     sherbet, *or* fresh fruit
   Powdered sugar
     (optional)   Oven 400°

In a medium saucepan combine margarine or butter, 1 cup *water,* and ⅛ teaspoon *salt.* Bring to boiling. Add flour all at once, stirring vigorously. Cook and stir till mixture forms a ball that doesn't separate. Remove from heat. Cool 10 minutes. Add eggs, one at a time, beating with a wooden spoon after each addition till smooth.

Drop batter by heaping tablespoons, 3 inches apart, onto a greased baking sheet. Bake in a 400° oven for 30 to 35 minutes or till golden. Cool on a wire rack. Split puffs and remove any soft dough from inside. Fill with the pudding, whipped cream, ice cream, sherbet, or fruit. Replace tops. Lightly sift powdered sugar over tops, if desired. Makes 10.

Éclairs: Prepare as above, *except* spoon batter into a pastry tube fitted with a Number 10 or larger tip. Slowly pipe strips of batter onto a greased baking sheet, making each strip about 4 inches long, ¾ inch wide, and 1 inch high. Bake, split, and cool as above. Fill with pudding or whipped cream. Frost with *Chocolate Glaze* (see recipe, page 89). Makes 12.

Dressing Up Pudding

Take your favorite pudding and create a whole new dessert with one of these easy-to-fix ideas.

● For cream tarts, spoon pudding into baked tart shells.

● For parfaits, layer pudding and canned fruit-pie filling in parfait glasses.

● For frozen pops, spoon pudding into 3-ounce paper cups. Cover with foil. Insert wooden sticks through the foil into the pudding. Freeze till firm.

● For sauce, stir additional milk into the pudding till of desired consistency. Serve over fruit or cake.

Chocolate Pots de Crème

Savor pot de crème (poh-duh-KREM), a very rich dessert, in small portions.

1 **cup light cream**
1 **4-ounce package German sweet**
     chocolate, coarsely chopped
2 **teaspoons sugar**
3 **beaten egg yolks**
½ **teaspoon vanilla**
   Whipped cream (optional)

In a heavy small saucepan combine light cream, chocolate, and sugar. Cook and stir over medium heat about 10 minutes or till mixture comes to a full boil and thickens. Gradually stir about *half* of the hot mixture into beaten egg yolks; return yolk mixture to saucepan. Cook and stir over low heat for 2 minutes more. Remove from heat. Stir in vanilla. Pour into 4 or 6 pot de crème cups or small dessert dishes. Cover and chill for 2 to 24 hours. Serve with whipped cream, if desired. Makes 4 or 6 servings.

Cream Cheese Hearts

End a meal in style with these creamy, rich treats.

6 **to 8 six-inch squares cheesecloth**
1 **8-ounce package cream cheese,**
     softened
½ **teaspoon vanilla *or* few drops**
     almond *or* lemon extract
⅓ **cup sifted powdered sugar**
¾ **cup whipping cream**
   Fruit Sauce (see recipe, page 139)
     ***or* fresh fruit**

Line six ½-cup or eight ⅓-cup heart-shape or other molds with *damp* cheesecloth squares, allowing the cheesecloth to hang over edges.

Beat cream cheese and vanilla with an electric mixer on medium speed till combined. Gradually add powdered sugar, beating till fluffy. Set aside.

In another bowl beat whipping cream till soft peaks form. Fold into the cream cheese mixture. Spoon into the prepared molds. Cover and chill for 6 to 24 hours.

To serve, invert molds onto a serving plate. Holding onto cheesecloth ends, lift molds from cheesecloth. Peel cheesecloth from shapes. Serve with Fruit Sauce or fruit. Serves 6 or 8.

Baked Custards

Caramel Flan, a dressed-up version of Baked Custards, is pictured below right.

> **3 beaten eggs**
> **1½ cups milk**
> **⅓ cup sugar**
> **1 teaspoon vanilla**
> **Ground nutmeg *or* cinnamon (optional)**   Oven 325°

Combine eggs, milk, sugar, and vanilla. Beat till well combined but not foamy. Place four 6-ounce custard cups or one 3½-cup soufflé dish in an 8x8x2-inch baking dish on an oven rack. Pour egg mixture into custard cups or dish. Sprinkle with nutmeg or cinnamon, if desired. Pour *boiling* water into the baking dish around custard cups or dish to a depth of 1 inch.

Bake in a 325° oven for 30 to 45 minutes for custard cups (50 to 60 minutes for dish) or till a knife inserted near the center or centers comes out clean. Serve warm or chilled. If desired, loosen edges of individual custards with a spatula or knife, slipping point of spatula down sides to let air in; invert onto dessert plates. Serves 4.

Microwave directions: In a 4-cup measure micro-cook milk, sugar, and vanilla, uncovered, on 100% power (high) for 3 to 5 minutes or till steaming and foamy but not boiling, stirring once. Stir milk mixture into beaten eggs. Pour into the custard cups in the baking dish. (Do not use soufflé dish.) Pour 2½ cups *boiling* water into the baking dish around the custard cups. Cook, uncovered, on high for 3 minutes, giving the dish a quarter-turn every minute. Rotate cups. Cook for 1 to 3 minutes more or till edges are set but centers still quiver. After 1 minute, check for doneness every 15 seconds, turning custards as necessary. Remove each when done.

Caramel Flan: Prepare as above, *except* in a heavy saucepan cook ⅓ cup *sugar* over medium-high heat (*do not stir*) till sugar begins to melt; shake saucepan occasionally. Reduce heat to low and cook till sugar is golden brown; stir frequently. Divide sugar mixture among custard cups. Tilt to coat bottoms. Let stand for 10 minutes. Add egg mixture. Bake individual custards as above. Remove from custard cups to serve.

Baked Rice Pudding: Prepare as above, *except* stir 1 cup *cooked rice* and ½ cup *raisins* into egg mixture. Pour into a 1½-quart casserole. Bake as above for 45 to 55 minutes, stirring after 30 minutes. Makes 6 servings. Do not use the microwave directions.

Add boiling water to the baking dish to keep the edges of the custards from overcooking.

When custards are done, a knife inserted near the centers will come out clean.

Bread Pudding

To dry bread cubes, bake them in a 300° oven about 15 minutes. Or, cut toasted bread slices into 1-inch cubes.

   4 **beaten eggs**
   2 **cups milk**
   ⅓ **cup sugar**
   ½ **teaspoon ground cinnamon**
   ½ **teaspoon vanilla**
   3 **cups (4 slices) dry bread cubes**
   ⅓ **cup raisins *or* other snipped dried
       fruit**
       **Whiskey Sauce (see recipe,
       page 140) (optional)**   Oven 325°

In a mixing bowl beat together eggs, milk, sugar, cinnamon, and vanilla. Place dry bread cubes in an 8x1½-inch round baking dish. Sprinkle raisins or dried fruit over bread. Pour egg mixture over all. Bake in a 325° oven for 35 to 40 minutes or till a knife inserted near the center comes out clean. Cool slightly. Serve warm with Whiskey Sauce, if desired. Makes 6 servings.

   Coconut Bread Pudding: Prepare as above, *except* sprinkle ¼ cup *coconut* over the raisins or dried fruit.

Stirred Custard

Serve this custard as a rich sauce over fresh fruit or cake.

   3 **beaten eggs**
   2 **cups milk *or* light cream**
   ¼ **cup sugar**
   1 **teaspoon vanilla**
       Sponge cake *or* fresh fruit

In a heavy medium saucepan combine eggs, milk or light cream, and sugar. Cook and stir over medium heat. Continue cooking egg mixture till it just coats a metal spoon. Remove from heat. Stir in vanilla. Quickly cool the custard by placing the saucepan in a sink or bowl of *ice* water for 1 to 2 minutes, stirring constantly. Pour custard mixture into a bowl. Cover surface with clear plastic wrap. Chill till serving time. Serve over cake slices or fruit. Makes 3 cups (6 servings).

   Amaretto Stirred Custard: Prepare as above, *except* substitute 2 to 3 tablespoons *amaretto, orange liqueur, coffee liqueur, rum, or brandy* for the vanilla.

Stirred Rice Pudding

   3 **cups milk**
   ⅓ **cup long grain rice**
   ⅓ **cup raisins**
   ¼ **cup sugar**
   1 **teaspoon vanilla**
   ¼ **teaspoon ground nutmeg**

In a heavy medium saucepan bring milk to boiling; stir in *uncooked* rice and raisins. Cover; cook over low heat, stirring occasionally, for 30 to 40 minutes or till most of the milk is absorbed. (Mixture may appear curdled.) Stir in sugar and vanilla. Spoon into dessert dishes. Sprinkle with nutmeg. Serve warm or chilled. Serves 5 or 6.

Trifle

Save a step and use a bakery sponge cake or ladyfingers for the base.

       Stirred Custard (see recipe, left)
       **Hot-Milk Sponge Cake (see recipe,
       page 85)**
   3 **tablespoons cream sherry *or* brandy**
   ¼ **cup strawberry preserves *or* currant
       jelly**
   2 **cups cut-up, peeled peaches *or* kiwi
       fruit; *or* strawberries,
       raspberries, *or* blueberries**
   2 **tablespoons toasted sliced almonds**
   ½ **cup whipping cream**
   1 **tablespoon sugar**
   ½ **teaspoon vanilla**

Prepare Stirred Custard and cool. Cut cake into 1-inch cubes (you should have 5 cups). Reserve remaining cake for another use. In a 2-quart serving bowl layer *half* of the cake cubes. Sprinkle with *half* of the sherry. Dot with *half* of the preserves. Top with *half* of the fruit and *half* of the almonds. Pour *half* of the Stirred Custard over all. Repeat layers. Cover and chill for 3 to 24 hours. To serve, beat whipping cream, sugar, and vanilla till soft peaks form. Spread over trifle. Serves 8.

   Shortcut Trifle: Prepare as above, *except* substitute one 4-serving-size package *instant vanilla pudding mix,* prepared according to package directions, for the Stirred Custard; one 3-ounce package (12) *ladyfingers* for the cake; and *half* of a 4-ounce container *frozen whipped dessert topping,* thawed, for the whipping cream, sugar, and vanilla. Chill up to 4 hours.

No-Cook Vanilla Ice Cream

Looks and tastes like soft-serve ice cream.

    3 cups light cream
 1½ cups sugar
    1 tablespoon vanilla
    3 cups whipping cream

In a large mixing bowl combine light cream, sugar, and vanilla. Stir till sugar dissolves. Stir in whipping cream. Freeze in a 4- or 5-quart ice-cream freezer according to the manufacturer's directions. Makes 2 quarts (16 to 20 servings).

   No-Cook Cherry-Nut Ice Cream: Prepare as above, *except* stir 1 cup chopped pitted *dark sweet cherries* and ¾ cup chopped *walnuts* into cream mixture before freezing.

   No-Cook Chocolate-Almond Ice Cream: Prepare as above, *except* reduce sugar to *1 cup.* Stir one 16-ounce can (1½ cups) *chocolate-flavored syrup* and ½ cup chopped toasted *almonds* into cream mixture before freezing.

   No-Cook Chocolate Chip and Mint Ice Cream: Prepare as above, *except* stir 1 cup *miniature semisweet chocolate pieces,* several drops of *mint extract,* and, if desired, a few drops of green or red food coloring into the cream mixture before freezing.

   No-Cook Strawberry Ice Cream: Prepare as above, *except,* in a blender container, blend 4 cups fresh *or* frozen-then-thawed unsweetened *strawberries or blueberries* till nearly smooth. (You should have 2 cups.) Stir blended berries into cream mixture before freezing.

   No-Cook Peach Ice Cream: Prepare as above, *except,* in a blender container, blend 4 cups cut-up, peeled *peaches* till nearly smooth. (You should have 2 cups.) Stir peaches into cream mixture before freezing.

   No-Cook Coffee Ice Cream: Prepare as above, *except* dissolve 2 to 3 tablespoons *instant coffee crystals* in the light cream mixture. Stir ½ cup miniature semisweet chocolate pieces into cream mixture before freezing, if desired.

   Butter-Pecan Ice Cream: Prepare as above, *except,* in a heavy skillet, cook ½ cup chopped *pecans,* ¼ cup *sugar,* and 1 tablespoon *margarine or butter* over medium-high heat (*do not stir*) till sugar begins to melt, shaking skillet occasionally. Reduce heat to low and cook till sugar turns golden, stirring frequently. Immediately spread on a baking sheet lined with greased foil. Cool; break into chunks. Stir nut mixture into cream mixture before freezing.

Vanilla Ice Cream

    2 cups sugar
    2 envelopes unflavored gelatin
    6 cups light cream
    6 beaten eggs
    2 cups whipping cream
    3 tablespoons vanilla

In a large saucepan combine sugar and gelatin. Stir in light cream. Cook and stir over medium heat till mixture almost boils and sugar dissolves. Stir about *1 cup* of the hot mixture into beaten eggs; return all to saucepan. Cook and stir for 2 minutes more. *Do not boil.* Stir in whipping cream and vanilla. Cool. Freeze in a 4- or 5-quart ice-cream freezer according to manufacturer's directions. Makes about 3 quarts (24 servings).

   Chocolate Ice Cream: Prepare as above, *except* stir 6 squares (6 ounces) *unsweetened chocolate,* melted and cooled, into gelatin mixture after heating. Beat with a rotary beater till combined. Stir 1 cup chopped toasted almonds into the cooled mixture, if desired.

Ripening Ice Cream

Let your homemade ice cream ripen for four hours to blend its flavors. To ripen the ice cream, remove the dasher, then cover the freezer can with waxed paper or foil. Plug the hole in the lid. Place it on the can. Pack the outer freezer bucket with enough ice and rock salt to cover the top of the freezer can. (Use 4 cups ice per 1 cup salt.)

Lemon Sherbet

We added just enough lemon peel to give a tangy, refreshing taste.

1½ cups sugar
1 envelope unflavored gelatin
1 teaspoon finely shredded lemon peel *or* orange peel
1 cup milk
¾ cup lemon juice
Few drops yellow food coloring

In saucepan mix sugar and gelatin; add 3 cups *water*. Cook and stir till sugar and gelatin dissolve. Remove from heat. Add lemon peel, milk, lemon juice, and food coloring. (Mixture will look curdled.) Transfer to a 9x9x2-inch baking pan. Cover; freeze 2 to 3 hours or till almost firm. (*Or,* after mixing ingredients, freeze in a 4- or 5-quart ice-cream freezer according to manufacturer's directions. Omit remaining steps.)

Break frozen mixture into small chunks. Transfer to a chilled bowl. Beat with an electric mixer till smooth but not melted. Return to pan. Cover; freeze till firm. Makes 2 quarts (serves 16 to 20).

Orange Sherbet: Prepare as above, *except* substitute 3¾ cups *orange juice* for water. Omit lemon juice. Substitute *orange food coloring* for yellow food coloring.

Pineapple Sherbet: Prepare as above, *except* substitute 3¾ cups unsweetened *pineapple juice* for water. Omit lemon juice.

Choose-a-Fruit Frozen Yogurt

 EASY

Double all the ingredients for a 4- or 5-quart ice-cream freezer.

2 cups fresh *or* frozen unsweetened strawberries, red raspberries, blueberries, *or* boysenberries; cut-up, peeled peaches *or* nectarines; *or* pitted dark sweet cherries
2 8-ounce cartons plain yogurt
½ to ¾ cup honey *or* sugar

In blender container blend fruit till smooth. Press through a sieve to remove seeds, if necessary. Stir in yogurt and honey. Pour into a 1- to 2-quart ice-cream freezer. Freeze according to manufacturer's directions. Let stand at room temperature for 20 minutes. Makes 1 quart (8 servings).

Fruit Ice

3 cups fresh *or* frozen unsweetened strawberries *or* raspberries, *or* sliced peaches *or* nectarines
1 cup orange juice
½ cup sugar
2 tablespoons orange liqueur (optional)
Orange juice

In a blender container combine fruit, orange juice, sugar, and, if desired, liqueur. Cover; blend till smooth. Press through a sieve to remove skin or seeds. Add additional orange juice to make *3 cups* mixture. Transfer to an 8x4x2-inch or 9x5x3-inch loaf pan. Cover; freeze 4 hours or till firm. Break frozen mixture into small chunks. Transfer to chilled bowl. Beat with an electric mixer till smooth but not melted. Return mixture to loaf pan. Cover; freeze till firm. To serve, scrape across top with a spoon and mound into dessert dishes. Makes 3 cups (6 to 8 servings).

Mocha Toffee Squares

1 cup finely crushed chocolate wafers
3 tablespoons margarine *or* butter, melted
2 teaspoons instant coffee crystals
¾ cup sugar
½ cup margarine *or* butter
4 egg yolks
1 square (1 ounce) unsweetened chocolate, melted and cooled
½ teaspoon vanilla
4 egg whites
2 1⅛-ounce bars chocolate-covered English toffee, crushed (½ cup)

For crust, combine crushed wafers and the melted margarine; press onto bottom of an 8x8x2-inch dish. Dissolve coffee crystals in 1 tablespoon *hot* water. Beat together ½ *cup* sugar and the ½ cup margarine till fluffy. Add egg yolks, one at a time, beating well after each. Add coffee, chocolate, and vanilla; beat till combined. Beat egg whites to soft peaks; gradually add remaining sugar, beating to stiff peaks. Fold chocolate mixture into egg whites. Spread over crust. Sprinkle toffee atop. Cover; freeze 6 hours or till firm. Let stand 5 minutes before serving. Serves 9.

Frosty Strawberry Squares

  1 **cup all-purpose flour**
  ½ **cup chopped walnuts**
  ½ **cup margarine *or* butter, melted**
  ¼ **cup packed brown sugar**
  2 **egg whites**
  2 **cups sliced strawberries***
  1 **cup sugar***
  2 **tablespoons lemon juice**
  1 **cup whipping cream**   Oven 350°

For crumb mixture, combine flour, nuts, margarine, and brown sugar. Spread evenly into a shallow baking pan. Bake in a 350° oven for 20 minutes; stir occasionally. Sprinkle *two-thirds* of the crumbs into a 13x9x2-inch baking pan.

In a large mixing bowl combine egg whites, strawberries, sugar, and lemon juice. Beat with an electric mixer on high speed about 10 minutes or till stiff peaks form (tips stand straight). In a small mixing bowl beat the whipping cream till soft peaks form. Fold whipped cream into strawberry mixture. Spoon evenly over crumbs in baking pan; sprinkle remaining crumbs on top. Cover; freeze at least 6 hours or till firm. Serves 12 to 16.

Frosty Cranberry Squares: Prepare as above, *except* substitute 1½ cups ground *cranberries* for strawberries and 1 tablespoon frozen *orange juice concentrate* for lemon juice.

***Note:** If desired, use one 10-ounce package frozen sliced strawberries, partially thawed, and ⅔ cup sugar.

Easy Ice-Cream Treats

Here are two soda-shop treats you can make at home.

Saucy Scoops: Top scoops of ice cream with a sauce from the opposite page, whipped cream, and nuts.

Banana Splits: For each serving, cut a banana in half lengthwise and place in a dessert dish. Add three scoops of ice cream. Top one with marshmallow creme, one with Hot Fudge Sauce (see recipe, opposite), and one with Fruit Sauce (see recipe, opposite). Top with whipped cream, nuts, and maraschino cherries.

Ice-Cream Torte

Combine cake and ice cream in one dessert.

  1 **10¾-ounce frozen loaf pound cake**
  1 **pint peppermint, cherry, *or* chocolate ice cream**
  1 **3-ounce package cream cheese**
  2 **tablespoons margarine *or* butter**
  ½ **teaspoon vanilla**
1½ **cups sifted powdered sugar**
  ¼ **cup crushed striped round peppermint candies, crushed chocolate-covered English toffee, *or* chopped nuts**

For torte, with a serrated knife, slice pound cake horizontally into two layers.

In a chilled mixing bowl stir ice cream just to soften. Place *bottom* cake layer on a baking sheet. Spread ice cream over cake. Top with remaining cake layer. Place torte in freezer.

For frosting, in a small mixing bowl beat cream cheese, margarine or butter, and vanilla with an electric mixer on medium speed for 30 seconds or till fluffy. Gradually add powdered sugar, beating till smooth.

Remove torte from the freezer. Trim ice cream to cake edge, if necessary. Pipe or spread frosting over top and sides of torte. Freeze torte till firm.

Place frozen torte in a moisture- and vapor-proof container. Seal and label. Freeze torte for up to 6 months.

To serve, remove torte from freezer and let stand, covered, at room temperature for 10 minutes. Unwrap and place on a serving platter. Sprinkle with crushed peppermint, crushed toffee, or chopped nuts. Makes 1 torte (8 servings).

Chocolaty Velvet Ice Cream

This nutty treat needs no ice-cream freezer.

  2 **cups whipping cream**
  ½ **of a 14-ounce can (⅔ cup) sweetened condensed milk**
  ⅔ **cup chocolate-flavored syrup**
  ⅓ **cup coarsely chopped walnuts**

Combine cream, sweetened condensed milk, and chocolate syrup. Beat with an electric mixer till soft peaks form. Fold in chopped nuts. Transfer to an 8x8x2-inch pan; freeze till firm. Makes 1 quart (8 servings).

Fruit Sauce

Sweeten to taste with 1 to 2 tablespoons sugar.

- ½ **teaspoon finely shredded orange peel**
- ¼ **cup orange juice**
- 1 **tablespoon cornstarch**
- ¼ **teaspoon ground cinnamon**
- 1 **8- to 8¾-ounce can fruit (unpeeled apricot halves, pitted light sweet cherries, fruit cocktail, peach slices, pear slices, *or* crushed pineapple) *or* one 10-ounce package frozen fruit, thawed (red raspberries, strawberries, *or* peach slices)**

In a saucepan mix orange peel, orange juice, cornstarch, and cinnamon. Stir in *undrained* fruit. Cook and stir till bubbly. Cook and stir 2 minutes more. Serve over ice cream, cake, cheesecake, or crepes. Makes 1⅓ cups (6 servings).

Microwave directions: In a 4-cup measure mix orange peel and juice, cornstarch, and cinnamon. Stir in *undrained* fruit. Micro-cook, uncovered, on 100% power (high) for 3 to 5 minutes or till bubbly; stir every minute till slightly thickened, then every 30 seconds. Cook 30 seconds more.

Orange Sauce

Tastes great with gingerbread or ice cream.

- ¼ **cup sugar**
- 1 **tablespoon cornstarch**
- ¼ **teaspoon finely shredded orange peel**
- ¾ **cup orange juice**
- 2 **teaspoons margarine *or* butter**

In a saucepan combine sugar, cornstarch, and orange peel. Stir in orange juice. Cook and stir till thickened and bubbly. Cook and stir 2 minutes more. Remove from heat; stir in margarine or butter. Serve warm. Makes ¾ cup (serves 4 to 6).

Microwave directions: In a 2-cup measure mix sugar, cornstarch, and orange peel. Stir in orange juice. Micro-cook, uncovered, on 100% power (high) for 2 to 3 minutes or till bubbly; stir once. Stir in margarine. Serve warm.

Lemon Sauce: Prepare as above, *except* substitute *lemon peel* for the orange peel and ½ cup *water* plus 1 tablespoon *lemon juice* for the orange juice. Makes ⅔ cup (4 servings).

Caramel Sauce

- ½ **cup packed brown sugar**
- 1 **tablespoon cornstarch**
- ⅓ **cup light cream**
- 2 **tablespoons light corn syrup**
- 1 **tablespoon margarine *or* butter**
- ½ **teaspoon vanilla**

In a heavy saucepan mix sugar and cornstarch. Stir in ¼ cup *water*. Stir in cream and corn syrup. Cook and stir till bubbly (mixture may appear curdled). Cook and stir for 2 minutes more. Remove from heat; stir in margarine and vanilla. Serve warm or cool over ice cream, fruit, cheesecake, or cake. Makes 1 cup (8 servings).

Microwave directions: In a 2-cup measure mix sugar and cornstarch. Stir in ¼ cup *water,* then cream and corn syrup. Micro-cook, uncovered, on 100% power (high) for 2 to 3 minutes or till bubbly, stirring every minute till slightly thickened, then every 30 seconds. Stir in margarine and vanilla. Serve as above.

Hot Fudge Sauce

To reheat ½ cup of the sauce in your microwave oven, allow 15 to 30 seconds on high power.

- ¾ **cup semisweet chocolate pieces**
- ¼ **cup margarine *or* butter**
- ⅔ **cup sugar**
- 1 **5-ounce can (⅔ cup) evaporated milk**

In a heavy small saucepan melt chocolate pieces and margarine or butter. Add the sugar; gradually stir in milk. Bring to boiling; reduce heat. Boil gently over low heat for 8 minutes, stirring frequently. Remove from heat. Serve warm over ice cream. Makes about 1½ cups (8 servings).

Peanut-Butter Fudge Sauce: Prepare as above, *except,* after cooking 8 minutes, stir in ¼ cup *peanut butter.* Then remove from heat.

Rhubarb Sauce

In a saucepan mix ½ to ⅔ cup *sugar,* ¼ cup *water,* and, if desired, 1 strip orange peel. Bring to boiling. Add 3 cups of ½-inch *rhubarb* slices. Reduce heat. Cover and simmer about 5 minutes or till rhubarb is tender. Remove peel. Serve over cake or ice cream. Makes 2 cups (8 servings).

Vanilla Sauce

Delicious with fresh or poached fruit.

  2 **beaten egg yolks**
  ⅓ **cup milk *or* light cream**
  3 **tablespoons sugar**
  ½ **cup whipping cream**
  1 **teaspoon vanilla**

In a small saucepan combine yolks, milk, and sugar. Cook and stir till mixture is thickened and bubbly. Remove from heat. Cool, then chill. To serve, whip cream and vanilla to soft peaks. Fold into yolk mixture. Makes 1½ cups (12 servings).

Whiskey Sauce

Southerners traditionally ladle this sauce over bread pudding.

  ¼ **cup margarine *or* butter**
  ½ **cup sugar**
  1 **beaten egg yolk**
  2 **tablespoons water**
  2 **tablespoons bourbon**

In a small saucepan melt margarine or butter. Stir in sugar, egg yolk, and water. Cook and stir constantly over medium-low heat for 5 to 6 minutes or till sugar dissolves and mixture boils. Remove from heat and stir in bourbon. Serve warm. Makes ⅔ cup (8 servings).

Freeze-Ahead Whipped Cream

When you've whipped more cream than you need, freeze the extra. Just spoon the whipped cream into mounds on a baking sheet lined with waxed paper. Freeze till firm, then transfer the mounds to a freezer container. Freeze up to 1 month. To serve, let stand 5 minutes, then place on top of dessert.

Whipped Cream

  1 **cup whipping cream**
  2 **tablespoons sugar**
  ½ **teaspoon vanilla**

In a chilled bowl combine whipping cream, sugar, and vanilla. Beat with chilled beaters of an electric mixer on medium speed till soft peaks form. Serve with pie, fruit desserts, cake, cream puffs, and hot drinks. Makes 2 cups (8 servings).

   Flavored Whipped Cream: Prepare as above, *except* add one of the following with the vanilla: 2 tablespoons *unsweetened cocoa powder* plus *1 tablespoon* additional sugar; 2 tablespoons *amaretto or coffee, hazelnut, orange, or praline liqueur;* 1 teaspoon *instant coffee crystals;* ½ teaspoon *almond extract;* ½ teaspoon finely shredded *lemon, orange, or lime peel;* or ¼ teaspoon ground *cinnamon, nutmeg, or ginger.*

Hard Sauce

Traditionally served with steamed puddings and warm gingerbread.

  ¼ **cup margarine *or* butter, softened**
  1 **cup sifted powdered sugar**
  ½ **teaspoon vanilla**

In a small mixer bowl beat together softened margarine or butter and powdered sugar with an electric mixer on medium speed for 3 to 5 minutes or till mixture is well combined. Beat in vanilla. Spoon into serving bowl. Chill to harden. Serve with plum pudding or warm gingerbread. Makes ⅔ cup (10 to 12 servings).

   Brandy Hard Sauce: Prepare as above, *except* substitute 1 tablespoon *brandy or rum* for the vanilla.

   Orange Hard Sauce: Prepare as above, *except* substitute ¼ teaspoon finely shredded *orange peel* and 1 tablespoon *orange juice or orange liqueur* for the vanilla.

Eggs, Cheese, & Legumes

Nutrition Analysis

	Servings Per Recipe	Calories	Protein (g)	Carbohydrate (g)	Fat (g)	Cholesterol (mg)	Sodium (mg)	Potassium (mg)	Protein	Vitamin A	Vitamin C	Thiamine	Riboflavin	Niacin	Calcium	Iron
	Per Serving								**Percent U.S. RDA Per Serving**							
Asparagus-Egg Casserole (p. 147)	3	357	17	18	25	298	590	486	27	40	56	18	29	9	28	15
Bacon-Asparagus Puffy Omelet (p. 151)	2	330	20	12	23	558	852	594	31	42	57	22	31	13	10	20
Baked Eggs (p. 147)	3	267	16	2	22	564	337	150	24	19	1	6	21	0	16	12
Bean and Cheese Burritos (p. 162)	3	582	27	61	26	59	1096	787	42	14	17	14	20	7	62	29
Bean and Cheese Chimichangas (p. 162)	3	820	28	66	51	59	1096	787	43	14	17	15	21	8	64	31
Beer Rarebit (p. 160)	4	378	21	19	23	126	532	192	32	16	11	17	20	13	37	9
Blue Cheese and Bacon Puff (p. 153)	4	535	31	18	37	268	938	378	48	75	7	16	34	9	58	17
Breakfast Pizza (p. 155)	6	325	15	20	21	260	733	200	23	64	4	12	20	7	25	11
Broccoli Puff (p. 153)	4	454	27	19	30	254	647	224	41	34	15	12	27	6	49	11
Bulgur Tacos (p. 162)	4	279	13	34	12	15	882	494	19	23	24	14	11	9	24	17
California-Style Egg-Salad Sandwiches (p. 147)	2	497	21	32	31	570	729	344	33	16	5	21	30	11	22	23
Cheese Fondue (p. 158)	5	359	21	6	22	75	232	129	32	17	0	4	12	2	70	3
Cheese French Omelet (p. 150)	1	373	19	2	32	579	447	164	30	26	0	6	24	0	26	13
Cheese-Herb Puffy Omelet (p. 151)	2	391	20	8	30	576	430	284	31	28	2	10	31	2	30	14
Cheese-Onion Scrambled Eggs (p. 148)	3	279	17	3	21	570	646	213	27	19	1	7	24	0	21	12
Cheese Soufflé (p. 152)	6	465	23	10	37	339	586	229	36	29	1	9	29	2	52	10
Cheese Strata (p. 159)	6	260	15	19	14	213	673	254	22	13	3	12	23	5	29	9
Cheese-Stuffed Manicotti (p. 159)	4	577	35	39	29	142	1026	480	54	32	15	26	41	12	88	15
Cheesy Brunch Roll-Ups (p. 155)	6	394	19	26	24	234	367	341	29	18	22	12	30	8	48	15
Choose-a-Flavor Quiche (p. 154)	6	406	20	26	24	181	331	236	31	10	2	16	24	15	37	11
Cream-Cheese Scrambled Eggs (p. 148)	3	305	15	3	25	583	459	208	24	23	0	7	24	0	11	14
Creamy Cheese Fondue (p. 159)	3	429	19	4	34	103	1169	206	29	26	0	2	19	0	49	5
Creamy Lasagna (p. 159)	4	610	36	46	30	142	1026	498	56	33	11	32	43	15	88	16
Creamy Poached Eggs (p. 143)	4	323	17	18	20	321	451	173	26	18	0	12	23	5	26	12
Denver Omelet (p. 150)	2	416	23	11	31	572	859	650	36	41	113	36	36	19	8	24
Denver Scrambled Eggs (p. 148)	3	307	17	5	24	560	544	279	26	22	15	16	23	5	10	14
Deviled Eggs (p. 146)	12	73	3	1	6	140	66	35	5	3	0	1	4	0	2	3
Egg-Pita Sandwiches (p. 149)	2	364	18	26	21	429	336	229	28	17	4	15	24	6	21	17
Egg-Salad Sandwiches (p. 147)	2	416	17	31	24	558	654	257	27	16	12	20	25	10	12	22
Eggs Benedict (p. 144)	4	358	21	17	23	401	873	243	32	17	12	35	20	20	10	14
Eggs in a Puff (p. 149)	6	441	18	20	32	560	630	232	27	42	34	18	28	7	16	19
Farmer's Breakfast (p. 148)	4	372	19	16	26	431	713	638	29	21	38	27	20	13	7	15
Fettuccine with Asparagus and Swiss Cheese Sauce (p. 158)	4	455	22	55	17	39	825	580	34	28	31	43	36	23	43	16
Fettuccine with Broccoli and Cheese Sauce (p. 158)	4	438	21	55	15	39	834	492	32	38	34	40	32	20	44	15
Fettuccine with Cheese Sauce (p. 158)	4	420	19	51	15	39	819	380	29	14	5	37	29	18	41	13
French Omelet (p. 150)	1	261	12	1	23	550	540	136	19	20	0	6	18	0	6	12
Fried Eggs (p. 146)	2	192	12	1	15	550	183	132	19	14	0	6	18	0	6	12
Fried-Rice Supper (p. 162)	4	454	24	64	12	69	594	1164	36	5	8	32	13	23	13	37
Frittata (p. 151)	3	229	15	5	16	553	266	227	24	25	43	9	24	2	16	15
Fruited French Omelet (p. 150)	1	391	14	19	29	563	561	311	21	25	48	7	23	1	12	15
Garbanzo Sandwich Spread (p. 162)	5	170	5	15	10	0	115	230	10	10	20	15	5	5	10	15
Greek Frittata (p. 151)	3	259	17	5	19	567	432	435	25	79	18	11	33	3	20	20
Greek-Style Egg-Salad Sandwiches (p. 147)	2	461	20	32	28	570	785	292	30	20	9	22	33	11	19	23
Ham-and-Cheese Puffy Omelet (p. 151)	2	422	24	10	31	585	746	365	37	27	5	20	33	7	30	16
Hard-Cooked Eggs (p. 146)	3	159	12	1	11	550	139	130	19	10	0	6	18	0	6	12
Herbed Scrambled Eggs (p. 148)	3	206	13	3	16	552	375	174	20	15	0	7	21	0	9	12
Huevos Rancheros (p. 145)	3	427	23	25	27	575	547	573	35	55	50	15	29	8	38	25
Indian-Style Deviled Eggs (p. 146)	12	90	4	1	8	140	61	56	6	3	0	2	4	2	2	3
Individual Quiche Casseroles (p. 154)	4	276	20	9	18	252	342	257	31	15	3	6	25	1	54	6

On the divider: Denver Omelet (p. 150).

Nutrition Analysis

	Servings Per Recipe	Calories	Protein (g)	Carbohydrate (g)	Fat (g)	Cholesterol (mg)	Sodium (mg)	Potassium (mg)	Protein	Vitamin A	Vitamin C	Thiamine	Riboflavin	Niacin	Calcium	Iron
	Per Serving								**Percent U.S. RDA Per Serving**							
Italian-Style Deviled Eggs (p. 146)	12	64	4	1	5	138	96	34	5	3	0	1	5	0	3	3
Macaroni and Cheese (p. 160)	4	426	21	28	25	68	1016	301	32	21	3	21	28	10	51	7
Meat Cheese Strata (p. 159)	6	294	19	20	15	225	864	321	30	13	7	24	25	10	29	11
Meatless Red Beans and Rice (p. 161)	4	317	15	62	1	0	404	633	23	1	4	28	8	12	9	28
Meatless Tacos (p. 162)	4	281	14	32	12	15	886	554	22	23	24	15	12	8	24	19
Meaty Red Beans and Rice (p. 161)	4	552	31	64	19	58	925	863	47	1	17	64	17	29	9	35
Mediterranean Sandwich (p. 162)	1	421	20	44	20	28	468	463	31	19	30	25	16	13	42	26
Mexican-Style Deviled Eggs (p. 146)	12	74	3	1	7	140	88	40	5	8	2	1	4	0	2	3
Mushroom French Omelet (p. 150)	1	368	13	2	34	581	659	226	20	29	1	8	24	5	7	13
Mushroom Scrambled Eggs (p. 148)	3	280	14	4	23	552	470	235	21	22	4	8	24	3	10	13
Onion-Cheese Fondue (p. 158)	5	367	21	8	22	75	236	182	32	78	4	5	13	2	70	4
Oven Frittata (p. 151)	3	229	15	5	16	553	266	227	24	25	43	9	24	2	16	15
Poached Eggs (p. 144)	1	159	12	1	11	550	139	130	19	10	0	6	18	0	6	12
Puffy Omelet (p. 151)	2	210	12	1	17	550	206	133	19	15	0	6	18	0	6	12
Quiche Lorraine (p. 154)	6	357	10	25	24	153	364	212	16	5	7	19	18	10	10	11
Red Beans and Corn Bread (p. 161)	4	414	20	73	5	67	942	751	31	6	4	31	21	13	16	30
Scrambled-Egg Casserole (p. 149)	4	331	16	10	25	436	576	243	25	25	21	9	24	3	24	12
Scrambled Eggs (p. 148)	3	206	13	3	16	552	375	174	20	15	0	7	21	0	9	12
Shortcut Macaroni and Cheese (p. 160)	4	426	21	28	25	68	1016	301	32	21	3	21	28	10	51	7
Soft-Cooked Eggs (p. 146)	3	159	12	1	11	550	139	130	19	10	0	6	18	0	6	12
Spinach-Egg Casserole (p. 155)	4	468	27	40	22	314	820	519	42	109	11	34	39	16	46	28
Spinach Manicotti (p. 159)	4	503	27	39	25	130	1032	640	42	110	8	21	46	14	73	22
Spinach Puff (p. 153)	4	451	26	18	30	254	659	29	41	67	5	12	29	6	51	15
Vegetable Cheese Strata (p. 159)	6	267	15	21	14	213	675	296	24	20	21	13	26	6	32	11
Vegetable French Omelet (p. 150)	1	383	15	3	35	551	714	287	23	38	18	9	22	3	11	14
Vegetable Macaroni and Cheese (p. 160)	4	480	24	40	25	68	1048	454	36	99	5	25	34	13	53	11
Vegetable Soufflé (p. 153)	4	325	16	13	24	240	497	268	25	31	31	10	26	4	36	11
Welsh Rarebit Breakfast (p. 160)	4	334	23	20	18	130	637	261	35	18	15	23	23	13	42	9

Eggs, Cheese, And Legumes

Whether you're scrambling eggs, making a soufflé, or baking a meatless legume dish, our how-to pictures and directions will assure you tasty results. Many of the egg and cheese recipes include make-ahead directions, so you can serve them for breakfast with little last-minute fuss. In each of the meatless recipes, the dried beans, lentils, or legumes are matched with eggs, nuts, grains, cheese, or milk for a flavor bonus and to provide a protein-rich main dish. Be sure to refer, too, to the cheese and legume identification photos.

Creamy Poached Eggs

2 English muffins or bagels, split
¾ cup shredded American cheese
1 3-ounce package cream cheese
   with chives, cut up
½ cup milk
4 eggs

Toast muffins or bagels. In a medium skillet combine cheeses, milk, and ⅛ teaspoon *pepper*. Cook and stir over medium heat till cheeses melt.

Break *1* egg into a cup. Carefully slide egg into cheese mixture. Repeat with remaining eggs. Cover; cook over medium-low heat for 3 to 5 minutes or to desired doneness. Top *each* muffin or bagel half with an egg. Stir cheese mixture with a wire whisk. Spoon over eggs. Serves 4.

Poached Eggs

Eggs Benedict (pictured below right) makes a spectacular brunch entrée. Serve fresh fruit and sparkling water or wine to complete the menu.

Cooking oil *or* shortening (optional)
1 to 2 teaspoons instant chicken
   bouillon granules (optional)
Eggs (2 per serving)

Lightly grease a saucepan, if desired, using a 2-quart pan for 3 or 4 eggs or a 1-quart pan for 1 or 2 eggs. Add water to half-fill the pan; stir in bouillon granules, if desired. Bring water to boiling. Reduce heat to simmering (bubbles should begin to break the surface of the water).

Break *1* egg into a measuring cup. Carefully slide egg into simmering water, holding the lip of the cup as close to the water as possible. Repeat with remaining eggs, allowing each egg an equal amount of space.

Simmer eggs, uncovered, for 3 to 5 minutes or to desired doneness. Remove with a slotted spoon. Season to taste with salt and pepper.

Poacher-cup directions: Grease each cup of an egg-poaching pan. Place poacher cups over the pan of *boiling* water (water should not touch bottoms of cups). Reduce heat to simmering.

Break *1* egg into a measuring cup. Carefully slide egg into a poacher cup. Repeat with remaining eggs. Cover and cook for 4 to 6 minutes or to desired doneness. Run a knife around edges to loosen eggs. Invert poacher cups to remove eggs.

Eggs Benedict: Prepare as above, *except*, before poaching eggs, split 2 *English muffins.* Place muffin halves and 8 slices *Canadian-style bacon* on a baking sheet. Bake in a 350° oven for 10 to 15 minutes or till muffins are toasted and bacon is hot. Keep warm.

Place 4 poached eggs in a large pan of *warm* water to keep warm while preparing *half* of a recipe of *Hollandaise Sauce* (see recipe, page 362) *or half* of a recipe of *Mock Hollandaise Sauce* (see recipe, page 363).

To serve, top each muffin half with 2 slices of bacon and an egg; spoon sauce over eggs. Sprinkle with paprika and garnish with orange slices and parsley, if desired. Serves 4.

To slip the egg into the simmering water, use a measuring cup with a handle.

Lift the poached egg from the water with a slotted spoon and let it drain for a few seconds.

Huevos Rancheros

Featuring poached eggs and tortillas topped with a chili-pepper-spiked sauce, Huevos Rancheros (WEH-vohs rahn-CHEH-rohs) is one hot dish.

½ **cup chopped onion**
1 **tablespoon cooking oil**
1 **16-ounce can tomatoes, cut up**
2 **tablespoons canned diced green chili peppers, rinsed**
1 **teaspoon chili powder**
⅛ **teaspoon garlic powder**
3 **6-inch corn tortillas**
1 **teaspoon cooking oil**
6 **eggs**
¾ **cup shredded Monterey Jack, Monterey Jack with jalapeño peppers, *or* American cheese**
   Bottled hot pepper sauce Oven 350°

In a large skillet cook chopped onion in the 1 tablespoon oil till tender. Stir in *undrained* tomatoes, chili peppers, chili powder, and garlic powder. Simmer, uncovered, for 5 to 10 minutes or till slightly thickened.

Meanwhile, place tortillas on a baking sheet; brush lightly with the 1 teaspoon oil. Bake in a 350° oven about 10 minutes or till crisp.

Break *1* egg into a measuring cup. Carefully slide egg into simmering tomato mixture. Repeat with remaining eggs. Simmer gently, covered, for 3 to 5 minutes or to desired doneness.

To serve, place tortillas on 3 plates. Top *each* tortilla with *2* eggs; spoon tomato mixture over eggs. Sprinkle with cheese. Pass hot pepper sauce. Makes 3 servings.

Microwave directions: In an 8x1½-inch round baking dish micro-cook onion and 1 tablespoon *water* (omit the 1 tablespoon cooking oil), covered, on 100% power (high) for 2 to 3 minutes or till tender. Stir in *undrained* tomatoes, chili peppers, chili powder, and garlic powder. Cook, covered with vented plastic wrap, on high for 6 to 8 minutes or till boiling over entire surface, stirring twice. Break *1* egg into a cup. Carefully slide egg into tomato mixture. Repeat with remaining eggs, placing eggs around the edge of dish. Prick each yolk and each white 3 times with a toothpick. Cook, covered, on high for 3 to 5 minutes or till eggs are nearly set, giving dish a quarter-turn every minute. Let stand, covered, for 2 minutes. To warm tortillas, place between paper towels (do not brush with oil); cook on high for 15 to 20 seconds. Serve as above.

Choosing and Using Eggs

Great-tasting egg dishes depend on good-quality eggs. To be sure your eggs are always in top condition, follow these shopping, storing, and serving guidelines.

● Purchase clean, fresh eggs from refrigerated display cases. When preparing our recipes, select large eggs. Take your choice of either white eggs or brown eggs. Their nutrition content is the same.

● When you come home from the store, refrigerate the eggs promptly with the large ends up. For the best quality, use your eggs within one week. You can store them, however, as long as five weeks.

● Always discard any eggs with broken or cracked shells. They may have become contaminated with harmful bacteria called salmonella.

● Serve hot egg dishes right away.

● Refrigerate chilled egg dishes immediately after mixing, and keep them cold until serving time.

● Chill leftovers or make-ahead dishes containing eggs promptly.

Note: Some experts believe using uncooked or slightly cooked eggs in recipes such as mayonnaise, meringue pie, or Caesar salad may be harmful to some people because of possible salmonella contamination. The same is true of over-easy eggs and sunny-side-up eggs. If you are elderly, ill, or otherwise at risk, you may wish to avoid these recipes. Check with your doctor to be sure.

Soft-Cooked Eggs and Hard-Cooked Eggs

Place 6 *eggs* in saucepan. Add enough *cold* water to cover eggs. Bring to boiling over high heat. Reduce heat so water is just below simmering; cover. For soft-cooked eggs, cook 4 to 6 minutes. For hard-cooked eggs, cook 15 minutes. Drain.

For soft-cooked eggs, add *cold* water to the pan just till eggs are cool enough to handle. Cut off tops and serve in egg cups. *Or,* cut eggs in half and use a spoon to scoop the eggs into dishes.

For hard-cooked eggs, fill the saucepan with *cold* water and let stand 2 minutes. To quickly cool, add a few *ice cubes.* Drain. Gently tap each egg on the countertop. Roll egg between palms of hands. Peel off eggshell, starting at the large end. Makes 3 servings.

Deviled Eggs

Four different flavors to choose from.

6 hard-cooked eggs
¼ cup mayonnaise *or* salad dressing
1 teaspoon prepared mustard
1 teaspoon vinegar
Paprika *or* parsley sprigs (optional)

Halve hard-cooked eggs lengthwise and remove yolks. Place yolks in a bowl; mash with a fork. Add mayonnaise, mustard, and vinegar; mix well. Season with salt and pepper, if desired. Stuff egg white halves with yolk mixture. Garnish with paprika or parsley, if desired. Makes 12 servings.

Italian-Style Deviled Eggs: Prepare as above, *except* omit mayonnaise, mustard, and vinegar. Add ¼ cup *creamy Italian salad dressing* and 2 tablespoons grated *Parmesan cheese* to mashed yolks; mix well.

Indian-Style Deviled Eggs: Prepare as above, *except* omit mustard and vinegar. Add ¼ cup finely chopped *peanuts* and ½ teaspoon *curry powder* to yolk mixture; mix well.

Mexican-Style Deviled Eggs: Prepare as above, *except* omit mustard and vinegar. Add 2 tablespoons canned diced *green chili peppers,* 1 tablespoon chopped pitted *ripe olives,* ½ teaspoon *chili powder,* and ⅛ teaspoon ground *red pepper* to yolk mixture; mix well. Stuff egg whites with yolk mixture. Garnish with sliced pitted ripe olives or cilantro and serve with salsa, if desired.

Fried Eggs

No need to turn the eggs with this simple method.

2 teaspoons margarine *or* butter, *or* nonstick spray coating
4 eggs

In a large skillet melt margarine or butter over medium heat. (*Or,* spray a *cold* skillet with nonstick coating, then heat.) Add eggs. When whites are set, add 1 teaspoon *water.* Cover skillet; cook eggs to desired doneness (about 2 minutes for soft or 4 minutes for firm). Makes 2 servings.

Note: For *1 or 2* eggs, use a small skillet and *1 teaspoon* margarine or butter.

◀ To quickly make Deviled Eggs, use two spoons to fill the egg white cavities with the yolk mixture.

Or, pipe the well-mashed yolk mixture into the cavities with a large star tip and a decorating bag.

Baked Eggs

Same great poached-egg taste, but less work.

   Margarine *or* butter
 6 **eggs**
   Snipped chives *or* desired herb
 6 **tablespoons shredded cheddar,**
   Swiss, *or* Monterey Jack cheese
   (optional)   Oven 325°

Generously grease three 10-ounce casseroles with margarine. Carefully break *2* eggs into *each* casserole; sprinkle with salt, pepper, and chives or herb. Set casseroles into a 13x9x2-inch baking pan; place on an oven rack. Pour *hot* water around casseroles in pan to a depth of 1 inch.

Bake in a 325° oven about 25 minutes or till eggs are firm and whites are opaque. If desired, after 20 minutes of cooking, sprinkle cheese atop eggs. Cook for 5 to 10 minutes more or till eggs are cooked and cheese melts. Serves 3.

Egg-Salad Sandwiches

 4 **hard-cooked eggs, chopped**
 2 **tablespoons finely chopped green**
   onion
 1 **tablespoon diced pimiento**
 2 **tablespoons mayonnaise *or* salad**
   dressing
 1 **tablespoon prepared mustard *or***
   Dijon-style mustard
 4 **slices bread, *or* 2 small pita bread**
   rounds *or* 2 bagels, split
   Lettuce leaves

In a bowl combine chopped eggs, green onion, and pimiento; stir in mayonnaise and mustard. Add salt and pepper to taste. Spread egg mixture on *2* slices of bread, in pita rounds, or on bagel bottoms. Top with lettuce and, if not using pitas, remaining bread slices or bagel tops. Serves 2.

Greek-Style Egg-Salad Sandwiches: Prepare as above, *except* omit the pimiento and mustard. Stir ¼ cup crumbled *feta cheese,* ¼ cup finely chopped *tomato,* and 2 tablespoons chopped pitted *ripe olives* into egg mixture.

California-Style Egg-Salad Sandwiches: Prepare as above, *except* omit pimiento. Stir ¼ cup chopped *avocado* and ¼ cup shredded *Monterey Jack cheese* into egg mixture. Substitute *alfalfa sprouts* for lettuce.

Asparagus-Egg Casserole

Next time, try frozen chopped broccoli in place of the asparagus.

 1 **10-ounce package frozen cut**
   asparagus
 ¼ **cup chopped onion**
 ¼ **cup chopped green pepper**
 2 **tablespoons margarine *or* butter**
 2 **tablespoons all-purpose flour**
 ½ **teaspoon dry mustard**
 ¼ **teaspoon salt**
 ¼ **teaspoon pepper**
 ¾ **cup milk**
 ½ **cup shredded cheddar cheese**
 3 **hard-cooked eggs, coarsely**
   chopped
 ¼ **cup crushed rich round *or* whole**
   wheat crackers (about 6 crackers)
 2 **teaspoons margarine *or***
   butter, melted   Oven 375°

Cook asparagus according to package directions; drain. For sauce, in a medium saucepan cook onion and green pepper in the 2 tablespoons margarine till tender. Stir in flour, dry mustard, salt, and pepper. Add milk. Cook and stir till thickened and bubbly. Add cheese; stir till melted.

Reserve ¼ *cup* asparagus. Stir remaining asparagus and chopped eggs into sauce. Pour into a 1-quart casserole. Bake, covered, in a 375° oven for 10 minutes. Arrange reserved asparagus on top. Combine crushed crackers with the melted margarine. Sprinkle atop casserole. Bake, uncovered, for 10 minutes more. Serves 3.

Microwave directions: Cook asparagus according to package microwave directions; drain.

For sauce, in a 2-cup measure combine onion, green pepper, and the 2 tablespoons margarine. Micro-cook, uncovered, on 100% power (high) for 1½ to 2½ minutes or till tender. Stir in flour, dry mustard, salt, and pepper. Add milk. Stir to combine. Cook, uncovered, on high for 2 to 3 minutes or till thickened and bubbly, stirring every minute. Stir in cheese till melted.

Reserve ¼ *cup* asparagus. In a 1-quart casserole combine remaining asparagus and chopped eggs. Stir in sauce. Cook, covered, on high for 1 to 2 minutes or till heated through. Top with reserved asparagus. Combine crushed crackers with the melted margarine. Sprinkle cracker mixture atop casserole. Cook, uncovered, on high for 30 seconds more.

Scrambled Eggs

6 **eggs**
⅓ **cup milk or light cream**
1 **tablespoon margarine or butter**

In a bowl beat together eggs, milk or light cream, ¼ teaspoon *salt,* and dash *pepper.* In a large skillet melt margarine over medium heat; pour in egg mixture. Cook, without stirring, till mixture begins to set on the bottom and around edge.

Using a large spoon or spatula, lift and fold partially cooked eggs so uncooked portion flows underneath. Continue cooking over medium heat for 2 to 3 minutes or till eggs are cooked throughout but are still glossy and moist. Remove from the heat *immediately.* Serves 3.

Microwave directions: In a 1½-quart casserole micro-cook margarine on 100% power (high) for 35 to 40 seconds or till melted. Beat together eggs, milk, ¼ teaspoon *salt,* and dash *pepper.* Pour into casserole with margarine. Cook, uncovered, on high for 4 to 5 minutes or till eggs are almost set, pushing cooked portions to the center after 1½ minutes, then every 30 seconds. Let stand about 1 minute or till set.

Herbed Scrambled Eggs: Prepare as above, *except* add 1 tablespoon snipped *parsley* and ⅛ teaspoon dried *thyme,* crushed, to the beaten egg mixture.

Cream-Cheese Scrambled Eggs: Prepare as above, *except* add one 3-ounce package *cream cheese with chives,* cut into small cubes, to the beaten egg mixture.

Cheese-Onion Scrambled Eggs: Prepare as above, *except* cook 1 *green onion,* sliced, in margarine 30 seconds. Then add egg mixture. Add ½ cup shredded *American cheese* after eggs begin to set. Do not use microwave directions.

Mushroom Scrambled Eggs: Prepare as above, *except* increase margarine to *2 tablespoons.* Cook ½ cup sliced fresh *mushrooms* and 1 tablespoon chopped *onion* in margarine. Add 1 tablespoon snipped *parsley,* ½ teaspoon *dry mustard,* and ¼ teaspoon *Worcestershire sauce* to beaten egg mixture. Do not use the microwave directions.

Denver Scrambled Eggs: Prepare as above, *except* omit salt and increase margarine to *2 tablespoons.* In the skillet cook ⅓ cup diced fully cooked *ham;* ¼ cup chopped *onion;* one 2-ounce can *mushroom stems and pieces,* drained; and 2 tablespoons finely chopped *green pepper* in margarine. Then add egg mixture. Do not use the microwave directions.

Farmer's Breakfast

For a quicker breakfast, substitute frozen hash brown potatoes for the fresh potatoes.

2 **medium potatoes, peeled and finely chopped (2 cups)**
¼ **cup sliced green onion**
⅓ **cup margarine or butter**
6 **eggs**
2 **tablespoons milk**
1 **cup diced fully cooked ham**

In a large nonstick or well-seasoned skillet cook potatoes and onion in margarine over medium heat for 8 to 10 minutes or till tender; stir often.

Beat together eggs, milk, and ¼ teaspoon *pepper;* stir in ham. Pour over potato mixture. Cook, without stirring, till mixture begins to set on the bottom and around edge. Using a large spoon, lift and fold partially cooked egg mixture so uncooked portion flows underneath. Continue cooking about 4 minutes or till eggs are cooked throughout but still glossy and moist. Serves 4.

Microwave directions: In a 1½-quart casserole micro-cook onion and *2 tablespoons* margarine or butter, uncovered, on 100% power (high) for 1 minute, stirring once. Add potatoes. Cook, covered, on high for 4 to 6 minutes or till potatoes are tender, stirring once.

Beat together eggs, milk, and ¼ teaspoon *pepper;* stir in ham. Pour over potato mixture. Cook on high for 4 to 5 minutes or till eggs are almost set, pushing cooked portions to center after 1½ minutes, then every 30 seconds. Let stand about 1 minute or till eggs are set.

◄ Gently lift and fold the mixture with a spoon or spatula so the uncooked egg flows underneath.

Scrambled-Egg Casserole

Use the make-ahead directions when you know your morning is going to be busy.

1/4 **cup chopped green pepper or sliced green onion**
3 **tablespoons margarine or butter**
6 **beaten eggs**
1 **tablespoon all-purpose flour**
2/3 **cup milk**
3/4 **cup shredded American or process Swiss cheese (3 ounces)**
2 **tablespoons diced pimiento**
1/4 **cup plain or seasoned fine dry bread crumbs**   Oven 350°

In a large skillet cook green pepper or onion in *1 tablespoon* of the margarine till tender. Add eggs; cook over medium heat without stirring till mixture begins to set on bottom and around edge. Lift and fold partially cooked eggs so uncooked portion flows underneath. Continue cooking till just set. Transfer to a 1-quart casserole.

In a small saucepan melt *1 tablespoon* of the margarine. Stir in flour and 1/8 teaspoon *pepper.* Add milk all at once. Cook and stir till thickened and bubbly. Stir in cheese till melted. Stir in pimiento. Fold cheese mixture into cooked eggs.

Melt remaining margarine; toss with crumbs. Sprinkle over egg mixture. Bake in a 350° oven for 15 to 20 minutes or till hot. Serves 4.

To make ahead: Prepare as above, *except* do not bake. Cover and refrigerate casserole for 3 to 24 hours. Bake, covered, 25 minutes. Uncover; bake 10 to 15 minutes more or till hot.

Microwave directions: In a 1-quart casserole micro-cook green pepper or onion and *1 tablespoon* margarine, covered, on 100% power (high) for 1 1/2 to 2 1/2 minutes or till tender. Add beaten eggs. Cook on high for 2 1/2 to 3 1/2 minutes or till just set, pushing cooked portions to the center after 1 1/2 minutes, then every 30 seconds.

In a 2-cup measure cook *1 tablespoon* margarine on high for 35 to 40 seconds or till melted. Stir in flour and 1/8 teaspoon *pepper.* Add 1/2 *cup* milk. Stir to combine. Cook on high for 2 to 4 minutes or till thickened and bubbly, stirring every minute till mixture begins to thicken, then every 30 seconds. Add cheese; stir till melted. Stir in pimiento. Fold cheese mixture into cooked eggs. Cook remaining margarine on high for 35 to 40 seconds or till melted; toss with crumbs. Sprinkle over egg mixture. Cook on high for 2 to 3 minutes or till heated through.

Eggs in a Puff

Cheesy eggs served in a cream-puff shell.

1/2 **cup margarine or butter**
1 **cup all-purpose flour**
12 **eggs**
1/3 **cup milk**
1/2 **of a 6-ounce package frozen pea pods, thawed**
1/2 **cup chopped green or sweet red pepper**
1 **tablespoon margarine or butter**
1/2 **cup shredded cheddar or Swiss cheese (4 ounces)**   Oven 400°

For cream-puff shell, combine the 1/2 cup margarine and 1 cup *water.* Bring to boiling. Add flour and 1/8 teaspoon *salt* all at once, stirring vigorously. Cook and stir till mixture forms a ball that doesn't separate. Remove from heat. Cool 5 minutes. Add *4 eggs,* one at a time, beating with a wooden spoon after each addition till smooth. Spread over bottom and up the sides of a greased 9-inch pie plate. Bake in a 400° oven for 25 to 30 minutes or till golden brown and puffy.

Meanwhile, beat together the remaining eggs, milk, 1/4 teaspoon *salt,* and dash *pepper.* Stir in pea pods and green or red pepper. In a large skillet melt the 1 tablespoon margarine. Pour in egg mixture. Cook, without stirring, till mixture begins to set on bottom and around edge; sprinkle with cheese. Lift and fold egg mixture till eggs are cooked but still glossy and moist, and cheese melts. Spoon into baked puff shell. Serves 6.

Egg-Pita Sandwiches

In a medium skillet cook 1/3 cup sliced fresh *mushrooms* and 1/4 cup sliced *green onion or* chopped *green pepper* in 1 tablespoon *margarine or butter* till tender. In a bowl beat together 3 *eggs;* 3 tablespoons *milk;* 1/8 teaspoon dried *basil,* crushed; dash *salt;* and dash *pepper.* Pour over mushroom mixture. Cook, without stirring, till eggs begin to set on bottom and around edge. Lift and fold partially cooked eggs so uncooked portion flows underneath. Continue cooking till thoroughly cooked but still glossy and moist.

Sprinkle 1/4 cup shredded *cheddar cheese* over eggs. Remove from heat. Let stand 1 minute or till cheese melts slightly. Halve 1 *pita bread round;* spoon egg mixture into halves. Serves 2.

French Omelet

The Vegetable French Omelet with zucchini and cheddar cheese is pictured below right.

  2 eggs
  1 tablespoon water
  ⅛ teaspoon salt
  1 tablespoon margarine or butter

In a bowl combine eggs, water, salt, and dash *pepper.* Using a fork, beat till combined but not frothy. In an 8- or 10-inch skillet with flared sides, heat margarine or butter till a drop of water sizzles. Lift and tilt the pan to coat the sides.

Add egg mixture to skillet; cook over medium heat. As eggs set, run a spatula around the edge of the skillet, lifting eggs and letting uncooked portion flow underneath. When eggs are set but still shiny, remove from the heat. Fold omelet in half. Transfer onto a warm plate. Serves 1.

Microwave directions: In a bowl combine *3* eggs, *2 tablespoons* water, salt, and dash *pepper.* In a 9-inch pie plate micro-cook *1 teaspoon* margarine or butter on 100% power (high) for 30 to 40 seconds or till melted. Spread margarine to coat plate. Add egg mixture. Cook, uncovered, on high for 2½ to 3½ minutes or till eggs are set but still shiny, pushing cooked portions toward center every 30 seconds. Fold and serve as above. Serves 1 or 2.

Mushroom French Omelet: Prepare as above, *except,* for filling, cook ⅓ cup sliced fresh *mushrooms* in 1 tablespoon *margarine* till tender. Spoon across center of omelet. Fold sides over.

Cheese French Omelet: Prepare as above, *except* omit salt. For filling, sprinkle ¼ cup shredded *cheddar, Swiss, Monterey Jack, or American cheese* across center of omelet. Fold sides over. Top with shredded *cheese* and snipped *parsley.*

Fruited French Omelet: Prepare as above, *except,* for filling, spread 2 tablespoons dairy *sour cream or yogurt* across center of omelet. Fold sides over. Top omelet with ¼ cup halved *strawberries;* sliced, peeled *peaches;* or *blueberries.* Sprinkle with 1 tablespoon *brown sugar.*

Vegetable French Omelet: Prepare as above, *except,* for filling, cook ⅓ cup *vegetables* (combination of sliced *asparagus,* sliced *zucchini,* sliced *green onion,* sliced *celery,* or chopped *green pepper)* and ⅛ teaspoon dried *basil,* crushed, in 1 tablespoon *margarine.* Spoon filling across center of omelet. Sprinkle grated *Parmesan,* shredded *cheddar,* or crumbled *feta cheese* atop filling before folding omelet.

Denver Omelet

Chock-full of bright garden vegetables and ham. (Pictured on page 141.)   Oven 325°

Prepare Puffy Omelet (see recipe, opposite). Prepare filling while omelet is baking.

For filling, in a skillet melt 2 tablespoons *margarine or butter.* Add 1 cup sliced fresh *mushrooms;* 1 medium *green pepper,* chopped; 4 *green onions,* bias sliced; and ¼ teaspoon dried *basil,* crushed. Cook till tender but not brown. Stir in 3 ounces fully cooked *ham,* cut into thin 1-inch-long strips (½ cup), and ½ cup *cherry tomatoes,* halved. Heat through. Remove omelet from the oven. Fill omelet with ham mixture before folding. Makes 2 or 3 servings.

Loosen the edges of the omelet and fold one side over the filling. Repeat with the other side.

Slide the omelet to the edge of the skillet. Tilt the skillet and gently push the omelet onto the plate.

Puffy Omelet

4 **egg whites**
4 **egg yolks, beaten**
1 **tablespoon margarine**
   or **butter**   Oven 325°

In a bowl beat egg whites till frothy. Add 2 table-spoons *water;* continue beating about 1½ minutes or till stiff peaks form (tips stand straight). Fold egg yolks into egg whites.

In a large ovenproof skillet heat margarine till a drop of water sizzles. Pour in egg mixture, mounding it slightly higher at the sides. Cook over low heat for 8 to 10 minutes or till puffed, set, and golden brown on the bottom. Then bake in a 325° oven for 8 to 10 minutes or till a knife inserted near the center comes out clean. Loosen sides of omelet with a metal spatula. Make a shallow cut slightly off center across the omelet. Fold smaller side over the larger side. Serves 2.

Cheese-Herb Puffy Omelet: Prepare as above, *except,* while omelet is baking, melt 1 tablespoon *margarine or butter* in a saucepan. Stir in 1 tablespoon all-purpose *flour,* 1 teaspoon snipped *chives,* and ¼ teaspoon dried *fines herbes,* crushed. Add ⅔ cup *milk.* Cook and stir till thickened and bubbly. Cook and stir 1 minute more. Stir in ⅓ cup shredded *cheddar or Swiss cheese* till melted. Pour over folded omelet.

Ham-and-Cheese Puffy Omelet: Prepare as above, *except,* while omelet is baking, melt 1 tablespoon *margarine or butter* in a saucepan. Stir in 1 tablespoon *all-purpose flour.* Add ⅔ cup *milk.* Cook and stir till thickened and bubbly. Cook and stir 1 minute more. Stir in ⅓ cup shredded *cheddar or Swiss cheese* till melted. Stir in ¼ cup diced fully cooked *ham* and one 2-ounce jar sliced *mushrooms,* drained. Heat through. Pour over folded omelet.

Bacon-Asparagus Puffy Omelet: Prepare as above, *except* place one 10-ounce package frozen cut *asparagus* in a colander. Run *hot* water over asparagus till thawed; drain. Stir together ¼ cup *cold water,* 1 tablespoon *soy sauce,* and 2 teaspoons *cornstarch;* set aside.

In a skillet cook 2 slices *bacon* till crisp; drain, reserving drippings. Crumble bacon; set aside. Cook ¼ cup chopped *onion* in drippings over medium heat till tender. Add asparagus; cook and stir for 3 minutes. Stir soy sauce mixture; add to skillet. Cook and stir till thickened and bubbly. Cook and stir 2 minutes more. Add bacon; spoon atop omelet before folding.

Frittata

An open-face omelet that's easy to whip up for a quick supper or breakfast.

6 **eggs**
¼ **cup chopped onion**
1 **clove garlic, minced**
1 **tablespoon margarine *or* butter**
¾ **cup chopped cooked vegetables**
   or **meat**
2 **tablespoons grated Parmesan**
   or **Romano cheese**

In a bowl beat eggs and ⅛ teaspoon *pepper;* set aside. In a 10-inch broilerproof or regular skillet cook onion and garlic in margarine or butter till tender. Stir in chopped vegetables or meat.

Pour egg mixture into skillet over vegetables or meat. Cook over medium heat. As mixture sets, run a spatula around edge of skillet, lifting egg mixture to allow uncooked portions to flow underneath. Continue cooking and lifting edges till egg mixture is almost set (surface will be moist).

Place broilerproof skillet under the broiler 4 to 5 inches from the heat. Broil for 1 to 2 minutes or till top is just set. (*Or,* if using a regular skillet, remove skillet from the heat; cover and let stand 3 to 4 minutes or till top is set.) Sprinkle with Parmesan cheese. Cut into wedges. Serves 3.

Microwave directions: In a 9-inch pie plate combine onion, garlic, and margarine. Micro-cook on 100% power (high) for 1 to 2 minutes or till onion is tender, stirring once. Stir in vegetables or meat. (If vegetables or meat are cold, cook mixture on high about 1 minute or till hot.) In a bowl beat together eggs and pepper. Pour into pie plate over hot vegetable or meat mixture. Cook on high for 3 to 5 minutes or till eggs are set but still shiny, lifting cooked edges every minute and letting uncooked portions flow underneath. Sprinkle with Parmesan cheese. Let stand for 5 minutes. Cut into wedges.

Greek Frittata: Prepare as above, *except* substitute 4 cups torn *fresh spinach* for the chopped cooked vegetables or meat. After adding spinach to onion and garlic in the skillet, cook for 2 to 3 minutes more or till spinach is limp. Substitute ½ cup crumbled *feta cheese* for Parmesan cheese. Do not use microwave directions.

Oven Frittata: Prepare as above, *except* use an *ovenproof* skillet. After pouring egg mixture into the skillet, bake in a 350° oven about 15 minutes or till a knife inserted near the center comes out clean.

Cheese Soufflé

Choose from four cheeses to make this melt-in-your-mouth dish.

 6 **tablespoons margarine *or* butter**
 ⅓ **cup all-purpose flour**
    Dash ground red pepper
1½ **cups milk**
 3 **cups shredded cheddar, process
    Swiss, Colby, *or* Havarti cheese
    (12 ounces)**
 6 **egg yolks**
 6 **egg whites**   Oven 350°

Fold some of the stiffly beaten egg whites into the cheese sauce to make the sauce lighter.

Measure enough foil to wrap around a 2-quart soufflé dish with 6 inches to spare. Fold foil into thirds lengthwise. Lightly butter one side. With buttered side in, position foil around dish, letting it extend 2 inches above the top. Fasten the foil.

For cheese sauce, in a saucepan melt margarine or butter; stir in flour and red pepper. Add milk all at once. Cook and stir till thickened and bubbly. Remove from the heat. Add cheese, *1 cup* at a time, stirring till melted. In a bowl beat yolks with a fork till combined. *Slowly* add cheese sauce to yolks, stirring constantly. Cool slightly.

In a bowl beat *egg whites* till stiff peaks form (tips stand straight). Gently fold about *2 cups* of the stiffly beaten whites into cheese sauce.

Gradually pour cheese sauce over remaining stiffly beaten whites, folding to combine. Pour into the *ungreased* soufflé dish. Bake in a 350° oven about 50 minutes or till a knife inserted near the center comes out clean. Gently peel off foil; serve soufflé *immediately.* Makes 6 servings.

Gradually pour the cheese sauce over the remaining egg whites. Fold the mixtures together.

Fit a foil collar around the top of the dish to support the high soufflé during cooking.

To serve, insert two forks into the soufflé and gently pull the soufflé apart.

Vegetable Soufflé

Puffs nicely in either a 10x6x2-inch dish or a soufflé dish.

- ¼ **cup chopped onion**
- 1 **clove garlic, minced**
- 3 **tablespoons margarine** *or* **butter**
- ¼ **cup all-purpose flour**
- ¾ **teaspoon fresh marjoram, basil, dill, or tarragon, snipped;** *or* **¼ teaspoon dried herb, crushed**
- ¼ **teaspoon salt**
- ⅛ **teaspoon pepper**
- 1 **cup milk**
- 1 **cup shredded cheddar** *or* **Swiss cheese (4 ounces)**
- 1 **cup finely chopped cooked broccoli, cauliflower, asparagus, carrot,** *or* **spinach**
- 3 **egg yolks**
- 3 **egg whites**   Oven 350°

In a medium saucepan cook onion and garlic in margarine or butter till tender. Stir in flour, desired herb, salt, and pepper. Add milk all at once. Cook and stir till thickened and bubbly. Remove from heat. Add shredded cheese and stir till melted. Stir in broccoli, cauliflower, asparagus, carrot, or spinach.

In a bowl beat egg yolks with a fork till combined. Gradually add vegetable mixture, stirring constantly. Set aside.

In a bowl beat egg whites till stiff peaks form (tips stand straight). Gently fold about *1 cup* of the beaten egg whites into vegetable mixture to lighten it. Gradually pour vegetable mixture over remaining beaten egg whites, folding to combine. Pour into an *ungreased* 1½-quart soufflé dish or a 10x6x2-inch baking dish.

Bake in a 350° oven about 40 minutes for the soufflé dish (25 to 30 minutes for the 10x6x2-inch baking dish) or till a knife inserted near the center comes out clean. Serve soufflé *immediately*. Makes 4 servings.

Spinach Puff

Serve this soufflélike dish as an entrée, or as a side dish with fish or roast beef.

- ½ **of a 10-ounce package frozen chopped spinach, thawed**
- 4 **teaspoons fine dry bread crumbs**
- 1 **cup cream-style cottage cheese**
- 3 **eggs**
- 1½ **cups shredded Swiss** *or* **cheddar cheese (6 ounces)**
- ½ **cup all-purpose flour**
- ¼ **cup margarine** *or* **butter, melted**
- ¼ **teaspoon onion salt**
- ⅛ **teaspoon finely shredded lemon peel**   Oven 350°

Drain spinach well in a colander, pressing out liquid with a spoon. Grease a 1-quart soufflé dish or casserole; sprinkle with crumbs. Set aside.

In a bowl, blender container, or food processor bowl, combine cottage cheese and eggs. Add shredded cheese, flour, margarine, onion salt, and peel. Beat with an electric mixer, or cover and blend or process till smooth. Stir in spinach.

Transfer mixture to the prepared dish. Bake in a 350° oven about 1 hour or till a knife inserted near the center comes out clean. Makes 4 main-dish servings or 8 side-dish servings.

Broccoli Puff: Prepare as above, *except* substitute frozen chopped *broccoli* for the spinach. Cook broccoli in boiling water for 4 to 5 minutes or till crisp-tender; drain well.

Blue Cheese and Bacon Puff: Prepare as above, *except* add ⅓ cup crumbled *blue cheese* with the shredded cheese. Stir in 4 slices crisp-cooked, crumbled *bacon* with the spinach.

Serving a Soufflé

A soufflé makes a great entrée when you're entertaining because it bakes for almost an hour, giving you time to socialize. Just make the salad and side dishes ahead, then pop the soufflé into the oven when your guests arrive.

Just before the soufflé finishes baking, gather everyone around the table. Then present the spectacular dish.

Choose-a-Flavor Quiche

Mix and match the meat and cheese to suit your fancy, or rely on the classic bacon and Swiss cheese combination in Quiche Lorraine.

> **Pastry for Single-Crust Pie (see recipe, page 293)**
> 3 **beaten eggs**
> 1½ **cups milk**
> ¼ **cup sliced green onion**
> ¼ **teaspoon salt**
> ⅛ **teaspoon pepper**
> **Dash ground nutmeg**
> ¾ **cup chopped cooked chicken, crabmeat, *or* ham**
> 1½ **cups shredded Swiss, cheddar, Monterey Jack, *or* Havarti cheese (6 ounces)**
> 1 **tablespoon all-purpose flour**

Oven 450°

Prepare Pastry for Single-Crust Pie. Line the un-pricked pastry shell with a double thickness of heavy-duty foil. Bake in a 450° oven for 5 minutes. Remove foil. Bake for 5 to 7 minutes more or till pastry is nearly done. Remove from the oven. Reduce oven temperature to 325°.

Meanwhile, in a bowl stir together eggs, milk, onion, salt, pepper, and nutmeg. Stir in chicken, crabmeat, or ham. Toss together shredded cheese and flour. Add to egg mixture; mix well.

Pour egg mixture into *hot* pastry shell. Bake in the 325° oven for 35 to 40 minutes or till a knife inserted near the center comes out clean. If necessary, cover edge of crust with foil to prevent over-browning. Let stand for 10 minutes. Serves 6.

Quiche Lorraine: Prepare as above, *except* omit green onion and chicken, crabmeat, or ham. Cook 6 slices *bacon* till crisp. Drain, reserving *2 tablespoons* drippings. Crumble bacon; set aside. Cook 1 medium *onion,* sliced, in drippings over medium heat till tender; drain. Add bacon, onion, and *Swiss-cheese*-flour mixture to egg mixture.

Individual Quiche Casseroles: Prepare as above, *except* omit pastry and chicken, crabmeat, or ham. Pour egg mixture into *four 10-ounce custard cups.* Place custard cups in a 13x9x2-inch baking pan on an oven rack. Pour *boiling* water around cups in the pan to a depth of 1 inch. Bake in a 325° oven for 20 to 25 minutes or till a knife inserted near centers comes out clean. Serves 4.

Choose-a-Flavor Quiche with ham

Spinach-Egg Casserole

  2 **tablespoons margarine or butter**
  2 **tablespoons all-purpose flour**
  1 **cup milk**
  1 **cup shredded American cheese**
  1 **10-ounce package frozen chopped
      spinach, thawed and well drained**
  ½ **cup chopped fully cooked ham**
  4 **hard-cooked eggs, halved**
  4 **English muffins, split and toasted,
      or toast points**   Oven 350°

For sauce, in a medium saucepan melt margarine. Stir in flour and ⅛ teaspoon *pepper*. Add milk. Cook and stir till thickened and bubbly. Add cheese. Cook and stir till cheese melts. Measure ⅔ *cup* sauce; set aside. Stir spinach and ham into sauce in the saucepan. Pour into a 1½-quart casserole. Place eggs atop mixture, pressing lightly. Pour reserved sauce over eggs. Bake in a 350° oven about 30 minutes or till heated through. Serve over muffins or toast. Serves 4.

To make ahead: Prepare as above, *except* do not bake. Cover casserole and refrigerate 2 to 24 hours. Bake, covered, in a 350° oven for 50 to 55 minutes or till heated through.

Breakfast Pizza

                               Oven 375°

For crust, unroll 1 package (8) refrigerated *crescent rolls;* separate into triangles. Place triangles on a lightly greased 12-inch pizza pan with points toward center. Press triangles together to cover bottom and ½ inch up sides of pan. Bake in a 375° oven for 10 to 12 minutes or till lightly browned. (Do not remove crust from the oven.)

Meanwhile, combine 5 beaten *eggs;* ¼ cup *milk;* ¼ teaspoon dried *oregano,* crushed; and ⅛ teaspoon *pepper.* When crust is lightly browned, leave on oven shelf (if necessary, press down any high spots in crust). Carefully pour egg mixture onto crust. Bake for 8 to 10 minutes more or till egg mixture is almost set.

Sprinkle with 1½ cups desired vegetables (sliced pitted *ripe olives;* sliced *avocado, green onion, or mushrooms;* or chopped *tomato*).

Sprinkle with 1½ cups shredded *cheddar, Swiss, or mozzarella cheese;* diced fully cooked *ham;* or chopped cooked *turkey or chicken.* Return to the oven and bake 3 to 5 minutes more or till cheese melts. Cut into wedges. Serves 6.

Cheesy Brunch Roll-Ups

  2   **cups sliced fresh mushrooms**
  ½   **cup sliced green onion**
  ½   **cup chopped green pepper**
  2   **tablespoons margarine or butter**
  8   **7-inch flour tortillas**
  1½ **cups shredded cheddar cheese**
  4   **beaten eggs**
  2   **cups milk**
  1   **tablespoon all-purpose flour**
  ¼   **teapoon garlic powder**
      Few drops bottled hot pepper sauce
  ½   **cup shredded cheddar
       cheese**   Oven 350°

In a saucepan cook mushrooms, onion, and green pepper in margarine till tender. Drain. Dividing mushroom mixture evenly, spoon along center of *each* tortilla. Divide the 1½ cups cheese among the tortillas. Roll up tortillas and place, seam side down, in a greased 12x7½x2-inch baking dish. In a bowl stir together eggs, milk, flour, garlic powder, and pepper sauce. Pour over rolled-up tortillas.

Bake in a 350° oven for 35 to 40 minutes or till set. Sprinkle the ½ cup cheese over top. Let stand 10 minutes. Cut into 6 squares. Serves 6.

To make ahead: Prepare as above, *except* do not bake. Cover and refrigerate 2 to 24 hours. Bake, uncovered, in a 350° oven for 45 to 50 minutes or till set.

When to Use Natural or Process Cheese

Whether to use natural or process cheese for a dish can sometimes be confusing. In our recipes, we specifically call for process cheese when we have found that it is necessary for easy, smooth melting. If the word "process" is not mentioned in the ingredient list (for example, ½ cup shredded Swiss cheese), you can use either process cheese or natural cheese successfully.

Cheeses

Soft

These cheeses range in texture from soft and smooth to grainy and dry.

Feta

Brie

Camembert

Boursin

Gourmandise

Ricotta

Chevret or chèvre

Cream cheese

Neufchâtel

Farmer cheese

Cottage cheese

Semisoft

These white or yellow cheeses are mild to mellow in flavor. They are used in cooking, salads, and desserts.

Havarti

Mozzarella

Scamorza

Brick

Monterey Jack

Muenster

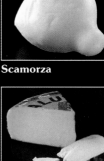
Port du Salut

Bel Paese

Fontina

Colby-Monterey Jack

American

Semisoft To Hard

These mild cheeses are usually compact and chewy in texture.

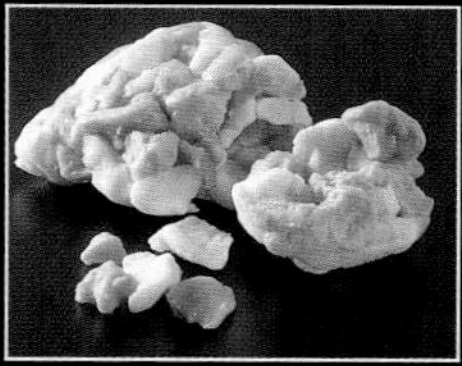

Curd cheese

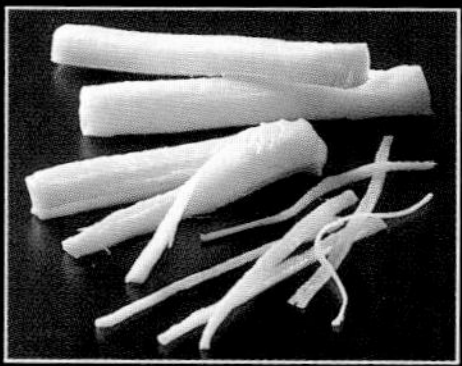

String cheese

Edam

Blue-Veined

Crumbly and pleasantly sharp or pungent, these cheeses are used in salads, dips, and cooking.

Gorgonzola

Roquefort

Blue cheese

Hard

Smooth textured, the cheeses in this category are used in recipes or sliced for snacking.

Asiago

Cheddar

Cheshire

Colby

Gjetost

Gloucester

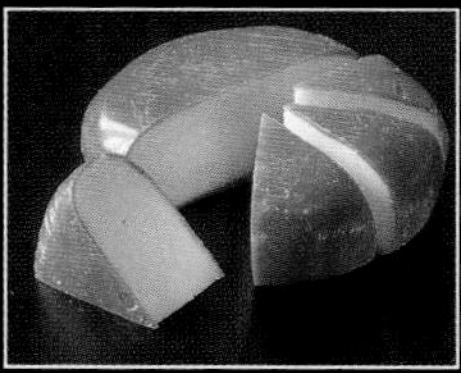

Gouda

Gruyère

Jarlsberg

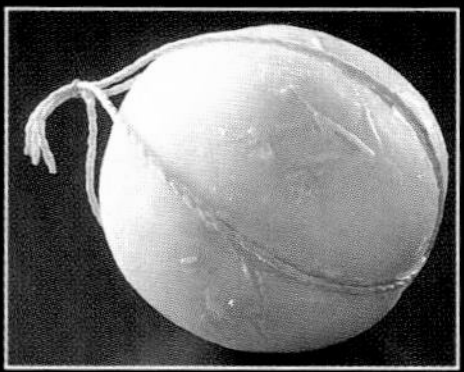

Provolone

Swiss

Very Hard

Sharp and granular, these cheeses are usually grated for cooking or for seasoning.

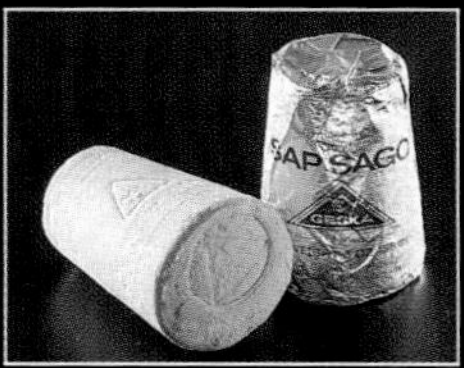

Sapsago

Parmesan

Romano

Fettuccine with Cheese Sauce

Elegant for entertaining.

  8 **ounces packaged fettuccine, linguine, *or* egg noodles**
  ½ **cup chopped onion**
  1 **or 2 cloves garlic, minced**
  1 **tablespoon margarine *or* butter**
  1 **tablespoon all-purpose flour**
  ½ **teaspoon instant chicken bouillon granules**
  ¼ **teaspoon pepper**
  1 **cup milk**
 1½ **cups shredded process Swiss, Gruyère, *or* American cheese (6 ounces)**
  2 **tablespoons snipped parsley Freshly ground pepper**

Cook fettuccine according to package directions (or see chart, page 278). Drain; keep warm.

For cheese sauce, in a saucepan cook onion and garlic in margarine till tender. Stir in flour, bouillon granules, and the ¼ teaspoon pepper. Add milk all at once. Cook and stir till thickened and bubbly. Cook and stir 1 minute more.

Stir in cheese. Cook and stir till cheese melts. Stir in parsley. If cheese sauce is too thick, stir in 1 to 2 tablespoons additional *milk*.

Serve cheese sauce over hot cooked pasta. Sprinkle with freshly ground pepper. Serves 4.

Microwave directions: Cook fettuccine as above. For cheese sauce, in a 4-cup measure micro-cook onion, garlic, and margarine or butter on 100% power (high) for 1½ to 2 minutes or till onion is tender. Stir in flour, bouillon granules, and the ¼ teaspoon pepper. Add milk. Stir to combine. Cook on high for 3 to 5 minutes or till thickened and bubbly, stirring every minute till the sauce starts to thicken, then every 30 seconds. Cook for 30 seconds more. Add cheese; stir till melted. If necessary, cook on high for 15 to 30 seconds or till cheese melts. Serve as above.

Fettuccine with Broccoli and Cheese Sauce: Prepare as above, *except* add one 10-ounce package frozen chopped *broccoli* to pasta after it has simmered for 5 minutes.

Fettuccine with Asparagus and Swiss Cheese Sauce: Prepare as above, *except* add one 10-ounce package frozen cut *asparagus* to pasta after it has simmered for 5 minutes. For sauce, use the process Swiss cheese. Substitute 2 tablespoons toasted sliced *almonds* for the freshly ground pepper.

Cheese Fondue

Also makes a great appetizer.

  3 **cups coarsely shredded Gruyère *or* Swiss cheese (12 ounces)**
  2 **tablespoons all-purpose flour**
  1 **clove garlic, halved**
 1¼ **cups dry white wine***
  1 **tablespoon kirsch *or* dry sherry**
       Dash ground nutmeg
       Dash pepper
       Dippers (cubed French *or* Italian bread *or* raw vegetables)

Bring shredded Gruyère or Swiss cheese to room temperature. Toss flour with cheese; set aside. Rub inside of a fondue pot with garlic halves; discard garlic. Set pot aside.

In a medium saucepan heat wine over medium heat till small bubbles rise to surface. Just before wine boils, reduce heat to low and stir in cheese mixture, a little at a time, stirring *constantly* and making sure cheese melts before adding more. Stir till mixture bubbles gently.

Stir in kirsch or sherry, nutmeg, and pepper. Transfer cheese mixture to the fondue pot; keep mixture bubbling gently over a fondue burner. Serve with bread cubes or raw vegetables. Makes 5 servings.

Onion-Cheese Fondue: Prepare as above, *except* stir ½ cup sliced *green onion* and ½ cup shredded *carrot* into the cheese mixture with the kirsch or sherry.

*****Note:** For a milder flavor, substitute ¼ cup *chicken broth or water* for *¼ cup* of the wine.

Creamy Cheese Fondue

If you don't have a fondue pot, just serve this creamy fondue from a casserole dish.

  ⅔ **cup dry white wine *or* apple juice**
  2 **cups shredded American cheese**
  ⅛ **teaspoon dry mustard**
  1 **3-ounce package cream cheese with chives, softened**
     Dippers (breadsticks, cubed French bread, fruit wedges, *or* vegetables)

In a medium saucepan heat wine or juice just till bubbling. Add American cheese and mustard, stirring till smooth and bubbly. Stir in cream cheese; cook and stir over low heat till smooth. Transfer mixture to a fondue pot. If desired, keep cheese mixture bubbling gently over a fondue burner. Serve with dippers. Serves 3.

Microwave directions: In 1-quart casserole mix ½ *cup* wine or juice, American cheese, mustard, and cream cheese. Micro-cook on 100% power (high) for 4 to 5 minutes or till melted and bubbly; stir every minute. Serve as above.

Cheese Strata

  6 **slices bread, halved diagonally**
  5 **1-ounce slices American *or* Swiss cheese**
  4 **eggs**
  2 **cups milk**
  ⅓ **cup sliced green onion**
  2 **teaspoons prepared mustard *or* Dijon-style mustard**
     Paprika   Oven 325°

In a greased 8x8x2-inch baking dish layer *8* bread-slice halves, the cheese slices, then the remaining bread-slice halves. Beat eggs; stir in milk, onion, mustard, ¼ teaspoon *salt,* and ¼ teaspoon *pepper.* Pour over bread and cheese layers. Sprinkle with paprika. Cover; chill in the refrigerator for 2 to 24 hours. Bake, uncovered, in a 325° oven for 45 to 50 minutes or till set and lightly browned. Let stand 10 minutes. Serves 6.

Vegetable Cheese Strata: Prepare as above, *except* layer 1 cup chopped cooked *broccoli or carrot* atop cheese slices.

Meat Cheese Strata: Prepare as above, *except* layer 1 cup diced fully cooked *ham or* 1 cup diced cooked *chicken or turkey* atop cheese slices. (If using ham, omit salt.)

Cheese-Stuffed Manicotti

  8 **manicotti shells**
  ¼ **cup sliced green onion**
  1 **clove garlic, minced**
  2 **tablespoons margarine *or* butter**
  2 **tablespoons all-purpose flour**
 1⅓ **cups milk**
  1 **cup shredded process Swiss cheese**
  ¼ **cup dry white wine**
  1 **beaten egg**
  1 **cup ricotta cheese**
  1 **cup shredded mozzarella cheese**
  ½ **cup grated Parmesan cheese**
  ⅓ **cup snipped parsley**
  ¼ **teaspoon finely shredded lemon peel**
  ⅛ **teaspoon ground nutmeg**   Oven 350°

Cook manicotti according to package directions (or see chart, page 278); drain. For sauce, in a saucepan cook onion and garlic in margarine till tender. Stir in flour. Add milk all at once. Cook and stir till thickened and bubbly. Add Swiss cheese and wine; stir till cheese melts.

In a bowl stir together egg, ricotta cheese, mozzarella cheese, Parmesan cheese, parsley, peel, and nutmeg. Fill manicotti with ricotta mixture. Arrange in a 12x7½x2-inch baking dish. Pour sauce over filled shells. Cover and bake in a 350° oven for 35 to 40 minutes or till hot. Serves 4.

Microwave directions: Cook manicotti as above. For sauce, in a 4-cup measure combine onion, garlic, and margarine. Micro-cook on 100% power (high) for 1½ to 2½ minutes or till onion is tender. Stir in flour. Add *1 cup* milk. Stir. Cook on high for 3 to 5 minutes or till thickened and bubbly, stirring every minute till sauce starts to thicken, then every 30 seconds. Add Swiss cheese and wine; stir till cheese melts.

Fill manicotti as above. Pour sauce atop. Cook, covered with vented clear plastic wrap, on high for 4 to 6 minutes or till heated through, turning dish once.

Spinach Manicotti: Prepare as above, *except* reduce ricotta to ½ *cup.* Omit mozzarella and parsley. Add ½ *cup* crumbled *feta cheese* and one 10-ounce package frozen chopped *spinach,* thawed and drained, to ricotta mixture.

Creamy Lasagna: Prepare as above, *except* substitute 8 *lasagna noodles* for the manicotti. Spread ¼ *cup* ricotta mixture over each cooked lasagna noodle. Roll up noodles and place, seam side down, in an 8x8x2-inch baking dish.

Macaroni and Cheese

For homemade flavor in a hurry, try the Shortcut Macaroni and Cheese.

> 1 **cup elbow macaroni (4 ounces)**
> ¼ **cup chopped onion**
> 1 **tablespoon margarine *or* butter**
> 1 **tablespoon all-purpose flour**
>   **Dash pepper**
> 1¼ **cups milk**
> 2 **cups shredded American cheese (8 ounces)**
> 1 **medium tomato, sliced (optional)**   Oven 350°

Cook macaroni according to package directions (or see chart, page 278); drain well.

Meanwhile, for cheese sauce, in a saucepan cook onion in margarine or butter till tender but not brown. Stir in flour and pepper. Add milk all at once. Cook and stir till slightly thickened and bubbly. Add shredded cheese; stir till melted.

Stir macaroni into cheese sauce. Transfer to a 1-quart casserole. Bake, uncovered, in a 350° oven for 25 to 30 minutes or till bubbly. During the last 5 minutes of baking, arrange tomato slices atop macaroni, if desired. Let stand 10 minutes. Makes 4 servings.

Microwave directions: Cook macaroni as above. For cheese sauce, in a *1½-quart* casserole micro-cook onion and margarine or butter on 100% power (high) for 1 to 2 minutes or till onion is tender. Stir in flour and pepper. Stir in *1 cup* milk.

Cook on high for 3 to 5 minutes or till slightly thickened and bubbly, stirring every minute. Stir in cheese; cook on high for 1 minute. Stir till cheese melts. Stir in cooked macaroni. Cook on high for 2½ to 3½ minutes or till heated through, stirring once. If desired, place tomato slices atop macaroni during the last minute of cooking. Let stand 10 minutes.

Vegetable Macaroni and Cheese: Prepare as above, *except* stir 2 cups frozen *mixed vegetables*, thawed, *or* one 16-ounce can *mixed vegetables*, drained, into cheese sauce with macaroni. Transfer to a *1½-quart* casserole.

Shortcut Macaroni and Cheese: Prepare as above, *except immediately* return the drained macaroni to the saucepan it was cooked in. Pour the cheese sauce over the macaroni; mix well. Cook over low heat for 3 to 5 minutes or till heated through, stirring frequently. Let stand for 10 minutes.

Welsh Rarebit Breakfast

This tangy cheese sauce also is good served over broccoli, cauliflower, and burgers.

> 2 **English muffins, split and toasted, *or* 4 slices bread, toasted**
> 4 **slices Canadian-style bacon, warmed, *or* 4 poached eggs (see recipe, page 144)**
> 4 **slices tomato**
> 1½ **cups shredded cheddar *or* American cheese (6 ounces)**
> ¾ **cup milk**
> 1 **teaspoon dry mustard**
> ½ **teaspoon Worcestershire sauce**
>   **Dash ground red pepper**
> 1 **beaten egg**

For English muffin or toast stacks, place muffin halves or toast slices on plates. Top *each* with a slice of Canadian-style bacon, then a tomato slice; or, if using poached eggs, top muffins or toast with tomato slices, then eggs. Set aside.

For cheese sauce, in a heavy medium saucepan combine cheese, milk, mustard, Worcestershire sauce, and red pepper. Cook over low heat, stirring constantly, till cheese melts.

Slowly stir about *half* of the hot cheese sauce into beaten egg; return all to the saucepan. Cook and stir over low heat till cheese sauce thickens slightly and just bubbles.

Serve cheese sauce *immediately* over English muffin or toast stacks. Makes 4 servings.

Microwave directions: Assemble English muffin or toast stacks as above. For sauce, in a 1-quart casserole combine cheese, milk, mustard, Worcestershire sauce, and red pepper. Micro-cook, covered, on 100% power (high) for 3 to 4 minutes or till cheese melts, stirring every minute.

Slowly stir about *half* of the hot cheese mixture into beaten egg; return all to casserole. Cook on 50% power (medium) for 1 to 3 minutes or till mixture thickens slightly and just bubbles, stirring every 30 seconds. Serve as above.

Beer Rarebit: Prepare as above, *except* substitute 8 slices crisp-cooked *bacon,* drained and halved crosswise, for the Canadian-style bacon or poached eggs. Substitute *beer* for the milk.

Legumes

Red kidney beans   Pinto beans   Navy beans   Black-eyed peas

Large lima beans   Red beans   Garbanzo beans   Soybeans

Lentils   Black beans   Split peas, yellow and green   Great northern beans

Meatless Red Beans and Rice

Adjust the amount of ground red pepper to give this dish the zing you like.

  1⅛ **cups dry red beans *or* dry red kidney beans (½ pound)**
  ½ **cup chopped onion**
  2 **cloves garlic, minced**
  1 **bay leaf**
  ¾ **teaspoon salt**
  ½ **teaspoon fennel seed, crushed**
  ¼ **to ½ teaspoon ground red pepper**
  2 **cups hot cooked rice**

Rinse beans. In a large saucepan combine beans and 3 cups *water*. Bring to boiling; reduce heat. Simmer for 2 minutes. Remove from heat. Cover and let stand 1 hour. (*Or,* soak by placing beans and 3 cups *water* in a bowl. Cover and set in a cool place for 6 to 8 hours or overnight.)

Drain beans in a colander and rinse. Return beans to the saucepan. Stir in onion, garlic, bay leaf, salt, fennel seed, red pepper, and 3 cups *fresh* water. Bring to boiling; reduce heat. Cover and simmer about 2½ hours or till beans are tender, adding more water, if necessary, and stirring occasionally.

Uncover and simmer, stirring occasionally, for 15 to 20 minutes more or till a thick gravy forms. Discard bay leaf. Serve over rice. Serves 4.

Meaty Red Beans and Rice: Prepare as above, *except* omit salt and fennel seed. Add ½ pound smoked *pork hocks or* meaty *ham bone* with onion. When beans are tender, remove hocks or ham bone. Cut meat from bones or bone. Discard bones or bone and return meat to bean mixture along with ½ pound smoked *sausage,* cut into bite-size pieces.

Red Beans and Corn Bread: Prepare as above, *except* omit rice and spoon bean mixture over squares of *corn bread.*

Meatless Tacos

¼ cup lentils
¼ cup chopped onion
1 8-ounce can tomato sauce
½ of a 1⅛- or 1¼-ounce envelope (5 teaspoons) taco seasoning mix
8 ounces tofu (fresh bean curd), drained and finely chopped
8 taco shells, warmed
1½ cups shredded lettuce
1 medium tomato, chopped
½ cup shredded cheddar cheese
Salsa

Rinse lentils; drain. In a medium saucepan combine lentils, onion, and ½ cup *water.* Bring to boiling; reduce heat. Cover and simmer about 30 minutes or till tender and liquid is absorbed.

Stir tomato sauce and seasoning mix into lentils. Simmer, uncovered, for 5 minutes. Stir in tofu; heat through. Spoon into taco shells. Top with lettuce, tomato, cheese, and salsa. Serves 4.

Bulgur Tacos: Prepare as above, *except* substitute *bulgur* for lentils. Cover and simmer bulgur, onion, and ¾ cup *water* about 10 minutes or till tender and liquid is absorbed.

Fried-Rice Supper

The rice is chilled to keep it from sticking.

1 teaspoon margarine *or* butter
1 beaten egg
5 green onions, sliced (⅓ cup)
1 clove garlic, minced
1 tablespoon margarine *or* butter
1½ cups cooked brown rice, chilled
1 15-ounce can dark red kidney beans, drained
2 tablespoons soy sauce
1 tablespoon dry sherry
¼ teaspoon sesame oil
Dash ground red pepper
⅓ cup coarsely chopped peanuts

In a large skillet melt the 1 teaspoon margarine. Add beaten egg. Cook egg without stirring till set. Invert skillet to remove egg; cut into strips. In the skillet cook onions and garlic in the 1 tablespoon margarine till tender. Add rice; cook and stir for 3 minutes. Stir in beans, soy sauce, sherry, oil, and red pepper. Cook and stir till heated through. Toss with nuts and egg strips. Serves 4.

Garbanzo Sandwich Spread

Serve this spread for lunch in pita bread or on bagels, or as an appetizer on party rye bread.

1 15-ounce can garbanzo beans, drained
¼ cup tahini* (sesame seed paste)
3 tablespoons lemon juice
1 tablespoon olive *or* salad oil
2 cloves garlic, quartered
¼ teaspoon paprika
½ cup snipped parsley
1 2-ounce jar diced pimiento, drained

In a blender container or food processor bowl combine beans, tahini, juice, oil, garlic, paprika, and ¼ teaspoon *salt.* Cover; blend or process till smooth, scraping sides as necessary. Transfer to a bowl. Stir in parsley and pimiento. Cover; chill 2 to 24 hours. Makes about 1⅔ cups (5 servings).

Mediterranean Sandwich: Spread about ⅓ cup cold *Garbanzo Sandwich Spread* on 1 slice *whole wheat bread.* Top with 2 *tomato slices,* 1 slice *Swiss or brick cheese,* and another slice *bread.* Makes 1 serving.

*****Tahini Substitute:** Stir together 3 tablespoons *creamy peanut butter* and 1 tablespoon *sesame oil* till well combined. Makes ¼ cup.

Bean and Cheese Burritos

Oven 350°

Stack six 8-inch *flour tortillas* and wrap in foil. Heat in a 350° oven for 10 minutes to soften. In a skillet cook 1 cup chopped *onion* in 1 tablespoon *cooking oil* till tender. Add one 16-ounce can *refried beans.* Cook and stir till heated through.

Spoon about ¼ cup bean mixture onto *each* tortilla just below center. Divide 1½ cups shredded *cheddar cheese* among tortillas. Fold edge nearest filling up and over just till mixture is covered. Fold in 2 sides just till they meet; roll up. Place on a baking sheet. Bake in a 350° oven about 10 minutes or till heated through. Serve with shredded *lettuce* and *salsa.* Serves 3.

Bean and Cheese Chimichangas: Prepare as above, *except* use *10-inch* flour tortillas and omit baking. Secure rolled-up tortillas with wooden toothpicks. In a 3-quart saucepan fry tortillas, 2 or 3 at a time, in 1 inch hot *cooking oil* (375°) about 1 minute on each side or till golden. Drain. Keep warm in a 300° oven. Remove picks. Pass dairy *sour cream* and *guacamole.*

Fish & Shellfish

Nutrition Analysis	Servings Per Recipe	Calories	Protein (g)	Carbohydrate (g)	Fat (g)	Cholesterol (mg)	Sodium (mg)	Potassium (mg)	Protein	Vitamin A	Vitamin C	Thiamine	Riboflavin	Niacin	Calcium	Iron
		Per Serving							**Percent U.S. RDA Per Serving**							
Baked Fish with Mushrooms (p. 171)	4	156	21	3	7	49	129	573	32	6	6	8	9	15	3	4
Blackened Redfish (p. 169)	4	195	24	1	10	42	307	494	36	9	0	4	1	2	5	3
Boiled Lobster (p. 184)	2	135	28	1	1	143	0	0	43	0	0	0	4	11	0	0
Broccoli-Stuffed Sole (p. 171)	4	460	34	24	25	130	730	619	52	37	19	15	21	23	24	11
Chilled Salmon Steaks (p. 173)	6	137	24	1	3	59	96	578	37	3	11	7	5	14	2	3
Citrus Baked Halibut (p. 170)	4	152	22	4	5	33	224	531	33	8	13	6	5	30	6	6
Clarified Butter (p. 184)	2	305	0	0	35	93	352	11	0	26	0	0	0	0	1	0
Coquilles Saint Jacques (p. 182)	4	350	23	13	22	132	380	526	35	18	3	8	16	13	9	8
Crab Cakes (p. 179)	6	241	13	13	15	181	634	117	19	15	1	8	8	8	6	9
Crab Mornay (p. 179)	4	498	20	25	34	50	887	361	31	13	2	20	24	9	39	9
Crab Newburg (p. 184)	4	598	22	22	45	231	1160	334	34	22	1	21	17	8	14	12
Crawfish Étouffée (p. 183)	4	390	19	40	17	128	668	592	30	14	43	15	5	22	11	18
Creamed Tuna (p. 175)	4	466	30	43	19	61	319	410	47	16	3	23	26	56	26	17
Curried Pan-Fried Fish (p. 174)	4	423	24	13	30	118	202	530	37	2	5	11	10	16	5	9
Curried Scallop Kabobs (p. 183)	4	170	20	15	3	37	442	552	31	45	92	6	8	10	4	6
Deviled Crab (p. 179)	4	281	15	13	19	99	767	285	24	16	7	7	17	6	24	7
Dijon-Mustard Fillets (p. 168)	4	132	21	1	4	56	181	502	32	4	3	6	6	11	4	3
Dill Smoked Cod (p. 169)	6	151	28	0	3	68	86	662	44	1	3	8	6	16	3	4
Dilly-of-a-Sauce (p. 177)	4	105	5	5	7	15	343	139	8	7	0	3	9	2	16	2
Extra-Creamy Tuna-Noodle Casserole (p. 176)	4	480	29	33	26	87	795	548	44	35	17	22	22	54	24	15
Fish and Chips (p. 175)	4	820	26	51	56	49	227	958	40	1	18	27	14	29	5	12
Fish Creole (p. 180)	4	283	19	36	7	37	580	769	29	27	55	18	8	19	7	14
Fish en Papillote (p. 172)	4	232	18	7	15	45	272	441	27	83	4	4	5	2	7	5
Fish Potpies (p. 170)	4	556	32	35	31	95	789	592	50	96	8	9	16	25	29	12
Fish Stacks (p. 170)	4	372	25	22	21	49	555	780	39	219	15	17	16	21	8	9
Fish with Beer-Cheese Sauce (p. 170)	4	229	25	5	12	64	347	564	38	10	4	8	11	13	15	4
French-Fried Shrimp (p. 181)	6	411	26	17	26	218	357	248	40	1	0	10	8	19	7	21
Fried Seafood (p. 183)	4	381	22	27	20	180	472	458	34	10	0	12	27	18	8	108
Halibut with Sherry Sauce (p. 168)	4	314	34	5	17	58	290	780	52	15	3	9	10	48	11	9
Herbed Sauce for Fish (p. 167)	4	78	0	0	9	0	101	13	0	7	2	0	0	0	0	0
Hot Tuna Sandwich Cups (p. 175)	6	350	25	15	21	66	493	305	38	13	6	12	12	47	16	12
Linguine with Red Clam Sauce (p. 182)	4	423	21	62	10	35	1665	1054	32	52	56	45	25	32	18	32
Linguine with White Clam Sauce (p. 182)	4	564	21	57	27	94	648	413	32	24	7	41	29	23	25	30
Lobster Mornay (p. 179)	4	501	21	25	34	58	663	400	32	14	2	19	24	9	39	9
Lobster Newburg (p. 184)	4	568	15	23	45	226	607	306	23	22	1	19	16	6	13	10
Marinated Salmon Steaks (p. 167)	4	181	22	1	10	63	58	406	34	4	3	14	9	30	1	3
Orange Swordfish Kabobs (p. 168)	4	148	17	5	7	30	107	476	26	7	14	7	18	48	1	8
Oysters au Gratin (p. 183)	4	295	15	17	18	77	464	472	23	14	3	7	25	15	22	51
Pan-Fried Fish (p. 174)	4	419	24	12	30	118	201	510	37	2	2	10	10	15	5	8
Poached Fish with Dill Sauce (p. 173)	6	183	29	2	6	114	154	665	45	5	2	9	7	16	3	5
Potato-Chip Pan-Fried Fish (p. 174)	4	427	23	7	34	118	144	667	35	2	8	8	7	14	3	5
Salmon Loaf (p. 177)	4	229	22	8	12	111	613	426	34	8	2	6	16	27	5	10
Salmon-Pasta Skillet (p. 177)	4	569	36	49	25	94	1077	749	55	77	4	35	37	49	20	21
Scallop Chow Mein (p. 180)	4	286	21	30	10	31	1499	540	32	2	19	9	13	16	6	11
Scallops in Garlic Butter (p. 181)	4	135	15	3	6	28	205	299	22	7	4	1	4	5	3	2
Shrimp Chow Mein (p. 180)	4	301	24	29	10	132	1488	424	37	2	19	10	12	21	8	21
Shrimp Creole (p. 180)	4	303	21	37	8	129	660	575	33	26	77	15	6	21	11	24
Shrimp in Garlic Butter (p. 181)	4	150	18	2	7	129	194	182	27	7	3	2	2	11	5	12
Shrimp Mornay (p. 179)	4	506	22	25	34	113	618	348	34	13	2	20	24	13	39	15
Shrimp Newburg (p. 184)	4	568	15	22	45	277	543	236	23	22	1	19	15	9	12	16

On the divider: Vegetable-Topped Fillets (p. 173).

Nutrition Analysis

	Per Serving								Percent U.S. RDA Per Serving							
	Servings Per Recipe	Calories	Protein (g)	Carbohydrate (g)	Fat (g)	Cholesterol (mg)	Sodium (mg)	Potassium (mg)	Protein	Vitamin A	Vitamin C	Thiamine	Riboflavin	Niacin	Calcium	Iron
Sole Amandine (p. 174)	4	395	26	14	26	124	319	516	41	7	3	15	15	22	7	9
Sweet-and-Sour Fish Kabobs (p. 169)	4	205	22	18	5	40	150	500	33	5	24	9	8	52	5	14
Sweet-and-Sour Stir-Fried Fish (p. 175)	4	490	26	68	12	52	1308	576	40	14	85	21	9	27	8	20
Sweet-Sour Sauce (p. 177)	8	43	0	11	0	0	88	46	0	1	3	2	1	1	1	2
Teriyaki Shark (p. 168)	4	142	22	1	5	52	368	183	34	5	0	3	4	16	4	6
Tex-Mex Sauce (p. 177)	4	24	1	6	0	0	597	252	0	62	37	3	3	4	0	3
Trout Amandine (p. 174)	4	528	38	15	35	162	309	684	58	9	5	46	41	5	12	20
Tuna-Biscuit Casseroles (p. 177)	6	325	24	28	13	46	521	445	37	40	6	15	21	49	16	14
Tuna-Broccoli Crepes (p. 176)	6	359	23	22	20	115	651	413	35	33	21	14	26	27	34	11
Tuna-Noodle Casserole (p. 176)	4	381	28	33	15	65	788	537	44	27	17	22	21	54	23	15
Vegetable-Topped Fillets (p. 173)	4	157	25	10	2	54	520	884	38	17	35	14	14	29	7	10
Vegetable Tuna-Noodle Casserole (p. 176)	4	413	31	38	15	65	822	604	47	33	21	29	23	57	24	19
Wild-Rice-Stuffed Fish (p. 171)	4	428	38	28	17	95	429	786	59	13	16	16	18	20	3	15

Fish and Shellfish

For quick cooking and light eating, choose a fish or shellfish dish. The pages immediately following include a variety of recipes for baking, poaching, frying, and broiling fresh or frozen fish. You'll also find recipes using convenient canned tuna and salmon. To cook shrimp, crab, oysters, and other shellfish, check out the basic cooking information and tantalizing recipes in the second section.

Freshness Counts

Accept nothing less than the very freshest when buying fish. Here's how to make sure the fish you buy is fresh. First, use your nose. Fresh fish in any form has a fresh and mild odor.

For whole, drawn, or dressed fish, look for shiny, taut, and bright skin. The eyes should be clear, bright, and often bulging. The gills should be bright red or pink and not slippery. The skin should be shiny, and the intestinal cavity clean and pink. The flesh should spring back and feel firm and elastic when pressed lightly.

Fillets and steaks should have a moist appearance with clean cuts. Ragged edges and discoloration indicate poor quality.

When buying frozen fish, be sure the flesh is frozen solid. Avoid packages with torn wrappers, or those with frost.

How to Store

Cook fresh fish as soon as possible, preferably the day you catch it or buy it. If you can't cook it right away, wrap it loosely in clear plastic wrap and refrigerate it up to two days. For longer storage, wrap fresh fish in moisture- and vaporproof wrap and freeze. Frozen fish will keep up to 3 months. Store leftover cooked fish, covered, in the refrigerator and use it within two days.

To thaw fish, place the unopened package in the refrigerator for 6 to 8 hours. Do not thaw fish at room temperature or in water because it will thaw unevenly and may spoil. Don't refreeze fish.

To thaw fish in a microwave oven, place 1 pound frozen fillets or steaks in a baking dish. Cover with vented clear plastic wrap. Micro-cook on 30% power (medium-low) for 6 to 8 minutes, turning and separating the fish after 3 minutes. Let fillets stand 10 minutes, and let steaks stand 15 minutes. The fish should be pliable and cold on the outside yet still slightly icy in the centers of thick areas. Rinse and pat dry.

Selecting Fish

Most of our recipes give several fish options. If none of the fishes listed is available, use this chart to choose a substitute fish that's similar in texture and flavor.

Use the following descriptions to help identify the market forms of fish. A *whole* or *round* fish is a fish as it comes from the water. A *drawn* fish is a whole fish with the internal organs removed and the scales left on. A *dressed* fish or *pan-dressed* small fish has had both its organs and scales removed. The head, tail and fins may or may not be removed. A fish *steak* is a crosscut slice (½ to 1 inch thick) from a large dressed fish. A *fillet* is a boneless piece cut lengthwise from the sides of the fish. Fillets may or may not be skinned.

Species	Market Forms	Texture	Flavor
Catfish	Dressed, steaks, fillets	Firm	Mild
Cod	Dressed, steaks, fillets	Firm	Delicate
Flounder	Dressed, fillets	Fine	Delicate
Haddock	Dressed, fillets	Firm	Delicate
Halibut	Dressed, steaks	Firm	Delicate
Lake trout	Dressed, steaks, fillets	Firm	Mild
Ocean perch	Dressed, fillets	Firm	Delicate
Orange roughy	Fillets	Firm	Delicate
Pike	Dressed, fillets	Firm	Mild
Rainbow trout	Drawn, drawn and partially boned, dressed, fillets	Firm	Delicate
Redfish	Dressed, fillets	Firm	Mild
Red snapper	Dressed, fillets	Firm	Mild
Salmon	Dressed, steaks, fillets	Firm	Mild to rich
Sole	Dressed, fillets	Fine	Delicate
Swordfish	Steaks	Firm, dense	Mild
Tuna	Dressed, steaks, fillets	Firm	Mild to rich
Whitefish	Dressed, steaks, fillets	Firm	Delicate

Marinated Salmon Steaks

The zesty marinade flavors and moistens the fish.

- **1 pound fresh *or* frozen salmon, swordfish, *or* halibut steaks, cut 1 inch thick**
- **½ teaspoon finely shredded lemon peel *or* lime peel**
- **¼ cup lemon juice *or* lime juice**
- **1 tablespoon cooking oil**
- **1 tablespoon Worcestershire sauce**
- **½ teaspoon dried rosemary *or* thyme, crushed**
- **1 clove garlic, minced**

Thaw fish, if frozen. Cut steaks into serving-size portions. For marinade, in a shallow dish combine lemon or lime peel, lemon or lime juice, oil, Worcestershire sauce, rosemary or thyme, garlic, and 1 tablespoon *water*. Add fish; turn to coat with marinade. Cover and marinate at room temperature for 30 minutes (or in the refrigerator for 2 hours), turning steaks occasionally.

Drain fish, reserving marinade. Place fish on greased unheated rack of broiler pan. Broil 4 inches from the heat for 5 minutes. Using a wide spatula, carefully turn fish over. Brush with marinade. Broil for 3 to 7 minutes more or till fish flakes easily with a fork. Makes 4 servings.

Grill directions: Marinate the fish as above. Drain fish, reserving marinade. Place fish steaks on a greased grill rack. Grill fish on an uncovered grill directly over *medium-hot* coals for 5 minutes. Using a wide spatula, carefully turn fish over. Brush with marinade. Grill for 3 to 7 minutes more or till fish flakes easily with a fork.

Herbed Sauce for Fish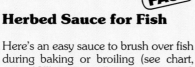

Here's an easy sauce to brush over fish during baking or broiling (see chart, page 185). In a small saucepan melt 3 tablespoons *margarine or butter.* Stir in 1 tablespoon *lemon juice;* ½ teaspoon dried *dillweed or* dried *basil, rosemary, or oregano,* crushed; and a dash *pepper.* Makes about ¼ cup sauce (enough for 1 pound of fillets).

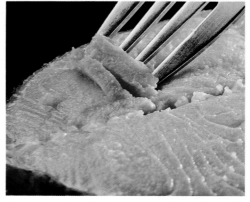

Properly cooked fish is opaque, with milky, white juices. The flesh flakes easily with a fork.

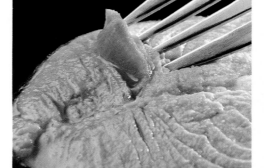

Undercooked fish is translucent, with clear juices. The flesh is firm and does not flake easily.

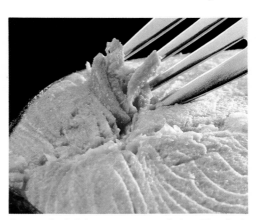

Overcooked fish is opaque and dry. The flesh flakes into little pieces when tested with a fork.

Halibut with Sherry Sauce

1½ to 2 pounds fresh *or* frozen halibut
   or other fish steaks, cut 1 inch
   thick
2 tablespoons margarine *or* butter,
   melted
4 green onions, sliced (¼ cup)
1 clove garlic, minced
1 tablespoon margarine *or* butter
4 teaspoons all-purpose flour
⅓ cup dairy sour cream
½ cup chicken broth
1 tablespoon dry sherry

Thaw fish, if frozen. Place on the greased unheated rack of a broiler pan. Brush with *half* of the melted margarine; sprinkle with pepper. Broil 4 inches from the heat 5 minutes; turn fish. Brush with remaining melted margarine. Broil 3 to 7 minutes more or till fish flakes easily with a fork.

For sauce, cook onions and garlic in the 1 tablespoon margarine till tender. Stir flour into sour cream; stir in broth. Add to onion mixture. Cook and stir till bubbly. Stir in sherry. Cook and stir 1 minute more. Serve over fish. Serves 4.

Grill directions: Thaw fish, if frozen. Place fish on a greased grill rack. Brush with *half* of the melted margarine; sprinkle with pepper. Grill on an uncovered grill directly over *medium-hot* coals for 5 minutes. Turn fish. Brush with remaining melted margarine. Grill for 3 to 7 minutes more. Meanwhile, prepare sauce as above. Serve with grilled fish.

Dijon-Mustard Fillets

1 pound fresh *or* frozen fish fillets
¼ cup dairy sour cream
1 tablespoon milk
1 tablespoon Dijon-style mustard
2 teaspoons snipped chives

Thaw fish, if frozen. Measure thickness of fish. Place fish on the unheated rack of a broiler pan. Broil 4 inches from the heat till fish flakes easily with a fork. (Allow 4 to 6 minutes per ½-inch thickness. Turn once if more than 1 inch thick.)

Meanwhile, in a small saucepan stir together sour cream, milk, mustard, chives, and a dash *pepper.* Cook till hot (*do not boil*). Serve over fish. Makes 4 servings.

Teriyaki Shark

Use 1 pound fresh or frozen *shark, tuna, or halibut steaks,* cut 1 inch thick. Thaw fish, if frozen. Place in a shallow dish. For marinade, stir together ½ cup *teriyaki sauce,* 2 tablespoons *dry sherry,* 1 teaspoon grated *gingerroot,* and 1 clove *garlic,* minced. Pour over fish. Turn fish to coat with marinade. Cover and marinate for 30 minutes (or in the refrigerator for 2 hours), turning the steaks occasionally.

Drain fish, reserving marinade. Place fish on the greased unheated rack of a broiler pan. Brush fish with some of the marinade. Broil 4 inches from the heat for 5 minutes. Turn fish over. Brush with marinade. Broil for 3 to 7 minutes more or till fish flakes easily with a fork. Serves 4.

Orange Swordfish Kabobs

Swordfish, tuna, and shark make great kabobs because of their firm flesh.

¾ pound fresh *or* frozen swordfish,
   tuna, *or* shark steaks, cut 1 inch
   thick
16 medium fresh mushrooms
4 large green onions, cut into 2-inch
   lengths
¼ cup cooking oil
¼ cup dry white wine
1 clove garlic, minced
½ teaspoon finely shredded orange *or*
   lemon peel
8 cherry tomatoes

Thaw fish, if frozen. Cut into 1-inch cubes. Place fish, mushrooms, and onions in a plastic bag; set bag into a bowl. Combine oil, wine, garlic, orange peel, and ¼ teaspoon *salt;* add to bag. Seal bag and marinate at room temperature for 30 minutes (or in the refrigerator for 2 hours), turning bag occasionally. Drain. On eight 12-inch skewers, alternately thread fish cubes, mushrooms, and onions, leaving about ¼ inch between pieces. Place on the greased unheated rack of a broiler pan. Broil 4 inches from the heat for 5 minutes. Turn kabobs over. Broil for 4 to 5 minutes more or till fish flakes easily with a fork. To serve, add a tomato to each skewer. Serves 4.

Grill directions: Assemble and marinate kabobs as above. On greased grill rack, grill kabobs, uncovered, directly over *medium-hot* coals for 8 to 12 minutes; turn once. Serve as above.

Sweet-and-Sour Fish Kabobs

Complete an Oriental theme with hot cooked rice and buttered snow peas.

- 1 **pound fresh *or* frozen swordfish, sea bass, shark, *or* tuna steaks, cut 1 inch thick**
- 2 **medium leeks *or* carrots, cut into 1-inch pieces**
- ¼ **cup pineapple preserves *or* orange marmalade**
- ¼ **cup catsup**
- 2 **tablespoons lemon juice**
- 1 **tablespoon cooking oil**
- 1 **8¼-ounce can pineapple chunks, drained**

Thaw fish, if frozen. Cut fish into 1-inch cubes. Cook leeks in a small amount of boiling water for 4 minutes or till tender. (Cook carrots for 10 to 12 minutes or till tender.) Drain and set aside.

For the sauce, in a bowl combine pineapple preserves or orange marmalade, catsup, lemon juice, and cooking oil.

For kabobs, on 4 long or 8 medium skewers, alternately thread fish cubes, leeks or carrots, and pineapple chunks, leaving about ¼ inch between pieces. Place kabobs on the greased unheated rack of a broiler pan. Broil 4 inches from the heat for 5 minutes. Turn kabobs over. Broil for 4 to 5 minutes more or till fish flakes easily with a fork, brushing with sauce during the last 2 minutes of broiling. Brush again with sauce before serving. Makes 4 servings.

Grill directions: Prepare sauce and assemble kabobs as above. Place the kabobs on a greased grill rack. Grill, uncovered, directly over *medium-hot* coals for 4 minutes. Turn kabobs over. Grill for 4 to 6 minutes more or till fish flakes easily with a fork, brushing with sauce during the last 2 minutes of grilling. Brush again with sauce before serving.

How Much Fish to Buy

As a general rule, allow 8 to 12 ounces of drawn or dressed fish per serving. Allow 4 to 8 ounces of fish steaks or fillets per serving.

Blackened Redfish

Stand back! This Cajun specialty really smokes as it cooks. That's why it's best to grill it.

- 4 **4-ounce fresh *or* frozen redfish *or* red snapper fillets**
- ½ **teaspoon onion powder**
- ½ **teaspoon garlic powder**
- ½ **teaspoon ground white pepper**
- ½ **teaspoon ground red pepper**
- ½ **teaspoon ground black pepper**
- ½ **teaspoon dried thyme, crushed**
- 3 **tablespoons margarine *or* butter, melted**

Thaw fish, if frozen. Measure thickness of fish. Combine onion powder, garlic powder, white pepper, red pepper, black pepper, thyme, and ¼ teaspoon *salt*. Brush fish with some of the melted margarine. Coat fillets evenly on both sides with pepper mixture.

Remove grill rack. Place a cast-iron 12-inch skillet directly on *hot* coals. Heat 5 minutes or till a drop of water sizzles in skillet. Add fish to skillet. Drizzle with remaining margarine. Cook, uncovered, 2 to 3 minutes per side for ½- to ¾-inch-thick fillets (3 to 4 minutes per side for 1-inch-thick fillets) or till fish flakes with a fork. Serves 4.

To cook indoors: Prepare as above, *except* cook in a well-ventilated area inside. Turn on exhaust fan. Heat the skillet till a drop of water sizzles before adding fish. *Avoid breathing fumes.*

Dill Smoked Cod

- 1 **3- to 4-pound fresh or frozen dressed cod *or* other fish**
- 2 **cups cherry *or* apple wood chips**
- 1 **tablespoon cooking oil**
- 1 **tablespoon snipped fresh dillweed *or* 1 teaspoon dried dillweed**

Thaw fish, if frozen. Soak wood chips in enough water to cover for 1 hour. Meanwhile, cut ½-inch-deep diagonal slits, 1 inch apart, into both sides of fish. Rub oil into slits. Then rub with dill, pressing into slits. Prick a few holes into a piece of *heavy* foil large enough to hold fish. Drain chips. In a covered grill arrange preheated coals around a foil drip pan. Test for *medium* coals. Place chips on coals. Place foil on rack above drip pan. Place the fish on foil. Grill fish, covered, 50 to 60 minutes or till fish flakes easily with a fork. Makes 6 to 8 servings.

Fish with Beer-Cheese Sauce

The tangy cheese sauce also tastes great over burgers and pork chops.

  1 **pound fresh *or* frozen fish fillets *or* steaks**
  ¼ **cup sliced green onion**
  2 **tablespoons margarine *or* butter**
  1 **tablespoon all-purpose flour**
  ½ **teaspoon dry mustard**
  ¼ **teaspoon caraway seed (optional)**
  ½ **cup milk**
  ½ **cup shredded American cheese**
  3 **tablespoons beer**   Oven 450°

Thaw fish, if frozen. Measure thickness of fish. In a lightly greased 10x6x2-inch baking dish arrange fish. (For fillets, tuck under thin edges.) Bake in a 450° oven till fish flakes with a fork. (Allow 4 to 6 minutes per ½-inch thickness of fish.)

Meanwhile, for sauce, cook onion in margarine till tender. Stir in flour, mustard, and, if desired, caraway seed. Add milk all at once. Cook and stir till thickened and bubbly. Cook and stir 1 minute more. Add cheese and beer. Cook and stir till cheese melts. Spoon over fish. Serves 4.

Fish Potpies

Oven 400°

Use 1 pound fresh or frozen *haddock, cod, or orange roughy fillets.* Thaw fish, if frozen. Let *half* of a 15-ounce package folded *refrigerated unbaked piecrusts* (1 crust) stand at room temperature for 15 to 20 minutes.

In a medium saucepan cook ¼ cup sliced *green onion* and 1 clove *garlic,* minced, in 2 tablespoons *margarine or butter* till tender. Stir in ¼ cup *all-purpose flour.* Add ¾ cup *milk* all at once. Cook and stir till thickened and bubbly. Add 1 cup shredded *American or process Swiss cheese,* ½ cup shredded *carrot,* 2 tablespoons snipped *parsley,* 1 tablespoon chopped *pimiento,* and ⅛ teaspoon *pepper.* Cook and stir till cheese melts. Remove from heat.

Cut fish into ½-inch pieces; stir into cheese mixture. Spoon into four greased 8- or 10-ounce casseroles. Cut pastry into 4 wedges. Center *one* wedge on *each* casserole; trim to fit. Cut slits into pastry. Place on a baking sheet. Bake in a 400° oven for 20 to 25 minutes or till brown. Let stand 10 minutes before serving. Makes 4 servings.

Citrus Baked Halibut

  1 **pound fresh *or* frozen halibut steaks, cut ¾ inch thick**
  ⅓ **cup finely chopped onion**
  1 **clove garlic, minced**
  1 **tablespoon margarine *or* butter**
  2 **tablespoons snipped parsley**
  ½ **teaspoon finely shredded orange peel**
  ¼ **cup orange juice**
  1 **tablespoon lemon juice**   Oven 400°

Thaw fish, if frozen. Arrange in an 8x8x2-inch baking dish. Cook onion and garlic in margarine till tender. Remove from heat. Stir in parsley, orange peel, ¼ teaspoon *salt,* and ⅛ teaspoon *pepper.* Spread over fish. Sprinkle orange and lemon juices over all. Bake, covered, in a 400° oven for 15 to 20 minutes or till fish flakes easily with a fork. Spoon pan juices over fish. Serves 4.

Microwave directions: Thaw fish, if frozen. Arrange in an 8x8x2-inch baking dish. In a 2-cup measure micro-cook onion, garlic, and margarine on 100% power (high) for 1½ to 2½ minutes or till tender; stirring once. Stir in parsley, peel, ¼ teaspoon *salt,* and ⅛ teaspoon *pepper.* Spread over fish. Sprinkle *2 tablespoons* orange juice and *1 teaspoon* lemon juice over all. Cover with vented clear plastic wrap. Cook on high for 7 to 9 minutes or till fish is done, giving dish a half-turn once. Serve as above.

Fish Stacks

Oven 350°

Thaw one 16-ounce package *frozen fish fillets.* Drain well. Cut into four 4x3-inch portions. Place in a shallow baking dish.

Cook 1 cup finely chopped *onion,* 1 cup finely chopped *carrot,* and 1 cup thinly sliced fresh *mushrooms* in 2 tablespoons *margarine or butter,* covered, about 5 minutes. Uncover; simmer for 2 to 4 minutes or till excess liquid evaporates. Remove from heat. Stir in *half* of an 8-ounce container *soft-style cream cheese,* ½ teaspoon dried *dillweed,* and ¼ teaspoon *pepper.* Spoon over each fish portion. Separate 1 package (4) *refrigerated crescent rolls* into 2 rectangles. Pinch perforations to seal. Cut each rectangle in half. Place one rectangle atop each fish portion. Brush dough with milk, if desired. Bake in a 350° oven for 20 to 25 minutes or till fish is done. Serves 4.

Broccoli-Stuffed Sole

4 **4-ounce fresh *or* frozen skinless
   sole, flounder, *or* other fish
   fillets (about ¼ inch thick)**
1 **cup frozen cut broccoli, thawed**
1 **beaten egg**
1 **8-ounce container soft-style cream
   cheese with chives and onion**
¼ **cup grated Parmesan cheese**
¾ **cup herb-seasoned stuffing mix**
2 **tablespoons milk**
2 **tablespoons dry
   white wine**   Oven 350°

Thaw fish, if frozen. For stuffing, drain broccoli, pressing out excess liquid. Combine egg, *half* of the cream cheese, and the Parmesan cheese. Stir in broccoli and stuffing mix. Spoon *one-fourth* of the stuffing onto one end of *each* fillet. Roll up; secure rolls with wooden toothpicks. Place in a 10x6x2-inch baking dish. Bake, covered, in a 350° oven for 30 to 35 minutes or till fish flakes easily with a fork.

Meanwhile, for sauce, in a saucepan cook remaining cream cheese, milk, and wine till heated through, stirring often. Serve over fish. Serves 4.

Microwave directions: Assemble fish rolls as above. Micro-cook fish rolls, covered with vented clear plastic wrap, on 100% power (high) for 3 to 5 minutes or till fish flakes easily with a fork, giving the dish a half-turn once. Prepare sauce as above. Serve sauce over fish.

Baked Fish with Mushrooms

1 **pound fresh *or* frozen fish fillets *or*
   steaks, cut ½ to ¾ inch thick**
1 **cup sliced fresh mushrooms**
½ **cup sliced green onion**
¼ **teaspoon dried tarragon, crushed**
2 **tablespoons margarine *or* butter
   Paprika**   Oven 450°

Thaw fish, if frozen. Arrange fish in a 12x7½x2-inch baking dish, turning under thin edges. Sprinkle with salt. Cook mushrooms, onion, and tarragon in margarine till tender. Spoon over fish; sprinkle with paprika. Bake, covered, in a 450° oven for 6 to 10 minutes or till fish flakes easily with a fork. Makes 4 servings.

Wild-Rice-Stuffed Fish

Two midwestern delights—whitefish from the Great Lakes and Minnesota's wild rice—combine to create this impressive dish.

1 **2- to 2½-pound fresh *or* frozen
   dressed whitefish *or* other fish**
⅔ **cup wild rice**
1 **cup sliced fresh mushrooms**
¼ **cup chopped onion**
1 **clove garlic, minced**
2 **tablespoons margarine *or* butter**
1¼ **cups chicken broth**
2 **tablespoons dry sherry**
1 **cup frozen peas**
2 **tablespoons chopped pimiento**
¼ **teaspoon finely shredded
   lemon peel**
1 **to 2 teaspoons
   cooking oil**   Oven 350°

Thaw fish, if frozen. Rinse rice thoroughly; drain.

For stuffing, in a medium saucepan cook mushrooms, onion, and garlic in margarine. Stir in broth, sherry, and rice. Cover and simmer for 45 to 50 minutes or till rice is tender and liquid is absorbed. Stir in peas, pimiento, and lemon peel.

Place fish in a well-greased shallow baking pan; sprinkle cavity lightly with salt. Spoon *half* of the stuffing into cavity; press lightly to flatten. Brush fish lightly with oil. Cover loosely with foil. Place remaining stuffing in a 1-quart casserole; cover. Bake fish and stuffing in a 350° oven for 30 to 40 minutes or till fish flakes easily with a fork. Use two large spatulas to transfer fish to a serving platter. Makes 4 or 5 servings.

Spoon stuffing into fish, then press lightly with the back of the spoon so the fish lies flat.

Fish en Papillote

"En papillote" (pahp-ee-YOHT) is French for "in paper." It's a simple yet elegant way to cook fish.

4 3-ounce fresh *or* frozen skinless pompano, perch, sole, *or* flounder fish fillets (about ½ inch thick)
Parchment paper *or* brown paper
1 cup water
2 lemon slices
1 bay leaf
1 teaspoon instant chicken bouillon granules
1 medium carrot, coarsely shredded (½ cup)
¼ cup sliced green onion
2 tablespoons margarine *or* butter
2 tablespoons all-purpose flour
1 teaspoon Dijon-style mustard
½ cup milk   Oven 400°

Thaw fish, if frozen. Cut 4 pieces of parchment paper or brown paper into heart shapes, 12 inches wide and 9 inches long.

In a large skillet bring water, lemon slices, bay leaf, and bouillon granules to boiling. Add fillets in a single layer. Return to boiling; reduce heat. Simmer, covered, for 4 to 6 minutes or till fish flakes easily with a fork. Using a slotted spoon, remove fish. Strain liquid; reserve ½ cup.

For sauce, in same skillet cook carrot and onion in margarine till tender. Stir in flour and mustard. Add reserved liquid and milk. Cook and stir till bubbly. Cook and stir 1 minute more.

To assemble *each* packet, place *one* fillet on half of *each* parchment heart. Top with *one-fourth* of the sauce. Fold the other half of the heart over fillet. Starting at the top, seal tightly by turning up edges of heart and folding in twice. At bottom, twist the tip of heart to seal. Place packets on a large baking sheet. Bake in a 400° oven for 10 to 12 minutes or till slightly puffed. Transfer to dinner plates. To serve, cut an X in top of each. Pull back the paper. Serves 4.

Chilled Salmon Steaks

Serve this luncheon specialty with Tartar Sauce (see recipe, page 364).

1½ **cups Court Bouillon *or* water**
2 **pounds fresh *or* frozen salmon steaks, cut 1 to 1¼ inches thick**
½ **cup lemon juice**
⅓ **cup sliced green onion**
¼ **cup cooking oil**
3 **tablespoons snipped parsley**
3 **tablespoons finely chopped green *or* sweet red pepper**
1 **tablespoon sugar**
2 **teaspoons dry mustard**
⅛ **teaspoon ground red pepper**

In large skillet bring Court Bouillon to boiling. Add fish. Cover; simmer 8 to 12 minutes (12 to 18 minutes for frozen) or till fish flakes with fork. Remove fish. For marinade, in screw-top jar mix lemon juice, onion, oil, parsley, sweet pepper, sugar, mustard, red pepper, and ½ teaspoon *salt*. Shake well. Pour over fish. Cover; chill 4 to 24 hours. Spoon marinade over fish often. Serves 6.

Court Bouillon: Simmer, covered, 8 cups *water;* 1 cup *dry white wine;* 2 medium *carrots,* sliced; 2 stalks *celery,* sliced; 1 medium *onion,* sliced; 2 *lemon slices;* 1 *bay leaf;* 3 whole *peppercorns;* and 2 teaspoons *salt* for 30 minutes. Strain through cheesecloth. Makes 8 cups.

Poached Fish with Dill Sauce

Use one 3-pound fresh *or* frozen *dressed fish.* Thaw fish, if frozen. In a fish poacher or a large roasting pan that has a wire rack with handles, add enough water to almost reach the rack. Remove and grease rack; set aside. Add 3 *lemon slices;* 1 *bay leaf;* ¼ teaspoon dried *tarragon,* crushed; and ½ teaspoon *salt* to water. Place pan over two burners on range top. Bring to boiling. Reduce heat. Lower fish on rack into pan. Simmer, covered, 35 to 40 minutes or till fish flakes easily with a fork. Remove fish; keep warm.

For dill sauce, strain cooking liquid; reserve *1 cup.* Melt 2 tablespoons *margarine or butter.* Stir in 4 teaspoons *all-purpose flour,* ½ teaspoon *sugar,* ½ teaspoon dried *dillweed,* and dash *salt.* Add reserved liquid. Cook and stir till bubbly. Gradually stir about ½ *cup* of the mixture into 1 beaten *egg yolk;* return to saucepan. Cook and stir 1 minute more. Pass sauce with fish. Serves 6.

Vegetable-Topped Fillets

Summer squash and zucchini make a colorful combo, but use just one type of squash if you wish. (Pictured on page 163.)

1 **pound fresh *or* frozen skinless sole *or* flounder fillets**
1 **small yellow summer squash**
1 **small zucchini**
1 **cup sliced fresh mushrooms**
½ **of a small onion, sliced and separated into rings**
1 **clove garlic, minced**
1 **14½-ounce can tomatoes, cut up**
1 **tablespoon cornstarch**
¼ **teaspoon dried basil, crushed**
¼ **teaspoon dried oregano, crushed**
  Dash bottled hot pepper sauce
1 **cup chicken broth**

For sauce, cut yellow squash and zucchini in half lengthwise, then crosswise into ¼-inch-thick slices. In a saucepan combine squash, zucchini, mushrooms, onion, garlic, ¼ cup *water,* and ⅛ teaspoon *salt.* Bring to boiling; reduce heat. Simmer, covered, 4 minutes or till vegetables are nearly tender. Drain. Mix *undrained* tomatoes, cornstarch, basil, oregano, and hot sauce. Stir into vegetables. Cook and stir till bubbly. Cook and stir 2 minutes more.

Meanwhile, measure thickness of fish. In a large skillet bring chicken broth just to boiling. Carefully add fish. Return just to boiling; reduce heat. Cover and simmer till fish flakes easily with a fork. (Allow 4 to 6 minutes per ½-inch thickness for fresh fish; 6 to 9 minutes per ½-inch thickness for frozen fish.) Serve sauce over fish. Garnish with fresh herbs, if desired. Serves 4.

Microwave directions: Use ½-inch-thick fish fillets. Thaw, if frozen. Cut squash and zucchini as above. In a 2-quart casserole mix squash, zucchini, mushrooms, onion, garlic, and 2 tablespoons *water.* Micro-cook, covered, on 100% power (high) for 4½ to 5 minutes or till vegetables are nearly tender; stir once. Drain. Mix *undrained* tomatoes, cornstarch, basil, oregano, and hot sauce. Stir into vegetables. Cook, uncovered, on high 4 to 6 minutes or till bubbly, stirring every 2 minutes. Cook 1 minute more. In an 8x8x2-inch baking dish arrange fish; turn under thin portions. Do not use chicken broth. Cover with vented clear plastic wrap. Cook on high 4 to 7 minutes or till fish flakes easily with a fork, giving dish a half-turn once. Serve sauce over fish.

Trout Amandine

The perfect recipe for freshly caught fish. If no one fishes in your family, buy your catch at the supermarket or fish market.

    4 **fresh *or* frozen pan-dressed trout *or* other pan-dressed fish (about 8 ounces each)**
    1 **beaten egg**
  ¼ **cup milk**
  ½ **cup all-purpose flour**
  ¼ **teaspoon salt**
  ¼ **cup cooking oil**
  ¼ **cup sliced almonds**
    2 **tablespoons margarine *or* butter**
    2 **tablespoons lemon juice**

Thaw fish, if frozen. Bone fish, if desired. Combine egg and milk. Stir together flour and salt. Coat fish with flour mixture, dip into egg mixture, then coat again with flour mixture. In a 12-inch skillet heat the oil. Fry *half* of the fish in hot oil for 5 to 6 minutes on each side or till golden and crisp and fish flakes easily with a fork. Remove fish from skillet and keep warm while cooking remaining fish. In a medium skillet cook sliced almonds in margarine or butter till golden. Remove from heat; stir in lemon juice. Place fish on a serving platter; spoon almond mixture over fish. Makes 4 servings.

Sole Amandine: Prepare as above, *except* substitute 1 pound fresh *or* frozen ½-inch-thick skinless *sole or flounder fillets* for the pan-dressed fish. Reduce lemon juice to *1 tablespoon*. Cook fillets for 3 to 4 minutes on each side.

Pan-Fried Fish

The crispy coating seals in the fresh fish flavor.

    1 **pound fresh *or* frozen fish fillets (½ to 1 inch thick)**
    1 **beaten egg**
  ⅔ **cup cornmeal *or* fine dry bread crumbs**
      Shortening *or* cooking oil for frying   Oven 300°

Thaw fish, if frozen. Measure thickness of fish. Cut into serving-size portions. Pat dry. In a shallow dish combine egg and 2 tablespoons *water.* In another dish mix cornmeal or bread crumbs, ½ teaspoon *salt,* and dash *pepper.* Dip fish into egg mixture, then coat with cornmeal mixture.

In a large skillet heat ¼ inch melted shortening or oil. Add *half* of the fish in a single layer. (If fillets have skin, fry skin side last.) Fry fish on one side till golden. Allow 3 to 4 minutes per side for ½-inch-thick fillets (5 to 6 minutes per side for 1-inch-thick fillets). Turn carefully. Fry till golden and fish flakes easily with a fork. Drain on paper towels. Keep warm in a 300° oven while frying remaining fish. Makes 4 servings.

Potato-Chip Pan-Fried Fish: Prepare as above, *except* substitute ⅔ cup finely crushed *potato chips or saltine crackers* for the cornmeal or bread crumbs and omit salt.

Curried Pan-Fried Fish: Prepare as above, *except* add 1 tablespoon *lime or lemon juice* to egg mixture and add 2 teaspoons *curry powder* to cornmeal mixture. Serve with *chutney.*

Dip both sides of the fish fillets into the egg mixture, then into the cornmeal mixture.

Fry the fish in hot oil on one side till golden. Turn and cook on the other side.

Sweet-and-Sour Stir-Fried Fish

    1 pound fresh *or* frozen monkfish,
         shark, sea bass, tuna, *or* cusk
         steaks *or* fillets
    1 15¼-ounce can pineapple chunks
         (juice pack)
    ¼ cup packed brown sugar
    ¼ cup catsup
    ¼ cup soy sauce
    3 tablespoons vinegar
    3 tablespoons dry sherry *or* orange
         juice
    2 tablespoons cornstarch
    2 tablespoons cooking oil
    1 medium green *or* sweet red pepper,
         cut into ¾-inch pieces
    2 cups hot cooked rice

Thaw fish, if frozen. Cut into 1-inch pieces. Drain pineapple, reserving *¾ cup* juice. For sauce, combine reserved juice, brown sugar, catsup, soy sauce, vinegar, sherry, and cornstarch. Set aside.

Preheat a wok or large skillet over high heat; add *1 tablespoon* cooking oil. Stir-fry sweet pepper for 1½ to 2 minutes or till crisp-tender. Remove pepper. Add remaining oil. Stir-fry fish for 3 to 5 minutes or till fish flakes easily. Remove fish. Stir sauce; add to wok. Cook and stir till bubbly. Stir in pineapple, fish, and sweet pepper. Heat for 1 minute. Serve over rice. Serves 4.

Fish and Chips

Oven 300°

Use 1 pound fresh *or* frozen *fish fillets.* Thaw fish, if frozen. For chips, cut 3 peeled medium *potatoes* lengthwise into ⅜-inch-wide sticks. Pat dry. In a heavy saucepan or deep-fat fryer heat 2 inches melted *shortening or cooking oil for deep-fat frying* to 375°. Fry potatoes in hot fat, about *one-third* at a time, for 4 to 6 minutes or till lightly browned. Remove and drain on paper towels. Keep warm in a 300° oven while frying fish.

Pat fish dry with paper towels. Cut into serving-size pieces. For batter, combine 1 cup *all-purpose flour,* ½ teaspoon *baking powder,* and ¼ teaspoon *salt.* Add 1 cup *beer or milk;* beat till smooth. Dip fish into batter. Fry fish in hot fat, 2 or 3 pieces at a time, about 2 minutes on each side or till golden brown. Drain; keep warm in oven while frying remaining fish. Serve with malt or cider vinegar, if desired. Serves 4.

Creamed Tuna

Try this richly sauced tuna over cooked noodles or rice, too.

    ¼ cup sliced green onion
    3 tablespoons margarine *or* butter
    3 tablespoons all-purpose flour
 1⅓ cups milk
    ½ cup dairy sour cream
    1 9¼-ounce can tuna, drained
    3 tablespoons dry white wine *or* milk
    4 English muffins, split and toasted,
         or toast points
    2 tablespoons sliced almonds, toasted

In a saucepan cook onion in margarine till tender. Stir in flour, ¼ teaspoon *salt,* and dash *pepper.* Add milk all at once. Cook and stir till thickened and bubbly. Stir about *1 cup* of the hot mixture into sour cream; return all to saucepan. Gently stir in tuna and wine or milk. Heat through (*do not boil*). Serve over muffin halves or toast points. Sprinkle with almonds. Serves 4.

Hot Tuna Sandwich Cups

    1 package (6) refrigerated biscuits
    ¼ cup sliced celery
    ¼ cup chopped onion
    1 tablespoon margarine *or* butter
    ⅓ cup mayonnaise *or* salad dressing
    1 teaspoon prepared mustard
    ½ teaspoon dried dillweed
    2 6½-ounce cans tuna (water pack),
         drained and flaked
    1 cup shredded cheddar cheese
    1 cup cooked peas
    6 thin tomato slices   Oven 400°

Separate biscuits. Grease the *outside* of six 6-ounce custard cups. Press *one* biscuit over bottom and halfway down side of *each* custard cup. Place cups, dough side up, on a 15x10x1-inch baking pan. Bake in a 400° oven 7 minutes or till lightly browned. Immediately remove biscuits from cups; place upright in baking pan.

Meanwhile, in saucepan cook celery and onion in margarine till tender. Stir in mayonnaise, mustard, and dillweed. Stir in tuna, *half* of the cheese, and the peas. Spoon into biscuit cups. Return to oven and bake 7 minutes or till heated. Top with tomato slices and remaining cheese. Bake 2 to 3 minutes more or till cheese melts. Serves 6.

Tuna-Noodle Casserole

Home-style cooking at its best.

 3 cups medium noodles (4 ounces)
   or 1 cup elbow macaroni
   (3½ ounces)
 1 cup chopped celery
 ¼ cup chopped onion
 2 tablespoons margarine **or** butter
 1 11-ounce can condensed cheddar
   cheese soup **or** one 10¾-ounce
   can condensed cream of
   mushroom soup
 ¾ cup milk
 1 9¼-ounce can tuna, drained and
   broken into chunks, **or** two 6¾-
   ounce cans skinless boneless
   salmon
 ¼ cup chopped pimiento
 2 tablespoons grated Parmesan
   cheese
   Parsley sprigs (optional)   Oven 375°

Cook noodles or macaroni according to package directions. Drain and set aside.

Meanwhile, in a saucepan cook celery and onion in margarine or butter till tender. Stir in soup and milk. Gently stir in tuna or salmon, pimiento, and the cooked noodles or macaroni. Transfer to a 1½-quart casserole. Sprinkle with Parmesan cheese. Bake in a 375° oven for 25 to 30 minutes or till heated through. Garnish with parsley sprigs, if desired. Makes 4 servings.

Microwave directions: Cook noodles or macaroni according to package directions. Drain; set aside. Meanwhile, in a 2-quart casserole micro-cook celery and onion in margarine or butter, covered, on 100% power (high) for 3 to 5 minutes or till tender, stirring once. Stir in soup and milk. Cook, uncovered, on high for 3½ to 5½ minutes or till mixture is hot and bubbly, stirring once. Gently stir in tuna or salmon, pimiento, and the cooked noodles or macaroni. Cook, uncovered, on high for 2 to 4 minutes or till mixture is heated through, stirring once. Sprinkle with Parmesan and, if desired, garnish with parsley.

Vegetable Tuna-Noodle Casserole: Prepare as above, *except* stir in 1 cup *cooked vegetables* with tuna; transfer to a *2-quart* casserole.

Extra-Creamy Tuna-Noodle Casserole: Prepare as above, *except* substitute one 8-ounce carton dairy *sour cream or plain yogurt* for the milk. Stir 1 to 2 tablespoons *milk* into mixture, if necessary, to obtain desired consistency.

Tuna-Broccoli Crepes

Special enough for company.

  1 10-ounce package frozen chopped
    broccoli
  ¼ cup chopped onion
  3 tablespoons margarine **or** butter
  3 tablespoons all-purpose flour
  1 tablespoon prepared mustard
  ⅛ teaspoon pepper
 1½ cups milk
 1½ cups shredded American cheese
    (6 ounces)
  1 6½-ounce can tuna, drained and
    broken into chunks, **or** one
    7½-ounce can salmon, drained,
    flaked, and skin and bones
    removed
 12 Crepes (see recipe, page 72)
    Milk
    Paprika
    Sliced **or** slivered almonds,
    toasted (optional)   Oven 375°

Cook broccoli according to package directions; drain. Cut up any large broccoli pieces. Set aside.

For cheese sauce, in a medium saucepan cook onion in margarine or butter till tender but not brown. Stir in flour, mustard, and pepper. Add the 1½ cups milk all at once. Cook and stir till thickened and bubbly. Add cheese. Cook and stir till melted. Remove from heat.

Combine tuna or salmon, broccoli, and *¾ cup* of the sauce. Spoon about *3 tablespoons* of the tuna-broccoli mixture onto the *unbrowned* side of *each* crepe; roll up. Place crepes, seam side down, in a 12x7½x2-inch baking dish. Bake, covered, in a 375° oven for 20 to 25 minutes or till heated through.

Reheat the remaining cheese sauce. Stir in additional milk, if necessary. To serve, spoon remaining cheese sauce over crepes. Sprinkle with paprika and, if desired, top with toasted almonds. Makes 6 servings.

Tuna-Biscuit Casseroles

Biscuits top these no-fuss potpies.

    ½ cup chopped onion
    ¼ cup margarine *or* butter
    ½ cup all-purpose flour
    2 teaspoons instant chicken bouillon
       granules
    ¼ teaspoon dried thyme, crushed
   2½ cups milk
    2 6½-ounce cans tuna, drained and
       broken into chunks
    1 cup cooked mixed vegetables
    3 tablespoons snipped parsley
    1 package (6) refrigerated
       biscuits   Oven 400°

Cook onion in margarine till tender. Stir in flour, bouillon granules, thyme, and ⅛ teaspoon *pepper*. Add milk. Cook and stir till thickened and bubbly. Stir in tuna, vegetables, and parsley. Cook and stir till heated through. Immediately pour into six 10-ounce casseroles. Quarter biscuits; place *four* pieces atop *hot* filling in *each* casserole. Bake in a 400° oven 10 to 12 minutes or till biscuits are lightly browned. Serves 6.

Salmon Loaf

No time for the sauce? Cook a package of frozen creamed peas and onions to ladle over the loaf.

    ¼ cup finely chopped onion
    1 teaspoon dried dillweed
    1 tablespoon margarine *or* butter
    1 slightly beaten egg
    1 cup soft bread crumbs
    ¼ cup milk
    1 15½-ounce can pink salmon,
       drained, flaked, and skin and
       bones removed; *or* two 6½-ounce
       cans tuna, drained and broken
       into chunks
       Cheese Sauce (see recipe, page 361)
       or 2 American cheese slices
       (optional)   Oven 350°

In a saucepan cook onion, dillweed, and a dash *pepper* in margarine till onion is tender. Combine egg, bread crumbs, milk, and onion mixture. Add salmon; mix well. Shape into a 6x3-inch loaf in a greased shallow baking pan. Bake in a 350° oven for 30 to 35 minutes. Top with Cheese Sauce or cheese slices, if desired. Makes 4 servings.

Salmon-Pasta Skillet

   1½ cups chicken broth
   1½ cups corkscrew macaroni
    1 10-ounce package frozen mixed
       vegetables
    2 3-ounce packages cream cheese
       with chives, cut into cubes
    ½ cup milk
    ¼ cup grated Parmesan cheese
    1 teaspoon prepared mustard
    ½ teaspoon dried basil, crushed
    1 15½-ounce can salmon, drained,
       flaked, and skin and bones
       removed

In a large skillet bring chicken broth to boiling. Add pasta and vegetables. Cover and simmer for 15 to 20 minutes or till pasta is just tender. Stir in cream cheese till combined. Stir in milk, Parmesan, mustard, basil, and dash *pepper*. Gently stir in salmon. Cook till heated through. Serves 4.

Fast Fish Fix-Ups

For a delicious dinner in a hurry, put frozen breaded fish portions, sticks, or fillets in the oven and stir up one of these easy sauces.

Dilly-of-a-Sauce: In a saucepan melt 1 tablespoon *margarine or butter*. Stir in 1 tablespoon *all-purpose flour* and ½ teaspoon dried *dillweed*. Add ¾ cup *milk*. Cook and stir till thickened and bubbly. Stir in one 2½-ounce jar sliced *mushrooms*, drained, and ½ cup shredded *process Swiss cheese*. Cook and stir till cheese melts.

Tex-Mex Sauce: Cook one 8-ounce can *tomato sauce;* one 4-ounce can *diced green chili peppers*, drained; ½ teaspoon *sugar;* ¼ teaspoon ground *coriander;* and a dash *bottled hot pepper sauce;* cook till heated.

Sweet-Sour Sauce: Cook one 10-ounce jar *sweet-and-sour sauce;* one 8-ounce can *pineapple tidbits,* drained; and half of a green *or* sweet red *pepper,* cut into strips, till heated through.

Shellfish

Whether you eat shellfish steamed or boiled, or use them in classic dishes like Crab Mornay or Lobster Newburg, you'll find them irresistible.

Buying

Shellfish are available live, partially prepared, cooked, frozen, and canned.

When buying live shellfish, look for oysters and hard-shell clams that close their shells when you tap them. Look for crabs and lobsters that move their legs and claws.

Buy partially prepared shellfish for easier eating and cooking. These shellfish include shelled scallops, oysters, clams, or mussels packed in clear liquid; peeled and unpeeled shrimp with heads removed; and whole cooked crabs, lobsters, or shrimp.

Frozen shellfish is available cooked or uncooked. Frozen shrimp may be in or out of the shell. As for canned seafood, it's sold in whole, chunk, and smoked forms.

How Much to Buy

For each serving, you'll need these amounts:
- 6 oysters or clams in the shell
- ½ cup shucked oysters or clams
- 12 mussels in the shell
- ½ to 1 whole Dungeness crab, 1 pound live blue crabs, ½ pound crab legs, or 3 to 4 ounces crabmeat
- 1 whole lobster or one 8-ounce lobster tail
- 3 to 4 ounces shucked scallops
- 6 ounces shrimp in shells or 3 to 4 ounces peeled shrimp
- 1 pound live crawfish

Storing and Freezing

Cook live shellfish the day you buy them or freeze them as follows:
- Shuck oysters, clams, and scallops; freeze immediately in freezer containers for up to three months.
- Cook crabs and lobsters as for eating. Cool; remove meat from shells. Freeze in freezer containers for up to one month.
- Remove the heads from shrimp, then freeze shrimp cooked or uncooked in freezer containers for up to three months.

How to Tell When Seafood Is Cooked

Shellfish can be boiled, broiled, baked, steamed, or fried. When done, shelled oysters, mussels, and clams become plump and opaque (or, if they're cooked in the shells, the shells open). Oysters curl around the edges. Lobsters and crawfish turn bright red, shrimp turn pink, and scallops turn opaque.

Clams

Crawfish

Lobster tails

Mussels

Oysters

Sea and bay scallops

Shrimp, in shells and peeled

Snow crab legs

Crab Mornay

Topping crab, shrimp, or lobster with a sherried cheese sauce makes for an easy, elegant dinner.

  1 **cup sliced fresh mushrooms**
  2 **tablespoons chopped onion**
  2 **tablespoons thinly sliced celery**
  2 **tablespoons margarine *or* butter**
  2 **tablespoons all-purpose flour**
    Dash ground red pepper
1¼ **cups milk**
  1 **cup shredded process Swiss *or***
    Gruyère cheese (4 ounces)
  1 **cup cooked crabmeat; one**
    7-ounce can crabmeat, drained,
    flaked, and cartilage removed;
    ***or* one 6-ounce package frozen**
    crabmeat, thawed and drained
  2 **tablespoons dry sherry *or* dry**
    white wine
  4 **baked patty shells *or* toast points**
    Paprika *or* snipped parsley
    (optional)

In a saucepan cook mushrooms, onion, and celery in margarine or butter till tender. Stir in flour, red pepper, and ⅛ teaspoon *salt*. Add milk all at once. Cook and stir till thickened and bubbly. Cook and stir 1 minute more. Reduce heat. Add cheese and stir till melted. Stir in crabmeat and sherry or white wine. Heat through; *do not boil*. Serve in patty shells or over toast points. Sprinkle with paprika or parsley, if desired. Serves 4.

Microwave directions: In a 1-quart casserole micro-cook mushrooms, onion, celery, and margarine or butter on 100% power (high) for 2 to 3 minutes or till tender. Stir in flour, red pepper, and ⅛ teaspoon *salt*. Stir in *1 cup* milk all at once. Cook, uncovered, on high for 4 to 6 minutes or till thickened and bubbly, stirring *every minute* till the sauce starts to thicken, then *every 30 seconds*. Cook, uncovered, for 30 seconds more. Add cheese; stir till melted. Stir in crabmeat and sherry or white wine. Cook, uncovered, about 2 minutes more or till heated through. Serve as above.

Shrimp Mornay: Prepare as above, *except* substitute 8 ounces cooked, peeled, and deveined *shrimp or* two 4½-ounce cans *shrimp,* rinsed and drained, for crabmeat.

Lobster Mornay: Prepare as above, *except* substitute 1 cup cooked *lobster or* one 6½-ounce can *lobster,* drained, broken into large pieces, and cartilage removed, for crabmeat.

Crab Cakes

Oven 300°

In a small saucepan cook ¼ cup finely chopped *onion* in 2 tablespoons *margarine or butter* till tender. In a medium mixing bowl combine 3 beaten *eggs,* ⅔ cup *fine dry bread crumbs,* 2 teaspoons *Worcestershire sauce,* and 1 teaspoon *dry mustard.* Stir in onion mixture and two 6-ounce cans *crabmeat,* drained, flaked, and cartilage removed.

Using about ⅓ *cup* crab mixture for *each,* shape into ½-inch-thick patties. Coat patties with ¼ cup *fine dry bread crumbs.* In a large skillet heat ¼ cup *shortening or cooking oil.* Add *half* of the patties. Cook over medium heat about 3 minutes per side or till golden brown. Drain on paper towels. Keep warm in a 300° oven while frying remaining patties. Serve warm with *lemon wedges.* Makes 6 servings.

Deviled Crab

  2 **tablespoons margarine *or* butter**
  2 **tablespoons all-purpose flour**
  1 **cup milk *or* light cream**
    Several dashes bottled hot pepper
    sauce
  1 **6-ounce can crabmeat, drained,**
    flaked, and cartilage removed
  1 **hard-cooked egg, chopped**
  ½ **cup shredded process Swiss cheese**
  2 **tablespoons chopped pimiento**
  1 **tablespoon Dijon-style mustard**
  ¼ **cup fine dry bread crumbs**
  1 **tablespoon margarine *or* butter,**
    melted
  ¼ **cup sliced almonds,**
    toasted   Oven 375°

In a saucepan melt the 2 tablespoons margarine. Stir in flour. Add milk and hot pepper sauce all at once. Cook and stir till thickened and bubbly. Cook and stir 1 minute more.

Stir in crabmeat, chopped egg, cheese, pimiento, and mustard. Spoon into four 10-ounce casseroles or coquille shells. Toss bread crumbs with the 1 tablespoon melted margarine; sprinkle over casseroles. Top with almonds. Bake in a 375° oven about 20 minutes or till tops brown. Makes 4 servings.

Shrimp Creole

This peppy New Orleans dish is the perfect match for a cool, crisp salad.

**12 ounces fresh *or* frozen peeled and
        deveined shrimp
½ cup chopped onion
½ cup chopped celery
½ cup chopped green pepper
2 cloves garlic, minced
2 tablespoons margarine *or* butter
1 16-ounce can tomatoes, cut up
2 tablespoons snipped parsley
½ teaspoon salt
½ teaspoon paprika
⅛ to ¼ teaspoon ground red pepper
1 bay leaf
2 tablespoons cold water
4 teaspoons cornstarch
2 cups hot cooked rice**

Thaw shrimp, if frozen. In a large skillet cook onion, celery, green pepper, and garlic in margarine or butter till tender but not brown. Stir in *undrained* tomatoes, parsley, salt, paprika, red pepper, and bay leaf. Bring to boiling; reduce heat. Cover and simmer for 15 minutes.

Stir together cold water and cornstarch. Stir cornstarch mixture and shrimp into tomato mixture. Cook and stir till thickened and bubbly. Cook and stir about 2 minutes more or till shrimp turn pink. Remove bay leaf. Serve over rice. Makes 4 servings.

Microwave directions: Thaw shrimp, if frozen. In a 2-quart casserole micro-cook onion, celery, green pepper, garlic, and margarine or butter, covered, on 100% power (high) for 3 to 5 minutes or till vegetables are tender. Stir in *undrained* tomatoes, parsley, salt, paprika, red pepper, and bay leaf. Cook, covered, on high for 4 to 7 minutes or till bubbly, stirring once. Stir together water and *2 tablespoons* cornstarch; stir into tomato mixture. Cook, uncovered, on high for 1 to 2 minutes or till thickened and bubbly. Stir in shrimp. Cook, covered, on high, stirring once, for 3 to 5 minutes more or till shrimp turn pink. Remove bay leaf. Serve over rice.

Fish Creole: Prepare as above, *except* substitute 12 ounces fresh *or* frozen *fish fillets* for the shrimp. Thaw fish, if frozen. Cut into 1-inch pieces. Add fish to the tomato mixture after the mixture is thickened and bubbly. Cook and stir about 3 minutes or till fish flakes with a fork.

Shrimp Chow Mein

**12 ounces fresh *or* frozen peeled and
        deveined shrimp
1 cup water
¼ cup soy sauce
2 tablespoons cornstarch
1 teaspoon instant chicken bouillon
        granules
1 teaspoon grated gingerroot *or*
        ¼ teaspoon ground ginger
1 tablespoon cooking oil
1 cup sliced fresh mushrooms
1 small onion, halved lengthwise and
        sliced
2 cloves garlic, minced
1 8-ounce can sliced water chestnuts
½ of a 14-ounce can bean sprouts,
        drained
1 6-ounce package frozen pea pods,
        thawed
2 cups chow mein noodles, warmed,
        or hot cooked rice**

Thaw shrimp, if frozen. Cut any large shrimp in half lengthwise. For sauce, combine water, soy sauce, cornstarch, bouillon granules, and gingerroot or ginger. Set aside.

Preheat a wok or large skillet over high heat; add cooking oil. (Add more oil as necessary during cooking.) Stir-fry mushrooms, onion, and garlic for 1 minute. Remove vegetables. Stir-fry shrimp for 2 to 3 minutes or till shrimp turn pink. Push to side of wok or skillet.

Stir sauce; add to center of wok. Cook and stir till thickened and bubbly. Add water chestnuts, bean sprouts, pea pods, and cooked vegetables. Stir ingredients together to coat with sauce. Heat through. Serve over warmed chow mein noodles or hot cooked rice. Serves 4.

Scallop Chow Mein: Prepare as above, *except* substitute 12 ounces fresh *or* frozen *scallops* for the shrimp. Thaw scallops, if frozen. Cut any large scallops into bite-size pieces. Stir-fry scallops for 2 to 3 minutes or till they turn opaque.

Shrimp in Garlic Butter

**12 ounces fresh *or* frozen peeled and
   deveined shrimp**
2 tablespoons margarine *or* butter
3 cloves garlic, minced
2 tablespoons snipped parsley
1 tablespoon dry sherry

Thaw shrimp, if frozen. In a large skillet heat
margarine or butter over medium-high heat. Add
shrimp and garlic. Cook, stirring frequently, for 1
to 3 minutes or till shrimp turn pink. Stir in parsley and sherry. Makes 4 servings.

Scallops in Garlic Butter: Prepare as
above, *except* substitute 12 ounces fresh *or* frozen *scallops* for the shrimp. Thaw scallops, if frozen. Cut any large scallops in half. Cook and stir
the scallops and garlic in margarine or butter for
3 to 5 minutes or till scallops turn opaque.

French-Fried Shrimp

*Patting the shrimp dry before dipping them into
the batter gives a more even coating.*

**2 pounds fresh *or* frozen shrimp in
   shells**
   **Shortening *or* cooking oil for deep-
   fat frying**
¾ cup all-purpose flour
¼ cup yellow cornmeal
½ teaspoon sugar
½ teaspoon salt
   Dash pepper
1 beaten egg
¾ cup cold water
2 tablespoons cooking oil
   **Cocktail Sauce (see recipe, page
   364) (optional)**   Oven 300°

Thaw shrimp, if frozen. Peel shrimp, leaving the
last few sections before the tails and the tails
intact. To devein shrimp, use a sharp knife to
make a shallow slit along the back of each
shrimp. Remove the sandy black vein, if present.
To butterfly shrimp, make a deeper slit along the
back of the shrimp, cutting almost all the way
through. Lay the shrimp on a flat surface so that
the sides open to resemble a butterfly. Rinse; pat
dry with paper towels. Set aside.

In a large deep saucepan or deep-fat fryer, heat
2 inches melted shortening or oil to 375°. Meanwhile, for batter, stir together flour, cornmeal,
sugar, salt, and pepper. Make a well in the center.
Combine egg, cold water, and the 2 tablespoons
oil; add to dry ingredients. Beat with a rotary
beater till smooth. Dip shrimp into batter.

Fry shrimp, a few at a time, in the hot fat for 2
to 3 minutes or till golden. Remove with a slotted
spoon; drain on paper towels. Keep warm in a
300° oven while frying remainder. Serve with
Cocktail Sauce, if desired. Makes 6 servings.

To devein a shrimp, use the tip of a knife to lift
out the black vein.

To butterfly the shrimp, make a deep cut down
the back. Do not cut all the way through.

Linguine with White Clam Sauce

The zesty red clam sauce in the alternate recipe features tomato sauce with tomato tidbits.

    8 ounces linguine
    2 6½-ounce cans minced clams
       Light cream or milk
    ½ cup chopped onion
    2 cloves garlic, minced
    2 tablespoons margarine or butter
    ¼ cup all-purpose flour
    ½ teaspoon dried oregano, crushed
    ¼ teaspoon salt
    ⅛ teaspoon pepper
    ¼ cup snipped parsley
    ¼ cup dry white wine
    ¼ cup grated Parmesan cheese

Cook linguine according to package directions; drain well. Set aside.

Meanwhile, drain clams, reserving liquid from *one* can. Add enough light cream or milk to the reserved liquid to make *2 cups.*

For sauce, in a medium saucepan cook onion and garlic in margarine or butter till tender. Stir in flour, oregano, salt, and pepper. Add cream mixture all at once. Cook and stir till thickened and bubbly. Cook and stir for 1 minute more. Stir in clams, parsley, and wine. Heat through.

Serve sauce over linguine. Sprinkle with Parmesan cheese. Makes 4 servings.

Linguine with Red Clam Sauce: Prepare as above, *except* omit reserved clam liquid, cream or milk, and flour. Stir two 15-ounce cans *tomato sauce with tomato tidbits,* oregano, salt, pepper, drained clams, parsley, and wine into cooked onion and garlic. Heat through. Serve sauce over linguine. Sprinkle with Parmesan cheese.

Coquilles Saint Jacques

    1 pound fresh or frozen scallops
    4 tablespoons margarine or butter
    1 cup chopped fresh mushrooms
    2 tablespoons thinly sliced green
       onion
    2 tablespoons all-purpose flour
    ⅛ teaspoon pepper
    ⅔ cup light cream
    1 egg yolk, slightly beaten
    3 tablespoons dry white wine
    ¾ cup soft bread crumbs (1 slice)
    1 tablespoon margarine or butter,
       melted
    1 tablespoon snipped
       parsley   Oven 400°

Thaw scallops, if frozen. Halve any large scallops. In a large skillet cook *half* of the scallops in *1 tablespoon* of the margarine or butter over medium heat for 1 to 3 minutes or till scallops turn opaque. Remove scallops with a slotted spoon. Drain, if necessary. Repeat with remaining scallops and *1 tablespoon* of the margarine.

In the same skillet, cook mushrooms and onion in *2 tablespoons* margarine till tender. Stir in flour and pepper. Add cream; cook and stir till thickened and bubbly. Gradually stir hot mixture into egg yolk. Stir in cooked scallops and wine.

Spoon scallop mixture into 4 coquille shells, au gratin dishes, or 6-ounce custard cups. Place in a shallow baking pan. Toss together bread crumbs, melted margarine, and parsley; sprinkle over scallop mixtures. Bake in a 400° oven for 7 to 9 minutes or till crumbs are brown. Serves 4.

Microwave directions: Thaw scallops, if frozen. Halve any large scallops. In a 1½-quart casserole, micro-cook ½ cup *water* on 100% power (high) for 2 to 4 minutes or till boiling. Add scallops. Cook, covered, on high for 2 to 5 minutes or till scallops are opaque, stirring once or twice. Drain well. Cook mushrooms, onion, and *2 tablespoons* margarine, covered, on high for 2 to 3 minutes or till tender. Stir in flour and pepper. Add cream. Cook, uncovered, on high for 2 to 4 minutes or till bubbly; stir *every* 30 seconds. Gradually stir hot mixture into egg yolk. Stir in cooked scallops and wine. Spoon into 4 coquille shells, au gratin dishes, or 6-ounce custard cups. Combine bread crumbs, melted margarine, and parsley; sprinkle over the scallop mixtures. Cook, uncovered, on high for 1½ to 2½ minutes or till heated; rearrange once.

Curried Scallop Kabobs

Use 1 pound fresh *or* frozen *scallops.* Thaw scallops, if frozen. Halve any large scallops. Place scallops in a plastic bag. Set bag into a bowl. For marinade, combine ¼ cup *soy sauce,* 2 tablespoons *cooking oil,* 2 tablespoons *honey,* 2 tablespoons *vinegar,* 1 teaspoon *toasted sesame seed,* 1 teaspoon *curry powder,* and ¼ teaspoon *pepper;* add to bag. Seal bag; marinate at room temperature 15 minutes, turning bag occasionally.

Meanwhile, cut 1 *green pepper* into 1-inch squares. Cook in boiling water 1 minute; drain. Drain scallops; reserve marinade. Quarter and core one small *pineapple.* Slice one quarter. (Reserve remaining pineapple for another use.) Pit and quarter 2 *plums.* Using eight 10-inch skewers, alternately thread fruit, scallops, and green pepper, leaving about ¼ inch between pieces. Place on greased unheated rack of broiler pan. Brush with marinade. Broil 4 inches from heat 8 to 10 minutes or till scallops are opaque, turning and brushing often with marinade. Serves 4.

Crawfish Étouffée

- 1 **pound fresh *or* frozen peeled crawfish tails *or* peeled and deveined shrimp**
- 2 **cups chopped onion**
- 1 **cup finely chopped celery**
- ½ **cup finely chopped green pepper**
- 2 **cloves garlic, minced**
- 3 **tablespoons cooking oil, margarine, *or* butter**
- 2 **tablespoons crawfish fat, margarine, *or* butter**
- 4 **teaspoons cornstarch**
- ½ **cup tomato sauce**
- ⅛ **to ¼ teaspoon ground red pepper**
- 2 **cups hot cooked rice**

Thaw crawfish tails or shrimp, if frozen. In a large saucepan cook onion, celery, green pepper, and garlic, covered, in cooking oil for 10 minutes or till tender. Add crawfish fat; stir till melted. Stir in cornstarch. Add tomato sauce, red pepper, 1 cup *water,* ½ teaspoon *salt,* and ¼ teaspoon *black pepper.* Cook and stir till bubbly.

Add crawfish tails or shrimp. Return to boiling; reduce heat. Simmer, uncovered, for 4 to 5 minutes or till crawfish are tender (shrimp turn pink). Season to taste. Serve with rice. Serves 4.

Fried Seafood

- 2 **pints shucked clams *or* oysters, *or* 2 pounds fresh *or* frozen scallops, thawed**
- ⅓ **cup all-purpose flour**
- ¼ **teaspoon salt**
- ⅛ **teaspoon pepper**
- 2 **beaten eggs**
- 1 **cup finely crushed saltine crackers *or* fine dry bread crumbs**
   Shortening *or* cooking oil for deep-fat frying   Oven 300°

Pat seafood dry with paper towels. (If scallops are large, cut in half.) In a shallow bowl stir together flour, salt, and pepper. In another bowl mix eggs with 2 tablespoons *water.* Roll seafood in flour mixture, then dip into egg mixture and roll in cracker or bread crumbs. Fry, a few at a time, in deep hot fat (375°) for 1 to 1½ minutes or till golden. Drain on paper towels. Keep warm in a 300° oven while frying remainder. Serve with tartar sauce or cocktail sauce, if desired. Serves 4.

Oysters au Gratin

- 2 **pints shucked oysters**
- 3 **tablespoons margarine *or* butter**
- 1 **cup sliced fresh mushrooms**
- 1 **clove garlic, minced**
- 2 **tablespoons all-purpose flour**
- ¾ **cup milk**
- ¼ **cup dry white wine**
- 2 **tablespoons snipped parsley**
- ½ **teaspoon Worcestershire sauce**
- ¾ **cup soft bread crumbs**
- ¼ **cup grated Parmesan cheese**
- 1 **tablespoon margarine *or* butter, melted**   Oven 400°

Pat oysters dry. In a large skillet cook and stir oysters in *1 tablespoon* of the margarine for 3 to 4 minutes or till oyster edges curl. Drain. Transfer oysters to four 10-ounce casseroles.

For sauce, in the same skillet cook mushrooms and garlic in *2 tablespoons* margarine till tender. Stir in flour. Add milk all at once. Cook and stir till thickened and bubbly. Stir in wine, parsley, and Worcestershire sauce. Spoon over oysters.

Mix crumbs, Parmesan, and melted margarine. Sprinkle over sauce. Bake in a 400° oven for 10 minutes or till crumbs are brown. Serves 4.

Lobster Newburg

The rich Madeira-flavored sauce enhances the delicate taste of lobster.

  2 tablespoons margarine *or* butter
  2 tablespoons all-purpose flour
 ¼ teaspoon salt
    Dash ground red pepper
1½ cups light cream *or* milk
  2 beaten egg yolks
  2 5-ounce cans lobster, drained, broken into large pieces, and cartilage removed; *or* 10 ounces cooked lobster
  3 tablespoons Madeira *or* dry sherry
  4 baked patty shells
    Paprika
    Parsley sprigs (optional)

In a saucepan melt margarine or butter. Stir in flour, salt, and red pepper. Add cream all at once. Cook and stir till thickened and bubbly. Cook and stir 1 minute more. Stir about *half* of the hot mixture into egg yolks; return all to saucepan. Cook and stir till mixture just bubbles. Reduce heat. Cook and stir 2 minutes more. Stir in lobster and Madeira; heat through. Spoon into patty shells. Sprinkle with paprika. Garnish with parsley sprigs, if desired. Makes 4 servings.

    Crab Newburg: Prepare as above, *except* substitute two 7-ounce cans *crabmeat,* drained, flaked, and cartilage removed, *or* two 6-ounce packages frozen *crabmeat,* thawed and drained, for the lobster.

    Shrimp Newburg: Prepare as above, *except* substitute 8 ounces frozen peeled, cooked *shrimp* (1⅓ cups), thawed, for the lobster.

Boiled Lobster

In a 12-quart Dutch oven bring 8 quarts *water* and 2 teaspoons *salt* to boiling. Use two 1- to 1½-pound live *lobsters.* Grasp each lobster just behind the eyes; rinse lobsters under cold running water. Quickly plunge lobsters headfirst into the boiling water. Return to boiling; reduce heat. Cover and simmer for 20 minutes. Drain lobsters; remove the bands or pegs on large claws.

Place each lobster on its back. With kitchen shears, cut the body in half lengthwise up to the tail. Cut away the membrane on the tail to expose the meat. Remove black vein running through the tail and the small sand sac near the head. Remove the green tomalley (liver) and coral roe (found only in females); reserve to serve with the lobster, if desired. Twist the large claws away from the body. Using a nutcracker, break open the claws. Remove the meat from the claws, tail, and body. If desired, serve with Clarified Butter, tomalley, and roe. Makes 2 servings.

    Clarified Butter: Melt ½ cup *butter* over very low heat without stirring; cool slightly. Pour off clear top layer; discard milky bottom layer. Makes 2 servings.

Using kitchen shears, halve the body lengthwise up to the tail.

Remove the green tomalley (liver). Set aside and serve with the lobster meat, if desired.

Cooking Fish

Fish in most of its forms makes a quick-cooking main dish. Follow the times and directions below, cooking the fish till it flakes easily when tested with a fork (see photos, page 167). Season the cooked fish to taste with salt and pepper. If desired, serve lemon wedges with the fish.

Cooking Method	Fresh Fillets or Steaks	Frozen Fillets or Steaks	Dressed
Bake: Place in a single layer in a greased shallow baking pan. For fillets, tuck under any thin edges. Brush with melted margarine or butter.	Bake, uncovered, in a 450° oven for 4 to 6 minutes per ½-inch thickness.	Bake, uncovered, in a 450° oven for 9 to 11 minutes per ½-inch thickness.	Bake, uncovered, in a 350° oven for 6 to 9 minutes per ½ pound.
Broil: Preheat broiler. Place fish on the greased unheated rack of a broiler pan. For fillets, tuck under any thin edges. Brush with melted margarine or butter.	Broil 4 inches from the heat for 4 to 6 minutes per ½-inch thickness. If fish is 1 inch or more thick, turn it over half-way through broiling.	Broil 4 inches from the heat for 6 to 9 minutes per ½-inch thickness. If fish is 1 inch or more thick, turn it over half-way through broiling.	Not recommended.
Poach: Add 1½ cups water, broth, or wine to a large skillet. Bring to boiling. Add fish. Return to boiling; reduce heat.	Simmer, covered, for 4 to 6 minutes per ½-inch thickness.	Simmer, covered, for 6 to 9 minutes per ½-inch thickness.	Simmer, covered, for 6 to 9 minutes per ½ pound.
Grill: Place fillets in a well-greased grill basket. Place steaks on a greased grill rack.	Grill on an uncovered grill directly over *medium-hot* coals for 4 to 6 minutes per ½-inch thickness, turning once. Brush with melted margarine or butter, if necessary.	Not recommended.	Grill on an uncovered grill directly over *medium-hot* coals for 7 to 9 minutes for a ½- to 1½-pound fish. Brush with melted margarine or butter, if necessary.
Micro-cook: Remove head and tail from dressed fish. Arrange fish in a single layer in a shallow baking dish. For fillets, tuck under any thin edges. Cover with vented clear plastic wrap.	Micro-cook on 100% power (high). For ½ pound of ½-inch-thick fillets, allow 3 to 4 minutes; for 1 pound of ½-inch-thick fillets, allow 4 to 7 minutes. For 1 pound of ¾- to 1-inch-thick steaks, allow 7 to 9 minutes.	Not recommended.	Micro-cook on 100% power (high). For two 8- to 10-ounce fish, allow 5 to 7 minutes; for one 1- to 1½-pound fish, allow 10 to 12 minutes, giving dish a half-turn once. Let stand for 5 minutes.

Preparing and Cooking Shellfish

Shellfish	Preparation Directions	Cooking Directions
Clams	Scrub live clams under cold running water. For 24 clams, in an 8-quart Dutch oven combine 4 quarts of cold water and ⅓ cup salt. Add clams and soak for 15 minutes. Drain and rinse. Discard water. Repeat twice.	For 24 clams in shells, add water to an 8-quart Dutch oven to ½-inch depth; bring to boiling. Place clams in a steamer basket. Steam, covered, 5 minutes or till clams open. Discard any that do not open. Serve with melted butter or margarine or use as cooked clams in a recipe.
Crawfish	Rinse live crawfish under cold running water. For 4 pounds live crawfish, in a 12- to 16-quart kettle combine 8 quarts cold water and ⅓ cup salt. Add crawfish and soak for 15 minutes; rinse. Drain.	For 4 pounds live crawfish, in a 12- to 16-quart kettle bring 8 quarts water and 2 teaspoons salt to boiling. Add crawfish. Return to boiling; reduce heat. Simmer, covered, 5 minutes or till shells turn bright red. Drain. Serve hot with a sauce or melted butter or margarine.
Lobster tails	Thaw frozen tails.	For 4 tails, in a 3-quart saucepan bring 6 cups water and 1½ teaspoons salt to boiling. Add tails; return to boiling. Simmer, uncovered, for 4 to 8 minutes for 3-ounce tails (6 to 10 minutes for 6-ounce tails; 8 to 12 minutes for 8-ounce tails) or till shells turn bright red and meat is tender. Drain. Serve with melted butter or margarine and lemon, or remove meat and use as cooked lobster in a recipe.
Mussels	Scrub live mussels under cold running water. Using your fingers, pull out the beards that are visible between the shells. Soak (see clams, above).	For 24 mussels, add water to an 8-quart Dutch oven to ½-inch depth; bring to boiling. Place mussels in a steamer basket. Steam, covered, for 3 to 5 minutes or till shells open. Discard any that do not open. Serve with melted butter or margarine.
Oysters	Scrub live oysters under cold running water. For easier shucking, chill them before opening. Shuck, reserving bottom shells, if desired.	For 24 shucked oysters, simmer, uncovered, in 2 cups water and ½ teaspoon salt for 1 to 4 minutes or till oysters begin to curl around edges. Drain and chill. Serve with lemon and black pepper or on the half shell with a sauce.
Scallops	Thaw shelled scallops, if frozen. Rinse scallops and cut large ones in half.	For 1 pound, simmer, uncovered, in 4 cups water and 1 teaspoon salt for 1 to 2 minutes or till opaque, stirring occasionally. Drain. Use as cooked scallops in a recipe or chill and serve with a sauce.
Shrimp (in shells or peeled and deveined)	Rinse shrimp in shells or peeled shrimp under cold running water and drain. Store in the refrigerator for up to 2 days if not to be used immediately.	For 1 pound, simmer, uncovered, in 4 cups water and 1 teaspoon salt for 1 to 3 minutes or till shrimp turn pink, stirring occasionally. Rinse under cold running water. Drain. Use as cooked shrimp in a recipe or chill and serve with a sauce.

Nutrition Analysis

	Servings Per Recipe	Calories	Protein (g)	Carbohydrate (g)	Fat (g)	Cholesterol (mg)	Sodium (mg)	Potassium (mg)	Protein	Vitamin A	Vitamin C	Thiamine	Riboflavin	Niacin	Calcium	Iron
	Per Serving								**Percent U.S. RDA Per Serving**							
Apple Butter (p. 204)	128	33	0	8	0	0	0	32	0	0	2	0	0	0	0	1
Berry Freezer Jam (p. 204)	64	13	0	4	0	0	0	18	0	0	4	0	0	0	0	0
Bread 'n' Butter Pickles (p. 201)	80	19	0	5	0	0	113	48	0	0	2	1	0	0	1	1
Catsup (p. 200)	64	23	0	6	0	0	104	110	1	12	11	2	2	2	1	2
Corn Relish (p. 201)	224	16	0	4	0	0	60	36	1	2	7	1	0	1	0	1
Dill Pickles (p. 201)	12	7	0	1	0	0	160	43	0	0	1	1	0	1	2	1
Fruit-Juice Jelly (p. 203)	96	43	0	11	0	0	0	13	0	0	1	0	0	0	0	0
Grape Jam (p. 203)	96	47	0	12	0	0	0	32	0	0	1	1	1	0	0	0
Harvest Applesauce (p. 204)	24	97	0	25	0	0	0	127	0	1	7	1	1	0	1	1
Horseradish Pickles (p. 201)	80	19	0	5	0	0	113	48	0	0	2	1	0	0	1	1
Kosher-Style Dill Pickles (p. 201)	12	7	0	1	0	0	160	43	0	0	1	1	0	1	2	1
Mustard Pickles (p. 201)	50	8	0	2	0	0	81	51	0	1	7	1	0	0	0	0
Orange Marmalade (p. 203)	96	2	0	1	0	0	0	15	0	0	4	0	0	0	0	0
Peach-Berry Jam (p. 203)	112	43	0	11	0	0	0	17	0	1	2	0	0	0	0	0
Peach Jam (p. 203)	112	43	0	11	0	0	0	16	0	1	1	0	0	0	0	0
Peach-Plum Jam (p. 203)	112	43	0	11	0	0	0	16	0	1	1	0	0	0	0	0
Rhubarb-Raspberry Jam (p. 204)	80	46	0	12	0	0	4	34	0	0	3	0	0	0	1	0
Tomato Juice (p. 198)	20	32	1	7	0	0	147	343	2	37	35	7	5	5	1	4
Tomato Juice Cocktail (p. 199)	16	47	2	11	0	0	167	458	3	47	64	9	6	6	2	6
Vegetable Relish (p. 202)	256	9	0	2	0	0	55	24	0	3	12	1	0	0	0	1

On the divider: Rhubarb-Raspberry Jam (p. 204), canned peaches (p. 194), Dill Pickles (p. 201), and corn on the cob (p. 198).

Freezing and Canning

Enjoy fresh foods all year long by freezing, canning, or pickling them, or by making them into jellies and jams. You'll have foods just the way your family likes them, and always within easy reach.

Freezing

Freezing is one of the simplest methods of preserving foods. Because it only preserves the food, though, and doesn't improve its quality, always start with garden-fresh produce and top-quality baked goods, prepared dishes, and meats. Also, be sure to select varieties of fruits and vegetables recommended for freezing (check seed catalogs or ask a county extension agent), and to freeze the food when it's young, tender, and at its peak of flavor and texture.

Equipment

A colander and a large kettle, Dutch oven, or saucepan with a wire basket are basic to freezing foods. A freezer thermometer, to help you regulate the temperature of your freezer, also is a good investment. For best results, keep your freezer at 0° or below. Food deteriorates at temperatures above 0°.

For liquid or semi-liquid foods, use rigid plastic freezer containers, freezer bags, or wide-top freezing or canning jars. For solid or dry-packed foods, use freezer bags, heavy foil, plastic wrap for the freezer, or laminated freezer wrap.

All wrapping used for freezing should be moistureproof and vaporproof, able to withstand temperatures of 0° or below for extended times, and capable of being tightly sealed.

General Freezing Steps

1. Wash fruits and vegetables well in cold water. Prepare them as specified in the charts on pages 194–199. Rinse again and drain. Keep your work area clean.

2. Blanch vegetables (and fruits when directed) to stop or slow the enzymes that can cause loss of flavor and color and toughen the food. Follow these steps for blanching:

In a large kettle or Dutch oven, bring at least 4 quarts of water to a rapid boil.

Place 1 pound of prepared food in a wire basket. Lower the food into the water; cover. Start timing *immediately*. Cook on high heat for the time specified in the charts. (Add one minute if you live 5,000 feet above sea level or higher.)

Remove the food and plunge it into cold water to chill it quickly. Chill the food for the same length of time it was boiled. Drain well.

3. Put the food into the freezer container, leaving the amount of headspace specified (see tip, page 193).

4. For fruits, add one of the following packs as specified in the chart on pages 194–195:

Unsweetened or dry pack: Add no sugar or liquid to the fruit.

Water pack: Cover the fruit with water. Do not use glass jars for this pack. Be sure to maintain the specified headspace.

Sugar pack: Sprinkle the fruit with granulated sugar. If the fruit tends to darken, sprinkle with an ascorbic-acid color-keeper solution first.

Syrup pack: Cover the fruit with a syrup of sugar and water (see tip, page 192).

If the fruit floats above the level of the water or syrup, place crumpled clear plastic wrap atop the fruit to hold it under the surface.

5. Wipe any spills from the rims of the containers and jars. Seal the containers according to the manufacturer's directions, pressing out as much air as possible. If necessary, use freezer tape around the edges of the lids to ensure a tight seal.

6. Label each container with contents, amount, and date of freezing.

7. Add the packages to the freezer in batches to make sure that the food freezes quickly and solidly. Leave space between the packages so air can circulate around them.

Using Frozen Foods

Use frozen vegetables and fruits within 8 to 10 months. Don't thaw vegetables before cooking. Thaw fruits in their sealed containers in the refrigerator or in a bowl of cool water. If the fruit is to be used in cooking, thaw it just enough to be separated. If the fruit will not be cooked, thaw it only until a few ice crystals remain.

Wrap solid blocks of food in freezer paper or foil. Fold the edges down in a series of locked folds.

Fold in the ends of the package, pressing out air and fitting snugly. Secure with freezer tape.

Freezing Prepared Food

Freeze extras of everything from breads to stews to have foods in reserve. Freeze most casseroles before baking. Cook casseroles first, though, that contain raw rice, raw vegetables, or raw meat that has been frozen and thawed. Follow the freezing directions on pages 188–189.

Food	Preparation for Freezing	How to Serve	Storage Time
Breads, rolls, biscuits	Bake and cool. Seal in a freezer bag or container.	Thaw in package 1 hour or reheat in foil in a 300° oven about 20 minutes.	3 months
Cakes, cupcakes	Bake, remove from pans, and cool. Freeze on a tray, then wrap.	Unwrap. Thaw at room temperature 1 to 2 hours.	6 months
Casseroles (fish, poultry, or meat with vegetables or pasta)	Use less seasoning (some intensify during freezing) and undercook slightly. Cool quickly. Pour into a freezer container, freezer bag, or freezer-to-oven casserole (seal lid with freezer tape).	Bake in a 400° oven for 1¾ hours per quart. Cover for first half of the baking time, then uncover.	2 to 4 weeks
Cookies	*Unbaked:* Drop dough and freeze on a tray till firm; put into freezer bags. Or, shape into rolls; wrap individually.	Bake dropped dough without thawing. Thaw rolls until just soft enough to slice; bake.	6 months
	Baked: Cool. Freeze in containers.	Thaw.	6 to 8 months
Leftovers (meat with gravy, stews)	Cool. Package in rigid freezer containers (leaving headspace) or freezer bags.	Thaw, covered, in the refrigerator. Reheat.	1 to 3 months
Pies	*Unbaked:* Do not freeze pecan pie. Treat light-colored fruit with ascorbic-acid color keeper. Prepare pie as usual but do not cut slits in top crust. Use a metal or freezer-to-oven pie plate. Cover with inverted paper plate to protect crust. Place in a freezer bag.	Unwrap; cut slits in top. Cover edge with foil. Bake frozen pie in a 450° oven for 15 minutes, then in a 375° oven for 15 minutes. Uncover; bake about 30 minutes more or till done.	2 to 4 months
	Baked: Do not freeze cream or custard pies. Bake pie and cool. Package as directed for unbaked pies.	Thaw in package at room temperature. Reheat.	6 to 8 months
Sandwiches	Spread bread with margarine. Use cheese, meat, poultry, tuna, salmon, or peanut butter filling. Wrap individually. *Not recommended:* Lettuce, tomatoes, celery, jelly, cooked egg whites, mayonnaise, or salad dressing.	Thaw meat, poultry, or fish sandwiches in wrap in the refrigerator for 1 to 2 hours. Thaw other sandwiches at room temperature.	2 months
Stews, soups	Use vegetables that freeze well (not potatoes). Omit salt and thickening if to be kept longer than 2 months. Undercook vegetables. Cool quickly. Pour into freezer containers or bags, leaving some headspace.	Place frozen food in a heavy saucepan. Cook over low heat, separating often with a fork till hot. Season and thicken.	1 to 3 months

Canning

Canning foods for year-round enjoyment takes a knowledge of canning basics, top-quality food, and the right equipment. Go over the following procedures for canning, then review each step so you'll be confident as you begin.

Select varieties of fruits and vegetables that are recommended for canning (check seed catalogs or ask a county extension agent). Be sure to select top-quality fruits and vegetables that are fresh, young, and tender because even a little poor-quality food may affect an entire batch. For best results, can food within 12 hours of harvest.

Equipment

Canner: A *boiling-water canner* is used for fruits, tomatoes, pickles, relishes, jellies, jams, and preserves. The 212° temperature of boiling water (for the specified time) provides sufficient heat for canning these high-acid foods.

A *pressure canner* is used for low-acid foods, such as vegetables, because these foods must be processed at 240° or 250° (for the specified time). This is done under pressure in a pressure canner with a dial or a weighted gauge.

With both types of canning, to get high-quality, *safe* home-canned food, it's essential to carefully follow our directions and those of the equipment manufacturer.

Jars: Use only standard canning jars. These jars are tempered, and their mouths are specially threaded for canning. Run your finger over the rims of the jars to check for any chips. Discard any jars with chips or cracks.

Do not use jars from commercially prepared foods. They may not seal properly and may break during processing.

Lids: Use screw bands and flat metal lids with built-in sealing compound. Carefully follow the manufacturer's directions when preparing the lids and bands. Lids are designed for one-time use, but you can reuse screw bands if they are not bent or rusty.

Other useful pieces of equipment are a large kettle or Dutch oven, wide-mouth funnel, jar lifter, and food mill, colander, or sieve.

General Canning Steps

Foods are packed into canning jars by either the *raw-pack* (cold-pack) or the *hot-pack* method. In raw packing, the uncooked food is packed into the canning jar and covered with boiling water, juice, or syrup (see tip, page 192). In hot packing, food is partially cooked, then packed into jars and covered with the cooking liquid. Follow these guidelines for both methods.

1. Wash the canning jars in hot sudsy water and rinse thoroughly. Pour boiling water over the jars and let them stand in hot water until you're ready to fill them. Prepare the lids according to the manufacturer's directions.

2. Prepare only one cannerful of food at a time. Work quickly, preparing the foods as specified in the charts on pages 194–199. Keep your work area clean.

3. Place the hot jars on cloth towels to prevent them from slipping during packing.

4. Pack the food into each jar, leaving the recommended headspace (see charts).

5. Ladle or pour boiling liquid over the food, keeping the specified headspace.

6. Release air bubbles in the jar by gently working a wooden spoon or nonmetallic utensil down the jar's sides. Add liquid if needed.

7. Wipe the jar rim with a clean, damp cloth. Food on the rim prevents a perfect seal.

8. Add the prepared lid. Screw the band onto the jar by hand following the manufacturer's directions.

9. Set each jar into the canner as it is filled, being sure the jars do not touch.

10. Process filled jars, following the specified procedures and recipe timings exactly.

11. Remove jars and place on a towel to cool. Leave at least 1 inch of space between jars to allow air to circulate, but keep the area free of drafts.

12. After the jars are completely cooled, press the center of each lid to check the seal. If the dip in the lid holds, the jar is sealed. If the lid bounces up and down, the jar isn't sealed.

If a jar isn't sealed, check it for flaws. Repack and reprocess the contents using a clean jar and a *new* lid, processing the food again for the full length of time specified. Or freeze the food (allowing 1½-inch headspace). If you plan to use the food within a day or two, you also can refrigerate it.

13. Wipe the jars and lids. Label jars with contents and date. Remove the screw bands. Store in a cool (50° to 70°), dry, dark place. Use the food within one year.

Pressure Canning

Use a pressure canner to process low-acid foods such as vegetables. Before pressure-canning, study the instructions packed with your pressure canner to become familiar with the canner's operation. Make sure all parts work properly and are clean. If your canner has a dial gauge, have it checked for accuracy once a year. Contact your county extension service office for the nearest testing location.

When you're ready to start canning, check to see that the steam vent is clear. Set the canner and rack on the range top, and add 2 to 3 inches of hot water, or the amount specified by the canner manufacturer. Turn the heat to low.

Next, prepare enough food for one canner load. Fill each jar and place it in the canner. When the last jar is added, cover and lock the canner. Turn the heat to high. When steam comes out the vent, reduce the heat until the steam flows freely at a moderate rate. Let the steam flow steadily for 10 minutes or more to release all the air from inside the canner.

Close the vent, or place the weighted gauge over the vent according to your canner's instructions. Start the timing when the recommended pressure is reached. Adjust the heat to maintain a constant pressure.

When the processing time is up, remove the canner from the heat and set out of drafts on a rack or wooden board. Do not run water over the canner or rush the cooling. Allow the pressure to return to normal on its own.

Follow the canner's instructions for opening the pressure canner. Be sure to lift the cover away from you to avoid a blast of steam. If food is still boiling vigorously in the jars, wait a few minutes before removing the jars from the canner. Do not tighten the lids at this time. Cool the jars 2 to 3 inches apart on a wooden board or towels in a draft-free area. When completely cool, check the seals of the jars.

Syrup for Fruit

Choose the syrup that best suits the fruit and your taste. The heavier syrups are for tart fruits; the thin syrups, for mild-flavored fruits.

Place the specified amounts of sugar and water in a large saucepan. Heat until the sugar dissolves. Skim off the top, if necessary. Use the syrup hot when canning, cool when freezing. Allow ½ to ⅔ cup syrup for each 2 cups of fruit.

Type of Syrup	Sugar	Water	Yield
Very thin	1 cup	4 cups	4¾ cups
Thin	2 cups	4 cups	5 cups
Medium	3 cups	4 cups	5½ cups
Heavy	4½ cups	4 cups	6½ cups

Canning at High Altitudes

Boiling-Water Canning: Times given in this chapter for boiling-water processing are for altitudes less than 1,000 feet above sea level. If you live at a higher altitude, you must use a longer processing time (call your county extension agent for detailed instructions).

Pressure Canning: For pressure canning, the processing times remain the same at higher altitudes. Different pressures must be used, however.

For *weighted-gauge* canners, use 10 pounds of pressure if you live up to 1,000 feet above sea level. Use 15 pounds of pressure above 1,000 feet.

For *dial-gauge* pressure canners, use 11 pounds of pressure if you live up to 2,000 feet above sea level; 12 pounds for 2,001 to 4,000 feet; 13 pounds for 4,001 to 6,000 feet; and 14 pounds for 6,001 to 8,000 feet.

Before eating a pressure-canned food, boil it for 10 minutes if you live less than 1,000 feet above sea level. If you live at a higher altitude, add one minute for each 1,000 feet of elevation.

Boiling-Water Canning

A boiling-water canner is used to process fruits, tomatoes, pickles, jams, and jellies. It consists of a large, deep kettle, a lid, and a rack or basket for holding the jars. Any large kettle will work if it's deep enough to allow at least one inch of water to boil freely over the tops of the jars and if it has a rack and lid.

Set the canner and rack on the range top. Fill the canner half full of water. Cover and heat over high heat. Heat additional water.

Next, if needed, prepare the syrup, keeping it warm but not boiling. Prepare the food. When the water is hot, fill each jar and place it on the rack in the canner. Replace the canner cover each time you add a jar. After the last jar has been added, fill the canner with boiling water so that the water reaches 1 inch over the jar tops. Cover and heat to a brisk, rolling boil. Now begin the processing timing. Times given in this chapter are for canning at altitudes up to 1,000 feet above sea level. For higher altitudes, see the "Special Helps" chapter.

Keep the water boiling gently during processing, adding more boiling water if the level drops. If the water stops boiling when you add more, stop counting the time, turn up the heat, and wait for a full boil before resuming counting. At the end of the processing time, turn off the heat and remove the jars. Cool on a board or towel. When completely cool, check the seals of the jars.

Detecting Spoilage

Like commercially canned food, home-canned food will spoil if it isn't properly processed. Always inspect each home-canned jar carefully before serving. If the jar has leaked, shows patches of mold, or has a swollen lid, or if the food has a foamy or murky appearance, *discard* the food and the jar. The odor from the opened jar should be pleasant. If the food doesn't look or smell right, don't use it.

NEVER taste low-acid foods (those that were pressure-canned) cold from the jar. If these foods didn't seal or were improperly processed, harmful toxins (which cause botulism) can form without changing the food's appearance or smell. To ensure that the food is safe to eat, bring low-acid foods to a boil and boil for 10 minutes (if you live more than 1,000 feet above sea level, see tip, opposite). If the food looks and smells good after boiling, it's safe to eat. If you have any doubts, destroy the food.

Add or remove liquid and solids until the headspace measures exactly the amount specified.

Leaving Headspace

Allowing space between the top of the food and the rim of the container is essential when canning or freezing.

In canning, headspace is necessary for a vacuum to form. Too little or too much headspace, however, can prevent a good seal. (See charts, pages 194–199, for recommended headspace.)

In freezing, headspace allows room for the food to expand without breaking the container. If you're using freezer bags, press out the air. Allow headspace according to these guidelines.

Sugar, syrup, or water pack: For wide-top containers with straight or slightly flared sides, leave a ½-inch headspace for pints and a 1-inch headspace for quarts.

For narrow-top containers and canning jars, leave a ¾-inch headspace for pints and a 1½-inch headspace for quarts.

Unsweetened or dry pack (no sugar or liquid): Leave a ½-inch headspace unless directed otherwise.

Canning and Freezing Fruits, Including Tomatoes

Food	Preparation	Boiling-Water Canning, Raw Pack
Apples	Allow 2½ to 3 pounds per quart. Peel and core; halve, quarter, or slice. Dip into ascorbic-acid color-keeper solution; drain.	Not recommended.
Apricots	Allow 1½ to 2½ pounds per quart. If desired, peel (see note, page 203). Prepare as for peaches, below.	See peaches, below.
Berries	Allow 1½ to 2½ pounds per quart for blackberries, blueberries, currants, huckleberries, gooseberries, elderberries, loganberries, raspberries, mulberries, strawberries, and boysenberries.	Not recommended for strawberries and boysenberries. Fill jars, shaking down gently. Add boiling syrup,° juice, or water, leaving a ½-inch headspace. Process pints for 15 minutes and quarts for 20 minutes.
Cherries	Allow 2 to 3 pounds per quart. If desired, pit and treat with ascorbic-acid color-keeper solution.	Fill jars, shaking down gently. Add boiling syrup° or water, leaving a ½-inch headspace. Process pints for 25 minutes.
Melons	Allow about 4 pounds per quart for honeydew, cantaloupe, and watermelon.	Not recommended.
Peaches, nectarines	Allow 2 to 3 pounds per quart. Peel (see note, page 203). Halve and pit. Slice, if desired. Treat with ascorbic-acid color-keeper solution; drain.	Fill jars. Add boiling syrup° or water, leaving a ½-inch headspace. Process pints for 25 minutes and quarts for 30 minutes. (Note: Hot pack gives a better product.)
Pears	Allow 2 to 3 pounds per quart. Peel, halve, and core. Treat with ascorbic-acid color-keeper solution; drain.	Not recommended.
Plums	Allow 1½ to 2½ pounds per quart. Prick skin on 2 sides. Freestone varieties may be halved and pitted.	Pack firmly into jars. Add boiling syrup,° leaving a ½-inch headspace. Process pints for 25 minutes and quarts for 30 minutes.
Rhubarb	Allow 1 to 2 pounds per quart. Discard leaves and woody ends. Cut into ½- to 1-inch pieces.	Not recommended.
Tomatoes	Allow 2½ to 3½ pounds per quart. Use underripe to ripe, unblemished tomatoes. Peel and core (see note, page 203). Cut large tomatoes into eighths. Remove seeds, if desired.	Not recommended.

°Note: See "Syrup for Fruit," page 192.

Boiling-Water Canning, Hot Pack	Freezing
Simmer in syrup* for 5 minutes. Fill jars with fruit and syrup, leaving a ½-inch headspace. Process quarts and pints for 20 minutes.	For a firmer texture, steam apple pieces on a rack over boiling water for ½ to 3 minutes. Cool in very cold water. Use syrup, sugar, or dry pack (see page 189), leaving the recommended headspace (see page 193).
See peaches, below.	Peel (see note, page 203). Use syrup pack, sugar pack, or water pack (see page 189), leaving the recommended headspace (see page 193).
Simmer blueberries, currants, elderberries, gooseberries, and huckleberries in water for 30 seconds. Drain. Fill jars with berries and hot syrup,* leaving a ½-inch headspace. Process quarts and pints for 15 minutes.	Use syrup, sugar, or dry pack (see page 189), leaving the recommended headspace (see page 193). Slice strawberries, if desired.
Add to hot syrup;* bring to boiling. Fill jars with fruit and syrup, leaving a ½-inch headspace. Process pints 15 minutes; quarts 20 minutes.	Use syrup pack, sugar pack, or dry pack (see page 189), leaving the recommended headspace (see page 193).
Not recommended.	Use dry or syrup pack (see page 189), leaving the recommended headspace (see page 193).
Add to hot syrup;* bring to boiling. Fill jars with fruit (in layers with cut side down) and syrup, leaving a ½-inch headspace. Process pints for 20 minutes and quarts for 25 minutes.	Use syrup pack, sugar pack, or water pack (see page 189), leaving the recommended headspace (see page 193).
Simmer fruit in syrup* for 5 minutes. Fill jars with fruit and syrup, leaving a ½-inch headspace. Process pints for 20 minutes; quarts 25 minutes.	Not recommended.
Simmer in syrup* for 2 minutes. Remove from heat. Let stand, covered, 20 to 30 minutes. Fill jars with fruit and syrup, leaving a ½-inch headspace. Process pints 20 minutes and quarts 25 minutes.	Halve and pit. Treat with ascorbic-acid color-keeper solution; drain well. Use dry pack, sugar pack, or syrup pack (see page 189), leaving the recommended headspace (see page 193).
In a saucepan sprinkle ½ cup sugar over each 4 cups fruit; mix well. Let stand till juice appears. Bring slowly to boiling, stirring gently. Fill jars with hot fruit and juice, leaving a ½-inch headspace. Process pints and quarts for 15 minutes.	Blanch for 1 minute; cool quickly. Drain. Use dry pack or syrup pack (see page 189), leaving the recommended headspace (see page 193). Or use a sugar pack of ½ cup sugar to 3 cups fruit.
Chop one-sixth of tomatoes. In large kettle, bring slowly to a boil. Add remaining tomatoes. Simmer 5 minutes. Add 1 tablespoon lemon juice to each pint jar or 2 tablespoons to each quart jar. Add ½ teaspoon salt to each pint jar and 1 teaspoon to each quart jar, if desired. Fill jars with hot tomatoes and liquid, leaving a ½-inch headspace. Process pints 35 minutes; quarts 45 minutes.	In a large kettle, simmer tomatoes for 10 minutes or till tender, stirring constantly. Set kettle into sink of ice water to cool. Pack tomatoes and liquid into freezer containers or jars, leaving the recommended headspace (see page 193). If desired, add ½ teaspoon salt to each pint jar and 1 teaspoon to each quart jar. (Use in casseroles, soups, and stews.)

Canning and Freezing Vegetables

Vegetable	Preparation	Pressure Canning, Raw Pack
Asparagus	Allow 2½ to 4½ pounds per quart. Wash; scrape off scales. Break off woody bases where spears snap easily. Wash again. Sort by thickness. Leave whole or cut into 1-inch lengths.	Not recommended.
Beans, green or wax	Allow 1½ to 2½ pounds per quart. Wash; remove ends and strings. Leave whole or snap or cut into 1-inch pieces.	Pack tightly in jars; add boiling water, leaving a 1-inch headspace. Process pints for 20 minutes and quarts for 25 minutes.
Beans, lima or butter	Allow 3 to 5 pounds unshelled beans per quart. Wash, shell, rinse, drain, and sort beans by size.	Fill jars with beans; do not shake down. Add boiling water, leaving a 1-inch headspace for pints, a 1¼-inch headspace for large beans in quarts, and a 1½-inch headspace for small beans in quarts. Process pints for 40 minutes and quarts for 50 minutes.
Beets	Allow about 3 pounds per quart. Rinse. Cut off all but 1 inch of tops. Leave roots. Scrub well.	Not recommended.
Broccoli	Allow about 1 pound per pint. Wash; remove outer leaves and tough parts of stalks. Wash again. Cut lengthwise into spears. Cut to fit containers.	Not recommended.
Carrots	Allow 2 to 3 pounds per quart. Rinse, trim, peel, and rinse again. Leave tiny ones whole. For larger ones, slice, dice, or cut into strips.	Pack tightly into jars; add boiling water, leaving a 1-inch headspace. Process pints for 25 minutes and quarts for 30 minutes.
Cauliflower	Allow 1 to 1½ pounds per pint. Wash; remove leaves and woody stems. Break into 1-inch pieces.	Not recommended.
Corn, cream-style	Allow 2 to 3 pounds per pint. Clean as for corn on the cob (see page 198).	Use a sharp knife to cut off just the kernel tips, then scrape corn with dull edge of knife. Pack loosely in pint jars (do not shake); add boiling water, leaving a 1-inch headspace. Process pints for 95 minutes. Quarts are not recommended.
Corn, whole kernel	Allow 4 to 5 pounds per quart. Clean as for corn on the cob (see page 198).	Cut corn from cobs at two-thirds depth of kernels; do not scrape. Pack loosely in jars (do not shake or press down). Add boiling water, leaving a 1-inch headspace. Process pints for 55 minutes and quarts for 85 minutes.

Pressure Canning, Hot Pack	Freezing
Not recommended.	Blanch small spears for 2 minutes, medium for 3 minutes, and large for 4 minutes. Cool quickly. Fill containers; shake down, leaving a ½-inch headspace.
Boil 5 minutes. Loosely fill jars with beans and cooking liquid, leaving a 1-inch headspace. Process pints for 20 minutes; quarts 25 minutes.	Blanch for 3 minutes; cool quickly. Fill containers; shake down, leaving a ½-inch headspace.
Cover beans with boiling water; return to boiling. Fill jars loosely with beans and cooking liquid, leaving a 1-inch headspace. Process pints for 40 minutes and quarts for 50 minutes.	Blanch small beans for 2 minutes and large beans for 4 minutes; cool quickly. Fill containers loosely, leaving a ½-inch headspace.
Boil 15 to 25 minutes or till skins slip off easily. Cool, peel, and trim. Cube, slice, or leave small ones whole. Pack into jars; fill with *fresh hot* water, leaving a 1-inch headspace. Process pints for 30 minutes and quarts for 35 minutes.	Boil for 25 to 50 minutes or till tender. Drain; cool. Slip off skins. Cube or slice. Fill containers loosely (shake lightly), leaving a ½-inch headspace.
Not recommended.	Blanch 3 minutes in boiling water or 5 minutes over steam; cool quickly. Package, leaving no headspace.
Simmer 5 minutes. Fill jars with carrots and cooking liquid, leaving a 1-inch headspace. Process pints for 25 minutes and quarts for 30 minutes.	Blanch tiny whole carrots for 5 minutes and cut-up carrots for 2 minutes; cool quickly. Pack closely into containers, leaving a ½-inch headspace.
Not recommended.	Blanch for 3 minutes; cool quickly. Package, leaving no headspace.
Use a sharp knife to cut off just the kernel tips, then scrape corn with a dull knife. Bring to boiling 2 cups water for each 4 cups corn. Add corn; return to boiling. Fill pint jars, leaving a 1-inch headspace. Process pints for 85 minutes. Quarts are not recommended.	Do not cut corn off cob. Blanch 6 ears at a time for 4 minutes. Cut off just the kernel tips; scrape cobs with a table knife. Fill containers, shaking down and leaving ½-inch headspace.
Cut corn from cobs at two-thirds depth of kernels; do not scrape. Bring to boiling 1 cup water for each 4 cups corn. Add corn; simmer 5 minutes. Fill jars with corn and liquid, leaving a 1-inch headspace. Process pints for 55 minutes and quarts 85 minutes.	Do not cut corn off cobs. Blanch 6 ears at a time for 4 minutes; cool quickly. Cut corn from cobs at two-thirds depth of kernels; do not scrape. Fill containers, shaking to pack lightly and leaving a ½-inch headspace.

Canning and Freezing Vegetables (Continued)

Vegetable	Preparation	Pressure Canning, Raw Pack
Corn on the cob	Remove husks. Scrub with a vegetable brush to remove silks. Wash and drain.	Not recommended.
Peas, green or English	Allow 2 to 2½ pounds per pint. Wash, shell, rinse, and drain.	Pack loosely in pint jars (do not shake or press down); add boiling water, leaving a 1-inch headspace. Process pints for 40 minutes. Quarts are not recommended.
Peppers, sweet	Wash. Remove stems, seeds, and membranes. Cut into large pieces or leave whole.	Not recommended.
Squash, winter, and pumpkin	Allow 1½ to 3 pounds per quart. Peel and cut into 1-inch cubes. *Do not can mashed squash or pumpkin.*	Not recommended.
Turnips, rutabagas	Rinse, trim, peel, and rinse again. Slice or cube.	Not recommended.

Safety Reminder

Always boil home-canned vegetables (except tomatoes) *before* tasting or using them. Bring the food to a boil and boil for 10 minutes if you live less than 1,000 feet above sea level. If you live more than 1,000 feet above sea level, add one additional minute for each 1,000 feet of elevation. Add water, if needed, to prevent sticking. If you smell an unnatural odor as the food heats, discard the food.

Tomato Juice

Thoroughly wash 8 pounds ripe but firm *tomatoes*. Remove stems. Core and cut into pieces; drain. Place tomatoes in an 8- or 10-quart kettle. Bring to boiling over low heat, stirring frequently. Cover and simmer about 15 minutes or till soft, stirring often. Press tomatoes through a food mill or sieve. Discard solids.

Return tomato juice to the kettle and bring to boiling. Boil gently, uncovered, for 5 minutes, stirring often. Makes about 5 pints (twenty ½-cup servings).

Boiling-Water Canning: Add 1 tablespoon *lemon juice* to each hot, clean pint jar or 2 tablespoons *lemon juice* to each hot, clean quart jar. If desired, add ¼ teaspoon salt to each pint or ½ teaspoon salt to each quart jar. Pour hot juice into jars, leaving a ½-inch headspace. Process pints for 35 minutes; quarts for 40 minutes.

Freezing: Cool tomato juice. Pour into wide-top freezer containers, leaving a ½-inch headspace. If desired, add ¼ teaspoon salt to pints or ½ teaspoon salt to quarts. Seal, label, and freeze.

Pressure Canning, Hot Pack	Freezing
Not recommended.	Blanch 6 ears at a time, allowing 7 minutes for small ears, 9 minutes for medium, and 11 minutes for large. Drain well. Wrap individually in foil, molding to the shape of the ear. Seal in a freezer bag. Use within 4 to 6 months. Cook, without thawing, in boiling water for 5 to 10 minutes.
Cover with boiling water. Simmer for 2 minutes. Fill pint jars loosely with peas; add cooking liquid, leaving a 1-inch headspace. Process pints for 40 minutes. Quarts are not recommended.	Blanch 1½ minutes; chill quickly. Fill containers, shaking down and leaving ½-inch headspace.
Not recommended.	Spread peppers in a single layer on a baking sheet; freeze firm. Fill container, shaking to pack closely and leaving no headspace.
Simmer 2 minutes in water to cover. Do not mash or puree. Fill jars with cubes and cooking liquid, leaving a 1-inch headspace. Process pints for 55 minutes and quarts for 90 minutes.	Simmer about 15 minutes or till tender. Drain; place pan in ice water to cool quickly. Mash. Fill containers, shaking to pack lightly and leaving a ½-inch headspace. Cook without thawing, covered, for 20 minutes, stirring occasionally.
Not recommended.	Blanch for 2 minutes; cool quickly. Fill containers, leaving no headspace.

Tomato Juice Cocktail

Start with the smaller amount of horseradish and add more until you get just the zest you like.

- **8 pounds tomatoes***
- **1 cup chopped celery**
- **½ cup chopped onion**
- **¼ cup lemon juice**
- **1 tablespoon sugar**
- **1 tablespoon Worcestershire sauce**
- **1 teaspoon salt**
- **1 to 2 teaspoons prepared horseradish**
- **¼ teaspoon bottled hot pepper sauce**

Thoroughly wash tomatoes. Remove stems. Cut out cores. Cut tomatoes into pieces; drain.

In an 8- or 10-quart kettle or Dutch oven combine *19 cups* tomato pieces, the celery, and on-ion. Bring to boiling over low heat, stirring frequently. Cover and simmer about 15 minutes or till soft; stir often to prevent sticking.

Press through a food mill or sieve to extract juice; measure *12 cups* juice. Discard solids. Re-turn juice to the kettle and bring to boiling. Boil gently, uncovered, for 15 minutes, stirring often. (You should have about 9½ to 10 cups juice.)

Stir in lemon juice, sugar, Worcestershire sauce, salt, prepared horseradish, and bottled hot pepper sauce. Simmer for 10 minutes. Makes about 4 pints (sixteen ½-cup servings).

Pressure Canning: Pour hot juice into hot, clean pint jars, leaving a ½-inch headspace. Pro-cess pints for 15 minutes.

Freezing: Cool juice. Pour into wide-top freezer containers, leaving a ½-inch headspace. Seal, label, and freeze.

***Note:** Tomatoes should be ripe but still firm.

Catsup

The fresh tomato flavor comes through in this thick catsup.

  1   **cup white vinegar**
1½   **inches stick cinnamon, broken**
1½   **teaspoons whole cloves**
  1   **teaspoon celery seed**
  8   **pounds tomatoes (24 medium)**
 ½   **cup chopped onion**
 ¼   **teaspoon ground red pepper**
  1   **cup sugar**
  1   **tablespoon salt**

In a saucepan combine vinegar, stick cinnamon, cloves, and celery seed. Bring to boiling. Remove from heat; set aside.

Wash, core, and quarter tomatoes. Drain in a colander; discard liquid. Place tomatoes in an 8- or 10-quart kettle or Dutch oven. Add onion and ground red pepper. Bring to boiling; cook 15 minutes, stirring often.

Put mixture through a food mill or sieve; discard seeds and skins. Return puree to kettle; add sugar. (Measure depth with a ruler at start and finish.) Bring to boiling; reduce heat. Simmer for 1½ to 2 hours or till reduced by half, stirring occasionally. Strain vinegar mixture into tomatoes; discard spices. Add salt. Simmer about 30 minutes or to desired consistency, stirring often. May be refrigerated up to 1 month. Makes 4 half-pints (sixty-four 1-tablespoon servings).

Boiling-Water Canning: Ladle hot catsup into hot, *sterilized* half-pint jars, leaving a ½-inch headspace. Adjust lids. Process in a boiling-water canner for 10 minutes.

Freezing: Set the kettle into a sink of *ice* water; cool. Ladle catsup into freezer containers, leaving a ½-inch headspace. Seal, label, and freeze for 8 to 10 months.

Pickles and Relishes

For full-flavored, homemade pickles, remember the following guidelines:

Start with cucumber varieties specially developed for pickling. These varieties yield the crunchiest pickles. Select top-quality, unwaxed cucumbers, and start your recipe as soon as possible after harvesting (within 12 hours). Be sure to remove the blossoms and a slice off the blossom end.

For pickles and relishes, use granulated pickling or canning salt. Iodized table salt may cause the pickles to darken, and uniodized table salt may make the brine cloudy. Choose a high-grade vinegar of 4 to 6 percent acid (40 to 60 grain). Cider vinegar is most often used for pickles, but white vinegar may be used when a lighter-colored product is desired. Never dilute the vinegar more than indicated in the recipe. Instead, for a less-sour product, add additional sugar.

To make sure your pickles and relishes don't spoil, process them in a boiling-water canner with standard canning jars and lids. Use stoneware, glass, aluminum, enameled ware, or stainless-steel utensils when preparing your pickles. Do not use copper, brass, zinc, galvanized, or iron utensils. Follow the general directions for processing in a boiling-water canner beginning on page 191. When making pickles, though, be sure to sterilize the jars by immersing them in boiling water for 10 minutes before filling.

Pickle Problems

Hollow pickles: cucumbers poorly developed or not fresh.

Shriveled pickles: salt, sugar, or vinegar solution too strong.

Soft or slippery pickles: too little salt or vinegar, an imperfect seal, or too little processing time.

Dill Pickles

The ingredients listed are for one quart. Multiply by the number of quarts you plan to make. (Pictured on page 187.)

½ **pound 4-inch pickling cucumbers (5 or 6 cucumbers)**
4 **to 6 heads fresh dill *or* 2 to 3 tablespoons dillseed**
1 **teaspoon mustard seed**
1¾ **cups water**
¾ **cup cider vinegar**
1 **tablespoon pickling salt**

Thoroughly rinse cucumbers. Remove stems and cut off a slice from each blossom end. Pack cucumbers loosely into a hot, *sterilized* quart jar, leaving a ½-inch headspace. Add dill and mustard seed. Make a brine by combining water, vinegar, and salt. Bring to boiling.

Pour hot brine over cucumbers, leaving a ½-inch headspace. Adjust lid. Process in a boiling-water canner for 15 minutes. Let stand 1 week before opening. Makes 1 quart (12 servings).

Kosher-Style Dill Pickles: Prepare as above, *except* substitute 2 cloves *garlic,* halved, for the mustard seed.

Bread 'n' Butter Pickles

4 **quarts sliced medium cucumbers**
8 **medium white onions, sliced**
⅓ **cup pickling salt**
3 **cloves garlic, halved**
   Cracked ice
5 **cups sugar**
3 **cups cider vinegar**
2 **tablespoons mustard seed**
1½ **teaspoons turmeric**
1½ **teaspoons celery seed**

In a large bowl combine cucumbers, onions, salt, and garlic. Stir in a large amount of cracked ice. Let stand 3 hours; drain well. Remove garlic. In a large kettle combine sugar, vinegar, mustard seed, turmeric, and celery seed. Add drained mixture. Bring to boiling. Pack cucumber mixture and liquid into hot, *sterilized* pint jars, leaving a ½-inch headspace. Adjust lids. Process 10 minutes. Makes 8 pints (80 servings).

Horseradish Pickles: Prepare as above, *except* add ½ cup prepared *horseradish* to the sugar mixture.

Mustard Pickles

2 **pounds medium pickling cucumbers or zucchini**
1 **1-pound head cauliflower, broken into flowerets**
2 **cups white vinegar**
1⅓ **cups sugar**
1 **tablespoon pickling salt**
1 **tablespoon dry mustard**
1 **tablespoon prepared horseradish**
1½ **teaspoons celery seed**

Cut cucumbers into ½-inch chunks or ¼-inch slices; measure 6 cups. Pack cucumbers and cauliflower into hot, *sterilized* pint jars, leaving a ½-inch headspace. In a saucepan mix remaining ingredients and 1⅓ cups *water.* Bring to a boil.

Pour hot liquid over vegetables, leaving the ½-inch headspace. (Liquid will be cloudy because of the mustard.) Adjust lids. Process in boiling-water canner 10 minutes. Makes 5 pints (50 servings).

Corn Relish

12 **to 16 fresh ears of corn**
3 **cups chopped celery (6 stalks)**
1½ **cups chopped sweet red pepper**
1½ **cups chopped green pepper**
1 **cup chopped onion (2 medium)**
2½ **cups vinegar**
1¾ **cups sugar**
2 **tablespoons pickling salt**
2 **teaspoons celery seed**
⅓ **cup all-purpose flour**
2 **tablespoons dry mustard**
1 **teaspoon ground turmeric**

Cut corn from cobs (*do not scrape cobs*). Measure *8 cups* cut corn. In an 8- or 10-quart kettle or Dutch oven combine corn and 2 cups *water.* Bring to boiling; reduce heat. Simmer, covered, about 12 minutes or till corn is nearly tender.

Add celery, red and green pepper, and onion. Stir in *2 cups* vinegar, sugar, pickling salt, and celery seed. Return to boiling. Boil, uncovered, 5 minutes, stirring occasionally. Stir together remaining vinegar, flour, dry mustard, and turmeric. Add to corn mixture. Cook and stir till bubbly; cook 1 minute more. Ladle into hot, *sterilized* pint jars, leaving a ½-inch headspace. Adjust lids. Process in a boiling-water canner for 15 minutes. Makes 7 pints (224 one-tablespoon servings).

Vegetable Relish

This sweet relish is great on burgers and hot dogs.

> 8 **medium tomatoes, peeled, cored,
>   and cut up (about 2¾ pounds)**
> 6 **medium zucchini, quartered
>   lengthwise (about 3 pounds)**
> 3 **large sweet red peppers, stems
>   and seeds removed, and cut up**
> 3 **large green peppers, stems and
>   seeds removed, and cut up**
> 2 **medium onions, quartered**
> 4 **cloves garlic**
> ¼ **cup pickling salt**
> 2 **cups sugar**
> 2 **cups vinegar**
> 1 **cup water**
> 2 **teaspoons dried thyme, crushed**
> ½ **teaspoon pepper**

Using the coarse blade of a food grinder, grind tomatoes, zucchini, red peppers, green peppers, onions, and garlic. Place in a colander to drain excess liquid. Place ground-vegetable mixture in a large *nonmetallic* container and sprinkle with the pickling salt. Let stand overnight.

Rinse ground-vegetable mixture. Drain well. In an 8- or 10-quart kettle or Dutch oven combine sugar, vinegar, water, thyme, and pepper. Bring to boiling, stirring to dissolve sugar. Stir in ground-vegetable mixture. Return mixture to boiling. Remove from heat. Makes about 8 pints (256 one-tablespoon servings).

Boiling-Water Canning: Ladle hot vegetable mixture into hot, *sterilized* pint jars, leaving a ½-inch headspace. Adjust lids. Process in a boiling-water canner for 10 minutes.

Freezing: Cool vegetable mixture quickly by setting kettle into a sink of *ice* water. Ladle relish into freezer containers, leaving a ½-inch headspace. Seal, label, and freeze.

Jellies and Jams

Jelly making is one canning process you can do year-round. By using either fresh produce or frozen or canned products, you can have delicious jams, jellies, and marmalades for your family and for gift giving anytime.

Equipment

To make jelly, you'll need a large kettle or Dutch oven. To allow for vigorous boiling, the jelly mixture should fill no more than one-third of the pan before it starts cooking.

Canning is necessary to prevent jellies and jams from molding during storage. If you don't have a standard boiling-water canner, you can substitute a large kettle and rack. Just be sure the kettle is deep enough to allow one inch of boiling water above the tops of the jars. You'll also need canning jars, canning lids and screw bands, a sieve or food mill, and a funnel.

Jelly-Making Procedure

Follow our recipes carefully. Note that liquid and powdered pectins are added differently to different mixtures. Prepare only one batch at a time. When the jelly is done, remove it from the heat. Skim the foam from the top with a large metal spoon and discard it. Follow the general procedures for canning beginning on page 191. When making jelly, though, you'll need to sterilize the jars by immersing them in boiling water for 10 minutes before filling them. Ladle the hot jelly into the jars. Wipe the rims of the jars carefully to remove all food. Adjust the lids and screw bands. Set the jars into the boiling-water canner. Begin timing when the water returns to a boil.

Terms to Know

Full Rolling Boil: A boil that is so rapid you can't stir it down with a spoon.

Sheets Off the Spoon: A test for the jellying point of jams and jellies. For this test, dip a metal spoon into the boiling mixture, then hold it over the kettle. If the mixture is done, two drops will hang off the edge of the spoon and then run together. If you have a candy thermometer, use it to find when the jellying point is reached (8° above the boiling point of water).

Pectin: A substance in some fruits, especially underripe fruit, that makes a fruit and sugar mixture gel or set up. Powdered, liquid, or light pectin are called for in a recipe if the fruit doesn't have enough natural pectin to gel. Be sure to use the type of pectin called for.

Fruit-Juice Jelly

    4 **cups unsweetened apple, grape, or**
       orange juice, or cranberry juice
       cocktail (not low calorie)
    ¼ **cup lemon juice**
    1 **1¾-ounce package powdered**
       fruit pectin
    4½ **cups sugar**

Pour fruit juice and lemon juice into an 8- or 10-quart kettle. Sprinkle with pectin. Let stand 1 or 2 minutes; stir to dissolve. Bring to a full rolling boil over medium-high heat; stir frequently. Stir in sugar. Return to a full rolling boil; stir often. Boil hard 1 minute, stirring constantly. Remove from heat; quickly skim off foam with a metal spoon.

Ladle into hot, *sterilized* half-pint jars, leaving a ¼-inch headspace. Adjust lids. Process in a boiling-water canner 5 minutes. Makes 6 half-pints (96 one-tablespoon servings).

Peach Jam

    2½ **to 3 pounds peaches (10 to 12)**
    1 **1¾-ounce package powdered**
       fruit pectin
    2 **tablespoons lemon juice**
    5½ **cups sugar**

Peel,* pit, and coarsely grind or mash peaches; measure *4 cups*. In an 8- or 10-quart kettle combine peaches, pectin, and lemon juice. Bring to a full rolling boil, stirring constantly. Stir in sugar.

Return to a full rolling boil. Boil hard for 1 minute, stirring constantly. Remove from heat; quickly skim off foam with a metal spoon. Ladle at once into hot, *sterilized* half-pint jars, leaving a ¼-inch headspace. Adjust lids. Process in boiling-water canner 5 minutes. Makes 7 half-pints (112 one-tablespoon servings).

Peach-Plum Jam: Prepare as above, *except* reduce peaches to *1½ pounds (2 cups ground)*. Add 1 pound fully ripe *Italian prune plums*, pitted and finely chopped (2 cups), with pectin.

Peach-Berry Jam: Prepare as above, *except* reduce peaches to *2 pounds (3 cups ground)*. Add 2 cups *strawberries, blackberries, or raspberries,* crushed (1 cup), with pectin.

*****Note:** To peel peaches, immerse in boiling water for 20 to 30 seconds or till skins start to crack; remove and plunge into *cold* water. (Also peel apricots, nectarines, and tomatoes this way.)

Grape Jam

One-fourth of the grapes should be underripe for best flavor and thickening.

    3½ **pounds Concord grapes**
    4½ **cups sugar**

Wash and stem grapes. Measure *10 cups*. Remove and set aside skins from *half* of the grapes. In an 8- or 10-quart kettle combine the skinned and unskinned grapes. Cover and cook about 10 minutes or till grapes are very soft. Sieve; discard seeds and cooked skins. Measure *3 cups* of strained pulp and return to kettle.

Stir in uncooked grape skins and 2 cups *water*. Cook, covered, for 10 minutes. Uncover; stir in sugar. Bring mixture to a full rolling boil, stirring often. Boil, uncovered, about 12 minutes or till jam sheets off a metal spoon. Remove from heat; quickly skim off foam with a metal spoon.

Ladle hot jam at once into hot, *sterilized* half-pint jars, leaving a ¼-inch headspace. Adjust lids. Process in a boiling-water canner for 5 minutes. Makes 6 half-pints (96 one-tablespoon servings).

Orange Marmalade

A beautiful gift for the holidays or any occasion.

    4 **medium oranges**
    1 **medium lemon**
    1½ **cups water**
    ⅛ **teaspoon baking soda**
    5 **cups sugar**
    ½ **of a 6-ounce package (1 foil pouch)**
       liquid fruit pectin

Score orange and lemon peels into 4 lengthwise sections. Remove peels; scrape off white portions. Cut peels into very thin strips. Combine peels, water, and baking soda. Bring to boiling. Cover; simmer for 20 minutes. *Do not drain.*

Remove membranes from fruits. Section fruits, reserving juices. Discard seeds. Add fruits and juices to peel mixture. Return to boiling. Cover and simmer for 10 minutes. Measure *3 cups.*

In an 8- or 10-quart kettle combine the 3 cups fruit mixture and sugar. Bring to a full rolling boil. Boil, uncovered, 1 minute. Remove from heat; stir in pectin. Skim off foam.

Ladle at once into hot, *sterilized* half-pint jars, leaving a ¼-inch headspace. Adjust lids. Process in a boiling-water canner for 15 minutes. Makes about 6 half-pints (96 one-tablespoon servings).

Rhubarb-Raspberry Jam

Eager for a taste of springtime fruit? Use frozen rhubarb and raspberries to make this refrigerator or freezer jam. (Pictured on page 187.)

>   6 cups fresh *or* frozen unsweetened
>   sliced rhubarb
>   4 cups sugar
>   2 cups raspberries *or* one 12-ounce
>   package frozen loose-pack
>   raspberries
>   1 3-ounce package raspberry-flavored
>   gelatin

In a large kettle or Dutch oven combine rhubarb and sugar. Let stand 15 to 20 minutes or till sugar is moistened. Bring to boiling. Boil, uncovered, for 10 minutes, stirring frequently.

Add raspberries; return to boiling. Boil hard for 5 to 6 minutes or till thick, stirring frequently. Remove from heat. Add gelatin; stir till dissolved.

Ladle into half-pint jars or freezer containers, leaving a ½-inch headspace. Seal; label. Let stand at room temperature several hours or till jam is set. Store up to 3 weeks in the refrigerator or 1 year in the freezer. Makes about 5 half-pints (eighty 1-tablespoon servings).

Berry Freezer Jam

>   4 cups blackberries, raspberries, *or*
>   strawberries, caps removed
>   4 cups sugar
>   ¼ teaspoon finely shredded lemon
>   peel *or* orange peel
>   ½ of a 6-ounce package (1 foil pouch)
>   liquid fruit pectin
>   2 tablespoons lemon juice

Crush berries. Measure *2 cups* blackberries or raspberries, or *1¾ cups* strawberries. In a bowl combine berries, sugar, and lemon peel or orange peel. Let stand 10 minutes.

Combine pectin and lemon juice. Add to berry mixture; stir for 3 minutes.

Ladle at once into jars or freezer containers, leaving a ½-inch headspace. Seal; label. Let stand at room temperature about 2 hours or till jam is set. Store up to 3 weeks in the refrigerator or 1 year in the freezer. Makes 4 half-pints (sixty-four 1-tablespoon servings).

Harvest Applesauce

>   8 pounds cooking apples, cored and
>   quartered (24 cups)
>   2 cups water
> 10 inches stick cinnamon (optional)
>   1 to 1½ cups sugar

In an 8- or 10-quart kettle combine apples, water, and, if desired, cinnamon. Bring to a boil; reduce heat. Simmer, covered, for 15 to 20 minutes, stirring often. Remove cinnamon. Press apples through a food mill or sieve. Return pulp to kettle. Stir in sugar. If necessary, add ½ to 1 cup *water* for desired consistency. Bring to a boil. Makes 6 pints (twenty-four ½-cup servings).

Boiling-Water Canning: Ladle hot sauce into hot, *sterilized* jars, leaving a ½-inch headspace. Adjust lids. Process in boiling water for 15 minutes for pints and for 20 minutes for quarts.

Freezing: Cool applesauce. Spoon into freezer containers, leaving the recommended headspace (see tip, page 193). Seal, label, and freeze.

Apple Butter

Freeze or can this spicy spread.

>   6 pounds tart cooking apples, cored
>   and quartered (18 cups)
>   6 cups apple cider *or* apple juice
>   3 cups sugar
>   2 teaspoons ground cinnamon
>   ½ teaspoon ground cloves
>   ½ teaspoon ground allspice

In an 8- or 10-quart kettle or Dutch oven combine apples and cider or juice. Bring to a boil; reduce heat. Cover; simmer for 30 minutes, stirring occasionally. Press through a food mill or sieve. (You should have about 13 cups pulp.)

Return pulp to kettle. Stir in sugar, cinnamon, cloves, and allspice. Bring to boiling; reduce heat. Simmer, uncovered, about 2 hours or till very thick, stirring often. Makes about 8 half-pints (128 one-tablespoon servings).

Boiling-Water Canning: Spoon hot apple butter into hot, *sterilized* pint jars, leaving a ¼-inch headspace. Adjust lids. Process in boiling-water canner for 5 minutes.

Freezing: Place kettle in a sink of *ice* water to cool apple butter. Spoon into freezer containers, leaving the recommended headspace (see tip, page 193). Seal, label, and freeze.

Meat

Nutrition Analysis

		Per Serving							Percent U.S. RDA Per Serving							
	Servings Per Recipe	Calories	Protein (g)	Carbohydrate (g)	Fat (g)	Cholesterol (mg)	Sodium (mg)	Potassium (mg)	Protein	Vitamin A	Vitamin C	Thiamine	Riboflavin	Niacin	Calcium	Iron
Apple-Stuffed Sausage Patties (p. 238)	5	389	19	21	25	67	910	350	30	6	7	28	15	23	5	14
Bacon and Onion Bratwursts (p. 238)	4	405	13	27	26	46	837	310	20	3	50	35	14	18	7	14
Barbecue-Style Pot Roast (p. 214)	8	235	26	6	11	77	348	324	40	9	4	7	14	17	2	19
Barbecue-Style Ribs (p. 230)	4	440	38	23	22	101	537	893	58	11	20	59	26	38	5	14
Barbecue-Style Sandwiches (p. 253)	4	279	22	31	7	56	625	509	35	17	26	16	17	22	4	22
Beef Fajitas (p. 220)	4	415	25	33	21	58	185	494	38	9	53	15	13	25	14	25
Beef Pot Roast (p. 214)	8	284	27	17	11	77	143	588	41	282	13	12	16	21	3	20
Beef Stroganoff (p. 221)	4	453	25	27	27	109	311	530	39	15	4	18	30	23	9	22
Beef Teriyaki Kabobs (p. 221)	4	158	21	2	7	54	392	320	32	0	0	5	9	20	1	11
Beef Wellington (p. 215)	8	487	27	22	30	160	243	320	42	7	2	16	29	32	3	31
Beer-Braised Rabbit (p. 240)	4	617	50	46	23	139	635	1733	77	410	48	22	15	106	8	23
Braised Pork Steaks Italian (p. 230)	4	506	34	32	26	123	410	506	52	8	12	59	30	36	3	19
British-Style Burgers (p. 243)	4	356	30	26	14	152	467	390	45	6	4	20	21	33	7	28
Burritos (p. 245)	4	437	27	32	23	91	532	373	42	65	25	12	17	27	24	27
Calzones (p. 247)	6	510	25	54	21	48	905	545	39	17	17	46	35	31	33	24
Caraway Pork Chops (p. 232)	4	349	33	4	20	107	192	557	51	61	3	69	23	32	3	7
Cashew Pork and Pea Pods (p. 234)	4	555	35	59	21	83	591	728	53	7	36	82	23	36	6	20
Cheeseburgers (p. 243)	4	457	35	26	23	178	897	394	54	9	0	19	27	33	24	27
Cheesy Pork Chops (p. 232)	4	384	36	5	23	117	253	624	56	65	3	70	28	31	13	7
Chili-Mac Skillet (p. 249)	6	388	27	38	15	59	740	1003	42	60	30	27	19	26	16	33
Chimichangas (p. 245)	4	919	27	32	77	91	532	373	42	65	25	13	17	27	24	27
Cider-Caraway Pot Roast (p. 212)	6	366	35	12	19	111	86	487	53	118	6	9	20	20	5	24
Citrus-Ginger Pot Roast (p. 212)	6	326	35	11	15	102	418	509	54	115	25	10	19	21	3	24
Citrus-Glazed Ribs (p. 230)	4	360	37	8	19	120	280	582	57	0	3	77	25	34	2	7
Coney Islands (p. 237)	6	483	23	42	25	55	1043	740	35	12	35	26	18	26	9	29
Corn Dogs (p. 237)	4	843	21	51	62	127	1316	350	32	5	34	23	22	25	16	20
Corned Beef and Cabbage (p. 216)	6	289	20	5	20	105	1219	318	31	1	28	4	12	17	4	14
Corned Beef Hash (p. 252)	4	224	16	18	10	48	580	372	24	7	16	7	9	15	2	16
Corn-Stuffed Pork Chops (p. 231)	4	363	34	10	20	90	392	572	52	7	24	50	22	32	3	9
Creamed Bratwurst (p. 237)	4	628	22	34	43	106	878	460	34	13	8	51	22	29	12	16
Creamed Dried Beef (p. 252)	2	399	23	27	22	41	2220	378	36	19	2	16	30	15	23	19
Creamy Herbed Pork Chops (p. 232)	4	356	34	5	21	110	210	617	53	63	3	70	26	31	8	7
Create-Your-Own Meat Loaf (p. 241)	4	287	23	6	19	147	440	200	35	4	2	8	15	24	5	18
Creole Stuffed Roast (p. 228)	10	235	29	1	12	80	44	448	44	1	13	33	16	27	2	7
Currant-Glazed Rack of Lamb (p. 224)	4	234	23	13	9	85	60	279	36	0	1	9	14	25	1	11
Curried Lamb (p. 224)	4	338	22	42	9	66	141	414	34	1	7	19	14	27	4	18
Curried Pork Chops (p. 232)	4	372	34	9	21	110	206	622	53	6	4	70	26	31	7	7
Deep-Dish Meat Pie (p. 251)	4	633	31	52	33	67	560	648	48	107	18	34	27	37	5	33
Fiesta Pork Kabobs (p. 233)	4	346	31	32	12	83	129	733	48	11	70	84	22	34	1	11
Five-Spice Beef Ribs (p. 217)	4	289	29	2	17	86	569	333	45	0	1	4	12	16	2	19
French Onion Sandwiches (p. 219)	4	425	36	24	20	100	586	362	56	7	1	15	24	24	17	24
Fruit-Stuffed Rib Crown Roast (p. 228)	6	541	39	52	19	118	278	815	60	7	1	84	24	38	4	16
Garden Burgers (p. 244)	4	450	26	27	26	152	625	391	40	18	17	19	20	31	7	25
German-Style Burgers (p. 243)	4	362	29	28	14	154	496	366	44	2	0	18	20	33	6	26
Ginger-Beef Stir-Fry (p. 221)	4	307	25	25	10	54	855	889	38	312	49	18	19	28	6	17
Glazed Ham Patties (p. 244)	4	297	24	20	13	137	760	376	37	2	18	34	15	24	4	18
Greek-Style Burgers (p. 243)	4	361	30	28	13	152	463	349	46	2	1	18	21	33	7	25
Hamburger Pie (p. 248)	4	387	24	34	18	77	630	630	37	16	74	21	16	34	6	26
Hamburgers (p. 243)	4	351	29	26	14	152	493	348	45	2	0	19	21	33	7	26
Ham Caribbean (p. 235)	6	243	23	27	5	51	1445	564	35	1	53	64	15	30	3	10
Ham Loaf (p. 241)	4	254	25	7	14	138	827	353	38	4	16	34	17	24	5	15

On the divider: Beef Pot Roast (p. 214).

Nutrition Analysis

	Per Serving							Percent U.S. RDA Per Serving							
	Servings Per Recipe	Calories	Protein (g)	Carbohydrate (g)	Fat (g)	Cholesterol (mg)	Sodium (mg)	Potassium (mg)	Protein	Vitamin A	Vitamin C	Thiamine	Riboflavin	Niacin	Calcium	Iron
Ham-Potato Scallop (p. 251)	4	360	19	42	13	48	1306	1159	30	18	52	39	19	25	15	16
Ham with Pineapple Sauce (p. 235)	16	262	24	20	9	60	1579	415	37	7	31	59	15	24	2	11
Harvest Pot Roast (p. 229)	8	442	44	27	17	125	263	1281	67	215	43	112	27	46	5	15
Herbed Rump Roast (p. 216)	10	234	27	4	11	82	78	298	42	0	2	6	14	18	1	19
Herb-Rubbed Leg of Lamb (p. 223)	12	173	26	0	6	92	134	306	41	1	1	10	16	29	2	12
Honey-Orange Pork Chops (p. 232)	4	347	34	13	17	107	592	621	52	1	18	70	23	32	3	7
Horseradish-Rubbed Roast (p. 212)	12	290	24	1	20	84	125	396	37	5	1	6	12	15	3	14
Indian-Style Burgers (p. 243)	4	386	30	29	16	152	500	396	47	2	0	20	21	37	7	27
Italian Sausage Sandwiches (p. 238)	4	454	27	33	23	66	1372	328	42	16	52	38	25	24	36	17
Italian-Style Burgers (p. 243)	4	371	30	28	15	154	636	376	47	5	2	19	21	34	11	27
Lamb Chops with Herb Sauce (p. 225)	4	242	21	5	15	82	251	325	33	5	4	10	15	23	5	12
Lamb Chops with Honey-Mustard Glaze (p. 225)	2	349	38	18	13	132	453	468	58	2	14	23	41	2	17
Lamb Shish Kabobs (p. 225)	4	170	21	7	7	66	121	650	33	10	15	15	32	37	2	15
Lasagna (p. 246)	8	398	30	27	19	102	890	656	46	31	22	19	27	21	51	20
Lemon-Marinated Chuck Steak (p. 217)	6	223	28	1	11	86	86	253	43	0	2	5	14	16	0	18
Liver and Onions (p. 239)	4	219	23	8	10	341	268	358	35	999	45	20	218	77	2	41
London Broil (p. 219)	4	232	21	0	16	58	100	339	32	0	0	6	9	20	0	12
Marinated Venison Chops (p. 240)	2	313	45	3	12	138	390	725	69	2	3	33	61	68	3	19
Meat and Bulgur Bake (p. 251)	4	322	32	23	11	79	602	666	49	19	25	14	19	24	21	25
Meat and Corn Bread Squares (p. 248)	6	506	25	40	27	164	983	580	40	62	31	19	24	26	28	23
Meat and Pasta Bake (p. 248)	5	571	29	38	34	110	934	528	44	64	5	25	30	29	27	23
Meat-Stuffed Pita Pockets (p. 253)	4	415	28	25	22	82	131	305	43	81	2	14	16	18	6	21
Meaty Noodle Casserole (p. 251)	4	475	32	31	25	122	812	526	49	26	8	21	28	25	19	23
Meaty Stuffed Potatoes (p. 252)	4	338	23	30	14	71	293	1068	35	7	36	13	16	22	11	17
Mexicali Pork Chops (p. 232)	4	588	44	57	21	107	1104	1515	68	75	54	92	32	47	13	32
Mexican-Style Burgers (p. 243)	4	350	29	26	14	151	555	369	44	18	5	19	21	34	6	26
Mint-Glazed Rack of Lamb (p. 224)	4	234	23	13	9	85	60	279	36	0	1	9	14	25	1	11
Moussaka (p. 250)	6	306	23	15	16	198	567	617	35	20	10	16	23	21	19	15
Muffuletta (p. 239)	6	599	24	57	31	61	1943	409	37	14	20	27	26	23	28	25
Mushroom-Onion Sauce (p. 243)	4	64	1	3	6	0	68	104	1	5	3	2	5	4	1	2
Mustard-Chive Sauce (p. 243)	4	57	2	3	4	3	233	78	3	5	1	2	5	1	6	0
New England Boiled Dinner (p. 216)	6	388	22	28	21	105	1240	901	35	204	52	13	16	24	7	18
Oriental-Style Burgers (p. 243)	4	364	30	28	14	151	1005	430	46	2	1	20	22	35	6	27
Pan Gravy for Roasted Meat (p. 214)	8	80	1	3	7	8	196	36	2	0	0	2	2	3	0	2
Parsley Pesto (p. 243)	4	167	4	4	16	5	129	211	6	33	32	3	4	2	14	12
Pastitsio (p. 250)	6	407	28	28	19	248	659	557	43	21	10	26	31	26	25	18
Pepper-Rubbed Steaks (p. 219)	4	243	24	1	15	84	90	360	37	4	0	6	18	15	2	18
Pizza (p. 247)	6	510	25	54	21	48	905	545	39	17	17	46	35	31	33	24
Popover Sausage (p. 239)	4	391	14	28	24	170	631	278	22	5	0	40	2	17	10	17
Porcupine Meatballs (p. 242)	4	302	27	20	12	149	619	454	41	10	47	13	16	32	3	26
Pork Chop Suey (p. 233)	4	434	34	43	13	83	966	840	52	1	16	81	32	42	5	20
Pork Chow Mein (p. 233)	4	432	35	32	18	86	1191	828	53	1	17	75	32	38	5	16
Pork Mediterranean (p. 233)	4	415	35	30	17	119	408	715	54	17	27	65	21	40	7	18
Pork with Apple-Nutmeg Sauce (p. 230)	8	309	29	11	16	81	128	534	45	2	6	45	20	28	2	7
Reuben Sandwiches (p. 253)	4	472	28	31	27	82	1356	209	43	14	6	12	22	17	34	23
Rice-Stuffed Rib Crown Roast (p. 228)	6	497	39	40	19	118	282	724	60	138	34	87	26	40	5	17
Roast Pork with Mushroom-Butter Sauce (p. 229)	8	505	29	11	37	156	392	638	45	57	8	61	28	32	6	12
Saucy Lamb Shanks (p. 224)	4	323	26	15	13	85	580	811	41	209	20	16	19	32	6	17
Sloppy Joes (p. 245)	6	299	17	26	14	53	468	329	27	9	27	17	14	23	5	19
Sour Cream and Cheese Sauce (p. 243)	4	93	3	1	9	21	60	50	4	6	0	1	4	0	9	0

Nutrition Analysis

	Per Serving								Percent U.S. RDA Per Serving							
	Servings Per Recipe	Calories	Protein (g)	Carbohydrate (g)	Fat (g)	Cholesterol (mg)	Sodium (mg)	Potassium (mg)	Protein	Vitamin A	Vitamin C	Thiamine	Riboflavin	Niacin	Calcium	Iron
Spaghetti and Meatballs (p. 242)	6	501	25	61	18	97	808	1002	38	36	62	48	32	47	10	35
Spaghetti Pie (p. 249)	4	470	32	32	23	198	861	491	50	15	17	23	27	22	29	17
Spaghetti Sauce (p. 242)	6	437	23	58	13	51	686	987	36	35	61	47	30	46	9	33
Spiced Tongue and Vegetables (p. 239)	6	444	34	22	24	133	822	879	52	203	23	12	28	35	4	24
Spinach-Stuffed Lamb Roast (p. 223)	12	253	29	10	10	136	235	438	45	34	4	14	22	30	10	19
Standing Rib Roast with Beef au Jus (p. 213)	12	232	24	0	14	80	82	358	37	0	0	6	11	15	0	13
Standing Rib Roast with Oven-Browned Potatoes (p. 213)	12	286	25	13	14	80	70	595	39	0	10	10	12	19	1	14
Standing Rib Roast with Yorkshire Pudding (p. 213)	12	364	29	18	18	174	154	462	45	3	0	17	23	21	7	21
Steak and Spinach Pinwheels (p. 218)	4	329	30	2	22	76	463	672	46	91	12	17	21	27	17	24
Stuffed Burgers (p. 244)	4	362	29	26	15	152	800	342	45	3	0	18	21	34	7	26
Stuffed Cabbage Rolls (p. 249)	4	337	21	28	17	67	1150	838	32	33	50	16	16	27	16	22
Stuffed Green Peppers (p. 249)	4	311	19	21	17	67	502	500	30	19	130	15	14	22	12	21
Stuffed Zucchini (p. 249)	4	309	20	20	16	67	503	661	31	19	25	16	14	23	14	19
Submarine Sandwich (p. 239)	6	539	23	46	29	61	1461	323	36	13	17	27	26	23	26	21
Swedish Meatballs (p. 241)	4	477	31	34	24	182	378	590	47	15	8	35	36	28	21	21
Sweet-and-Sour Pork (p. 234)	4	726	34	75	32	152	706	731	52	209	72	85	24	36	5	20
Swiss Steak (p. 217)	4	356	29	38	9	67	385	751	45	115	24	22	18	36	6	26
Tacos (p. 245)	4	394	23	25	23	77	649	385	36	56	20	12	15	26	7	21
Tortilla Roll-Ups (p. 252)	4	302	24	18	15	69	370	243	37	5	1	6	14	13	18	7
Veal Cordon Bleu (p. 219)	4	442	35	13	27	179	609	383	54	12	8	24	24	32	17	23
Veal Marsala (p. 220)	4	285	22	2	20	82	281	330	34	8	2	5	17	26	2	16
Vegetable-Lamb Skillet (p. 224)	4	313	26	22	14	85	352	839	40	9	35	18	20	32	7	18
Vegetable-Stuffed Rolled Roast (p. 215)	8	211	24	3	11	61	114	411	37	71	5	8	9	17	2	10
Venison Pot Roast (p. 240)	8	328	28	24	12	105	282	516	44	49	7	28	39	43	4	15
Zesty Short Ribs (p. 216)	4	376	30	25	17	86	697	697	46	13	14	8	14	20	9	27

Meat

Whether for grilling, braising, roasting, or micro-cooking, the recipes on the following pages bring out the best in beef, veal, pork, and lamb.

Recognizing Meat Cuts
Our recipes list the most common names for meat cuts. Your butcher, however, may use different names. To be sure you're buying the right cut of meat, refer to the identification pictures in this chapter. Also on these picture pages, we list the best ways to cook each cut of meat. To learn the definitions of these cooking methods, see the "Special Helps" chapter. To find out how long to roast, grill, broil, micro-cook, panfry, or panbroil each meat cut, use the charts on pages 254–260.

Handling and Storing Meat
Be sure to follow these rules for meat safety.
● Freeze raw meats you don't plan to use in one to two days. Wrap meats in freezer paper or bags.
● Thaw meat overnight in the refrigerator, *not* at room temperature.
● Thoroughly wash your hands and utensils after handling raw meat.
● Never leave raw or cooked meat at room temperature for more than two hours.

Use the Hot Line
Do you have questions about storing and preparing meat? Call the toll-free Meat and Poultry Hotline (800/535-4555). Home economists from the U.S. Department of Agriculture answer calls from 10 a.m. to 4 p.m. eastern time.

Veal

Match the wholesale cuts on the drawing with the retail cuts in the same-numbered picture (reading left to right).

Shoulder
1

Rib
2

Loin
3

Sir-
loin
4

Round
5

Foreshank & Breast
6

1
Blade steak
Braise, panfry
Boneless shoulder steak
Braise, panfry
Boneless shoulder roast
Braise, roast

2, 3
Loin roast (3)
Roast
Loin chop (3)
Braise, broil, panfry
Rib roast (2)
Roast
Rib chop (2)
Braise, broil, panfry

4, 5
Top round steak (5)
Braise, panfry
Cutlet (5)
Braise, broil, panfry
Boneless sirloin steak (4)
Braise, broil, panfry

6
Riblet
Braise, cook in liquid
Boneless breast roast
Braise, roast
Shank crosscut
Braise, cook in liquid

Beef

Match the wholesale cuts on the drawing with the retail cuts in the same-numbered pictures (reading left to right).

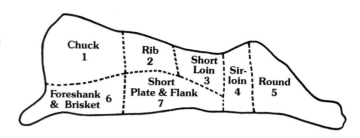

Chuck 1 | Rib 2 | Short Loin 3 | Sir-loin 4 | Round 5
Foreshank & Brisket 6 | Short Plate & Flank 7

1
Mock tender roast
  Braise
Boneless top blade roast
  Braise
Boneless shoulder pot roast
  Braise

1
Boneless arm pot roast
  Braise
7-bone pot roast
  Braise
Short ribs
  Braise, cook in liquid

2
Rib roast
  Roast
Rib eye roast/steak
  Roast: roast
  Steak: broil, panbroil, panfry
Back ribs
  Braise, cook in liquid, roast

3
Top loin steak
  Broil, panbroil, panfry
Tenderloin roast/steak
  Roast: roast, broil
  Steak: broil, panbroil, panfry
T-bone steak
  Broil, panbroil, panfry

4

Bottom and top sirloin steak
  Broil, panbroil, panfry
Sirloin steak
  Broil, panbroil, panfry
Top sirloin roast
  Roast

5

Tip steak
  Broil, panbroil, panfry
Round steak
  Braise, panfry

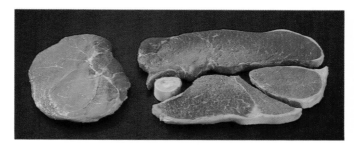

5

Bottom round roast
  Braise, roast
Top round roast
  Roast
Tip roast
  Roast, braise
Eye round roast
  Braise, roast

6

Corned beef brisket
  Braise, cook in liquid
Fresh beef brisket
  Braise, cook in liquid
Shank crosscut
  Braise, cook in liquid

7

Flank steak
  Broil, braise, panfry
Skirt steak
  Braise, broil, panbroil,
  panfry
Flank steak roll
  Braise, broil, panbroil,
  panfry

How Much Meat to Buy

When buying meat, remember that cuts with large amounts of bone and fat will give fewer servings per pound. To calculate the cost per serving, divide the cost per pound of meat by the number of servings you expect to get from each pound. The chart below shows how many servings you'll get from meat cuts with different amounts of bone.

Type of Meat	Servings Per Pound
Boneless meat—ground meats, meats for soups and stews, boneless roasts and steaks, variety meats	4 or 5
Cuts with little bone—beef round or ham center cuts, lamb or veal cutlets	3 or 4
Cuts with a medium amount of bone—whole or end cuts of beef round; bone-in ham; loin, rump, rib, or chuck roasts; steaks and chops	2 or 3
Cuts with much bone—shanks, spareribs, short ribs	1 or 2

Cider-Caraway Pot Roast

    1   2½- to 3-pound beef chuck pot roast
    2   tablespoons cooking oil
    2   medium onions, sliced and
           separated into rings
    1   cup apple cider or apple juice
    1   cup sliced carrot
    1   teaspoon caraway seed
    2   cloves garlic, minced
    ½   cup dairy sour cream
    4   teaspoons cornstarch

Trim fat from roast. If desired, sprinkle with salt and pepper. In a Dutch oven brown roast on all sides in hot oil. Drain fat. Add onions, apple cider, carrot, caraway seed, and garlic. Bring to boiling; reduce heat. Cover and simmer for 1½ to 2 hours or till tender. Remove meat and vegetables from pan.

For gravy, skim fat from pan juices. Measure juices. If necessary, add water to equal 1¼ cups. Combine sour cream and cornstarch. Stir into juices; return to pan. Cook and stir till thickened and bubbly. Cook and stir 2 minutes more. Season to taste. Makes 6 to 8 servings.

Citrus-Ginger Pot Roast: Prepare as above, *except* substitute *orange juice* for the apple cider and 2 teaspoons grated *gingerroot* (or ½ teaspoon ground *ginger*) for the caraway seed. For gravy, omit sour cream and stir cornstarch into 2 tablespoons *soy sauce*. Stir into pan juices; return to pan. Cook and stir till thickened and bubbly. Cook and stir for 2 minutes more.

Horseradish-Rubbed Roast

    1   4- to 6-pound beef rib eye roast
    ⅓   cup prepared horseradish
    1   teaspoon finely shredded
           lemon peel
    1   tablespoon lemon juice
    ¼   cup margarine or butter, softened
    ½   cup dairy sour cream or ¼ cup
           whipping cream, whipped
    1   tablespoon snipped
           parsley   Oven 325°

Cut 1-inch-wide pockets into roast at 3-inch intervals. If desired, sprinkle roast with salt and pepper. In a mixing bowl combine horseradish, lemon peel, and lemon juice. Reserve *2 tablespoons* of the horseradish mixture. Stir margarine into remaining horseradish mixture. Rub margarine mixture onto roast and into pockets.

Place meat, fat side up, on a rack in a shallow roasting pan. Insert a meat thermometer. Roast in a 325° oven for 1¼ to 2 hours for rare (140°), 1¼ to 2¼ hours for medium (160°), or 1½ to 2½ hours for well-done (170°). Cover with foil and let stand for 15 minutes before carving.

Meanwhile, stir together reserved horseradish mixture, sour cream or whipped cream, and parsley. Pass with meat. Makes 12 to 14 servings.

How to Use a Meat Thermometer

You'll be guaranteed perfect roasts every time if you use a meat thermometer to determine exactly when your meat is done. To be sure you get an accurate temperature reading, insert the thermometer into the center of the largest muscle or thickest portion of the meat. The thermometer should not touch any fat or bone or the bottom of the pan.

When the meat reaches the desired doneness (see charts, pages 254–260), push the thermometer into the meat a little farther. If the temperature drops, continue cooking. If the temperature stays the same, remove the roast. Cover the meat and let it stand about 15 minutes before carving. (The meat will continue to cook slightly while standing. If you like, remove the roast when the thermometer registers 5 degrees below the desired doneness.)

Standing Rib Roast

For a perfect accompaniment to roast beef, make Oven-Browned Potatoes, Yorkshire Pudding, or Beef au Jus.

1 4- to 6-pound beef rib roast
   Oven-Browned Potatoes, Yorkshire
   Pudding, or Beef au Jus
   Oven 325°

Place meat, fat side up, in a 15½x10½x2-inch roasting pan. Insert a meat thermometer. Roast in a 325° oven for 1¾ to 3 hours for rare (140°), 2¼ to 3¾ hours for medium (160°), or 2¾ to 4¼ hours for well-done (170°). Prepare Oven-Browned Potatoes, Yorkshire Pudding, or Beef au Jus. Remove meat from pan. Cover with foil and let stand 15 minutes before carving. Makes 12 to 14 servings.

Oven-Browned Potatoes: Peel and quarter 5 medium *potatoes.* Cook in boiling salted water for 10 minutes. Drain. About 30 to 40 minutes before roast is done (the roast temperature should be about 100°), add ½ cup *water* to pan. Arrange potatoes around roast, turning to coat.

Yorkshire Pudding: After removing meat from the oven, increase oven temperature to 450°. Measure pan drippings. If necessary, add *cooking oil* to drippings to equal ¼ *cup;* return to pan. In a bowl combine 4 *eggs* and 2 cups *milk.* Add 2 cups *all-purpose flour* and ¼ teaspoon *salt.* Beat with an electric mixer or rotary beater till smooth. Stir into drippings in roasting pan. Bake for 20 to 25 minutes or till puffy and golden. Cut into squares. Serve at once with roast.

Beef au Jus: After removing meat from the oven, remove pan drippings from pan; skim fat. Add 2 cups *boiling water* to pan, stirring and scraping crusty browned bits off the bottom. Stir in pan drippings. Cook and stir till bubbly. For a richer flavor, stir in 2 teaspoons *instant beef bouillon granules.* Season to taste.

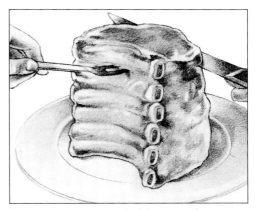

To carve roast, insert a fork between the top two ribs. Slice from the fat side across to the rib bone.

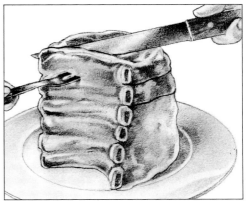

Cut along the rib bone with the knife tip to loosen each slice, keeping the knife close to the bone.

Beef Pot Roast

Pictured on page 205.

  1   **2½- to 3-pound beef chuck pot roast**
  2   **tablespoons cooking oil**
  ¾   **cup water, dry wine, or tomato juice**
  1   **tablespoon Worcestershire sauce**
  1   **teaspoon instant beef bouillon
        granules**
  1   **teaspoon dried basil, crushed**
 12   **ounces whole tiny new potatoes,
        2 medium potatoes, or 2 medium
        sweet potatoes**
  8   **small carrots or parsnips**
  2   **small onions, cut into wedges**
  2   **stalks celery, bias-sliced into 1-inch
        pieces**
  ¼   **cup all-purpose flour**

Trim fat from roast. In a Dutch oven brown roast on all sides in hot oil. Drain fat. Combine water, Worcestershire sauce, bouillon granules, and basil. Pour over roast. Bring to boiling; reduce heat. Cover and simmer for 1 hour.

Remove a narrow strip of peel from the center of each new potato, or peel and quarter each medium potato. Add potatoes, carrots, onions, and celery to meat. Cover; simmer 45 to 60 minutes or till tender, adding additional water if necessary. Remove meat and vegetables from pan.

For gravy, measure pan juices; skim fat. If necessary, add water to equal *1½ cups*. Combine flour and ½ cup *cold water*. Stir into juices; return to pan. Cook and stir till thickened and bubbly. Cook and stir 1 minute more. Season to taste. Makes 8 to 10 servings.

Microwave directions: Trim fat from roast. In a 3-quart casserole combine water, Worcestershire sauce, bouillon granules, and basil. Add roast. Micro-cook, covered, on 100% power (high) for 5 minutes. Cook, covered, on 50% power (medium) for 25 minutes. Turn roast over. Prepare potatoes as above. Add vegetables. Cook, covered, on medium for 25 to 40 minutes or till tender. Remove meat and vegetables.

Pour pan juices into a 4-cup measure; skim fat. If necessary, add water to equal *1½ cups*. Combine flour and ½ cup *cold water*. Stir into juices. Cook, uncovered, on high for 5 to 7 minutes or till thickened and bubbly, stirring every minute. Cook 30 seconds more. Season to taste.

Crockery-cooker directions: Trim the fat from roast and brown as above. *Thinly* slice vegetables and place in the bottom of a 3½- or 4-quart electric crockery cooker. Cut roast to fit cooker; place atop vegetables. Combine water, Worcestershire sauce, bouillon granules, and basil. Pour over meat and vegetables. Cover; cook on low-heat setting for 10 to 12 hours. Prepare gravy as above, using a saucepan.

Oven directions: Trim fat from roast and brown meat as above. Combine water, Worcestershire sauce, bouillon granules, and basil. Pour over roast. Bake, covered, in a 325° oven for 1 hour. Prepare potatoes as above. Add vegetables. Bake for 45 to 60 minutes more or till tender. Continue as above.

Barbecue-Style Pot Roast

  1   **2½- to 3-pound beef chuck pot roast**
  2   **tablespoons margarine or butter**
  2   **medium onions, sliced and
        separated into rings**
  2   **cloves garlic, minced**
  ¾   **cup bottled barbecue sauce**
  1   **4-ounce can sliced mushrooms,
        drained**
  1   **tablespoon dry mustard**
  1   **teaspoon chili powder**

Trim fat from meat. Sprinkle with salt and pepper. In a Dutch oven brown meat on all sides in margarine. Remove meat. Add onions and garlic. Cook till tender but not brown. Stir in barbecue sauce, mushrooms, dry mustard, chili powder, and ½ cup *water*. Add meat. Bring to boiling; reduce heat. Cover; simmer for 1½ to 2 hours or till meat is tender. Remove meat; boil pan juices gently, uncovered, for 3 to 5 minutes or to desired consistency, stirring often. Serves 8 to 10.

Pan Gravy for Roasted Meat

After removing roasted meat from pan, pour drippings into a large measuring cup, scraping out the crusty browned bits. Skim fat, reserving ¼ *cup* fat. (To skim fat, tilt measuring cup and spoon off the oily liquid that rises to the top.) Reserve all the drippings.

In a medium saucepan combine reserved fat and ¼ cup *all-purpose flour*. Add enough *beef broth or water* to reserved drippings in the measuring cup to equal *2 cups* liquid. Add all at once to flour mixture. Cook and stir till thickened and bubbly. Cook and stir for 1 to 2 minutes more. Season to taste. Makes 2 cups (8 servings).

Beef Wellington

  1 **2- to 2¼-pound beef tenderloin**
1½ **cups all-purpose flour**
 ½ **cup shortening**
  1 **beaten egg yolk**
  3 **tablespoons cold water**
 ½ **cup deli or canned liver pâté**
  1 **beaten egg white**
     Bordelaise Sauce   Oven 425°

If roast is long and thin, fold narrow ends under and tie. If roast is flat and wide, tie crosswise in 2 or 3 places to form a rounder roast. (Finished shape should be about 7x3½ inches.) Place meat on a rack in a shallow roasting pan. Roast in a 425° oven for 30 minutes for a 2-pound roast (35 minutes for a 2¼-pound roast). Remove from pan. (Remove strings, if tied.) Refrigerate about 10 minutes to cool surface.

Meanwhile, for pastry, combine flour and ⅛ teaspoon *salt.* Cut in shortening till pieces are the size of small peas. Combine egg yolk and water. Add to flour mixture, tossing with a fork till all is moistened. (If necessary, add 1 to 2 tablespoons additional *water* to moisten.) Form into a ball. On a floured surface, roll into a 14x12-inch rectangle. Spread pastry with pâté to within 1½ inches of edges. Center meat atop pastry. Wrap pastry around meat, overlapping long sides. Brush edges with beaten egg white and seal. Trim excess pastry from ends; fold up. Brush with egg white and seal. Place seam side down in a greased shallow baking pan. Reroll trimmings to make cutouts. Place cutouts on pastry-covered meat. Brush remaining egg white over pastry.*

Bake in a 425° oven about 25 minutes or till pastry is golden. Serve with Bordelaise Sauce. If desired, garnish with parsley sprigs. Serves 8.

Bordelaise Sauce: In a medium saucepan combine 1½ cups *water;* ¾ cup *dry red wine;* 2 tablespoons finely chopped *shallot or onion;* 1 teaspoon *instant beef bouillon granules;* ½ teaspoon *dried thyme,* crushed; and 1 *bay leaf.* Bring to boiling; reduce heat. Simmer for 15 to 20 minutes. (You should have about 1⅓ cups.) Remove bay leaf. Stir together 3 tablespoons softened *margarine or butter* and 2 tablespoons *all-purpose flour.* Add to wine mixture. Cook and stir till thickened and bubbly. Cook and stir for 1 minute more. Stir in 1 tablespoon snipped *parsley.* Makes about 1 cup.

*__Note:__ If desired, insert a meat thermometer into pastry-wrapped meat. Roast to 140°.

◄Wrap pastry around meat, brushing egg white on the edges of pastry to hold seams in place.

Vegetable-Stuffed Rolled Roast

Impress your guests with this elegant entrée.

  1 **2- to 3-pound beef eye of round roast**
  4 **slices bacon**
  1 **cup chopped onion**
  1 **cup shredded carrot or parsnip**
  2 **cloves garlic, minced**
  1 **teaspoon dried basil,**
     crushed   Oven 325°

To butterfly the roast, make a single lengthwise cut down the center of the meat, cutting to within ½ inch of the other side. Spread the meat open. At the center of the roast, make one perpendicular slit to the right of the V and one perpendicular slit to the left. Cover roast with clear plastic wrap. Pound with a meat mallet to ½- to ¾-inch thickness. Set aside.

Cook bacon till crisp. Drain, reserving *2 tablespoons* drippings. Crumble bacon; set aside. Cook onion, carrot, garlic, and basil in reserved drippings over medium heat till tender. Remove from heat. Stir in bacon.

Remove plastic wrap from roast. Spread bacon mixture over roast. Roll up from one of the short sides. Tie with string to secure. Place meat on a rack in a shallow roasting pan. Insert a meat thermometer. Roast in a 325° oven for 1¼ to 1¾ hours or till meat thermometer registers 140°. Cover with foil and let stand for 15 minutes before carving. Makes 8 to 10 servings.

New England Boiled Dinner

Serving Corned Beef and Cabbage is a great way to celebrate Saint Patrick's Day.

- 1 **2- to 2½-pound corned beef brisket**
- 1 **teaspoon whole black peppers**
- 2 **bay leaves**
- 2 **medium potatoes, peeled and quartered**
- 3 **medium carrots, quartered**
- 2 **medium parsnips or 1 medium rutabaga, peeled and cut into chunks**
- 1 **medium onion, cut into 6 wedges**
- 1 **small cabbage, cut into 6 wedges**

Trim fat from meat. Place in a Dutch oven; add juices and spices from package. Add water to cover meat. Add peppers and bay leaves. (If your brisket comes with an additional packet of spices, add it and omit the peppercorns and bay leaves.) Bring to boiling; reduce heat. Cover and simmer about 2 hours or till almost tender.

Add potatoes, carrots, parsnips, and onion. Return to boiling; reduce heat. Cover and simmer 10 minutes. Add cabbage. Cover; cook for 15 to 20 minutes more or till tender. Discard bay leaves. Remove meat and vegetables. Slice meat across the grain. Season to taste. If desired, serve with prepared horseradish or mustard. Serves 6.

Corned Beef and Cabbage: Prepare as above, *except* omit the potatoes, the carrots, and the parsnips.

Herbed Rump Roast

- 1 **3- to 4-pound boneless beef round rump roast**
- 2 **tablespoons cooking oil**
- 1 **cup chopped onion**
- 1 **teaspoon instant beef bouillon granules**
- 1 **teaspoon dried marjoram, crushed**
- 1 **teaspoon dried thyme, crushed**
- 1 **bay leaf**
- 1 **clove garlic, halved**
- ¼ **cup all-purpose flour**
- 1 **tablespoon snipped parsley**

Trim fat from roast. In a Dutch oven brown roast in hot oil. Drain fat. Combine onion, bouillon granules, marjoram, thyme, bay leaf, garlic, ½ cup *water,* and ¼ teaspoon *pepper.* Add to

Dutch oven. Bring to boiling; reduce heat. Cover; simmer 1¾ to 2¼ hours or till meat is tender. Remove meat from pan. Discard bay leaf.

For gravy, measure pan juices; skim fat. If necessary, add water to equal *1¾ cups.* Combine flour, parsley, and ½ cup *water.* Stir into juices. Return to pan. Cook and stir till thickened and bubbly. Cook and stir for 1 minute more. Season to taste. If desired, sprinkle with additional snipped parsley. Makes 10 to 12 servings.

Crockery-cooker directions: Untie and trim fat from roast. Brown as above. Arrange the pieces in the bottom of a 3½- or 4-quart electric crockery cooker. Add onion, bouillon granules, marjoram, thyme, bay leaf, garlic, ½ cup *water,* and ¼ teaspoon *pepper.* Cover; cook on low-heat setting for 10 to 12 hours. Prepare gravy as above, using a saucepan.

Oven directions: Trim fat from roast. Brown meat as above, using an ovenproof Dutch oven. Combine onion, bouillon granules, marjoram, thyme, bay leaf, garlic, ½ cup *water,* and ¼ teaspoon *pepper.* Add to Dutch oven. Bake, covered, in a 350° oven for 1¾ to 2¼ hours or till tender. Continue as above.

Zesty Short Ribs

- 3 **to 4 pounds beef short ribs, cut into serving-size pieces**
- ⅓ **cup catsup**
- ⅓ **cup chili sauce**
- ¼ **cup molasses**
- 3 **tablespoons lemon juice**
- 2 **tablespoons prepared mustard**

Trim fat from meat. Place in a Dutch oven. Add water to cover meat. Cover and simmer about 1½ hours or till tender. Drain.

For sauce, combine catsup, chili sauce, molasses, lemon juice, and mustard. Place ribs on the unheated rack of a broiler pan. Brush with sauce. Broil 4 to 5 inches from the heat for 10 to 15 minutes or till heated through, turning often and brushing with sauce. Heat any remaining sauce and pass with ribs. Makes 4 servings.

Grill directions: Simmer meat and prepare sauce as above. In a covered grill arrange *medium-slow* coals around a drip pan. Test for *slow* heat above pan. Place cooked ribs on grill rack over drip pan but not over coals. Brush with sauce. Lower grill hood. Grill 20 to 25 minutes or till heated through, turning and brushing occasionally with the sauce. Heat remaining sauce.

Five-Spice Beef Ribs

If you like, use 2 teaspoons purchased five-spice powder instead of the fennel, cinnamon, aniseed, pepper, and cloves.

> **3** **to 4 pounds beef short ribs, cut into serving-size pieces**
> ½ **cup soy sauce**
> ¼ **cup dry sherry *or* orange juice**
> **6** **cloves garlic, minced**
> **1** **tablespoon sugar**
> **1** **tablespoon lemon juice**
> ½ **teaspoon fennel seed, crushed**
> ½ **teaspoon ground cinnamon**
> ½ **teaspoon aniseed, crushed**
> ½ **teaspoon Szechwan peppercorns, crushed, *or* ¼ teaspoon pepper**
> ¼ **teaspoon ground cloves**   Oven 350°

Place ribs in a plastic bag set into a deep bowl. For marinade, combine soy sauce, sherry or orange juice, garlic, sugar, lemon juice, fennel seed, cinnamon, aniseed, pepper, and cloves. Pour mixture over ribs. Seal bag. Marinate in the refrigerator 6 to 24 hours, turning bag occasionally.

Remove ribs from bag, reserving marinade. Place ribs, bone side down, in a shallow roasting pan. Pour marinade over ribs. Bake, covered, in a 350° oven for 2 to 2½ hours or till tender. Makes 4 servings.

Lemon-Marinated Chuck Steak

> **1** **1½- to 1¾-pound beef chuck steak, cut 1 inch thick**
> **1** **teaspoon finely shredded lemon peel**
> ⅓ **cup lemon juice**
> ¼ **cup cooking oil**
> ¼ **cup chopped onion**
> **1** **tablespoon sugar**
> **1** **tablespoon Worcestershire sauce**
> **1** **teaspoon prepared mustard**

Slash fat on edges of roast. Place meat in a plastic bag set into a shallow dish. For marinade, combine lemon peel, lemon juice, cooking oil, onion, sugar, Worcestershire sauce, mustard, ¼ teaspoon *salt,* and ¼ teaspoon *pepper.* Pour over roast. Seal bag. Marinate in the refrigerator for 6 to 24 hours, turning bag occasionally.

Remove roast from bag, reserving marinade. Place meat on the unheated rack of a broiler pan. Broil 3 inches from the heat for 6 minutes. Turn, brush with marinade, and broil to desired doneness, allowing 6 to 8 minutes more for medium. Brush occasionally with reserved marinade. To serve, thinly slice meat across the grain. Serves 6.

Grill directions: Marinate steak as above. Grill marinated steak on an uncovered grill directly over *medium* coals for 9 minutes. Turn and grill to desired doneness, allowing 9 to 11 minutes more for medium. Brush occasionally with reserved marinade. Continue as above.

Swiss Steak

> **1** **pound beef round steak, cut ¾ inch thick**
> **2** **tablespoons all-purpose flour**
> **1** **tablespoon cooking oil**
> **1** **16-ounce can tomatoes, cut up**
> **1** **small onion, sliced and separated into rings**
> ½ **cup sliced celery**
> ½ **cup sliced carrot**
> ½ **teaspoon dried thyme, crushed**
> **2** **cups hot cooked rice *or* noodles**

Cut meat into 4 serving-size pieces. Trim fat. Combine the flour, ¼ teaspoon *salt,* and ¼ teaspoon *pepper.* With a meat mallet, pound flour mixture into meat. In a large skillet brown meat on both sides in hot oil. Drain fat.

Add *undrained* tomatoes, onion, celery, carrot, and thyme. Cover and cook over low heat about 1¼ hours or till meat is tender. Skim fat. Serve with hot rice or noodles. Makes 4 servings.

Crockery-cooker directions: Cut meat into 4 pieces. Trim fat. Omit flouring and pounding meat. Brown meat in hot oil. In a 3½- or 4-quart electric crockery cooker place onion, celery, and carrot. Sprinkle with thyme, 2 tablespoons *quick-cooking tapioca,* ¼ teaspoon *salt,* and ¼ teaspoon *pepper.* Pour *undrained* tomatoes over vegetables. Add meat. Cover; cook on low-heat setting for 10 to 12 hours. Continue as above.

Oven directions: Cut meat into 4 pieces. Trim fat, pound, and brown in the skillet as above. Transfer meat to an 8x8x2-inch baking dish. In the same skillet combine *undrained* tomatoes, onion, celery, carrot, and thyme. Bring to boiling, scraping up any browned bits in the pan. Pour over meat. Cover and bake in a 350° oven about 1 hour or till tender. Continue as above.

Steak and Spinach Pinwheels

8 slices bacon
1 1- to 1½-pound beef flank steak *or*
    beef top round steak
1 10-ounce package frozen chopped
    spinach, thawed and well drained
¼ cup grated Parmesan cheese
    **Mock Hollandaise Sauce (see
    recipe, page 363) (optional)**

In a large skillet cook bacon till just done but not crisp. Drain on paper towels. Score steak by making shallow cuts at 1-inch intervals diagonally across steak in a diamond pattern. Repeat on second side. With a meat mallet, pound steak into a 12x8-inch rectangle, working from center to edges. Sprinkle with salt and pepper. Arrange bacon lengthwise on steak.

Spread spinach over bacon. Sprinkle with Parmesan cheese. Roll up from a short side. Secure with wooden picks at 1-inch intervals, starting ½ inch from one end. Cut between picks into eight 1-inch slices.

Place, cut side down, on the unheated rack of a broiler pan. Broil 3 inches from the heat for 6 minutes. Turn; broil for 6 to 8 minutes more for medium doneness. Remove picks. If desired, serve with Mock Hollandaise Sauce. Serves 4.

Grill directions: Prepare meat as above. Thread *two* slices onto *each* of four long skewers. Grill slices on an uncovered grill directly over *medium* coals for 6 minutes. Turn and grill to desired doneness, allowing 6 to 8 minutes more for medium. Serve as above.

Score the steak by making shallow diagonal cuts about 1 inch apart in a diamond pattern.

Using a sharp knife, cut the meat roll between the picks into eight 1-inch slices.

London Broil

This American creation often is served with a béarnaise or bordelaise sauce.

1 **1- to 1½-pound beef flank steak or top round steak**
¼ **cup cooking oil**
2 **tablespoons vinegar *or* lemon juice**
1 **clove garlic, minced**

Score meat by making shallow cuts at 1-inch intervals diagonally across steak in a diamond pattern. Repeat on second side. Place meat in a plastic bag set into a shallow dish. For marinade, combine oil, vinegar, garlic, ¼ teaspoon *salt,* and ¼ teaspoon *pepper.* Pour over meat. Seal bag. Marinate at room temperature *up to* 1 hour or in refrigerator up to 24 hours; turn bag occasionally.

Remove meat from marinade and place on the unheated rack of a broiler pan. Broil 3 inches from heat for 6 minutes. Turn and broil 5 to 6 minutes more for rare or 7 to 8 minutes more for medium-rare. Season to taste. To serve, thinly slice diagonally across the grain. Serves 4 to 6.

Grill directions: Prepare and marinate steak as above. Grill marinated steak on an uncovered grill directly over *medium* coals for 6 minutes. Turn and grill to desired doneness, allowing 5 to 6 minutes more for rare or 7 to 8 minutes more for medium-rare. Continue as above.

Pepper-Rubbed Steaks

4 **beef top loin *or* tenderloin steaks, cut 1 inch thick (1¼ pounds)**
2 **teaspoons cracked whole black pepper**
1 **tablespoon margarine *or* butter**
¼ **cup brandy**
½ **cup light cream**

Slash fat on edges of steaks at 1-inch intervals. Sprinkle both sides of steak with cracked pepper, pressing into surface. In a 12-inch skillet melt margarine. Cook steaks over medium-high heat for 7 minutes. Turn and cook 7 to 9 minutes more for medium doneness. Remove meat. Reduce heat to low. Cool pan 1 minute. Gradually pour brandy into skillet. Cook for 1 minute on low heat, stirring to scrape up crusty browned bits. Stir cream into skillet. Bring to boiling; reduce heat. Simmer for 1½ to 2½ minutes or till slightly thickened. Pour over steaks. Serves 4.

French Onion Sandwiches

Tastes like French onion soup over steak.

2 **tablespoons margarine *or* butter**
4 **4-ounce beef cubed steaks**
1 **medium onion, sliced and separated into rings**
1 **cup beef broth**
1 **tablespoon cornstarch**
2 **teaspoons Worcestershire sauce**
⅛ **teaspoon garlic powder**
4 **1-inch slices French bread, toasted**
2 **1-ounce slices Swiss cheese, halved**

In a large skillet melt margarine. Add steaks and cook over medium-high heat for 2 to 3 minutes on each side or till done. Remove from skillet, reserving drippings. Cook onion in drippings till tender. Combine broth, cornstarch, Worcestershire sauce, garlic powder, and a dash *pepper.* Add to skillet. Cook and stir till bubbly. Cook and stir 2 minutes more. Place steaks on bread. Top with cheese and onion mixture. Serves 4.

Veal Cordon Bleu

4 **slices fully cooked ham**
1 **pound boneless veal leg top round steak, cut ¼ inch thick**
½ **cup shredded Swiss cheese**
⅓ **cup fine dry bread crumbs**
1 **tablespoon snipped parsley**
¼ **cup all-purpose flour**
1 **beaten egg**
3 **tablespoons margarine *or* butter**

Cut ham into strips. Cut veal into 4 pieces. With a meat mallet, pound each veal piece to ⅛-inch thickness. Place some ham and cheese in center of each veal piece. Fold in sides, then overlap ends, forming bundles. Secure with wooden picks. Combine bread crumbs, parsley, and ⅛ teaspoon *pepper.* Roll meat bundles in flour, egg, then crumb mixture. In a large skillet melt margarine. Cook meat bundles over medium heat for 14 to 17 minutes or till golden brown, turning occasionally. (Reduce heat to medium-low if browning too quickly.) Serves 4.

Oven directions: Prepare meat bundles as above. In a large skillet brown meat bundles in melted margarine for 5 minutes. Transfer to a 12x7½x2-inch baking dish. Bake in a 400° oven for 18 to 20 minutes or till done.

Veal Marsala

1 **pound boneless veal leg top round steak, veal sirloin steak, *or* pork tenderloin, cut ¼ inch thick**
3 **tablespoons margarine *or* butter**
1 **cup sliced fresh mushrooms**
½ **cup water**
¼ **cup dry marsala *or* dry sherry**
1 **teaspoon instant chicken bouillon granules**
1 **tablespoon snipped parsley**
   Hot cooked noodles (optional)

Cut veal into 4 pieces. With a meat mallet, pound each piece to ⅛-inch thickness. If desired, sprinkle with salt and pepper.

In a large skillet melt *1 tablespoon* of the margarine or butter. Cook *half* of the veal over medium-high heat for 1 to 2 minutes on each side or till done. Remove from skillet; keep warm. Repeat with remaining veal and another *1 tablespoon* of the margarine or butter.

Cook mushrooms in remaining margarine or butter till tender. Stir in water, marsala or dry sherry, and bouillon granules. Bring to boiling. Boil rapidly for 3 to 4 minutes. (You should have about ⅓ cup mixture.) Stir in parsley. Pour over veal. If desired, serve with hot cooked noodles. Makes 4 servings.

Marinating the Easy Way

Marinating is a cinch if you use a plastic bag. The meat stays in the marinade and it's easy to turn and rearrange. Cleanup is easy, too. Just toss the bag.

Beef Fajitas

Serve the meat sizzling hot for a typical South Texas fajita.

1 **pound boneless beef plate skirt steaks, beef flank steak, *or* beef round steak**
½ **cup Italian salad dressing**
½ **cup Salsa (see recipe, page 368) *or* bottled salsa**
2 **tablespoons lime *or* lemon juice**
1 **teaspoon Worcestershire sauce**
8 **7-inch flour tortillas**
1 **tablespoon cooking oil**
1 **medium onion, thinly sliced and separated into rings**
1 **medium green *or* sweet red *or* yellow pepper, cut into thin strips**
1 **medium tomato, chopped**
   Guacamole (see recipe, page 13) *or* one 6-ounce container frozen avocado dip, thawed (optional)
   Dairy sour cream (optional)
   Shredded cheddar *or* Monterey Jack cheese (optional)
   Salsa (see recipe, page 368) *or* bottled salsa (optional)   Oven 350°

Partially freeze beef. Thinly slice across the grain into bite-size strips. Place strips in a plastic bag set into a deep bowl. For marinade, in a mixing bowl stir together salad dressing, the ½ cup Salsa, the lime juice, and Worcestershire sauce. Pour mixture over meat. Seal bag. Marinate in the refrigerator for 6 to 24 hours, stirring occasionally.

Wrap tortillas in foil. Heat in a 350° oven for 10 minutes to soften. Meanwhile, preheat a large skillet over high heat; add oil. Cook and stir onion rings in hot oil for 1½ minutes. Add sweet pepper strips; cook and stir about 1½ minutes or till crisp-tender. Remove vegetables from skillet.

Add *half* of the *undrained* beef strips to the hot skillet. Cook and stir for 2 to 3 minutes or till done. Remove beef and drain well. Repeat with remaining beef. Return all beef and vegetables to skillet. Add chopped tomato. Cook and stir for 1 to 2 minutes or till heated through.

To serve, immediately fill warmed tortillas with beef-vegetable mixture. If desired, add Guacamole or avocado dip, sour cream, cheese, and additional Salsa. Roll up fajitas. Makes 4 servings.

Beef Stroganoff

 1 **pound beef tenderloin steak** *or*
   sirloin steak
 2 **tablespoons all-purpose flour**
 1 **8-ounce carton dairy sour cream**
 2 **teaspoons instant beef**
   bouillon granules
 2 **tablespoons margarine** *or* **butter**
1½ **cups sliced fresh mushrooms**
 ½ **cup chopped onion**
 1 **clove garlic, minced**
 2 **cups hot cooked noodles**

Partially freeze beef. Thinly slice across the grain into bite-size strips. Combine flour and sour cream. Stir in bouillon granules, ½ cup *water,* and ¼ teaspoon *pepper*. Set aside. In a large skillet cook and stir *half* of the meat in margarine over high heat till done. Remove. Add remaining meat, mushrooms, onion, and garlic. Cook and stir till meat is done and onion is tender. Return all meat to skillet. Add sour cream mixture. Cook and stir over medium heat till bubbly. Cook and stir 1 minute more. Serve over noodles. Serves 4.

Beef Teriyaki Kabobs

 1 **pound boneless beef sirloin steak**
 ⅓ **cup soy sauce**
 2 **tablespoons dry sherry**
   or apple juice
 1 **tablespoon molasses**
 2 **teaspoons dry mustard**
 1 **teaspoon grated gingerroot** *or*
   ¼ teaspoon ground ginger
 1 **clove garlic, minced**

Partially freeze beef. Thinly slice across the grain into long strips ⅛ inch thick. For marinade, combine soy sauce, sherry, molasses, mustard, gingerroot, garlic, and ⅓ cup *water*. Pour over meat. Marinate for 15 minutes at room temperature.

Drain meat, reserving marinade. On 8 long skewers, loosely thread meat accordion-style.

Place skewers on the unheated rack of a broiler pan. Broil 3 inches from the heat 5 to 6 minutes or to desired doneness, turning and brushing occasionally with marinade. Makes 4 servings.

Grill directions: Cut, marinate, and skewer meat as above. Place on uncovered grill directly over *hot* coals 5 to 6 minutes or to desired doneness. Turn and brush with marinade often.

Ginger-Beef Stir-Fry

 1 **6-ounce package frozen pea pods**
 1 **pound boneless beef sirloin steak** *or*
   top round steak
 ¼ **cup dry sherry**
 3 **tablespoons soy sauce**
 1 **tablespoon cornstarch**
 1 **tablespoon grated gingerroot** *or*
   ½ teaspoon ground ginger
 1 **tablespoon cooking oil**
 2 **cloves garlic, minced**
 3 **medium carrots, thinly bias sliced**
 1 **cup broccoli flowerets**
 1 **medium onion, cut into thin wedges**
 1 **8-ounce can sliced water chestnuts**
   or bamboo shoots, drained

Thaw pea pods. Partially freeze beef. Thinly slice across the grain into bite-size strips. For sauce, combine sherry, soy sauce, cornstarch, ground ginger (if using), and ⅓ cup *water*. Set aside.

Preheat a wok or large skillet over high heat; add oil. (Add more oil as necessary during cooking.) Stir-fry garlic and gingerroot (if using) in hot oil 15 seconds. Add carrots; stir-fry 2 minutes. Add broccoli and onion; stir-fry about 3 minutes or till crisp-tender. Remove vegetables from wok.

Add *half* of the beef to the hot wok. Stir-fry for 2 to 3 minutes or till done. Remove. Repeat with remaining beef. Return all beef to wok. Push from center of wok. Stir sauce; add to center of wok. Cook and stir till bubbly. Cook and stir 2 minutes more. Stir in pea pods, vegetables, and water chestnuts. Cover; cook 1 minute or till hot. If desired, serve with hot cooked rice. Serves 4.

Stir-Frying Hints

There's no mystery to stir-frying if you follow these hints.
● Use a spatula or a long-handled spoon to gently lift and turn the food with a folding motion.
● Use high heat, but keep the food moving so it won't burn.
● If you need to add more oil during cooking, bring it to frying temperature before adding more food.

Lamb

Match the wholesale cuts on the drawing with the retail cuts in the same-numbered pictures (reading left to right).

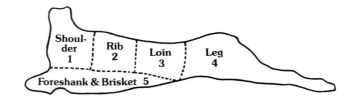

Shoulder 1 | Rib 2 | Loin 3 | Leg 4

Foreshank & Brisket 5

1

Arm chop
  Braise, broil, panbroil, panfry
Boneless shoulder roast
  Roast, braise
Blade chop
  Braise, broil, panbroil, panfry

2, 3

Rib chop (2)
  Broil, panbroil, panfry, roast
Rib roast (2)
  Roast
Loin chop (3)
  Broil, panbroil, panfry
Loin roast (3)
  Roast

4

Sirloin chop
  Braise, broil, panbroil, panfry
Boneless leg roast
  Roast, broil (if butterflied)
Whole leg
  Roast

5

Shank
  Braise, cook in liquid
Spareribs
  Braise, broil, roast
Riblet
  Braise, cook in liquid, broil

Spinach-Stuffed Lamb Roast

If your meat market doesn't regularly carry this cut, order it a few days early from your butcher.

- ¾ **cup chopped onion**
- ⅓ **cup chopped celery**
- 2 **cloves garlic, minced**
- 2 **tablespoons margarine *or* butter**
- 2 **beaten eggs**
- 1 **10-ounce package frozen chopped spinach, thawed and drained**
- 3 **tablespoons snipped fresh basil *or* 1 tablespoon dried basil, crushed**
- 1 **teaspoon snipped fresh marjoram *or* ¼ teaspoon dried marjoram, crushed**
- 3 **cups plain croutons**
- ¼ **cup grated Parmesan cheese**
- 1 **4- to 6-pound leg of lamb, boned and butterflied**   Oven 325°

For stuffing, in a small saucepan cook onion, celery, and garlic in margarine or butter till tender but not brown. In a mixing bowl combine onion mixture, eggs, spinach, basil, and marjoram. Stir in croutons and Parmesan cheese. Add ¼ cup *water,* tossing lightly. Set aside.

Remove fell (paper-thin, pinkish red layer) from outer surface of meat. Trim fat. With boned side up, pound meat with a meat mallet to an even thickness. If desired, sprinkle with salt and pepper. Spread stuffing over roast. Roll up; tie securely. Place roast, seam side down, on a rack in a shallow roasting pan. Insert meat thermometer into thickest portion of meat. Roast in a 325° oven for 1¾ to 2½ hours or till thermometer registers 150°. Let stand 15 minutes before carving. Remove strings. If desired, garnish with fresh basil and marjoram. Makes 12 to 16 servings.

Herb-Rubbed Leg of Lamb

- 1 **5- to 7-pound leg of lamb**
  Lemon juice
- 1 **tablespoon dried parsley flakes**
- 1 **teaspoon dried mint *or* basil, crushed**
- ½ **teaspoon onion salt**
- ½ **teaspoon dried rosemary, crushed**
- ¼ **teaspoon pepper**
- 1 **to 2 cloves garlic, slivered**
  Mint jelly (optional)   Oven 325°

Remove fell (paper-thin, pinkish red layer) from outer surface of meat. Trim fat from meat. Cut ½-inch-wide pockets into roast at 1-inch intervals. Brush meat and pockets with lemon juice. Combine parsley flakes, mint or basil, onion salt, rosemary, and pepper. Rub over meat and into pockets. Insert garlic slivers into meat pockets.

Place meat, fat side up, on a rack in a shallow roasting pan. Insert a meat thermometer. Roast in a 325° oven for 1¾ to 3 hours for rare (140°), 2 to 3 hours for medium (160°), or 2½ to 4½ hours for well-done (170°). Let stand 15 minutes before carving. Serve with mint jelly, if desired. Makes 12 to 16 servings.

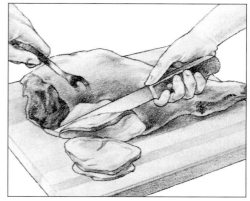

To carve a leg of lamb, cut 3 slices from the thin side parallel to the bone. Rest the leg on this base.

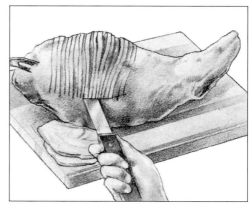

Beginning at the wide end, cut ¼-inch slices down to leg bone. Cut along bone to free slices.

Currant-Glazed Rack of Lamb

The rib bones are the rack. Oven 325°

Trim fat from one 1¾- to 2-pound *lamb rib roast* (6 to 8 ribs) with backbone loosened. For glaze, in a small saucepan combine ¼ cup *currant jelly,* 1 tablespoon *dry white wine or apple juice,* and ¼ teaspoon *dried tarragon,* crushed. Heat till smooth. Place meat, rib side down, in a shallow roasting pan. Roast in a 325° oven 1¼ to 1½ hours for medium (160°). Brush with glaze the last 30 minutes of roasting. Makes 4 servings.

Mint-Glazed Rack of Lamb: Prepare as above, *except* substitute *mint jelly* for currant jelly and finely shredded *orange peel* for tarragon.

Curried Lamb

1 **pound boneless lamb, cut into ¾-inch cubes**
1 **tablespoon cooking oil**
1 **cup coarsely chopped onion**
3 **to 4 teaspoons curry powder**
2 **cloves garlic, minced**
2 **medium apples, peeled, cored, and thinly sliced**
1 **teaspoon instant chicken bouillon granules**
2 **tablespoons all-purpose flour**
2 **cups hot cooked rice**

In a large saucepan brown *half* of the meat in hot oil. Remove meat. Brown remaining meat with onion, curry powder, and garlic till onion is tender. Return all meat to pan. Stir in apples, bouillon granules, and ¾ cup *water.* Cover; simmer for 30 to 40 minutes or till tender. Stir ¼ cup *cold water* into flour; stir into saucepan. Cook and stir till thickened and bubbly. Cook and stir 1 minute more. Season to taste. Serve over rice. If desired, pass chutney, sliced green onion, raisins, shredded coconut, or chopped peanuts. Serves 4.

Microwave directions: Omit cooking oil. In a 2-quart casserole micro-cook lamb, onion, curry powder, and garlic, covered, on 100% power (high) 5 minutes. Stir in apples, bouillon granules, and ¾ cup *water.* Cook, covered, on 50% power (medium) 15 minutes or till tender, stirring every 5 minutes. Stir ¼ cup *cold water* into flour; stir into casserole. Cook on high 3 to 5 minutes or till thickened and bubbly, stirring every minute. Cook 30 seconds more. Continue as above.

Vegetable-Lamb Skillet

A saucy meal in a pan.

1 **9-ounce package frozen Italian-style green beans or frozen cut green beans**
4 **lamb shoulder chops, cut ½ inch thick**
1 **medium onion, sliced and separated into rings**
1 **tablespoon cooking oil**
2 **teaspoons instant chicken bouillon granules**
¼ **teaspoon dried basil, crushed**
¼ **teaspoon dried oregano, crushed**
2 **cups sliced, peeled potatoes**
1 **2-ounce jar diced pimiento, drained**
2 **teaspoons cornstarch**
¼ **cup sliced pitted ripe olives**

Run *cold* water over beans to separate; set aside. Trim fat from meat. If desired, sprinkle with salt and pepper. In a large skillet brown chops and onion in hot oil. Drain fat.

Combine bouillon granules, basil, oregano, 1 cup *water,* and ⅛ teaspoon *pepper.* Pour over chops. Add beans, potatoes, and pimiento. Cover; simmer for 20 to 25 minutes or till tender. Remove meat and vegetables.

For sauce, skim fat from pan juices. Add water to pan juices to equal ¾ cup. Return to skillet. Combine 1 tablespoon *cold water* and cornstarch; stir into juices. Cook and stir till thickened and bubbly. Cook and stir 2 minutes more. Pour sauce over chops; sprinkle with olives. Serves 4.

Saucy Lamb Shanks

Cut 3½ to 4 pounds *lamb shanks* (4) *or beef short ribs* (10 to 12) into 1-rib portions. In a 12-inch skillet brown shanks or ribs in 2 tablespoons hot *cooking oil;* drain fat.

Combine 1 cup finely chopped *onion,* 1 cup finely chopped *carrot,* 1 cup chopped *celery,* 1 cup *dry red wine,* one 8-ounce can *tomato sauce,* ¼ teaspoon *salt,* ¼ teaspoon *pepper,* 2 cloves minced *garlic,* and 1 *bay leaf.* Pour over shanks or ribs. Cover; simmer for 1¼ to 1½ hours or till tender. Remove shanks or ribs.

For sauce, boil pan juices rapidly for 6 to 8 minutes. (You should have about 3 cups.) Discard bay leaf. Skim fat. Serve sauce over shanks or ribs and 2 cups hot cooked *noodles.* Serves 4.

Lamb Chops with Herb Sauce

> 4 **lamb shoulder chops or sirloin chops, cut ½ inch thick (1¼ to 1½ pounds)**
> 1 **tablespoon cooking oil**
> ¼ **cup finely chopped celery**
> ¼ **cup sliced green onion**
> 1 **teaspoon instant beef bouillon granules**
> ¼ **teaspoon pepper**
> ⅓ **cup dairy sour cream or plain yogurt**
> 1 **tablespoon all-purpose flour**
> ½ **teaspoon dried thyme, crushed, or dried dillweed**
> 1 **2½-ounce jar sliced mushrooms, drained**
> 2 **tablespoons snipped parsley**

Trim fat from meat. If desired, sprinkle with salt and pepper. In a large skillet brown chops in hot oil. Drain fat.

Combine celery, onion, bouillon granules, pepper, and ¾ cup *water*. Pour over chops. Bring to boiling; reduce heat. Cover and simmer for 10 to 15 minutes or till tender. Remove meat. Skim fat from juices. Reserve ½ cup juices; set aside.

For sauce, combine sour cream or yogurt, flour, and thyme or dillweed. Stir in the reserved juices. Add to skillet. Add mushrooms and parsley. Cook and stir till thickened and bubbly. Cook and stir 1 minute more. Pass sauce with chops. Makes 4 servings.

Microwave directions: Trim fat from meat. If desired, sprinkle with salt and pepper. In a 12x7½x2-inch baking dish micro-cook lamb chops, covered with waxed paper, on 100% power (high) for 3 minutes, turning once. Drain.

Meanwhile, combine celery, onion, bouillon granules, pepper, and ½ cup *water;* pour over chops. Cook, covered, on high for 5 minutes. Cook, covered, on 50% power (medium) for 9 to 11 minutes or till tender, rearranging and turning chops over once. Remove lamb. Skim fat from juices. Reserve ½ cup juices; set aside.

For sauce, in a 2-cup measure combine sour cream or yogurt, flour, thyme or dillweed, mushrooms, and parsley. Stir in reserved juices. Cook on high for 3 to 4 minutes or till thickened and bubbly, stirring *every* minute. Pass sauce with lamb chops.

Lamb Chops with Honey-Mustard Glaze

Trim fat from 4 *lamb loin chops*, cut 1 inch thick. If desired, sprinkle with salt and pepper. Place chops on the unheated rack of a broiler pan. Broil 3 inches from the heat for 5 minutes. Turn; broil 5 minutes more for medium. Meanwhile, combine 2 tablespoons *honey* and 4 teaspoons *Dijon-style mustard.* Brush each side of chops with honey mixture. Broil 1 minute more on each side. Brush any remaining honey mixture over chops before serving. Sprinkle with 1 tablespoon snipped parsley and 1 tablespoon finely chopped walnuts or pecans, if desired. Makes 2 servings.

Grill directions: Trim fat from meat. Place chops on an uncovered grill directly over *medium* coals for 7 minutes. Turn and grill for 7 minutes more for medium. Combine honey and mustard. Brush chops with honey mixture; grill 1 minute more on each side. Continue as above.

Lamb Shish Kabobs

Serve with another Middle Eastern dish, rice pilaf.

> 1 **pound boneless lamb round steak or sirloin steak, cut ¾ inch thick**
> ½ **cup chopped onion**
> ¼ **cup lemon juice**
> 2 **tablespoons olive oil or cooking oil**
> ½ **teaspoon garlic powder**
> ½ **teaspoon dried thyme, crushed**
> 1 **large zucchini, sliced ½ inch thick**
> 16 **large fresh mushrooms**
> 1 **large tomato, cut into 8 wedges, or 8 cherry tomatoes**

Partially freeze lamb. Cut into 3-inch-long strips about ¼ inch thick. For marinade, in a bowl combine onion, lemon juice, oil, garlic powder, thyme, 2 tablespoons *water,* ½ teaspoon *salt,* and ¼ teaspoon *pepper.* Add meat. Cover; marinate in the refrigerator for 4 to 24 hours.

Drain meat, reserving marinade. Cook zucchini in boiling water 2 minutes; add mushrooms and cook 1 minute more. Drain. On four long skewers, alternately thread meat, accordion-style, zucchini, and mushrooms. Place on the unheated rack of a broiler pan. Broil 3 inches from the heat for 6 to 8 minutes for medium, brushing with marinade and turning skewers often. Add *two* tomato wedges or cherry tomatoes to *each* skewer the last 1 minute of broiling. Makes 4 servings.

Pork and Ham

Match the wholesale cuts on the drawing, with the retail cuts in the same-numbered pictures (reading left to right).

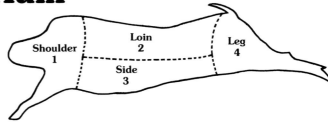

1
Blade steak
   Braise, broil, panbroil, panfry
Blade roast
   Roast, braise
Boneless blade roast
   Roast, braise

1
Smoked picnic
   Roast, cook in liquid
Smoked hock
   Braise, cook in liquid
Smoked shoulder roll
   Roast, cook in liquid

2
Boneless loin roast
   Roast
Top loin roast (double)
   Roast
Tenderloin
   Roast

2
Butterfly chop
   Broil, panbroil, panfry, braise
Top loin chop
   Broil, panbroil, panfry, braise
Loin chop
   Broil, panbroil, panfry, braise

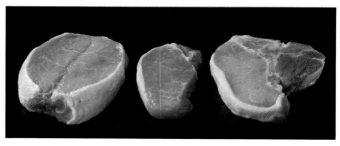

2

Boneless blade roast
 Roast, braise
Top loin roast
 Roast
Rib crown roast
 Roast

2

Rib chop
 Broil, panbroil, panfry,
 braise
Sirloin cutlet
 Braise, broil, panbroil,
 panfry
Sirloin chop
 Braise

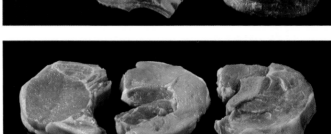

2, 3

Spareribs (3)
 Roast, broil, cook in liquid,
 braise
Country-style ribs (2)
 Roast, braise, broil, cook
 in liquid
Back ribs (2)
 Roast, broil, braise, cook
 in liquid

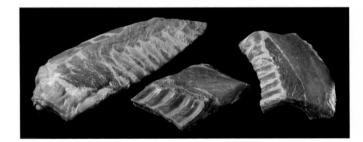

4

Ham shank/center slice
 Shank: roast
 Slice: broil, panbroil, roast
**Boneless smoked ham
(whole muscle)**
 Roast
**Boneless smoked ham
(sectioned and formed)**
 Roast

2, 3

Canadian bacon (2)
 Roast, broil, panbroil,
 panfry
Smoked loin chop (2)
 Roast, broil, panbroil,
 panfry
Bacon (3)
 Panfry, broil, bake

Creole Stuffed Roast

½ **cup finely chopped onion**
½ **cup finely chopped green pepper**
2 **cloves garlic, minced**
½ **teaspoon celery seed**
¼ **to ½ teaspoon black pepper**
¼ **teaspoon ground red pepper**
1 **3- to 4-pound boneless pork
   top loin roast (double
   loin tied)**   Oven 325°

For stuffing, in a mixing bowl combine onion, green pepper, garlic, celery seed, black pepper, and red pepper. Set aside. Trim fat from meat. Cut about 20 deep slits, 1 inch wide, randomly around the pork roast. Untie roast and separate.

Fill slits with some of the stuffing. Pat remaining stuffing onto the flat side of one half of roast. Top with remaining half; retie roast. Place meat on a rack in a shallow roasting pan. Insert a meat thermometer. Roast in a 325° oven for 1¾ to 2¼ hours or till meat thermometer registers 170° (well-done). Cover and let stand 15 minutes before carving. Makes 10 to 12 servings.

Rice-Stuffed Rib Crown Roast

Slabs of ribs form this impressive roast.

4 **pounds pork loin back ribs
   (16 to 20 ribs)**
1 **clove garlic, halved**
¼ **cup light corn syrup**
2 **cups water**
1 **cup long grain rice**
1 **cup shredded carrot**
½ **cup chopped onion**
½ **cup chopped green pepper**
¾ **teaspoon dried Italian seasoning**
½ **teaspoon salt**
⅛ **teaspoon pepper**   Oven 450°

To form the crown roast, tie the 2 or 3 slabs of ribs together, rib side out, forming a circle and leaving a center 5 inches in diameter. Place in a shallow roasting pan. Rub garlic on the inside of the crown. If desired, sprinkle with a little salt and pepper. Insert a meat thermometer. Roast in a 450° oven for 20 minutes. Reduce oven temperature to 350°. Brush roast with corn syrup. Roast for 1 to 1¼ hours more or till thermometer registers 170° (well-done).

Meanwhile, for stuffing, in a saucepan combine water, rice, carrot, onion, green pepper, Italian seasoning, the ½ teaspoon salt, and the ⅛ teaspoon pepper. Bring to boiling; reduce heat. Cover; simmer for 15 minutes. Remove from heat. Cover and let stand for 15 minutes.

To serve, transfer meat to a serving platter. Remove strings. Spoon stuffing into the center of the crown. Using a fork to steady the crown, cut between the ribs. Makes 6 to 8 servings.

Fruit-Stuffed Rib Crown Roast: Prepare as above, *except* omit carrot, onion, green pepper, Italian seasoning, and pepper. Increase water to *2¾ cups* and add one 6-ounce package (1⅓ cups) *mixed dried fruit bits* and ⅛ teaspoon ground *cinnamon* with the rice.

With the rib side of the uncooked roast out, arrange the rib slabs in a circle and tie with string.

Steady the cooked roast with a carving fork and cut between the ribs. Allow 2 to 3 ribs per serving.

Harvest Pot Roast

1   3- to 3½-pound boneless pork
      shoulder roast
2   tablespoons cooking oil
1   medium onion, cut into thin wedges
1   tablespoon instant beef bouillon
      granules
1   teaspoon dried basil, crushed, *or*
      dried dillweed
1   bay leaf
1   medium acorn squash
4   medium potatoes, peeled and
      quartered (1½ pounds)
3   large carrots, thinly sliced
¼   cup all-purpose flour

Trim fat from meat. If desired, sprinkle with salt and pepper. In a Dutch oven brown meat on all sides in hot oil. Drain fat. Add onion, bouillon, herb, bay leaf, 1½ cups *water,* and ¼ teaspoon *pepper.* Bring to boiling; reduce heat. Cover and simmer for 1¼ hours. Cut squash in half lengthwise; discard seeds. Cut each half into 4 pieces. Add squash, potatoes, and carrots to meat. Return to boiling; reduce heat. Simmer for 25 to 30 minutes or till tender. Remove meat and vegetables from pan. Discard bay leaf.

For sauce, skim fat from pan juices. Measure 1½ cups juices. Stir ½ cup *cold water* into flour; stir into reserved juices. Cook and stir till thickened and bubbly. Cook and stir 1 minute more. Season to taste. Pass with meat. Serves 8.

Crockery-cooker directions: Trim the fat from a 1½- to 2-pound boneless pork shoulder roast. If desired, sprinkle with salt and pepper. Brown meat on all sides in hot oil. Drain. Cut meat, if necessary, to fit into a 3½- or 4-quart electric crockery cooker. Place potatoes and carrots in the bottom of the cooker. (Omit squash.) Add onion, seasonings, meat, 1½ cups *water,* and ⅛ teaspoon *pepper.* Cover; cook on low-heat setting for 10 to 12 hours. Make sauce as above. Makes 4 servings.

Roast Pork with Mushroom-Butter Sauce

2   cups finely chopped fresh
      mushrooms
1¾ cups finely chopped green onions
¼   cup margarine *or* butter
¼   cup dry white wine
¾   cup soft bread crumbs
½   cup shredded carrot
1   4- to 5-pound pork loin
      center rib roast, backbone
      loosened (8 ribs)
      Mushroom-Butter Sauce   Oven 325°

For stuffing, cook mushrooms and green onions in margarine till tender. Stir in wine. Bring to boiling; reduce heat. Simmer 5 minutes or till liquid evaporates. Remove from heat. Stir in bread crumbs, carrot, ¼ teaspoon *salt,* and ⅛ teaspoon *pepper.* Place roast, rib side down, in a shallow roasting pan. On meaty side, cut a pocket above each rib. Spoon stuffing into pockets. Insert meat thermometer. Roast in a 325° oven 2 to 3 hours or till thermometer registers 170°. Cover loosely with foil after 1 hour. Cover; let stand 15 minutes before carving. Slice between ribs. Serve with Mushroom-Butter Sauce. Serves 8.

Mushroom-Butter Sauce: Combine 1 cup sliced fresh *mushrooms,* ¼ cup dry *white wine,* and 1 teaspoon *fines herbes.* Bring to boiling; reduce heat. Simmer 5 to 7 minutes or till most liquid is evaporated. Stir in ½ cup *whipping cream,* 1 teaspoon *instant chicken bouillon granules,* and ⅛ teaspoon *pepper.* Heat through. Remove from heat. Using a wire whisk, stir in ½ cup *butter,* 1 tablespoon at a time, till melted. Stir in 2 teaspoons *lemon juice.* Keep sauce warm for up to 30 minutes, but *do not boil.* Makes 1⅓ cups.

Checking Pork Doneness

Pork cooked with bacon, spinach, tomatoes, or onion sometimes remains pink even when well-done. The same is true of grilled or smoked pork. So, when cooking pork mixtures with the ingredients above, or grilling or smoking pork, use a meat thermometer.

Pork with Apple-Nutmeg Sauce

Unpeeled red apples make a colorful sauce.

 1 **4- to 5-pound pork loin center rib roast, backbone loosened**
 2 **cups chopped apple**
 ½ **cup finely chopped onion**
 1 **small clove garlic, minced**
 1 **tablespoon margarine *or* butter**
 1 **tablespoon cornstarch**
 1 **teaspoon instant chicken bouillon granules**
 ¼ **teaspoon ground nutmeg**
 ⅛ **teaspoon white pepper**
1¼ **cups apple juice *or* apple cider**   Oven 325°

Trim fat from meat. If desired, sprinkle with salt and pepper. Place roast, rib side down, in a shallow roasting pan. Insert a meat thermometer. Roast in a 325° oven for 1½ to 3 hours or till thermometer registers 170° (well-done). Cover with foil and let stand 15 minutes before carving.

For sauce, in a saucepan cook apple, onion, and garlic in margarine till tender. Stir in cornstarch, bouillon granules, nutmeg, and pepper. Add apple juice all at once. Cook and stir till bubbly. Cook and stir 1 minute more. To serve, slice between ribs; pass sauce. Serves 8 to 10.

Citrus-Glazed Ribs

Oven 350°

Cut 2½ to 3 pounds *pork loin back ribs or pork spareribs* into serving-size pieces. Place ribs, bone side down, on a rack in a shallow roasting pan. Roast in a 350° oven for 1 hour. Drain.

Meanwhile, for glaze, combine ½ cup *orange marmalade,* 3 tablespoons *soy sauce,* 2 tablespoons *lemon juice,* and ¾ teaspoon *ground ginger.* Brush ribs with some of the glaze. Roast 30 to 45 minutes more or till well-done, brushing occasionally with glaze. Brush with any remaining glaze before serving. Makes 4 servings.

Grill directions: Cut ribs into serving-size pieces. In a covered grill arrange *medium-hot* coals around a drip pan. Test for *medium* heat above pan. Place ribs on grill rack over drip pan but not over coals. Lower grill hood. Grill for 1 hour. Prepare glaze as above. Brush ribs with glaze. Grill ribs 15 to 20 minutes more or till well-done, brushing occasionally with glaze. Brush with any remaining glaze before serving.

Barbecue-Style Ribs

2½ **to 3 pounds pork country-style ribs**
 1 **cup chopped onion**
 1 **clove garlic, minced**
 1 **tablespoon cooking oil**
 1 **8-ounce can tomato sauce**
 ¼ **cup packed brown sugar**
 3 **tablespoons lemon juice**
 2 **tablespoons Worcestershire sauce**
 1 **tablespoon prepared mustard**
 ½ **teaspoon celery seed**   Oven 350°

Place ribs, bone side down, on a rack in a shallow roasting pan. Bake in a 350° oven 1 hour. Drain.

Meanwhile, for sauce, in a medium saucepan cook onion and garlic in hot oil till tender. Stir in tomato sauce, brown sugar, lemon juice, Worcestershire sauce, mustard, celery seed, ½ cup *water,* and ¼ teaspoon *pepper.* Simmer for 15 minutes, stirring occasionally. Spoon sauce over ribs. Bake ribs, covered, 30 to 60 minutes more or till well-done, spooning sauce over ribs occasionally. Pass remaining sauce with ribs. Serves 4.

Grill directions: In a covered grill arrange *medium-hot* coals around a drip pan. Test for *medium* heat above pan. Place ribs on grill rack over drip pan but not over coals. Lower grill hood. Grill for 1 hour. Prepare sauce as above. Brush ribs with sauce. Grill ribs about 30 minutes more or till well-done, brushing occasionally with sauce. Pass remaining sauce with ribs.

Braised Pork Steaks Italian

 4 **pork shoulder blade steaks, cut ½ inch thick (2 to 2½ pounds)**
 1 **tablespoon cooking oil**
 1 **medium onion, sliced and separated into rings**
 1 **8-ounce can pizza sauce**
 2 **to 3 cups hot cooked rice *or* noodles**

Trim fat from meat. In a large skillet brown 2 steaks in hot oil over medium heat about 5 minutes on each side. Remove steaks. Brown remaining 2 steaks and remove. Add onion to oil; cook for 2 minutes. Drain fat. Return steaks to skillet. Add pizza sauce. Cover and cook over low heat about 30 minutes or till no pink remains. Remove steaks. Skim fat from pan juices. If necessary, continue cooking juices to thicken slightly. Spoon over meat. Serve with rice. Serves 4 to 6.

Corn-Stuffed Pork Chops

Serve with poached apple slices or applesauce.

4 pork loin rib chops, cut 1¼ inches thick (about 2 pounds)
¼ cup chopped onion
¼ cup chopped green pepper
1 tablespoon margarine *or* butter
¾ cup corn-bread stuffing mix *or* herb-seasoned stuffing mix
½ cup cooked whole kernel corn
2 tablespoons chopped pimiento
¼ teaspoon salt
⅛ teaspoon pepper
⅛ to ¼ teaspoon ground cumin   Oven 375°

Trim fat from chops. Cut a pocket in each chop by cutting from fat side almost to bone. For stuffing, in a small saucepan cook onion and green pepper in margarine till tender but not brown. Stir in stuffing mix, corn, pimiento, salt, pepper, and cumin. Spoon *one-fourth* of the stuffing into *each* pork chop. Secure pockets with wooden toothpicks. Place chops on a rack in a shallow roasting pan. Bake in a 375° oven for 40 to 50 minutes or till no pink remains. Remove wooden toothpicks. Makes 4 servings.

Grill directions: Assemble chops as above. In a covered grill arrange *medium-hot* coals around a drip pan. Test for *medium* heat above pan. Place chops on rack over drip pan but not over coals. Lower hood. Grill for 40 to 45 minutes or till no pink remains. Remove picks.

Cut from the fat side of the chop nearly to the bone to make a pocket for the stuffing.

For the stuffing, cook vegetables in margarine till tender but not brown, stirring occasionally.

Mexicali Pork Chops

- **4 pork loin chops, cut ¾ inch thick (about 1½ pounds)**
- **1 tablespoon cooking oil**
- **2 14½-ounce cans stewed tomatoes, cut up**
- **1 8-ounce can whole kernel corn, drained**
- **1 8-ounce can red kidney beans, drained**
- **½ cup long grain rice**
- **1 4-ounce can diced green chili peppers, drained, *or* 1 teaspoon chili powder**
- **¼ teaspoon salt**
- **Few dashes bottled hot pepper sauce**   Oven 350°

Trim fat from meat. In a large skillet brown chops in hot oil about 5 minutes on each side. Remove from skillet. Drain fat. In the same skillet combine *undrained* tomatoes, corn, kidney beans, rice, chili peppers or chili powder, salt, and hot pepper sauce. Bring to boiling; boil for 1 minute.

Transfer tomato mixture to a 12x7½x2-inch baking dish. Arrange chops on top. If desired, sprinkle chops lightly with salt and pepper.

Bake, covered, in a 350° oven for 30 minutes. Uncover; bake about 10 minutes more or till rice is tender and pork is no longer pink. Serves 4.

Creamy Herbed Pork Chops

- **4 pork chops, cut ¾ inch thick**
- **1 tablespoon margarine *or* butter**
- **⅓ cup finely chopped carrot**
- **1 tablespoon snipped parsley**
- **2 teaspoons all-purpose flour**
- **½ teaspoon dried basil, thyme, *or* tarragon, crushed**
- **½ teaspoon instant beef bouillon granules**
- **⅔ cup milk *or* light cream**
- **2 tablespoons dry white wine *or* water**

Trim fat from meat. If desired, sprinkle with salt and pepper. In a large skillet cook chops in margarine or butter over medium heat for 5 minutes. Turn chops and add carrot. Cook for 5 to 7 minutes more or till no pink remains. Remove chops, reserving drippings and carrot.

For sauce, stir parsley; flour; basil, thyme, or tarragon; bouillon granules; and ¼ teaspoon *pepper* into drippings and carrot. Add milk or light cream all at once. Cook and stir till thickened and bubbly. Stir in wine or water. Return chops to skillet and heat through. To serve, spoon sauce over chops. Makes 4 servings.

Cheesy Pork Chops: Prepare as above, *except* stir ¼ cup shredded *cheddar or Swiss cheese* into sauce after thickened. Stir till melted.

Curried Pork Chops: Prepare as above, *except* omit carrot. After removing chops from skillet, add 1 cored, thinly sliced *apple* to skillet and cook for 1 minute. Substitute ½ to 1 teaspoon *curry powder* for the herb.

Caraway Pork Chops: Prepare as above, *except* substitute *caraway seed* for the herb and ¾ cup *beer* for the milk and wine.

Honey-Orange Pork Chops

A blend of fruit flavors enhances the chops.

- **¼ teaspoon finely shredded orange peel**
- **½ cup orange juice**
- **¼ cup pineapple juice**
- **2 tablespoons soy sauce**
- **1 tablespoon honey**
- **⅛ teaspoon pepper**
- **2 cloves garlic, minced**
- **4 pork loin chops, cut ¾ inch thick (about 1½ pounds)**
- **1 tablespoon cornstarch**

Trim fat from chops. For marinade, in a shallow baking dish combine orange peel, orange juice, pineapple juice, soy sauce, honey, pepper, and garlic. Add meat, turning to coat. Cover; marinate in the refrigerator for 6 to 24 hours, turning once.

Remove meat from marinade, reserving marinade. Place meat on the unheated rack of a broiler pan. Broil 4 to 5 inches from the heat for 12 to 14 minutes or till no pink remains, turning once.

Transfer marinade to a saucepan. Stir in cornstarch. Cook and stir till thickened and bubbly. Cook and stir 2 minutes more. Pass with chops. Makes 4 servings.

Grill directions: Prepare chops as above. Grill on an uncovered grill directly over *medium-hot* coals for 12 to 14 minutes or till no pink remains; turn once. Continue as above.

Fiesta Pork Kabobs

2 **fresh ears of corn, cut into 1-inch pieces**
1 **pound boneless pork, cut into 1-inch cubes**
1 **large green *or* sweet red pepper, cut into 1-inch pieces**
¼ **cup taco sauce**
2 **tablespoons margarine *or* butter, melted**
1 **tablespoon snipped cilantro *or* parsley**
2 **teaspoons lime juice *or* lemon juice**
1 **teaspoon sugar**

Cook corn in boiling water for 5 minutes. Drain. On 4 long skewers, alternately thread meat, sweet pepper, and corn.

For sauce, mix taco sauce, margarine, cilantro, lime juice, and sugar. Brush some of the sauce onto kabobs. Place kabobs on the unheated rack of a broiler pan. Broil 4 to 5 inches from the heat for 15 to 18 minutes or till meat is no longer pink. Turn and brush with sauce occasionally. Serves 4.

Grill directions: Assemble the kabobs and sauce as above. Grill kabobs on an uncovered grill directly over *medium-hot* coals about 15 minutes or till meat is no longer pink, turning and brushing with sauce occasionally.

Pork Chop Suey

1 **pound lean boneless pork**
3 **tablespoons soy sauce**
2 **tablespoons dry sherry *or* water**
2 **tablespoons cornstarch**
1 **teaspoon instant chicken bouillon granules**
¼ **teaspoon pepper**
1 **tablespoon cooking oil**
2 **teaspoons grated gingerroot**
1 **cup celery, thinly bias sliced**
2 **cups sliced fresh mushrooms**
2 **cups fresh bean sprouts *or* one 16-ounce can bean sprouts, drained**
10 **green onions, bias-sliced into 1-inch pieces (1 cup)**
1 **8-ounce can sliced water chestnuts *or* bamboo shoots, drained**
2 **to 3 cups hot cooked rice**

Partially freeze pork. Thinly slice across the grain into bite-size strips. For sauce, combine soy sauce, sherry, cornstarch, bouillon granules, pepper, and ¾ cup *water.* Set aside.

Preheat a wok or large skillet over high heat; add oil. (Add more oil as necessary.) Stir-fry gingerroot in hot oil for 15 seconds. Add celery; stir-fry 2 minutes. Add mushrooms; fresh bean sprouts, if using; and green onions. Stir-fry 1 to 2 minutes or till celery is crisp-tender. Remove vegetables from wok. Add *half* of the pork to hot wok. Stir-fry for 2 to 3 minutes or till no pink remains. Remove from wok. Stir-fry remaining pork for 2 to 3 minutes or till no pink remains. Return all meat to wok. Push from center of wok.

Stir sauce; add to center of wok. Cook and stir till thickened and bubbly. Add vegetables, water chestnuts, and, if using, canned bean sprouts. Cook and stir till heated through. Serve with hot cooked rice. Makes 4 to 6 servings.

Pork Chow Mein: Prepare as above, *except* substitute *chow mein noodles* for the rice.

Pork Mediterranean

1 **pound boneless pork, cut into ¾-inch cubes**
1 **tablespoon cooking oil**
1 **large onion, sliced and separated into rings**
2 **cloves garlic, minced**
1 **16-ounce can tomatoes, cut up**
1 **teaspoon instant chicken bouillon granules**
1 **teaspoon dried thyme, crushed**
1 **3-ounce can sliced mushrooms, drained**
¼ **cup sliced pitted ripe olives (optional)**
2 **tablespoons snipped parsley**
1 **tablespoon all-purpose flour**
2 **cups hot cooked noodles**

In a large skillet brown *half* of the pork in hot oil. Brown remaining pork with onion rings and garlic. Return all pork to skillet. Stir in *undrained* tomatoes, bouillon granules, thyme, and ⅛ teaspoon *pepper.* Bring to boiling; reduce heat. Cover; simmer 45 minutes or till tender.

Skim fat, if necessary. Stir in mushrooms; olives, if desired; and parsley. Combine flour and ¼ cup *cold* water; stir into pork mixture. Cook and stir till thickened and bubbly. Cook and stir for 1 minute more. Serve over noodles. Serves 4.

Sweet-and-Sour Pork

A combination that can't be beat: deep-fried, batter-coated pork with vegetables and pineapple

 1 8-ounce can pineapple chunks
   (juice pack)
 ⅓ cup sugar
 ¼ cup vinegar
 2 tablespoons cornstarch
 2 tablespoons soy sauce
 1 teaspoon instant chicken bouillon
   granules
 1 beaten egg
 ¼ cup cornstarch
 ¼ cup all-purpose flour
 ¼ cup water
 ⅛ teaspoon ground red *or* black
   pepper
 1 pound boneless pork, cut into
   ¾-inch cubes
   Shortening *or* cooking oil for
   deep-fat frying
 1 tablespoon cooking oil
 2 medium carrots, thinly bias sliced
 2 cloves garlic, minced
 1 large green *or* sweet red pepper,
   cut into ½-inch pieces
 2 cups hot cooked rice

For sauce, drain pineapple, reserving juice. Add water to reserved juice to equal *1½ cups.* Stir in sugar, vinegar, the 2 tablespoons cornstarch, the soy sauce, and bouillon granules; set sauce aside.

 For batter, in a bowl combine egg, the ¼ cup cornstarch, the flour, water, and pepper. Stir till smooth. Dip pork cubes into batter. Fry *one-third* at a time in the hot shortening or oil (365°) for 4 to 5 minutes or till pork is no longer pink and batter is golden. Drain on paper towels.

 Preheat a wok or large skillet over high heat; add the 1 tablespoon oil. (Add more oil as necessary during cooking.) Stir-fry carrots and garlic in hot oil for 1 minute. Add sweet pepper; stir-fry for 1 to 2 minutes or till crisp-tender. Push from center of wok.

 Stir sauce and pour into center of wok. Cook and stir till thickened and bubbly. Cook and stir 1 minute more. Stir in pork and pineapple. Stir together all ingredients to coat with sauce; heat through. Serve over rice. Makes 4 servings.

Cashew Pork and Pea Pods

Look for bean threads in large supermarkets or Oriental food stores.

 1 pound boneless pork
 ½ cup orange juice
 ¼ cup orange marmalade
 2 tablespoons soy sauce
 1 tablespoon cornstarch
 ½ teaspoon ground ginger
 1 tablespoon cooking oil
 2 cups fresh pea pods *or* one 6-ounce
   package frozen pea pods, thawed
 2 medium peaches, peeled and cubed;
   1 small papaya, peeled, seeded,
   and cubed; 2 medium nectarines,
   cubed (about 1½ cups); *or* 1½
   cups frozen peach slices, thawed
 ½ cup cashews *or* peanuts
   Fried bean threads* *or* hot
   cooked rice

Partially freeze meat. Thinly slice across the grain into bite-size strips. For sauce, combine orange juice, orange marmalade, soy sauce, cornstarch, and ginger. Set aside.

 Preheat a wok or large skillet over high heat; add cooking oil. (Add more oil as necessary during cooking.)

 Add *half* of the pork to the wok or skillet and stir-fry for 2 to 3 minutes or till no pink remains. Remove pork from wok. Add remaining pork and stir-fry for 2 to 3 minutes or till no pink remains. Return all meat to wok. Stir in pea pods and peaches, papaya, or nectarines. Push from the center of the wok.

 Stir sauce and pour into center of wok. Cook and stir till thickened and bubbly. Cook and stir 2 minutes more. Add cashews or peanuts. Stir together all ingredients to coat with sauce. Serve over fried bean threads or rice. Serves 4.

 ***Note:** For fried bean threads, fry 1 ounce *bean threads (cellophane noodles),* a few at a time, in *shortening or cooking oil for deep-fat frying* (375°) about 5 seconds or till bean threads puff and rise to top. Drain on paper towels.

Ham with Pineapple Sauce

Next time, serve your ham with the Cherry Sauce on page 366.

  1 **4- to 6-pound fully cooked boneless ham**
  ½ **cup finely chopped onion**
  ¼ **cup margarine *or* butter**
  1 **cup catsup**
  1 **cup pineapple *or* apricot preserves, *or* orange marmalade**
  2 **teaspoons dry mustard**   Oven 325°

Place ham on a rack in a shallow baking pan. If desired, score top of ham in a diamond pattern, making cuts about ¼ inch deep. Insert a meat thermometer. Bake in a 325° oven for 1¼ to 2½ hours or till thermometer registers 140°.

Meanwhile, for sauce, in a medium saucepan cook onion in margarine till tender but not brown. Stir in catsup, preserves, and dry mustard. Heat through. Brush some sauce onto ham before serving; pass remaining. Serves 16 to 24.

Grill directions: In a covered grill arrange *medium-hot* coals around a drip pan. Test for *medium* heat above pan. Place ham on grill rack over drip pan but not over coals. Insert meat thermometer. Lower grill hood. Grill for 1¼ to 2½ hours or till meat thermometer registers 140°. Prepare and serve sauce as above.

Ham Caribbean

  1 **1½-pound fully cooked center-cut ham slice, cut 1 inch thick**
  1 **8-ounce can pineapple chunks (juice pack)**
  ¼ **cup packed brown sugar**
  1 **tablespoon cornstarch**
  ⅛ **teaspoon ground cloves *or* nutmeg**
  ⅓ **cup orange juice *or* ¼ cup orange juice plus 2 tablespoons rum**
  ½ **cup light raisins**   Oven 350°

Trim fat from ham. Slash edges of ham at 1-inch intervals. Place on a rack in a shallow baking pan. Bake in a 350° oven for 30 minutes.

Meanwhile, drain pineapple chunks, reserving juice. If necessary, add water to reserved juice to measure ⅓ cup. In a small saucepan combine brown sugar, cornstarch, and cloves. Stir in pineapple juice, orange juice, and, if using, rum. Cook and stir till thickened and bubbly. Cook and stir 2 minutes more. Stir in pineapple chunks and raisins. Heat through. Spoon over ham. Serves 6.

Microwave directions: Trim fat from ham. Slash edges of ham at 1-inch intervals. Place ham slice in an 8x8x2-inch baking dish. Micro-cook, covered with waxed paper, on 100% power (high) for 9 to 12 minutes, turning meat over once. Cover and keep warm. Meanwhile, drain pineapple chunks, reserving juice. If necessary, add water to reserved juice to measure ⅓ cup. In a 2-cup measure combine brown sugar, cornstarch, and cloves. Stir in pineapple juice, orange juice, and, if using, rum. Cook on high for 2 to 3 minutes or till thickened and bubbly, stirring after 1 minute, then every 30 seconds. Stir in pineapple chunks and raisins. Cook on high for 1 minute more or till heated through. Spoon over ham.

Identifying Hams

If you find yourself confused by the different kinds of ham available at your local supermarket, just remember these handy definitions.

The most popular kind of ham is *fully cooked ham*. It is ready to eat when you buy it. If you want to serve the ham hot, just heat it to 140° (see chart, page 255).

Hams labeled *cook before eating* are not completely cooked during processing and should be cooked to 160°. (If you're unsure whether a ham you've bought is fully cooked, cook it to 160°.)

Country or country-style hams are distinctively flavored and specially processed. They are cured, may or may not be smoked, and are usually aged. Country hams generally are saltier than other hams, and often are named for the city where they are processed. Follow package directions for these hams.

Turkey ham is skinless, boneless turkey thigh meat that is smoked and cured to taste like pork ham. It's available in large pieces or as cold cuts. To serve it hot, heat it to 140°.

Sausage

Frankfurter, knockwurst
(Top row, left to right)
Smoked sausage, smoked bratwurst
(Bottom row, left to right)

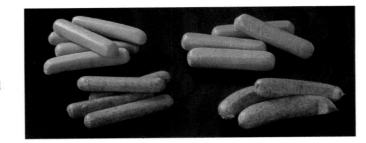

Bratwurst, Italian sausage, pork patty
(Top row, left to right)
Boudin, pork link, chorizo
(Bottom row, left to right)

Liver sausage, braunschweiger, fully cooked bratwurst, blood sausage

Bologna, Polish sausage, cooked salami

Cervelat, Genoa salami, pepperoni link and slices
(Top row, left to right)
Hard salami, summer sausage
(Bottom row, left to right)

Corn Dogs

1   **1-pound package frankfurters
    (8 to 10)**
1   **cup all-purpose flour**
⅔   **cup cornmeal**
2   **tablespoons sugar**
1½ **teaspoons baking powder**
½   **teaspoon dry mustard**
1   **beaten egg**
¾   **cup milk**
2   **tablespoons cooking oil
    Shortening *or* cooking oil for
    deep-fat frying**

Pat frankfurters dry with paper towels. If desired, insert a wooden skewer into *one* end of *each* frankfurter. Set aside. Combine flour, cornmeal, sugar, baking powder, and dry mustard. Combine egg, milk, and the 2 tablespoons oil. Add to dry ingredients; mix well. (Batter will be thick.)

Coat frankfurters with batter. In a large skillet fry franks, three at a time, in ¾ inch hot shortening (375°), turning with tongs after 10 seconds to prevent batter from sliding off. Cook 3 minutes more; turn again after 1½ minutes. Serve with catsup and mustard, if desired. Serves 4 or 5.

Creamed Bratwurst

1   **cup chopped onion**
1   **teaspoon dry mustard**
2   **tablespoons margarine *or* butter**
1   **pound fully cooked bratwurst, bias-
    sliced into ¾-inch pieces**
1   **cup beer**
1   **4-ounce can sliced mushrooms,
    drained**
¼   **cup beef broth**
2   **teaspoons sugar**
2   **tablespoons all-purpose flour**
½   **cup dairy sour cream**
2   **cups hot cooked noodles**
2   **tablespoons snipped parsley**

Cook onion and mustard in margarine till tender. Stir in bratwurst, beer, mushrooms, beef broth, sugar, and ¼ teaspoon *pepper*. Simmer 5 minutes. Stir flour into sour cream. Stir some pan juices into sour cream mixture to thin. Stir into bratwurst mixture. Cook and stir till thickened and bubbly. Cook and stir 1 minute more. Serve over noodles. Sprinkle with parsley. Serves 4.

Coney Islands

½   **pound ground beef**
½   **cup chopped onion**
¼   **cup chopped green pepper**
1   **8-ounce can tomato sauce**
1   **8-ounce can red kidney beans,
    drained**
1½ **to 2 teaspoons chili powder**
6   **frankfurters**
6   **frankfurter buns, split and toasted**

In a large skillet cook ground beef, onion, and green pepper till meat is brown. Drain fat. Stir in tomato sauce, beans, and chili powder. Bring to boiling; reduce heat. Simmer for 5 minutes.

Meanwhile, in a saucepan cover frankfurters with *cold* water. Bring to boiling; reduce heat. Simmer 5 minutes. To serve, place frankfurters in buns and top with some of the meat mixture. Serve with shredded cheddar cheese, chopped onion, and pickle relish, if desired. Serves 6.

Cooking Sausages

Different sausages are cooked differently. Here's how to cook each one.

Uncooked patties: Place ½-inch-thick sausage patties in an unheated skillet. Cook over medium-low heat 10 to 12 minutes or till juices run clear, turning once. Drain well. Or, arrange ½-inch-thick patties on a rack in a shallow baking pan. Bake in a 400° oven about 15 minutes or till juices run clear.

Uncooked links: Place 1- to 1¼-inch-diameter sausage links in an unheated skillet. Add ½ inch water. Bring to boiling; reduce heat. Cover and simmer 15 minutes or till juices run clear. Drain. Cook for 1 to 2 minutes more or till browned, turning often.

Place ¾-inch-diameter links in an unheated skillet. Cook over medium-low heat 10 to 15 minutes; turn often.

Fully cooked links: Place in a saucepan. Cover with *cold* water. Bring to boiling; reduce heat. Simmer 5 to 10 minutes or till heated through.

Italian Sausage Sandwiches

Feature these hearty sandwiches the next time friends come to watch a game on TV.

- **1 pound bulk Italian sausage**
- **1 8-ounce can pizza sauce**
- **1 4-ounce can mushroom stems and pieces, drained**
- **4 French-style rolls, split lengthwise**
- **1 medium green pepper, cut into rings**
- **6 ounces sliced mozzarella cheese** Oven 375°

In a skillet cook sausage till no pink remains. Drain fat. Stir in pizza sauce and mushrooms; heat through. Hollow out bottom halves of rolls. Spoon in meat mixture. Top with pepper rings and cheese. Cover with bun tops. Place sandwiches in a shallow baking pan or on a baking sheet. Cover tightly with foil and heat in a 375° oven for 15 minutes or till cheese melts and sandwiches are hot. Makes 4 servings.

Microwave directions: In a 1½-quart casserole micro-cook sausage, covered, on 100% power (high) for 4 to 6 minutes or till no pink remains, stirring twice. Drain fat. Stir in pizza sauce and mushrooms. Cook, uncovered, on high for 2 to 3 minutes or till heated through. Assemble and bake sandwiches as above.

Bacon and Onion Bratwursts

- **2 slices bacon**
- **2 medium onions, sliced and separated into rings**
- **1 medium green pepper, cut into strips**
- **1 tablespoon Dijon-style mustard**
- **4 links fully cooked bratwurst or knockwurst, or 4 frankfurters (½ pound)**
- **4 frankfurter buns, split and toasted Dijon-style mustard**

In a large skillet cook bacon till crisp. Drain bacon, reserving *2 tablespoons* drippings. Crumble bacon and set aside.

Cook onions and green pepper in reserved drippings, covered, over medium heat about 5 minutes or till tender, stirring occasionally. Stir in the 1 tablespoon mustard. Score bratwurst ¼ inch deep at 1-inch intervals; add to onion mixture. Cover and cook for 10 to 12 minutes or till heated through.

Spread buns with additional mustard. Place bratwurst in buns. Top with onions and green pepper. Sprinkle with bacon. Makes 4 servings.

Microwave directions: In a 2-quart casserole micro-cook bacon, covered with paper towels, on 100% power (high) for 2½ to 3½ minutes or till crisp. Drain bacon, reserving *2 tablespoons* drippings. Crumble bacon and set aside. Cook onions and green pepper in reserved drippings, covered, on high for 4 to 5 minutes or till tender, stirring once. Stir in the 1 tablespoon mustard. Score bratwurst ¼ inch deep at 1-inch intervals; add to casserole. Cook, covered, on high for 3 to 4 minutes or till heated through, stirring once. Assemble sandwiches as above.

Apple-Stuffed Sausage Patties

The stuffing stands in for the bun in this burger.

- **1 pound bulk pork sausage**
- **½ pound ground beef**
- **¼ cup finely chopped celery**
- **¼ cup finely chopped onion**
- **2 tablespoons margarine or butter**
- **¼ cup apple juice or water**
- **¾ cup herb-seasoned stuffing mix**
- **½ cup finely chopped peeled apple**
- **2 tablespoons snipped parsley**
- **¼ teaspoon dry mustard**
- **¼ teaspoon pepper** Oven 375°

Combine sausage and beef; shape into ten ¼-inch-thick patties.

In a saucepan cook celery and onion in margarine till tender but not brown. Remove from heat. Add apple juice or water. Stir in stuffing mix, apple, parsley, mustard, and pepper. Place about ¼ *cup* stuffing atop each of *five* patties. Spread to within ½ inch of edges. Top with remaining patties. Press meat around edges to seal.

Place on a rack in a shallow baking dish or pan. Bake in a 375° oven for 35 to 40 minutes or till no pink remains. Makes 5 servings.

Submarine Sandwich

Named for its traditionally long shape.

- 1 16-ounce loaf unsliced French bread, one 9-inch round loaf unsliced Italian bread, *or* 6 French-style rolls
- ¼ cup mayonnaise *or* salad dressing
- 2 tablespoons prepared mustard
- 6 lettuce leaves
- 12 ounces thinly sliced salami, pepperoni, summer sausage, fully cooked ham, *or* prosciutto, *or* a combination
- 6 ounces sliced provolone, Swiss, *or* mozzarella cheese
- 2 medium tomatoes, sliced

Split bread loaf or rolls in half horizontally. Spread mayonnaise or salad dressing on the cut side of the bottom(s); spread mustard on the cut side of the top(s). On bottom(s), layer lettuce, desired meat and cheese, and tomatoes. Add top(s) and secure with wooden picks or skewers. Slice loaf into 6 portions. Makes 6 servings.

Muffuletta: Prepare as above, *except* combine 1 cup chopped, well-drained *pickled mixed vegetables* and ½ cup chopped, well-drained *pimiento-stuffed olives*. Layer mixture atop lettuce.

Popover Sausage

Top this hearty main dish with Cheese Sauce (see recipe, page 361) for brunch.

- 1 8-ounce package brown-and-serve sausage links
- 2 beaten eggs
- 1 cup milk
- 1 tablespoon cooking oil
- 1 cup all-purpose flour
- ¼ teaspoon salt   Oven 400°

Grease bottom and 1 inch up the sides of an 8x8x2-inch baking dish. Set aside.

Slice sausage into ½-inch pieces. In a large skillet brown sausage. Drain on paper towels. Meanwhile, combine eggs, milk, and oil. Stir in flour and salt. Beat with an electric mixer or rotary beater till smooth. Pour batter into prepared dish. Arrange sausage pieces in batter.

Bake in a 400° oven about 35 minutes or till puffed and golden. Serve immediately with maple-flavored syrup or honey, if desired. Serves 4.

Liver and Onions

- 1 medium onion, sliced and separated into rings
- 2 tablespoons margarine *or* butter
- 1 pound sliced beef liver
- 2 teaspoons water
- 2 teaspoons lemon juice
- 1 teaspoon Worcestershire sauce

In a large skillet cook onion in margarine till tender but not brown. Remove from skillet. Add liver and sprinkle with salt and pepper. Cook over medium heat for 3 minutes. Turn liver over and return onion to skillet. Cook for 2 to 3 minutes more or till liver is slightly pink in center. Remove liver and onion from skillet. Stir water, lemon juice, and Worcestershire sauce into pan drippings; heat through. Pour over liver and onion. Makes 4 servings.

Spiced Tongue and Vegetables

- 2 cups water
- ¼ cup soy sauce
- ¼ teaspoon garlic powder
- ¼ teaspoon ground ginger
- ¼ teaspoon ground cloves
- ¼ teaspoon pepper
- 1 2½- to 3-pound fresh beef tongue
- 3 medium potatoes, quartered
- 3 medium carrots, cut into 1½-inch pieces
- 3 stalks celery, bias-sliced into 1½-inch pieces
- ¼ cup cold water
- 2 tablespoons cornstarch

In a Dutch oven combine the 2 cups water, the soy sauce, garlic powder, ginger, cloves, and pepper. Add tongue. Bring to boiling; reduce heat. Cover; simmer about 2 hours or till nearly tender.

Remove skin from tongue. Return tongue to pan; add potatoes, carrots, and celery. Return to boiling; reduce heat. Cover and simmer for 15 to 20 minutes more or till tender. Remove tongue and vegetables from pan; keep warm.

For sauce, skim fat from pan juices. If necessary, add water to juices to equal *1½ cups*. Mix the ¼ cup cold water and the cornstarch; stir into pan juices. Cook and stir till thickened and bubbly. Cook and stir 2 minutes more. Slice tongue thinly; serve with sauce and vegetables. Serves 6.

Venison Pot Roast

1 **2- to 3-pound venison shoulder** *or*
   rump roast
2 **tablespoons cooking oil**
1 **6-ounce can (¾ cup) tomato juice**
½ **cup finely chopped onion**
½ **cup finely chopped carrot**
2 **teaspoons instant beef bouillon**
   granules
3 **tablespoons all-purpose flour**
½ **cup dairy sour cream** *or* **plain yogurt**
4 **cups hot cooked noodles**

In a Dutch oven brown meat on all sides in hot oil. Drain fat. Stir in tomato juice, onion, carrot, and bouillon granules. Bring to boiling; reduce heat. Cover and simmer for 1½ to 2 hours or till meat is tender. Remove meat from pan.

For sauce, add enough water to pan juices and vegetables to equal *2 cups*. Return mixture to pan. Stir flour into sour cream or yogurt. Add to pan juices. Cook and stir till thickened and bubbly. Cook and stir 1 minute more. Season to taste. Slice venison thinly; spoon sauce over. Serve with noodles. Makes 8 servings.

Marinated Venison Chops

4 **single** *or* **2 double venison chops** *or*
   steaks, cut ¾ inch thick (about
   1¼ pounds)
¼ **cup vinegar**
¼ **cup catsup**
2 **tablespoons cooking oil**
2 **tablespoons Worcestershire sauce**
¾ **teaspoon dry mustard**
2 **cloves garlic, minced**
¼ **teaspoon salt**
¼ **teaspoon pepper**
   Snipped parsley (optional)

Place chops or steaks in a plastic bag set into a shallow dish. For marinade, combine vinegar, catsup, oil, Worcestershire sauce, dry mustard, garlic, salt, and pepper. Pour over meat; close bag. Marinate in the refrigerator for 6 to 24 hours, turning bag occasionally.

Remove venison from bag, reserving marinade. Place meat on the unheated rack of a broiler pan. Broil 3 inches from the heat for 7 minutes. Turn and brush meat with marinade.

Broil 5 to 7 minutes more for medium or 7 to 9 minutes more for well-done. Sprinkle with snipped parsley, if desired. Makes 2 to 4 servings.

Grill directions: Marinate the meat as above. Grill meat on an uncovered grill directly over *medium-hot* coals for 8 minutes. Turn and brush with reserved marinade. Grill for 6 to 8 minutes more for medium or 8 to 10 minutes more for well-done. Sprinkle with snipped parsley, if desired.

Beer-Braised Rabbit

1 **2½- to 3-pound domestic rabbit,**
   cut up
2 **tablespoons cooking oil**
4 **medium potatoes, quartered**
4 **medium carrots, cut into ½-inch**
   pieces
1 **medium onion, sliced and separated**
   into rings
1 **12-ounce can beer** *or* **1½ cups apple**
   juice
¼ **cup chili sauce**
½ **teaspoon salt**
¼ **cup cold water**
2 **tablespoons all-purpose flour**

If desired, sprinkle rabbit with salt and pepper. In a 12-inch skillet brown rabbit on all sides in hot oil. Drain fat. Add potatoes, carrots, and onion to skillet. Combine beer, chili sauce, and salt. Pour over rabbit and vegetables in skillet. Bring to boiling; reduce heat. Cover and simmer for 35 to 45 minutes or till tender. Remove rabbit and vegetables from skillet. Keep warm.

For sauce, skim fat from pan juices. If necessary, add water to juices to equal *1½ cups*. Return pan-juices mixture to skillet. Combine water and flour; stir into pan juices. Cook and stir till thickened and bubbly. Cook and stir for 1 minute more. Serve sauce with rabbit and vegetables. Makes 4 servings.

Create-Your-Own Meat Loaf

Use your microwave to cut the cooking time by more than half.

　1　**beaten egg**
　¾　**cup soft bread crumbs (1 slice) or**
　　　¼ cup fine dry bread crumbs
　¼　**cup milk, beer, apple juice, or water**
　¼　**cup finely chopped onion or 1**
　　　tablespoon dried minced onion
　¼　**cup finely chopped celery or green**
　　　pepper, or shredded carrot; or
　　　one 2-ounce can mushrooms,
　　　drained and chopped (optional)
　2　**tablespoons snipped parsley**
　　　(optional)
　½　**teaspoon dried sage, thyme, basil,**
　　　or oregano, crushed; or dried
　　　dillweed
　½　**teaspoon salt**
　¼　**teaspoon pepper**
　1　**pound ground beef or ground lamb**
　2　**tablespoons bottled barbecue**
　　　sauce, chili sauce,
　　　or catsup 　　　　　　　Oven 350°

In a mixing bowl combine egg; bread crumbs; milk; onion; celery and parsley, if desired; herb; salt; and pepper. Add ground meat and mix well.

In a shallow baking dish pat mixture into a 7x3x2-inch loaf. *Or,* shape into a circle with a 6-inch diameter. Form a 2-inch-diameter hole in the center of the circle.

Bake in a 350° oven for 45 to 50 minutes for the loaf (25 to 30 minutes for the ring) or till no pink remains. Transfer to a serving plate. Spoon barbecue sauce over meat. Makes 4 servings.

Microwave directions: In a mixing bowl combine egg; bread crumbs; milk; onion; celery and parsley, if desired; herb; salt; and pepper. Add ground meat and mix well. Shape into a circle with a 6-inch diameter. Form a 2-inch-diameter hole in the center of the circle. Place ring in a 9-inch pie plate. Cover with waxed paper. Micro-cook on 100% power (high) for 8 to 10 minutes or till no pink remains, giving the dish a quarter-turn every 3 minutes. Transfer to a serving plate. Spoon barbecue sauce over meat.

Ham Loaf: Prepare as above, *except* use soft bread crumbs. Substitute *dry mustard* for the herb and omit salt. Reduce ground beef or lamb to *½ pound* and add ½ pound ground *ham.* Bake 50 minutes or till juices run clear.

Swedish Meatballs

Robust, fluffy-textured meatballs served along with noodles and a creamy sauce.

　1　**beaten egg**
　2¼　**cups milk or light cream**
　¾　**cup soft bread crumbs (1 slice)**
　½　**cup finely chopped onion**
　¼　**cup snipped parsley**
　¼　**teaspoon pepper**
　⅛　**teaspoon ground allspice or ground**
　　　nutmeg
　½　**pound ground beef or ground veal**
　½　**pound ground pork or ground lamb**
　1　**tablespoon margarine or butter**
　2　**tablespoons all-purpose flour**
　2　**teaspoons instant beef bouillon**
　　　granules
　⅛　**teaspoon pepper**
　2　**to 3 cups hot cooked noodles**

In a mixing bowl combine egg, ¼ *cup* of the milk, the bread crumbs, onion, parsley, the ¼ teaspoon pepper, and the allspice or nutmeg. Add meat; mix well. Shape into 30 meatballs. In a large skillet cook meatballs in margarine or butter, *half* at a time, over medium heat about 10 minutes or till no pink remains, turning to brown evenly. Remove meatballs from skillet, reserving *2 tablespoons* drippings. Drain the meatballs on paper towels.

Stir flour, bouillon granules, and the ⅛ teaspoon pepper into reserved drippings. Add remaining milk. Cook and stir till thickened and bubbly. Cook and stir 1 minute more. Return meatballs to skillet. Heat through. Serve with noodles. Makes 4 to 6 servings.

Microwave directions: In a mixing bowl combine egg, ¼ *cup* of the milk, the bread crumbs, onion, parsley, the ¼ teaspoon pepper, and the allspice or nutmeg. Add meat; mix well. Shape into 30 meatballs. In a dish or plate micro-cook *half* of the meatballs, covered with vented plastic wrap, on 100% power (high) for 3½ to 5½ minutes or till no pink remains, rearranging once. Drain meatballs on paper towels. Repeat with remaining meatballs. In a 2-quart casserole cook *2 tablespoons* margarine 40 to 50 seconds or till melted. Stir in flour, bouillon granules, and the ⅛ teaspoon pepper. Stir in remaining milk. Cook on high 4 to 6 minutes or till thickened and bubbly, stirring every minute. Add meatballs. Cook on high about 1 minute more or till heated through. Serve with noodles.

Spaghetti Sauce

If you prefer meatballs in your sauce, try the Spaghetti and Meatballs version.

 1 **pound ground beef** *or* **ground pork**
 1½ **cups sliced fresh mushrooms**
 ½ **cup chopped onion**
 ½ **cup chopped green pepper**
 2 **cloves garlic, minced**
 2 **16-ounce cans tomatoes, cut up**
 1 **6-ounce can tomato paste**
 1 **teaspoon sugar**
 1 **teaspoon dried oregano, crushed**
 1 **teaspoon dried basil, crushed**
 ½ **teaspoon dried thyme, crushed**
 1 **bay leaf**
 6 **cups hot cooked spaghetti**

In a Dutch oven cook meat, mushrooms, onion, green pepper, and garlic till meat is brown. Drain fat. Stir in *undrained* tomatoes, tomato paste, sugar, oregano, basil, thyme, bay leaf, ½ teaspoon *salt,* and ¼ teaspoon *pepper.* Bring to boiling; reduce heat. Cover; simmer 30 minutes. Uncover; simmer 10 to 15 minutes more or to desired consistency, stirring occasionally. Discard bay leaf. Serve over spaghetti. If desired, pass grated Parmesan cheese. Makes 6 servings.

Microwave directions: In a 3-quart casserole micro-cook meat, mushrooms, onion, green pepper, and garlic on 100% power (high) 6 to 8 minutes or till no pink remains, stirring twice. Drain. Stir in *one* 16-ounce can *undrained* tomatoes, cut up; one 7½-ounce can *tomatoes,* cut up; tomato paste; sugar; oregano; basil; thyme; bay leaf; ½ teaspoon *salt;* and ¼ teaspoon *pepper.* Cook, covered, on high for 10 to 12 minutes or till boiling. Cook, uncovered, on 50% power (medium) about 20 minutes or to desired consistency, stirring once. Discard bay leaf. Serve as above.

Spaghetti and Meatballs: Prepare as above, *except* in a Dutch oven cook mushrooms, onion, green pepper, and garlic in 1 tablespoon *cooking oil.* Continue cooking sauce as above. Meanwhile, combine 1 beaten *egg,* ¾ cup *soft bread crumbs* (1 slice), ¼ cup finely chopped *onion,* and ¼ teaspoon *salt.* Add ground meat; mix well. Shape into 48 meatballs. In a large skillet cook meatballs, *half* at a time, in 1 tablespoon hot *cooking oil* about 8 minutes or till no pink remains. Drain. (*Or,* place meatballs in a 15x10x1-inch baking pan. Bake in a 375° oven about 20 minutes or till no pink remains. Drain.) Add meatballs to the sauce after uncovering. Do not use microwave directions.

Porcupine Meatballs

The rice pokes out like a porcupine's quills.

 1 **beaten egg**
 1 **10¾-ounce can condensed tomato soup**
 ¼ **cup long grain rice**
 ¼ **teaspoon onion powder**
 ¼ **teaspoon pepper**
 1 **pound lean ground beef**
 1 **teaspoon Worcestershire sauce**
 ½ **teaspoon dried oregano, crushed**

Combine egg, ¼ cup of the soup, *uncooked* rice, onion powder, and pepper. Add beef; mix well. Shape into 20 meatballs. Place in a large skillet. Mix the remaining soup with Worcestershire sauce, oregano, and ½ cup *water;* pour over meatballs. Bring to boiling; reduce heat. Cover; simmer, stirring often, about 20 minutes or till no pink remains in meat and rice is tender. Skim fat. Pass Parmesan cheese, if desired. Serves 4 or 5.

Microwave directions: Combine egg, ¼ cup of the soup, ½ cup uncooked *quick-cooking rice,* the onion powder, and pepper. Add beef; mix well. Shape into 20 meatballs. In an 8x8x2-inch baking dish micro-cook meatballs, covered, on 100% power (high) for 6 minutes, rearranging once. Drain well. Mix the remaining soup with Worcestershire sauce, oregano, and ½ cup *water.* Pour over meatballs. Cook, covered, on high, stirring twice, for 3 to 5 minutes more or till no pink remains in meatballs and rice is tender.

◀ Shape meat mixture into an 8x6-inch rectangle. Divide into 48 pieces. Roll into meatballs.

Hamburgers

1 **beaten egg**
2 **tablespoons milk *or* water**
¾ **cup soft bread crumbs (1 slice) *or***
  ¼ **cup fine dry bread crumbs**
2 **tablespoons chopped onion *or***
  ¼ **teaspoon onion powder**
1 **tablespoon prepared mustard *or***
  ½ **teaspoon dry mustard**
1 **clove garlic, minced, *or* ⅛ teaspoon**
  garlic powder (optional)
1 **pound ground beef, ground pork,**
  ground veal, *or* ground lamb
4 **or 6 hamburger buns, split and**
  toasted

In a mixing bowl combine egg and milk or water. Stir in bread crumbs; onion; mustard; garlic, if desired; ¼ teaspoon *salt;* and ¼ teaspoon *pepper.* Add meat; mix well. Shape meat mixture into four ¾-inch-thick or six ½-inch-thick patties.

Place patties on the unheated rack of a broiler pan. Broil 3 to 4 inches from the heat for 15 to 18 minutes for ¾-inch patties (10 to 12 minutes for ½-inch patties) or till no pink remains. Turn once. Serve patties on buns. Serves 4 or 6.

Cheeseburgers: Prepare as above, *except* place *one* slice *American, Swiss, cheddar, mozzarella, Monterey Jack, Monterey Jack with jalapeño peppers, or Muenster cheese* atop *each* patty at the end of cooking time. Broil about 1 minute more or till cheese begins to melt.

Italian-Style Burgers: Prepare as above, *except* substitute *catsup* for the milk. Stir in 2 tablespoons grated *Parmesan cheese* and ¾ teaspoon *Italian seasoning* with bread crumbs.

Mexican-Style Burgers: Prepare as above, *except* substitute *salsa or taco sauce* for the milk and omit the mustard. Stir in 2 tablespoons canned diced *green chili peppers* and 1 teaspoon *chili powder* with the bread crumbs. Serve with additional salsa or taco sauce, if desired.

Greek-Style Burgers: Prepare as above, *except* substitute *plain yogurt* for the milk and ¼ cup *cracked wheat* for the bread crumbs. Stir in ½ teaspoon dried *mint,* crushed, or ¼ teaspoon dried *oregano,* crushed, with the cracked wheat. If desired, serve with additional plain yogurt and crumbled feta cheese.

Indian-Style Burgers: Prepare as above, *except* stir in 2 tablespoons chopped *peanuts,* 1 tablespoon chopped *chutney,* and 1 teaspoon *curry powder* with the bread crumbs.

German-Style Burgers: Prepare as above, *except* substitute *beer or apple juice* for the milk and ¼ cup crushed *gingersnaps* for the bread crumbs. Stir in ½ teaspoon *caraway seed* with the crushed gingersnaps.

British-Style Burgers: Prepare as above, *except* substitute ¼ cup *quick-cooking rolled oats* for the bread crumbs. Stir in ¼ cup snipped *parsley* and 1 tablespoon *prepared horseradish* with the oats.

Oriental-Style Burgers: Prepare as above, *except* substitute *soy sauce* for the milk. Stir in ¼ cup chopped *water chestnuts* and 1 teaspoon grated *gingerroot or* ¼ teaspoon ground *ginger* with the bread crumbs.

Steak and Burger Toppings

Dress up your steaks and burgers with one of these savory sensations. Each makes enough for 4 servings.

Mushroom-Onion Sauce: Cook 1 cup sliced fresh *mushrooms;* ½ cup sliced *green onion;* and 1 clove *garlic,* minced, in 2 tablespoons *margarine or butter* till tender. Season to taste.

Sour Cream and Cheese Sauce: Combine ½ cup dairy *sour cream* and ¼ cup shredded *cheddar or Swiss cheese or* 2 tablespoons crumbled *blue cheese or feta cheese.* If desired, add 1 tablespoon snipped parsley.

Mustard-Chive Sauce: In a saucepan melt 1 tablespoon *margarine or butter.* Stir in 2 teaspoons *all-purpose flour* and ⅛ teaspoon *salt.* Add ¾ cup *milk.* Cook and stir till bubbly. Cook and stir 1 minute more. Remove from heat. Stir in 1 tablespoon *Dijon-style mustard,* 1 teaspoon snipped *chives,* and 1 teaspoon drained *capers.*

Parsley Pesto: In a blender container place 3 tablespoons *cooking oil.* Add 2 cups lightly packed snipped *parsley,* 2 tablespoons chopped *walnuts,* 1 teaspoon dried *basil,* and 1 clove *garlic,* quartered. Cover and blend till nearly smooth. Stir in ¼ cup grated *Parmesan cheese.*

Stuffed Burgers

1 beaten egg
¼ cup fine dry bread crumbs
1 tablespoon milk
½ teaspoon dried basil, thyme, sage,
    or oregano, crushed
1 pound ground beef, ground pork,
    ground veal, or ground lamb
¼ cup finely chopped pimiento-stuffed
    olives, pitted ripe olives, green
    pepper, or canned sliced
    mushrooms; or ¼ cup shredded
    zucchini, carrot, or cheese
4 hamburger buns, split and toasted

In a mixing bowl combine egg, bread crumbs, milk, basil, ½ teaspoon *salt,* and ⅛ teaspoon *pepper.* Add meat and mix well. Shape meat mixture into eight ¼-inch-thick patties. Place about *1 tablespoon* olives, vegetables, or cheese atop each of *four* patties. Spread to within ½ inch of edges. Top with remaining patties. Press meat around edges to seal.

Place patties on the unheated rack of a broiler pan. Broil 3 inches from the heat for 15 to 18 minutes or till no pink remains, turning once. Serve patties on buns. Makes 4 servings.

Glazed Ham Patties

1 beaten egg
¾ cup soft bread crumbs (1 slice)
⅓ cup raisins or snipped dried apricots
    (optional)
¼ cup chopped green onion
½ pound ground fully cooked ham
½ pound lean ground beef
¼ cup packed brown sugar
1 teaspoon all-purpose flour
2 tablespoons orange juice
    or water   Oven 375°

Combine egg; bread crumbs; raisins, if desired; onion; and ¼ teaspoon *pepper.* Add meat and mix well. Shape meat mixture into four ½-inch-thick patties. For glaze, in an 8x8x2-inch baking dish combine brown sugar and flour. Stir in orange juice or water. Place patties in dish with glaze. Bake in a 375° oven for 25 to 30 minutes or till juices run clear, spooning glaze over patties after 15 minutes. Remove patties from dish. Stir glaze and spoon over meat. Makes 4 servings.

Garden Burgers

1 beaten egg
1 tablespoon catsup
½ teaspoon dried basil, crushed
½ teaspoon onion salt
¼ teaspoon pepper
1 cup frozen loose-pack chopped
    broccoli or shredded hash brown
    potatoes, thawed; or shredded
    carrot or zucchini
¼ cup soft bread crumbs
1 pound ground beef, ground pork,
    or ground lamb
    Catsup or bottled barbecue sauce
4 hamburger buns, split and toasted
    Mayonnaise or salad dressing
    Leaf lettuce

Combine egg, the 1 tablespoon catsup, the basil, onion salt, and pepper. Stir in vegetable and bread crumbs. Add meat; mix well. Shape into four ¾-inch-thick patties.

Place patties on the unheated rack of a broiler pan. Broil 3 inches from the heat for 15 to 18 minutes or till no pink remains, turning and brushing with additional catsup once. Brush again with catsup before serving.

Serve patties on buns with mayonnaise and lettuce. Makes 4 servings.

Microwave directions: Assemble meat patties as above. Arrange in an 8x8x2-inch baking dish. Cover with waxed paper. Micro-cook on 100% power (high) for 3 minutes. Give dish a half-turn, turn patties over, spoon off fat, and brush with additional catsup. Cook on high for 3 to 5 minutes more or till no pink remains. Brush again with catsup before serving. Serve as above.

Judging Ground Meat Doneness

For safety's sake, we recommend cooking all meat loaves and meat-loaf-type ground-meat patties to 170° or till no pink remains. Ground-meat patties with no other ingredients added, however, may be cooked till their centers are brownish pink (medium doneness).

Tacos

- 12 **taco shells**
- 1 **pound ground beef *or* ground pork**
- ½ **cup chopped onion**
- 2 **cloves garlic, minced**
- 1 **4-ounce can diced green chili peppers, drained**
- 1 **to 2 teaspoons chili powder**
  Several dashes bottled hot pepper sauce (optional)
- 1½ **cups shredded lettuce**
- 1 **cup chopped tomatoes**
- 1 **cup shredded sharp cheddar *or* Monterey Jack cheese**   Oven 350°

Heat taco shells according to package directions. For filling, in a large skillet cook meat, onion, and garlic till meat is brown and onion is tender. Drain fat. Stir in chili peppers; chili powder; hot pepper sauce, if desired; and ¼ teaspoon *salt*. Heat through. Fill each taco shell with some of the meat mixture. Top with lettuce, tomatoes, and cheese. If desired, serve with taco sauce, sour cream, and guacamole. Makes 4 servings.

Microwave directions: Heat taco shells according to package directions. In a 1½-quart casserole micro-cook the meat, onion, and garlic, covered, on 100% power (high) for 4 to 6 minutes or till no pink remains, stirring once. Drain. Stir in chili peppers; chili powder; hot pepper sauce, if desired; and ¼ teaspoon *salt*. Cook on high about 1 minute more or till heated through. Serve as above.

Chimichangas: Prepare as above, *except* substitute eight 10-inch *flour tortillas* for taco shells. Wrap tortillas tightly in foil and heat in a 350° oven for 10 minutes. Spoon about ⅓ *cup* meat mixture down the center of *each* tortilla. If desired, top *each* with *2 tablespoons* chopped tomato and *2 tablespoons* shredded cheddar or Monterey Jack cheese. Fold opposite sides of the tortilla in over the filling. Fold up the tortilla, starting from the bottom. Secure with wooden picks. In a heavy 3-quart saucepan heat 1 inch of *cooking oil for deep-fat frying* to 375°. Fry filled tortillas, two or three at a time, about 1 minute on each side or till crisp and golden brown. Drain on paper towels. Keep chimichangas warm in a 300° oven while frying remaining ones. Remove wooden picks. Serve on lettuce and top with tomatoes and cheese. If desired, pass taco sauce, sour cream, and guacamole. Do not use microwave directions.

Burritos: Prepare as above, *except* substitute eight 10-inch *flour tortillas* for taco shells. Wrap tortillas tightly in foil and heat in a 350° oven 10 minutes. Spoon about ⅓ *cup* meat mixture onto *each* tortilla just below center. If desired, top *each* with *2 tablespoons* chopped tomato and *2 tablespoons* shredded cheddar or Monterey Jack cheese. Fold bottom edge of each tortilla up and over filling, just till mixture is covered. Fold opposite sides of each tortilla in, just till they meet. Roll up tortillas from the bottom. Secure with wooden picks, if necessary. Arrange on a baking sheet. Bake in a 350° oven for 10 to 12 minutes or till heated through. Remove wooden picks. Serve on lettuce; top with tomatoes and cheese. If desired, pass taco sauce, sour cream, and guacamole. Do not use microwave directions.

Sloppy Joes

The rolled oats give the meat mixture just the right thickness for clinging to the buns.

- 1 **pound ground beef, ground pork, *or* bulk pork sausage***
- ½ **cup chopped onion**
- ½ **cup chopped green pepper**
- 1 **8-ounce can tomatoes, cut up**
- 2 **tablespoons quick-cooking rolled oats**
- 1 **to 1½ teaspoons chili powder**
- 1 **to 2 teaspoons Worcestershire sauce**
- ½ **teaspoon garlic salt**
  Dash bottled hot pepper sauce
- 6 **hamburger buns, split and toasted**

In a large skillet cook meat, onion, and green pepper till meat is brown. Drain fat. Stir in *undrained* tomatoes, oats, chili powder, Worcestershire sauce, garlic salt, hot pepper sauce, and ¼ cup *water*. Bring to boiling; reduce heat. Simmer for 5 to 10 minutes or till mixture is of desired consistency. Serve in hamburger buns. Serves 6.

Microwave directions: In a 1½-quart casserole micro-cook meat, onion, and green pepper, covered, on 100% power (high) for 4 to 6 minutes or till no pink remains, stirring once. Drain fat. Stir in *undrained* tomatoes, oats, chili powder, Worcestershire sauce, garlic salt, hot pepper sauce, and 2 tablespoons *water*. Cook, covered, on high for 3 to 5 minutes or till hot. Serve in hamburger buns.

***Note:** If using sausage, omit garlic salt.

Lasagna

For a cheesy, vegetarian lasagna, see page 159.

¾ **pound ground beef, ground pork,
bulk pork sausage, *or* bulk
Italian sausage**
1 **cup chopped onion**
2 **cloves garlic, minced**
1 **7½-ounce can tomatoes, cut up**
1 **8-ounce can tomato sauce**
1 **6-ounce can tomato paste**
2 **teaspoons dried basil, crushed**
1 **teaspoon dried oregano, crushed**
1 **teaspoon fennel seed, crushed
(optional)**
½ **teaspoon salt**
½ **teaspoon pepper**
5 **ounces lasagna noodles (6 noodles)**
1 **beaten egg**
2 **cups ricotta cheese *or* cream-style
cottage cheese, drained**
½ **cup grated Parmesan *or* Romano
cheese**
1 **tablespoon dried parsley flakes**
1 **8-ounce package sliced
mozzarella cheese**   Oven 375°

For meat sauce, in a large saucepan cook meat, onion, and garlic till meat is brown and onion is tender. Drain fat. Stir in *undrained* tomatoes; tomato sauce; tomato paste; basil; oregano; fennel, if desired; salt; and pepper. Bring to boiling; reduce heat. Cover and simmer for 15 minutes; stir occasionally. Meanwhile, cook lasagna noodles according to package directions. Drain.

For filling, combine egg, ricotta or cottage cheese, ¼ *cup* of the Parmesan or Romano cheese, and the parsley flakes.

Layer *half* of the cooked noodles in a 12x7½x2-inch baking dish. Spread with *half* of the filling. Top with *half* of the meat sauce and *half* of the mozzarella cheese. Repeat layers. Sprinkle the remaining Parmesan cheese atop.

Bake in a 375° oven for 30 to 35 minutes or till heated through. Let stand 10 minutes. Serves 8.

To make ahead: Prepare as above, *except,* after assembling, cover with plastic wrap and refrigerate up to 24 hours. Remove plastic wrap and cover with foil. Bake in a 375° oven for 35 minutes. Uncover and bake about 20 minutes more or till heated through.

Pizza on the Double

For a quick, fuss-free version of the pizza recipe opposite, make the dough from one of the convenience products listed below. Unless otherwise specified, just shape, assemble, and bake according to the instructions for the homemade dough. (To speed your pizza even more, use canned pizza sauce, the fully cooked meat options, and purchased shredded cheese.)

● One 16-ounce loaf frozen bread dough, thawed and halved.

● Two 10-ounce packages refrigerated bread dough. Do not use for Thin Pizzas. Omit the second rising time for Pan Pizzas.

● Two 10-ounce packages refrigerated pizza dough. Omit the second rising time for Pan Pizzas.

● One 16-ounce package hot roll mix. Prepare according to package directions for pizza dough.

● Packaged biscuit mix. Prepare according to package directions for pizza crust, making enough for two crusts.

● Sixteen English muffin halves. Top with sauce, meat, vegetables, and cheese. Bake in a 425° oven about 10 minutes or till heated through.

● Eight 8-inch flour tortillas. Top with sauce, meat, vegetables, and cheese. Bake the tortillas, *half* at a time, in a 425° oven about 10 minutes or till hot.

Pizza

2¾ to 3¼ cups all-purpose flour
1 package active dry yeast
1 cup warm water (120° to 130°)
2 tablespoons cooking oil
    Pizza Sauce
1 pound bulk Italian sausage, ground
    beef, *or* ground pork, cooked and
    drained; 6 ounces sliced
    pepperoni; *or* 1 cup cubed fully
    cooked ham *or* Canadian-style
    bacon
½ cup sliced green onion *or* pitted ripe
    olives
1 cup sliced fresh mushrooms *or*
    chopped green pepper
2 to 3 cups shredded mozzarella
    cheese   Oven 425° or 375°

In a large bowl combine *1¼ cups* of the flour, the yeast, and ¼ teaspoon *salt.* Add warm water and oil. Beat with an electric mixer on low speed for 30 seconds, scraping bowl constantly. Beat on high speed for 3 minutes. Using a spoon, stir in as much of the remaining flour as you can. Turn out onto a lightly floured surface. Knead in enough remaining flour to make a moderately stiff dough that is smooth and elastic (6 to 8 minutes total). Divide in half. Cover; let rest 10 minutes.

Thin Pizzas: Make Pizza Sauce. Grease two 12-inch pizza pans or baking sheets. If desired, sprinkle with cornmeal. On a lightly floured surface, roll each half of dough into a 13-inch circle. Transfer to pans. Build up edges slightly. *Do not let rise.* Bake in a 425° oven about 12 minutes or till browned. Spread Pizza Sauce over hot crust. Sprinkle meat, vegetables, and cheese atop. Bake 10 to 15 minutes more or till bubbly. Serves 6.

Pan Pizzas: Grease two 11x7x1½-inch or 9x9x2-inch baking pans. If desired, sprinkle with cornmeal. With greased fingers, pat dough into bottoms and halfway up sides of prepared pans. Cover;* let rise in a warm place till nearly double (30 to 45 minutes). Bake in a 375° oven 20 to 25 minutes or till lightly browned. Meanwhile, make Pizza Sauce. Spread Pizza Sauce over hot crust. Sprinkle meat, vegetables, and cheese atop. Bake 15 to 20 minutes more or till bubbly. Serves 6.

Pizza Sauce: In a medium saucepan combine one 8-ounce can *tomato sauce;* one 7½-ounce can *undrained tomatoes,* cut up; ½ cup chopped *onion;* 1 tablespoon dried *basil,* crushed; 1 teaspoon *sugar;* 1 teaspoon dried *oregano,* crushed; 2 cloves *garlic,* minced; and ¼ teaspoon *pepper.* Bring to boiling; reduce heat. Cover and simmer about 10 minutes or till onion is tender. (If desired, substitute one 15-ounce can pizza sauce for the homemade sauce.)

Calzones: Prepare as above for Thin Pizzas, *except,* after transferring to prepared pans, spoon sauce and meat on *half* of *each* circle to within 1 inch of edge. Sprinkle with vegetables and cheese. Moisten edges of dough with water. Fold dough in half over filling. Seal edge by pressing with tines of a fork. Prick top. Brush top with *milk.* If desired, sprinkle with grated Parmesan cheese. Bake in a 375° oven for 30 to 35 minutes or till crust is lightly browned. Serves 6.

*__Note:__ If desired, cover and refrigerate 2 to 24 hours. Bake as directed, omitting rising.

Layer sauce, meat, vegetables, and cheese onto *half* of the dough. Fold dough over.

Meat and Corn Bread Squares

- 1 **pound ground beef, ground pork,**
  or bulk pork sausage*
- 1 **tablespoon cornstarch**
- 1 **tablespoon dried minced onion**
- 1 **to 2 teaspoons chili powder**
- ½ **teaspoon garlic salt**
- 1 **16-ounce can tomatoes, cut up**
- 1 **4-ounce can diced green chili**
  peppers, drained
- ¾ **cup all-purpose flour**
- ¾ **cup cornmeal**
- 2 **teaspoons baking powder**
- 2 **beaten eggs**
- 1 **8¾-ounce can cream-style corn**
- ½ **cup milk**
- 3 **tablespoons cooking oil**
- 1 **cup shredded cheddar cheese**
  or Monterey Jack cheese
  with jalapeño peppers
  (4 ounces)   Oven 375°

In a skillet cook meat till brown. Drain fat. Stir in cornstarch, onion, chili powder, and garlic salt. Stir in *undrained* tomatoes and chili peppers. Cook and stir till thickened and bubbly.

Combine flour, cornmeal, and baking powder. Combine eggs, corn, milk, and cooking oil; stir into dry ingredients. Add cheese. Stir just till moistened. Spread *half* of the batter into a greased 9x9x2-inch baking pan. Spoon meat mixture atop. Top with remaining batter.

Bake in a 375° oven about 30 minutes or till golden brown. Let stand 5 minutes. Cut into squares. If desired, serve with salsa. Serves 6.

***Note:** If using sausage, omit garlic salt.

Meat and Pasta Bake

- 4 **ounces small shell macaroni *or***
  elbow macaroni (1 cup)
- 1 **pound ground beef *or* ground pork**
- ½ **cup chopped onion**
- 1 **10¾-ounce can condensed cream of**
  onion, mushroom, *or* celery soup
- 1 **cup shredded American cheese**
- 1 **8-ounce carton dairy sour cream**
- ¼ **cup milk**
- 1 **teaspoon Worcestershire sauce**
- ¾ **teaspoon dried thyme, marjoram,**
  or savory, crushed

- 1 **10-ounce package frozen mixed**
  vegetables
- ¼ **cup crushed rich round crackers**
  (7 crackers)   Oven 375°

Cook pasta according to package directions. Drain; set aside. In a large skillet cook meat and onion till meat is brown. Drain fat. Stir in soup, cheese, sour cream, milk, Worcestershire sauce, and herb. Stir in vegetables and pasta. Transfer to a 2-quart casserole. Bake, covered, in a 375° oven for 30 minutes. Stir. Sprinkle with crushed crackers. Bake, uncovered, for 5 to 10 minutes more or till heated through. Serves 5 or 6.

Hamburger Pie

This classic also is known as shepherd's pie.

- 1 **10-ounce package frozen cut green**
  beans, whole kernel corn, peas,
  or mixed vegetables
- 1 **pound ground beef, ground pork,**
  or ground lamb
- ½ **cup chopped onion**
- 1 **10¾- to 11-ounce can condensed**
  tomato *or* cheddar cheese soup
- 1 **teaspoon Worcestershire sauce**
- ¼ **teaspoon dried thyme, crushed**
  Packaged instant mashed
  potatoes (enough for
  4 servings)   Oven 375°

Run *cold* water over vegetables to separate. In a large skillet cook meat and onion till meat is brown. Drain. Stir vegetables and ¼ cup *water* into skillet. Cook, covered, 5 to 10 minutes or till tender. Stir in soup, Worcestershire sauce, thyme, and ¼ teaspoon *pepper*. Transfer to a 1½-quart casserole. Prepare potatoes according to package directions. Drop in mounds atop hot mixture. If desired, sprinkle with paprika. Bake in a 375° oven for 25 to 30 minutes or till hot. Serves 4.

Microwave directions: Run *cold* water over vegetables to separate. In a 1½-quart casserole micro-cook meat and onion, covered, on 100% power (high) for 4 to 6 minutes or till no pink remains; stir once. Drain. Stir in vegetables, soup, Worcestershire sauce, thyme, ¼ cup *water,* and ¼ teaspoon *pepper.* Cook, covered, on high for 6 to 8 minutes or till vegetables are tender; stir once. Prepare potatoes according to package directions. Drop potatoes in mounds atop hot mixture. If desired, sprinkle with paprika. Cook, uncovered, on high for 1 to 2 minutes or till hot.

Spaghetti Pie

> 4 ounces spaghetti
> 1 beaten egg
> ⅓ cup grated Parmesan cheese
> 1 tablespoon margarine *or* butter
> 1 cup cream-style cottage cheese
> 1 beaten egg
> ½ pound ground beef *or* bulk Italian
>   sausage
> ½ cup chopped onion
> ¼ cup chopped green pepper
> ¾ cup spaghetti sauce
> ½ cup shredded mozzarella
>   cheese (2 ounces)   Oven 350°

For crust, cook spaghetti according to package directions. Drain. Combine 1 egg, Parmesan cheese, and margarine. Stir in hot spaghetti. Press mixture evenly into bottom and up sides of a 9-inch pie plate. Drain cottage cheese; combine with 1 egg. Spread over crust. Set aside. In a large skillet cook meat, onion, and green pepper till meat is brown. Drain fat. Stir in spaghetti sauce. Heat through. Spoon over cottage cheese mixture. Bake in a 350° oven 20 minutes. Sprinkle with mozzarella cheese. Bake about 5 minutes more or till cheese melts and crust sets. Let stand 5 minutes. Cut into wedges. Serves 4 or 5.

Chili-Mac Skillet

> 1 pound ground beef
> ¾ cup chopped onion
> 1 15½-ounce can red kidney beans,
>   drained
> 1 8-ounce can tomato sauce
> 1 7½-ounce can tomatoes, cut up
> ½ cup elbow macaroni
> 1 4-ounce can diced green chili
>   peppers, drained
> 2 to 3 teaspoons chili powder
> ½ teaspoon garlic salt
> ½ cup shredded Monterey Jack *or*
>   cheddar cheese (2 ounces)

In a large skillet cook meat and onion till meat is brown. Drain fat. Stir in beans, tomato sauce, *undrained* tomatoes, *uncooked* pasta, green chilies, chili powder, garlic salt, and ¼ cup *water*. Bring to boiling; reduce heat. Cover; simmer 20 minutes, stirring often. Top with cheese. Cover; heat 2 minutes or till cheese melts. Serves 6.

Stuffed Green Peppers

> 2 large green peppers
> ¾ pound ground beef, ground pork,
>   ground lamb, *or* bulk pork
>   sausage
> ⅓ cup chopped onion
> 1 7½-ounce can tomatoes, cut up
> ⅓ cup long grain rice
> 1 tablespoon Worcestershire sauce
> ½ teaspoon dried basil *or* dried
>   oregano, crushed
> ½ cup shredded American
>   cheese (2 ounces)   Oven 375°

Halve peppers lengthwise, removing stem ends, seeds, and membranes. Immerse peppers into *boiling* water for 3 minutes. Sprinkle insides with salt. Invert on paper towels to drain well.

In a skillet cook meat and onion till meat is brown and onion is tender. Drain fat. Stir in *undrained* tomatoes, *uncooked* rice, Worcestershire, basil, ½ cup *water,* ¼ teaspoon *salt,* and ¼ teaspoon *pepper.* Bring to boiling; reduce heat. Cover and simmer for 15 to 18 minutes or till rice is tender. Stir in ¼ cup of the cheese. Fill peppers with meat mixture. Place in an 8x8x2-inch baking dish with any remaining meat mixture.

Bake in a 375° oven about 15 minutes or till heated through. Sprinkle with remaining cheese. Let stand 1 to 2 minutes. Makes 4 servings.

Stuffed Zucchini: Prepare as above, *except* substitute 4 medium *zucchini* for the green peppers. Cut a thin lengthwise slice from each zucchini. Scoop out, leaving shells. Immerse into *boiling* water for 2 minutes. Continue as above.

Stuffed Cabbage Rolls: Prepare as above, *except* substitute 8 medium to large *cabbage leaves* for green peppers. Remove center veins from cabbage leaves, keeping each leaf in 1 piece. Immerse leaves, four at a time, into *boiling* water about 3 minutes or till limp. Drain well. Place about ⅓ *cup* meat mixture on *each* cabbage leaf; fold in sides. Starting at an unfolded edge, carefully roll up each leaf, making sure folded sides are included in roll.

Combine one 15-ounce can *tomato sauce,* 1 teaspoon *sugar,* and ½ teaspoon dried *basil,* crushed. Pour *half* of the tomato mixture into the baking dish. Add cabbage rolls. Spoon remaining tomato mixture atop. Bake, covered, in a 350° oven for 25 to 30 minutes or till heated through. Sprinkle with remaining cheese.

Pastitsio

Two home-style casseroles from Greece.

   **1   pound ground lamb, ground beef,
         or ground pork**
   ½   cup chopped onion
   2   cloves garlic, minced
   1   8-ounce can tomato sauce
   ¼   cup dry red wine
   2   tablespoons snipped parsley
   ½   teaspoon dried oregano, crushed
   ¼   teaspoon salt
   ¼   teaspoon ground cinnamon
   4   eggs, beaten individually
   3   tablespoons margarine *or* butter
   3   tablespoons all-purpose flour
   ¼   teaspoon pepper
 1¾   cups milk
   ½   cup grated Parmesan cheese
   **1   cup elbow macaroni, cooked
         and drained**   Oven 350°

In a large skillet cook meat, onion, and garlic till meat is brown and onion is tender. Drain fat. Stir in tomato sauce, wine, parsley, oregano, salt, and cinnamon. Bring to boiling; reduce heat. Simmer for 10 minutes. Gradually stir meat mixture into *one* of the eggs; set aside.

For sauce, in a medium saucepan melt margarine. Stir in flour and pepper. Add *1½ cups* of the milk all at once. Cook and stir till thickened and bubbly. Cook and stir 1 minute more. Gradually stir sauce into *two* of the beaten eggs. Stir in *half* of the Parmesan cheese. Toss macaroni with the remaining egg, milk, and Parmesan cheese.

To assemble, in an 8x8x2-inch baking dish layer *half* of the macaroni mixture, all of the meat mixture, remaining macaroni mixture, and all of the sauce. Sprinkle with additional cinnamon, if desired. Bake in a 350° oven for 30 to 35 minutes or till set. Let stand 5 minutes. Serves 6.

Moussaka: Prepare as above, *except* omit the macaroni and the egg, milk, and Parmesan cheese that are tossed with it. In a large skillet cook 1 large *eggplant,* peeled and cut into ½-inch slices, in a small amount of boiling water for 3 to 4 minutes or till just tender. Drain well.

To assemble Moussaka, in an 8x8x2-inch baking dish layer *half* of the eggplant, all of the meat mixture, remaining eggplant, and all of the sauce. Bake and serve as above.

Pastitsio

Deep-Dish Meat Pie

Pastry for Single-Crust Pie
    (see recipe, page 293)
1 cup chopped potato
½ cup chopped onion
3 tablespoons margarine *or* butter
⅓ cup all-purpose flour
½ teaspoon dried thyme, savory, *or*
    sage, crushed
1¼ cups beef broth
1½ cups loose-pack frozen peas and
    carrots
2 cups cubed cooked beef,
    pork, lamb, *or* veal   Oven 425°

Prepare pastry. Roll pastry into a 12-inch circle. Cover and set aside. In a medium saucepan cook potato and onion in margarine over medium heat, stirring constantly, for 5 to 6 minutes or till onion is tender but not brown. Stir in flour, herb, and ⅛ teaspoon *pepper*. Add broth all at once. Stir in peas and carrots. Cook and stir till bubbly.

    Stir in meat. Transfer mixture to a 1½-quart casserole. Top with pastry; trim pastry to ½ inch beyond rim. Turn under and flute edges of pastry. Cut slits for steam. Place on a baking sheet. Bake in a 425° oven for 25 to 30 minutes or till golden. Let stand 10 minutes. Makes 4 servings.

Ham-Potato Scallop

1½ cups cubed fully cooked ham
½ cup chopped onion
4 medium potatoes, peeled and thinly
    sliced (4 cups)
1 10¾- to 11-ounce can condensed
    cheddar cheese soup, *or* cream
    of mushroom *or* celery soup
½ cup milk
¼ cup fine dry bread crumbs
2 tablespoons snipped parsley
1 tablespoon margarine
    or butter, melted   Oven 350°

In a 1½-quart casserole layer *half* of the ham, *half* of the onion, and *half* of the potatoes. Repeat layers. Mix soup, milk, and ¼ teaspoon *pepper.* Pour over potatoes. Bake, covered, in a 350° oven about 1 hour or till potatoes are almost tender. Mix crumbs, parsley, and margarine. Sprinkle atop casserole. Bake, uncovered, for 15 minutes more. Let stand 10 minutes. Serves 4.

Meaty Noodle Casserole

3 ounces medium noodles (1¾ cups)
1 11-ounce can condensed cheddar
    cheese soup
½ cup milk
½ cup dairy sour cream
½ cup thinly sliced celery
1 2½-ounce jar sliced mushrooms,
    drained
2 tablespoons chopped pimiento
1 teaspoon dried parsley flakes
1 teaspoon dried minced onion
2 cups diced cooked beef, pork, *or*
    ham (10 ounces)
¼ cup fine dry bread crumbs
1 tablespoon margarine
    or butter, melted   Oven 375°

Cook noodles according to package directions. Drain well. Combine soup, milk, and sour cream. Stir in the celery, mushrooms, pimiento, parsley flakes, and onion. Stir in cooked noodles and meat. Transfer to a 2-quart casserole. Combine bread crumbs and margarine. Sprinkle over casserole. Bake in a 375° oven for 35 to 40 minutes or till heated through. Makes 4 or 5 servings.

    Microwave directions: Cook noodles according to package directions. Drain. In a 2-quart casserole mix soup, milk, and sour cream. Stir in celery, mushrooms, pimiento, parsley flakes, and onion. Stir in cooked noodles and meat. Microcook, uncovered, on 100% power (high) 10 to 12 minutes or till hot, stirring twice. Combine bread crumbs and margarine. Sprinkle over casserole. Cook on high 30 seconds more.

Meat and Bulgur Bake

Oven 375°

In a 1½-quart casserole combine 2 cups cubed cooked *beef, pork, or lamb;* one 16-ounce can *undrained tomatoes,* cut up; 1 medium *zucchini,* halved lengthwise and sliced; ½ cup *bulgur;* ½ cup chopped *onion;* ½ teaspoon *salt;* ½ teaspoon dried *oregano, basil, or mint,* crushed; and ¼ teaspoon *pepper.* Bake, covered, in a 375° oven 45 to 50 minutes or till bulgur is tender. Sprinkle with ¾ cup shredded *mozzarella cheese.* Bake, uncovered, 1 minute more or till cheese melts. Makes 4 servings.

Corned Beef Hash

Stir in some beef gravy for moister hash.

- 2 **tablespoons margarine *or* butter**
- 2 **cups finely chopped cooked potato *or* loose-pack frozen hash brown potatoes, thawed**
- 1½ **cups finely chopped cooked corned beef *or* beef**
- ½ **cup chopped onion**
- 2 **tablespoons snipped parsley**
- 1 **to 2 teaspoons Worcestershire sauce**
- 2 **tablespoons milk (optional)**

In a large skillet melt margarine. Stir in potatoes, meat, onion, parsley, Worcestershire sauce, and ⅛ teaspoon *pepper*. Spread evenly into skillet. Cook over medium heat for 8 to 10 minutes or till browned on bottom, turning occasionally. Stir in milk, if desired, and heat through. Serves 4.

Microwave directions: In a 1½-quart casserole micro-cook onion and margarine, covered, on 100% power (high) for 2 minutes. Stir in remaining ingredients except milk. Cook, covered, on high for 5 to 7 minutes or till hot; stir twice. Add milk as above, if desired.

Oven directions: Cook onion in margarine till tender. Stir in remaining ingredients except milk. Transfer to an 8x1½-inch round baking dish. Bake, covered, in a 375° oven for 30 minutes or till hot. Add milk as above, if desired.

Meaty Stuffed Potatoes

- 4 **medium baking potatoes (6 to 8 ounces each)**
- 1½ **cups cubed cooked beef, pork, *or* ham***
- ½ **cup dairy sour cream**
- ¼ **cup sliced green onion**
- 3 **tablespoons milk**
- ¼ **teaspoon garlic powder**
- ¼ **teaspoon salt**
- ¼ **teaspoon pepper**
- ¼ **cup shredded American, Swiss, Monterey Jack, *or* cheddar cheese**   Oven 425°

Scrub potatoes; prick with a fork. Bake in a 425° oven for 50 to 60 minutes or till tender. When cool enough to handle, slice off tops of potatoes. Scoop out centers, leaving ¼-inch-thick shells. In a mixing bowl mash the potato centers. Stir in meat, sour cream, onion, milk, garlic powder, salt, and pepper. Fill potato shells with meat mixture. Place in a shallow baking dish.

Bake for 25 to 30 minutes or till heated through. Sprinkle with cheese. Bake for 2 to 3 minutes more or till cheese melts. Serves 4.

Microwave directions: Scrub the potatoes and prick with a fork. Micro-cook, uncovered, on 100% power (high) for 14 to 17 minutes or till tender, rearranging once. Stuff the potatoes as above. Arrange potatoes in an 8x8x2-inch baking dish. Cook on high for 7 to 9 minutes or till heated through. Sprinkle with cheese. Cook on high 1 to 2 minutes more or till cheese melts.

Note: If using ham, omit salt.

Creamed Dried Beef

- 1 **3- or 4-ounce package sliced dried *or* smoked beef, snipped**
- ½ **cup chopped green pepper (optional)**
- 2 **tablespoons margarine *or* butter**
- 2 **tablespoons all-purpose flour**
- ⅛ **teaspoon pepper**
- 1⅓ **cups milk**
- ¼ **teaspoon Worcestershire sauce Toast***

If using dried beef, rinse and drain well. In a large skillet cook and stir beef and, if desired, green pepper in margarine about 3 minutes or till edges of beef curl. Stir in flour and pepper. Add milk and Worcestershire sauce all at once. Cook and stir till thickened and bubbly. Cook and stir 1 minute more. Spoon over toast. Serves 2.

Note: To make toast points, spread *one* side of each toast slice with margarine or butter, if desired. Cut each slice into 2 triangles. Cut again to form 4 triangles.

Tortilla Roll-Ups

Cut into 1-inch pieces for bite-size appetizers.

Spread *one* side of *four* 6- to 7-inch *flour tortillas* with *half* of an 8-ounce container (½ cup) *sour cream dip or half* of a 6-ounce container (⅓ cup) *frozen avocado dip,* thawed. Drizzle with 2 tablespoons *taco sauce or salsa.* Top with ½ pound thinly sliced cooked *beef, pork, or ham;* 4 thin slices *cheddar, Swiss, or Monterey Jack cheese* (about 3 ounces)*;* and 4 *lettuce leaves.* Roll up tortillas. Makes 4 servings.

Reuben Sandwiches

Originally, Reubens were made with Russian dressing, but today most versions use Thousand Island dressing.

- **8 slices dark rye *or* pumpernickel bread**
- **3 tablespoons margarine *or* butter, softened**
- **¼ cup Thousand Island *or* Russian salad dressing**
- **½ pound thinly sliced cooked corned beef, beef, pork, *or* ham**
- **4 slices Swiss cheese (1½ ounces)**
- **1 cup sauerkraut, well drained**

Spread *one* side of *each* slice of bread with margarine and the other side with salad dressing. With the margarine side down, top *four* slices of bread with meat, cheese, and sauerkraut. Top with remaining bread slices, dressing side down.

In a large skillet cook 2 sandwiches over medium-low heat for 4 to 6 minutes or till bread toasts and cheese melts, turning once. Repeat with remaining sandwiches. Makes 4 servings.

Barbecue-Style Sandwiches

- **1 8-ounce can tomato sauce**
- **½ cup chopped onion**
- **¼ cup finely chopped green pepper**
- **1 tablespoon brown sugar**
- **2 tablespoons vinegar**
- **1 tablespoon Worcestershire sauce**
- **1½ teaspoons dry mustard**
- **1 teaspoon chili powder**
- **¼ teaspoon celery seed**
- **1 clove garlic, minced**
- **½ pound thinly sliced cooked beef, pork, *or* lamb**
- **4 French-style rolls, split and toasted**

In a medium saucepan combine tomato sauce, chopped onion, chopped green pepper, and brown sugar. Stir in vinegar, Worcestershire sauce, mustard, chili powder, celery seed, and garlic. Bring to boiling; reduce heat. Stir in meat. Cover and simmer for 15 minutes.

Spoon some of the meat mixture onto bottom half of each roll. Top with other half of roll. Makes 4 servings.

Meat-Stuffed Pita Pockets

- **¼ cup dairy sour cream**
- **¼ cup mayonnaise *or* salad dressing**
- **1 tablespoon prepared horseradish *or* prepared mustard**
- **2 cups coarsely chopped cooked beef, pork, ham, *or* lamb**
- **½ cup shredded carrot *or* chopped celery**
- **2 large pita bread rounds**
- **½ cup alfalfa sprouts *or* 4 lettuce leaves**

Combine sour cream, mayonnaise, and horseradish. Stir in meat and carrot. Halve pita bread crosswise. Line each half with alfalfa sprouts or lettuce. Spoon in meat mixture. Serves 4.

Brown-Bag Pointers

Follow these easy steps to keep your brown-bag lunches fresh and safe, from the time you leave home till mealtime.

- ● Make sure *everything* that touches the food is clean.
- ● Seal foods in clean airtight containers or clear plastic storage bags.
- ● Pack hot foods in preheated vacuum bottles.
- ● Chill cold foods overnight. In the morning, pack them in prechilled vacuum bottles or in insulated lunch boxes with frozen ice packs.
- ● To preheat (prechill) a vacuum bottle, fill the container with hot (cold) tap water. Cover tightly with the lid and let stand 5 minutes. Empty the bottle, shaking out the excess moisture. Immediately fill with hot (cold) food.
- ● For sandwiches, pack moist fillings separately from the bread. Pack lettuce and tomato slices in separate clear plastic bags. Use small airtight containers to carry condiments.
- ● Keep your lunch in a cool, dry place.

Roasting and Indirect-Grilling Meat

To roast: Place meat, fat side up, on a rack in a shallow roasting pan. (Rib roasts do not need a rack.) For ham, if desired, score the top in a diamond pattern. Insert a meat thermometer.

Do not add water or liquid and do not cover. Roast in a 325° oven, unless chart or recipe says otherwise, for the time given or till the thermometer registers the specified temperature.

Cut	Weight (Pounds)	Doneness	Roasting Time (Hours)	Indirect-Grilling Time (Hours)
Beef				
Boneless rolled rump roast	4 to 6	150° to 170°	1½ to 3	1¼ to 2½
Boneless sirloin roast	4 to 6	140° rare	2¼ to 2¾	1¾ to 2¼
		160° medium	2¾ to 3¼	2¼ to 2¾
		170° well-done	3¼ to 3¾	2½ to 3
Eye round roast	2 to 3	140° rare	1¼ to 1¾	1 to 1½
		160° medium	1¾ to 2¼	1½ to 2
		170° well-done	2¼ to 2¾	1¾ to 2¼
Rib eye roast (roast at 350°)	4 to 6	140° rare	1¼ to 2	1 to 1½
		160° medium	1¼ to 2¼	1½ to 2
		170° well-done	1½ to 2½	2 to 2½
Rib roast	4 to 6	140° rare	1¾ to 3	2¼ to 2¾
		160° medium	2¼ to 3¾	2¾ to 3¼
		170° well-done	2¾ to 4¼	3¼ to 3¾
Tenderloin roast				
Half	2 to 3	140° rare	¾ to 1	¾ to 1
Whole	4 to 6	140° rare	¾ to 1	1¼ to 1½
(roast at 425° or test for *medium-hot* heat above the pan)				
Tip roast	3 to 5	140° to 170°	1¾ to 3¼	1¼ to 2½
	6 to 8	140° to 170°	3 to 4½	2 to 3¼
Top round roast	4 to 6	140° to 170°	1½ to 3	1 to 2
Veal				
Boneless rolled breast roast	2½ to 3½	170° well-done	1¾ to 2¼	1¾ to 2¼
Boneless rolled shoulder roast	3 to 5	170° well-done	2¾ to 3¼	2¼ to 2¾
Loin roast	3 to 5	170° well-done	2 to 2½	2¼ to 2¾
Rib roast	3 to 5	170° well-done	1¾ to 2¾	2¼ to 2¾

Roasting and Indirect-Grilling Meat (Continued)

To grill indirect: In a covered grill arrange *medium* coals around a drip pan. Test for *medium-low* heat above the pan, unless chart says otherwise. Place meat, fat side up, on grill rack over drip pan but not over coals.

Insert a meat thermometer. Lower the grill hood. Grill for the time given or till thermometer registers desired temperature. Add more coals to maintain heat as necessary.

Cut	Weight (Pounds)	Doneness	Roasting Time (Hours)	Indirect-Grilling Time (Hours)
Lamb				
Boneless leg roast	4 to 7	160° medium	2 to 4	2¼ to 2¾
Boneless rolled shoulder roast	2 to 3	160° medium	1½ to 3¼	1¾ to 2¼
Rib crown roast	3 to 4	140° rare	1 to 1¼	¾ to 1
		160° medium	1¼ to 1¾	¾ to 1
		170° well-done	1½ to 2	1 to 1¼
Whole leg roast	5 to 7	140° rare	1¾ to 3	1¾ to 2¼
		160° medium	2 to 3	2¼ to 2½
		170° well	2½ to 4½	2½ to 3
Pork				
Boneless top loin roast				
Single loin	2 to 4	170° well-done	1 to 2¼	1 to 2¼
Double loin, tied	3 to 5	170° well-done	1¾ to 3¼	1½ to 3
Loin back ribs, spareribs, country-style ribs (roast at 350° or test for *medium* heat above the pan)	2 to 4	Well-done	1½ to 2	1 to 2
Loin blade or sirloin roast	3 to 4	170° well-done	2 to 3	1¾ to 3
Loin center rib roast (backbone loosened)	3 to 5	170° well-done	1½ to 3	1½ to 3
Rib crown roast	4 to 6	170° well-done	1¾ to 3	1¾ to 3
Tenderloin	¾ to 1	170° well-done	½ to 1	½ to ¾
Ham (fully cooked)				
Boneless half	4 to 6	140°	1¼ to 2½	1¼ to 2½
Boneless portion	3 to 4	140°	1½ to 2¼	1½ to 2¼
Smoked picnic	5 to 8	140°	2 to 4	2 to 3

Direct-Grilling Meat

Test for the desired coal temperature (see "Grilling Techniques," page 442). Place the desired meat on the grill rack directly over the preheated coals.

Grill the meat, uncovered, for the time specified in the chart or recipe or till done, turning the meat over after half of the cooking time.

Cut	Thickness (Inches)	Coal Temperature	Doneness	Time (Minutes)
Beef				
Flank steak	¾	Medium	Medium	12 to 14
Steak (chuck, blade, top round)	1	Medium	Rare	14 to 16
			Medium	18 to 20
			Well-done	22 to 24
	1½	Medium	Rare	19 to 26
			Medium	27 to 32
			Well-done	33 to 38
Steak (top loin, tenderloin, T-bone, porterhouse, sirloin, rib, ribeye)	1	Medium-hot	Rare	8 to 12
			Medium	12 to 15
			Well-done	16 to 20
	1½	Medium-hot	Rare	14 to 18
			Medium	18 to 22
			Well-done	24 to 28
Veal				
Chop	¾	Medium-hot	Well-done	10 to 12
Lamb				
Chop	1	Medium	Rare	10 to 14
			Medium	14 to 16
			Well-done	16 to 20
Pork				
Blade steak	½	Medium-hot	Well-done	10 to 12
Canadian-style bacon	¼	Medium-hot	Heated	3 to 5
Chop	¾	Medium-hot	Well-done	12 to 14
	1¼ to 1½	Medium	Well-done	35 to 45
Ham slice	1	Medium-hot	Heated	20 to 25
Miscellaneous				
Bratwurst, fresh		Medium-hot	Well-done	12 to 14
Frankfurters		Medium-hot	Heated	3 to 5
Ground-meat patties (beef, lamb, pork)	¾ (4 to a pound)	Medium	Medium*	12 to 14
			Well-done	15 to 18

Serve ground pork well-done only.

Broiling Meat

Place meat on the unheated rack of a broiler pan. For cuts less than 1½ inches thick, broil 3 inches from the heat. For cuts 1½ inches thick or thicker, broil 4 to 5 inches from the heat. Broil for the time given or till done, turning meat over after half of the broiling time.

Cut	Thickness (Inches)	Doneness	Time (Minutes)
Beef			
Flank steak	¾	Medium	12 to 14
Steak (chuck, blade, top round)	1	Rare	16 to 20
		Medium	22 to 24
		Well-done	26 to 28
	1½	Rare	18 to 25
		Medium	26 to 30
		Well-done	31 to 36
Steak (top loin, tenderloin, T-bone, porterhouse, sirloin, rib, rib eye)	1	Rare	8 to 12
		Medium	13 to 17
		Well-done	18 to 22
	1½	Rare	14 to 18
		Medium	19 to 22
		Well-done	23 to 28
Veal			
Chop	¾	Well-done	8 to 10
Lamb			
Chop	1	Rare	8 to 10
		Medium	10 to 12
		Well-done	14 to 16
Pork			
Blade steak	½	Well-done	12 to 14
Canadian-style bacon	¼	Heated	3 to 5
Chop	¾	Well-done	12 to 14
	1¼ to 1½	Well-done	24 to 28
Ham slice	1	Heated	14 to 18
Miscellaneous			
Bratwurst, fresh		Well-done	10 to 12
Frankfurters		Heated	3 to 5
Ground-meat patties (beef, lamb, pork)	¾ (4 to a pound)	Medium°	12 to 14
		Well-done	15 to 18

°Serve ground pork well-done only.

Micro-Cooking Beef, Pork, or Lamb Cubes

Cut meat into ¾-inch cubes. Place in a 1½-quart casserole. (Add ½ cup water to the beef.) Cover and micro-cook on the suggested power level(s) for the cooking time(s) specified or till tender and no pink remains, stirring every 10 minutes for beef (stirring every 5 minutes for lamb or pork).

Meat	Amount	Power/Cooking Time
Beef stew meat	1 pound	Cook on 100% power (high) for 5 minutes, then on 50% power (medium) for 40 minutes.
Lamb cubes	1 pound	Cook on 100% power (high) for 5 minutes, then on 50% power (medium) for 3 to 5 minutes.
Pork cubes	1 pound	Cook on 50% power (medium) for 10 to 15 minutes.

Micro-Cooking Bacon

Place on a rack or paper plate. Cover with microwave-safe paper towels. Micro-cook on 100% power (high) for time specified or till done.

Meat	Amount	Cooking Time
Bacon	2 slices	1½ to 2 minutes
	4 slices	2½ to 3½ minutes
	6 slices	4 to 5 minutes

Micro-Cooking Fully Cooked Ham

Place the meat in an 8x8x2-inch baking dish. (Add ½ cup water to canned ham.) Cover with waxed paper. Micro-cook on the suggested power level(s) for the cooking time(s) specified or till heated through, turning meat occasionally. If necessary, shield any parts that are overcooking with small pieces of foil. (Check your owner's manual to see if you can use foil in your microwave oven.)

Meat	Amount	Power/Cooking Time
1-inch slice	One 2-pound	Cook on 100% power (high) for 8 to 10 minutes.
Canned ham	One 3-pound	Cook on 100% power (high) for 5 minutes, then on 50% power (medium) for 40 to 50 minutes.
	One 5-pound	Cook on 100% power (high) for 7 minutes, then on 50% power (medium) for 50 to 60 minutes.

Micro-Cooking Meatballs, Meat Ring, and Patties

Combine 1 beaten egg, ¼ cup fine dry bread crumbs, ¼ cup milk, and desired seasonings. Add 1 pound ground beef; mix well. Shape as indicated. Arrange meat in an 8x8x2-inch baking dish. Cover with waxed paper. Micro-cook on 100% power (high) for time specified or till no pink remains, giving the dish a half-turn and turning patties or meatballs over once.

Meat	Amount	Cooking Time
Meatballs	Twenty-four 1-inch	4 to 6 minutes
Meat ring	One 6-inch	6 to 8 minutes
Patties	One ¾-inch-thick Two ¾-inch-thick Four ¾-inch-thick	2 to 3 minutes 3 to 5 minutes 6 to 8 minutes

Micro-Cooking Ground Meat

Crumble meat into a 1½-quart casserole. Cover; micro-cook on 100% power (high) for the time specified or till no pink remains, stirring once or twice. Drain fat.

Meat	Amount	Cooking Time
Ground beef	1 pound	4 to 6 minutes
Ground pork	1 pound	6 to 8 minutes

Micro-Cooking Sausages

Arrange links or patties in a baking dish. Cover frankfurters with waxed paper and sausage links or patties with microwave-safe paper towels. Micro-cook on 100% power (high) for time specified or till heated through. Rearrange once if cooking 4 or more pieces. Drain cooked sausage on paper towels.

Meat	Amount	Cooking Time
Frankfurters	1 link 2 links 4 links 6 links 8 links	20 to 40 seconds 30 to 45 seconds 1½ to 2½ minutes 2½ to 3 minutes 3 to 3½ minutes
Pork sausage links	2 links 4 links 6 links 8 links	1 to 1½ minutes 1½ to 2 minutes 2 to 3 minutes 3 to 4 minutes
Pork sausage patties	2 patties 4 patties 6 patties	1½ to 2 minutes 3 to 4 minutees 4 to 6 minutes

Panbroiling and Panfrying Meat

To panbroil these meats, preheat a heavy skillet over high heat till very hot. Do not add water or fat. (For beef steaks and veal, brush skillet lightly with cooking oil.) Add meat. Do not cover. Reduce heat to medium and cook for the time given or till done, turning meat over after half of the cooking time. If meat browns too quickly, reduce heat to medium-low. Spoon off fat and juices as they accumulate during cooking.

To panfry these meats, in a heavy skillet melt 1 to 2 tablespoons margarine or butter over medium-high heat. Add meat. Do not cover. Reduce heat to medium and cook for time given or till done, turning meat over after half of the cooking time.

Cut	Thickness (Inches)	Doneness	Panbroiling Time	Panfrying Time
Beef				
Cubed steak	½	Well-done	5 to 8	6 to 8
Steak (sirloin, top loin, tenderloin, rib eye, top round)	1	Rare Medium Well-done	6 to 8 9 to 12 14 to 18	8 to 11 12 to 14 15 to 17
Veal				
Cutlet	¼	Well-done	3 to 5	4 to 6
Lamb				
Chop	1	Medium Well-done	8 to 10 11 to 13	7 to 9 10 to 13
Pork				
Chop	¾	Well-done	10 to 12	10 to 12

To panbroil these meats, place meat in a cool skillet. (If using an electric range, preheat the burner for 2 to 4 minutes.) Turn heat to medium.

Turn meat halfway through cooking time (for bacon, turn occasionally). If meat browns too quickly, reduce heat slightly.

Cut	Thickness (Inches)	Doneness	Panbroiling Time
Pork			
Bacon	Slices	Crisp	8 to 10
Canadian-style bacon	¼	Heated	3 to 5
Ham slice	1	Heated	16 to 18
Miscellaneous			
Ground-meat patties (beef, lamb, pork)	¾ (4 to a pound)	Medium* Well-done	8 to 10 10 to 12

*Serve ground pork well-done only.

Pasta, Rice, & Grains

Nutrition Analysis

	Per Serving							Percent U.S. RDA Per Serving							
	Servings Per Recipe	Calories	Protein (g)	Carbohydrate (g)	Fat (g)	Cholesterol (mg)	Sodium (mg)	Potassium (mg)	Protein	Vitamin A	Vitamin C	Thiamine	Riboflavin	Niacin	Calcium	Iron
Apple-Cinnamon Granola (p. 274)	15	186	3	22	11	0	7	132	5	0	0	6	4	3	4	6
Baked Gnocchi (p. 275)	5	231	12	20	11	72	447	214	18	11	2	11	19	4	30	6
Boiled Gnocchi (p. 275)	5	231	12	20	11	72	447	214	18	11	2	11	19	4	30	6
Brown and Wild Rice Pilaf (p. 273)	4	191	5	29	5	3	243	191	8	3	5	12	8	12	2	6
Bulgur Pilaf (p. 273)	4	165	5	25	5	3	241	203	7	3	5	9	5	10	2	9
Cheesy Grits (p. 274)	4	226	10	17	13	95	589	91	15	10	0	10	13	5	18	6
Choose-a-Grain Casserole (p. 275)	5	226	6	19	14	12	465	148	9	71	50	7	6	4	13	6
Cinnamon-Raisin Oatmeal (p. 273)	4	325	7	64	7	0	144	464	11	0	1	20	5	3	6	15
Confetti Rice Mold (p. 272)	4	140	3	31	0	0	143	70	5	19	1	11	2	7	1	7
Cornmeal Mush (p. 274)	4	110	3	23	1	0	272	76	4	3	6	1	3	0	3	0
Couscous and Tomatoes (p. 269)	4	116	4	23	1	0	603	287	6	16	21	5	3	6	5	8
Curried Rice Pilaf (p. 273)	4	240	4	45	5	3	198	253	7	3	5	15	3	9	3	9
Egg Noodles (p. 266)	8	159	5	27	3	103	147	45	8	2	0	16	10	9	2	11
Fettuccine Alfredo (p. 270)	4	190	7	22	8	14	192	80	11	5	0	17	9	9	13	5
Fettuccine Alfredo with Mushrooms (p. 270)	4	197	8	24	8	14	193	180	12	5	0	19	16	14	14	7
Fettuccine with Marinara Sauce (p. 268)	8	180	5	31	4	0	318	454	8	88	26	23	10	15	5	11
Fried Mush (p. 274)	7	115	2	13	6	0	155	43	2	2	0	3	0	2	0	2
Fried Rice (p. 273)	4	306	11	40	11	147	717	242	17	16	17	23	10	14	6	15
Granola (p. 274)	12	227	4	24	14	3	143	0	7	0	0	9	5	3	5	8
Grits (p. 274)	2	148	4	32	0	0	268	65	5	0	0	17	9	10	0	9
Ham Pasta Primavera (p. 268)	4	475	21	49	22	24	669	638	32	225	70	53	23	26	17	24
Herb-Buttered Pasta (p. 267)	4	156	4	21	6	0	101	65	6	5	0	17	6	9	0	5
Herb-Garlic Gnocchi (p. 275)	5	232	12	20	11	72	525	224	18	11	2	11	19	4	31	6
Herb Pasta (p. 266)	8	145	6	26	3	69	154	150	10	1	0	14	5	8	2	8
Homemade Pasta (p. 266)	8	145	6	26	3	69	154	150	10	1	0	14	5	8	2	8
Lemon-Chive Pasta (p. 267)	4	156	4	22	6	0	101	67	6	9	3	17	7	9	1	5
Mexican Rice (p. 272)	6	128	3	29	0	0	539	373	5	52	32	11	4	10	5	10
Nutty Cheese Pasta (p. 267)	4	266	7	24	16	2	160	138	11	6	0	21	8	9	7	7
Oven-Cooked Rice (p. 272)	4	152	2	28	3	0	277	34	4	2	0	10	0	6	1	6
Oven-Cooked Rice Pilaf (p. 272)	4	174	4	30	4	0	328	172	7	45	2	12	3	13	2	7
Parsley Rice Mold (p. 272)	4	127	2	28	0	0	137	52	4	4	4	10	0	6	0	7
Pasta Primavera (p. 268)	8	212	7	24	10	2	124	267	10	112	31	18	9	9	8	10
Pasta with Carbonara Sauce (p. 268)	3	313	13	29	15	114	386	165	21	9	5	28	15	15	14	10
Peppery Rice Mold (p. 272)	4	132	3	29	0	0	386	73	4	52	17	10	1	7	1	6
Pesto for Pasta (p. 269)	4	179	6	22	7	3	125	116	9	8	11	18	8	9	8	9
Pesto Spaetzle (p. 263)	4	262	9	30	12	74	288	147	13	13	8	18	14	10	11	14
Polenta (p. 274)	6	134	2	15	8	0	181	50	3	2	0	4	0	2	0	2
Potluck Pasta (p. 270)	10	158	5	19	7	15	323	202	8	46	13	13	9	7	9	5
Raisin-Date Granola (p. 274)	16	200	4	26	10	0	3	178	5	0	0	8	4	3	4	7
Rice Mold (p. 272)	4	126	2	28	0	0	135	32	4	0	0	10	0	6	0	6
Rice Pilaf (p. 273)	4	187	4	31	5	3	242	146	6	3	5	14	4	10	2	7
Risotto (p. 272)	4	214	5	28	7	2	393	145	8	7	19	11	3	11	6	8
Spaetzle (p. 263)	4	188	6	28	5	70	163	86	9	4	0	16	13	10	4	10
Spanish Rice (p. 272)	6	144	3	27	3	0	223	376	5	21	48	12	4	10	5	10
Spinach Gnocchi (p. 275)	5	234	13	21	11	71	472	401	19	83	6	13	24	5	35	14
Spinach Pasta (p. 266)	10	147	5	27	2	55	130	93	8	18	2	16	11	9	3	12
Spinach Pesto for Pasta (p. 269)	4	179	6	22	7	3	127	127	9	10	4	18	8	9	8	8
Vegetable Fried Rice (p. 273)	4	294	8	42	10	37	527	219	13	19	17	9	12	6	15	6
Whole Wheat Pasta (p. 266)	8	141	6	25	3	69	154	146	10	1	0	14	5	8	2	8
Whole Wheat Spaetzle (p. 263)	4	181	6	27	5	70	163	127	10	5	0	11	10	9	5	9

On the divider: Fettuccine with Marinara Sauce (p. 268).

Pasta, Rice, And Grains

Whether you're looking for old-fashioned goodness, new ideas, or healthy high-fiber foods, this chapter has what you want.

To discover the vast selection of pasta, rice, and grains available today, check the identification photos on pages 264, 265, and 271, and the up-to-date recipes throughout the chapter. Then explore your supermarket's shelves, refrigerated cases, and freezer sections, or your local import shop, to find the different forms.

After purchasing, store dried pasta, rice (except brown rice), and whole grains in tightly covered containers in a cool, dry place. Refrigerate brown rice. Refrigerate or freeze grains if they will not be used within five months. Store refrigerated and frozen products according to package directions.

Pasta Perfection

Use these handy tips when cooking and eating pasta.
● To make 2½ cups of cooked elbow macaroni or shell macaroni, use 1 cup (4 ounces) of uncooked packaged elbow or shell macaroni.
● To make 3 cups of cooked noodles, use 3 cups (4 ounces) of uncooked packaged medium noodles.
● To make 2 cups of cooked spaghetti, use 4 ounces of uncooked spaghetti. (Held together in a bunch, 4 ounces of 10-inch-long spaghetti has about a 1-inch diameter.)
● To eat spaghetti or other long pasta, catch a few strands on a fork; then, with the tines rested against a large spoon, twist the fork to wrap up the pasta. Or, with the tines rested against the plate, twirl the fork and the pasta together.

Spaetzle

Serve spaetzle (SHPETS-luh) with sauces or in soups as you would noodles. Or serve it with sauerbraten, the traditional German way.

- **1 cup all-purpose flour**
- **⅛ teaspoon salt**
- **1 egg**
- **⅓ cup milk**
- **1 tablespoon margarine *or* butter**
- **3 tablespoons fine dry bread crumbs**

In a large saucepan or Dutch oven bring about 3 quarts *lightly salted water* to boiling.

Meanwhile, for spaetzle batter, in a bowl stir together flour and salt. In another bowl stir together egg and milk. Stir egg mixture into the flour mixture.

Set a colander with large holes (at least 3/16-inch diameter) on a large piece of waxed paper. (*Or,* use a spaetzle maker according to manufacturer's directions.)

Pour the spaetzle batter into the colander. Immediately hold the colander over the pan of boiling water; press the batter through the colander with a wooden spoon to form the spaetzle. Cook about 5 minutes or till done, stirring occasionally. Drain well.

Melt margarine or butter; toss with bread crumbs. Sprinkle crumb mixture over the hot spaetzle. Makes 4 servings.

Whole Wheat Spaetzle: Prepare as above, *except* reduce all-purpose flour to ½ *cup* and add ½ cup *whole wheat flour.*

Pesto Spaetzle: Prepare as above, *except* omit margarine and crumbs. Toss hot cooked spaetzle with 1 portion (about ¼ cup) *Pesto for Pasta* (see recipe, page 269).

Pasta

Acini di pepe

Alphabets

Bean threads

Bow ties, tiny

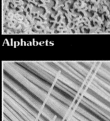

Bow ties (farfalle)

Capellini

Capellini, nested

Cavatelli

Chow mein noodles

Couscous

Ditalini (thimbles)

Egg roll wrappers

Fettuccine

Gemelli

Kluski

Lasagna

Linguine

Macaroni, elbow

Macaroni, four-color

Mafalda

Manicotti

Mostaccioli

Noodles, fine

Noodles, medium

Noodles, spinach

Noodles, whole wheat

Noodles, wide

Orzo (rosamarina)

Ravioli

Rice sticks

Rigatoni

Rings

Rotini

Rotini, tricolor

Shells, jumbo

Shells, large

Shells, medium

Shells, small

Spaetzle

Spaghetti

Spaghetti, thin

Spaghetti, twisted

Stars

Tortellini

Homemade Pasta

In recipes that call for packaged pasta, substitute half of this recipe for each 4 ounces of the packaged product. Cut dough into desired shape.

- **2⅓ cups all-purpose flour**
- **½ teaspoon salt**
- **2 beaten eggs**
- **⅓ cup water**
- **1 teaspoon cooking oil *or* olive oil**

In a large mixing bowl stir together *2 cups* of the flour and the salt. Make a well in the center of the mixture. In a bowl combine *eggs, water,* and *oil.* Add to flour mixture; mix well.

Sprinkle kneading surface with the remaining flour. Turn dough out onto floured surface. Knead till dough is smooth and elastic (8 to 10 minutes total). Cover and let rest for 10 minutes.

Divide dough into fourths. On a lightly floured surface, roll *each* fourth into a 12x12-inch square (about ⅟₁₆ inch thick). Let stand 20 minutes. Cut as desired (see tip and photos, opposite).

Or, if using a pasta machine, pass dough through machine according to manufacturer's directions till ⅟₁₆ inch thick. Cut as desired.

Cook pasta (see chart, page 278), allowing a few more minutes for dried or frozen pasta. Drain well. Makes 1 pound fresh pasta (8 servings).

To store: After cutting and shaping the pasta, hang it from a pasta drying rack or clothes hanger, or spread it on a wire cooling rack. Let dry overnight or till completely dry. Place in an airtight container and refrigerate for up to 3 days.

Or, dry the pasta for at least 1 hour. Seal it in a freezer bag or freezer container. Freeze for up to 8 months.

Whole Wheat Pasta: Prepare as above, *except* substitute *whole wheat flour* for the all-purpose flour.

Spinach Pasta: Prepare as above, *except* increase all-purpose flour to *2¾ cups,* reduce water to *¼ cup,* and add ¼ cup very finely chopped cooked *spinach,* well drained, to the egg mixture. Makes 1¼ pounds fresh pasta (10 servings).

Herb Pasta: Prepare as above, *except* add 1 teaspoon dried *basil, marjoram, or sage,* crushed, to flour mixture.

Egg Noodles: Prepare as above, *except* substitute 1 *egg* plus 2 *egg yolks* for the 2 eggs. Reduce flour to *1¾ cups* in flour mixture and ¼ cup for kneading. Cut dough into ¼-inch-wide strips, then cut into 2- to 3-inch lengths.

To knead, push down and away with the heel of your hand, give the dough a turn, and fold it over.

Pass dough through machine according to manufacturer's directions till it's ⅟₁₆ inch thick.

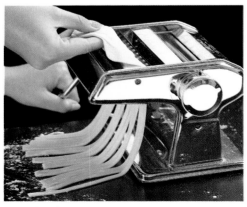

Pass the dough through the machine's cutting blades to cut it to the desired width.

Shaping Pasta

Knead and roll the Homemade Pasta dough (see recipe, opposite), then cut it into one of the following pasta shapes:

Lasagna: Cut into 2½-inch-wide strips. Cut into desired lengths.

Bow ties (farfalle): Cut into 2x1-inch rectangles. Pinch the centers to form bow-tie shapes.

Tripolini: Cut into 1-inch circles. Pinch centers, forming butterfly shapes.

Linguine or tagliatelle: After rolling dough and letting it stand, roll up dough loosely; cut into ⅛-inch-wide slices for linguine or ½-inch-wide slices for tagliatelle. Shake strands to separate. Cut into 12-inch lengths.

Fettuccine or noodles: After rolling dough and letting it stand, roll up dough loosely; cut into ¼-inch-wide slices. Shake the strands to separate. Cut into 12-inch lengths for fettuccine or 2-inch lengths for noodles.

◀ For linguine, cut the roll of dough into ⅛-inch slices. For fettuccine, cut it into ¼-inch slices.

For lasagna, use a fluted pastry wheel or a sharp knife to cut the dough into 2½-inch-wide strips.

Herb-Buttered Pasta

- **4** ounces packaged spaghetti, linguine, *or* fettuccine
- **2** tablespoons margarine *or* butter, cut up
- **½** teaspoon dried basil, oregano, thyme, *or* marjoram, crushed; dried dillweed; *or* caraway seed

Cook pasta (see chart, page 278). Drain well. Return to hot saucepan. Add margarine and desired herb. Toss gently till pasta is well coated. Season to taste with salt and pepper. Serves 4.

Lemon-Chive Pasta: Prepare as above, *except* omit herb and add ¼ cup snipped *chives* and 1 teaspoon finely shredded *lemon peel* with margarine or butter.

Nutty Cheese Pasta: Prepare as above, *except* omit herb and add ½ cup chopped *walnuts, pecans, or almonds* and 2 tablespoons grated *Parmesan or Romano cheese* with margarine.

For bow ties (farfalle), pinch the centers of the small rectangles to make bow-tie shapes.

Pasta Primavera

> 6 ounces packaged linguine *or* fettuccine
> 3 tablespoons margarine *or* butter
> 2 cups broccoli flowerets
> 1 cup bias-sliced carrots
> 1 medium onion, cut into thin wedges
> 1 clove garlic, minced
> 1 cup fresh *or* frozen pea pods
> ½ cup cashews *or* almonds
> ¼ cup dry white wine
> 1 teaspoon dried thyme, crushed
> ¼ teaspoon pepper
> ¼ cup grated Parmesan cheese

Cook pasta (see chart, page 278). Drain well. Meanwhile, in a large skillet melt *2 tablespoons* of the margarine. Stir in broccoli, carrots, onion, and garlic. Cook and stir over medium-high heat about 3 minutes or till broccoli is crisp-tender.

Stir in pea pods. Cook 2 minutes more. Stir in cooked linguine or fettuccine, remaining margarine, the cashews or almonds, wine, thyme, and pepper. Cover and cook 1 minute more. Transfer to a warm serving plate. Sprinkle with Parmesan cheese. Makes 8 servings.

Ham Pasta Primavera: Prepare as above, *except* stir 1 cup cubed fully cooked *ham* into vegetable mixture with the pea pods. Makes 4 main-dish servings.

Using a Food Processor To Make Pasta

Preparing Homemade Pasta (see recipe, page 266) is a cinch when you mix and knead the dough with a food processor. Begin by placing the steel blade in the food processor bowl. Add *all* of the dry ingredients and eggs. Cover and process until the mixture forms fine crumbs about the consistency of cornmeal. With the processor running, slowly pour the liquid ingredients through the feed tube. Continue processing *just* till the dough forms a ball. Let the dough rest 10 minutes. Then roll and shape as directed in the recipe.

Fettuccine with Marinara Sauce

Choose plain or spinach fettuccine to go with this rich tomato sauce. And, for a special treat, add sautéed shrimp. (Pictured on page 261.)

> 1 cup chopped onion
> ½ cup finely chopped carrot
> 2 large cloves garlic, minced
> 2 tablespoons cooking oil
> 1 28-ounce can tomatoes, cut up
> ½ of a 6-ounce can (⅓ cup) tomato paste
> 1 teaspoon sugar
> 1 teaspoon dried oregano, crushed
> ¼ teaspoon salt
> 8 ounces packaged fettuccine, spinach fettuccine, or spaghetti

For marinara sauce, in a medium saucepan cook onion, carrot, and garlic in hot oil till tender but not brown. Stir in *undrained* tomatoes, tomato paste, sugar, oregano, salt, and dash *pepper.* Bring to boiling; reduce heat. Simmer, uncovered, about 30 minutes or to desired consistency.

Meanwhile, cook pasta (see chart, page 278). Drain well. Serve with marinara sauce. Serves 8.

Pasta with Carbonara Sauce

Bits of bacon highlight the cheesy sauce.

> 1 egg
> 1 tablespoon whipping cream, light cream, *or* milk
> 1 tablespoon margarine *or* butter
> 4 slices bacon, cut into 1-inch pieces
> 4 ounces packaged fettuccine *or* spaghetti
> ¼ cup grated Parmesan *or* Romano cheese
> 1 tablespoon snipped parsley

Let egg, cream or milk, and margarine or butter stand at room temperature for 1 hour. Cook bacon till crisp. Drain bacon on paper towels.

Meanwhile, cook pasta (see chart, page 278). Drain well. Return pasta to saucepan and place over low heat. Toss margarine with pasta. Beat together egg and cream just till combined. Pour egg mixture over pasta; toss till well coated. Add bacon, cheese, and parsley; toss to mix. Season with coarsely ground *pepper.* Transfer to a warm serving dish. Serve immediately. Serves 3 or 4.

Pesto for Pasta

Toss one portion with hot pasta now and freeze the remaining two. Pesto also is good in soups, vegetables, sauces, and dips.

> 1 **cup firmly packed fresh basil leaves**
> ½ **cup firmly packed parsley sprigs**
>   **with stems removed**
> ½ **cup grated Parmesan *or* Romano**
>   **cheese**
> ¼ **cup pine nuts, walnuts, *or* almonds**
> 1 **large clove garlic, quartered**
> ¼ **cup olive oil *or* cooking oil**
> 4 **ounces packaged fettuccine,**
>   **spaghetti, *or* other pasta**

For pesto, in a blender container or food processor bowl combine basil leaves, parsley, Parmesan or Romano cheese, nuts, garlic, and ¼ teaspoon *salt.* Cover and blend or process with several on-off turns till a paste forms, stopping the machine several times and scraping the sides.

With the machine running slowly, gradually add oil and blend or process to the consistency of soft butter. Divide into 3 portions (about ¼ *cup* each) and place in small airtight containers. Refrigerate for 1 or 2 days or freeze up to 1 month.

To serve, thaw *1 portion* pesto, if frozen. Bring to room temperature. Cook pasta (see chart, page 278). Drain well. Return pasta to pan. Toss pesto with pasta. Serve immediately. Serves 4.

Spinach Pesto for Pasta: Prepare the pesto as above, *except* substitute torn fresh *spinach* for the fresh basil and add 1 teaspoon *dried basil,* crushed.

Couscous and Tomatoes

Try quick-cooking rice in place of the couscous.

> 1 **14½-ounce can stewed tomatoes**
> ¼ **cup chopped onion**
> ⅛ **to ¼ teaspoon ground red pepper**
> ⅛ **teaspoon garlic powder**
> ⅔ **cup couscous**
> ¼ **cup sliced pitted ripe olives**
> ¼ **cup snipped parsley**

In a saucepan combine *undrained* stewed tomatoes, onion, pepper, garlic powder, 1 cup *water,* and ½ teaspoon *salt.* Bring to boiling. Stir in couscous. Cover; remove from heat. Let stand 5 minutes. Stir in olives and parsley. Serves 4.

Pasta, Rice, and Grains On Call

When you're cooking pasta, rice, or grains, make some extra to put in the freezer. The frozen portions are great for rounding out last-minute meals or for making just a few servings. Here's what to do.

Cook pasta, rice, or grain as usual and drain. Rinse and drain pasta again.

For *individual servings,* place the cooked pasta, rice, or grain into 6-ounce custard cups, cover, and freeze till firm. Remove the food from the cups and place in a freezer bag. Seal, label, and freeze for up to 6 months.

For *family-size servings,* place the pasta, rice, or grain in a freezer container. Seal and label the container. Freeze for up to 6 months.

To quickly thaw and cook the frozen food, use one of these suggestions.

● Place rice in a saucepan, adding about 1 tablespoon water for every ½ cup of cooked rice. Cover and cook over low heat till heated through.

● Using a large spoon, carefully lower frozen pasta into a saucepan of boiling water. Return water to boiling and cook for 1 minute. Drain.

● Place frozen wheat berries in a colander and rinse under hot water for a few minutes.

● Use your microwave. For individual servings, return the frozen food to the custard cups. Do not add water. Micro-cook, covered with waxed paper, on 100% power (high) till heated through. For 1 portion, allow 1½ to 2 minutes; for 2 portions, allow 2 to 2½ minutes; for 4 portions allow 4 to 4½ minutes.

For family-size servings, transfer the frozen food to a casserole. Add 2 tablespoons water for each 2 cups of food. Cook, covered, on 100% power (high) about 5 minutes for each 2 cups of food or till heated through; stir once.

Fettuccine Alfredo

Simple yet elegant.

3 tablespoons light cream *or* whipping cream
4 ounces packaged fettuccine
⅓ cup grated Parmesan cheese
1 tablespoon margarine *or* butter
Coarsely cracked black pepper
Ground nutmeg

Let cream come to room temperature. Cook fettuccine (see chart, page 278). Drain well. Return fettuccine to the hot saucepan. Add cream, Parmesan cheese, and margarine or butter. Toss gently till fettuccine is well coated. Transfer to a warm serving dish. Sprinkle with pepper and nutmeg. Serve immediately. Makes 4 servings.

Fettuccine Alfredo with Mushrooms: Prepare as above, *except* cook 1½ cups sliced fresh *mushrooms* and 1 clove *garlic,* minced, in the margarine or butter till tender. Add to cooked fettuccine with cream and Parmesan cheese.

Keeping Pasta Hot

Here's how to serve pasta at its best—piping hot.

● Warm the serving dish by running hot water into it and letting it stand a few minutes. Drain the pasta in a colander. Give the colander a few firm shakes to speed draining. Dry the dish and add the pasta. Serve immediately.

● When adding other ingredients to the cooked pasta, first return the pasta to the pan it was cooked in, then add the ingredients. The heat of the pan will warm the new ingredients.

● If after draining the cooked pasta you face a short delay, return the pasta to the pan it was cooked in. Or, for a slightly longer delay, leave the pasta in, or transfer it to, a *metal* colander, then place the colander over a pan containing a small amount of boiling water. Coat the pasta with a little margarine to prevent sticking. Cover the colander. Serve as soon as possible.

Potluck Pasta

Transform this side dish into a main dish just by adding tuna, ham, or cooked chicken or turkey.

2 cups large shells, rotini, *or* elbow macaroni
1 10-ounce package frozen chopped broccoli, peas, *or* mixed vegetables
⅓ cup chopped onion
1 10¾-ounce can condensed cream of celery, chicken, *or* mushroom soup; *or* one 11-ounce can condensed cheddar cheese soup
1 8-ounce carton dairy sour cream
1 4-ounce can mushroom stems and pieces, drained
½ cup milk
½ cup shredded carrot
1 teaspoon dried oregano *or* basil, crushed, *or* dried dillweed
¼ teaspoon pepper
2 tablespoons grated Parmesan cheese

In a large saucepan cook pasta (see chart, page 278), adding frozen vegetable and onion the last 6 minutes. Drain in a colander.

In the same saucepan stir together condensed soup; sour cream; mushrooms; milk; carrot; oregano, basil, or dillweed; and pepper. Cook and stir over medium heat till heated through.

Stir in drained pasta mixture; heat through. Transfer to a warm serving dish. Sprinkle with Parmesan cheese and serve immediately. Makes 10 servings.

To make ahead: Prepare as above, *except* omit heating the macaroni-soup mixture. Transfer mixture to a 2-quart casserole. Sprinkle with Parmesan cheese. Cover and chill for 3 to 24 hours. To serve, bake, covered, in a 350° oven about 55 minutes or till heated through.

Barley, pearl
Barley, quick cooking
Buckwheat flour
Buckwheat groats
Bulgur
Cornmeal, white
Cornmeal, yellow
Farina
Hominy grits
Millet
Oats, rolled, quick
Oats, rolled, regular
Rice, brown
Rice, long grain
Rice, medium grain
Rice, quick cooking
Rice, wild |
Rye berries |
Rye flour |
Wheat, cracked |

Rice Mold

Plain or perked up, rice shaped into a mold turns an ordinary meal into a special dinner.

 1½ **cups water *or* chicken broth**
 ¾ **cup long grain rice *or* brown rice**
 ¼ **teaspoon salt**
 ½ **teaspoon dried basil, thyme,
    or oregano, crushed (optional)**

In a saucepan combine water or broth, rice, and salt. If desired, add herb. Bring to boiling; reduce heat. Cover and simmer about 15 minutes for long grain rice (35 minutes for brown rice) or till rice is tender and liquid is absorbed. Remove from heat. Let stand, covered, for 5 minutes.

Press hot rice into a buttered 3-cup mold or bowl. Unmold at once. Makes 4 servings.

Parsley Rice Mold: Prepare as above, *except* stir ¼ cup snipped *parsley* into cooked rice. Omit herb.

Confetti Rice Mold: Prepare as above, *except* stir in ½ cup frozen *mixed vegetables* and ¼ teaspoon dried *dillweed* with the uncooked long grain rice. Omit herb. (*Or,* for brown rice, stir in vegetables and dillweed after 20 minutes of cooking. Return to boiling. Reduce heat and continue as above.)

Peppery Rice Mold: Prepare as above, *except* stir in one 4-ounce can diced *green chili peppers,* drained, and ⅛ teaspoon ground *red pepper* with the uncooked rice. Omit herb.

Oven-Cooked Rice

 1½ **cups boiling water**
 1 **tablespoon margarine *or* butter**
 ¾ **cup long grain rice *or*
    quick-cooking barley**   Oven 350°

In a 1-quart casserole combine boiling water and margarine or butter; stir till melted. Stir in rice or barley and ½ teaspoon *salt.* Cover; bake in a 350° oven about 35 minutes or till tender and liquid is absorbed. Fluff with a fork. Serves 4.

Oven-Cooked Rice Pilaf: Prepare as above, *except* substitute boiling *chicken broth* for the water. Omit salt and stir in ¼ cup sliced *green onion,* ¼ cup chopped *celery,* and ¼ cup chopped *carrot* with uncooked rice or barley.

Risotto

Parmesan flavors this creamy rice dish.

 1 **cup sliced fresh mushrooms**
 ⅔ **cup long grain rice**
 ⅓ **cup chopped green pepper**
 2 **tablespoons margarine *or* butter**
 1 **cup chicken broth**
 ½ **cup water**
 ¼ **cup dry sherry**
 ¼ **teaspoon dried sage, crushed**
 2 **tablespoons grated Parmesan
    cheese**

In a medium saucepan cook mushrooms, rice, and green pepper in margarine till green pepper is tender. Remove from heat. Stir in broth, water, sherry, sage, and ⅛ teaspoon *pepper.* Bring to boiling; reduce heat. Cover and simmer about 15 minutes or till tender. Remove from heat. Let stand, covered, for 5 minutes. Fluff with a fork. Sprinkle with Parmesan cheese. Serves 4.

Spanish Rice

 ½ **cup chopped onion**
 ½ **cup chopped green pepper**
 1 **clove garlic, minced**
 1 **tablespoon cooking oil**
 1 **28-ounce can tomatoes, cut up**
 ¾ **cup long grain rice**
 1 **teaspoon sugar**
 1 **teaspoon chili powder**
 ⅛ **teaspoon pepper**
    **Several dashes bottled hot pepper
    sauce**
 ½ **cup shredded cheddar cheese
    (2 ounces) (optional)**

In a large skillet cook onion, green pepper, and garlic in oil till tender but not brown. Stir in *undrained* tomatoes, rice, sugar, chili powder, pepper, hot pepper sauce, and 1 cup *water.* Bring to boiling; reduce heat. Cover and simmer for 20 to 25 minutes or till rice is tender and most of the liquid is absorbed. Sprinkle with shredded cheddar cheese, if desired. Makes 6 to 8 servings.

Mexican Rice: Prepare as above, *except* omit onion, green pepper, garlic, and cooking oil. Substitute *stewed tomatoes,* undrained, for the tomatoes. Stir one 4-ounce can diced *green chili -peppers,* drained, and 1 tablespoon *Worcestershire sauce* into the uncooked rice mixture.

Rice Pilaf

Add a nutty flavor to the rice by browning it lightly in a tablespoon of margarine or butter before beginning the recipe.

  ½ cup chopped onion
  ½ cup sliced fresh mushrooms
  ¼ cup chopped celery *or* green pepper
  1 clove garlic, minced
  1 tablespoon margarine *or* butter
  ¾ cup long grain rice
  1½ teaspoons instant chicken *o*beef
      bouillon granules
  ⅛ teaspoon pepper
  2 slices bacon, crisp-cooked, drained,
      and crumbled

In a saucepan cook onion, mushrooms, celery or green pepper, and garlic in margarine or butter till tender but not brown. Stir in rice, bouillon granules, pepper, and 1½ cups *water*. Bring to boiling; reduce heat. Cover and simmer about 15 minutes or till rice is tender and liquid is absorbed. Stir in crumbled bacon. Makes 4 servings.

Curried Rice Pilaf: Prepare as above, *except* omit mushrooms and add ½ to 1 teaspoon *curry powder* with onion. Stir in ½ cup *raisins* with rice.

Brown and Wild Rice Pilaf: Prepare as above, *except,* instead of cooking the celery or green pepper with the mushrooms, add with the water. Substitute ½ cup *brown rice* and ¼ cup *wild rice* for the long grain rice. If desired, add 2 tablespoons dry sherry to the uncooked rice mixture. Cook rice mixture about 40 minutes.

Bulgur Pilaf: Prepare as above, *except* substitute *bulgur* for the long grain rice.

Making Toasty Oats

Give a nutty flavor to cereals and cookies by using toasted rolled oats. To toast oats, just spread the oats in a shallow layer in a baking pan. Then bake in a 350° oven for 15 to 20 minutes or till lightly browned, stirring occasionally. Cool. Store tightly covered.

Try this idea with millet, rye berries, and other grains, too.

Fried Rice

  2 tablespoons cooking oil
  2 beaten eggs
  ½ cup diced fully cooked ham
  ¼ cup finely chopped fresh
      mushrooms
  ¼ cup thinly sliced green onion
  ½ to 1 teaspoon grated gingerroot
      Dash ground red pepper
  3 cups unsalted cooked rice, chilled
  2 cups chopped Chinese cabbage
  2 tablespoons soy sauce

In a large skillet heat *1 tablespoon* of the oil over medium heat. Add eggs and cook without stirring till set. Loosen eggs and invert skillet over cutting board to remove; cut into short, narrow strips.

In the skillet heat the remaining oil over medium heat. Cook ham, mushrooms, onion, gingerroot, and red pepper in the hot oil for 3 minutes.

Stir in cooked rice, cabbage, and egg strips; sprinkle with soy sauce and 1 tablespoon *water*. Cook for 3 to 5 minutes or till heated through, tossing gently to coat with soy sauce. Serves 4.

Vegetable Fried Rice: Prepare as above, *except* omit ham and stir ½ cup frozen *peas,* thawed, into the skillet with the rice.

Cinnamon-Raisin Oatmeal

This ready-to-cook mixture of oats, fruit, and spices can be made one bowl at a time.

Stir together 1½ cups *quick-cooking rolled oats,* 1 cup *raisins or mixed dried fruit bits,* ¼ cup chopped *nuts,* ¼ cup packed *brown sugar,* ½ teaspoon ground *cinnamon,* ¼ teaspoon *salt,* and ¼ teaspoon ground *nutmeg.* Store in an airtight container at room temperature.

In a medium saucepan bring 3 cups *water* to boiling. Slowly add oat mixture to water, stirring constantly. (For 1 serving, use ¾ cup *water* and ⅔ *cup* oat mixture.) Cook, stirring constantly, for 1 minute. Cover; remove from heat. Let stand 1 to 3 minutes or till of desired consistency. Serve with milk, if desired. Serves 4.

Microwave directions: Assemble as above. For 1 serving, in a 2-cup measure micro-cook ¾ cup *water* on 100% power (high) for 1¾ to 2¾ minutes or till boiling. Slowly add ⅔ *cup* oat mixture, stirring constantly. Cook, uncovered, on high for 30 seconds, stirring once. Let stand 1 minute. Serve with milk, if desired.

Granola

Choose your favorite nuts and fruits to make this crispy snack or cereal.

> **2 cups regular rolled oats**
> ½ **cup coconut**
> ½ **cup coarsely chopped slivered *or* sliced almonds, *or* chopped peanuts**
> ½ **cup sunflower nuts**
> ¼ **cup sesame seed**
> ½ **cup honey *or* maple-flavored syrup**
> ⅓ **cup cooking oil**   Oven 300°

In a bowl stir together rolled oats, coconut, almonds or peanuts, sunflower nuts, and sesame seed. In another bowl combine honey or syrup and oil; stir into oat mixture. Spread mixture evenly into a greased 15x10x1-inch baking pan. Bake in a 300° oven for 30 to 35 minutes or till lightly browned, stirring after 20 minutes.

Remove from the oven and immediately turn out onto a large piece of foil. Cool, then break into clumps. Store in tightly covered jars or plastic bags at room temperature for up to 2 weeks. For longer storage, seal in freezer bags and freeze. Makes about 6 cups (12 servings).

Microwave directions: In a 2½-quart bowl combine oats, coconut, almonds or peanuts, sunflower nuts, and sesame seed. Combine honey or syrup and oil; stir into oat mixture. Micro-cook on 100% power (high) for 8 to 10 minutes or till lightly browned, stirring *every* 2 minutes for the first 4 minutes, then *every* minute.

Immediately turn out onto a large piece of foil. Cool, then break into clumps. Store in tightly covered jars or plastic bags at room temperature for up to 2 weeks. For longer storage, seal in freezer bags and freeze.

Apple-Cinnamon Granola: Prepare as above, *except* reduce rolled oats to *1½ cups.* Stir 1 teaspoon ground *cinnamon* into honey-oil mixture. Just before serving, stir in 1 cup coarsely chopped dried *apple.* Makes about 7½ cups (15 servings).

Raisin-Date Granola: Prepare as above, *except,* after removing granola from the oven, stir in ½ cup *raisins* and ½ cup snipped pitted whole *dates.* Makes about 8 cups (16 servings).

Cornmeal Mush

Serve the mush plain as a cereal, fried for breakfast, or baked and topped with a sauce for a dinner side dish.

> **1 cup cornmeal**
> ½ **teaspoon salt**

Bring 2¾ cups *water* to boiling. In a bowl combine cornmeal, salt, and 1 cup *cold water.* Slowly add cornmeal mixture to boiling water, stirring constantly. Cook and stir till mixture returns to boiling. Reduce heat; cook over low heat for 10 to 15 minutes or till mixture is very thick, stirring occasionally. If desired, serve with milk, margarine, butter, honey, or sugar. Makes 4 servings.

Fried Mush: Prepare as above, *except* pour hot mush into a 7½x3½x2-inch loaf pan. Cool; cover and chill for several hours or overnight. Turn out of the pan and cut into ½-inch-thick slices. In a large skillet heat 3 tablespoons *cooking oil, margarine, or butter* over medium heat. Add *five* slices of the mush and fry for 10 to 12 minutes on each side or till brown and crisp. Repeat with remaining slices of mush. Serve with *margarine or butter* and *honey or maple-flavored syrup.* Makes 7 servings.

Polenta: Prepare as above, *except* pour hot mush into a 9-inch pie plate. Cover and chill about 30 minutes or till firm. Bake in a 350° oven about 20 minutes or till hot. Cut into wedges. If desired, serve with spaghetti sauce, pizza sauce, or taco sauce, and sprinkle with grated Parmesan cheese. Makes 6 servings.

Grits

In a saucepan bring 2 cups *water or chicken broth* and ¼ teaspoon *salt* to boiling. Slowly add ½ cup *quick-cooking grits,* stirring constantly. Cook and stir till boiling. Reduce heat; cook and stir for 5 to 6 minutes or till water is absorbed and mixture is thick. Serve with margarine, butter, or milk, if desired. Makes 2 servings.

Cheesy Grits: Prepare as above, *except* omit salt. Stir 1 cup shredded *American or cheddar cheese* and 1 tablespoon *margarine or butter* into hot grits till melted. Gradually stir about ½ *cup* of the hot grits into 1 beaten *egg.* Return all to the saucepan and stir to combine. Pour into a greased 1-quart casserole. Bake in a 325° oven about 25 minutes or till nearly set. Let stand 5 minutes. Makes 4 servings.

Baked Gnocchi

Baking makes the Parmesan-flavored gnocchi (NAH-key) extra crisp.

1½ cups milk
 2 tablespoons margarine *or* butter
 ¾ cup milk
 ½ cup quick-cooking farina
 ¼ teaspoon salt
 1 beaten egg
 ⅓ cup grated Parmesan cheese
 ¼ cup grated Parmesan
    cheese   Oven 425°

In a medium saucepan heat the 1½ cups milk and the margarine or butter to boiling. In a bowl mix the ¾ cup milk, the farina, and salt. Slowly add farina mixture to boiling milk, stirring constantly. Cook and stir 3 to 4 minutes or till thick.

Remove from heat; stir about ½ *cup* of the hot mixture into egg. Return all to the saucepan; stir in the ⅓ cup Parmesan cheese. Pour into a well-buttered 10x6x2-inch baking dish. Chill about 1 hour or till firm.

Turn out of baking dish onto a cutting board. Cut into 3x1-inch rectangles. Sprinkle tops with the ¼ cup Parmesan cheese. Place on a well-greased baking sheet. Bake in a 425° oven about 25 minutes or till golden. Serve warm. Serves 5.

Spinach Gnocchi: Prepare as above, *except* reduce the 1½ cups milk to *1¼ cups.* Cook one 10-ounce package frozen chopped *spinach* according to package directions. Drain in a colander, pressing out as much liquid as possible with a spoon. Stir spinach into hot farina mixture with the ⅓ cup Parmesan cheese.

Boiled Gnocchi: Prepare as above, *except* do not pour into baking dish. Cool slightly. With lightly floured hands, shape mixture into compact balls, using about *1 tablespoon* farina mixture for *each* ball. Drop balls, several at a time, into a large amount of *gently boiling* water. Cook about 4 minutes or till gnocchi rises to the surface. Remove and drain on paper towels. Sprinkle with the ¼ cup Parmesan cheese.

Herb-Garlic Gnocchi: Prepare as above, *except* omit salt and stir in 1 teaspoon dried *basil, oregano, or marjoram,* crushed, and ½ teaspoon *garlic salt* with the farina.

Choose-a-Grain Casserole

Great with baked chicken or fish.

 ½ cup chopped green *or* sweet red
    pepper
 ½ cup chopped onion
 ½ cup chopped celery *or* one 4-ounce
    can diced green chili peppers,
    drained
 1 clove garlic, minced
 1 tablespoon margarine *or* butter
1½ cups cooked rice, bulgur, wheat
    berries, *or* barley
 ½ of an 8-ounce container (½ cup)
    soft-style cream cheese
 ¼ teaspoon salt
 ¼ teaspoon pepper
 ¼ teaspoon ground cumin, ground
    coriander, *or* dried basil, crushed
 Milk
 ½ cup shredded cheddar cheese
    (2 ounces)   Oven 375°

In a small saucepan cook green or red pepper, onion, celery (if using instead of chili peppers), and garlic in margarine or butter till tender.

Meanwhile, in a bowl combine cooked rice, bulgur, wheat berries, or barley; cream cheese; chili peppers (if using); salt; pepper; and cumin. Stir in onion mixture. Transfer to a 1-quart casserole. Bake, covered, in a 375° oven about 25 minutes or till heated through.

If mixture seems stiff, stir in milk, a tablespoon at a time, to moisten. Sprinkle with cheese. Bake 2 to 3 minutes more or till cheese melts. Makes 5 or 6 servings.

Microwave directions: In a 1-quart casserole micro-cook green or red pepper, onion, celery (if using instead of chili peppers), garlic, and margarine or butter, covered, on 100% power (high) for 1½ to 2½ minutes or till tender, stirring once. Stir in cooked rice, bulgur, wheat berries, or barley; cream cheese; chili peppers (if using); salt; pepper; and cumin. Cook, covered, on high for 3 to 5 minutes or till heated through, stirring once. If mixture seems stiff, stir in milk, a tablespoon at a time, to moisten. Sprinkle with cheese. Cover and let stand till cheese melts.

Cooking Rice and Grains

Use this chart as a guide when cooking rice and grains. Measure the amount of water into a medium saucepan and bring to a full boil (unless chart indicates to add the grain to cold water). If desired, add ¼ to ½ teaspoon salt to the water.

Slowly add the rice or grain and return to boiling. Cover and simmer for the time specified or till tender (pinch a kernel or grain between your thumb and finger; if the core is hard, it is not done) and most of the water is absorbed.

Rice or Grain and Amount	Amount of Water	Cooking Directions	Yield
Barley, pearl ¾ cup	3 cups	Simmer about 45 minutes. Drain, if necessary.	3 cups
Barley, quick cooking 1 cup	1½ cups	Simmer for 10 to 12 minutes.	2½ cups
Buckwheat groats or kasha ⅔ cup	1½ cups	Add to *cold* water. Bring to boiling. Cover and simmer for 10 to 12 minutes.	2 cups
Bulgur ⅔ cup	1⅓ cups	Add to *cold* water. Bring to boiling. Cover and simmer for 12 to 15 minutes.	2 cups
Cornmeal 1 cup	2¾ cups	Combine cornmeal and 1 cup *cold* water. Add to the 2¾ cups boiling water. Cover and simmer about 10 minutes.	3½ cups
Farina, quick cooking ¾ cup	3½ cups	Simmer for 2 to 3 minutes, stirring constantly.	3 cups
Hominy grits, quick cooking ¾ cup	3 cups	Simmer about 5 minutes.	3 cups
Millet ¾ cup	2 cups	Simmer for 15 to 20 minutes. Let stand, covered, for 5 minutes.	3 cups
Oats, rolled, quick cooking 1 cup	2 cups	Simmer for 1 minute. Let stand, covered, for 3 minutes.	2 cups
Oats, rolled, regular 1¼ cups	2½ cups	Simmer for 5 to 7 minutes. Let stand, covered, for 3 minutes.	2¼ cups

Cooking Rice and Grains (Continued)

Rice or Grain and Amount	Amount of Water	Cooking Directions	Yield
Oats, steel cut 1 cup	2½ cups	Simmer for 20 to 25 minutes.	2½ cups
Rice, brown 1 cup	2 cups	Simmer about 35 minutes.	2⅔ cups
Rice, long grain 1 cup	2 cups	Simmer about 15 minutes.	3 cups
Rice, quick cooking 1 cup	1 cup	Add to boiling water. Remove from heat. Let stand, covered, for 5 minutes.	2 cups
Rice, wild 1 cup	2 cups	Rinse rice well. Add to boiling water. Simmer about 40 minutes. Drain, if necessary.	2⅔ cups
Rye berries 1 cup	3 cups	Add to *cold* water. Bring to boiling. Cover and simmer about 1 hour. Drain. *Or,* for quicker cooking, soak berries in the 3 cups water in the refrigerator for 6 to 24 hours. Do not drain. Bring to boiling; reduce heat. Cover and simmer for 30 minutes.	2½ cups
Wheat, cracked ⅔ cup	1½ cups	Add to *cold* water. Bring to boiling. Cover and simmer for 12 to 15 minutes. Let stand, covered, for 5 minutes.	2 cups
Wheat berries ¾ cup	2½ cups	Add to *cold* water. Bring to boiling. Cover and simmer for 45 to 60 minutes. Drain. *Or,* for quicker cooking, see rye berries, above.	2 cups

Cooking Pasta

In a large saucepan or Dutch oven bring water (about 3 quarts of water for 4 to 8 ounces of pasta) to boiling. If desired, add 1 teaspoon salt and 1 tablespoon olive oil or cooking oil to help keep the pasta separated. Add the pasta a little at a time so the water does not stop boiling. Hold long pasta, such as spaghetti, at one end and dip the other end into the water. As the pasta softens, gently curl it around the pan and down into the water. Reduce the heat slightly and boil, uncovered, for the time specified or till the pasta is al dente (tender but still firm). Stir occasionally. Test often for doneness near the end of the cooking time. Drain in a colander.

Homemade Pasta	Cooking Time°	Homemade Pasta	Cooking Time°
Bow ties, tiny	2 to 3 minutes	Noodles	1½ to 2 minutes
Bow ties (farfalle)	2 to 3 minutes	Ravioli	6 to 8 minutes
Fettuccine	1½ to 2 minutes	Spaetzle	5 to 10 minutes
Lasagna	2 to 3 minutes	Tagliatelle	1½ to 2 minutes
Linguine	1½ to 2 minutes	Tortellini	8 to 10 minutes
Manicotti	2 to 3 minutes	Tripolini	2 to 3 minutes

Packaged Pasta	Cooking Time	Packaged Pasta	Cooking Time
Acini di pepe	5 to 6 minutes	Orzo (rosamarina)	5 to 8 minutes
Alphabets	5 to 8 minutes	Rigatoni	15 minutes
Bow ties, tiny	5 to 6 minutes	Rings	9 to 10 minutes
Bow ties (farfalle)	10 minutes	Rotini	8 to 10 minutes
Capellini	5 to 6 minutes	Shells, jumbo	23 to 25 minutes
Cavatelli	12 minutes	Shells, large	12 to 14 minutes
Ditalini (thimbles)	7 to 9 minutes	Shells, small	8 to 9 minutes
Fettuccine	8 to 10 minutes	Spaetzle	10 to 12 minutes
Gemelli	10 minutes	Spaghetti	10 to 12 minutes
Lasagna	10 to 12 minutes	Spaghetti, thin	8 to 10 minutes
Linguine	8 to 10 minutes	Spaghetti, twisted	15 minutes
Macaroni, elbow	10 minutes	Stars	5 to 8 minutes
Mafalda	10 to 12 minutes	Tortellini	15 minutes
Manicotti	18 minutes	Vermicelli	5 to 7 minutes
Mostaccioli	14 minutes	Wagon wheels	12 minutes
Noodles	6 to 8 minutes	Ziti	14 to 15 minutes

°*If homemade pasta is dried or frozen, allow a few more minutes.*

Pies

Nutrition Analysis	Servings Per Recipe	Calories	Protein (g)	Carbohydrate (g)	Fat (g)	Cholesterol (mg)	Sodium (mg)	Potassium (mg)	Protein	Vitamin A	Vitamin C	Thiamine	Riboflavin	Niacin	Calcium	Iron
				Per Serving							**Percent U.S. RDA Per Serving**					
Banana Cream Pie (p. 289)	8	419	9	65	15	144	165	371	13	8	6	13	21	7	13	9
Berry Glacé Pie (p. 285)	8	261	3	43	9	0	69	266	5	0	100	10	10	7	2	8
Black-Bottom Pie (p. 290)	8	425	9	56	20	141	128	213	14	6	0	12	16	6	10	11
Brown Sugar and Rhubarb Pie (p. 287)	8	340	5	56	11	103	104	305	8	3	5	12	10	7	9	14
Cheese Pastry (p. 294)	8	318	7	24	22	15	222	44	10	3	0	14	10	8	11	8
Cherry Lattice Pie (p. 285)	8	425	4	62	18	0	159	142	6	18	3	15	10	9	2	16
Chocolate Chiffon Pie (p. 290)	8	304	7	38	15	136	99	109	10	3	0	10	10	6	2	10
Chocolate-Wafer Crust (p. 294)	8	160	1	14	11	7	126	29	2	8	0	4	3	2	1	3
Cinnamon Pastry (p. 293)	8	148	2	15	9	0	67	20	3	0	0	8	5	5	0	5
Cocoa Pastry (p. 293)	8	197	2	19	13	0	77	27	4	0	0	8	5	5	0	6
Coconut Cream Pie (p. 289)	8	437	9	60	19	144	167	237	13	8	0	12	18	6	13	10
Coconut Crust (p. 294)	8	127	1	8	11	0	55	67	1	4	0	0	0	0	0	2
Coconut Custard Pie (p. 286)	8	294	8	33	14	143	175	186	12	6	0	12	16	6	11	8
Coconut-Oatmeal Pie (p. 287)	8	478	5	69	21	103	213	91	8	8	0	12	9	6	4	18
Creamy Key Lime Pie (p. 288)	8	393	8	46	20	107	159	259	13	9	6	13	21	6	17	7
Crumb-Topped Apple Pie (p. 282)	8	349	3	60	12	0	105	169	5	3	4	13	7	8	2	10
Crumb-Topped Apricot Pie (p. 282)	8	427	5	78	12	0	106	310	7	43	9	16	10	11	3	13
Crumb-Topped Blackberry Pie (p. 282)	8	374	4	65	12	0	105	220	6	5	15	15	9	10	4	13
Crumb-Topped Blueberry Pie (p. 282)	8	350	4	59	12	0	110	143	6	4	10	15	10	9	2	11
Crumb-Topped Cherry Pie (p. 282)	8	414	4	75	12	0	108	248	7	27	10	16	10	10	3	12
Crumb-Topped Gooseberry Pie (p. 282)	8	394	4	70	12	0	106	228	6	7	25	15	9	10	4	12
Crumb-Topped Nectarine Pie (p. 282)	8	372	4	64	12	0	105	348	6	21	8	15	10	14	2	11
Crumb-Topped Peach Pie (p. 282)	8	364	4	63	12	0	105	329	6	16	10	14	10	14	2	11
Crumb-Topped Pear Pie (p. 282)	8	369	4	64	12	0	105	233	6	3	6	15	11	9	3	12
Crumb-Topped Raspberry Pie (p. 282)	8	347	4	58	12	0	105	195	6	4	22	15	11	12	3	13
Crumb-Topped Rhubarb Pie (p. 282)	8	374	4	65	12	0	108	255	6	4	6	14	9	9	7	11
Crunchy Peach Pie (p. 284)	8	365	7	41	20	72	170	275	10	23	6	13	14	12	4	12
Custard Pie (p. 286)	8	271	8	31	13	143	174	170	12	6	0	12	16	6	11	8
Dark-Chocolate Cream Pie (p. 289)	8	455	9	63	20	144	165	283	14	8	0	12	19	6	14	12
Deep-Dish Apple Pie (p. 284)	8	251	2	42	0	9	67	116	4	0	4	10	6	6	0	6
Deep-Dish Peach Pie (p. 284)	8	258	3	44	9	0	67	273	5	14	10	11	8	12	1	6
Double-Crust Apple Pie (p. 282)	8	359	4	49	17	0	134	124	5	0	4	15	8	9	0	8
Double-Crust Apricot Pie (p. 282)	8	437	5	67	17	0	135	265	8	40	9	17	10	12	2	11
Double-Crust Blackberry Pie (p. 282)	8	384	4	55	17	0	134	175	6	2	20	16	10	11	2	11
Double-Crust Blueberry Pie (p. 282)	8	360	4	49	17	0	138	98	6	1	11	17	10	10	1	9
Double-Crust Cherry Pie (p. 282)	8	424	5	64	17	0	137	203	7	25	11	17	11	12	2	11
Double-Crust Gooseberry Pie (p. 282)	8	404	4	59	17	0	135	183	7	4	25	17	10	10	3	10
Double-Crust Nectarine Pie (p. 282)	8	382	5	53	18	0	134	303	7	19	8	16	11	15	1	9
Double-Crust Peach Pie (p. 282)	8	374	4	53	17	0	134	284	7	14	10	16	11	15	1	9
Double-Crust Pear Pie (p. 282)	8	380	4	54	17	0	134	188	6	0	6	17	11	10	2	10
Double-Crust Raspberry Pie (p. 282)	8	357	4	47	17	0	134	150	7	2	22	16	12	12	2	11
Double-Crust Rhubarb Pie (p. 282)	8	384	4	54	17	0	137	209	7	1	6	16	9	10	6	9
Four-Egg-White Meringue (p. 288)	8	56	2	13	0	0	25	23	3	0	0	0	3	0	0	0
French Silk Pie (p. 292)	10	382	5	34	27	120	216	110	7	12	0	8	8	5	2	9
Fruity Cream Pie (p. 289)	8	271	4	33	13	3	146	151	6	12	1	10	9	6	6	7
Fudge Ribbon Pie (p. 292)	8	503	8	69	24	35	197	279	12	9	0	11	21	6	15	8
Gingersnap Crust (p. 294)	8	150	1	14	10	7	200	85	2	7	0	3	2	2	2	3
Graham Cracker Crust (p. 294)	8	151	1	16	10	0	189	56	2	7	0	1	5	2	1	3
Grasshopper Pie (p. 292)	8	478	3	44	34	89	163	81	4	25	3	4	7	2	6	3
Key Lime Pie (p. 288)	8	388	9	55	15	122	162	257	13	6	6	13	21	6	17	8
Lemon Chess Pie (p. 286)	8	385	5	54	17	138	170	63	8	7	2	10	9	5	2	8

On the divider: Grasshopper Pie (p. 292) and Crumb-Topped Raspberry Pie (p. 282).

Nutrition Analysis

	Servings Per Recipe	Calories	Protein (g)	Carbohydrate (g)	Fat (g)	Cholesterol (mg)	Sodium (mg)	Potassium (mg)	Protein	Vitamin A	Vitamin C	Thiamine	Riboflavin	Niacin	Calcium	Iron
	Per Serving								**Percent U.S. RDA Per Serving**							
Lemon Chiffon Pie (p. 290)	8	315	6	35	17	157	103	80	10	8	8	10	11	5	3	8
Lemon Meringue Pie (p. 288)	8	404	5	67	14	103	143	62	7	4	6	11	9	6	2	8
Maple Pecan Pie (p. 287)	8	518	6	60	30	103	187	183	9	9	0	22	11	6	6	12
Meringue for Pie (p. 288)	8	42	1	9	0	0	19	17	2	0	0	0	2	0	0	0
Milk-Chocolate Cream Pie (p. 289)	8	428	9	59	19	144	165	259	14	8	0	12	19	6	14	11
Mince-Apple Pie (p. 281)	8	513	4	86	18	0	396	324	7	0	6	14	8	9	5	19
Mocha Chiffon Pie (p. 290)	8	304	7	38	15	136	98	119	10	3	0	10	11	6	2	10
Oil Pastry (p. 294)	8	254	4	28	14	0	70	50	6	0	0	16	10	10	2	8
Orange Meringue Pie (p. 288)	8	406	5	68	14	103	143	70	7	5	6	11	9	6	2	8
Parfait Pie (p. 290)	8	307	5	33	18	35	136	132	7	7	4	10	10	5	6	5
Pastry for Double-Crust Pie (p. 294)	8	261	3	24	17	0	134	30	5	0	13	7	8	0	8	0
Pastry for Lattice-Top Pie (p. 294)	8	261	3	24	17	0	134	30	5	0	13	7	8	0	8	0
Pastry for Single-Crust Pie (p. 293)	8	145	2	15	9	0	67	19	3	0	0	8	5	5	0	5
Peach Glacé Pie (p. 285)	8	271	3	47	9	0	67	270	5	14	10	10	8	11	1	6
Peanut Pie (p. 287)	8	556	10	66	29	103	308	207	16	8	0	14	9	22	6	19
Pecan Pastry (p. 293)	8	170	2	16	11	0	67	33	4	0	0	10	5	5	0	5
Pecan Pie (p. 287)	8	538	6	65	30	103	211	115	9	9	0	19	9	6	4	18
Pumpkin Pie (p. 286)	8	291	7	39	12	110	123	241	10	254	4	11	15	7	10	12
Raisin Pie (p. 284)	8	501	6	75	22	0	145	437	9	0	10	20	10	11	5	16
Raspberry Chiffon Pie (p. 291)	8	301	3	40	16	20	209	139	5	12	17	2	9	4	3	4
Sour Cream and Raisin Cream Pie (p. 289)	8	469	9	70	18	151	175	352	14	10	2	14	20	6	16	10
Strawberry Chiffon Pie (p. 291)	8	296	3	39	15	20	209	158	5	12	30	2	9	3	3	4
Vanilla Cream Pie (p. 289)	8	378	8	54	15	144	164	194	13	8	0	12	18	6	13	8
Vanilla-Wafer Crust (p. 294)	8	160	1	13	11	7	146	17	2	8	0	3	3	2	1	2

Pies

For your eating pleasure, here's a taste-tempting array of recipes for fruit, custard, cream, refrigerated, and frozen pies.

Nothing sets off a filling better than a beautifully finished pastry edge. Here are a couple of tips to help you get a perfect fluted edge every time.

To retain a pie's shape during baking, hook the fluted edge over the side of the plate all the way around, or press each flute firmly against the rim.

To keep the edge from burning, cover it with foil during the first part of baking. Start by folding a 12-inch square of aluminum foil into quarters. Cut a quarter circle from the folded corner. Unfold; mold over the edge of the pie. Or mold long narrow strips around the edge. Remove the foil at the time specified in the recipe. Pies that bake 30 minutes or less do not need to be shielded.

Mince-Apple Pie

3 cups thinly sliced, peeled cooking apples (3 medium)
1 28- or 29-ounce jar mincemeat
¼ cup packed brown sugar
2 tablespoons orange juice or brandy
Pastry for Double-Crust Pie (see recipe, page 294)
Milk (optional)
Sugar (optional)
Hard Sauce (see recipe, page 140) (optional)   Oven 375°

Stir together apples, mincemeat, brown sugar, and orange juice. Transfer to a pastry-lined 9-inch pie plate. Cut slits in top crust. Adjust top crust. Seal and flute edge. Brush crust with milk and sprinkle with sugar, if desired. Cover edge of pie with foil. Bake in a 375° oven for 25 minutes. Remove foil. Bake for 25 to 30 minutes more or till pastry is golden and apples are tender. Serve with Hard Sauce, if desired. Makes 8 servings.

Double-Crust Fruit Pie

Fruit-Pie Filling (see chart, opposite)
Flavoring (optional)
Pastry for Double-Crust Pie (see recipe, page 294)
Sugar (optional)   Oven 375°

Mix ingredients for filling, adding flavoring, if desired. Transfer to a pastry-lined 9-inch pie plate. Cut slits in top crust. Adjust top crust. Seal and flute edge. Sprinkle with sugar, if desired. Cover edge with foil. Bake in a 375° oven 25 minutes. Remove foil. Bake for 20 to 25 minutes more or till the top is golden and fruit is tender. (Bake cherry pie for 50 to 60 minutes total.) Serves 8.

Flavoring: Add *one* of the following to filling with the flour: ½ teaspoon *finely shredded lemon peel,* ¼ to ½ teaspoon ground *cinnamon,* ¼ teaspoon ground *allspice or ginger, or* ⅛ teaspoon ground *nutmeg. Or,* add ¼ teaspoon *almond extract* to filling with the fruit.

Crumb-Topped Fruit Pie

Use the smallest amount of sugar recommended for your fruit because the brown-sugar topping also sweetens the pie. (Crumb-Topped Raspberry Pie is pictured on page 279.)

Fruit-Pie Filling (see chart, opposite)
Flavoring (see above) (optional)
Pastry for Single-Crust Pie (see recipe, page 293)
½ **cup all-purpose flour**
½ **cup packed brown sugar**
2 **tablespoons margarine or butter**
   Powdered Sugar Icing (see recipe, page 88) (optional)   Oven 375°

Mix ingredients for filling, adding flavoring, if desired. Transfer filling to a pastry-lined 9-inch pie plate. Combine flour and brown sugar. Cut in margarine till mixture resembles coarse crumbs; sprinkle over filling. Cover edge with foil. Bake in a 375° oven 25 minutes. Remove foil. Bake 20 to 25 minutes more or till top is golden and fruit is tender. (Bake cherry pie for 50 to 60 minutes total.) If desired, drizzle with icing. Serves 8.

For a fluted edge, press with thumb from outside the pie against other thumb and forefinger.

For rope edge, pinch dough, pushing forward at a slant with bent finger and pulling with thumb.

For a petal edge, flute as directed in top photo. Press fork tines lightly into center of each flute.

Making Fruit-Pie Fillings

Use this chart to make fillings for either Double-Crust Fruit Pie or Crumb-Topped Fruit Pie, opposite. For the desired fruit filling, in a large mixing bowl stir together the sugar and flour. Add the fruit and toss till the fruit is coated with the sugar mixture. Continue as directed in recipe.

When making blackberry, blueberry, cherry, peach, raspberry, or rhubarb pies, *frozen* fruit also may be used. If using frozen fruit, toss it with the sugar-flour mixture, then let the mixture stand for 15 to 30 minutes or till the fruit is partially thawed but still icy. Stir well. Transfer to the pastry-lined pie plate. Top filling with pastry or crumb topping as directed in the recipe. Cover edge with foil. Bake for 50 minutes. Remove foil; bake for 20 to 30 minutes more or till the top is golden and the fruit is tender.

Fruit	Amount of Fruit	Sugar	All-Purpose Flour
Apples, peeled, cored, and thinly sliced	6 cups	½ to ¾ cup	1 tablespoon
Apricots, pitted and sliced	4 cups	1¼ cups	⅓ cup
Blackberries	4 cups	¾ to 1 cup	¼ cup
Blueberries	4 cups	½ to ¾ cup	3 tablespoons
Cherries, tart red, pitted	4 cups	1 to 1¼ cups	¼ cup
Gooseberries, stemmed	4 cups	1 cup	¼ cup flour
Nectarines, pitted and thinly sliced	6 cups	½ to ¾ cup	3 tablespoons
Peaches, peeled, pitted, and thinly sliced	6 cups	½ to ¾ cup	3 tablespoons
Pears, peeled, cored, and thinly sliced	6 cups	⅓ to ½ cup	¼ cup
Raspberries	5 cups	½ to ¾ cup	3 tablespoons
Rhubarb, cut into 1-inch pieces	4 cups	1 cup	¼ cup

Deep-Dish Apple Pie

Just spoon the filling into a casserole and top it with pastry for this old-time dessert.

- ½ to ¾ cup sugar
- 3 tablespoons all-purpose flour
- ½ teaspoon ground cinnamon
- ⅛ teaspoon ground allspice
- 6 cups thinly sliced, peeled cooking apples (about 2¼ pounds)
    Pastry for Single-Crust Pie
    (see recipe, page 293)   Oven 375°

In a mixing bowl combine sugar, flour, cinnamon, and allspice. Add apples; toss to coat fruit. Transfer to a 1½-quart casserole.

Prepare Pastry for Single-Crust Pie, *except* roll pastry 1 inch larger than top of casserole. Cut slits in pastry. Place pastry atop apples. Seal and flute to rim of casserole. Cover edges of pie with foil. Place on a baking sheet. Bake in a 375° oven for 25 minutes. Remove foil. Bake for 30 to 35 minutes more or till crust is golden and filling is bubbly. Serve warm or cool. Makes 8 servings.

Deep-Dish Peach Pie: Prepare as above, *except* omit cinnamon and allspice. Substitute 6 cups sliced, peeled *peaches* (3 pounds) for the apples. Sprinkle peaches with ¼ teaspoon *almond extract;* toss with the sugar and flour.

Making Fruit Pies

Follow these simple tips for delicious, picture-perfect fruit pies.
- To avoid messy spills in your oven, set the pie plate on a baking sheet or pizza pan.
- For a prettier double-crust pie, brush the unbaked top with milk, water, or melted margarine or butter, then sprinkle lightly with sugar. Or brush the unbaked top lightly with a beaten egg or milk and skip the sugar.
- Store fruit pies at room temperature up to one day. Refrigerate for longer storage. Cover and refrigerate any pies that contain eggs or dairy products.

Crunchy Peach Pie

Almonds in the crumb topping add the crunch.

- ¾ cup finely crushed vanilla wafers (about 20 wafers)
- ½ cup chopped almonds
- 3 tablespoons margarine *or* butter, melted
    Pastry for Single-Crust Pie
    (see recipe, page 293)
- 2 eggs
- 1 tablespoon lemon juice
- ¼ cup sugar
- 3 16- *or* 17-ounce cans peach slices, pear slices, *or* unpeeled apricot halves, drained and coarsely chopped   Oven 450°

Mix crushed wafers, almonds, and margarine; set aside. Line the bottom of a pastry-lined 9-inch pie plate with a double thickness of foil. Bake in a 450° oven for 5 minutes. Remove foil. Bake 5 minutes more. Meanwhile, beat together eggs and lemon juice; stir in sugar. Fold fruit into egg mixture. Transfer fruit mixture to the partially baked pastry shell. Sprinkle with wafer mixture. Cover edge with foil. Reduce oven temperature to 375°. Bake for 20 minutes. Remove foil; bake for 15 to 20 minutes more or till set. Cool on a wire rack. Cover and chill to store. Serves 8.

Raisin Pie

- ⅔ cup packed brown sugar
- 2 tablespoons cornstarch
- 2 cups raisins
- 1 teaspoon finely shredded orange peel
- ½ cup orange juice
- 2 tablespoons lemon juice
- ½ cup chopped walnuts
    Pastry for Double-Crust Pie
    (see recipe, page 294)   Oven 375°

In a saucepan mix brown sugar and cornstarch. Stir in raisins, peel, orange juice, lemon juice, and 1⅓ cups *cold water.* Cook and stir till bubbly; cook and stir 2 minutes more. Remove from heat; stir in nuts. Transfer to a pastry-lined 9-inch pie plate. Cut slits in top crust. Adjust top crust. Seal and flute edge. Cover edge with foil. Bake in a 375° oven 25 minutes. Remove foil; bake 20 to 25 minutes more or till crust is golden. Serves 8.

Berry Glacé Pie

The flavor of just-picked fruit awaits you in this delicious glazed pie.

8   **cups medium strawberries, *or* 3 cups red raspberries *and* 3 cups sliced, peeled peaches**
⅔   **cup water**
⅔   **cup sugar**
2   **tablespoons cornstarch**
     Several drops red food coloring (optional)
     Baked Pastry Shell (see recipe, page 293)
     Whipped cream (optional)

Remove stems from strawberries. Cut any large strawberries in half lengthwise. Set aside.

For glaze, in a blender container or food processor bowl combine *1 cup* of the strawberries or raspberries and the water. Cover and blend or process till smooth. (If using raspberries, press through a sieve after blending to remove seeds.) Add enough additional water to equal *1½ cups*. In a medium saucepan combine sugar and cornstarch. Stir in blended berry mixture. Cook and stir over medium heat till mixture is thickened and bubbly. Cook and stir for 2 minutes more. Stir in red food coloring, if desired. Cool for 10 minutes without stirring.

Spread about ¼ *cup* of the glaze over bottom and sides of the Baked Pastry Shell. Arrange *half* of the remaining strawberries, stem end down, in pastry shell (or *half* of the remaining raspberries and *half* of the peaches). Carefully spoon *half* of the remaining glaze over fruit, thoroughly covering each piece of fruit. Arrange remaining fruit over first layer. Spoon remaining glaze over fruit, covering each piece. Chill for 1 to 2 hours. (After 2 hours, filling may begin to water out.) Garnish with whipped cream, if desired. Makes 8 servings.

Microwave directions: Prepare strawberries as above. For glaze, blend berries as above. In a 1½-quart casserole combine sugar and cornstarch. Stir in blended berry mixture. Micro-cook, uncovered, on 100% power (high) for 3 to 5 minutes or till thickened and bubbly, stirring every minute. Cook, uncovered, on high for 30 seconds more. Stir in red food coloring, if desired. Cool for 10 minutes without stirring. Assemble and chill pie as above.

Peach Glacé Pie: Prepare as above, *except* substitute 6 cups sliced, peeled peaches for the fruit and omit food coloring.

Cherry Lattice Pie

A ruby red filling enticingly peeks through the lattice crust.

2   **16-ounce cans pitted tart red cherries (water pack)**
1   **cup sugar**
¼   **cup cornstarch**
1   **tablespoon margarine *or* butter**
3   **to 4 drops almond extract**
10 **drops red food coloring (optional)**
     Pastry for Lattice-Top Pie (see recipe, page 294)   Oven 375°

Drain cherries, reserving *1 cup* liquid. In a large saucepan combine ¾ *cup* of the sugar and the cornstarch. Stir in reserved cherry liquid. Cook and stir over medium heat till thickened and bubbly. Cook and stir for 2 minutes more. Remove from heat. Stir in the remaining sugar, margarine or butter, almond extract, and, if desired, food coloring. Stir in cherries. Cool slightly.

Fill a pastry-lined 9-inch pie plate with cherry mixture. Top with lattice crust. Cover edge of pie with foil. Bake in a 375° oven for 25 minutes. Remove foil; bake for 25 to 30 minutes more or till crust is golden. Cool on a wire rack before serving. Makes 8 servings.

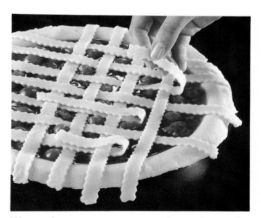

Weave the crosswise strips under and over the lengthwise strips to form a lattice.

Custard Pie

Sweet, silky, and scrumptious.

> **Pastry for Single-Crust Pie
> (see recipe, page 293)**
> 4 **eggs**
> ½ **cup sugar**
> 1 **teaspoon vanilla**
> ⅛ **teaspoon salt**
> 2½ **cups milk**
> **Ground nutmeg**   Oven 450°

Bake pastry shell in a 450° oven for 5 minutes.

For filling, in a bowl beat eggs slightly with a rotary beater or fork till combined. Stir in sugar, vanilla, and salt. Gradually stir in milk. Mix well.

Place the partially baked pastry shell on oven rack. Pour the filling into the pastry shell. Sprinkle with nutmeg. Cover edge of pie with foil. Reduce oven temperature to 350° and bake for 25 minutes. Remove foil. Bake for 15 to 20 minutes more or till a knife inserted near the center comes out clean. Cool pie on a wire rack. Cover and chill to store. Makes 8 servings.

Coconut Custard Pie: Prepare as above, *except* stir in ½ cup toasted *coconut* with the milk. Mix well.

Making Custard Pies

For delicious, velvety, and fuss-free fillings, follow these tips when making custard pies.

● To avoid spills, place the pie shell on the oven rack before adding the filling.
● To check for doneness, gently shake the pie. If the liquid area in the center is smaller than a quarter, the pie is done. The filling will continue to set after you remove the pie from the oven. *Or,* insert a knife near the pie's center. If the knife comes out clean, the pie is done. The knife test may cause the filling to crack.
● After the pie cools, cover and refrigerate till serving time. Cover and chill leftovers, too.

Lemon Chess Pie

This sweet yet tart pie hails from the South.

> **Pastry for Single-Crust Pie
> (see recipe, page 293)**
> 4 **eggs**
> 1½ **cups sugar**
> ¼ **cup margarine *or* butter, melted**
> 2 **teaspoons finely shredded lemon
>   peel**
> 2 **tablespoons lemon juice**
> 1 **tablespoon cornmeal**
> 1½ **teaspoons vanilla**   Oven 450°

Line bottom of a pastry-lined 9-inch pie plate with a double thickness of foil. Bake in a 450° oven for 5 minutes. Remove foil. Bake for 5 minutes more.

For filling, in a bowl beat eggs lightly till combined. Stir in sugar, margarine, peel, lemon juice, cornmeal, and vanilla. Mix well. Place pastry shell on the oven rack. Pour filling into shell.

Cover edge of pie with foil. Reduce oven temperature to 350° and bake for 20 minutes. Remove foil. Bake for 15 to 20 minutes more or till a knife inserted near the center comes out clean. Cool on a rack. Cover and chill to store. Serves 8.

Pumpkin Pie

> 1 **16-ounce can pumpkin**
> ⅔ **cup sugar**
> 1 **teaspoon ground cinnamon**
> ½ **teaspoon ground ginger**
> ½ **teaspoon ground nutmeg**
> 3 **eggs**
> 1 **5-ounce can (⅔ cup) evaporated
>   milk**
> ½ **cup milk**
> **Pastry for Single-Crust Pie
> (see recipe, page 293)**   Oven 375°

For filling, in a mixing bowl combine pumpkin, sugar, cinnamon, ginger, and nutmeg. Add eggs. Beat lightly with a rotary beater or fork. Gradually stir in evaporated milk and milk. Mix well.

Place a pastry-lined 9-inch pie plate on the oven rack; pour in filling. Cover edge with foil. Bake in a 375° oven for 25 minutes. Remove foil; bake about 25 minutes more or till a knife inserted near the center comes out clean. Cool on a wire rack. Serve with whipped cream, if desired. Cover and chill to store. Makes 8 servings.

Brown Sugar and Rhubarb Pie

Pastry for Single-Crust Pie
(see recipe, page 293)
1 to 1¼ cups packed brown sugar
¼ cup all-purpose flour
4 cups finely chopped rhubarb
(1 pound) *or* one 16-ounce
package frozen unsweetened
sliced rhubarb
3 eggs
Meringue for Pie (see
recipe page 288)   Oven 450°

Bake pastry in a 450° oven for 5 minutes.

For filling, in a mixing bowl combine brown sugar and flour. Add rhubarb; toss to coat. Let stand for 15 minutes (30 minutes for frozen rhubarb), stirring once or twice.

Separate egg yolks from whites; set whites aside for meringue. Beat egg yolks slightly with a fork. Stir yolks into rhubarb mixture. Transfer rhubarb mixture to the partially baked pastry shell. Cover edge of pie with foil. Reduce oven temperature to 375°. Bake for 25 minutes. (If using frozen rhubarb, bake 45 minutes.) Remove foil; bake for 20 to 25 minutes more or till filling is nearly set. (Pie will appear soft in the center but will become firmer upon cooling.)

Spread meringue over hot filling, sealing to edge of pastry. Reduce oven temperature to 350°. Bake for 12 to 15 minutes or till golden. Cool on rack. Cover and chill to store. Serves 8.

Easy as Pie

For easy pies, use frozen fruit and partially prepared pastries.

Packaged frozen fruit comes already peeled, sliced, or pitted. And with frozen fruit, you can enjoy a fresh-baked fruit pie anytime of the year.

Check your supermarket, too, for frozen unbaked pastry shells and folded frozen or refrigerated piecrusts. Each package of pastry shells has two shells and each package of frozen or refrigerated piecrusts contains enough for one double-crust pie or two one-crust pies.

Pecan Pie

We offer three variations of this favorite pie— Maple Pecan, Peanut, and Coconut-Oatmeal. (Pecan Pie is pictured below.)

3 eggs
1 cup corn syrup
⅔ cup sugar
⅓ cup margarine *or* butter, melted
1 teaspoon vanilla
1¼ cups pecan halves
Pastry for Single-Crust
Pie (see recipe,
page 293)   Oven 350°

For filling, in a mixing bowl beat eggs lightly with a rotary beater or a fork till combined. Stir in corn syrup, sugar, margarine or butter, and vanilla. Stir well. Stir in pecan halves.

Place a pastry-lined 9-inch pie plate on the oven rack. Pour the filling into the pastry-lined pie plate. Cover edge of pie with foil. Bake in a 350° oven for 25 minutes.

Remove foil; bake for 20 to 25 minutes more or till a knife inserted near the center comes out clean. Cool pie on a wire rack. Cover and chill to store. Makes 8 servings.

Maple Pecan Pie: Prepare as above, *except* substitute *maple syrup or maple-flavored syrup* for the corn syrup.

Peanut Pie: Prepare as above, *except* substitute coarsely chopped *peanuts, macadamia nuts, or cashews* for the pecans.

Coconut-Oatmeal Pie: Prepare as above, *except* substitute ¾ cup *coconut* and ½ cup *quick-cooking rolled oats* for the pecans.

Lemon Meringue Pie

A refreshingly tangy dessert.

1½ **cups sugar**
 3 **tablespoons all-purpose flour**
 3 **tablespoons cornstarch**
 3 **eggs**
 2 **tablespoons margarine *or* butter**
 1 **to 2 teaspoons finely shredded**
    lemon peel
 ⅓ **cup lemon juice**
    Baked Pastry Shell
    (see recipe, page 293)
    Meringue for Pie (see
    recipe, below right)   Oven 350°

For filling, in a medium saucepan combine sugar, flour, cornstarch, and dash *salt*. Gradually stir in 1½ cups *water*. Cook and stir over medium-high heat till thickened and bubbly. Reduce heat; cook and stir for 2 minutes more. Remove from heat.

Separate egg yolks from whites; set whites aside for meringue. Beat egg yolks slightly. Gradually stir *1 cup* of the hot filling into yolks; return all to saucepan. Bring to a gentle boil. Cook and stir 2 minutes more. Remove from heat. Stir in margarine and lemon peel. Gradually stir in lemon juice, gently mixing well. Pour hot filling into Baked Pastry Shell. Spread meringue over hot filling; seal to edge. Bake in a 350° oven for 12 to 15 minutes or till meringue is golden. Cool on a wire rack. Cover and chill to store. Serves 8.

Orange Meringue Pie: Prepare as above, *except* substitute 1 tablespoon *finely shredded orange peel* for the lemon peel and *orange juice* for the lemon juice. If desired, add 2 drops red food coloring and 1 drop yellow food coloring with the orange juice.

Serving Cream Pies

Cool cream pies for four to six hours before serving. For longer storage, cover and refrigerate. To cover meringue-topped pies, insert toothpicks halfway between the centers and edges of the pies. Loosely cover with clear plastic wrap. When cutting cream pies, dip your knife into water.

Key Lime Pie

Although named for a variety of lime grown on the Florida Keys, our version tastes great with any type of lime.

 3 **eggs**
 1 **14½-ounce can (1¼ cups)**
    ***sweetened condensed* milk**
1½ **teaspoons finely shredded lime peel**
 ⅓ **cup lime juice**
    Baked Pastry Shell
    (see recipe, page 293)
    Meringue for Pie
    (see recipe, below)   Oven 350°

Separate egg yolks from whites; set whites aside for meringue. In a bowl beat yolks till thick and lemon colored. Stir in condensed milk and lime peel. Gradually add lime juice, beating at low speed just till combined. *Do not overbeat.* Stir in green food coloring, if desired.

Spoon lime mixture into pastry shell. Spread meringue over filling; seal to edge. Bake in a 350° oven for 12 to 15 minutes or till meringue is golden. Cool. Cover and chill to store. Serves 8.

Creamy Key Lime Pie: Prepare as above, *except* substitute 2 *whole eggs* for the yolks and omit meringue. Beat eggs till slightly thickened. Stir in condensed milk, peel, and juice. Spoon into pastry shell. Cover and chill about 4 hours or till firm. Serve with whipped cream, if desired.

Meringue for Pie

 3 **egg whites**
 ½ **teaspoon vanilla**
 ¼ **teaspoon cream of tartar**
 6 **tablespoons sugar**

Bring egg whites to room temperature. In a mixing bowl combine egg whites, vanilla, and cream of tartar. Beat with an electric mixer on medium speed about 1 minute or till soft peaks form (tips curl). Gradually add sugar, *1 tablespoon* at a time, beating on high speed about 4 minutes more or till mixture forms stiff, glossy peaks and sugar dissolves. Immediately spread meringue over pie, carefully sealing to edge of pastry to prevent shrinkage. Bake as directed in pie recipe.

Four-Egg-White Meringue: Prepare as above, *except* use *4* egg whites, *1 teaspoon* vanilla, *½ teaspoon* cream of tartar, and *½ cup* sugar. Beat about 5 minutes till stiff, glossy peaks form.

Vanilla Cream Pie

If you like, skip the meringue and top the filling with whipped cream.

¾ **cup sugar**
¼ **cup cornstarch *or* ½ cup all-purpose flour**
3 **cups milk**
4 **eggs**
1 **tablespoon margarine *or* butter**
1½ **teaspoons vanilla**
**Baked Pastry Shell
(see recipe, page 293)
Four-Egg-White Meringue
(see recipe, opposite)**   Oven 350°

For filling, in a medium saucepan combine sugar and cornstarch or flour. Gradually stir in milk. Cook and stir over medium-high heat till mixture is thickened and bubbly. Reduce heat; cook and stir for 2 minutes more. Remove from heat.

Separate egg yolks from whites; set whites aside for meringue. Beat egg yolks lightly with a fork. Gradually stir about *1 cup* of the hot filling into yolks. Return all to saucepan; bring to a gentle boil. Cook and stir for 2 minutes more. Remove from heat. Stir in margarine or butter and vanilla. Pour the hot filling into Baked Pastry Shell. Spread meringue over hot filling; seal to edge. Bake in a 350° oven for 12 to 15 minutes or till golden. Cool on a wire rack. Cover and chill to store. Makes 8 servings.

Coconut Cream Pie: Prepare as above, *except* stir in 1 cup flaked *coconut* with margarine or butter and vanilla. Sprinkle another ⅓ cup flaked *coconut* over meringue before baking.

Banana Cream Pie: Prepare as above, *except,* before adding filling, spread 3 medium *bananas,* sliced (about 2¼ cups), into the bottom of the Baked Pastry Shell.

Dark-Chocolate Cream Pie: Prepare as above, *except* increase the sugar to *1 cup.* Stir in 3 squares (3 ounces) *unsweetened chocolate,* chopped, with the milk.

Milk-Chocolate Cream Pie: Prepare as above, *except* stir in 3 squares (3 ounces) *semisweet chocolate,* chopped, with the milk.

Sour Cream and Raisin Cream Pie: Prepare as above, *except* increase cornstarch to ⅓ cup (or increase flour to ⅔ cup). Fold in 1 cup *raisins* and ½ cup dairy *sour cream* with the margarine or butter and vanilla.

Fruity Cream Pie

In a medium saucepan cook one 4-serving-size package *regular vanilla pudding mix* according to package directions, *except* use only 1¼ cups *milk.* Remove from heat. Drain and chop one 8¾-ounce can unpeeled *apricot* halves *or peach* slices, *or* drain one 8¼-ounce can crushed *pineapple.* Stir drained fruit and 2 tablespoons light *rum or brandy* into pudding. Cover surface with clear plastic wrap; cool to room temperature without stirring. Fold one 4-ounce container frozen *whipped dessert topping,* thawed, into pudding mixture. Pour into a *Baked Pastry Shell* (see recipe, page 293). Cover and chill several hours. If desired, garnish with toasted coconut. Serves 8.

◄ Pour the filling from the saucepan into the Baked Pastry Shell.

Using a spatula, spread the meringue over the hot filling, sealing it to the pastry shell.

Black-Bottom Pie

1 **envelope unflavored gelatin**
1 **cup sugar**
1 **tablespoon cornstarch**
2 **cups milk**
4 **slightly beaten egg yolks**
1 **teaspoon vanilla**
1 **6-ounce package (1 cup)**
   semisweet chocolate pieces
   Baked Pastry Shell
   (see recipe, page 293)
2 **tablespoons rum** *or* **½ teaspoon**
   rum extract
4 **egg whites**

Soften gelatin in ¼ cup *cold water;* set aside. In a saucepan combine ½ *cup* of the sugar and the cornstarch. Stir in milk and egg yolks. Cook and stir till bubbly. Cook and stir 2 minutes more. Remove from heat; stir in vanilla. Divide mixture in half. Add chocolate to one portion, stirring till melted. Pour into pastry shell. Chill. Stir softened gelatin into remaining *hot* mixture till gelatin dissolves. Stir in rum. Chill to the consistency of corn syrup, stirring occasionally. Remove from refrigerator (gelatin mixture will continue to set). Immediately beat egg whites till soft peaks form. Gradually add remaining sugar, beating till stiff peaks form. When gelatin is partially set (consistency of unbeaten egg whites), fold in stiff-beaten whites. Chill till mixture mounds when spooned. Spoon into shell. Chill 8 hours or till set. Serves 8.

Lemon Chiffon Pie

In a saucepan combine 1 envelope *unflavored gelatin* and ½ cup *sugar.* Beat together 4 slightly beaten *egg yolks,* ½ cup *water,* and ½ cup *lemon juice.* Stir into gelatin mixture. Cook and stir till mixture boils and gelatin dissolves. Remove from heat. Stir in 1 teaspoon *finely shredded lemon peel.* Chill to consistency of corn syrup, stirring occasionally. Remove from refrigerator (mixture will continue to set). Immediately beat 4 *egg whites* till soft peaks form. Gradually add ¼ cup *sugar,* beating till stiff peaks form. When gelatin is partially set (consistency of unbeaten egg whites), fold in stiff-beaten whites. Beat ½ cup *whipping cream* till soft peaks form. Fold into gelatin mixture. Chill till mixture mounds when spooned. Spoon into *Baked Pastry Shell* (see recipe, page 293). Chill for 4 hours or till firm. Serves 8.

Chocolate Chiffon Pie

4 **egg yolks**
1 **teaspoon vanilla**
½ **cup sugar**
1 **envelope unflavored gelatin**
2 **squares (2 ounces) unsweetened**
   chocolate, melted
4 **egg whites**
⅓ **cup sugar**
   Baked Pastry Shell
   (see recipe, page 293)

Beat egg yolks and vanilla about 5 minutes or till thick and lemon colored. In a saucepan combine the ½ cup sugar and gelatin. Stir in ¾ cup *cold water.* Cook and stir till gelatin dissolves. Stir in chocolate. Cook and stir till mixture boils and is smooth. Pour gelatin mixture in a thin stream into yolk mixture, beating constantly. Chill to consistency of corn syrup, stirring occasionally.

Remove from refrigerator (gelatin mixture will continue to set). Immediately beat egg whites till soft peaks form. Gradually add the ⅓ cup sugar, beating till stiff peaks form. When gelatin is partially set (consistency of unbeaten egg whites), fold in stiff-beaten whites. Chill till mixture mounds when spooned. Spoon into pastry shell. Cover and chill for 8 hours or till set. Serves 8.

Mocha Chiffon Pie: Prepare as above, *except* stir in 3 to 4 teaspoons *instant coffee crystals* with the water.

Parfait Pie

1 **teaspoon finely shredded**
   orange peel
¼ **cup orange juice**
1 **3-ounce package flavored**
   gelatin (any flavor)
1 **pint vanilla ice cream**
½ **cup whipping cream**
   Baked Pastry Shell
   (see recipe, page 293)

Bring orange juice and ½ cup *water* to boiling. Add gelatin; stir to dissolve. Stir in orange peel. Add ice cream, a spoonful at a time, stirring till melted. Chill, if necessary, till partially set (consistency of unbeaten egg whites). Whip cream; fold into gelatin mixture. Chill till the mixture mounds when spooned. Spoon into pastry shell. Chill for 5 to 24 hours or till set. Serves 8.

Strawberry Chiffon Pie

Sample the summertime pleasure of fresh berries and cream in this light and airy pie.

2½ cups fresh strawberries
¼ cup sugar
1 tablespoon lemon juice
¼ cup sugar
1 envelope unflavored gelatin
⅔ cup water
2 egg whites
¼ cup sugar
½ cup whipping cream
Graham Cracker Crust (see recipe, page 294) *or* Baked Pastry Shell (see recipe, page 293)
Whipped cream (optional)

Reserve a few strawberries for garnish.

In a mixing bowl crush enough of the remaining strawberries with a potato masher, pastry blender, or fork to measure *1¼ cups. (Do not use a food processor or blender.)* Stir in ¼ cup sugar and the lemon juice; set aside.

In a small saucepan stir together ¼ cup sugar and the gelatin. Stir in the water. Cook and stir over low heat till sugar and gelatin dissolve. Remove from heat. Cool.

Stir the cooled gelatin mixture into the strawberry mixture. Chill to the consistency of corn syrup, stirring occasionally (about 1 hour). Remove from the refrigerator (gelatin mixture will continue to set).

Immediately beat the egg whites with an electric mixer on high speed till soft peaks form (tips curl). Gradually add ¼ cup sugar, beating till stiff peaks form (tips stand straight). When gelatin is partially set (the consistency of unbeaten egg whites), fold in the stiff-beaten egg whites.

Beat the ½ cup whipping cream till soft peaks form. Fold whipped cream into strawberry mixture. Chill till mixture mounds when spooned (about 1 hour). Pile into Graham Cracker Crust or Baked Pastry Shell. Chill pie about 8 hours or till firm. Garnish with the reserved strawberries. Serve with additional whipped cream, if desired. Makes 8 servings.

Raspberry Chiffon Pie: Prepare as above, *except* substitute fresh *red raspberries* for the strawberries.

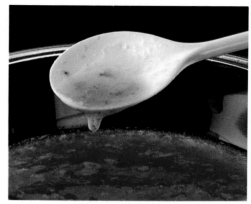

Chill the strawberry-gelatin mixture till it's as thick as corn syrup. Remove from the refrigerator.

Let the mixture stand at room temperature till it's the consistency of unbeaten egg whites.

Chill the filling till it mounds when dropped from a spoon. Pile filling into the cooled crust.

Fudge Ribbon Pie

> 2 squares (2 ounces) unsweetened
>   chocolate, cut up
> 2 tablespoons margarine *or* butter
> 1 cup sugar
> 1 5-ounce can (⅔ cup) evaporated
>   milk
> 1 teaspoon vanilla
> 1 quart peppermint ice cream
>   Baked Pastry Shell
>   (see recipe, opposite)
>   Meringue for Pie
>   (see recipe, page 288)
> ¼ cup crushed peppermint
>   candy   Oven 475°

For sauce, melt chocolate and margarine. Stir in sugar. Gradually stir in evaporated milk. Heat just to boiling; reduce heat. Boil gently about 5 minutes or till slightly thickened, stirring often. Stir in vanilla. Cover with plastic wrap; cool.

Stir ice cream to soften. Spoon *half* of the ice cream into the pastry shell. Spread *half* of the sauce over the ice-cream layer. Repeat layers. Cover; freeze at least 8 hours.

To serve, prepare meringue. Fold *3 tablespoons* of the crushed candy into meringue. Spread meringue over frozen pie, carefully sealing to pastry edge. Bake in a 475° oven for 3 to 5 minutes or till golden. Sprinkle with remaining candy. Serve *immediately.* Makes 8 servings.

French Silk Pie

Tastes like chocolate fudge in a pie shell.

> 1 cup sugar
> ¾ cup butter (*not* margarine)
> 3 squares (3 ounces) unsweetened
>   chocolate, melted and cooled
> 1 teaspoon vanilla
> 3 eggs
>   Baked Pastry Shell
>   (see recipe, opposite)

In a bowl beat sugar and butter with an electric mixer on medium speed about 4 minutes or till fluffy. Stir in chocolate and vanilla. Add eggs, one at a time, beating on high speed after each addition and scraping sides of bowl constantly. Transfer to Baked Pastry Shell. Cover; chill for 5 to 24 hours or till set. If desired, top with unsweetened whipped cream and chocolate curls. Serves 10.

Grasshopper Pie

For easier serving, wrap a warm, damp cloth around the pie plate to loosen the crumb crust. (Pictured on page 279.)

>   Chocolate-Wafer Crust (see recipe,
>   page 294)
> 1 7-ounce jar marshmallow creme
> ¼ cup green crème de menthe
> 2 tablespoons white crème de cacao
> 2 cups whipping cream
>   Whipped cream (optional)
>   Chocolate curls (optional)

Chill Chocolate-Wafer Crust at least 30 minutes. Meanwhile, in a mixing bowl combine the marshmallow creme, crème de menthe, and crème de cacao. Beat with an electric mixer on low speed till smooth. Whip cream till soft peaks form. Fold whipped cream into marshmallow creme mixture. Spoon filling into chilled crust. Freeze at least 5 hours (pie will not freeze firm). Garnish with additional whipped cream and chocolate curls, if desired. Makes 8 servings.

Pastry Know-How

Before picking up your rolling pin, read these tips.
- For a pie or crust that will be baked, select a glass pie plate or dull metal pie pan. Use shiny metal pans, which keep crusts from browning properly, only for crumb crusts that are not baked.
- Measure accurately. Too much flour makes pastry tough, too much shortening makes pastry greasy and crumbly, and too much water makes pastry tough and soggy.
- To roll the dough with little sticking, use a stockinette cover for your rolling pin and a pastry cloth.
- If the pastry is baked without filling, prick it well with a fork. This prevents it from puffing up. (Do not prick pastry if the filling is baked in the crust.)
- After baking, cool pie on a wire rack. Allowing air to circulate under the pie keeps the crust from becoming soggy.

Pastry for Single-Crust Pie

1¼ cups all-purpose flour
¼ teaspoon salt
⅓ cup shortening or lard
3 to 4 tablespoons cold water

In a mixing bowl stir together flour and salt. Cut in shortening or lard till pieces are the size of small peas.

Sprinkle *1 tablespoon* of the water over part of the mixture; gently toss with a fork. Push to side of bowl. Repeat till all is moistened. Form dough into a ball.

On a lightly floured surface, flatten dough with hands. Roll dough from center to edges, forming a circle about 12 inches in diameter. Wrap pastry around rolling pin. Unroll onto a 9-inch pie plate. Ease pastry into pie plate, being careful not to stretch pastry.

Trim to ½ inch beyond edge of pie plate; fold under extra pastry. Make a fluted, rope-shape, or scalloped edge. *Do not prick pastry.* Bake as directed in individual recipes.

Microwave Pastry for Single-Crust Pie: In a mixing bowl stir together flour, ¼ teaspoon *baking powder,* and salt. Prepare, roll, and trim pastry as above. Prick bottom and sides generously with the tines of a fork. Prick where bottom and sides meet all around pie shell.

Micro-cook, uncovered, on 100% power (high) for 5 to 7 minutes or till pastry is dry and air bubbles form, giving dish a quarter-turn once. Cool on a wire rack. Use in recipes calling for a baked pastry shell.

Baked Pastry Shell: Prepare as above, *except* prick bottom and sides of pastry generously with the tines of a fork. Prick where bottom and sides meet all around pie shell. Bake in a 450° oven for 10 to 12 minutes or till golden. Cool on a wire rack.

Pecan Pastry: Prepare as above, *except,* before adding water, stir ¼ cup finely chopped *pecans* into flour mixture.

Cocoa Pastry: Prepare as above, *except* stir 2 tablespoons *unsweetened cocoa powder* and 2 tablespoons *sugar* in with the flour and salt. Increase shortening to ½ cup.

Cinnamon Pastry: Prepare as above, *except* stir 1 teaspoon ground *cinnamon* in with the flour and salt.

Use a pastry blender to cut in the shortening or lard till the pieces are the size of small peas.

Loosely unroll pastry from the rolling pin, easing it into the pie plate. Avoid stretching the pastry.

Trim pastry to ½ inch beyond edge of pie plate. Fold under the extra pastry to build up the edge.

Pastry for Double-Crust Pie

      2 **cups all-purpose flour**
    ½ **teaspoon salt**
    ⅔ **cup shortening *or* lard**
      6 **to 7 tablespoons cold water**

In a mixing bowl stir together flour and salt. Cut in shortening or lard till pieces are the size of small peas. Sprinkle *1 tablespoon* of the water over part of mixture; gently toss with a fork. Push to side of bowl. Repeat till all is moistened. Divide dough in half. Form each half into a ball.

On a lightly floured surface, flatten one ball of dough with hands. Roll dough from center to edges, forming a circle about 12 inches in diameter. Wrap pastry around rolling pin. Unroll onto a 9-inch pie plate. Ease pastry into pie plate, being careful not to stretch pastry. Trim pastry even with rim of pie plate .

For top crust, roll remaining dough. Cut slits to allow steam to escape. Fill pastry in pie plate with desired filling. Place top crust on filling. Trim top crust ½ inch beyond edge of plate. Fold top crust under bottom crust; flute edge. Bake as directed in individual recipes.

Electric-Mixer Pastry for Double-Crust Pie: In a mixing bowl combine flour and the salt; add shortening. Beat with an electric mixer on low speed till pieces are the size of small peas. Add *6 tablespoons cold* water; beat at low speed just till dough clings together (15 to 20 seconds). Continue as above.

Pastry for Lattice-Top Pie: Prepare as above, *except* trim bottom pastry to ½ inch beyond edge of pie plate. Cut top pastry into ½-inch-wide strips. Fill pastry in pie plate with desired filling. Weave strips atop filling to make a lattice. Press ends of strips into rim of crust. Fold bottom pastry over strips; seal and flute edge. Bake as directed in individual recipes.

Cheese Pastry: Prepare as above, *except* add 1 cup shredded *cheddar cheese* to flour.

Coconut Crust

Oven 325°

Mix 2 cups flaked *coconut* and 3 tablespoons melted *margarine or butter*. Press firmly onto bottom and sides of a 9-inch pie plate. Bake in a 325° oven 20 minutes or till edge is golden. Cool before filling. Use for chiffon or ice-cream pies.

Oil Pastry

    2¼ **cups all-purpose flour**
    ¼ **teaspoon salt**
    ½ **cup cooking oil**
    ⅓ **cup cold milk**

In a mixing bowl stir together flour and salt. Pour oil and milk into a measuring cup (*do not stir*); add all at once to flour mixture. Stir lightly with a fork. Form into 2 balls; flatten slightly with hands.

Cut waxed paper into four 12-inch squares. Place each ball of dough between 2 squares of paper. Roll each ball of dough into a circle to edges of paper. (Dampen work surface with a little water to prevent paper from slipping.)

Peel off top papers and fit dough, paper side up, into 9-inch pie plates. (*Or,* reserve one portion for use as a top crust.) Remove paper. Continue as directed for Pastry for Double- or Single-Crust Pie (see recipes, left and page 293). Makes one 9-inch double-crust pastry or two 9-inch single-crust pastries.

Graham Cracker Crust

    ⅓ **cup margarine *or* butter**
    ¼ **cup sugar**
    1¼ **cups finely crushed graham**
          crackers (about
          18 crackers)   Oven 375°

Melt margarine or butter. Stir in sugar. Add crushed graham crackers. Toss to mix well. Spread mixture evenly into a 9-inch pie plate. Press onto bottom and sides to form a firm, even crust. Chill about 1 hour or till firm. (*Or,* bake in a 375° oven for 4 to 5 minutes or till edge is lightly browned. Cool on a wire rack before filling.)

Chocolate-Wafer Crust: Prepare as above, *except* omit the sugar and substitute 1½ cups finely crushed *chocolate wafers* (25 wafers) for the crushed graham crackers. *Do not bake.*

Gingersnap Crust: Prepare as above, *except* omit the sugar and substitute 1¼ cups finely crushed *gingersnaps* (20 to 22 cookies) for the crushed graham crackers.

Vanilla-Wafer Crust: Prepare as above, *except* omit the sugar and substitute 1½ cups finely crushed *vanilla wafers* (36 to 40 wafers) for the crushed graham crackers. Chill about 1 hour or till firm. (*Or,* bake in a 375° oven for 7 to 10 minutes or till edge is golden. Cool on a wire rack before filling.)

Poultry

Nutrition Analysis

	Per Serving							Percent U.S. RDA Per Serving							
	Servings Per Recipe / Calories	Protein (g)	Carbohydrate (g)	Fat (g)	Cholesterol (mg)	Sodium (mg)	Potassium (mg)	Protein	Vitamin A	Vitamin C	Thiamine	Riboflavin	Niacin	Calcium	Iron
Apricot-Wild-Rice Stuffing (p. 324)	6	88	3	20	0	0	105	308	4	16	3	6	10	11	2	7
Beer Batter-Fried Chicken (p. 310)	6	367	26	14	22	118	472	232	40	2	0	11	14	42	2	10
Biscuit-Topped Chicken Potpies (p. 316)	6	358	27	24	17	65	880	463	41	86	18	20	20	48	9	15
Bulgur Pilaf Stuffing (p. 324)	6	85	4	11	3	7	218	209	6	58	6	8	3	6	2	4
Cheesy Chicken à la King (p. 316)	4	484	34	22	29	97	1181	554	52	27	15	16	34	45	35	13
Cheesy Chicken Kiev (p. 304)	4	376	43	11	17	181	262	347	66	9	2	12	15	82	18	12
Chestnut Stuffing (p. 323)	8	284	6	36	13	1	457	255	8	11	14	15	10	10	5	10
Chicken à la King (p. 316)	4	379	28	21	20	71	777	508	43	20	15	15	28	45	17	13
Chicken and Dumplings (p. 315)	6	296	27	21	11	73	292	448	41	231	8	16	16	45	9	13
Chicken and Noodles (p. 315)	6	263	27	20	7	107	605	345	42	116	4	16	16	44	4	14
Chicken-Asparagus Stacks (p. 319)	4	466	36	27	24	347	886	651	56	32	28	16	33	40	19	17
Chicken Cacciatore (p. 313)	6	306	29	23	9	77	515	580	44	13	15	14	17	50	5	14
Chicken-Cheese Crepes (p. 318)	6	397	27	25	21	125	640	472	41	59	25	20	26	31	30	14
Chicken Country Captain (p. 314)	6	277	26	23	8	73	387	434	40	14	31	12	11	44	5	15
Chicken Dijon (p. 304)	4	406	30	31	17	98	412	312	46	11	0	16	10	65	6	11
Chicken Divan (p. 319)	4	387	25	10	27	94	397	368	39	41	38	8	19	29	29	9
Chicken Enchiladas (p. 317)	4	576	33	39	33	104	936	456	51	71	22	14	24	42	43	20
Chicken Fricassee (p. 312)	6	308	29	20	12	99	296	368	47	17	20	14	18	50	4	13
Chicken Jambalaya (p. 318)	4	339	25	31	12	62	829	583	39	20	34	17	12	48	7	16
Chicken Kabobs (p. 301)	4	333	30	42	3	72	595	488	46	48	103	19	9	67	4	16
Chicken Kiev (p. 304)	4	419	39	11	24	197	332	340	59	14	2	11	13	82	4	12
Chicken Livers Stroganoff (p. 307)	4	499	29	34	26	528	305	564	44	475	50	27	149	66	10	62
Chicken Marsala (p. 306)	4	266	28	8	12	72	300	337	43	9	3	9	13	65	2	9
Chicken Nuggets (p. 303)	4	505	43	35	22	103	639	364	66	9	0	23	19	89	15	16
Chicken Paprikash (p. 312)	6	365	29	19	18	109	213	391	45	20	4	13	17	46	7	12
Chicken Potpies (p. 316)	6	633	30	46	37	65	817	485	46	86	25	33	27	55	9	22
Chicken Saltimbocca (p. 305)	4	583	44	27	33	151	563	517	68	28	8	25	28	71	40	13
Chicken Submarines (p. 319)	4	478	29	36	24	92	829	474	45	22	7	21	25	38	25	16
Chicken with Cashews (p. 308)	4	558	36	45	26	72	588	694	55	2	4	20	18	72	5	25
Chicken with Papaya (p. 310)	4	473	31	38	22	72	349	543	47	16	37	18	9	67	6	14
Chicken with Walnuts (p. 308)	4	553	35	39	29	72	840	593	53	7	92	24	12	69	6	21
Chili Chicken Nuggets (p. 303)	4	379	41	16	16	103	486	369	63	16	1	10	11	80	14	10
Coq au Vin (p. 313)	6	389	29	21	17	94	192	442	44	120	7	14	17	48	4	14
Corn Bread and Bacon Stuffing (p. 324)	8	201	7	26	7	99	528	201	12	5	6	11	11	9	7	10
Cornmeal Batter-Fried Chicken (p. 311)	6	402	27	17	24	120	274	272	42	4	0	12	16	42	6	11
Cranberry-Sauced Turkey Steaks (p. 302)	4	257	27	19	8	71	380	331	41	5	14	5	9	33	3	9
Cream Gravy (p. 324)	6	89	3	5	6	9	96	108	4	3	1	3	7	1	8	1
Crispy Barbecue-Style Oven-Fried Chicken (p. 303)	6	258	25	7	14	73	534	225	38	10	1	6	11	40	3	8
Crisp-Fried Chicken (p. 307)	6	215	24	4	11	73	251	212	37	5	0	6	10	39	2	7
Curried Chicken à la King (p. 316)	4	387	28	24	20	71	784	524	43	20	15	15	28	45	18	14
Curry-and-Parsley Oven-Fried Chicken (p. 303)	6	266	25	7	15	73	263	227	38	8	0	7	11	40	2	10
Four-Way Chicken with Barbecue Sauce (p. 299)	6	259	26	16	10	73	557	370	38	14	10	6	11	39	3	10

On the divider: Four-Way Chicken (grilled version) with Ginger-Honey Glaze (p. 299).

		Per Serving							Percent U.S. RDA Per Serving							

Nutrition Analysis

	Servings Per Recipe	Calories	Protein (g)	Carbohydrate (g)	Fat (g)	Cholesterol (mg)	Sodium (mg)	Potassium (mg)	Protein	Vitamin A	Vitamin C	Thiamine	Riboflavin	Niacin	Calcium	Iron
Four-Way Chicken with Cumberland Sauce (p. 299)	6	242	24	11	10	73	140	243	36	4	8	5	9	37	2	7
Four-Way Chicken with Ginger-Honey Glaze (p. 299)	6	227	24	10	10	73	209	262	36	4	0	16	11	37	1	6
Fruit-Sauced Chicken Breasts (p. 306)	4	376	29	43	9	72	198	465	45	20	27	12	7	65	3	13
Garlic Chicken (p. 308)	4	365	31	35	10	72	583	515	47	0	6	16	15	70	5	14
Garlic Chicken with Zucchini (p. 308)	4	370	31	36	10	72	584	596	48	3	9	18	15	71	5	15
Giblet Gravy (p. 325)	8	84	2	3	7	28	20	13	3	8	1	2	4	2	0	3
Giblet Stuffing (p. 323)	8	254	10	22	14	84	467	168	15	34	2	12	17	13	5	15
Ginger Chicken (p. 309)	4	375	31	35	10	72	618	561	48	197	41	20	12	69	10	17
Glazed Chicken and Vegetables (p. 320)	6	408	26	49	13	73	426	721	40	410	20	13	13	45	5	12
Harvest Stuffing (p. 323)	8	331	8	35	18	2	563	247	12	87	4	17	11	13	8	13
Herb and Onion Stuffing (p. 323)	8	226	5	23	13	1	444	130	7	12	5	12	7	8	5	9
Herb-Crumb-Topped Chicken Potpies (p. 316)	6	407	29	31	19	66	991	487	44	90	18	20	21	48	11	16
Herbed Batter-Fried Chicken (p. 311)	6	402	27	17	24	120	274	272	42	4	0	12	16	42	6	11
Herbed Chicken à la King (p. 316)	4	381	28	22	20	71	778	526	43	21	22	16	29	46	18	13
Herb-Marinated Chicken (p. 300)	6	170	24	0	7	73	105	209	36	1	0	4	9	37	2	6
Honey and Spice Duckling (p. 321)	3	300	25	25	11	89	1464	331	38	2	0	18	29	28	3	20
Lemon-Mustard Chicken (p. 300)	6	168	24	0	7	73	257	205	36	1	0	4	9	37	1	6
Mediterranean Chicken (p. 314)	6	323	21	28	14	56	472	364	33	31	54	23	11	34	5	15
Mushroom Stuffing (p. 323)	8	221	4	22	13	1	432	155	7	10	2	12	9	10	5	8
Old-Fashioned Bread Stuffing (p. 323)	8	221	4	22	13	1	456	129	7	10	2	12	7	8	5	8
Orange Chicken with Walnuts (p. 308)	4	578	35	47	29	72	840	727	54	10	138	28	14	70	9	21
Oven-Fried Chicken (p. 303)	6	266	25	10	14	73	296	220	38	17	7	13	18	47	2	10
Oyster Stuffing (p. 323)	8	261	8	24	14	34	499	260	13	10	2	11	13	12	8	30
Pan Gravy (p. 325)	8	86	2	3	7	6	191	55	2	0	0	2	2	5	0	2
Parmesan Batter-Fried Chicken (p. 311)	6	424	29	17	26	124	198	294	45	6	2	12	17	42	13	11
Parmesan Oven-Fried Chicken (p. 303)	6	318	29	12	17	80	519	241	45	9	1	7	13	41	15	9
Peanut Stuffing (p. 323)	8	325	9	25	22	1	534	255	14	10	2	15	8	22	6	10
Pepper-Lime Chicken (p. 300)	6	161	24	0	7	73	93	203	36	1	1	4	9	37	1	6
Pick-a-Butter Chicken Kiev (p. 304)	4	368	39	11	18	181	290	340	59	10	1	11	13	82	4	12
Potato-Chip Oven-Fried Chicken (p. 303)	6	232	25	8	11	73	140	392	38	1	7	5	9	40	2	6
Raisin Stuffing (p. 323)	8	248	5	29	13	1	457	197	7	10	2	12	7	9	5	9
Roast Herb Chicken (p. 321)	6	192	24	1	10	73	115	217	36	0	4	9	9	38	2	6
Saucy Chicken Livers (p. 307)	4	421	28	41	15	501	894	758	43	476	48	20	138	62	9	59
Sesame-Soy Chicken Nuggets (p. 303)	4	365	38	14	16	96	486	307	59	8	0	8	11	78	2	10
Skillet-Fried Chicken (p. 307)	6	215	24	4	11	73	251	212	37	5	0	6	10	39	2	7
Stewed Chicken (p. 315)	6	154	24	0	6	72	426	198	36	0	0	4	8	38	1	6
Stuffed Cornish Game Hens (p. 321)	4	469	36	20	25	113	452	475	56	84	25	17	17	58	5	13
Sweet-and-Sour Glazed Chicken (p. 301)	6	304	25	35	6	73	245	272	39	0	5	9	10	42	3	11
Taco Batter-Fried Chicken (p. 311)	6	409	28	18	25	120	370	281	43	4	0	12	16	42	7	11
Turkey Gruyère (p. 306)	4	447	38	20	23	232	688	386	59	21	13	13	20	38	27	18
Turkey Manicotti (p. 302)	4	574	51	44	20	172	1168	891	78	28	9	25	35	38	53	20
Turkey-Rice Skillet (p. 311)	4	352	33	36	8	99	432	607	52	25	18	17	21	33	22	21
Turkey Ring (p. 302)	4	220	28	10	7	133	666	380	43	11	7	7	13	26	6	15
Wild Rice Stuffing (p. 324)	6	63	2	13	0	0	104	159	3	0	2	6	9	9	1	4

Poultry

Easy to cook, low in calories, and versatile, poultry fits today's menus perfectly. Whether you want fried chicken pieces, sautéed turkey breasts, or a roasted and stuffed bird, you'll find the recipe you need here.

Poultry Pointers

For the best flavor and quality, use these tips when preparing and serving poultry.
● Refrigerate poultry promptly after purchasing. Keep it in the coldest section of your refrigerator for up to two days. For longer storage, freeze the poultry (see tip, page 306).
● Because bacteria can develop on poultry at room temperature, never thaw poultry on the countertop or in the sink. Thaw it in your refrigerator in a pan of cold water (change the water every 30 minutes), or in your microwave oven (see chart, page 326).
● Wash your hands, utensils, and work surfaces with hot, soapy water after handling raw poultry to prevent spreading bacteria to other foods.
● Cut raw and cooked poultry on an acrylic cutting board instead of a wooden board. Porous wooden boards are difficult to thoroughly wash.
● Use one dish for the raw food and another for the cooked food.
● Poultry is done when the thickest part of the meat near the bone is no longer pink, the juices run clear, the drumsticks twist easily in their sockets, and a meat thermometer inserted in the thickest part of the thigh registers 180° to 185° (white meat pieces should read 170°).
● Never leave poultry or other perishable foods at room temperature for more than two hours.
● Reheat leftovers to bubbling (about 185°) for best taste and maximum food safety.

Poultry Hot Line

For answers to your questions about poultry handling or safety, call the U.S. Department of Agriculture's Meat and Poultry Hotline. The toll-free number is 800/535-4555. (In the Washington, D.C., area, call 447-3333.) Home economists at the hot line take calls from 10 a.m. to 4 p.m. eastern time (the hours usually are extended around Thanksgiving).

Cutting Up Poultry

Follow these steps when cutting up a whole or a partially cut-up bird.
● With a sharp knife, cut the skin between the body and one thigh. Pull the thigh out and down until the bone pops out of the hip joint. Cut through the broken hip joint as close to the backbone as possible. Repeat on other side.
● To separate the thigh from the drumstick, cut through the skin at the knee joint. Bend the joint backward until the thigh and the drumstick touch. Cut through the knee joint. Repeat.
● To remove a wing, cut through the skin on the inside of the wing at the joint. Pull the wing out and down until the joint breaks. Cut through the joint. Repeat on the other side.
● To divide the body, turn the bird on its side and cut between the breast ribs and back ribs on each side. Bend the back in half to break it at the joint; cut through the broken joint. Cut off the tail, if desired.
● Divide the breast in half by cutting lengthwise along the breastbone.

To check for doneness, cut into the poultry up to the bone. If no pink remains, the poultry is done.

Four-Way Chicken

Broil, grill, micro-cook, or micro-cook and grill the chicken. (Grilled chicken with Ginger-Honey Glaze is pictured on page 295.)

1 **2½- to 3-pound broiler-fryer chicken, quartered or cut up**
   Melted margarine *or* butter, *or* cooking oil
   Barbecue Sauce, Cumberland Sauce, *or* Ginger-Honey Glaze

Rinse chicken; pat dry. If using a quartered chicken, break wing, hip, and drumstick joints so bird will lie flat during cooking. Twist wing tips under back. Brush chicken with margarine, butter, or oil. Sprinkle with salt and pepper.

Place chicken, skin side down, on the unheated rack of a broiler pan. Place under broiler 4 to 5 inches from the heat. (If broiler compartment does not allow enough distance, remove rack and place chicken directly in broiler pan.) Broil about 20 minutes or till lightly browned. Brush occasionally with margarine, butter, or oil.

Turn chicken, skin side up, and broil for 5 to 15 minutes more or till tender and no longer pink. During the last 5 minutes of cooking, brush occasionally with Barbecue Sauce, Cumberland Sauce, or Ginger-Honey Glaze. Heat the remaining sauce or glaze; pass with chicken. Serves 6.

Microwave directions: Use cut-up chicken. Rinse pieces; pat dry. In a 12x7½x2-inch baking dish arrange chicken, skin side down, with meaty portions toward the edges of the dish. (Omit brushing with margarine.) Micro-cook, covered with waxed paper, on 100% power (high) for 10 minutes, giving dish a half-turn and rearranging pieces after 5 minutes. Drain well. Brush chicken with Barbecue Sauce, Cumberland Sauce, or Ginger-Honey Glaze. Turn pieces over; brush again. Cook, covered, on high for 2 to 5 minutes more or till tender and no longer pink. Heat remaining sauce or glaze; pass with chicken.

Microwave-and-grill directions: Use cut-up chicken. Rinse pieces; pat dry. In a 12x7½x2-inch baking dish arrange chicken, skin side down, with meaty portions toward the edges of the dish. (Omit brushing with margarine.) Micro-cook, covered with waxed paper, on 100% power (high) for 8 to 10 minutes or till no longer pink on surface of chicken, giving dish a half-turn after 5 minutes. Immediately place chicken on grill rack, skin side down, directly over *medium* coals. Grill for 6 minutes. Brush with Barbecue Sauce, Cumberland Sauce, or Ginger-Honey Glaze. Turn; brush with sauce or glaze. Grill for 8 to 10 minutes more or till tender and no longer pink, brushing often with sauce or glaze. Heat remaining sauce or glaze; pass with chicken.

Grill directions: Rinse, dry, and season quartered or cut-up chicken as above. Place chicken, skin side down, on an uncovered grill directly over *medium* coals. Grill for 20 minutes. Turn; grill for 15 to 25 minutes more or till tender and no longer pink. Brush often with Barbecue Sauce, Cumberland Sauce, or Ginger-Honey Glaze during the last 10 minutes of grilling. Heat remaining sauce or glaze; pass with chicken.

Barbecue Sauce: In a saucepan stir together ½ cup *catsup*, ¼ cup chopped *onion*, 2 tablespoons *brown sugar*, 1 tablespoon *prepared mustard*, 1 tablespoon *water*, 1 teaspoon *Worcestershire sauce*, ¼ teaspoon *garlic powder*, and ¼ teaspoon crushed *red pepper*. Cook 2 minutes or till onion is tender. Makes ¾ cup (6 servings).

Cumberland Sauce: In a saucepan stir together 1½ teaspoons *cornstarch*, ¼ teaspoon dry *mustard*, dash ground *nutmeg*, and dash ground *ginger*. Stir in ⅓ cup *port or red wine*, ¼ cup *currant jelly*, 1 tablespoon frozen *orange juice concentrate*, and 1½ teaspoons *lemon juice*. Cook and stir till bubbly. Cook and stir for 2 minutes more. Makes about ½ cup (6 servings).

Ginger-Honey Glaze: In a saucepan stir together ½ teaspoon finely shredded *orange peel*, ½ cup *orange juice*, ¼ cup sliced *green onion*, 2 tablespoons *honey*, 1 tablespoon *soy sauce*, 2 teaspoons *cornstarch*, and 1 teaspoon grated *gingerroot*. Cook and stir till bubbly. Cook and stir for 2 minutes more. Makes ¾ cup (6 servings).

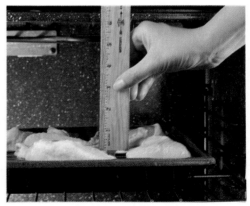

Adjust the broiler pan until the top of the chicken is 4 to 5 inches from the heating unit.

Pepper-Lime Chicken

This tangy chicken is good hot or cold.

  2 to 2½ pounds meaty chicken pieces
       (breasts, thighs, and drumsticks)
  ½ teaspoon finely shredded lime peel
  ¼ cup lime juice
  1 tablespoon cooking oil
  2 cloves garlic, minced
  1 teaspoon coarsely ground black
       pepper
  1 teaspoon dried thyme *or* basil,
       crushed
  ¼ teaspoon salt

Rinse chicken; pat dry. Place chicken pieces, skin side down, on the unheated rack of a broiler pan. Broil 4 to 5 inches from the heat about 20 minutes or till lightly browned.

Meanwhile, for lime glaze, in a bowl stir together lime peel, lime juice, oil, garlic, black pepper, thyme or basil, and salt. Brush chicken with lime glaze. Turn chicken; brush with more glaze. Broil for 5 to 15 minutes more or till tender and no longer pink, brushing often with glaze during the last 5 minutes of cooking. Makes 6 servings.

Microwave directions: Skin chicken. Rinse; pat dry. In a 12x7½x2-inch baking dish arrange chicken, skin side down, with meaty portions toward the edges of the dish. Micro-cook, covered with vented clear plastic wrap, on 100% power (high) for 10 minutes, giving the dish a half-turn and rearranging pieces after 5 minutes. Drain well.

Prepare glaze as above. If desired, add several dashes ground turmeric. Brush chicken with glaze. Turn pieces over; brush with more glaze. Cook, covered, on high 2 to 5 minutes more or till tender and no longer pink. Brush with glaze.

Grill directions: Rinse chicken; pat dry. Prepare glaze as above. Grill chicken, skin side down, on an uncovered grill directly over *medium* coals for 20 minutes. Turn and grill for 15 to 25 minutes more or till tender and no longer pink, brushing often with lime glaze during the last 10 minutes of cooking.

Lemon-Mustard Chicken: Prepare as above, *except* substitute the following glaze for lime glaze: In a small bowl stir together 2 tablespoons *cooking oil;* 1 tablespoon *Dijon-style mustard;* 1 tablespoon *lemon juice;* 1½ teaspoons *lemon-pepper seasoning;* 1 teaspoon dried *oregano or basil,* crushed; ¼ teaspoon *onion salt;* and ⅛ teaspoon ground *red pepper.*

Herb-Marinated Chicken

  2 to 2½ pounds meaty chicken pieces
       (breasts, thighs, and drumsticks)
  ½ cup white wine
  2 tablespoons olive oil *or* cooking oil
  1 tablespoon vinegar
  2 teaspoons dried basil, crushed
  1 teaspoon dried oregano *or* tarragon,
       crushed
  ½ teaspoon onion salt
  2 cloves garlic, minced

Skin chicken, if desired. Rinse chicken. Place in a heavy plastic bag set into a large mixing bowl. For marinade, in a bowl combine wine, oil, vinegar, basil, oregano or tarragon, onion salt, and garlic. Pour over chicken in bag. Close bag and turn chicken to coat well. Marinate for 5 to 24 hours in the refrigerator, turning bag occasionally.

Drain chicken, reserving marinade. Place the chicken, skin side down, on the unheated rack of a broiler pan. Brush with some of the marinade. Broil 4 to 5 inches from the heat about 20 minutes or till lightly browned, brushing often with marinade. Turn chicken, skin side up, and broil for 5 to 15 minutes more or till tender and no longer pink, brushing often with the marinade. Makes 6 servings.

Microwave directions: Skin chicken, if desired. Rinse and marinate chicken as above. Drain, reserving marinade. In a 12x7½x2-inch baking dish arrange drained chicken, skin side down, with meaty portions toward the edges of the dish. Brush with marinade. Micro-cook, covered with waxed paper, on 100% power (high) for 5 minutes. Give dish a half-turn, turn and rearrange the pieces, and brush with marinade. Cook, covered, on high 5 minutes. Turn dish; brush again. Cook, covered, on high for 2 to 5 minutes more or till chicken is tender and no longer pink.

Grill directions: Do not skin chicken. Rinse and marinate chicken as above. Drain, reserving marinade. Grill drained chicken pieces, skin side down, on an uncovered grill directly over *medium* coals for 20 minutes, brushing occasionally with marinade. Turn chicken and grill for 15 to 25 minutes more or till tender and no longer pink, brushing often with marinade.

Sweet-and-Sour Glazed Chicken

Pineapple preserves make an easy base for the sweet-and-sour sauce.

> 2 to 2½ pounds meaty chicken pieces (breasts, thighs, and drumsticks)
> ½ cup pineapple preserves
> 2 tablespoons red wine vinegar
> 1 tablespoon soy sauce
> ½ teaspoon grated gingerroot *or*
>   ⅛ teaspoon ground ginger
> ⅛ teaspoon onion powder
> ⅛ teaspoon ground red pepper
> 4 green onions, bias-sliced into 1-inch pieces
> 2 cups hot cooked rice

Rinse chicken; pat dry. Place chicken pieces, skin side down, on the unheated rack of a broiler pan. Broil 4 to 5 inches from the heat about 20 minutes or till lightly browned. Turn chicken pieces, skin side up, and broil for 5 to 15 minutes more or till tender and no longer pink.

Meanwhile, for glaze, in a small saucepan stir together pineapple preserves, vinegar, soy sauce, gingerroot or ground ginger, onion powder, and red pepper. Heat through; keep warm.

Stir green onions into hot cooked rice. Place rice mixture on a platter. Place chicken atop; spoon glaze over chicken. Makes 6 servings.

Microwave directions: Rinse chicken; pat dry. In a 12x7½x2-inch baking dish arrange chicken, skin side down, with meaty portions toward the edges of the dish. Micro-cook, covered with waxed paper, on 100% power (high) for 12 to 15 minutes or till tender and no longer pink, giving dish a half-turn and rearranging pieces after 5 minutes. Drain. Cover and keep warm. In a 1-cup measure combine pineapple preserves, red wine vinegar, soy sauce, gingerroot or ground ginger, onion powder, and red pepper. Cook, uncovered, on high for 1½ to 2½ minutes or till heated through. Stir green onions into hot cooked rice. Serve as above.

Grill directions: Rinse chicken; pat dry. Grill chicken, skin side down, on an uncovered grill directly over *medium* coals for 20 minutes. Turn chicken over and grill for 15 to 25 minutes more or till tender and no longer pink. Meanwhile, prepare glaze as above. Stir green onions into hot cooked rice. Serve as above.

Chicken Kabobs

> ¼ teaspoon finely shredded orange peel
> ¼ cup orange juice
> ¼ cup dry sherry
> ¼ cup soy sauce
> 2 teaspoons grated gingerroot *or*
>   ½ teaspoon ground ginger
> 2 cloves garlic, minced
> 2 whole medium chicken breasts (1½ pounds total), skinned and boned
> 1 medium onion, cut into 4 wedges
> 1 large green *or* sweet red pepper, cut into 1-inch pieces
> 1 8¼-ounce can pineapple chunks
> 1 tablespoon cornstarch
> 2 cups hot cooked rice

For marinade, in a bowl stir together orange peel, orange juice, sherry, soy sauce, gingerroot or ginger, and garlic. Rinse chicken; pat dry. Cut each breast half into 4 lengthwise strips. Add chicken to marinade, stirring to coat well. Cover. Let stand at room temperature for 30 minutes.

In a medium saucepan bring ½ cup *water* to boiling. Add onion. Return to boiling; reduce heat. Cover and simmer for 1 minute. Add green or red pepper and simmer for 2 minutes more. Drain. Drain pineapple, reserving juice.

Drain chicken, reserving marinade. Add ¼ cup marinade to reserved pineapple juice; set aside.

On four 15-inch skewers, alternately thread chicken, accordion style, with onion, green or red pepper, and pineapple. Place skewers on the unheated rack of a broiler pan. Broil 4 to 5 inches from the heat about 5 minutes or till lightly browned, brushing often with marinade. Turn; brush with marinade. Broil for 3 to 5 minutes or till chicken is tender and no longer pink and vegetables are crisp-tender, brushing with marinade.

For sauce, add water to pineapple juice mixture to equal *1¼ cups.* In a small saucepan stir together juice mixture and cornstarch. Cook and stir till bubbly. Cook and stir for 2 minutes more. Serve with kabobs and rice. Makes 4 servings.

Grill directions: Marinate meat, cook vegetables, and assemble kabobs as above. Grill kabobs on an uncovered grill directly over *medium-hot* coals for 8 to 10 minutes or till chicken is no longer pink and vegetables are crisp-tender, turning once and brushing often with marinade. Prepare sauce as above. Serve as above.

Cranberry-Sauced Turkey Steaks

Ready in only 20 minutes.

> 2 tablespoons margarine *or* butter, melted
> 1 tablespoon soy sauce
> 4 turkey breast tenderloin steaks (about 1 pound total)
> ½ cup cranberry-orange sauce
> ¼ cup orange juice
> 1 teaspoon cornstarch
> ⅛ teaspoon ground cinnamon
> 2 tablespoons toasted sliced almonds

In a bowl stir together margarine or butter and soy sauce. Rinse turkey; pat dry. Place turkey on the unheated rack of a broiler pan; brush with soy mixture. Broil 4 to 5 inches from the heat for 5 minutes; turn and brush with soy mixture. Broil for 4 to 6 minutes more or till turkey is tender and no longer pink.

Meanwhile, for sauce, in a small saucepan stir together cranberry-orange sauce, orange juice, cornstarch, and cinnamon. Cook and stir over medium heat till thickened and bubbly. Cook and stir for 2 minutes more. Spoon sauce over turkey steaks. Sprinkle with almonds. Makes 4 servings.

Microwave directions: Stir together margarine or butter and soy sauce. Rinse turkey; pat dry. Place turkey in a 12x7½x2-inch baking dish; drizzle with soy mixture, turning turkey to coat evenly. Micro-cook, covered with waxed paper, on 100% power (high) for 5 to 8 minutes or till tender and no longer pink, turning steaks over and rearranging once.

Meanwhile, for sauce, in a 2-cup measure stir together cranberry-orange sauce, orange juice, cornstarch, and cinnamon. Cook, uncovered, on high for 2 to 3 minutes or till thickened and bubbly, stirring every minute till sauce starts to thicken, then every 30 seconds. Spoon sauce over turkey steaks. Sprinkle with almonds.

Grill directions: Stir together margarine or butter and soy sauce. Rinse turkey; pat dry. Grill turkey on an uncovered grill directly over *medium* coals for 8 minutes. Turn. Grill for 4 to 7 minutes more or till tender and no longer pink, brushing often with soy mixture. Prepare sauce as above. Spoon sauce over turkey steaks. Sprinkle with almonds.

Turkey Manicotti

> 8 manicotti shells
> 1 pound ground raw turkey
> 1 15½-ounce jar chunky garden-style meatless spaghetti sauce
> 1 beaten egg
> 1 cup ricotta cheese *or* cream-style cottage cheese, drained
> 1 cup shredded mozzarella cheese
> ½ cup snipped parsley
> ¼ cup grated Parmesan cheese   Oven 350°

Cook manicotti in *boiling* water about 18 minutes or till tender but still firm. Drain well.

In a large skillet cook turkey till no longer pink. Drain. Stir in sauce; heat through. Mix together egg, ricotta, mozzarella, parsley, and Parmesan. Stuff cheese mixture into shells. Spoon *one-third* of the sauce mixture into a 12x7½x2-inch baking dish. Place shells atop. Top with remaining sauce mixture, covering shells. Bake, covered, in a 350° oven for 25 to 30 minutes or till hot. Serves 4.

Microwave directions: Cook manicotti as above. In a 1½-quart casserole crumble turkey. Micro-cook, covered, on 100% power (high) for 5 to 7 minutes or till no longer pink, stirring once. Drain. Stir in sauce. Cook, covered, 4 to 5 minutes or till hot, stirring once. Assemble as above. Cook, covered with vented plastic wrap, on high for 10 to 12 minutes or till heated through, giving dish a half-turn once.

Turkey Ring

Oven 350°

In a bowl combine 1 beaten *egg,* ⅓ cup chopped *onion,* ¼ cup fine dry *bread crumbs,* ¼ cup snipped *parsley,* 1 teaspoon prepared *mustard,* ½ teaspoon *salt,* ½ teaspoon *poultry seasoning,* and ¼ teaspoon *pepper.* Add 1 pound ground raw *turkey;* mix well. In a 9-inch pie plate shape mixture into a 6-inch ring, 2 inches wide. Bake in a 350° oven for 40 to 50 minutes or till no longer pink. In a saucepan heat ½ cup bottled *barbecue or pizza sauce;* serve with turkey. Serves 4.

Microwave directions: Assemble the turkey ring as above. Micro-cook, covered with waxed paper, on 100% power (high) for 7 to 9 minutes or till no pink remains, giving dish a quarter-turn twice. In a bowl cook barbecue sauce on high for 1½ to 2 minutes or till hot. Serve with turkey.

Oven-Fried Chicken

Crispy fried chicken the easy way.

> 3 **cups cornflakes *or* ½ cup fine dry bread crumbs**
> 1 **teaspoon dried basil, oregano, *or* Italian seasoning, crushed; *or* ½ teaspoon dried thyme, sage, fines herbes, *or* marjoram, crushed**
> 1 **2½- to 3-pound broiler-fryer chicken, cut up**
> ¼ **cup margarine *or* butter, melted** Oven 375°

If using cornflakes, crush finely enough to make *1 cup* crumbs. For coating mixture, on a sheet of waxed paper, mix cornflake or bread crumbs with desired herb; set aside.

Rinse chicken; pat dry. If desired, sprinkle with salt and pepper. Brush chicken with melted margarine or butter. Roll chicken pieces in coating mixture. In a 15x10x1-inch or 13x9x2-inch baking pan arrange chicken pieces, skin side up, so pieces don't touch. Drizzle any remaining margarine or butter atop.

Bake in a 375° oven for 45 to 55 minutes or till tender and no longer pink. *Do not turn.* Serves 6.

Potato-Chip Oven-Fried Chicken: Prepare as above, *except* omit cornflakes or bread crumbs, salt, and melted margarine or butter. For the coating mixture, combine 1½ cups finely crushed *potato chips* with desired herb. Brush *each* piece of chicken with *milk*.

Parmesan Oven-Fried Chicken: Prepare as above, *except* omit cornflakes or bread crumbs, herb, and salt. For coating mixture, combine ⅔ cup crushed *herb-seasoned stuffing mix,* ½ cup grated *Parmesan cheese,* and 1 tablespoon dried *parsley flakes.*

Curry-and-Parsley Oven-Fried Chicken: Prepare as above, *except* omit cornflakes or bread crumbs, herb, and salt. For coating mixture, combine ⅔ cup finely crushed *saltine crackers,* 1 tablespoon dried *parsley,* 1½ teaspoons *curry powder,* and ⅛ teaspoon *onion powder.*

Crispy Barbecue-Style Oven-Fried Chicken: Prepare as above, *except* use bread crumbs. For the herb and salt, substitute a mixture of 1 teaspoon *garlic salt,* 1 teaspoon *chili powder,* ¼ teaspoon *celery seed,* and ⅛ teaspoon ground *red pepper.*

Chicken Nuggets

Serve bottled barbecue sauce, honey, or sweet-and-sour sauce with these morsels.

> 3 **tablespoons margarine *or* butter, melted**
> 2 **teaspoons Worcestershire sauce**
> 2 **whole large chicken breasts (about 2 pounds total), skinned, boned, and cut into 1-inch pieces**
> 50 **wheat wafers, finely crushed**
> ⅓ **cup grated Parmesan cheese** Oven 450°

In a bowl stir together margarine or butter and Worcestershire sauce. Add chicken and toss to coat. In a plastic bag stir together crushed wafers and Parmesan cheese. Add chicken pieces, a few at a time, closing bag and shaking to coat pieces well. Place chicken pieces in a single layer in a 15x10x1-inch pan.

Bake in a 450° oven for 7 to 9 minutes or till no longer pink. Makes 4 servings.

Chili Chicken Nuggets: Prepare as above, *except* substitute ⅔ cup *cornmeal* for wafers. Add 1 teaspoon *chili powder,* ¼ teaspoon garlic *salt,* ⅛ to ¼ teaspoon ground *red pepper,* and ⅛ teaspoon ground *cumin* to cornmeal-Parmesan mixture.

Sesame-Soy Chicken Nuggets: Prepare as above, *except* substitute *soy sauce* for Worcestershire sauce. Substitute 20 *sesame crackers* for wheat wafers and omit Parmesan cheese. Stir ⅛ teaspoon ground *ginger* into crushed crackers.

◄For oven-fried chicken recipes, roll chicken pieces in the coating mixture to cover all sides.

Chicken Dijon

The cream, lemon-pepper seasoning, and Dijon-style mustard provide a superb balance of flavor.

¾ **cup long grain rice *or* one 4.5-ounce package herb-flavored rice mix**
2 **whole medium chicken breasts (1½ pounds total), skinned, boned, and halved lengthwise**
1 **teaspoon lemon-pepper seasoning**
¼ **teaspoon onion powder**
2 **tablespoons margarine *or* butter Light cream *or* milk**
2 **teaspoons all-purpose flour**
1 **tablespoon Dijon-style mustard Tomato wedges (optional) Parsley (optional)**

Cook rice or herb-flavored rice mix according to package directions.

Meanwhile, rinse chicken; pat dry. Sprinkle both sides of chicken with lemon-pepper seasoning and onion powder. In a skillet cook chicken in margarine or butter over medium heat about 20 minutes or till tender and no longer pink, turning once. Transfer to a platter; keep warm.

For sauce, measure pan juices; add light cream or milk to make ⅔ cup liquid. Return to the skillet. Stir ¼ *cup* light cream or milk into flour; add to juices mixture. Cook and stir till thickened and bubbly. Cook and stir for 1 to 2 minutes more. Stir in mustard. Spoon some sauce over chicken; pass remaining sauce. If desired, garnish with tomato wedges and snipped parsley. Serve with hot rice. Makes 4 servings.

Microwave directions: Cook rice or rice mix according to the package directions. Rinse chicken; pat dry. In a 10x6x2-inch baking dish place chicken. Sprinkle with lemon-pepper seasoning and onion powder. Omit the margarine or butter. Micro-cook, covered with waxed paper, on 100% power (high) for 4 to 6 minutes or till tender and no longer pink, turning pieces over and rearranging once. Transfer chicken to a platter; keep warm.

For sauce, measure pan juices into a 2-cup measure; add light cream or milk to make ½ cup liquid. Stir ¼ *cup* light cream into the flour; add to juices mixture. Cook, uncovered, on high for 2½ to 4 minutes or till thickened and bubbly, stirring every 30 seconds. Stir in the mustard. Serve as above.

Chicken Kiev

2 **whole large chicken breasts (2 pounds total), skinned, boned, and halved lengthwise**
1 **tablespoon chopped green onion**
1 **tablespoon snipped parsley**
1 **clove garlic, minced**
½ **of a ¼-pound stick of butter, chilled**
1 **beaten egg**
¼ **cup all-purpose flour**
¼ **cup fine dry bread crumbs**
1 **tablespoon butter**
1 **tablespoon cooking oil**   Oven 400°

Rinse chicken; pat dry. Place *each* breast half, boned side up, between 2 pieces of clear plastic wrap. Working from the center to the edges, pound lightly with the flat side of a meat mallet to ⅛-inch thickness. Remove plastic wrap. Sprinkle with salt and pepper. Combine onion, parsley, and garlic; sprinkle on chicken.

Cut *chilled* butter into four 2½x½-inch sticks. Place *one* piece in the center of *each* chicken piece. Fold in sides; roll up jelly-roll style, pressing edges to seal. Stir together egg and 1 tablespoon *water*. Coat rolls with flour, dip into egg mixture, then coat with crumbs. Cover; chill 1 to 24 hours.

In a large skillet melt the 1 tablespoon butter; add oil. Add chilled chicken rolls; cook over medium-high heat about 5 minutes or till golden brown, turning to brown all sides. Transfer to a 12x7½x2-inch baking dish. Bake in a 400° oven for 15 to 18 minutes or till no longer pink. Spoon drippings over rolls. Makes 4 servings.

Microwave directions: Rinse chicken; pat dry. Pound chicken as above. Assemble, coat, and chill chicken rolls as above, *except* coat rolls on *3 sides only.* Place chilled rolls, uncoated side down, on a rack in an 8x8x2-inch baking dish. Micro-cook, covered with waxed paper, on 100% power (high) for 7 to 9 minutes or till no longer pink, giving dish a half-turn and rearranging rolls after 4 minutes. *Do not turn rolls over.*

Cheesy Chicken Kiev: Prepare as above, *except,* for the butter in chicken rolls, substitute four 2x½-inch sticks of *caraway cheese, Gruyère cheese, blue cheese, Camembert* (rind removed), *Brie* (rind removed), *or cheddar cheese.*

Pick-a-Butter Chicken Kiev: Prepare as above, *except,* for the butter in the chicken rolls, substitute ¼ cup (½ recipe) *parsley butter or lemon-tarragon butter* (see tip, page 368), shaped into four 2½x½-inch sticks and chilled.

Chicken Saltimbocca

**2 whole medium chicken breasts
(1½ pounds total), skinned,
boned, and halved lengthwise**
**4 thin slices prosciutto _or_ fully
cooked ham**
**4 slices Gruyère _or_ Swiss cheese
(4 ounces)**
**1 small tomato, peeled, seeded,
and chopped**
¼ cup margarine _or_ butter
1 cup sliced fresh mushrooms
2 cloves garlic, minced
½ cup milk
½ cup dairy sour cream _or_ plain yogurt
2 tablespoons all-purpose flour
¼ teaspoon paprika
⅛ teaspoon ground nutmeg
2 cups hot cooked noodles

Rinse chicken; pat dry. Place _each_ breast half, boned side up, between 2 pieces of clear plastic wrap. Working from the center to the edges, pound lightly with the flat side of a mallet to form ⅛-inch-thick rectangles. Remove plastic wrap.

For each roll, place 1 slice of prosciutto or ham on a chicken piece, folding if necessary to fit. Place 1 slice of cheese atop prosciutto or ham near one edge. Top with some of the tomato. Fold in long sides of chicken and roll up jelly-roll style, starting from the edge with the cheese. Secure with wooden toothpicks.

In a large skillet cook chicken rolls in _2 table-spoons_ of the margarine over medium-low heat for 25 to 30 minutes or till no longer pink, turning to brown evenly. Remove toothpicks.

For sauce, in a medium saucepan melt remaining margarine. Add mushrooms and garlic. Cook till tender. Remove from heat. Stir together milk, sour cream, flour, paprika, nutmeg, ⅛ teaspoon _salt,_ and ⅛ teaspoon _pepper._ Add to sauce. Cook and stir till thickened and bubbly. Cook and stir 1 minute more. Arrange noodles and chicken on a platter. Pour sauce over all. Serves 4.

Microwave directions: Rinse chicken; pat dry. Pound chicken as above. Assemble chicken rolls as above. Place rolls, seam side down, in an 8x8x2-inch baking dish. Micro-cook, covered, on 100% power (high) for 6 to 8 minutes or till no longer pink, rearranging rolls after 4 minutes. Continue as above.

Pound the boned chicken breasts lightly with the flat side of a meat mallet.

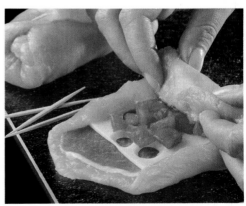

Fold the longer sides in over the filling. Then roll, starting from the short end with the cheese.

Boning Chicken Breasts

Skin the chicken breast, if desired. Using a thin sharp knife, cut as close to the breastbone as possible with a sawing motion. Press flat side of knife against rib bones, using your free hand to gently pull meat away from the rib bones. Repeat on other side of breastbone. Remove white tendon from each breast half by pulling on one end of the tendon, scraping off the meat as you pull.

Chicken Marsala

2 **whole medium chicken breasts (1½ pounds total), skinned, boned, and halved lengthwise**
¼ **cup all-purpose flour**
¼ **teaspoon dried marjoram, crushed**
1 **cup sliced fresh mushrooms**
2 **tablespoons sliced green onion**
3 **tablespoons margarine or butter**
¼ **cup chicken broth**
¼ **cup dry marsala or dry sherry**

Rinse chicken; pat dry. Place *each* breast half, boned side up, between 2 pieces of clear plastic wrap. Working from the center to edges, pound lightly with the flat side of a mallet till ⅛ inch thick. Remove the plastic wrap. Stir together flour, marjoram, ⅛ teaspoon *salt*, and ⅛ teaspoon *pepper*. Lightly press chicken pieces into flour mixture on both sides; shake off excess.

In a large skillet cook mushrooms and green onion in *1 tablespoon* of the margarine till tender; remove from skillet. In the same skillet cook chicken pieces in remaining margarine over medium-high heat for 4 minutes, turning to brown evenly. Remove skillet from heat. Return mushrooms and onion to skillet. Carefully add broth and marsala. Cook, uncovered, 2 to 3 minutes or till mushroom mixture thickens slightly, stirring occasionally. Transfer chicken to a serving platter. Spoon mushroom mixture over. Sprinkle with snipped parsley, if desired. Serves 4.

Freezing Poultry

Place uncooked whole birds in freezer bags, padding the ends with freezer paper to prevent bag punctures. Press out the air and seal. Spread uncooked pieces or cubed cooked poultry on a tray, freeze firm, then transfer to freezer bags. Press out air and seal.

For the best quality, keep frozen uncooked whole turkeys, whole chickens, or chicken pieces no longer than a year; frozen uncooked turkey pieces no longer than six months; or frozen cooked poultry no longer than four months.

Turkey Gruyère

Try skinned, boned, and lightly pounded chicken breasts in this recipe, too.

8 **turkey breast slices (about 1 pound total)**
⅓ **cup all-purpose flour**
2 **teaspoons lemon-pepper seasoning**
¼ **teaspoon ground nutmeg**
2 **beaten eggs**
1 **tablespoon dry sherry or white wine**
¾ **cup finely shredded natural Gruyère, Jarlsberg, or Swiss cheese (3 ounces)**
½ **cup fine dry seasoned bread crumbs**
¼ **cup snipped parsley**
¼ **cup margarine or butter**

Rinse turkey and pat dry. Stir together flour, lemon-pepper seasoning, and nutmeg; set aside. In a shallow dish stir together eggs and dry sherry or wine; set aside. Stir together shredded cheese, dry bread crumbs, and parsley. Coat turkey slices with flour mixture. Dip slices into egg mixture, then into cheese mixture, coating evenly.

In a 12-inch skillet melt *2 tablespoons* of the margarine. Cook turkey over medium heat about 4 minutes or till light brown and no longer pink, turning once. Add remaining margarine as needed. Serve with lemon wedges, if desired. Serves 4.

Fruit-Sauced Chicken Breasts

2 **whole medium chicken breasts (1½ pounds total), skinned, boned, and halved lengthwise**
2 **tablespoons margarine or butter**
1 **5½-ounce can apricot nectar**
⅓ **cup chicken broth**
2 **teaspoons cornstarch**
1 **teaspoon lemon juice**
½ **cup mixed dried fruit bits**
2 **cups hot cooked rice**

Rinse chicken; pat dry. In a large skillet cook chicken in margarine over medium heat for 8 to 10 minutes or till tender and no longer pink, turning once. For sauce, in a small saucepan stir together apricot nectar, broth, cornstarch, and lemon juice. Stir in fruit bits. Cook and stir till bubbly. Cook and stir for 2 minutes more. Serve sauce with chicken and rice. Makes 4 servings.

Chicken Livers Stroganoff

The sour cream sauce is loaded with mushrooms and bacon.

  1 **pound chicken livers, cut in half**
1½ **cups sliced fresh mushrooms**
  ½ **cup chopped onion**
  2 **tablespoons cooking oil**
  1 **8-ounce carton dairy sour cream *or*
       plain yogurt**
  ½ **cup water**
  2 **tablespoons all-purpose flour**
  2 **tablespoons dry sherry *or* milk**
  1 **teaspoon instant chicken bouillon
       granules**
  3 **slices bacon, crisp-cooked, drained,
       and crumbled**
  2 **cups hot cooked fettuccine *or* rice
       Snipped parsley (optional)**

Rinse livers; pat dry. In a large skillet cook livers, mushrooms, and onion in hot oil over medium-high heat about 5 minutes or till liver centers are only slightly pink and onion is tender. Drain; remove mixture from skillet.

In a bowl stir together sour cream or yogurt, water, flour, sherry or milk, and bouillon granules. Add to the skillet. Cook and stir till thickened and bubbly. Stir in chicken-liver mixture and bacon; heat through. Season to taste with salt and pepper. Serve atop hot fettuccine or rice. Sprinkle with parsley, if desired. Serves 4.

Saucy Chicken Livers

  1 **pound chicken livers, quartered**
  ½ **cup chopped onion**
  2 **tablespoons cooking oil**
  1 **15½-ounce jar spaghetti sauce with
       green peppers and mushrooms**
  2 **tablespoons dry white *or* red wine
       (optional)**
  2 **cups hot cooked spaghetti
       Grated Parmesan cheese**

Rinse livers; pat dry. In a large skillet cook livers and onion in hot oil about 5 minutes or till the liver centers are only slightly pink. Remove from skillet; keep warm.

In the same skillet combine spaghetti sauce, and, if desired, wine. Cook and stir till heated through. Stir in livers; heat through. Serve over hot spaghetti. Pass Parmesan cheese. Serves 4.

Skillet-Fried Chicken

  1 **2½- to 3-pound broiler-fryer
       chicken, cut up**
  ¼ **cup all-purpose flour *or* ½ cup
       fine dry bread crumbs**
  1 **teaspoon paprika, curry powder,
       poultry seasoning, chili powder,
       or dried basil *or* marjoram,
       crushed; *or* ½ teaspoon garlic
       powder *or* onion powder**
  2 **tablespoons cooking oil**

Rinse chicken; pat dry. In a plastic bag combine flour, paprika or other seasoning, ½ teaspoon *salt*, and ¼ teaspoon *pepper*. Add chicken pieces, a few at a time, shaking to coat.

In a 12-inch skillet heat oil. Add chicken, placing meaty pieces toward the center of the skillet. Cook, uncovered, over medium heat for 15 minutes, turning to brown evenly. Reduce heat; cover tightly. Cook for 25 minutes. Uncover; cook for 5 to 10 minutes more or till tender and no longer pink. Drain on paper towels. Makes 6 servings.

Oven directions: Rinse chicken; pat dry. Coat chicken as above. Brown chicken in a 12-inch *ovenproof* skillet. (Or, brown chicken in a regular skillet, then transfer, skin side up, to a 15x10x1-inch baking pan.) Place in a 375° oven. Bake, uncovered, for 35 to 40 minutes or till no longer pink. *Do not turn.*

Crisp-Fried Chicken: Prepare as above, *except,* after browning for 15 minutes, cook, *uncovered,* over medium-low heat for 35 to 40 minutes more or till no longer pink, turning often.

Once lightly browned on one side, turn the chicken with tongs to evenly brown the other side.

Garlic Chicken

Bottled minced garlic gives great fresh flavor but requires no peeling and mincing.

- ½ cup water
- 2 tablespoons soy sauce
- 1 tablespoon dry white wine
- 1 teaspoon cornstarch
- 2 whole medium chicken breasts (1½ pounds total), skinned and boned
- 2 tablespoons cooking oil
- 10 green onions, bias-sliced into 1-inch pieces (1¼ cups)
- 1 cup thinly sliced fresh mushrooms
- 10 cloves garlic, peeled and finely chopped (3 tablespoons), or 2 to 3 tablespoons bottled minced garlic
- ½ cup sliced water chestnuts
- 2 cups hot cooked rice or fried rice sticks

For marinade, in a bowl stir together water, soy sauce, white wine, and cornstarch. Rinse chicken and pat dry. Cut chicken into ½-inch pieces. Add chicken to marinade; stir to coat. Let stand at room temperature for 30 minutes. Drain chicken, reserving marinade.

Preheat a wok or large skillet over high heat; add oil. (Add more oil as necessary during cooking.) Stir-fry green onions, mushrooms, and garlic in hot oil for 1 to 2 minutes or till tender. Remove from wok or skillet. Add chicken to wok or skillet; stir-fry for 2 to 3 minutes or till no longer pink. Push chicken from the center of the wok or skillet. Stir reserved marinade; add to center of the wok or skillet. Cook and stir till thickened and bubbly. Add onion mixture and water chestnuts. Cook and stir about 1 minute or till heated through. Serve with hot cooked rice or rice sticks. Makes 4 servings.

Garlic Chicken with Zucchini: Prepare as above, *except,* before cooking chicken, stir-fry 1 medium *zucchini,* halved lengthwise and cut into ¼-inch-thick slices (about 1¼ cups), for 3 minutes. Remove from wok or skillet. Return zucchini to wok with onion mixture.

Chicken with Cashews: Prepare as above, *except* stir ½ teaspoon crushed *red pepper* into marinade. Reduce garlic to *2* cloves (or *1½ teaspoons* bottled minced garlic). Stir-fry 1 cup *raw cashews* with onion mixture.

Chicken with Walnuts

- 3 tablespoons soy sauce
- 2 tablespoons dry sherry
- 2 teaspoons cornstarch
- 1 teaspoon sugar
- ½ teaspoon crushed red pepper (optional)
- 2 whole medium chicken breasts (1½ pounds total), skinned and boned
- 2 tablespoons cooking oil
- 1 cup broken walnuts
- 1 teaspoon grated gingerroot
- 2 medium green peppers, cut into ¾-inch pieces
- 4 green onions, bias-sliced into 1-inch pieces
- 2 cups hot cooked rice
    Fresh kumquats (optional)

For sauce, in a bowl stir together soy sauce, sherry, cornstarch, sugar, and, if desired, red pepper. Set aside. Rinse chicken and pat dry. Cut into 1-inch pieces; set aside.

Preheat a wok or large skillet over high heat; add oil. (Add more oil as necessary during cooking.) Stir-fry walnuts in hot oil about 1 minute or till lightly toasted. Remove from wok or skillet. Add gingerroot; stir-fry for 15 seconds. Add green peppers and green onions; stir-fry about 3 minutes or till crisp-tender. Remove vegetables from the wok or skillet.

Add the chicken to the wok or skillet; stir-fry for 2 to 3 minutes or till no longer pink. Push chicken from the center of the wok. Stir sauce; add to center of wok. Cook and stir till thickened and bubbly. Stir in walnuts and vegetables; and cook and stir for 1 to 2 minutes more or till heated through. Serve with hot rice and, if desired, garnish with kumquats. Makes 4 servings.

Orange Chicken with Walnuts: Prepare as above, *except* substitute *orange juice* for the sherry and add ½ teaspoon finely shredded *orange peel* to the sauce. Stir in two *oranges,* peeled and sectioned, just before serving.

Ginger Chicken

Nicely hot! If you prefer a milder dish, omit the bean sauce or bean paste.

> 3 **tablespoons dry sherry**
> 2 **tablespoons soy sauce**
> 2 **tablespoons hot bean sauce *or* bean paste (optional)**
> 1 **tablespoon water**
> 1 **teaspoon cornstarch**
> 2 **whole medium chicken breasts (1½ pounds total), skinned and boned**
> 2 **tablespoons cooking oil**
> 1 **tablespoon grated gingerroot**
> 1 **cup bias-sliced carrots**
> 3½ **cups sliced bok choy *or* chopped Chinese cabbage**
> 2 **cups fresh pea pods, tips and strings removed, *or* one 6-ounce package frozen pea pods, thawed**
> 3 **green onions, bias-sliced into 1-inch pieces**
> 2 **cups hot cooked rice**

Stir together sherry; soy sauce; bean sauce, if desired; water; and cornstarch. Set aside. Rinse chicken and pat dry. Cut into thin bite-size strips.

Preheat a wok or large skillet over high heat; add *1 tablespoon* of the oil. (Add remaining oil as necessary during cooking.) Stir-fry gingerroot in hot oil for 15 seconds. Add carrots; stir-fry for 2 minutes. Add bok choy or cabbage, pea pods, and onions; stir-fry for 2 to 3 minutes or till crisp-tender. Remove vegetables from wok or skillet.

Add chicken to wok or skillet; stir-fry for 2 to 3 minutes or till no longer pink. Push chicken from the center of the wok or skillet. Stir soy sauce mixture; add to center of wok or skillet. Cook and stir till thickened and bubbly. Return vegetables to wok or skillet; stir to coat with sauce. Cook and stir about 1 minute or till heated through. Serve with hot rice. Makes 4 servings.

Stir the soy sauce mixture to remix the ingredients, then add it to the center of the wok or skillet.

Chicken with Papaya

Peaches make a good substitute for the papaya.

- ½ teaspoon finely shredded orange peel
- ⅓ cup orange juice
- 1 tablespoon soy sauce
- 2 teaspoons honey
- 1½ teaspoons grated gingerroot
- 2 whole medium chicken breasts (1½ pounds total), skinned and boned
- 2 teaspoons cornstarch
- 2 tablespoons cooking oil
- 1 cup thinly bias-sliced celery
- 1 small papaya, halved, seeded, peeled, and cut into bite-size pieces (1 cup)
- ½ cup macadamia nuts *or* toasted blanched whole almonds
- 2 cups hot cooked rice

For marinade, in a bowl stir together orange peel, orange juice, soy sauce, honey, and gingerroot. Rinse chicken; pat dry. Cut into 1-inch pieces. Add chicken to marinade, stirring to coat. Cover and marinate at room temperature for 30 minutes or in the refrigerator for 2 hours, stirring occasionally.

Drain chicken, reserving marinade. Combine cornstarch and reserved marinade. Set aside.

Preheat a wok or large skillet over high heat; add cooking oil. (Add more oil as necessary during cooking.) Stir-fry celery in hot oil for 3 to 4 minutes or till crisp-tender. Remove celery from the wok or skillet.

Add chicken to the wok or skillet; stir-fry for 2 to 3 minutes or till no longer pink. Push chicken from the center of the wok or skillet. Stir marinade mixture; add to center of the wok or skillet. Cook and stir till thickened and bubbly.

Return celery to the wok or skillet; add papaya. Stir to coat well. Cook, covered, about 1 minute or till heated through. Stir in nuts. Serve with hot cooked rice. Makes 4 servings.

Beer Batter-Fried Chicken

- 1 2½- to 3-pound broiler-fryer chicken, cut up
- 1 cup packaged biscuit mix
- ½ teaspoon onion salt
- ¼ teaspoon garlic powder
- ¼ to ½ teaspoon ground red pepper
- 1 beaten egg
- ½ cup beer
  Shortening *or* cooking oil for deep-fat frying

Skin chicken, if desired. Rinse chicken. In a large saucepan cover chicken with lightly salted water. Bring to boiling; reduce heat. Cover and simmer for 20 minutes. Drain. Pat dry with paper towels.

For batter, in a bowl combine biscuit mix, onion salt, garlic powder, and ground red pepper. In another bowl stir together egg and beer; add to biscuit mixture. Beat till smooth.

Meanwhile, in a heavy 3-quart saucepan or deep-fat fryer heat 1¼ inches of shortening or oil to 365°. Dip chicken pieces, one at a time, into batter, gently shaking off excess batter. Carefully lower into the hot oil. Fry, two or three pieces at a time, for 2 to 3 minutes or till golden, turning once. Drain well. Keep warm. Makes 6 servings.

To Skin or Not to Skin

Our recipes deal with chicken skin in three ways. In some recipes, we call for the skin to be left on, either because it is too difficult to remove or because it is necessary to keep the chicken from overcooking. In other recipes, we give you a choice. Remove the skin if you wish to save calories and cut down on fat. Finally, in still other recipes, we tell you to remove the skin. In these dishes, the skin develops an unpleasant texture if it is left on. Keep these guidelines in mind when you're trying to decide whether to skin chicken for your own recipes. One last tip: If you're micro-cooking skinned chicken, be sure to cover the baking dish with vented clear plastic wrap to keep the chicken moist.

Cornmeal Batter-Fried Chicken

The crisp golden coating is like a hush puppy wrapped around each piece of chicken.

> 1   2½- to 3-pound broiler-fryer chicken, cut up
> ⅔   cup all-purpose flour
> ⅓   cup cornmeal
> ½   teaspoon baking powder
> ½   teaspoon garlic salt
> ½   teaspoon poultry seasoning
> ⅛   teaspoon ground red pepper
> 1   beaten egg
> ½   cup milk
> 2   tablespoons cooking oil
>   Shortening *or* cooking oil for deep-fat frying

Skin chicken, if desired. Rinse chicken. In a large saucepan cover chicken with *lightly salted* water. Bring to boiling; reduce heat. Cover and simmer for 20 minutes. Drain. Pat chicken pieces dry with paper towels.

For batter, in a mixing bowl combine flour, cornmeal, baking powder, garlic salt, poultry seasoning, and red pepper. Stir together egg, milk, and the 2 tablespoons oil. Add to flour mixture; beat till smooth.

Meanwhile, in a heavy 3-quart saucepan or deep-fat fryer heat 1¼ inches shortening or oil to 365°. Dip chicken pieces, one at a time, into batter, gently shaking off excess batter. Carefully lower into the hot oil. Fry, two or three pieces at a time, for 2 to 3 minutes or till golden, turning once. Carefully remove; drain well. Keep warm while frying remaining chicken. Makes 6 servings.

Herbed Batter-Fried Chicken: Prepare as above, *except* omit poultry seasoning. Stir 1 teaspoon dried *thyme, savory, marjoram, Italian seasoning, or sage,* crushed, into flour mixture.

Taco Batter-Fried Chicken: Prepare as above, *except* omit poultry seasoning. Stir one 1¼-ounce envelope *taco seasoning mix* into flour mixture. Increase milk to ⅔ *cup.*

Parmesan Batter-Fried Chicken: Prepare as above, *except* omit garlic salt and poultry seasoning. Stir ¼ cup grated *Parmesan cheese,* 2 tablespoons snipped *parsley,* and ¼ teaspoon *garlic powder* into the flour mixture. Increase milk to ⅔ *cup.*

Turkey-Rice Skillet

If your family likes hot and spicy foods, use Monterey Jack cheese with jalapeño peppers.

In a large skillet cook 1 pound ground raw *turkey* till brown. Drain well.

Stir in one 14½-ounce can stewed *tomatoes,* undrained; 1 cup *water;* ⅔ cup *long grain rice;* 2 teaspoons *chili powder;* and ⅛ teaspoon *pepper.* Bring to boiling; reduce heat. Cover and simmer about 20 minutes or till rice is tender.

Stir together ¾ cup *milk* and 1 tablespoon all-purpose *flour;* add to skillet. Cook and stir till thickened and bubbly. Cook and stir 1 minute more. Add ½ cup shredded *Monterey Jack cheese;* stir till melted. Makes 4 servings.

◄ Dip boiled chicken pieces into the batter to coat. Parmesan Batter-Fried Chicken is shown.

Use tongs to carefully lower the chicken into the hot oil and to remove the pieces when golden.

Chicken Fricassee

This braised chicken, with its rich, creamy sauce, represents country cooking at its best.

- ¼ cup all-purpose flour
- 1 teaspoon paprika
- ¼ teaspoon salt
- ¼ teaspoon pepper
- 2 to 2½ pounds meaty chicken pieces (breasts, thighs, and drumsticks)
- 1 tablespoon cooking oil *or* shortening
- 1 cup halved fresh mushrooms
- ⅓ cup chopped green *or* sweet red pepper *or* celery
- ⅓ cup sliced green onion
- 1 cup chicken broth
- ¼ teaspoon dried basil, marjoram, oregano, *or* thyme, crushed
- ¼ cup light cream *or* milk
- 1 tablespoon all-purpose flour
- 2 cups hot cooked noodles *or* spaetzle

In a plastic or paper bag combine the ¼ cup flour, paprika, salt, and pepper.

Skin chicken, if desired. Rinse chicken; pat dry. Add chicken, two or three pieces at a time, to the bag, shaking to coat well.

In a 12-inch skillet cook chicken in hot oil about 15 minutes or till lightly browned, turning to brown evenly. Remove chicken; set aside.

Drain fat, reserving *2 tablespoons* of the dripping in the skillet (add more oil, if necessary). Add mushrooms, green or red pepper or celery, and green onion to skillet. Cook and stir for 2 minutes. Stir in chicken broth and basil, marjoram, oregano, or thyme.

Bring to boiling, scraping up browned bits from the bottom of the skillet. Return chicken to the skillet. Bring to boiling; reduce heat. Cover and simmer for 35 to 40 minutes or till chicken is tender and no longer pink.

Transfer chicken and vegetables to a platter; keep warm. Skim fat from pan juices; measure ¾ *cup* of the pan juices and return to the skillet. Stir cream or milk into the 1 tablespoon flour. Stir into pan juices. Cook and stir till thickened and bubbly. Cook and stir for 1 minute more.

Spoon some of the sauce over chicken; pass remaining sauce. Serve with hot noodles or spaetzle. Makes 6 servings.

Chicken Paprikash

- 2 to 2½ pounds meaty chicken pieces (breasts, thighs, and drumsticks)
- 1 tablespoon cooking oil
- 1 cup chopped onion
- 3 to 4 teaspoons paprika
- ¾ cup chicken broth
- ¼ cup dry white wine
- 1 8-ounce carton dairy sour cream
- 2 tablespoons all-purpose flour
- 2 cups hot cooked noodles *or* rice

Skin chicken, if desired. Rinse and pat dry. In a 12-inch skillet cook chicken in hot oil about 15 minutes or till lightly browned, turning to brown evenly. Sprinkle with salt and pepper. Remove chicken; set aside.

Add onion and paprika to skillet; cook till onion is tender. Add chicken, turning pieces to coat with paprika mixture. Add broth and wine. Bring to boiling; reduce heat. Cover; simmer 40 minutes or till chicken is tender and no longer pink.

Transfer chicken to a platter; keep warm. For sauce, skim fat from pan juices. Measure *1½ cups* juices, adding water, if necessary. In a bowl stir together sour cream and flour; gradually stir in juices mixture. Pour into skillet. Cook and stir till thickened and bubbly; cook and stir for 1 minute more. Spoon some sauce over chicken; pass remainder. Serve with hot cooked noodles or rice. Makes 6 servings.

Microwave directions: Skin chicken. Rinse; pat dry. In a 12x7½x2-inch baking dish micro-cook oil, onion, and paprika, covered with waxed paper, on 100% power (high) for 5 to 6 minutes or till onion is tender. Add chicken, turning to coat and arranging meaty portions toward the edges of the dish. Cook, covered, on high for 11 to 14 minutes or till no pink remains, giving dish a half-turn every 4 minutes. Transfer chicken to a platter; cover.

For sauce, skim fat from pan juices. Add broth to juices to make *1¼ cups;* add *2 tablespoons* wine. In a 4-cup measure stir together sour cream and flour. Slowly stir in the juices mixture. Cook, uncovered, on high for 6 to 8 minutes or till thickened and bubbly, stirring every minute. Cook 30 seconds more. Serve as above.

Chicken Cacciatore

2 to 2½ pounds meaty chicken pieces
   (breasts, thighs, drumsticks)
½ cup chopped onion
2 cloves garlic, minced
1 tablespoon cooking oil
1 cup sliced fresh mushrooms
1 8-ounce can tomato sauce
1 7½-ounce can tomatoes, cut up
½ cup dry white wine
½ cup chicken broth
1½ to 2 teaspoons dried basil, crushed
1 bay leaf
4 teaspoons cornstarch
2 cups hot cooked fettuccine

Skin chicken, if desired. Rinse and pat dry. In a large skillet cook chicken, onion, and garlic in hot oil about 15 minutes or till chicken is lightly browned, turning to brown evenly. Drain off fat.

Stir together mushrooms, tomato sauce, *undrained* tomatoes, wine, broth, basil, bay leaf, ¼ teaspoon *salt,* and ¼ teaspoon *pepper.* Pour over chicken in the skillet. Bring to boiling; reduce heat. Cover and simmer for 30 to 35 minutes or till chicken is tender and no longer pink.

Transfer chicken to a platter. Cover; keep warm. Discard bay leaf. Skim fat from tomato mixture. Stir together cornstarch and 2 tablespoons *cold water;* stir into tomato mixture. Cook and stir till bubbly; cook and stir 2 minutes more. Serve over chicken and noodles. Serves 6.

Microwave directions: In a 1½-quart casserole micro-cook onion, garlic, and oil, uncovered, on 100% power (high) about 2 minutes or till onion is tender. Add mushrooms, tomato sauce, *undrained* tomatoes, wine, broth, basil, bay leaf, ¼ teaspoon *salt,* and ¼ teaspoon *pepper.* Cook on high for 5 to 6 minutes or till boiling, stirring once. Cook on 50% power (medium) for 5 minutes. Discard bay leaf.

Skin chicken, if desired. Rinse; pat dry. In a 12x7½x2-inch baking dish arrange the chicken pieces, skin side down, with meaty portions toward the edges of the dish. Cook, covered with waxed paper, on high for 12 to 14 minutes or till tender and no longer pink, turning pieces over and giving dish a half-turn after 6 minutes. Drain fat; keep chicken warm. Combine *2 tablespoons* cornstarch and 2 tablespoons *cold water.* Add to tomato mixture; cook, uncovered, on high for 2 to 4 minutes or till thickened and bubbly, stirring every minute. Serve as above.

Coq au Vin

The rich burgundy sauce will impress your guests and family.

2 to 2½ pounds meaty chicken pieces
   (breasts, thighs, and drumsticks)
2 tablespoons cooking oil
12 to 18 pearl onions or shallots,
   peeled
1¼ cups burgundy
1 cup whole fresh mushrooms
1 cup thinly sliced carrot
1 tablespoon snipped parsley
2 cloves garlic, minced
½ teaspoon dried marjoram, crushed
½ teaspoon dried thyme, crushed
1 bay leaf
2 tablespoons all-purpose flour
2 tablespoons margarine or butter,
   softened
2 slices bacon, crisp-cooked, drained,
   and crumbled
   Snipped parsley (optional)
2 cups hot cooked noodles

Skin chicken, if desired. Rinse and pat dry. In a 12-inch skillet cook chicken pieces in hot oil about 15 minutes or till lightly browned, turning to brown evenly. Sprinkle with salt and pepper. Add onions or shallots, burgundy, mushrooms, carrot, the 1 tablespoon parsley, garlic, marjoram, thyme, and bay leaf. Bring to boiling; reduce heat. Cover and simmer for 35 to 40 minutes or till chicken is tender and no longer pink.

Transfer chicken and vegetables to a serving platter. Cover and keep warm. Discard bay leaf. In a bowl stir together flour and softened margarine or butter to make a smooth paste. Stir into burgundy mixture in the skillet. Cook and stir till thickened and bubbly. Cook and stir 1 minute more. Season to taste with salt and pepper.

Pour burgundy mixture over chicken and vegetables. Sprinkle with bacon and, if desired, additional parsley. Serve with hot noodles. Makes 6 servings.

Mediterranean Chicken

This combination of chicken, rice, and peas is reminiscent of paella and arroz con pollo.

1½ pounds meaty chicken pieces
      (breasts, thighs, and drumsticks)
  2 tablespoons cooking oil
  6 ounces bulk chorizo *or* bulk Italian
      sausage
  2 medium onions, cut into wedges
  3 cloves garlic, minced
2¼ cups water
  ¾ cup long grain rice
  1 tablespoon instant chicken bouillon
      granules
  ½ teaspoon dried oregano, crushed
  ¼ teaspoon pepper
  1 10-ounce package frozen peas,
      thawed
  1 medium green *or* sweet red pepper,
      cut into 1-inch squares
  8 cherry tomatoes, halved, *or*
      1 medium tomato, cut into
      6 wedges
  ½ cup sliced ripe olives

Rinse chicken; pat dry. In a 4½-quart Dutch oven cook chicken in hot oil, uncovered, over medium heat about 15 minutes or till lightly browned, turning to brown evenly. Remove chicken and set aside. Discard drippings.

In the same pan cook sausage, onions, and garlic over medium heat for 8 to 10 minutes or till sausage is no longer pink. Drain; return to pan. Add water, rice, bouillon granules, oregano, and pepper. Bring to boiling, scraping up the browned bits. Place chicken pieces atop the sausage mixture. Reduce heat. Cover and simmer about 15 minutes or till chicken is nearly tender, turning chicken once.

Add peas and green or red pepper to chicken mixture. Cook, covered, about 5 minutes more or till chicken is tender and no longer pink. Gently stir in tomatoes and olives. Makes 6 servings.

Chicken Country Captain

  1 2½- to 3-pound broiler-fryer
      chicken, cut up
  ¼ cup chopped onion
  ¼ cup chopped green pepper
  1 clove garlic, minced
  1 tablespoon margarine *or* butter
  1 14½-ounce can tomatoes, cut up
  ¼ cup snipped parsley
  2 tablespoons currants *or* raisins
  1 tablespoon curry powder
  ½ teaspoon salt
  ½ teaspoon ground mace *or* nutmeg
  ¼ teaspoon sugar
  ⅛ teaspoon pepper
  1 tablespoon cornstarch
  2 cups hot cooked rice
  2 tablespoons toasted sliced almonds
      (optional)

Skin chicken, if desired. Rinse and pat dry. In a large skillet cook onion, green pepper, and garlic in margarine or butter till tender but not brown. Remove from heat. Stir in *undrained* tomatoes, parsley, currants or raisins, curry powder, salt, mace, sugar, and pepper. Bring to boiling.

Add chicken pieces to the skillet, turning to coat. Bring to boiling; reduce heat. Cover and simmer for 35 to 45 minutes or till tender and no longer pink, turning chicken once. Remove chicken from the skillet; keep warm.

For sauce, skim fat from tomato mixture. Stir together cornstarch and 1 tablespoon *cold water;* add to tomato mixture. Cook and stir till thickened and bubbly. Cook and stir for 2 minutes more. Serve chicken and sauce with rice. If desired, sprinkle with almonds. Makes 6 servings.

Microwave directions: Skin chicken. Rinse and pat dry. Arrange in a 12x7½x2-inch baking dish with meaty portions toward the edges of the dish. Micro-cook, covered with vented plastic wrap, on 100% power (high) for 12 to 15 minutes or till tender and no longer pink, turning pieces over and rearranging after 5 minutes. Transfer chicken to a platter. Cover; keep warm.

For sauce, in a 4-cup measure combine onion, green pepper, garlic, and margarine. Cook, uncovered, on high 2 to 3 minutes or till tender. Stir in cornstarch. Add *undrained* tomatoes, parsley, currants, curry powder, salt, mace, sugar, and pepper. Cook, uncovered, on high 4 to 6 minutes or till thickened and bubbly, stirring every minute. Cook 30 seconds more. Serve as above.

Stewed Chicken

Use this chicken and its broth in recipes that call for cooked chicken or broth.

- 1 **2½- to 3-pound broiler-fryer chicken, cut up**
- 3 **stalks celery with leaves, cut up**
- 2 **carrots, cut up**
- 1 **large onion, quartered**
- 2 **sprigs parsley**
- 1 **teaspoon salt**
- ½ **teaspoon dried thyme, sage, *or* basil, crushed**
- ¼ **teaspoon pepper**
- 2 **bay leaves**
- 6 **cups water**

Skin chicken, if desired. Rinse. In a 4½-quart Dutch oven combine chicken; celery; carrots; onion; parsley; salt; thyme, sage, or basil; pepper; and bay leaves. Add water. Bring to boiling; reduce heat. Cover and simmer for 40 minutes.

Remove chicken. Strain broth through a large sieve lined with 2 layers of cheesecloth. Discard solids. If using broth while hot, skim off fat. (*Or,* if storing broth for later use, chill broth in a bowl for 6 hours. Lift off fat. Pour broth into airtight containers, discarding residue in the bottom of the bowl. Seal containers. Chill up to 2 days or freeze up to 3 months.)

When chicken is cool enough to handle, remove meat from bones; discard skin and bones. Chop meat and use immediately. (*Or,* if storing meat for later use, place in airtight containers; seal. Chill up to 3 days or freeze up to 3 months.) Makes about 5½ cups broth and 2½ cups chopped meat.

Chicken and Noodles: Prepare as above, *except* pour *4 cups* of the *hot* broth into the Dutch oven. (Freeze remaining broth for another use.) Bring to boiling. Add 6 ounces (2½ cups) dried *Homemade Pasta* (see recipe, page 266), 6 ounces (3 cups) packaged *noodles, or* one 8-ounce package frozen *noodles.* Stir in 1 cup thinly sliced *carrots;* ½ cup sliced *celery;* ½ cup chopped *onion;* ½ teaspoon dried *thyme, sage, or basil,* crushed; ½ teaspoon *salt;* and ¼ teaspoon *pepper.* Return to boiling; reduce heat. Cover and simmer for 10 to 15 minutes or till noodles and vegetables are tender. Slowly stir ⅓ cup *cold water* into 3 tablespoons *all-purpose flour.* Add to broth. Cook and stir till thickened and bubbly. Cook and stir 1 minute more. Stir in the chopped chicken. Heat through. Serves 6.

Chicken and Dumplings

Old-fashioned goodness ready to eat in an hour.

- 1 **2½- to 3-pound broiler-fryer chicken, cut up**
- ½ **cup chopped onion**
- ½ **teaspoon poultry seasoning *or* dried sage *or* thyme, crushed**
- ¼ **teaspoon salt**
- ¼ **teaspoon pepper**
- 2 **cups sliced carrot**
- 1 **cup sliced celery**
  Dumplings for Stew (see recipe, page 378)
- ¼ **cup all-purpose flour**

Skin chicken, if desired. Rinse. In a 4½-quart Dutch oven combine chicken, onion, poultry seasoning, salt, and pepper. Add 3 cups *water.* Bring to boiling; reduce heat. Cover and simmer for 25 minutes. Add carrot and celery. Simmer, covered, for 10 minutes more.

Prepare Dumplings for Stew, omitting the herb. Drop from a tablespoon into *six* mounds directly onto chicken (*do not drop batter into liquid*). Cover; simmer about 12 minutes or till a toothpick inserted into dumplings comes out clean. Using a slotted spoon, transfer chicken, dumplings, and vegetables to a platter; cover.

For gravy, skim fat from broth; discard fat. Measure *2 cups* broth into the Dutch oven. Slowly stir ½ cup *cold water* into flour. Stir into broth. Cook and stir till bubbly. Cook and stir 1 minute more. Season to taste with salt and pepper. Serve gravy over chicken and dumplings. Serves 6.

Microwave directions: Skin chicken, if desired. Rinse. In a 3-quart casserole combine chicken, onion, poultry seasoning, salt, pepper, and 2½ cups *water.* Micro-cook, covered, on 100% power (high) for 10 minutes, stirring once. Add carrot and celery. Cook, covered, on 50% power (medium) for 15 to 20 minutes or till chicken is no longer pink and vegetables are tender, stirring once. Prepare and drop Dumplings for Stew as above. Cook, covered, on high for 4 to 5 minutes or till a toothpick inserted into dumplings comes out clean. Transfer chicken, dumplings, and vegetables to a platter; cover.

Skim fat from broth; discard. Measure *2 cups* broth into the same casserole. Slowly stir ½ cup *cold water* into flour; stir into broth in casserole. Cook, uncovered, on high for 5 to 6 minutes or till thickened and bubbly, stirring every minute. Cook 1 minute more. Season; serve as above.

Chicken Potpies

Use pastry, crumbs, or biscuits to top these tasty minicasseroles.

Pastry for Double-Crust Pie (see recipe, page 294)
1 **10-ounce package frozen peas and carrots**
½ **cup chopped onion**
½ **cup chopped fresh mushrooms**
¼ **cup margarine *or* butter**
⅓ **cup all-purpose flour**
½ **teaspoon salt**
½ **teaspoon dried sage, marjoram, *or* thyme, crushed**
⅛ **teaspoon pepper**
2 **cups chicken broth**
¾ **cup milk**
3 **cups cubed cooked chicken *or* turkey**
¼ **cup snipped parsley**
¼ **cup chopped pimiento**   Oven 450°

Prepare pastry; set aside. Cook peas and carrots according to package directions; drain. In a saucepan cook onion and mushrooms in margarine or butter till tender. Stir in flour; salt; sage, marjoram, or thyme; and pepper. Add chicken broth and milk all at once. Cook and stir till thickened and bubbly. Stir in drained peas and carrots, chicken or turkey, parsley, and pimiento; heat till bubbly. Pour chicken mixture into six 10-ounce round casseroles. (*Or,* use a 12x7½x2-inch baking dish.)

Roll pastry into a 15x10-inch rectangle. Cut into six 5-inch circles and place atop the 10-ounce casseroles. (*Or,* roll pastry into a 13x9-inch rectangle. Place over the 12x7½x2-inch baking dish.) Flute edges of pastry and cut slits in the top for steam to escape. Bake in a 450° oven for 12 to 15 minutes or till pastry is golden brown. Makes 6 servings.

Herb-Crumb-Topped Chicken Potpies: Prepare as above, *except* omit pastry. Stir together 1 cup *herb-seasoned stuffing croutons* and 2 tablespoons melted *margarine or butter.* Sprinkle atop chicken mixture in casseroles or dish.

Biscuit-Topped Chicken Potpies: Prepare as above, *except* omit pastry. Cut 1 package (6) refrigerated *biscuits* into quarters and arrange atop *bubbly* chicken mixture in casseroles or dish. Bake in a 400° oven about 15 minutes or till biscuits are golden.

Chicken à la King

A great way to use leftover chicken or turkey.

¼ **cup margarine *or* butter**
1 **cup sliced fresh mushrooms *or* one 4-ounce can mushroom stems and pieces, drained**
⅓ **cup all-purpose flour**
1¾ **cups milk**
1 **cup chicken broth**
2 **cups cubed cooked chicken *or* turkey**
¼ **cup chopped pimiento**
2 **tablespoons dry sherry (optional)**
8 **toast points *or* 4 baked patty shells**

In a saucepan melt margarine. If using fresh mushrooms, add mushrooms and cook till tender. Stir in flour, ½ teaspoon *salt,* and ¼ teaspoon *pepper.* Add milk and chicken broth all at once. Cook and stir till thickened and bubbly. Cook and stir for 1 minute more. Add canned mushrooms, if using. Stir in chicken or turkey, pimiento, and, if desired, dry sherry. Heat through. Spoon atop toast points. Serves 4.

Microwave directions: Do not use fresh mushrooms. In a 2-quart casserole micro-cook margarine, uncovered, on 100% power (high) for 30 to 45 seconds or till melted. Stir in flour, salt, and pepper. Add milk and ½ cup chicken broth all at once. Stir to combine. Cook, uncovered, on high for 5 to 7 minutes or till thickened and bubbly, stirring every minute till mixture starts to thicken, then every 30 seconds. Stir in canned mushrooms, chicken or turkey, pimiento, and, if desired, sherry. Cook, covered, on high for 2 to 4 minutes or till heated through; stir once. Serve as above. Do not micro-cook recipes below.

Cheesy Chicken à la King: Prepare as above, *except* add 1 cup shredded *American or process Swiss cheese* to the thickened mixture before adding the chicken or turkey. Stir till cheese melts.

Curried Chicken à la King: Prepare as above, *except* add 1 teaspoon *curry powder* to melted margarine or butter; cook for 1 minute. Omit dry sherry. If desired, add 1 tablespoon chutney with chicken or turkey.

Herbed Chicken à la King: Prepare as above, *except* cook 2 tablespoons finely chopped *green pepper or* sliced *green onion;* 1 clove *garlic,* minced; and ½ teaspoon dried *basil,* crushed, in melted margarine or butter till tender.

Chicken Enchiladas

- **8 6-inch tortillas**
- **½ cup chopped onion**
- **4 cloves garlic, minced**
- **1 teaspoon ground coriander**
- **¼ teaspoon pepper**
- **2 tablespoons margarine *or* butter**
- **3 tablespoons all-purpose flour**
- **1 8-ounce carton dairy sour cream**
- **2 cups chicken broth**
- **1 or 2 canned jalapeño chili peppers, rinsed, seeded, and chopped; *or* one 4-ounce can diced green chili peppers, drained**
- **1 cup shredded Monterey Jack cheese (4 ounces)**
- **2 cups chopped cooked chicken *or* turkey**
- **Sliced pitted ripe olives (optional)**
- **Chopped tomatoes (optional)**
- **Sliced green onions (optional)** Oven 350°

Wrap tortillas in foil. Heat in a 350° oven for 10 to 15 minutes or till softened.

For sauce, in a saucepan cook onion, garlic, coriander, and pepper in margarine or butter till onion is tender. Stir flour into sour cream; add to onion mixture. Stir in broth and chili peppers all at once. Cook and stir till thickened and bubbly. Remove from heat; stir in ½ *cup* of the cheese.

For filling, stir ½ *cup* of the sauce into chicken. Place about ¼ *cup* filling atop *each* tortilla; roll up. Arrange rolls, seam side down, in a lightly greased 12x7½x2-inch baking dish. Top with remaining sauce. Bake, covered, in a 350° oven about 35 minutes or till heated through.

Sprinkle with remaining cheese. Bake, uncovered, about 5 minutes more or till cheese melts. If desired, sprinkle with olives, tomatoes, and green onions. Let stand 10 minutes. Makes 4 servings.

Microwave directions: In a 1½-quart casserole micro-cook onion, garlic, coriander, pepper, and margarine or butter, uncovered, on 100% power (high) for 2 to 3 minutes or till tender. Stir flour into sour cream; add to onion mixture. Stir in 1¾ *cups* chicken broth and chili peppers. Cook, uncovered, on high for 5 to 7 minutes or till thickened and bubbly, stirring every minute. Stir in ½ *cup* of the cheese.

Wrap tortillas in paper towels and cook on high for 30 to 60 seconds or till softened. Assemble filling and enchiladas as above. Arrange rolls, seam side down, in a lightly greased 12x7½x2-inch baking dish. Top with remaining sauce. Cook, covered with vented plastic wrap, on high for 12 to 14 minutes or till heated through, giving the dish a half-turn once. Sprinkle with remaining cheese. If desired, sprinkle with olives, tomatoes, and green onions. Let stand 10 minutes.

Chicken Jambalaya

Complete the menu with a tossed salad, French bread, and sherbet or ice cream.

- ⅓ cup chopped celery
- ¼ cup chopped onion
- ¼ cup chopped green pepper
- 2 tablespoons margarine *or* butter
- 1 14½-ounce can tomatoes, cut up
- 1½ cups chicken broth
- ⅔ cup long grain rice
- 1 teaspoon dried basil *or* thyme, crushed
- ½ teaspoon garlic salt
- ¼ teaspoon pepper
- ¼ to ½ teaspoon bottled hot pepper sauce
- 1 bay leaf
- 2 cups cubed cooked chicken *or* turkey

In a large skillet cook celery, onion, and green pepper in margarine or butter till vegetables are tender. Stir in the *undrained* tomatoes, chicken broth, rice, basil or thyme, garlic salt, pepper, hot pepper sauce, and bay leaf. Bring to boiling; reduce heat. Cover and simmer about 20 minutes or till rice is tender. Stir in chicken; cook till heated through. Discard bay leaf. Makes 4 servings.

Quick Cooked Chicken

If you need cooked chicken for a recipe but don't have time to stew a bird, poach some chicken breasts. To get two cups of cubed, cooked chicken, start with two whole medium chicken breasts (about 1½ pounds), halved and skinned, if desired, or ¾ pound skinned and boned chicken breasts.

Place the chicken breasts in a large skillet with 1⅓ cups water. Bring to boiling; reduce heat. Cover and simmer for 18 to 20 minutes for breast halves with bones (12 to 14 minutes for boneless pieces) or till tender and no longer pink. Drain and cut into cubes.

Chicken-Cheese Crepes

- 12 Crepes (see recipe, page 72)
- 1 cup frozen peas and carrots
- ½ cup chopped onion
- ½ cup chopped green pepper
- ¼ cup margarine *or* butter
- ¼ cup all-purpose flour
- 1½ cups milk
- ½ cup chicken broth
- ½ cup shredded process Swiss, Gruyère, *or* American cheese
- 2 tablespoons dry sherry (optional)
- 2 tablespoons snipped parsley
  Several dashes bottled hot pepper sauce
- 1 2½-ounce jar sliced mushrooms
- 2 cups chopped cooked chicken *or* turkey   Oven 375°

Prepare Crepes. Cook frozen peas and carrots according to package directions. Drain and season to taste with salt and pepper; set aside.

For sauce, in a medium saucepan cook onion and green pepper in margarine till tender. Stir in flour. Add milk and broth all at once. Cook and stir till bubbly. Cook and stir 1 minute more. Stir in cheese; sherry, if desired; parsley; and hot pepper sauce. Remove *1 cup* of the sauce; set aside. Drain mushrooms; stir into remaining sauce.

For filling, combine cooked peas and carrots, the 1 cup sauce, and chicken or turkey. Spread ¼ *cup* filling over the *unbrowned* side of *each* crepe, leaving a ¼-inch rim around edge. Roll up crepes. Place, seam side down, in a 12x7½x2-inch baking dish. Cover; bake in a 375° oven for 15 to 18 minutes or till heated through. Reheat remaining sauce; drizzle some over crepes. Pass remaining sauce. Makes 6 servings.

Microwave directions: Prepare Crepes and vegetables as above. For sauce, in a 1½-quart casserole micro-cook onion, green pepper, and margarine, covered, on 100% power (high) for 2 to 4 minutes or till tender. Stir in flour. Add milk and broth all at once; stir to combine. Cook, uncovered, on high for 5 to 6 minutes or till thickened and bubbly, stirring every minute. Cook for 1 minute more. Stir in cheese; sherry, if desired; parsley; and hot pepper sauce. Reserve *1 cup* sauce. Prepare filling, roll crepes, and place in baking dish as above. Cook, covered with waxed paper, on high for 4 to 6 minutes or till heated through, giving dish a half-turn once. Reheat remaining sauce on high for 1 to 2 minutes. Serve as above.

Chicken Divan

Parmesan cheese and a hint of wine will tingle your taste buds.

> 2 **cups frozen chopped broccoli**
> 3 **tablespoons margarine *or* butter**
> 3 **tablespoons all-purpose flour**
> ⅛ **teaspoon pepper**
> **Dash ground nutmeg**
> ¾ **cup light cream *or* milk**
> ½ **cup chicken broth**
> ½ **cup shredded Swiss cheese**
> 2 **tablespoons dry white wine**
> 1½ **cups cubed cooked chicken *or* turkey**
> 3 **tablespoons grated Parmesan cheese**
> **Paprika**　　　　　　Oven 350°

Cook broccoli according to package directions; drain. Arrange in a 10x6x2-inch baking dish.

Meanwhile, for sauce, in a medium saucepan melt margarine or butter. Stir in flour, pepper, and nutmeg. Add cream or milk and chicken broth all at once. Cook and stir till thickened and bubbly. Add Swiss cheese and wine, stirring till cheese melts.

Pour *half* of the sauce over broccoli. Top with chicken or turkey, then the remaining sauce. Sprinkle with Parmesan cheese and paprika. Bake in a 350° oven about 20 minutes or till heated through. Makes 4 servings.

Microwave directions: Cook broccoli according to package microwave directions; drain. Arrange in a 10x6x2-inch baking dish. In a 4-cup measure micro-cook margarine or butter, uncovered, on 100% power (high) for 30 to 45 seconds or till melted. Stir in flour, pepper, and nutmeg. Add cream or milk and broth. Stir to combine. Cook on high for 3 to 5 minutes or till thickened and bubbly, stirring every minute till sauce starts to thicken, then every 30 seconds. Stir in Swiss cheese and wine. Assemble as above. Cook, uncovered, on 70% power (medium-high) for 6 to 8 minutes or till heated through, giving the dish a half-turn every 2 minutes.

Chicken-Asparagus Stacks

> 1 **10-ounce package frozen asparagus *or* broccoli spears**
> ½ **cup sliced green onion**
> 2 **tablespoons margarine *or* butter**
> 1 **10¾-ounce can condensed cream of chicken soup**
> 1 **8-ounce carton plain yogurt**
> 2 **cups cubed cooked chicken *or* turkey**
> ¼ **cup toasted slivered almonds (optional)**
> 8 **rusks *or* 4 English muffins, split and toasted**
> 4 **hard-cooked eggs, sliced**

Cook asparagus or broccoli according to package directions. Drain; keep warm.

In a saucepan cook onion in margarine till onion is tender. Stir in condensed soup and yogurt till smooth. Stir in chicken. Heat through. If desired, stir in almonds. Top rusks or muffin halves with the asparagus or broccoli, chicken mixture, and egg slices. Makes 4 servings.

Microwave directions: Cook asparagus or broccoli according to package microwave directions. Drain; keep warm. In a 1½-quart casserole micro-cook onion in margarine, uncovered, on 100% power (high) for 1½ to 2 minutes or till onion is tender, stirring once. Stir in soup, yogurt, and chicken. Cook, covered, on high for 5 to 7 minutes or till heated through, stirring 2 or 3 times. If desired, stir in almonds. Serve as above.

Chicken Submarines

In a bowl mix ½ cup dairy *sour cream, plain yogurt, mayonnaise, or salad dressing;* 2 teaspoons *prepared mustard;* ½ teaspoon dried *basil,* crushed; and ⅛ teaspoon *garlic powder.* Halve, seed, peel, and thinly slice 1 small *avocado.* If desired, brush avocado with lemon juice.

Split 4 individual *French rolls* and scoop out some of the center of each half. Spread both halves of rolls with some of the yogurt mixture. On the bottom half of *each* roll, layer 1 leaf *lettuce;* 2 slices cooked *chicken or turkey;* 1 slice *American, Swiss, cheddar, or Monterey Jack cheese;* 3 thin slices *tomato or* 6 thin slices *cucumber;* and the avocado slices. If desired, top with alfalfa sprouts. Replace roll tops. Serves 4.

Stuffed and Roasted Bird

To prepare a whole bird for cooking, rinse the bird well on the outside, as well as inside the body and neck cavities. Pat the bird dry with paper towels. If desired, rub salt inside the body cavity.

For an *unstuffed bird,* place quartered onions and celery in the body cavity, if desired. Pull the neck skin to the back and fasten with a small skewer. If a band of skin crosses the tail, tuck the drumsticks under the band. If there is no band, tie the drumsticks securely to the tail. Twist the wing tips under the back.

For a *stuffed bird,* do not stuff until just before cooking. To stuff, spoon some of the stuffing loosely into the neck cavity; fasten the neck skin as for an unstuffed bird. Lightly spoon stuffing into the body cavity. (Put any remaining stuffing into a casserole and refrigerate. Bake the stuffing in a 325° oven for 40 to 45 minutes or in a 375° oven for 20 to 30 minutes.) Secure the drumsticks and wings as for an unstuffed bird.

Place the unstuffed or stuffed bird, breast side up, on a rack in a shallow roasting pan. Except when cooking a domestic duckling or goose, brush the bird with cooking oil or melted margarine or butter. (Prick the skin of a duckling or goose well all over to allow fat to drain during roasting.) If using a meat thermometer, insert it into the center of one of the inside thigh muscles. The bulb should not touch the bone.

Cover Cornish game hen, quail, squab, and turkey with foil, leaving an air space between the bird and the foil. Press the foil lightly at the ends of the drumsticks and the neck. Leave all other birds uncovered.

Roast in an uncovered pan for the time given in the chart on pages 328–329. Baste occasionally with pan drippings, if desired. When the bird is two-thirds done, cut the band of skin or string between the drumsticks so the thighs will cook evenly. Except when cooking quail, uncover the bird for the last 45 minutes of cooking. (Leave quail covered for the entire cooking time.)

Continue roasting until the meat thermometer registers 180° to 185°. At this time, the drumsticks should move easily in their sockets and the thickest parts of the drumsticks should feel very soft when pressed.

When the bird is done, remove it from the oven and cover it with foil. Let large birds stand for 15 to 20 minutes before carving.

Be sure to store leftover poultry and stuffing *separately* as soon as possible.

Glazed Chicken and Vegetables

1 2½- to 3-pound broiler-fryer chicken
   Cooking oil
2 medium potatoes, peeled and quartered, *or* 6 new potatoes
6 medium carrots, bias-sliced into ½-inch pieces
½ cup honey
¼ cup prepared mustard
2 tablespoons margarine *or* butter
2 tablespoons finely chopped onion
2 teaspoons curry powder
½ teaspoon garlic salt
¼ teaspoon crushed red pepper
¼ teaspoon ground ginger
2 medium apples, cored   Oven 375°

Rinse chicken and pat dry. Skewer neck skin to back. Tie legs to tail. Twist wing tips under back. Place, breast side up, on a rack in a shallow roasting pan. Brush with oil. Roast chicken, uncovered, in a 375° oven for 1 hour.

Cook potatoes and carrots in boiling water for 20 to 25 minutes or till nearly tender. Drain.

For glaze, in a saucepan combine honey, mustard, margarine, onion, curry powder, garlic salt, red pepper, and ginger. Bring to boiling, stirring constantly. Remove from heat; set aside.

Discard fat in roasting pan. Cut apples into wedges. Arrange potatoes, carrots, and apples around chicken in the pan. Spoon glaze over poultry, vegetables, and apples. Roast for 15 to 20 minutes more or till chicken is no longer pink, the drumsticks move easily in their sockets, and the vegetables are tender. Makes 6 servings.

Microwave directions: In a 4-cup measure combine honey, mustard, margarine, onion, curry powder, garlic salt, red pepper, and ginger. Micro-cook, uncovered, on 100% power (high) for 2½ to 3½ minutes or till boiling, stirring every minute. Rinse chicken; pat dry. Skewer neck skin to back. Tie legs to tail. Twist wing tips under back. In a 3-quart casserole place chicken, breast side down. Cook, covered, on high for 10 minutes. Drain. Turn chicken over. *Thinly* slice carrots. Arrange *uncooked* carrots and potatoes around chicken. Cook, covered, on 50% power (medium) for 25 minutes. Carefully drain off liquid. Quarter apples; add to casserole. Spoon honey mixture over all. Cook, covered, on medium for 15 to 20 minutes more or till chicken is no longer pink and vegetables are tender.

Roast Herb Chicken

When micro-cooking or grilling chicken, brush this tangy herb mixture on the bird.

    1 2½- to 3-pound broiler-fryer
         chicken
    2 tablespoons margarine *or* butter
    3 tablespoons lemon juice
    1 teaspoon dried tarragon, oregano,
         basil, thyme, savory, *or* sage,
         crushed; *or* 3 cloves garlic,
         minced   Oven 375°

Rinse chicken and pat dry. Skewer neck skin to back; tie legs to tail. Twist wings under back. Place, breast side up, on a rack in a shallow roasting pan. Melt margarine or butter; stir in lemon juice and a herb or garlic. Brush over chicken. Roast, uncovered, in a 375° oven for 1¼ to 1½ hours or till no longer pink and the drumsticks move easily in their sockets, brushing occasionally with drippings. Season to taste with salt and pepper. Makes 6 servings.

Honey and Spice Duckling

    1 3- to 5-pound domestic duckling
    2 teaspoons Szechwan pepper,
         coarsely ground, *or* 1 teaspoon
         whole pepper, coarsely ground
    1 teaspoon salt
    1 teaspoon ground ginger
    ½ teaspoon five-spice powder
    ¼ cup honey
    2 tablespoons soy sauce   Oven 375°

Rinse duck; pat dry. In a bowl combine pepper, salt, ginger, and five-spice powder. Sprinkle body cavity of duck with some of the salt mixture; rub remaining mixture on skin of duck. Skewer neck skin to back; tie legs to tail. Twist wing tips under back. Prick skin all over with a fork.

Place duckling, breast side up, on a rack in a shallow roasting pan. Roast in a 375° oven for 1¾ to 2¼ hours or till the drumsticks move easily in their sockets and duck is no longer pink, spooning off fat occasionally. Meanwhile, mix honey and soy sauce; baste duck with honey mixture once or twice during the last 10 minutes of roasting. Makes 3 or 4 servings.

Stuffed Cornish Game Hens

    3 slices bacon
    ½ cup shredded carrot
    2 tablespoons snipped parsley
    ¼ teaspoon dried savory, crushed
         Dash pepper
  1½ cups dry bread cubes
    ¼ teaspoon instant chicken bouillon
         granules
    2 1- to 1½-pound Cornish game hens
         Cooking oil
    ¼ cup dry red *or* white wine
    1 tablespoon margarine *or* butter,
         melted
    2 tablespoons orange juice
         Orange juice
    1 tablespoon cornstarch
    1 tablespoon brown sugar
    ½ teaspoon instant chicken
         bouillon granules   Oven 375°

Cook bacon till crisp. Remove bacon; drain and crumble. Cook carrot in drippings over medium heat till tender; remove from heat. Stir in bacon, parsley, savory, and pepper. Stir in bread cubes. Dissolve the ¼ teaspoon bouillon granules in 2 tablespoons *hot water*. Drizzle over bread mixture, tossing lightly.

Rinse hens; pat dry. Season cavities with salt. Lightly stuff hens with bread mixture. Pull neck skin, if present, to back of each hen. Twist wing tips under back, holding skin in place. Tie legs to tail. Place hens, breast side up, on a rack in a shallow roasting pan. Brush with oil; cover loosely with foil. Roast in a 375° oven for 30 minutes.

Stir together wine, melted margarine or butter, and the 2 tablespoons orange juice; brush on hens. Roast hens, uncovered, about 1 hour more or till tender and no longer pink, brushing with wine mixture twice.

For sauce, add additional orange juice to remaining wine mixture to make ¾ *cup*. In a small saucepan combine cornstarch, brown sugar, and the ½ teaspoon bouillon granules. Stir in wine mixture. Cook and stir till thickened and bubbly. Cook and stir 2 minutes more. Serve sauce with hens. Makes 4 servings.

Carving a Roasted Bird

To carve poultry with confidence, use a sharp knife and these directions.

● When the bird is done, remove it from the oven and cover it with foil. Let it stand for 15 to 20 minutes before beginning to carve. Standing lets the bird's flesh firm up, meaning the carved slices will hold together better.

● Place the bird on a cutting board. Remove the stuffing. Grasp the tip of one drumstick and pull it away from the body. Cut through the skin and meat between the thigh and the body. Repeat on the other side.

● With the tip of the knife, separate the thighbone from the backbone by cutting through the joint. Repeat on the other side.

● To separate the thighs and drumsticks, cut through the joints where the drumstick bones and thighbones meet.

● To carve the meat from the drumsticks, hold each drumstick vertically by the tip with the large end resting on the cutting board. Slice the meat parallel to the bone and under some tendons, turning the leg to get even slices. Slice the thigh meat the same way.

● To carve the breast meat, make a deep horizontal cut into the breast above each wing. This cut marks one end of each breast meat slice. Beginning at the outer edge of one side of each breast, cut slices from the top of the breast down to the horizontal cut. Cut the final smaller slices following the curve of the breastbone.

● Remove wings by cutting through the joints where the wing bones and backbone meet.

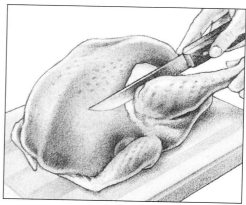

Pulling the leg away from the bird, cut through the meat between the thigh and the body.

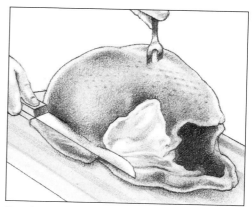

Steadying the bird with a large fork, make a deep cut into the breast just above each wing.

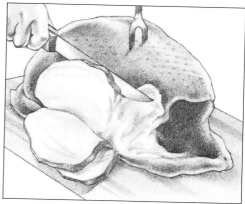

Cutting from the top down to the deep horizontal cut, cut thin, even slices from the breast.

Old-Fashioned Bread Stuffing

  1   **cup finely chopped celery**
  ½   **cup chopped onion**
  ½   **cup margarine *or* butter**
  1   **teaspoon poultry seasoning *or* dried
        sage leaves, crushed**
  8   **cups dry bread cubes**
  ¾   **to 1 cup chicken broth *or* water**

In a small saucepan cook celery and onion in margarine or butter till tender but not brown; remove from heat. Stir in poultry seasoning or sage, ¼ teaspoon *pepper,* and ⅛ teaspoon *salt.*
   Place dry bread cubes in a bowl. Add onion mixture. Drizzle with enough broth or water to moisten, tossing lightly. Use to stuff one 8- to 10-pound turkey. Makes 8 to 10 servings.
   Microwave directions: In a 1-quart casserole micro-cook celery, onion, and margarine, covered, on 100% power (high) for 6 to 8 minutes or till tender, stirring after 4 minutes. Continue as above.
   Mushroom Stuffing: Prepare as above, *except* cook 1 cup sliced fresh *mushrooms* with the celery mixture, *or* add two 4-ounce cans sliced *mushrooms,* drained, with seasonings. If using fresh mushrooms, reduce broth to *½ to ¾ cup.*
   Giblet Stuffing: Prepare as above, *except* add chopped, cooked *poultry giblets* (see Giblet Gravy, page 325) with the seasonings. If desired, substitute giblet cooking broth for the chicken broth or water.
   Oyster Stuffing: Prepare as above, *except* add 1 pint shucked *oysters,* drained and chopped, *or* two 8-ounce cans whole *oysters,* drained and chopped, with the seasonings. Reduce broth to ½ to ¾ cup. If desired, substitute oyster liquid for chicken broth or water.
   Chestnut Stuffing: Prepare as above, *except,* with a knife, cut an X in the shells of 1 pound fresh *chestnuts* (3 cups). Roast chestnuts on a baking sheet in a 400° oven for 15 minutes; cool. Peel and coarsely chop. (*Or,* use one 8-ounce jar whole peeled *chestnuts,* chopped.) Add with seasonings.
   Peanut or Raisin Stuffing: Prepare as above, *except* add 1 cup chopped *peanuts or* ½ cup *raisins or currants* with seasonings.
   Herb and Onion Stuffing: Prepare as above, *except* omit celery and increase onion to 1½ cups. Use sage. Add ¼ cup snipped *parsley;* ½ teaspoon dried *thyme,* crushed; and ¼ teaspoon dried *marjoram,* crushed, with seasonings.

Harvest Stuffing

Flavored with apples and walnuts.

  1   **cup shredded carrots**
  1   **cup chopped celery**
  ½   **cup chopped onion**
  ½   **cup margarine *or* butter**
  ¼   **teaspoon ground nutmeg**
  8   **cups dry bread cubes**
  2   **cups finely chopped peeled apple**
  ½   **cup chopped walnuts**
  ¼   **cup toasted wheat germ**
  ½   **to 1 cup chicken broth**

In a large skillet cook carrots, celery, and onion in margarine or butter till tender. Stir in nutmeg, ¼ teaspoon *salt,* and ¼ teaspoon *pepper.* In a bowl combine bread cubes, apple, walnuts, and wheat germ. Add carrot mixture. Drizzle with enough broth to moisten, tossing lightly. Use to stuff one 8- to 10-pound turkey. Makes 8 to 10 servings.

Stuffing Tips

● To make dry bread cubes for stuffing, cut bread into ½-inch cubes. (Use 16 slices of bread for 8 cups of dry cubes.) Spread into a single layer in a 15½x10½x2-inch baking pan. Bake in a 300° oven 10 to 15 minutes or till dry; stir twice. *Or,* let stand, covered, at room temperature for 8 to 12 hours.
● Halve the ingredients for Old-Fashioned Bread Stuffing or Harvest Stuffing (see recipes, above), or for Corn Bread and Bacon Stuffing (see recipe, page 324), for one 5-pound roasting chicken, two 2- to 3-pound wild geese, three 2-pound pheasant or ducks, or six 1- to 1½-pound Cornish game hens.
● Stuffing temperatures should reach at least 165°. To check, insert a meat thermometer through the body cavity into the thickest part of the stuffing and let stand for 5 minutes.
● If desired, bake the stuffing mixture separately in a casserole, covered, in a 325° oven for 40 to 45 minutes or in a 375° oven for 20 to 30 minutes.

Corn Bread and Bacon Stuffing

   4 slices bacon, chopped
   1 cup chopped celery
   1 cup chopped onion
   2 beaten eggs
   2 tablespoons snipped parsley
   1 teaspoon poultry seasoning
   ¼ teaspoon pepper
   3 cups coarsely crumbled Corn Bread
      (see recipe, page 59)
   3 cups dry bread cubes
   ½ to ¾ cup chicken broth

In a skillet cook chopped bacon, celery, and on-ion over medium heat till bacon is crisp and vege-tables are tender. *Do not drain.*

   Meanwhile, in a bowl combine eggs, parsley, poultry seasoning, and pepper. Add Corn Bread and bread cubes; toss lightly till mixed. Add ba-con mixture. Drizzle with enough of the broth to moisten, tossing lightly till mixed. Use to stuff one 8- to 10-pound turkey or domestic goose. Makes 8 to 10 servings.

Bulgur Pilaf Stuffing

   ½ cup chicken broth
   2 teaspoons Worcestershire sauce
   ⅓ cup bulgur
   4 ounces pork sausage *or* ground
      turkey sausage
   1 cup chopped onion
   1 cup chopped celery
   ½ cup shredded carrot

In a small saucepan bring broth and Worcester-shire sauce to boiling. Add bulgur. Remove from heat. Cover and let stand for 15 minutes.

   In a medium skillet crumble sausage; add on-ion, celery, and carrot. Cook about 6 minutes or till sausage is no longer pink and vegetables are tender, stirring often to break up large pieces. Drain. Stir in bulgur mixture. Use to stuff one 2½- to 3-pound broiler-fryer chicken. Serves 6.

   Microwave directions: In a 1-cup measure micro-cook *⅓ cup* chicken broth and Worcester-shire sauce, uncovered, on 100% power (high) 1 to 2 minutes or till boiling. Add bulgur; cover and let stand 15 minutes. In a 1-quart casserole cook sausage, onion, celery, and carrot, covered, on high 3 to 5 minutes or till sausage is no longer pink. Drain. Stir in bulgur mixture.

Wild Rice Stuffing

This delicious, nutty stuffing or dressing goes great with a chicken or Cornish game hens.

   ¼ cup wild rice
   ¼ cup brown rice
   1½ teaspoons instant chicken bouillon
      granules
   ⅛ teaspoon ground sage *or* nutmeg
   2 cups sliced fresh mushrooms
   ½ cup chopped celery
   3 green onions, sliced
   ¼ cup toasted slivered almonds *or*
      pine nuts (optional)   Oven 375°

Rinse wild rice in a strainer under *cold* water about 1 minute. In a medium saucepan combine wild rice, brown rice, bouillon granules, sage or nutmeg, and 1 cup *water*. Bring to boiling; reduce heat. Cover and simmer for 45 minutes.

   Add mushrooms, celery, and green onions. Cook, covered, over medium-low heat for 10 to 20 minutes more or till vegetables are just tender, stirring frequently. Stir in nuts, if desired. Use to stuff one 2½- to 3-pound broiler-fryer chicken. (*Or,* add ¼ cup *water* and transfer to a 1-quart casserole. Bake in a 375° oven for 25 to 30 minutes.) Makes 6 servings.

   Apricot-Wild-Rice Stuffing: Prepare as above, *except* use nutmeg and 1¼ cups *water*. Add ½ cup snipped dried *apricots or apples* to cooked rice with mushrooms.

Cream Gravy

Gravy is the perfect crowning touch for a fried poultry dinner.

      Fried poultry drippings
   2 tablespoons all-purpose flour
   1 teaspoon instant chicken bouillon
      granules
   ⅛ teaspoon pepper
   1⅔ cups milk

After frying poultry, transfer poultry to a platter; keep warm. Reserve *2 tablespoons* of the drip-pings in the skillet (discard remaining drippings). Stir in flour, bouillon granules, and pepper. Add milk all at once. Cook and stir over medium heat till thickened and bubbly. Cook and stir for 1 minute more. If necessary, thin with a little addi-tional *milk*. Makes 1⅔ cups (6 or 7 servings).

Pan Gravy

Pan drippings from roast poultry
¼ cup all-purpose flour
Chicken broth *or* water

After transferring roast poultry to a serving platter, pour pan drippings into a large measuring cup. Also scrape the browned bits into the cup. Skim and reserve fat from drippings.

Place *¼ cup* of the fat in a medium saucepan (discard remaining fat). Stir in flour. Add enough broth or water to remaining drippings in the measuring cup to equal *2 cups*. Add all at once to flour mixture. Cook and stir over medium heat till thickened and bubbly. Cook and stir 1 minute more. Season to taste with salt and pepper. Makes 2 cups (8 to 10 servings).

Giblet Gravy

For extra gravy to serve with leftover turkey, double this recipe.

¼ pound turkey *or* chicken giblets and neck
1 stalk celery with leaves, cut up
½ small onion, cut up
Pan drippings from roast turkey *or* chicken
¼ cup all-purpose flour
1 hard-cooked egg (optional)

Rinse giblets and neck. Refrigerate liver till needed. In a medium saucepan combine remaining giblets, neck, celery, onion, and *lightly salted* water to cover. Bring to boiling; reduce heat. Cover and simmer about 1 hour or till tender. Add liver; simmer 20 to 30 minutes more for turkey (5 to 10 minutes more for chicken) or till tender. Remove and finely chop giblets. Discard neck bones. Strain broth. Discard vegetables. Chill chopped giblets and broth till needed.

After transferring roast turkey or chicken to a platter, pour pan drippings into a large measuring cup. Skim and reserve fat from pan drippings. Pour *¼ cup* of the fat into the saucepan (discard remaining fat). Stir in flour, ¼ teaspoon *salt,* and ⅛ teaspoon *pepper.* Add reserved broth to the drippings to measure *1½ cups*. Add broth mixture all at once to flour mixture. Cook and stir till bubbly. Cook and stir 1 minute more. Stir in giblets. If desired, chop egg and stir in. Heat through. Makes 2 cups (8 to 10 servings).

To skim the fat from the pan drippings, tilt the cup and spoon off the oily layer on the top.

Using a wooden spoon, stir the reserved fat and flour together until well blended.

Cook and stir gently until the gravy looks thickened, and bubbles appear across its surface.

Defrosting Poultry in the Microwave

Place whole bird, unwrapped, breast side down, in a baking dish. Remove the metal clamp, if present, and the giblets packet as soon as possible. Place poultry pieces, unwrapped, in a baking dish.

Defrost on 30% power (medium-low) for the time specified. After half of the defrosting time, turn whole bird breast side up. (Or, separate, rearrange, and turn pieces over, putting icy parts near the dish edges.) If some areas thaw faster,

shield them with small pieces of foil (check your owner's manual to see if foil is allowed in your oven). If the poultry starts to cook on the edges, immediately remove it from the oven and place it in cold water for the specified standing time. (Some birds and roasts need additional defrosting time after standing, as indicated.*) Poultry must be completely thawed before cooking. It should feel soft and moist but still cold.

Type of Bird	Amount	Defrosting Time	Standing Time
Chicken, broiler-fryer, cut up	One 2½- to 3-pound bird	15 to 17 minutes	10 minutes
Chicken, broiler-fryer, whole	One 2½- to 3-pound bird	20 to 25 minutes	30 minutes
Chicken, roasting, whole	One 3½- to 4-pound bird	25 to 30 minutes	30 minutes
Chicken breasts, whole	One 12-ounce breast Two 12-ounce breasts	6 to 7 minutes 12 to 14 minutes	15 minutes 15 minutes
Chicken drumsticks	2 drumsticks 6 drumsticks	5 to 7 minutes 10 to 12 minutes	5 minutes 5 minutes
Chicken pieces, about ¾ inch thick	1 pound	8 to 12 minutes	
Cornish game hen, whole	One 1- to 1½-pound bird Two 1- to 1½-pound birds	8 to 10 minutes 12 to 15 minutes	30 minutes 30 minutes
Duckling, domestic, whole	One 4- to 5-pound bird	25 minutes	30 minutes*
Turkey, ground raw	1 pound	10 to 12 minutes	5 minutes
Turkey, whole	One 8-pound bird One 10-pound bird	25 minutes 30 minutes	30 minutes* 30 minutes*
Turkey breast half	One 3- to 4-pound half	20 to 25 minutes	40 to 45 minutes
Turkey breast tenderloin steaks	Four 4-ounce steaks	8 to 10 minutes	
Turkey drumstick	One 1-pound drumstick	9 to 11 minutes	
Turkey roast, boneless	3- to 3½-pound roast	20 to 25 minutes	15 minutes*

*Note: After standing, defrost these birds for additional time: 4- to 5-pound duckling, 10 to 15 minutes; 3- to 3½-pound turkey roast, 10 to 15 minutes; 10-pound turkey, 30 minutes; 8-pound turkey, 20 minutes. Turn halfway through both defrosting cycles. Let stand approximately as long as the first standing time.

Broiling and Direct-Grilling Poultry

Remove the skin from the poultry, if desired. Rinse and pat dry with paper towels. If desired, sprinkle with salt and pepper

To broil: Remove the broiler pan and preheat the broiler for five to 10 minutes. Arrange the poultry on the unheated rack of the broiler pan with the bone side up. If desired, brush with cooking oil. Place the pan under the broiler so the surface of the poultry is 4 to 5 inches from the heat. (Chicken and Cornish game hen halves should be 5 to 6 inches from the heat.) Turn the pieces over when browned on one side, usually after half of the broiling time. Chicken halves and meaty pieces should be turned after 20 minutes.

Brush again with oil. The poultry is done when the meat is tender (the dark meat will not become tender as quickly as the white meat) and no longer pink. Brush with a sauce the last five minutes of cooking, if desired.

To grill direct: Test for desired temperature of the coals (see "Grilling Techniques," page 442). Place poultry on the grill rack, bone side up, directly over the preheated coals. (For ground turkey patties, use a grill basket.) Grill, uncovered, for the specified time or till tender and no longer pink. Turn the poultry over after half of the grilling time. During the last 10 minutes, brush often with a sauce, if desired.

Type of Bird	Weight	Broiling Time	Coal Temperature	Grilling Time
Chicken, broiler-fryer, half	1¼ to 1½ pounds	28 to 32 minutes	Medium	40 to 50 minutes
Chicken breast, skinned and boned	4 to 5 ounces	12 to 15 minutes	Medium-hot	15 to 18 minutes
Chicken breast halves, thighs, and drumsticks	2 to 2½ pounds total	25 to 35 minutes	Medium	35 to 45 minutes
Chicken kabobs (boneless breast, cut into 2x½-inch strips and threaded loosely onto skewers)	1 pound	8 to 10 minutes	Medium-hot	8 to 10 minutes
Cornish game hen half	½ to ¾ pound	30 to 40 minutes	Medium-hot	45 to 50 minutes
Turkey breast steak or slice	2 ounces	6 to 8 minutes		Not recommended
Turkey breast tenderloin steak	4 to 6 ounces	8 to 10 minutes	Medium	12 to 15 minutes
Turkey drumstick	½ to 1½ pounds	Not recommended	Medium	¾ to 1¼ hours
Turkey hindquarter	2 to 4 pounds	Not recommended	Medium	1¼ to 1½ hours
Turkey patties (ground raw turkey)	¾ inch thick	10 to 12 minutes	Medium-hot	15 to 18 minutes
Turkey thigh	1 to 1½ pounds	Not recommended	Medium	50 to 60 minutes

Roasting and Indirect-Grilling Poultry

To roast: Prepare the bird according to the directions given in Stuffed and Roasted Bird, page 320.

To grill indirect: Prepare unstuffed poultry as for roasting (grilling a stuffed bird is not recommended). In a covered grill arrange *medium-hot* coals around a drip pan. Test for *medium* heat above the pan (see "Grilling Techniques," page 442). Place the poultry, breast side up, on the grill rack over the drip pan but not over the preheated coals. Lower the grill hood. Grill for the time specified. Add more coals to maintain heat as necessary.

To smoke: Soak wood chunks or chips in enough water to cover for one hour. Prepare grill for indirect grilling, adding one inch of water to the drip pan. Drain chunks or chips and place on top of preheated coals. Grill as for indirect grilling, adding more chunks or chips every 15 to 20 minutes and more water to drip pan as necessary.

Type of Bird	Weight	Oven	Roasting Time	Indirect-Grilling Time
Capon	5 to 7 pounds	325°	1¾ to 2½ hours	Not recommended
Chicken, broiler-fryer, whole	2½ to 3 pounds	375°	1 to 1¼ hours	1 to 1¼ hours
	3½ to 4 pounds	375°	1¼ to 1¾ hours	1½ to 1¾ hours
	4½ to 5 pounds	375°	1½ to 2 hours	1¾ to 2 hours
Chicken, roasting, whole	5 to 6 pounds	325°	1¾ to 2½ hours	Not recommended
Cornish game hen	1 to 1½ pounds	375°	1 to 1¼ hours	1 to 1¼ hours
Duckling, domestic	3 to 5 pounds	375°	1¾ to 2¼ hours	Not recommended
Goose, domestic	7 to 8 pounds	350°	2 to 2½ hours	Not recommended
	8 to 10 pounds	350°	2½ to 3 hours	Not recommended
	10 to 12 pounds	350°	3 to 3½ hours	Not recommended
Pheasant	2 to 3 pounds	350°	1½ to 1¾ hours	1 to 1½ hours

Note: Birds vary in size, shape, and tenderness. Use these times as general guides.

Roasting and Indirect-Grilling Poultry (Continued)

Type of Bird	Weight	Oven	Roasting Time	Indirect-Grilling Time
Quail	4 to 6 ounces each	375°	30 to 50 minutes	25 to 35 minutes
Squab	12 to 14 ounces each	375°	45 to 60 minutes	45 to 60 minutes
Turkey, boneless, whole	2½ to 3½ pounds	325°	2 to 2½ hours	1¾ to 2¼ hours
	4 to 6 pounds	325°	2½ to 3½ hours	2½ to 3½ hours
Turkey, unstuffed*	6 to 8 pounds	325°	3 to 3½ hours	1¾ to 2¼ hours
	8 to 12 pounds	325°	3 to 4 hours	2½ to 3½ hours
	12 to 16 pounds	325°	4 to 5 hours	3 to 4 hours
	16 to 20 pounds	325°	4¼ to 5 hours	Not recommended
	20 to 24 pounds	325°	5 to 6 hours	Not recommended
Turkey breast, whole	4 to 6 pounds	325°	1½ to 2¼ hours	1¾ to 2¼ hours
	6 to 8 pounds	325°	2¼ to 3¼ hours	2½ to 3½ hours
Turkey drumstick	1 to 1½ pounds	325°	1¼ to 1¾ hours	Not recommended
Turkey thigh	1½ to 1¾ pounds	325°	1½ to 1¾ hours	Not recommended

Note: Birds vary in size, shape, and tenderness. Use these times as general guides.
*Stuffed birds generally require 30 to 45 minutes more roasting time than unstuffed birds.

Micro-Cooking Poultry

To micro-cook a *whole bird,* rinse thoroughly and pat the bird dry. Tie the legs to the tail and twist the wing tips under the back. Place the bird, breast side down, on a rack in a baking dish. Brush with melted margarine or butter. Cover with waxed paper. Micro-cook on the power specified and for the time given or till done. After half of the cooking time, turn the breast side up and brush again with melted margarine or butter. (If desired, insert a temperature probe into the thigh, not touching the bone.)

The bird is done when the drumsticks move easily in their sockets, the temperature is 185° in several spots, no pink remains, and the juices run clear. If the wing and leg tips or other areas are done before the rest, shield these areas with small pieces of foil (check your owner's manual to see if foil is allowed in your oven). Let cooked birds weighing more than 2 pounds stand, covered with foil, for 15 minutes.

To micro-cook *poultry parts,* rinse thoroughly and pat dry. Arrange in a baking dish with meaty portions toward edges of dish, tucking under thin boneless portions. If pieces are crowded in the dish, omit the neck, back, and wings. Cover with waxed paper. (*Or,* for skinless poultry, cover with a lid or vented clear plastic wrap.) Micro-cook on the power level specified and for the time given or till done, rearranging, stirring, and turning pieces over after half of the cooking time.

Type of Bird	Amount	Power Level	Cooking Time
Chicken, broiler-fryer, cut up	One 2½- to 3-pound bird	100% (high)	12 to 17 minutes
Chicken, broiler-fryer, whole	One 2½- to 3-pound bird	50% (medium)	32 to 37 minutes
Chicken breasts, halved	Two 12-ounce breasts Two 16-ounce breasts	100% (high) 100% (high)	8 to 10 minutes 8 to 11 minutes
Chicken breast, whole	One 12-ounce breast Two 12-ounce breasts	100% (high) 100% (high)	5 to 7 minutes 13 to 15 minutes
Chicken drumsticks	2 drumsticks 6 drumsticks	100% (high) 100% (high)	3 to 5 minutes 8 to 10 minutes
Chicken pieces	1 pound	100% (high)	3 to 5 minutes
Cornish game hen, whole	One 1- to 1½-pound bird Two 1- to 1½-pound birds	100% (high) 100% (high)	7 to 10 minutes 13 to 18 minutes
Turkey, ground raw	1 pound	100% (high)	5 to 7 minutes
Turkey breast half	One 3- to 4-pound half	50% (medium)	40 to 55 minutes
Turkey breast tenderloin steaks	Four 4-ounce steaks	100% (high)	6 to 8 minutes
Turkey drumstick	One 1-pound drumstick	100% (high)	7 to 9 minutes
Turkey roast, boneless	One 3- to 3½-pound roast	50% (medium)	50 to 60 minutes
Turkey thigh	One 1¼-pound thigh	100% (high)	11 to 13 minutes

Salads & Dressings

	Per Serving							Percent U.S. RDA Per Serving							

Nutrition Analysis

	Servings Per Recipe	Calories	Protein (g)	Carbohydrate (g)	Fat (g)	Cholesterol (mg)	Sodium (mg)	Potassium (mg)	Protein	Vitamin A	Vitamin C	Thiamine	Riboflavin	Niacin	Calcium	Iron
Apricot-Nectar Dressing (p. 358)	16	13	0	3	0	0	6	30	0	2	7	0	1	0	2	0
Apricot-Pecan Mold (p. 353)	5	158	4	26	6	1	67	232	6	24	38	6	4	2	4	2
Avocado-Shrimp Salad (p. 340)	6	265	20	8	17	120	292	571	31	24	22	8	14	13	26	14
Barley Salad (p. 347)	6	240	7	30	11	0	303	233	11	55	9	6	3	18	3	7
Basil Mayonnaise (p. 336)	4	247	1	1	27	17	200	22	0	3	4	0	0	0	1	1
Bean and Sausage Bowl (p. 338)	3	530	27	32	33	324	689	912	41	13	15	24	25	10	26	33
Beef-Asparagus Salads (p. 336)	4	538	32	13	41	99	294	912	50	38	85	17	27	29	5	26
Berry Salad (p. 352)	8	160	3	40	0	0	70	138	4	1	47	1	2	1	1	3
Blender Mayonnaise (p. 355)	16	126	0	0	14	17	21	5	0	0	0	0	0	0	0	0
Blue Cheese Dressing (p. 357)	20	45	2	1	4	6	103	33	3	1	0	0	2	0	4	0
Bratwurst and Pasta Salad (p. 339)	4	564	19	31	41	67	654	613	29	35	89	43	20	23	11	17
Buttermilk Dressing (p. 356)	24	70	0	1	8	6	63	12	1	1	0	0	1	0	1	0
Caesar Salad (p. 342)	6	110	5	4	8	53	202	201	8	26	22	4	6	3	9	5
Cajun-Style Rice Salad (p. 347)	6	163	8	20	6	74	180	178	12	15	50	8	6	8	4	11
Carrot-Raisin Salad (p. 346)	6	140	1	13	10	7	85	203	1	203	9	3	2	2	2	2
Cheddar-Macaroni Salad (p. 348)	6	258	8	24	15	25	293	159	12	8	27	18	11	9	14	7
Chef's Salad (p. 334)	4	438	19	12	36	178	536	515	29	52	108	24	20	10	32	14
Cherry-Apple Salad Mold (p. 352)	4	270	5	44	10	0	124	337	7	8	7	5	4	2	4	5
Chicken and Garbanzo Bean Salad (p. 339)	4	559	31	24	38	99	534	566	48	20	80	12	17	31	26	21
Chicken Salad (p. 340)	4	291	17	8	21	187	275	363	27	20	26	7	11	23	4	10
Choose-a-Fruit Salad (p. 350)	4	322	2	29	24	0	12	679	3	9	58	8	8	8	2	5
Chutney-Fruit Rice Salad (p. 350)	6	334	6	32	21	12	196	286	9	3	25	9	5	12	7	6
Cinnamon Fruit Salad (p. 349)	6	78	1	20	0	0	3	250	2	12	79	6	4	2	3	3
Citrus and Poppy Seed Vinaigrette (p. 358)	12	89	0	2	9	0	0	12	0	0	6	0	0	0	0	0
Citrus Blender Mayonnaise (p. 355)	16	129	0	1	14	17	17	4	0	0	1	0	0	0	0	0
Coleslaw (p. 346)	4	232	1	8	22	17	173	199	2	105	64	3	2	2	3	4
Cooked Salad Dressing (p. 355)	16	19	1	2	1	35	73	21	1	1	0	1	2	0	2	1
Crab Louis (p. 340)	4	404	19	11	32	249	1068	500	29	52	49	13	14	11	10	13
Cranberry Relish Ring (p. 354)	12	123	2	31	0	0	45	85	2	1	16	2	1	1	1	1
Creamy Cucumber Mold (p. 353)	4	413	6	14	38	30	380	312	8	23	22	4	7	2	10	4
Creamy Cucumbers (p. 344)	6	55	1	4	4	9	367	117	2	4	5	2	2	0	3	1
Creamy French Dressing (p. 357)	22	75	0	1	8	0	26	5	0	2	0	0	0	0	0	0
Creamy Fruit Salad (p. 352)	8	226	5	21	14	93	100	264	8	16	26	6	8	2	6	4
Creamy Garlic Dressing (p. 356)	16	84	0	1	9	8	78	11	0	1	0	0	0	0	1	0
Creamy Italian Dressing (p. 356)	16	84	0	1	9	8	78	11	0	1	0	0	0	0	1	0
Creamy Onion Oil-Free Dressing (p. 357)	12	0	3	0	0	4	17	0	0	0	0	0	0	0	0	0
Creamy Parmesan Dressing (p. 356)	16	89	1	1	9	9	84	12	1	1	0	0	1	0	2	0
Creamy Potato Salad (p. 346)	12	278	5	17	22	151	376	364	8	5	38	8	6	6	3	6
Creamy Three-Bean Salad (p. 344)	6	187	7	19	10	7	145	429	10	4	35	10	5	3	6	15
Croutons (p. 357)	16	38	0	2	3	0	59	6	1	2	0	1	1	1	0	1
Five-Cup Salad (p. 351)	6	211	2	21	14	17	27	217	4	13	25	8	5	1	6	4
Fluffy Fruit Dressing (p. 358)	16	14	0	2	1	0	6	21	1	0	1	0	1	0	1	0
French Vinaigrette (p. 358)	12	85	0	1	9	0	0	3	0	0	0	0	0	0	0	0
Frosty Cranberry-Date Salad (p. 354)	8	295	3	26	21	72	96	225	5	19	34	4	7	2	6	3
Frozen Black Cherry Cups (p. 354)	12	107	2	12	6	9	24	205	4	5	7	5	6	2	6	2
Fruit-Filled Melons (p. 349)	4	284	6	54	7	7	108	1176	9	178	255	12	13	11	14	6
Fruity Pasta Salad (p. 348)	6	123	3	25	2	91	13	224	4	6	53	8	6	5	2	5
Fruity Slaw (p. 350)	4	78	2	18	1	1	24	399	3	2	101	8	6	3	7	4
Garlic Vinaigrette (p. 358)	12	86	0	2	9	0	0	4	0	0	1	0	0	0	0	0
Gazpacho-Style Salad (p. 342)	6	109	1	6	9	0	7	220	2	15	63	4	3	3	2	4
German-Style Potato Salad (p. 347)	4	284	7	38	12	81	545	672	11	3	43	17	6	14	3	7

On the divider: Marinated Potato Salad (p. 346).

Nutrition Analysis

	Per Serving							Percent U.S. RDA Per Serving							
	Servings Per Recipe	Calories	Protein (g)	Carbohydrate (g)	Fat (g)	Cholesterol (mg)	Sodium (mg)	Potassium (mg) · Protein	Vitamin A	Vitamin C	Thiamine	Riboflavin	Niacin	Calcium	Iron
Ginger Vinaigrette (p. 358)	12	85	0	1	9	0	0	2	0	0	0	0	0	0	0	0
Greek-Style Salads (p. 339)	3	419	21	10	34	74	310	547	32	40	41	14	24	21	14	14
Green Goddess Dressing (p. 356)	16	47	0	1	5	5	33	30	1	4	4	0	1	0	1	1
Greens with Basil Vinaigrette (p. 342)	4	69	1	9	4	0	36	236	2	11	14	4	5	3	2	2
Ham and Rice Salad (p. 338)	4	603	17	45	40	59	981	552	27	20	83	41	13	22	7	18
Ham Salad (p. 340)	4	280	15	9	21	176	867	394	23	19	45	31	13	13	4	11
Herb Blender Mayonnaise (p. 355)	16	125	0	0	14	17	19	5	0	0	0	0	0	0	0	0
Herb Vinegar (p. 341)	32	2	0	1	0	0	0	17	0	0	0	0	0	0	0	1
Honey-Lime Dressing (p. 358)	21	86	0	5	8	0	0	6	0	0	2	0	0	0	0	0
Horseradish Dressing (p. 356)	20	54	0	1	6	6	36	17	0	2	0	0	1	0	1	0
Italian-Style Pasta Toss (p. 338)	6	520	20	33	35	46	580	422	30	32	84	17	19	13	38	16
Italian Vinaigrette (p. 358)	12	91	0	2	9	1	20	5	0	0	0	0	0	0	2	0
Louis Dressing (p. 340)	4	264	1	4	27	37	279	86	2	9	24	2	2	1	2	2
Marinated Cucumbers (p. 344)	6	26	1	7	0	0	357	90	0	0	5	1	1	1	1	1
Marinated Mushroom Salad (p. 342)	4	107	2	10	7	0	183	525	4	219	31	10	19	15	3	7
Marinated Potato Salad (p. 346)	4	382	4	30	29	0	110	635	6	14	101	12	9	11	4	9
Marinated Steak Salads (p. 336)	4	393	27	13	27	63	331	858	42	121	34	14	23	31	6	20
Marinated Vegetable Salad (p. 343)	8	60	2	8	3	0	81	301	2	108	84	6	4	4	3	5
Mayonnaise (p. 355)	32	125	0	0	14	17	17	1	0	0	0	0	0	0	0	0
Nut-Flavored Oil (p. 334)	40	51	1	1	5	0	0	19	1	0	0	1	0	0	1	1
Nutty Citrus Coleslaw (p. 346)	5	245	2	13	22	13	139	254	3	85	74	6	3	2	4	5
Oil-Free Dressing (p. 357)	8	7	0	2	0	0	0	3	0	0	0	0	0	0	0	0
Onion Vinaigrette (p. 358)	12	86	0	1	9	0	0	4	0	0	0	0	0	0	0	0
Peach-Berry Frozen Salad (p. 354)	9	268	7	20	19	2	100	292	11	15	9	4	15	4	15	4
Pea-Cheese Salad (p. 345)	6	229	9	8	18	118	356	143	14	15	21	10	10	4	16	8
Pineapple-Lemon Squares (p. 351)	9	281	5	41	12	71	139	197	7	12	14	6	7	2	5	2
Red Wine Vinaigrette (p. 358)	12	87	0	2	9	0	0	5	0	0	0	0	0	0	0	0
Reuben Salads (p. 339)	4	515	21	19	40	78	1149	480	33	31	24	9	17	7	34	16
Russian Dressing (p. 358)	11	56	0	3	5	0	118	27	0	3	3	0	0	0	0	0
Rye Croutons (p. 339)	4	47	1	7	2	0	92	19	2	2	0	2	2	2	1	2
Salad Niçoise (p. 341)	4	456	20	20	33	236	151	718	31	40	103	14	16	37	8	18
Salmon Pasta Salad (p. 341)	6	528	22	19	41	44	669	514	34	26	10	10	19	31	33	10
Salmon Salad (p. 340)	4	285	15	5	23	167	435	417	23	22	26	6	12	22	17	8
Salmon Salad Niçoise (p. 341)	4	491	19	20	38	226	418	778	29	41	103	14	19	27	21	17
Shortcut Cranberry Relish Ring (p. 354)	12	179	2	45	0	0	60	72	2	0	17	2	1	1	1	1
Spinach and Garbanzo Bean Salad (p. 343)	6	274	10	21	18	98	149	779	16	63	42	14	17	9	12	19
Spinach-Orange Toss (p. 344)	4	167	4	16	11	0	45	537	6	77	88	9	15	7	10	11
Sunflower-Nut Dressing (p. 355)	16	18	1	1	1	1	11	46	2	0	0	2	2	0	3	1
Tabbouleh (p. 348)	6	168	3	19	10	0	84	218	4	13	28	7	3	6	2	9
Taco Salads (p. 337)	6	431	28	22	26	91	900	773	43	40	57	17	24	20	35	25
Thousand Island Dressing (p. 356)	24	74	0	1	8	17	111	20	0	2	3	0	0	0	0	1
Three-Bean Salad (p. 344)	6	204	6	25	10	0	63	427	10	3	35	10	5	3	6	15
Tomato-Vegetable Aspic (p. 353)	8	311	3	6	0	0	426	221	4	10	21	3	2	4	1	3
Tortilla Cups (p. 337)	6	177	2	21	10	0	0	0	3	0	0	4	1	2	9	8
Tuna-Melon Plates (p. 341)	4	417	25	15	29	70	311	610	39	67	92	10	11	48	18	10
Tuna Salad (p. 340)	4	260	17	8	18	177	223	368	26	20	26	6	9	33	4	10
24-Hour Fruit Salad (p. 351)	8	199	2	29	9	123	30	201	4	10	44	9	5	2	5	4
24-Hour Vegetable Salad (p. 345)	6	357	11	8	32	127	459	246	16	115	18	11	10	6	17	7
Vegetable-Pasta Salad (p. 348)	8	179	4	25	7	0	121	167	6	1	6	18	9	11	2	7
Vinaigrette (p. 358)	12	85	0	1	9	0	0	2	0	0	0	0	0	0	0	0
Vinaigrette Coleslaw (p. 346)	4	140	1	12	10	0	13	188	1	104	63	3	2	2	2	3
Waldorf Salad (p. 350)	4	283	2	19	23	35	95	221	3	8	9	4	3	1	3	3
Wilted Spinach Salad (p. 344)	4	147	9	6	10	83	480	634	15	112	50	14	19	13	9	17

Salads and Dressings

From simple tossed greens to elegant Crab Louis, salads have become an important part of meals everywhere.

Supermarkets today provide better-quality fresh produce in more variety than ever before. So take advantage of this bounty and enjoy a salad often. Our main-dish salads make cool and delicious one-dish meals. For example, try attractive Beef-Asparagus Salads or super-simple Bean and Sausage Bowl. For a salad on the side, choose from Caesar Salad, German-Style Potato Salad, or the many others we offer. Or opt for torn greens with one of our many dressings, from easy Vinaigrette to creamy Sunflower-Nut Dressing.

Nut-Flavored Oil

Nut-flavored oil adds zest to many salads and dressings. To make flavored oil, place 1½ cups unblanched shelled whole *hazelnuts, almonds, or walnuts* in a blender container or food processor bowl. Cover; blend or process till chopped. With blender on slow speed, gradually add ½ cup *salad oil* through opening in lid. Blend till the nuts are finely chopped. Transfer mixture to a small saucepan. Place a candy thermometer in the pan. Cook over low heat, stirring often, till thermometer registers 160°. Remove from heat; cool slightly. Combine mixture with 2 cups *salad oil.* Cover tightly; let stand in a cool place for 1 to 2 weeks.

Line a colander with several layers of cheesecloth. Pour mixture through colander; let drain in a bowl. Discard nut paste. Pour strained oil into a 1½-pint jar; cover tightly. Store in the refrigerator up to 3 months. Makes 2½ cups (forty 1-tablespoon servings).

Chef's Salad

Your options are wide open. Choose the meat, poultry, and cheese that you like best.

- 3 cups torn iceberg *or* leaf lettuce
- 3 cups torn romaine *or* spinach
- 4 ounces fully cooked ham, chicken, turkey, beef, pork, *or* lamb, cut into thin strips
- 1 cup cubed Swiss, cheddar, American, provolone, *or* Gruyère cheese *or* crumbled blue cheese (4 ounces)
- 2 hard-cooked eggs, sliced
- 2 medium tomatoes, cut into wedges, *or* 8 cherry tomatoes, halved
- 1 small green *or* sweet red pepper, cut into rings
- 3 green onions, sliced
- 1 cup Croutons (see tip, page 357) *or* purchased croutons (optional)
- ¾ cup Creamy French Dressing (see recipe, page 357), Buttermilk Dressing (see recipe, page 356), Creamy Italian Dressing (see recipe, page 356), *or* other salad dressing

In a large salad bowl toss together lettuce and romaine or spinach. Arrange meat or poultry, cheese, hard-cooked eggs, tomatoes, pepper rings, and green onions over the greens. Sprinkle with Croutons, if desired. Pour Creamy French Dressing or other salad dressing over all. Toss to coat. Makes 4 main-dish servings.

Note: To serve Chef's Salad as individual salads, toss together lettuce and romaine or spinach and divide among four individual salad bowls. Top *each* serving with *one-fourth* of the meat or poultry, cheese, hard-cooked eggs, tomatoes, pepper rings, and green onions. Sprinkle *each* with Croutons, if desired. Pass Creamy French Dressing or other salad dressing.

Look for these salad greens in your grocery store. To add flavor and interest to your salads, use a combination of two or more greens.

Arugula

Beet greens

Belgian endive

Bok choy

Boston lettuce

Chinese cabbage

Collard greens

Curly endive

Escarole

Green cabbage

Iceberg lettuce

Kale

Leaf lettuce

Mustard greens

Radicchio

Red cabbage

Red-tip leaf lettuce

Romaine

Savoy cabbage

Beef-Asparagus Salads

A great way to use leftover beef.

⅓ cup olive oil *or* salad oil
¼ cup lemon juice
3 tablespoons dry sherry *or* red wine
   vinegar
1 teaspoon lemon-pepper seasoning
12 ounces sliced cooked beef *or* turkey,
   cut into thin strips (about 2½
   cups)
½ cup chopped onion
¾ pound asparagus spears *or* one
   10-ounce package frozen
   asparagus spears
   Leaf lettuce
4 small tomatoes, sliced
1 medium cucumber, thinly sliced
1 cup sliced fresh mushrooms
   Fresh basil (optional)
   Basil Mayonnaise

For marinade, in a screw-top jar combine oil, lemon juice, sherry or vinegar, and lemon-pepper seasoning. Cover and shake well. In a mixing bowl combine beef or turkey and onion. Add marinade. Toss lightly to coat. Let stand at room temperature for 20 minutes.

Meanwhile, cook asparagus in boiling salted water for 10 to 15 minutes or till nearly tender. (*Or*, cook frozen asparagus according to package directions.) Drain asparagus. Rinse with *cold* water. Let stand, covered with *cold* water.

Drain beef and onion, reserving *3 tablespoons* of the marinade for Basil Mayonnaise. For salads, line 4 salad plates with lettuce. Cut the tomato slices in half. Around the outer edge of *each* plate, alternately arrange *one-fourth* of the tomatoes and *one-fourth* of the cucumber, overlapping as necessary. (Place the rounded edges of tomatoes toward the outer edges of the plates, forming petallike shapes.) Then, using *one-fourth* of the mushrooms, arrange a ring inside the cucumber-tomato ring. Drain asparagus spears. Arrange *one-fourth* of the asparagus and *one-fourth* of the beef mixture in the center of each plate. Garnish with fresh basil, if desired. Serve with Basil Mayonnaise. Makes 4 main-dish servings.

Basil Mayonnaise: Mix together ½ cup *mayonnaise or salad dressing,* 3 tablespoons *reserved marinade,* and 1 tablespoon snipped *fresh basil or* 1 teaspoon *dried basil,* crushed.

Marinated Steak Salads

The steak marinates in a tangy herb-flavored dressing after you cook it.

1 pound boneless beef sirloin steak,
   cut 1 inch thick
1 9-ounce package frozen artichoke
   hearts, thawed
10 cherry tomatoes, halved
1 medium carrot, thinly bias sliced
4 green onions, sliced
⅓ cup olive oil *or* salad oil
¼ cup red wine vinegar
½ teaspoon finely shredded lemon
   peel
2 tablespoons lemon juice
1 teaspoon dried thyme, crushed
½ teaspoon garlic salt
½ teaspoon dried marjoram, crushed
½ teaspoon cracked black pepper
4 cups torn salad greens
1 cup sliced fresh mushrooms

Slash fat edges of steak at 1-inch intervals, being careful not to cut into meat. Place steak on the unheated rack of a broiler pan. Broil 3 inches from the heat for 6 minutes. Turn steak. Broil to desired doneness (allow 6 to 9 minutes more for medium). Cool slightly; cut into thin slices. Place steak slices in a plastic bag; place bag in a bowl.

Cut any large artichoke hearts in half. Add artichoke hearts, cherry tomatoes, carrot, and green onions to the plastic bag. Set aside.

For marinade, in a screw-top jar combine olive or salad oil, vinegar, lemon peel and juice, thyme, garlic salt, marjoram, and pepper. Cover and shake well. Pour marinade over steak and vegetables in the bag. Seal bag. Marinate in the refrigerator for 6 to 24 hours, turning bag occasionally.

For salad, toss together greens and mushrooms. Place greens and mushrooms on 4 salad plates. Drain steak and vegetables, reserving marinade, if desired. Arrange steak and vegetables over greens on plates. Drizzle with reserved marinade, if desired. Makes 4 main-dish servings.

Taco Salads

In a hurry? Skip the Tortilla Cups and serve the salad with tortilla chips or corn chips.

- 1 **pound ground beef, ground raw turkey, or bulk pork sausage**
- 3 **cloves garlic, minced**
- 1 **16-ounce can dark red kidney beans**
- 1 **8-ounce jar taco sauce**
- 1 **tablespoon chili powder**
- 6 **cups torn iceberg lettuce**
- 4 **medium tomatoes, chopped**
- 2 **cups shredded cheddar cheese**
- 1 **cup chopped green pepper**
- ½ **cup sliced pitted ripe olives**
- 4 **green onions, sliced**
  Tortilla Cups (optional)
- 1 **medium avocado, pitted, peeled, and sliced (optional)**
  Dairy sour cream (optional)
  Taco sauce or salsa (optional)

For meat mixture, in a large skillet cook meat and garlic till meat is no longer pink. Drain off fat. Stir in *undrained* kidney beans, taco sauce, and chili powder. Bring to boiling; reduce heat. Cover; simmer for 10 minutes.

Meanwhile, for salads, combine lettuce, tomatoes, cheese, green pepper, olives, and green onions. Add hot meat mixture. Toss to mix. Divide among Tortilla Cups or individual salad plates. Garnish with avocado, if desired. Serve with sour cream and additional taco sauce or salsa, if desired. Makes 6 main-dish servings.

Microwave directions: For meat mixture, in a 1½-quart casserole crumble meat. Add garlic. Micro-cook, covered, on 100% power (high) for 4 to 6 minutes or till no pink remains in meat. Drain off fat. Stir in *undrained* kidney beans, taco sauce, and chili powder. Cook, uncovered, on high for 4 to 6 minutes or till bubbly, stirring once. Assemble salads as above.

Tortilla Cups: In a heavy 3-quart saucepan heat 2 inches *cooking oil or melted shortening for deep-fat frying* to 375°. Place one 7-inch *flour tortilla* on top of hot oil. Using a metal ladle, press tortilla into fat, forming the tortilla into a cup. Fry for 40 to 60 seconds or till golden. Remove with tongs. Drain on paper towels. Repeat with *five* more tortillas.

Using a ladle, press the tortilla completely into the fat, forming the tortilla into a cup.

Bean and Sausage Bowl

3 ounces thinly sliced salami,
    pepperoni, *or* summer sausage
2 cups torn iceberg lettuce
1 8-ounce can red kidney beans,
    drained
3 hard-cooked eggs, cut into wedges
1 stalk celery, sliced
½ cup shredded cheddar cheese
    (2 ounces)
2 green onions, sliced
¼ cup mayonnaise *or* salad dressing
1 tablespoon milk
2 teaspoons prepared mustard
1 teaspoon prepared horseradish

Cut salami, pepperoni, or summer sausage slices into quarters. In a large bowl toss together meat, lettuce, kidney beans, hard-cooked eggs, celery, cheese, and green onions. For dressing, stir together mayonnaise or salad dressing, milk, mustard, and horseradish; pour over meat mixture. Toss to coat. Makes 3 main-dish servings.

Ham and Rice Salad

Easy, colorful, and tasty!

1 10-ounce package frozen succotash
2 cups cold cooked long grain *or*
    brown rice
1½ cups cubed fully cooked ham
½ cup chopped green pepper
1 medium tomato, coarsely chopped
¼ cup chopped onion
¼ cup snipped parsley
1 cup Creamy Italian Dressing (see
    recipe, page 356) *or* other
    creamy salad dressing
    Leaf lettuce (optional)
2 hard-cooked eggs, sliced (optional)

Cook succotash according to package directions. Drain. In a large bowl stir together succotash, rice, ham, green pepper, tomato, onion, and parsley. Pour salad dressing over rice mixture. Toss to coat. Cover and chill for 4 to 24 hours. Serve on lettuce-lined salad plates and garnish with sliced egg, if desired. Makes 4 main-dish servings.

Italian-Style Pasta Toss

7 ounces corkscrew macaroni *or* one
    7-ounce package tortellini
1½ cups cubed Swiss *or* provolone
    cheese (6 ounces)
6 ounces sliced salami, cut into strips
1 cup cauliflower flowerets, thinly
    sliced
1 small zucchini, thinly sliced (1 cup)
½ cup chopped green *or* sweet red
    sweet pepper
1 small onion, thinly sliced and
    separated into rings
½ cup sliced pitted ripe olives
¼ cup grated Parmesan cheese
¼ cup snipped parsley
½ cup olive oil *or* salad oil
¼ cup wine vinegar
2 cloves garlic, minced
2 teaspoons dried basil, crushed
1 teaspoon dried oregano, crushed
½ teaspoon pepper
2 medium tomatoes, cut into wedges

Cook pasta according to package directions. Drain pasta. Rinse with *cold* water; drain again.

For salad, in a bowl toss together pasta, cubed cheese, salami, cauliflower, zucchini, green or red pepper, onion rings, olives, Parmesan cheese, and parsley.

For dressing, in a screw-top jar combine oil, vinegar, garlic, basil, oregano, and pepper. Cover and shake well. Pour over salad. Toss to coat. Cover; chill 4 to 24 hours. To serve, add tomatoes; toss gently. Makes 6 main-dish servings.

Bratwurst and Pasta Salad

  4 ounces cavatelli, medium shell
      macaroni, *or* corkscrew macaroni
10 ounces fresh broccoli *or* one
      10-ounce package frozen cut
      broccoli
12 ounces fully cooked smoked
      bratwurst, halved lengthwise and
      sliced
  2 small tomatoes, cut into wedges
  4 green onions, sliced
  1 teaspoon dried Italian seasoning
  ½ cup Creamy Italian Dressing (see
      recipe, page 356) or other
      creamy salad dressing
      Leaf lettuce (optional)
      Grated Parmesan cheese (optional)

Cook pasta according to package directions. Drain pasta; rinse with *cold* water. Drain again.

    Cut broccoli into 1-inch pieces. Cook broccoli in boiling salted water for 7 to 9 minutes or till crisp-tender. (*Or,* cook frozen broccoli according to package directions.) Drain.

    Toss together pasta, broccoli, bratwurst, tomatoes, and green onions. Stir Italian seasoning into salad dressing. Pour dressing mixture over salad. Toss to coat. Cover; chill for 4 to 24 hours. Serve over lettuce and sprinkle with Parmesan cheese, if desired. Makes 4 main-dish servings.

Reuben Salads

  8 cups torn leaf lettuce
  1 8-ounce can sauerkraut, chilled,
      drained, and snipped
  6 ounces cooked corned beef, cut into
      strips (1 cup)
  1 cup cubed Swiss cheese (4 ounces)
      Rye Croutons
  ¾ cup Thousand Island salad dressing
  ¾ teaspoon caraway
      seed   Oven 300°

Divide lettuce among 4 salad plates. Arrange sauerkraut, beef, cheese, and croutons over lettuce. Combine salad dressing and caraway seed. Serve with salads. Makes 4 main-dish servings.

    Rye Croutons: Brush both sides of 2 slices *rye bread* with 4 teaspoons softened *margarine or butter.* Cut into ½-inch cubes. In a shallow baking pan spread bread cubes. Bake in a 300° oven for 15 to 18 minutes or till dry, stirring once.

Greek-Style Salads

  3 cups torn curly endive *or* romaine
1½ cups torn iceberg lettuce *or* spinach
  6 ounces cooked lamb, pork, chicken,
      turkey, *or* beef, cut into strips
  1 medium tomato, chopped
  ½ of a small cucumber, thinly sliced
  ½ cup crumbled feta cheese (2 ounces)
  2 green onions, sliced
  6 radishes, sliced
  2 tablespoons sliced pitted ripe olives
  ½ cup Vinaigrette (see recipe,
      page 358)
  3 anchovy fillets, drained, rinsed, and
      patted dry (optional)

Toss together curly endive or romaine and lettuce or spinach. Divide greens among 3 salad plates. Arrange meat, tomato, cucumber, feta cheese, green onions, radishes, and olives over greens. Drizzle with Vinaigrette. Top with anchovies, if desired. Makes 3 main-dish servings.

Chicken and Garbanzo Bean Salad

Chili powder gives a south-of-the-border flavor.

  2 cups cubed cooked chicken, turkey,
      or beef
  1 15-ounce can garbanzo beans,
      drained
  1 cup cubed cheddar *or* Monterey
      Jack cheese (4 ounces)
  2 stalks celery, sliced
  1 small green pepper, chopped
  2 green onions, sliced
  ½ cup mayonnaise *or* salad dressing
  2 tablespoons lemon juice
  ½ teaspoon chili powder
  ¼ teaspoon garlic powder
      Leaf lettuce
  1 medium tomato, cut into wedges

In a medium bowl combine chicken, garbanzo beans, cheese, celery, green pepper, and green onions. For dressing, stir together mayonnaise, lemon juice, chili powder, garlic powder, ¼ teaspoon *salt,* and ¼ teaspoon *pepper.* Stir into chicken mixture. Cover and chill for 2 to 24 hours. Before serving, stir mixture. Serve on lettuce-lined salad plates. Garnish with tomato wedges. Makes 4 or 5 main-dish servings.

Chicken Salad

1½ cups finely chopped cooked chicken
 or turkey, *or* one 6¾-ounce can
 chunk-style chicken, drained
1 stalk celery, chopped
4 green onions, sliced
1 tablespoon lemon juice
2 hard-cooked eggs, chopped
⅓ cup mayonnaise *or* salad dressing
2 tablespoons sweet pickle relish *or*
 chopped green pepper
2 teaspoons prepared mustard
3 medium tomatoes *or* leaf lettuce

Combine chicken, celery, green onions, lemon juice, and ⅛ teaspoon *pepper*. Stir in eggs, mayonnaise, pickle relish, and mustard. Cover; chill at least 1 hour. Meanwhile, if using tomatoes, cut a thin slice off stem end of *each* tomato. Using a spoon, scoop out the centers of tomatoes, leaving ¼- to ½-inch-thick shells. Reserve pulp for another use. Serve salad in tomato shells or on lettuce leaves. Makes 4 main-dish servings.

Tuna Salad: Prepare as above, *except* substitute one 6½-ounce can *tuna,* drained and broken into chunks, for the chicken. Omit mustard.

Salmon Salad: Prepare as above, *except* substitute one 7¾-ounce can *salmon,* drained, flaked, and skin and bones removed, for the chicken. Omit pickle relish and mustard; add ½ teaspoon dried *dillweed* with the eggs.

Ham Salad: Prepare as above, *except* substitute finely chopped fully cooked *ham* for the chopped chicken.

Use a spoon to scoop out the tomato pulp and seeds, leaving ¼- to ½-inch-thick shells.

Avocado-Shrimp Salad

1 small avocado, halved, pitted,
 peeled, and cut up
½ cup buttermilk
1 3-ounce package cream cheese
1 tablespoon lemon juice
1 clove garlic
¼ teaspoon salt
 Dash bottled hot pepper sauce
1 pound peeled and deveined shrimp,
 cooked and chilled
18 cherry tomatoes, halved
4 ounces Swiss *or* Gruyère cheese,
 cut into julienne strips
6 cups torn lettuce

For dressing, in a blender container combine avocado, buttermilk, cream cheese, lemon juice, garlic, salt, and hot sauce. Cover and blend till smooth. Arrange shrimp, tomatoes, and cheese over lettuce. If desired, sprinkle with pepper. Drizzle with dressing. Makes 6 main-dish servings.

Crab Louis

1 medium head iceberg lettuce
2 6-ounce packages frozen crabmeat,
 thawed, *or* two 7-ounce cans
 crabmeat, chilled, drained, and
 cartilage removed
2 large tomatoes, cut into wedges
2 hard-cooked eggs, cut into wedges
 Louis Dressing
 Paprika
1 lemon, cut into wedges

Remove 4 large leaves from lettuce head. Set aside. Tear remaining lettuce into bite-size pieces. On *each* of 4 salad plates, place *one* lettuce leaf. Top with torn lettuce. Reserve *four* large pieces of crabmeat. Flake remaining crabmeat. Arrange flaked crabmeat, tomatoes, and eggs on lettuce. Drizzle with Louis Dressing. Sprinkle with paprika. Garnish with the reserved crabmeat and lemon. Makes 4 main-dish servings.

Louis Dressing: Mix ½ cup *mayonnaise or salad dressing,* ¼ cup finely chopped *green pepper,* ¼ cup finely chopped *green onion,* 2 tablespoons *chili sauce,* 1 tablespoon *milk,* ½ teaspoon *lemon juice,* and dash *Worcestershire sauce.* Beat ¼ cup *whipping cream* to soft peaks. Fold whipped cream into mayonnaise mixture.

Salad Niçoise

Buttery and slightly sweet, Boston and Bibb lettuce are varieties of butterhead lettuce.

- 2 **cups torn romaine**
- 2 **cups torn Boston *or* Bibb lettuce**
- 1 **6½-ounce can chunk white tuna (water pack), chilled**
- 1 **cup frozen cut green beans, cooked, drained, and chilled**
- 3 **hard-cooked eggs, chilled and cut into wedges**
- 1 **medium potato, cooked, chilled, and sliced**
- 10 **cherry tomatoes, halved**
- 1 **small green pepper, cut into strips**
- 1 **small onion, sliced and separated into rings**
- ¼ **cup pitted ripe olives, chilled**
- 4 **anchovy fillets, drained, rinsed, and patted dry (optional)**
  Vinaigrette (see recipe, page 358) *or* other oil and vinegar salad dressing

Toss together romaine and lettuce. Arrange greens on a large platter. Drain tuna; break tuna into chunks. Mound in center of greens. Arrange green beans, hard-cooked eggs, potato slices, cherry tomatoes, green pepper, onion, olives, and, if desired, anchovies around tuna. Drizzle with Vinaigrette. Makes 4 main-dish servings.

Salmon Salad Niçoise: Prepare as above, *except* substitute one 7¾-ounce can chunk *salmon,* drained, flaked, and skin and bones removed, for the tuna.

Tuna-Melon Plates

Mix together 2 cups cubed *cantaloupe or honey-dew melon;* one 11-ounce can *mandarin orange sections,* drained; ¾ cup cubed *brick, mozzarella, or Monterey Jack cheese* (3 ounces); and ½ cup chopped *celery.* Drain and flake one 9¼-ounce can chunk white *tuna.* Line 4 salad plates with *leaf lettuce.* Arrange melon mixture and tuna over lettuce. For dressing, stir together ½ cup *mayonnaise or salad dressing,* 1 tablespoon *milk,* 1 tablespoon *lemon juice,* and ¼ teaspoon *onion powder.* Drizzle dressing over fruit mixture and tuna. Sprinkle with 2 tablespoons toasted broken *pecans.* Makes 4 main-dish servings.

Salmon Pasta Salad

- 1¾ **cups corkscrew, medium shell, *or* wagon wheel macaroni**
- 1 **8-ounce container soft-style cream cheese**
- 1 **cup Buttermilk Dressing (see recipe, page 356) *or* other buttermilk salad dressing**
- 1 **cup milk**
- 1 **tablespoon snipped dill *or* 1 teaspoon dried dillweed**
- 1 **15½-ounce can salmon, drained, flaked, and skin and bones removed**
- 1 **small cucumber, seeded and chopped (about 1 cup)**
- 1 **medium tomato, seeded and chopped**
- 4 **green onions, sliced**

Cook macaroni according to package directions. Drain. Immediately transfer hot macaroni to a large bowl. Add cream cheese and Buttermilk Dressing. Toss till the macaroni is coated and mixture is blended. Stir in milk and dill. Add salmon, cucumber, tomato, and green onions. Toss lightly to mix. Cover and chill for 4 to 24 hours. Makes 6 main-dish servings.

Herb Vinegar

Herb vinegar gives salads a gourmet touch. To make herb vinegar, place 2 cups packed fresh *tarragon, thyme, dill, mint, or basil* into a hot, clean 1-quart jar. In a stainless steel or enamel saucepan heat 2 cups *wine vinegar* till hot but not boiling. Pour hot vinegar into the jar over the herb. Cover loosely with lid or plastic wrap till mixture cools, then cover tightly with the lid. (If using metal lid, cover jar with plastic wrap, then lid.) Let stand in a cool, dark place 1 week. Remove herb from jar. Transfer vinegar to a clean 1-pint jar. Add a sprig of fresh herb, if desired. Cover as above. Store in a cool, dark place up to 3 months. Makes 2 cups (thirty-two 1-tablespoon servings).

Caesar Salad

1 egg
1 clove garlic, halved
2 tablespoons olive *or* salad oil
2 tablespoons lemon *or* lime juice
  Few dashes Worcestershire sauce
  Dash bottled hot pepper sauce
5 cups torn romaine
½ cup Croutons (see tip, page 357) *or* purchased croutons
¼ cup grated Parmesan cheese
  Dash pepper
1 2-ounce can anchovy fillets, drained, rinsed, and patted dry

Allow egg to come to room temperature. To coddle egg, add egg in shell to a small saucepan of *boiling* water. Remove from heat; let stand 1 minute. Remove egg from water and cool slightly.

Cut garlic clove in half lengthwise. Rub a large wooden salad bowl with cut sides of the garlic clove. Discard garlic. Add oil, lemon or lime juice, Worcestershire sauce, and hot pepper sauce to bowl. Break the coddled egg into the bowl. Using a fork or a wire whisk, beat till creamy. Add romaine. Toss to coat. Sprinkle with croutons, Parmesan cheese, and pepper; toss to mix. Top with anchovy fillets. Makes 6 side-dish servings.

Greens with Basil Vinaigrette

Pineapple juice gives the vinaigrette a delicate fruity flavor.

4 cups torn salad greens
1 apple, quartered, cored, and sliced
½ cup sliced fresh mushrooms
¼ cup unsweetened pineapple juice
1 tablespoon white wine vinegar
1 tablespoon salad oil
½ teaspoon snipped fresh basil *or* ⅛ teaspoon dried basil, crushed
  Dash salt
  Dash pepper

For salad, place salad greens in a large salad bowl. Top with apple and mushroom slices. For vinaigrette, in a screw-top jar combine pineapple juice, vinegar, salad oil, basil, salt, and pepper. Cover and shake well. Drizzle vinaigrette over salad. Toss to mix. Makes 4 side-dish servings.

Gazpacho-Style Salad

We borrowed the vegetables from the popular cold soup for this refreshing salad.

3 medium tomatoes, cut into 8 wedges
1 medium cucumber, thinly sliced
1 medium green pepper, coarsely chopped
1 small red onion, thinly sliced and separated into rings
3 tablespoons snipped parsley
¼ cup salad oil
3 tablespoons vinegar
1½ teaspoons sugar
1 clove garlic, minced
¾ teaspoon snipped fresh basil *or* ¼ teaspoon dried basil, crushed
¼ teaspoon ground cumin
⅛ teaspoon dry mustard
  Dash bottled hot pepper sauce

In a mixing bowl combine tomatoes, cucumber, green pepper, onion, and parsley. For dressing, in a screw-top jar combine oil, vinegar, sugar, garlic, basil, cumin, mustard, and hot pepper sauce. Cover and shake well. Pour over vegetable mixture; toss lightly to coat. Cover and chill for 2 to 3 hours, stirring occasionally. Transfer to a salad bowl. Garnish with croutons and avocado slices, if desired. Makes 6 side-dish servings.

Marinated Mushroom Salad

2 tablespoons lemon juice
2 tablespoons salad oil
1 teaspoon Dijon-style mustard
½ teaspoon sugar
¼ teaspoon salt
¼ teaspoon dried basil, crushed
⅛ teaspoon pepper
3 cups sliced fresh mushrooms
3 cups torn Boston *or* Bibb lettuce
12 cherry tomatoes, halved
2 medium carrots, shredded

For dressing, in a screw-top jar combine lemon juice, salad oil, mustard, sugar, salt, basil, and pepper. Cover and shake well. Pour dressing over mushrooms; toss to coat. Cover and chill for 4 to 24 hours. To serve, in a large salad bowl combine lettuce, cherry tomatoes, and carrots. Top with mushroom mixture. Toss to coat all with dressing. Makes 4 to 6 side-dish servings.

Spinach and Garbanzo Bean Salad

>   1 large avocado, halved, seeded, and peeled
> ⅓ cup dairy sour cream
> 1½ teaspoons lemon juice
> ¼ teaspoon celery salt
> ¼ teaspoon bottled hot pepper sauce
> ¼ to ⅓ cup milk
>   4 cups torn fresh spinach
>   1 15-ounce can garbanzo beans, chilled and drained
>   8 cherry tomatoes, halved
> ½ small cucumber, thinly sliced
> ½ cup cauliflower flowerets
> ½ cup sliced fresh mushrooms
> ½ small red onion, thinly sliced and separated into rings
> ½ cup coarsely chopped walnuts
>   2 hard-cooked eggs, chilled

For dressing, mash *half* of the avocado. Stir together mashed avocado, sour cream, lemon juice, celery salt, and hot pepper sauce. Stir in milk till desired consistency. Cover and chill while preparing salad.

For salad, combine spinach, garbanzo beans, tomatoes, cucumber, cauliflower, mushrooms, onion, and walnuts. Slice *one* hard-cooked egg. Slice remaining avocado half; brush with additional lemon juice, if desired. Add sliced egg and avocado to salad. Top with dressing; toss to mix. Cut the remaining egg into wedges. Garnish salad with egg wedges. Makes 6 side-dish servings.

Marinated Vegetable Salad

Cook 2 cups small *cauliflower flowerets;* 2 cups bias-sliced *green beans,* cut into 1-inch pieces; 2 medium *carrots,* thinly sliced; 1 cup coarsely chopped *green pepper;* and 1 medium onion, sliced and separated into rings, in a small amount of boiling water for 5 minutes or till crisp-tender. Drain; transfer to a bowl. Stir in 1 small *zucchini,* thinly sliced, and ¼ cup halved pitted ripe *olives.*

For marinade, in a screw-top jar combine ½ cup white wine *vinegar;* ⅓ cup *salad oil;* 2 teaspoons *sugar;* 1½ teaspoons dried *oregano,* crushed; ½ teaspoon *salt;* and ¼ teaspoon *pepper.* Cover and shake well. Pour marinade over hot vegetables. Cover; chill for 4 to 24 hours, stirring occasionally. Serve with a slotted spoon. Makes 8 side-dish servings.

Create a Tossed Salad

Be an artist and design your own tossed salad. Just combine your favorite greens with the vegetables, fruits, and cheeses you like best. Then add some garnishes for interest. Finally, toss with your favorite homemade or bottled salad dressing.

● **Salad greens:** For each serving allow 1 cup salad greens. Choose one or more of the following: iceberg lettuce, romaine, curly endive, leaf lettuce, spinach, Boston lettuce, Bibb lettuce, Chinese cabbage, escarole, watercress, Swiss chard, mustard greens, beet greens, or kale.

● **Salad ingredients:** Select a combination of fresh or cooked vegetables, fruits, and cheeses.

Fresh vegetables: Tomato wedges, halved cherry tomatoes, sliced cucumber, sliced mushrooms, sliced celery, sliced radishes, shredded carrot, sliced cauliflower or broccoli flowerets, onion rings, sliced green onion, sliced zucchini, chopped red cabbage, bean sprouts, alfalfa sprouts, sliced water chestnuts, sliced avocado, or sliced pitted ripe or pimiento-stuffed olives.

Cooked vegetables: Brussels sprouts, peas, beans (garbanzo, cut green, lima, pinto, or kidney), or artichoke hearts.

Cheeses: American, cheddar, Monterey Jack, Swiss, Muenster, Colby, brick, or Gruyère cheese, cut into julienne strips or cubes; or crumbled feta cheese or blue cheese.

● **Salad garnishes:** Top your salad with one of the following: Croutons, toasted pumpkin seed, broken pecans or walnuts, crumbled crisp-cooked bacon, parsley sprigs, sieved hard-cooked egg yolks, carrot curls, anchovy fillets, coarsely chopped or sliced hard-cooked eggs, snipped chives, cubed tofu, or raisins.

Spinach-Orange Toss

Perfect for brunch.

4 cups torn fresh spinach
2 oranges, peeled and sectioned
¾ cup sliced fresh mushrooms
2 tablespoons salad oil
1 tablespoon lemon juice
1 tablespoon honey
¼ teaspoon poppy seed
⅛ teaspoon garlic powder
¼ cup toasted slivered almonds

Place spinach in a large salad bowl. Add oranges and mushrooms. Toss lightly to mix.

For dressing, in a screw-top jar combine salad oil, lemon juice, honey, poppy seed, and garlic powder. Cover and shake well. Pour the dressing over the salad. Toss lightly to coat. Sprinkle with toasted almonds. Makes 4 to 6 side-dish servings.

Wilted Spinach Salad

Leaf lettuce makes a tasty alternative to the fresh spinach.

6 cups torn fresh spinach
1 cup sliced fresh mushrooms
¼ cup sliced green onion
3 slices bacon
2 tablespoons vinegar
1 teaspoon sugar
1 hard-cooked egg, chopped

Combine spinach, mushrooms, and green onion. If desired, sprinkle with pepper. Set aside.

In a 12-inch skillet cook bacon till crisp. Remove bacon, reserving drippings in skillet. Crumble bacon; set aside. Stir vinegar, sugar, and ¼ teaspoon *salt* into drippings. Heat to boiling; remove from heat. Add the spinach mixture. Toss till coated. Transfer to a serving dish. Top with chopped egg and bacon. Serve immediately. Makes 4 side-dish servings.

Microwave directions: Combine spinach, mushrooms, and onion. If desired, sprinkle with pepper. Set aside. In a 2-quart casserole microcook bacon, covered, on 100% power (high) for 3 to 5 minutes or till crisp. Remove bacon, reserving drippings in casserole. Crumble, bacon; set aside. Stir vinegar, sugar, and salt into drippings. Cook, covered, for 30 to 45 seconds or till boiling. Add spinach mixture. Toss till coated. Top with chopped egg and bacon. Serve immediately.

Three-Bean Salad

Store any leftovers in the refrigerator for up to three days.

1 8-ounce can cut wax beans *or* one
8½-ounce can lima beans,
drained
1 8-ounce can cut green beans,
drained
1 8-ounce can red kidney beans,
drained
½ cup chopped onion
½ cup chopped green pepper
½ cup vinegar
¼ cup salad oil
3 tablespoons sugar
1 teaspoon celery seed
1 clove garlic, minced

Combine wax beans, green beans, red kidney beans, onion, and green pepper. For dressing, in a screw-top jar combine vinegar, oil, sugar, celery seed, and garlic. Cover and shake well. Add to vegetables; stir lightly. Cover; chill for 4 to 24 hours, stirring often. Makes 6 side-dish servings.

Creamy Three-Bean Salad: Prepare as above, *except* omit salad oil and sugar. For dressing, combine ⅓ cup *mayonnaise or salad dressing, 1 tablespoon* vinegar, celery seed, 1 teaspoon prepared *mustard,* and garlic.

Creamy Cucumbers

½ cup dairy sour cream *or* plain yogurt
1 tablespoon vinegar *or* lemon juice
1 teaspoon sugar
¼ teaspoon dried dillweed (optional)
1 large cucumber, halved lengthwise
and thinly sliced (about 3 cups)
1 small onion, thinly sliced and
separated into rings

Stir together sour cream; vinegar; sugar; dillweed, if desired; 1 teaspoon *salt;* and dash *pepper.* Add cucumber and onion slices; toss to coat. Cover; chill for 2 to 48 hours, stirring often. Stir before serving. Makes 6 side-dish servings.

Marinated Cucumbers: Prepare as above, *except* omit sour cream and dillweed. Increase vinegar or lemon juice to ¼ *cup* and sugar to *2 tablespoons.* If desired, stir ½ teaspoon celery seed into vinegar mixture. Cover and chill for 2 hours or up to 5 days, stirring occasionally.

Pea-Cheese Salad

This multicolored salad is even more showy when served in tomatoes.

- 1 10-ounce package frozen peas *or* one 17-ounce can peas
- 1 cup cubed cheddar cheese (4 ounces)
- 2 hard-cooked eggs, chopped
- ¼ cup chopped celery
- 2 tablespoons chopped onion
- 2 tablespoons diced pimiento *or* sweet red pepper
- ⅓ cup mayonnaise *or* salad dressing
- ¼ teaspoon salt
- ⅛ teaspoon pepper
- 6 medium tomatoes (optional)
  Leaf lettuce (optional)

Cook frozen peas according to package direction. Thoroughly drain the cooked or canned peas. Cool cooked peas.

In a large bowl combine peas, cheese cubes, hard-cooked eggs, celery, onion, and pimiento or sweet red pepper. Combine mayonnaise or salad dressing, salt, and pepper. Add to pea mixture; toss to mix. Cover and chill for 4 to 24 hours. Stir mixture well. If desired, cut *each* tomato into 8 wedges, cutting to, but not through, the bottom. Place tomatoes atop lettuce. Fill tomatoes with pea mixture. Makes 6 side-dish servings.

24-Hour Vegetable Salad

- 4 cups torn iceberg lettuce, romaine, leaf lettuce, Bibb lettuce, *or* fresh spinach
- 1 cup sliced fresh mushrooms *or* broccoli flowerets, *or* 1 cup frozen peas
- 1 cup shredded carrot
- 2 hard-cooked eggs, sliced
- 6 slices bacon, crisp-cooked, drained, and crumbled (¼ pound)
- ¾ cup shredded Swiss, American, *or* cheddar cheese (3 ounces)
- 2 green onions, sliced
- ¾ cup mayonnaise *or* salad dressing
- 1½ teaspoons lemon juice
- ½ teaspoon dried dillweed (optional)

Place lettuce or spinach in the bottom of a bowl, about 8 inches in diameter. If desired, sprinkle with salt and pepper. Layer mushrooms, broccoli, or peas atop. Then layer carrots. Arrange egg slices and bacon over vegetables. Top with ½ *cup* of the cheese and the green onions. For dressing, combine mayonnaise, lemon juice, and, if desired, dillweed. Spread dressing over top of salad, sealing to edge of bowl. Sprinkle with remaining cheese. Cover and chill for 2 to 24 hours. Before serving, toss to coat the vegetables. Sprinkle with additional sliced green onion, if desired. Makes 6 to 8 side-dish servings.

24-Hour Vegetable Salad

Coleslaw

2 cups shredded cabbage
1 medium carrot, shredded
½ small green *or* sweet red pepper, finely chopped
2 green onions, sliced
½ cup mayonnaise *or* salad dressing
1 tablespoon vinegar
2 teaspoons sugar
½ teaspoon celery seed

In a mixing bowl combine cabbage, carrot, green or sweet red pepper, and green onions. For dressing, stir together mayonnaise or salad dressing, vinegar, sugar, and celery seed. Pour the dressing over the cabbage mixture; toss to coat. Cover and chill for 1 to 24 hours. Makes 4 side-dish servings.

Vinaigrette Coleslaw: Prepare as above, *except* substitute vinaigrette for dressing. For vinaigrette, in a screw-top jar combine ¼ cup *vinegar,* 3 tablespoons *salad oil,* 2 to 3 tablespoons *sugar,* and, if desired, several dashes bottled hot pepper sauce. Cover and shake well.

Nutty Citrus Coleslaw: Prepare as above, *except* omit green onions. Add 1 small *orange,* peeled, sliced, and chopped; ¼ cup chopped *walnuts;* and 2 tablespoons *raisins* to the cabbage mixture. Makes 5 side-dish servings.

Carrot-Raisin Salad

Raisins and apples naturally sweeten this salad.

3 medium carrots, shredded (1½ cups)
1 small apple, chopped (¾ cup)
⅓ cup raisins
1 teaspoon lemon juice
⅓ cup mayonnaise *or* salad dressing
Milk (optional)
¼ cup toasted slivered almonds (optional)

In a mixing bowl combine carrots, apple, and raisins. Sprinkle with lemon juice. Add mayonnaise or salad dressing. Stir gently to coat well. Cover and chill for 2 to 24 hours. (If dressing becomes too thick, stir in a little milk.) Before serving, sprinkle with toasted almonds, if desired. Makes 6 side-dish servings.

Creamy Potato Salad

For a tangier dressing, substitute plain yogurt or sour cream for ½ cup of the mayonnaise.

6 medium potatoes (2 pounds)
2 stalks celery, thinly sliced
1 medium green pepper, chopped
⅓ cup chopped onion
1¼ cups mayonnaise *or* salad dressing
1 tablespoon vinegar
2 teaspoons Dijon-style mustard *or* prepared mustard
1 teaspoon salt
½ teaspoon pepper
6 hard-cooked eggs, coarsely chopped

In a covered saucepan cook potatoes in boiling water for 20 to 25 minutes or till just tender; drain well. Peel and cube potatoes.

In a very large bowl combine celery, green pepper, onion, mayonnaise or salad dressing, vinegar, mustard, salt, and pepper. Add potatoes and eggs. Toss lightly to mix. Cover and chill for 6 to 24 hours. Makes 12 side-dish servings.

Marinated Potato Salad

An elegant way to dress up spuds. (Pictured on page 331.)

¾ pound whole tiny new potatoes
¾ cup Vinaigrette (see recipe, page 358) *or* other oil and vinegar dressing
1 13¾-ounce can artichoke hearts, drained and halved
1 small green pepper, cut into strips
6 cherry tomatoes, halved
½ of a small red onion, sliced and separated into rings
¼ cup pitted ripe olives, halved
¼ cup snipped parsley
1 kale leaf (optional)

In a covered saucepan cook potatoes in boiling salted water for 15 to 20 minutes or just till tender; drain well. Cut potatoes into quarters. In a large bowl pour dressing over potatoes. Add artichoke hearts, green pepper, tomatoes, onion, olives, and parsley. Toss gently to mix. Cover and chill for 4 to 24 hours, stirring occasionally. Transfer to a serving bowl. Garnish with kale leaf, if desired. Makes 4 or 5 side-dish servings.

German-Style Potato Salad

4 medium potatoes
  (about 1¼ pounds)
4 slices bacon
½ cup chopped onion
1 tablespoon all-purpose flour
1 tablespoon sugar
¾ teaspoon salt
½ teaspoon celery seed
⅛ teaspoon pepper
½ cup water
¼ cup vinegar
1 hard-cooked egg, chopped;
  2 tablespoons snipped parsley; or
  2 slices bacon, cooked, drained,
  and crumbled (optional)

In a covered saucepan cook potatoes in boiling salted water for 20 to 25 minutes or till just tender; drain well. Cool slightly. Peel and slice potatoes. Set aside while preparing dressing.

For dressing, in a large skillet cook 4 slices bacon till crisp. Drain and crumble, reserving *2 tablespoons* drippings. Set the bacon aside. Add chopped onion to reserved drippings. Cook till tender. Stir in flour, sugar, salt, celery seed, and pepper. Stir in water and vinegar. Cook and stir till thickened and bubbly. Stir in potatoes and bacon. Cook for 2 to 3 minutes more or till heated through, stirring gently. Season to taste. Transfer to a serving bowl. Garnish with hard-cooked egg, parsley, or additional bacon, if desired. Makes 4 side-dish servings.

Microwave directions: Peel and slice *uncooked* potatoes ¼ inch thick. In a 1½-quart casserole combine potatoes and ½ cup *water*. Micro-cook, covered, on 100% power (high) for 8 to 10 minutes or till the potatoes are just tender, stirring twice. Let stand, covered, while preparing the dressing.

For dressing, place 4 slices bacon in a 2-quart casserole. Cover with white paper towels. Cook on high for 3 to 5 minutes or till crisp, stirring once. Drain and crumble, reserving *2 tablespoons* drippings. Set bacon aside. Add onion to reserved drippings. Cover and cook on high for 2 to 3 minutes or till tender. Stir in flour, sugar, salt, celery seed, and pepper. Stir in the ½ cup water and the vinegar. Cook, uncovered, on high for 2 to 3 minutes or till thickened and bubbly, stirring every 30 seconds. Drain the potatoes. Stir potatoes and bacon into dressing. Cook, covered, on high for 1 to 2 minutes or till heated through, stirring once. Serve as above.

Cajun-Style Rice Salad

2 cups cooked rice
1 medium green pepper, chopped
1 4½-ounce can shrimp, rinsed and
  drained
½ cup sliced fresh mushrooms
1 hard-cooked egg, finely chopped
2 tablespoons snipped parsley
¼ cup salad oil
¼ cup vinegar
¼ cup water
2 teaspoons paprika
2 teaspoons prepared horseradish
½ teaspoon onion salt
⅛ teaspoon ground red pepper
6 lettuce leaves

In a mixing bowl gently stir together rice, green pepper, shrimp, mushrooms, hard-cooked egg, and parsley. Set aside.

For dressing, in a screw-top jar combine salad oil, vinegar, water, paprika, horseradish, onion salt, and red pepper. Cover and shake well. Pour dressing over rice mixture. Toss to coat. Cover and chill for 4 to 24 hours. Serve on lettuce leaves. Makes 6 side-dish servings.

Barley Salad

Chopped peanuts and a hint of lemon flavor this nutty-tasting salad.

1¼ cups chicken broth
 1 cup quick-cooking barley
 ½ cup shredded carrot
 ¼ cup snipped parsley
 2 tablespoons water
 2 tablespoons salad oil
 2 tablespoons lemon juice
1½ teaspoons fresh snipped basil *or*
   ½ teaspoon dried basil, crushed
 ½ cup chopped peanuts *or* cashews, *or*
   toasted slivered almonds

In a saucepan combine chicken broth and barley. Bring to boiling; reduce heat. Cover and simmer for 10 to 12 minutes or till liquid is absorbed.

In a mixing bowl combine barley, carrot, and parsley. For dressing, in a screw-top jar combine water, salad oil, lemon juice, basil, ¼ teaspoon *salt*, and ¼ teaspoon *pepper*. Cover and shake well. Pour dressing over barley mixture. Toss to coat. Cover and chill for 4 to 24 hours. Stir in nuts before serving. Makes 6 side-dish servings.

Cheddar-Macaroni Salad

1 cup elbow *or* medium shell
   macaroni
¾ cup cubed cheddar *or* American
   cheese (3 ounces)
1 stalk celery, sliced
½ small green pepper, chopped
½ cup frozen peas, thawed
⅓ cup chopped onion
¼ cup mayonnaise *or* salad dressing
¼ cup dairy sour cream
2 tablespoons milk
2 tablespoons sweet pickle relish

Cook macaroni according to package directions. Drain macaroni; rinse with *cold* water. Drain again. In a mixing bowl combine macaroni, cheese, celery, green pepper, peas, and onion. Stir gently to combine.

For dressing, mix mayonnaise or salad dressing, sour cream, milk, pickle relish, and ¼ teaspoon *salt*. Toss dressing with macaroni mixture. Cover and chill for 4 to 24 hours. Stir in additional milk, if necessary. Makes 6 side-dish servings.

Fruity Pasta Salad

2 slightly beaten egg yolks
⅓ cup orange juice
3 tablespoons honey
2 tablespoons lemon juice
⅛ teaspoon ground cardamom
1 cup bow tie *or* ⅔ cup wagon wheel
   macaroni (about 2 ounces)
1 cup sliced, peeled peaches *or*
   orange sections, *or* cubed
   cantaloupe *or* honeydew melon
½ cup sliced celery
½ cup sliced strawberries
1 kiwi fruit, peeled and sliced

For dressing, in a small saucepan mix egg yolks, orange juice, honey, lemon juice, and cardamom. Cook and stir over medium heat till thickened and bubbly. Cool slightly. Cover and chill.

Cook pasta according to package directions. Drain pasta; rinse with *cold* water. Drain again. Combine pasta; peaches, orange sections, or melon; and celery. Add dressing; toss to coat. Cover; chill for 4 to 24 hours.

Before serving, stir in strawberries and kiwi fruit. Makes 6 side-dish servings.

Vegetable-Pasta Salad

1½ cups medium shell *or* corkscrew
   macaroni
⅓ cup vinegar
¼ cup olive oil *or* salad oil
1 teaspoon sugar
1 teaspoon dried savory, crushed
½ teaspoon garlic salt
¼ teaspoon dried dillweed
¼ teaspoon pepper
1 medium cucumber, seeded and
   coarsely chopped
1 cup sliced fresh mushrooms
1 stalk celery, thinly sliced
¼ cup sliced radishes
4 green onions, sliced

Cook macaroni according to package directions. Drain; rinse with *cold* water. Drain again.

For dressing, in a screw-top jar combine vinegar, oil, sugar, savory, garlic salt, dillweed, pepper, and 2 tablespoons *water*. Cover; shake well.

In a bowl mix macaroni, cucumber, mushrooms, celery, radishes, and onions. Add dressing. Toss to coat. Cover; chill for 4 to 24 hours, stirring occasionally. Makes 8 side-dish servings.

Tabbouleh

Tabbouleh (tuh-BOO-luh), a classic salad from the Middle East, features bulgur (precooked cracked wheat).

¾ cup bulgur
½ medium cucumber, seeded and
   coarsely chopped (1 cup)
½ cup snipped parsley
6 green onions, sliced
¼ cup olive oil *or* salad oil
¼ cup lemon juice
1 teaspoon dried mint, crushed
¼ teaspoon garlic salt
⅛ teaspoon pepper
2 medium tomatoes, chopped

Rinse bulgur in a colander with *cold* water. Drain. Combine bulgur, cucumber, parsley, and onions.

For dressing, in a screw-top jar combine oil, lemon juice, mint, garlic salt, and pepper. Cover; shake to mix. Pour over bulgur mixture. Toss to coat. Cover and chill 4 to 24 hours. Before serving, stir in tomatoes. Makes 6 side-dish servings.

Cinnamon Fruit Salad

1 8-ounce can unpeeled apricot halves
2 teaspoons sugar
2 teaspoons lemon juice
2 inches stick cinnamon, broken
  Dash ground nutmeg
2 medium oranges, peeled and sliced
1 8-ounce can pineapple chunks (juice
  pack), drained
1 cup strawberries, halved
  Leaf lettuce
  Fresh mint sprigs (optional)

For dressing, in a blender container or food processor bowl place *undrained* apricots. Cover and blend or process till smooth.

In a saucepan combine blended apricots, sugar, lemon juice, cinnamon, and nutmeg. Bring to boiling; reduce heat. Cover and simmer for 10 minutes. Remove cinnamon.

Meanwhile, in a mixing bowl stir together orange slices and pineapple chunks. Add dressing, stirring carefully to coat. Cover and chill for several hours.

Just before serving, stir in strawberry halves. Spoon fruit mixture onto 6 lettuce-lined plates. If desired, garnish with fresh mint sprigs. Makes 6 side-dish servings.

Fruit-Filled Melons

2 large cantaloupes
1 medium orange, peeled and
  sectioned
1 medium apple, cored and coarsely
  chopped*
1 medium peach, peeled, pitted and
  thinly sliced*
1 cup blueberries
½ cup strawberries, hulled and halved
1 8-ounce carton pineapple yogurt
2 tablespoons mayonnaise *or* salad
  dressing
2 teaspoons brown sugar
1 teaspoon grated gingerroot *or*
  ¼ teaspoon ground ginger
  Leaf lettuce

Cut each cantaloupe in half and remove the seeds. Use a melon baller to scoop out pulp, reserving shells. Set aside *2 cups* melon balls; reserve remaining melon for another use. Trim a thin slice from the bottom of each melon shell.

In a bowl mix the 2 cups melon balls, orange, apple, peach, blueberries, and strawberries. For dressing, stir together yogurt, mayonnaise, brown sugar, and gingerroot. Line each melon shell with lettuce leaves. Divide fruit among melon shells. Top *each* with *one-fourth* of the dressing. Makes 4 side-dish servings.

*****Note:** If desired, sprinkle with lemon juice to keep fruit from darkening (see tip, page 351).

Fruit-Filled Melons

Chutney-Fruit Rice Salad

To add an extra-special touch to this curried salad, use mango chutney in the dressing.

1½ cups cooked rice
  1 medium orange, peeled and cut into bite-size pieces
  1 cup chopped apple
  ½ cup seedless grapes, halved
  ½ cup plain yogurt
  ½ cup mayonnaise *or* salad dressing
  ¼ cup chutney, chopped
  ½ to 1 teaspoon curry powder
  ⅛ teaspoon garlic powder
  ⅛ teaspoon pepper
    Milk (optional)
  ½ cup coarsely chopped peanuts
    Leaf lettuce

In a mixing bowl combine rice, orange, apple, and grapes. For dressing, combine yogurt, mayonnaise, chutney, curry powder, garlic powder, and pepper. Pour over fruit mixture; toss to coat. Cover and chill for 4 to 24 hours. If necessary, add milk to moisten. Before serving, stir in peanuts. Serve on lettuce. Makes 6 side-dish servings.

Waldorf Salad

Spreading the dressing over the fruit mixture before it's chilled seals out air and helps keep the fruit fresh longer.

  2 cups chopped apple
1½ teaspoons lemon juice
  ¼ cup chopped celery
  ¼ cup chopped walnuts *or* pecans
  ¼ cup raisins *or* snipped pitted whole dates
  ¼ cup seedless green grapes, halved (optional)
  ⅓ cup whipping cream *or* ⅔ cup frozen whipped dessert topping, thawed
  ¼ cup mayonnaise *or* salad dressing
    Ground nutmeg

In a bowl toss apple with lemon juice. Stir in celery, nuts, raisins, and, if desired, grapes.

For dressing, if using whipping cream, in a chilled mixing bowl whip cream to soft peaks. Fold mayonnaise into the whipped cream or dessert topping. Spread dressing over the top of the apple mixture. Sprinkle with nutmeg. Cover and chill for 2 to 24 hours. To serve, fold dressing into fruit mixture. Makes 4 to 6 side-dish servings.

Choose-a-Fruit Salad

  4 cups desired fruit (see below)
    Lemon juice
    Leaf lettuce
  ½ cup Honey-Lime Dressing, Apricot-Nectar Dressing, *or* Fluffy Fruit Dressing (see recipes, page 358)

If necessary, brush fruits with lemon juice to prevent darkening (see tip, below). On a lettuce-lined platter, arrange fruit. Serve with Honey-Lime Dressing, Apricot-Nectar Dressing, or Fluffy Fruit Dressing. Makes 4 side-dish servings.

Fruit options: Choose any combination of peeled and sliced or cut-up avocados, bananas, kiwi fruits, mangoes, melons, papayas, peaches, or pineapples; sliced or cut-up apples, apricots, nectarines, pears, or plums; peeled and sectioned oranges, tangerines, or grapefruit; berries (halve any large strawberries); halved and pitted dark sweet cherries; or halved seedless grapes.

Fruity Slaw

Yogurt makes an easy salad dressing for the cabbage and fruit.

  2 cups shredded cabbage, Chinese cabbage, *or* savoy cabbage
  1 cup cubed honeydew melon *or* cantaloupe
  1 8¼-ounce can pineapple chunks, drained
  1 cup halved strawberries
  ¼ teaspoon poppy seed (optional)
  ⅓ cup pineapple, lemon, *or* vanilla yogurt

In a mixing bowl combine shredded cabbage, cubed honeydew melon or cantaloupe, pineapple chunks, strawberries, and, if desired, poppy seed. Cover and chill up to 3 hours. Just before serving, add pineapple, lemon, or vanilla yogurt. Toss gently till the cabbage and fruit are coated. Transfer slaw to a salad bowl, if desired. Makes 4 side-dish servings.

24-Hour Fruit Salad

  1 **20-ounce can pineapple chunks (juice pack)**
  3 **slightly beaten egg yolks**
  2 **tablespoons sugar**
  1 **tablespoon margarine *or* butter**
1½ **cups tiny marshmallows**
  2 **oranges, peeled, sectioned, and drained**
  1 **cup seedless grapes, halved**
  ½ **cup whipping cream**

Drain pineapple, reserving ¼ *cup* juice. For custard, in a small heavy saucepan combine reserved juice, egg yolks, sugar, and margarine or butter. Cook and stir over low heat about 6 minutes or till mixture thickens slightly and coats a metal spoon. Cool to room temperature.

Meanwhile, in a bowl combine pineapple, marshmallows, oranges, and grapes. Whip cream till soft peaks form. Fold into custard. Pour over fruit and mix gently. Transfer to a serving bowl. Cover and refrigerate for 4 to 24 hours. Stir gently before serving. Makes 8 side-dish servings.

Microwave directions: Drain pineapple, reserving ¼ *cup* juice. For custard, in a 2-cup measure combine reserved pineapple juice, sugar, and margarine or butter. Micro-cook, uncovered, on 100% power (high) for 1 to 1½ minutes or till bubbly, stirring once. Gradually stir hot mixture into egg yolks. Return all to the measuring cup. Cook on high for 45 to 60 seconds more or till mixture thickens slightly and coats a metal spoon, stirring every 10 seconds. Cool to room temperature. Continue as above.

Preventing Browned Fruit

Fruit is much more appealing when it looks freshly cut. To keep fruits such as apples, pears, peaches, apricots, and nectarines from turning brown after they're cut, dip the fruit into, or brush it with, lemon juice or a mixture of lemon juice and water. A mixture of water and ascorbic-acid color keeper, mixed according to package directions, works well, too.

Five-Cup Salad

  1 **8¼-ounce can pineapple chunks**
  1 **11-ounce can mandarin orange sections, drained**
  1 **cup coconut**
  1 **cup tiny marshmallows**
  1 **8-ounce carton dairy sour cream**
  2 **tablespoons chopped pecans**

Drain pineapple chunks, reserving *1 tablespoon* syrup. Combine pineapple chunks, reserved syrup, mandarin orange sections, coconut, marshmallows, and sour cream. Cover and chill for 2 to 24 hours. Before serving, sprinkle with pecans. Makes 6 side-dish servings.

Pineapple-Lemon Squares

  1 **15¼-ounce can crushed pineapple**
  1 **6-ounce package lemon-flavored gelatin**
1½ **cups lemon-lime carbonated beverage**
  2 **cups coarsely chopped pitted plums or cored pears**
  ¼ **cup sugar**
  2 **tablespoons all-purpose flour**
  1 **slightly beaten egg**
  1 **cup whipping cream**
  ⅓ **cup shredded American cheese**

Drain pineapple, reserving juice. Set aside. Dissolve gelatin in 2 cups *boiling water*. Add carbonated beverage. Chill till mixture is partially set (the consistency of unbeaten egg whites). Fold in pineapple and plums or pears. Pour into a 12x7½x2-inch baking dish. Chill till almost firm.

Meanwhile, in a saucepan combine sugar and flour. Add enough water to reserved pineapple juice to equal *1 cup*. Stir into sugar mixture. Cook and stir till thickened and bubbly. Gradually stir about *half* of the hot mixture into egg. Return mixture to saucepan. Cook and stir till nearly bubbly; reduce heat. Cook and stir about 1 to 2 minutes more, but *do not boil*. Remove from heat. Cover surface with clear plastic wrap. Cool to room temperature.

Beat whipping cream till soft peaks form. Fold egg mixture into whipped cream. Spread evenly atop gelatin layer. Sprinkle with cheese. Chill for 4 to 24 hours. Makes 9 side-dish servings.

Cherry-Apple Salad Mold

> 1 **cup frozen unsweetened pitted dark sweet cherries**
> 1½ **cups apple cider or apple juice**
> 1 **3-ounce package cherry-flavored gelatin**
> ½ **cup applesauce**
> ¼ **cup chopped celery**
> ¼ **cup chopped walnuts**
> **Apple cider *or* apple juice**
> ½ **cup soft-style cream cheese**

Let cherries stand at room temperature while preparing gelatin mixture. In a saucepan bring the 1½ cups apple cider to boiling; remove from heat. Add gelatin; stir till dissolved. Chill till partially set (the consistency of unbeaten egg whites). Halve partially thawed cherries. Stir cherries, applesauce, celery, and nuts into gelatin mixture. Pour into a 3- or 3½-cup mold. Chill till firm. Unmold onto a lettuce-lined plate, if desired.

For sauce, stir enough apple cider or apple juice (3 to 4 tablespoons) into cream cheese to make a sauce of spooning consistency. Pass sauce with salad. Makes 4 or 5 side-dish servings.

Creamy Fruit Salad

> 1 **11-ounce can mandarin orange sections**
> **Orange juice**
> 1 **3-ounce package lemon-flavored gelatin**
> 2 **beaten eggs**
> 1 **8-ounce carton dairy sour cream**
> 1 **3-ounce package cream cheese, cubed and softened**
> 1 **medium banana, sliced**
> ⅓ **cup chopped walnuts**

Drain orange sections, reserving syrup. Add enough orange juice to syrup to measure *1 cup*. In a medium saucepan bring mixture to boiling. Remove from heat. Add gelatin; stir till dissolved. Gradually stir about *1 cup* of the hot mixture into eggs. Return mixture to saucepan. Cook and stir till nearly bubbly; reduce heat. Cook and stir for 1 to 2 minutes more, but *do not boil*. Remove from heat. Add sour cream and cream cheese. Beat till smooth. Chill till partially set (the consistency of unbeaten egg whites). Fold in oranges, banana, and nuts. Transfer to a 10x6x2-inch dish. Chill till firm. Makes 8 side-dish servings.

◄ When the gelatin has chilled to the consistency of unbeaten egg whites, stir in the solids.

Place the salad in a bowl or sink of warm water just till the edges are loosened from the mold.

Berry Salad

Drain one 10-ounce package frozen sliced *strawberries,* thawed, and one 10-ounce package frozen *red raspberries,* thawed; reserve syrup from each. Dissolve one 6-ounce package *strawberry-* or *raspberry-flavored gelatin* in 1¼ cups *boiling water.* Stir in reserved syrup, ½ cup *cranberry juice cocktail or apple juice,* and 1 tablespoon *lemon juice.* Chill till partially set (the consistency of unbeaten egg whites). Fold in berries. Pour into a 5- or 5½-cup mold. Cover; chill till firm. Unmold onto a plate lined with *leaf lettuce.* Makes 8 side-dish servings.

Apricot-Pecan Mold

  1 **3-ounce package apricot- *or* orange-flavored gelatin**
  1 **cup boiling water**
  1 **5½-ounce can apricot nectar**
  2 **tablespoons lemon juice**
  ⅓ **cup plain yogurt**
  4 **apricots, peeled, pitted and chopped (about ⅔ cup), *or* one 8¾-ounce can apricots, drained and chopped**
  ⅓ **cup chopped pecans**

In a mixing bowl dissolve gelatin in boiling water. Stir in apricot nectar and lemon juice. Chill till partially set (the consistency of unbeaten egg whites). Beat with a rotary beater till fluffy and light in color (1 to 2 minutes). Beat in yogurt. If necessary, chill till the mixture mounds when spooned. Fold in apricots and pecans. Carefully spoon gelatin mixture into a 5½- or 6-cup mold. Chill till firm. Unmold onto a plate lined with leaf lettuce, if desired. Makes 5 or 6 side-dish servings.

Creamy Cucumber Mold

  2 **tablespoons sugar**
  1 **envelope unflavored gelatin**
  ¼ **teaspoon salt**
  2 **tablespoons lemon juice**
  ½ **of an 8-ounce container soft-style cream cheese**
  ½ **cup mayonnaise or salad dressing**
  ½ **cup dairy sour cream**
  1 **cup finely chopped, seeded, peeled cucumber**
  ¼ **cup snipped parsley**
  2 **tablespoons finely chopped green onion**

In a medium saucepan combine sugar, gelatin, salt, and ⅔ cup *water.* Let stand 5 minutes. Cook and stir over low heat till gelatin dissolves. Stir in lemon juice. With a rotary beater, gradually beat hot gelatin mixture into cream cheese till smooth. Beat in mayonnaise and sour cream. Stir cucumber, parsley, and onion into cream cheese mixture. Pour into a 3½-cup mold. Chill till firm. Unmold onto a lettuce-lined plate and garnish with cucumber slices, if desired. Makes 4 to 6 side-dish servings.

Tomato-Vegetable Aspic

The flavor will remind you of a Bloody Mary.

  2 **envelopes unflavored gelatin**
  1 **cup beef broth**
  3 **cups tomato juice**
  ½ **cup chopped cucumber, celery, *or* green pepper**
  ¼ **cup chopped onion**
  1 **tablespoon brown sugar**
  1 **teaspoon dried basil or tarragon, crushed**
  2 **teaspoons Worcestershire sauce**
  1 **bay leaf**
  2 **tablespoons lemon juice**
     Dash bottled hot pepper sauce
     Leaf lettuce

In a small saucepan combine gelatin and ½ *cup* of the beef broth. Let stand 5 minutes.

Meanwhile, in a medium saucepan combine *1 cup* of the tomato juice, the cucumber, onion, brown sugar, and basil. Add Worcestershire sauce and bay leaf. Simmer for 5 minutes. Strain mixture through several layers of cheesecloth. Discard vegetables and seasonings.

Add gelatin mixture to hot tomato-juice mixture; stir to dissolve. Stir in remaining beef broth and tomato juice, the lemon juice, and hot pepper sauce. Pour into a 4- or 4½-cup mold. Cover and chill for 6 to 24 hours. Unmold onto a lettuce-lined plate. Makes 8 to 10 side-dish servings.

Unmolding Salads

Removing your salad from its mold needn't be tricky. Just dip the mold into warm water for a few seconds to loosen the salad's edges. Then center a plate upside down over the mold. Holding the mold and plate together, invert them. Shake the mold gently until you feel the salad loosen, then carefully lift the mold off. If the salad doesn't unmold, repeat these steps.

Cranberry Relish Ring

½ cup sugar
1 3-ounce package cherry-flavored gelatin
1 3-ounce package raspberry-flavored gelatin
1½ cups boiling water
1 12-ounce can lemon-lime carbonated beverage
1 8¼-ounce can crushed pineapple
1 small orange, quartered and seeded
2 cups cranberries

Dissolve sugar and gelatins in boiling water. Add carbonated beverage and *undrained* pineapple. Chill till partially set (the consistency of unbeaten egg whites). Using a food processor or food grinder with a coarse blade, grind *unpeeled* orange and cranberries. Fold cranberry mixture into gelatin. Pour into a 6½-cup ring mold or a 12x7½x2-inch dish. Chill till firm. Makes 12 side-dish servings.

Shortcut Cranberry Relish Ring: Prepare as above, *except* reduce sugar to ¼ *cup* and substitute two 10-ounce packages frozen *cranberry-orange relish,* thawed, for the ground orange and cranberries.

Peach-Berry Frozen Salad

1 8-ounce container soft-style cream cheese *or* one 8-ounce package Neufchâtel cheese, softened
2 8-ounce cartons peach yogurt
1 4-ounce container frozen whipped dessert topping, thawed
1 cup chopped peeled fresh *or* frozen unsweetened peaches *or* one 8¾-ounce can peach slices, drained and chopped
1 cup fresh *or* frozen unsweetened raspberries *or* blueberries
¼ cup toasted slivered almonds

In a mixing bowl combine cream cheese and yogurt. Beat with an electric mixer till smooth. Stir in whipped topping, peaches, raspberries, and almonds. Pour into an 8x8x2-inch baking dish. Cover; freeze 8 to 24 hours or till firm.

To serve, let stand at room temperature about 30 minutes to thaw slightly. Cut into squares. Serve on lettuce-lined plates, if desired. Makes 9 side-dish servings.

Frosty Cranberry-Date Salad

1 cup cranberries, finely chopped
⅓ cup sugar
2 medium oranges
1 teaspoon vanilla
1 8-ounce package cream cheese, softened
1 small apple, finely chopped
½ cup snipped pitted whole dates
1 cup whipping cream
Leaf lettuce

Combine cranberries and sugar; let stand 10 minutes. Meanwhile, peel and section *one* of the oranges; reserve juice. Finely chop orange sections; set aside. Squeeze remaining orange to make ⅓ cup juice, adding reserved juice, if necessary.

Gradually beat orange juice and vanilla into cream cheese. Stir in cranberry mixture, chopped orange sections, apple, and dates. Whip cream till soft peaks form. Fold into cream cheese mixture. Spoon into an 8x4x2-inch loaf pan, 5-cup mold, or 10 to 12 paper bake cups in muffin pans. Cover and freeze till firm.

To serve, let salad stand at room temperature for 15 to 20 minutes to thaw slightly. Unmold from pan or mold, or remove paper bake cups. Serve on lettuce-lined plates. If desired, garnish with additional orange sections. Makes 8 to 12 side-dish servings.

Frozen Black Cherry Cups

1 8¼-ounce can crushed pineapple, drained
1 8-ounce carton dairy sour cream
1 8-ounce carton vanilla yogurt
1 tablespoon lemon juice
1 16-ounce can pitted dark sweet cherries, drained
1 medium banana, peeled and coarsely chopped
¼ cup toasted pecans, chopped
Leaf lettuce

Combine pineapple, sour cream, yogurt, and lemon juice. Gently stir in cherries, banana, and pecans. Spoon into 12 paper bake cups in muffin pans. Cover and freeze for 2 to 24 hours.

To serve, let stand at room temperature about 20 minutes to thaw slightly. Remove paper bake cups. Place on lettuce-lined salad plates. Makes 12 side-dish servings.

Mayonnaise

½ **teaspoon dry mustard**
¼ **teaspoon salt**
¼ **teaspoon paprika (optional)**
⅛ **teaspoon ground red pepper**
2 **egg yolks**
2 **tablespoons vinegar or lemon juice**
2 **cups salad oil**

In a small mixer bowl combine mustard; salt; paprika, if desired; and red pepper. Add egg yolks and vinegar or lemon juice. Beat with an electric mixer on medium speed till combined.

With mixer running, add the oil, 1 teaspoon at a time, till *2 tablespoons* oil have been added. Add the remaining oil in a thin, steady stream. (This should take about 5 minutes.) Cover and store in the refrigerator up to 2 weeks. Makes about 2 cups (thirty-two 1-tablespoon servings).

Food-processor directions: In a food processor bowl combine all ingredients except oil; process till combined. With the processor running, add oil in a thin, steady stream. (When necessary, stop the processor and use a rubber scraper to scrape the sides.)

Blender Mayonnaise: Prepare as above, *except* use *half* of *each* ingredient and substitute 1 *whole egg* for the 2 egg yolks. In a blender container combine all ingredients except oil. Cover and blend for 5 seconds. With blender running slowly, add oil in a thin, steady stream. (When necessary, stop blender and use a rubber scraper to scrape the sides.) Makes 1 cup (sixteen 1-tablespoon servings).

Herb Blender Mayonnaise: Prepare Blender Mayonnaise as above. To prepared mayonnaise, stir in 2 tablespoons sliced *green onion;* 1 tablespoon snipped *basil, oregano, or parsley* (*or* ½ teaspoon crushed *dried herb*); 1 tablespoon *dry sherry* (optional); ½ teaspoon *Worcestershire sauce;* and 1 clove *garlic,* minced. Makes 1 cup (sixteen 1-tablespoon servings).

Citrus Blender Mayonnaise: Prepare Blender Mayonnaise as above, *except* omit red pepper. To prepared mayonnaise, stir in 4 teaspoons *sugar,* 1½ teaspoons finely shredded *orange or lime peel,* 1 tablespoon *orange or lime juice,* and, if desired, ¼ teaspoon *poppy seed.* Makes 1 cup (sixteen 1-tablespoon servings).

◄While continuing to beat the mixture, gradually add oil in a thin stream about ⅛ inch in diameter.

Cooked Salad Dressing

Use the full 2 tablespoons of sugar when you need a topping for fruit.

1 **to 2 tablespoons sugar**
1 **tablespoon all-purpose flour**
½ **teaspoon salt**
½ **teaspoon dry mustard**
  Dash ground red pepper
¾ **cup milk**
2 **slightly beaten egg yolks**
¼ **cup vinegar**

In a saucepan combine sugar, flour, salt, mustard, and red pepper. Stir in milk and egg yolks. Cook and stir till thickened and bubbly. Cook and stir 1 minute more. Stir in vinegar till smooth. Cool. Cover; store in refrigerator up to 2 weeks. Makes 1 cup (sixteen 1-tablespoon servings).

Sunflower-Nut Dressing

In a blender container or food processor bowl blend or process ¼ cup *sunflower nuts* to a very fine powder. Add one 8-ounce carton *plain yogurt or* dairy *sour cream,* 2 tablespoons *milk,* ⅛ teaspoon *garlic powder,* ⅛ teaspoon *dry mustard,* and ⅛ teaspoon *pepper.* Blend or process till smooth. Cover and store in the refrigerator up to 2 weeks. If necessary, stir in additional milk to make desired consistency. Makes 1 cup (sixteen 1-tablespoon servings).

Green Goddess Dressing

To transform this salad dressing into a refreshing vegetable dip, just omit the milk.

- ¾ **cup packed parsley leaves**
- ⅓ **cup mayonnaise *or* salad dressing**
- ⅓ **cup dairy sour cream *or* plain yogurt**
- 1 **green onion, cut up**
- 1 **tablespoon vinegar**
- 1 **teaspoon anchovy paste *or* 1 anchovy fillet, cut up**
- ¼ **teaspoon dried basil, crushed**
- ⅛ **teaspoon garlic powder**
- ⅛ **teaspoon dried tarragon, crushed**
- 1 **to 2 tablespoons milk**

In a blender container or food processor bowl combine parsley, mayonnaise, sour cream, onion, vinegar, anchovy paste, basil, garlic powder, and tarragon. Cover and blend or process till smooth. Cover and store in the refrigerator up to 2 weeks. Before serving, stir in milk to make of desired consistency. Makes about 1 cup (sixteen 1-tablespoon servings).

Creamy Italian Dressing

- ¾ **cup mayonnaise or salad dressing**
- ¼ **cup dairy sour cream**
- 2 **teaspoons white wine vinegar *or* white vinegar**
- ¼ **teaspoon dry mustard**
- ¼ **teaspoon dried basil, crushed**
- ¼ **teaspoon dried oregano, crushed**
- ⅛ **teaspoon salt**
- ⅛ **teaspoon garlic powder**
- 1 **to 2 tablespoons milk (optional)**

In a mixing bowl stir together mayonnaise or salad dressing, sour cream, vinegar, mustard, basil, oregano, salt, and garlic powder. Cover and store in the refrigerator up to 2 weeks. If necessary, stir in milk to make of desired consistency. Makes 1 cup (sixteen 1-tablespoon servings).

Creamy Garlic Dressing: Prepare as above, *except* omit oregano and garlic powder. Add 2 cloves *garlic,* minced.

Creamy Parmesan Dressing: Prepare as above, *except* omit the dry mustard, dried oregano, and salt. Stir in 3 tablespoons grated *Parmesan cheese* and, if desired, ½ teaspoon cracked black pepper.

Thousand Island Dressing

For a dressing with less fat, use one 8-ounce carton plain yogurt instead of the mayonnaise.

- 1 **cup mayonnaise *or* salad dressing**
- ¼ **cup chili sauce**
- 1 **hard-cooked egg, finely chopped**
- 2 **tablespoons finely chopped pimiento-stuffed olives**
- 2 **tablespoons finely chopped green *or* sweet red pepper**
- 2 **tablespoons finely chopped onion**
- 1 **teaspoon Worcestershire sauce *or* prepared horseradish (optional)**
- 1 **to 2 tablespoons milk (optional)**

Combine mayonnaise and chili sauce. Stir in egg, olives, sweet pepper, onion, and, if desired, Worcestershire sauce. Cover; store in the refrigerator up to 1 week. If necessary, stir in milk to make of desired consistency. Makes 1½ cups (twenty-four 1-tablespoon servings).

Buttermilk Dressing

- 1 **cup mayonnaise *or* salad dressing**
- ½ **cup buttermilk *or* plain yogurt**
- 1 **tablespoon grated Parmesan cheese**
- 1 **tablespoon snipped fresh chives, parsley, *or* dillweed; 1 teaspoon dried chives *or* parsley; *or* ½ teaspoon dried dillweed**
- ¼ **teaspoon garlic powder**
- ¼ **teaspoon onion powder**
- ⅛ **teaspoon pepper**
- 1 **to 2 tablespoons milk (optional)**

Stir together mayonnaise or salad dressing and buttermilk. Stir in cheese, herb, garlic powder, onion powder, and pepper. Cover and store in refrigerator up to 2 weeks. If necessary, stir in milk to make of desired consistency. Makes 1½ cups (twenty-four 1-tablespoon servings).

Horseradish Dressing

Combine ½ cup *mayonnaise or salad dressing,* ½ cup dairy *sour cream,* 3 tablespoons *milk,* 2 tablespoons snipped *chives or green onion tops,* and 1 to 2 tablespoons *prepared horseradish.* Cover and store in the refrigerator up to 2 weeks. Makes 1¼ cups (twenty 1-tablespoon servings).

Creamy French Dressing

    2 tablespoons sugar
    3 tablespoons vinegar
    2 teaspoons paprika
    1 teaspoon Worcestershire sauce
        (optional)
    ¼ teaspoon salt
    ¼ teaspoon dry mustard
    ⅛ teaspoon garlic powder
        Dash ground red pepper
    ¾ cup salad oil or olive oil

In a small mixer bowl, blender container, or food processor bowl, combine sugar; vinegar; paprika; Worcestershire sauce, if desired; salt; mustard; garlic powder; and red pepper.

With mixer, blender, or food processor running, add oil in a thin, steady stream. (This should take 2 to 3 minutes.) Continue mixing, blending, or processing till mixture is thick. Cover and store in the refrigerator up to 2 weeks. Stir before serving. Makes about 1⅓ cups (twenty-two 1-tablespoon servings).

Oil-Free Dressing

Heavy on the herb flavor, light on the fat.

    1 tablespoon powdered fruit pectin
    ¾ teaspoon fresh or ¼ teaspoon dried
        oregano, basil, thyme, tarragon,
        savory, or dillweed, crushed
    ½ teaspoon sugar
    ⅛ teaspoon dry mustard
    ⅛ teaspoon pepper
    ¼ cup water
    1 tablespoon vinegar
    1 small clove garlic, minced

In a mixing bowl combine pectin, desired herb, sugar, mustard, and pepper. Stir in water, vinegar, and garlic. Cover and store in the refrigerator up to 3 days. Makes about ½ cup (eight 1-tablespoon servings).

Creamy Onion Oil-Free Dressing: Prepare as above, *except* increase sugar to *1 tablespoon*. Stir in ¼ cup sliced *green onion* and ¼ cup *plain yogurt* with the water. Makes ¾ cup (twelve 1-tablespoon servings).

Blue Cheese Dressing

    ½ cup plain yogurt or dairy sour cream
    ¼ cup cream-style cottage cheese
    ¼ cup mayonnaise or salad dressing
    ¾ cup crumbled blue cheese
    2 to 3 tablespoons milk (optional)

In a blender container or food processor bowl combine yogurt or sour cream, cottage cheese, mayonnaise, and ¼ *cup* of the blue cheese. Cover and blend or process till smooth. Stir in remaining blue cheese. If necessary, stir in milk to make of desired consistency. Cover and store in the refrigerator up to 2 weeks. Makes 1¼ cups (twenty 1-tablespoon servings).

Croutons

To complete your salads' fresh taste, make some homemade croutons. And while you're at it, make a double batch—half for salads, half for snacks.

Cut four ½-inch-thick slices *French bread* into ¾-inch cubes. In a large skillet melt ¼ cup *margarine or butter*. Remove from heat. Stir in ⅛ teaspoon *garlic powder*. Add bread cubes and stir till coated with mixture. Spread cubes into a single layer in a shallow baking pan. Bake in a 300° oven for 10 minutes. Stir. Bake about 5 minutes more or till bread cubes are dry and crisp. Makes about 2 cups (sixteen 2-tablespoon servings).

For variety, make the croutons with other breads such as *whole wheat, pumpernickel, or sourdough.* Or try omitting the garlic powder and stirring 3 tablespoons *Parmesan cheese* or 1 teaspoon dried *dillweed* into the melted margarine or butter.

Vinaigrette

½ cup salad oil
⅓ cup white wine vinegar *or* vinegar
1 tablespoon sugar
2 teaspoons snipped fresh thyme, oregano, *or* basil; *or* ½ teaspoon dried thyme, oregano, *or* basil, crushed
½ teaspoon paprika
¼ teaspoon dry mustard *or* 1 teaspoon Dijon-style mustard (optional)
⅛ teaspoon pepper

In a screw-top jar mix oil; vinegar; sugar; herb; paprika; mustard, if desired; and pepper. Cover; shake well. Store in the refrigerator up to 2 weeks. Shake before serving. Makes ¾ cup (twelve 1-tablespoon servings).

French Vinaigrette: Prepare as above, *except* omit herb. Use mustard and add a dash ground *red pepper.*

Italian Vinaigrette: Prepare as above, *except* use oregano for herb and use mustard. Add 2 tablespoons grated *Parmesan cheese,* ¼ teaspoon *celery seed,* and 1 clove *garlic,* minced.

Red Wine Vinaigrette: Prepare as above, *except* reduce vinegar to *3 tablespoons.* Use *half* thyme and *half* oregano for the herb. Add 2 tablespoons *dry red wine* and 1 clove *garlic,* minced.

Garlic Vinaigrette: Prepare as above, *except* omit herb and paprika. Add 2 large cloves *garlic,* minced.

Onion Vinaigrette: Prepare as above, *except* add 2 tablespoons sliced *green onion.*

Ginger Vinaigrette: Prepare as above, *except* omit herb and mustard. Add 1 teaspoon grated *gingerroot.*

Citrus and Poppy Seed Vinaigrette: Prepare as above, *except* substitute *lemon or lime juice* for the vinegar and *honey* for the sugar. Omit herb. Add 1 teaspoon *poppy seed.*

Honey-Lime Dressing

In a small mixer bowl combine ⅓ cup *honey,* ½ teaspoon finely shredded *lime peel,* ¼ cup *lime juice,* and ⅛ teaspoon ground *nutmeg.* Beating with an electric mixer on medium speed, add ¾ cup *salad oil* to honey mixture in a thin, steady stream. Continue beating till mixture is thick. Cover and store in the refrigerator up to 2 weeks. Serve with fruit. Makes about 1⅓ cups (twenty-one 1-tablespoon servings).

Russian Dressing

¼ cup salad oil
¼ cup catsup
1 tablespoon sugar
1 tablespoon white wine vinegar or vinegar
1 tablespoon lemon juice
1 teaspoon Worcestershire sauce
½ teaspoon paprika
¼ teaspoon salt
⅛ teaspoon pepper

In a screw-top jar combine oil, catsup, sugar, vinegar, lemon juice, Worcestershire sauce, paprika, salt, and pepper. Cover and shake well. Store in the refrigerator up to 2 weeks. Shake before serving. Makes ⅔ cup (eleven 1-tablespoon servings).

Apricot-Nectar Dressing

Enjoy as a topping on a bowl of fresh fruit.

1 tablespoon brown sugar
½ cup plain yogurt
½ cup apricot nectar
⅛ teaspoon ground cinnamon
Dash ground nutmeg

Stir brown sugar into yogurt. Add apricot nectar, cinnamon, and nutmeg. Stir till smooth. Cover and store in the refrigerator up to 2 weeks. Makes 1 cup (sixteen 1-tablespoon servings).

Fluffy Fruit Dressing

½ cup vanilla-flavored yogurt
½ cup frozen whipped dessert topping, thawed
½ teaspoon finely shredded orange *or* lemon peel
2 to 3 tablespoons orange juice

In a mixing bowl combine yogurt, dessert topping, and orange or lemon peel. Add orange juice to make desired consistency. Cover and store in the refrigerator up to 3 days. Makes 1 cup (sixteen 1-tablespoon servings).

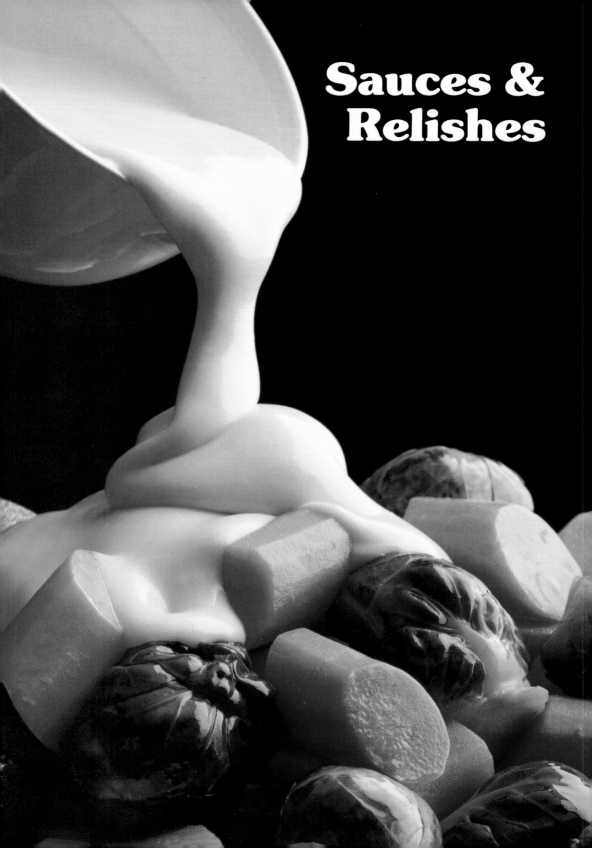

Sauces & Relishes

Nutrition Analysis

	Servings Per Recipe	Calories	Protein (g)	Carbohydrate (g)	Fat (g)	Cholesterol (mg)	Sodium (mg)	Potassium (mg)	Protein	Vitamin A	Vitamin C	Thiamine	Riboflavin	Niacin	Calcium	Iron
	Per Serving								**Percent U.S. RDA Per Serving**							
Almond Cranberry Sauce (p. 365)	8	121	1	28	2	0	3	61	1	0	5	1	2	1	1	2
Almond Sauce (p. 361)	16	25	1	1	2	1	38	32	1	1	0	1	2	1	2	1
Bacon and Sour Cream Sauce (p. 364)	20	19	1	1	2	2	67	12	1	1	1	1	1	0	1	0
Basic Barbecue Sauce (p. 364)	28	13	0	3	0	0	127	40	0	3	2	1	0	1	0	1
Béarnaise Sauce (p. 363)	12	91	1	0	10	91	93	17	2	10	0	1	2	0	1	2
Caraway-Cheese Sauce (p. 364)	24	26	1	1	2	3	105	23	1	3	0	0	1	0	2	0
Cheese Sauce (p. 361)	16	32	2	1	2	5	87	30	3	2	0	1	2	0	6	0
Cherry Sauce (p. 366)	36	14	0	4	0	0	1	30	0	0	4	0	0	0	0	1
Cocktail Sauce (p. 364)	16	15	0	4	0	0	179	54	1	4	5	1	1	1	0	1
Cranberry-Orange Relish (p. 366)	15	139	1	33	1	0	1	65	1	1	23	2	1	1	1	1
Cranberry Sauce (p. 365)	8	110	0	28	0	0	1	21	0	0	4	1	0	0	0	0
Creamy Mushroom Sauce (p. 363)	24	21	1	1	2	3	33	32	1	1	0	1	2	1	2	0
Cucumber Relish (p. 367)	10	23	0	3	1	0	28	63	0	0	3	1	0	1	1	1
Curry Sauce (p. 361)	12	21	1	2	1	1	43	29	1	1	0	1	2	0	2	0
Herb-Garlic Sauce (p. 361)	12	19	1	1	1	1	41	26	1	1	0	1	2	0	2	0
Hollandaise Sauce (p. 362)	12	84	1	0	9	68	103	9	1	8	1	1	1	0	1	1
Horseradish Sauce (p. 364)	16	26	0	0	3	10	5	11	0	2	0	0	0	0	1	0
Hot-Style Barbecue Sauce (p. 364)	28	13	0	3	0	0	127	40	0	3	2	1	0	1	0	1
Lemon-Chive Sauce (p. 361)	12	19	1	1	1	1	41	26	1	2	1	1	2	0	2	0
Low-Calorie White Sauce (p. 361)	12	8	1	1	0	0	29	26	1	1	0	1	1	0	2	0
Low-Fat Tartar Sauce (p. 364)	20	30	0	2	2	3	69	18	0	1	2	0	1	0	1	0
Mexicali Sauce (p. 361)	12	19	1	1	1	1	60	30	1	6	1	1	2	0	2	0
Mock Hollandaise Sauce (p. 363)	8	66	1	1	7	7	47	14	1	2	1	0	1	0	1	0
Molded Cranberry Sauce (p. 365)	8	110	0	28	0	0	1	21	0	0	4	1	0	0	0	0
Mustard-Dill Sauce (p. 364)	21	17	0	1	1	0	126	15	1	0	0	0	1	0	1	0
Mustard Sauce (p. 364)	16	28	0	0	3	10	58	8	0	2	0	0	0	0	0	0
Oriental-Style Mustard Sauce (p. 365)	16	10	0	0	1	0	33	8	0	0	0	0	0	0	1	1
Papaya-Apple Chutney (p. 367)	36	23	0	6	0	0	16	54	0	4	9	0	0	0	1	1
Parmesan Sauce (p. 361)	12	28	1	1	2	3	58	27	2	2	0	1	2	0	5	0
Pickled Beets (p. 366)	8	41	1	10	0	0	92	121	0	0	5	1	0	1	1	2
Pineapple-Date Chutney (p. 367)	36	27	0	7	0	0	16	51	0	0	4	1	1	1	1	1
Plum Sauce (p. 365)	12	43	0	10	0	0	173	28	1	0	1	0	0	1	0	1
Refrigerator Corn Relish (p. 367)	10	61	1	15	0	0	59	115	2	7	19	4	1	2	1	3
Salsa (p. 368)	32	4	0	1	0	0	60	35	0	9	9	0	0	1	0	1
Salsa Verde (p. 368)	32	4	0	1	0	0	60	35	0	9	9	0	0	1	0	1
Sauce Provençale (p. 363)	20	21	0	2	1	0	16	58	0	6	5	1	1	1	0	1
Sauce Véronique (p. 365)	20	8	0	1	0	0	40	25	1	0	0	1	1	1	1	0
Sauerkraut Relish (p. 368)	32	8	0	2	0	0	35	15	0	1	5	0	0	0	0	0
Sherry Sauce (p. 361)	12	20	1	1	1	1	41	26	1	1	0	1	2	0	2	0
Spiced Apple Rings (p. 366)	6	94	0	24	0	0	10	88	0	1	5	1	0	1	1	1
Sweet-Sour Sauce (p. 363)	20	26	0	7	0	0	54	38	0	1	5	0	0	1	1	2
Tangy Mustard Barbecue Sauce (p. 364)	28	14	0	3	0	0	140	42	0	3	2	1	0	1	0	1
Tartar Sauce (p. 364)	20	84	0	1	9	6	84	13	0	1	2	0	0	0	0	1
White Sauce (p. 361)	12	18	1	1	1	1	41	25	1	1	0	0	2	0	2	0
Wine-Mushroom Sauce (p. 362)	16	13	0	1	1	0	26	31	0	1	0	1	2	1	0	1
Yogurt-Chili Sauce (p. 365)	16	11	1	2	0	1	39	42	1	1	1	1	2	0	3	0
Yogurt-Chutney Sauce (p. 365)	16	15	1	3	0	1	15	40	1	0	0	0	2	0	3	0
Yogurt-Cucumber-Mint Sauce (p. 365)	16	10	1	1	0	1	10	41	1	0	1	1	2	0	3	0
Yogurt-Dill Sauce (p. 365)	16	9	1	1	0	1	10	36	1	0	0	0	2	0	3	0
Zesty Orange-Grape Sauce (p. 366)	21	16	0	3	1	0	15	30	0	1	8	1	0	0	1	0
Zesty Orange-Raisin Sauce (p. 366)	16	27	0	5	1	0	21	50	0	1	5	1	0	0	1	1
Zesty Orange Sauce (p. 366)	16	17	0	3	1	0	20	31	0	1	10	1	0	0	1	0

On the divider: Cheese Sauce (p. 361).

Sauces and Relishes

Sauces and relishes add a twist to everyday meat and vegetables. Whether you top your food with basic Cheese Sauce, classic Hollandaise Sauce, or tangy Cucumber Relish, you'll savor the flavors of the endless combinations you can create.

White Sauce

Cheese Sauce is pictured on page 359.

> 1 **tablespoon margarine *or* butter**
> 1 **tablespoon all-purpose flour**
> ⅛ **teaspoon salt**
>   **Dash pepper**
> ¾ **cup milk**

In a small saucepan melt margarine or butter. Stir in flour, salt, and pepper. Add milk all at once. Cook and stir over medium heat till thickened and bubbly. Cook and stir 1 minute more. Makes ¾ cup (twelve 1-tablespoon servings).

Microwave directions: In a 2-cup measure micro-cook margarine or butter, uncovered, on 100% power (high) for 30 to 40 seconds or till melted. Stir in flour, salt, and pepper. Add ⅔ cup milk all at once and stir to combine. Cook, uncovered, on high for 2 to 4 minutes or till thickened and bubbly, stirring every 30 seconds.

Low-Calorie White Sauce: Prepare as above, *except* omit margarine or butter and substitute *skim milk* for the milk. In a screw-top jar combine flour, salt, pepper, and milk. Shake till blended. Cook as above.

Almond Sauce: Prepare as above, *except* toast ¼ cup slivered *almonds* in the melted margarine or butter. Omit salt and add 1 teaspoon instant *chicken bouillon granules* with the flour. Serve with vegetables or fish. Makes 1 cup (sixteen 1-tablespoon servings). Do not use microwave directions.

Cheese Sauce: Prepare as above, *except* omit salt. Over low heat, stir ¾ cup shredded process *Swiss, American, or Gruyère cheese or* ¼ cup crumbled *blue cheese* into the *cooked* sauce till melted. Serve with vegetables. Makes about 1 cup (sixteen 1-tablespoon servings).

Curry Sauce: Prepare as above, *except* cook ½ to 1 teaspoon *curry powder* in the melted margarine or butter for 1 minute. If desired, stir 1 tablespoon chopped chutney into the *cooked* sauce. Serve with fish or poultry. Do not use microwave directions.

Herb-Garlic Sauce: Prepare as above, *except* cook 1 clove *garlic,* minced, in the melted margarine or butter. Stir in ¼ teaspoon *caraway seed or celery seed, or* dried *basil, oregano, or sage,* crushed, with the flour. Serve with vegetables or poultry.

Lemon-Chive Sauce: Prepare as above, *except* stir in 1 tablespoon snipped *chives* and ½ teaspoon finely shredded *lemon peel* with the flour. Serve with vegetables, poultry, or fish.

Mexicali Sauce: Prepare as above, *except* cook ½ teaspoon *chili powder* in melted margarine or butter for 30 seconds. Stir 2 tablespoons diced *green chili peppers* into *cooked* sauce. Serve with beef or pork. Do not use microwave directions.

Parmesan Sauce: Prepare as above, *except* omit salt. Over low heat, stir ¼ cup grated *Parmesan cheese* into *cooked* sauce till melted. Serve with beef, pork, poultry, or vegetables.

Sherry Sauce: Prepare as above, *except* stir 1 to 2 tablespoons *dry sherry or dry white wine* into *cooked* sauce. Serve with veal.

Successful Sauces

For a perfect sauce every time, closely follow the recipe directions and remember these tips.

● Prevent lumps in cornstarch- or flour-thickened sauces by stirring constantly. If lumps do form, beat the sauce briskly with a wire whisk or a rotary beater.

● Cook sauces over low to medium heat unless the recipe says otherwise. And cook your sauces no longer than the time specified. High heat and lengthy cooking can cause sauces to curdle or break down.

● If you have to leave the sauce while it's cooking, remove it from the heat.

Wine-Mushroom Sauce

Toss with pasta for an impressive side dish.

  1½ **cups sliced fresh mushrooms**
  2   **tablespoons sliced green onion**
  1   **clove garlic, minced**
  1   **tablespoon margarine or butter**
  1   **teaspoon cornstarch**
  ¼   **teaspoon dried thyme or basil,
        crushed**
  ⅛   **teaspoon salt**
       Dash pepper
  ⅓   **cup dry white wine**

In a medium saucepan cook mushrooms, onion, and garlic in margarine till tender. Stir in cornstarch, herb, salt, and pepper. Stir in wine and ¼ cup *water* all at once. Cook and stir till thickened and bubbly. Cook and stir for 2 minutes more. Serve with meat or toss with pasta. Makes 1 cup (sixteen 1-tablespoon servings).

Microwave directions: In a 2-cup measure micro-cook mushrooms, onion, and garlic in margarine, uncovered, on 100% power (high) 2 to 3 minutes or till tender. Stir in cornstarch, herb, salt, and pepper. Stir in wine and ¼ cup *water* all at once. Cook, uncovered, on high 2 to 4 minutes or till thickened and bubbly; stir every 30 seconds.

Hollandaise Sauce

A classic creamy sauce with a rich lemon flavor.

  ½   **cup margarine or butter**
  3   **beaten egg yolks**
  1   **tablespoon water**
  1   **tablespoon lemon juice**
       Dash white pepper

Cut margarine or butter into thirds and bring it to room temperature.

In the top of a double boiler combine egg yolks, water, lemon juice, pepper, and dash *salt*. Add *one piece* of the margarine or butter. Place over *boiling* water (upper pan should not touch water). Cook, stirring rapidly, till margarine melts and sauce begins to thicken.

Add the remaining margarine or butter, a piece at a time, stirring constantly. Cook and stir till sauce thickens (1 to 2 minutes). Immediately remove from heat. If sauce is too thick or curdles, immediately beat in 1 to 2 tablespoons *hot tap water*. Serve the sauce with cooked vegetables, poultry, fish, or eggs. Makes about ¾ cup (twelve 1-tablespoon servings).

Microwave directions: In a 2-cup measure combine margarine or butter, water, lemon juice, pepper, and dash *salt*. Micro-cook, uncovered, on 100% power (high) for 1 to 1½ minutes or till margarine melts. Stir.

Place egg yolks in a bowl. Gradually add margarine mixture, beating constantly with a wire whisk. Beat till smooth. Cook, uncovered, on high for 30 to 45 seconds or till thickened, stirring every 10 seconds.

The sauce should still be thin after the second piece of margarine is added to the pan.

After all the margarine is added and melted, the sauce should be thick.

Mock Hollandaise Sauce

In a small saucepan combine ¼ cup dairy *sour cream,* ¼ cup *mayonnaise or salad dressing,* 1 teaspoon *lemon juice,* and ½ teaspoon *prepared mustard.* Cook and stir over low heat till hot. Serve with vegetables, poultry, fish, or eggs. Makes ½ cup (eight 1-tablespoon servings).

Béarnaise Sauce

- **½ cup margarine *or* butter**
- **3 tablespoons white wine vinegar**
- **1 teaspoon finely chopped green onion**
- **1 teaspoon snipped fresh tarragon *or* ¼ teaspoon dried tarragon, crushed**
- **¼ teaspoon snipped fresh chervil *or* pinch dried chervil, crushed**
- **⅛ teaspoon white pepper**
- **4 beaten egg yolks**

Cut margarine into thirds and bring it to room temperature. In a small saucepan combine vinegar, onion, tarragon, chervil, and pepper. Bring to boiling; boil 2 minutes on high or till reduced by about half. In the top of a double boiler combine yolks, 1 tablespoon *water,* and vinegar mixture. Add *one piece* of the margarine. Place over *boiling* water (upper pan should not touch water). Cook, stirring rapidly, till margarine melts and sauce begins to thicken. Add remaining margarine, a piece at a time, stirring constantly. Cook and stir till thickened (1 to 2 minutes). Immediately remove from heat. If sauce is too thick or curdles, immediately beat in 1 to 2 tablespoons *hot tap water.* Serve with beef, pork, or poultry. Makes ¾ cup (twelve 1-tablespoon servings).

Sauce Provencale

Peel, seed, and chop 3 medium *tomatoes* (about 1 pound). Sprinkle tomatoes with ½ teaspoon *sugar;* set aside. Cook ¼ cup sliced *green onion* and 1 clove *garlic,* minced, in 2 tablespoons *margarine or butter* till tender but not brown. Add tomato mixture, ½ cup *dry white wine,* and 2 tablespoons snipped *parsley.* Bring to boiling; reduce heat. Boil gently 10 minutes (you should have about 1¼ cups). Serve with beef or pork. Makes 1¼ cups (twenty 1-tablespoon servings).

Creamy Mushroom Sauce

- **1 cup sliced fresh mushrooms**
- **¼ cup chopped onion**
- **1 tablespoon margarine *or* butter**
- **1 tablespoon all-purpose flour**
- **¼ teaspoon salt**
- **⅛ teaspoon pepper**
- **⅔ cup milk**
- **½ cup dairy sour cream *or* plain yogurt**

In a medium saucepan cook mushrooms and onion in margarine till tender. Stir in flour, salt, and pepper. Stir in milk all at once. Cook and stir till thickened and bubbly. Cook and stir 1 minute more. Stir in sour cream; heat through, but *do not boil.* Serve with beef or poultry. Makes about 1½ cups (twenty-four 1-tablespoon servings).

Microwave directions: In a 2-cup measure micro-cook mushrooms, onion, and margarine, uncovered, on 100% power (high) for 2 to 3 minutes or till tender. Stir in flour, salt, and pepper. Stir in milk all at once. Cook, uncovered, on high for 2 to 4 minutes or till thickened and bubbly, stirring every 30 seconds. Stir in sour cream. Cook about 30 seconds more or till heated through, stirring once. *Do not boil.*

Sweet-Sour Sauce

- **½ cup packed brown sugar**
- **1 tablespoon cornstarch**
- **⅓ cup red wine vinegar**
- **⅓ cup unsweetened pineapple juice**
- **¼ cup finely chopped green pepper**
- **2 tablespoons chopped pimiento**
- **1 tablespoon soy sauce**
- **¼ teaspoon garlic powder**
- **¼ teaspoon ground ginger**

In a small saucepan combine brown sugar and cornstarch. Stir in vinegar, pineapple juice, green pepper, pimiento, soy sauce, garlic powder, and ginger. Cook and stir till thickened and bubbly. Cook and stir 2 minutes more. Serve warm with spareribs, egg rolls, or fried wontons. Makes about 1¼ cups (twenty 1-tablespoon servings).

Microwave directions: In a 2-cup measure combine all ingredients. Micro-cook, uncovered, on 100% power (high) for 3 to 5 minutes or till thickened and bubbly, stirring every minute till mixture starts to thicken, then every 30 seconds. Cook 30 seconds more. Serve warm.

Cocktail Sauce

In a bowl combine ¾ cup *chili sauce;* 2 table-spoons *lemon juice;* 1 tablespoon *prepared horseradish;* 2 teaspoons *Worcestershire sauce;* 1 *green onion,* sliced, *or* ¼ teaspoon *dried minced onion;* and several dashes *bottled hot pepper sauce.* Cover and store in the refrigerator up to 2 weeks. Serve with fish or seafood. Makes about 1 cup (sixteen 1-tablespoon servings).

Basic Barbecue Sauce

Vary the hotness by adjusting the amount of hot pepper sauce.

> 1 **cup catsup**
> ¼ **cup finely chopped onion *or* 1 tablespoon dried minced onion**
> ¼ **cup vinegar**
> 1 **to 2 tablespoons sugar**
> 1 **tablespoon Worcestershire sauce**
> ¼ **teaspoon celery seed**
> **Several dashes bottled hot pepper sauce**

In a saucepan combine catsup, onion, vinegar, sugar, Worcestershire sauce, celery seed, hot pep-per sauce, ½ cup *water,* and ¼ teaspoon *salt.* Bring to boiling; reduce heat. Simmer 10 to 15 minutes or to desired consistency. Brush on beef, pork, or poultry during the last 10 to 20 minutes of grilling or roasting. If desired, pass remaining sauce. Makes 1¾ cups (twenty-eight 1-table-spoon servings).

Hot-Style Barbecue Sauce: Prepare as above, *except* add 1 teaspoon *chili powder* and ½ teaspoon ground *red pepper* with the catsup.

Tangy Mustard Barbecue Sauce: Prepare as above, *except* omit celery seed. Add 2 table-spoons *prepared mustard* and ¼ teaspoon *garlic powder* with the catsup.

Horseradish Sauce

Fluffy and full of flavor.

Beat ½ cup *whipping cream* till soft peaks form. Fold in 2 to 3 tablespoons *prepared horseradish.* Serve with beef or pork. Cover and store in the refrigerator up to 3 days. Makes 1 cup (sixteen 1-tablespoon servings).

Mustard Sauce: Prepare as above, *except* substitute 2 tablespoons *Dijon-style mustard* for the horseradish. Serve with beef or pork.

Tartar Sauce

In a mixing bowl combine 1 cup *mayonnaise or salad dressing;* ¼ cup finely chopped *sweet or dill pickle or sweet or dill pickle relish,* drained; 1 tablespoon finely chopped *onion;* 1 tablespoon snipped *parsley;* 1 tablespoon diced *pimiento;* and 1 teaspoon *lemon juice.* Cover and chill for at least 2 hours before serving. Store in the refrig-erator up to 2 weeks. Serve with fish or seafood. Makes 1¼ cups (twenty 1-tablespoon servings).

Low-Fat Tartar Sauce: Prepare as above, *except* substitute ⅔ cup *reduced-calorie mayon-naise or salad dressing* and ⅓ cup plain *yogurt* for the mayonnaise. Omit lemon juice.

EASY

Sauces from Soups

Dress up canned soups to make these quick and easy sauces.

Bacon and Sour Cream Sauce: In a saucepan combine one 7½-ounce can semicondensed *cream of mush-room soup* and 2 tablespoons *milk.* Add ¼ cup dairy *sour cream or plain yogurt* and 3 slices *bacon,* crisp-cooked, drained, and crumbled. Cook and stir till heated through. Serve with beef or toss with hot pasta. Makes 1¼ cups (twenty 1-tablespoon servings).

Caraway-Cheese Sauce: In a saucepan stir together one 11-ounce can condensed *cheddar cheese soup* and ¼ cup *milk.* Add ¼ cup soft-style *cream cheese* and ½ teaspoon *cara-way seed,* crushed. Cook and stir till heated through and the cheese melts. Serve with beef or toss with hot pasta. Makes 1½ cups (twenty-four 1-table-spoon servings).

Mustard-Dill Sauce: In a sauce-pan combine one 10¾-ounce can con-densed *cream of celery, chicken, or mushroom soup,* ¼ cup *milk,* 1 tea-spoon *Dijon-style mustard,* and ½ tea-spoon dried *dillweed.* Cook and stir till heated through. Serve with beef, pork, or fish. Makes 1⅓ cups (twenty-one 1-tablespoon servings).

Yogurt-Dill Sauce

- 1 **8-ounce carton plain yogurt**
  or dairy sour cream
- 1 **tablespoon snipped fresh dillweed**
  or 1 teaspoon dried dillweed
- ¼ **teaspoon pepper**
- ⅛ **teaspoon garlic powder**

In a mixing bowl combine yogurt, dillweed, pepper, and garlic powder. Chill till serving time. Serve with fish, seafood, or lamb. Makes about 1 cup (sixteen 1-tablespoon servings).

Yogurt-Cucumber-Mint Sauce: Prepare as above, *except* omit dillweed. Pat ½ cup shredded *cucumber* with a paper towel to remove excess liquid. Stir into yogurt mixture along with ¼ teaspoon dried *mint,* crushed.

Yogurt-Chutney Sauce: Prepare as above, *except* omit dillweed. Stir 3 tablespoons chopped *chutney* into yogurt mixture.

Yogurt-Chili Sauce: Prepare as above, *except* omit dillweed. Stir 2 tablespoons *chili or barbecue sauce* and several dashes bottled *hot pepper sauce* into yogurt mixture.

Sauce Véronique

In a medium saucepan bring 1 cup *chicken broth* to boiling; reduce heat. Boil gently 4 to 5 minutes (you should have ½ cup). Combine ⅓ cup *milk or light cream,* 1 tablespoon *all-purpose flour,* ¼ teaspoon finely shredded *lemon peel,* and a dash ground *nutmeg.* Add to broth. Cook and stir over medium heat till bubbly. Stir in ½ cup seedless *green or red grapes,* halved. Cook and stir 1 minute more. Serve with fish or poultry. Makes 1¼ cups (twenty 1-tablespoon servings).

Plum Sauce

In a saucepan combine ½ cup *red plum jam,* ¼ cup sliced *green onion,* and 1 tablespoon *cornstarch.* Add 2 tablespoons *dry sherry,* 2 tablespoons *soy sauce,* and 1 tablespoon *vinegar.* Cook and stir till bubbly. Cook and stir 2 minutes more. Serve with beef, lamb, pork, or poultry. Makes ¾ cup (twelve 1-tablespoon servings).

Microwave directions: In a 2-cup measure combine all ingredients. Micro-cook on 100% power (high) for 2 to 4 minutes or till thickened and bubbly, stirring every 30 seconds.

Oriental-Style Mustard Sauce

A tongue-tingling sauce for egg rolls or wontons.

- ¼ **cup dry mustard**
- 2 **teaspoons cooking oil**
- ¼ **teaspoon salt**

In a bowl combine mustard, oil, and salt. Stir in ¼ cup *boiling water.* Serve with wontons or egg rolls. Makes ⅓ cup (sixteen 1-teaspoon servings).

Cranberry Sauce

- 1 **cup sugar**
- 2 **cups cranberries (8 ounces)**

In a saucepan combine sugar and 1 cup *water.* Bring to boiling, stirring to dissolve sugar. Boil rapidly for 5 minutes. Add cranberries. Return to boiling; reduce heat. Boil gently over medium-high heat for 3 to 4 minutes or till skins pop, stirring occasionally. Remove from heat. Serve warm or chilled with beef, pork, or poultry. Makes about 2 cups (eight ¼-cup servings).

Molded Cranberry Sauce: Prepare as above, *except* cook cranberry mixture for 13 to 16 minutes or till a drop gels on a cold plate. Pour into a 1½-cup mold; chill till firm. Unmold.

Almond Cranberry Sauce: Prepare as above, *except* substitute ½ cup *honey* for the sugar. Boil 8 minutes before adding cranberries. After removing from heat, stir in ¼ cup *apricot or peach preserves or orange marmalade* and ¼ cup toasted sliced *almonds.*

Zesty Orange Sauce

> **2 medium oranges**
> **1 tablespoon cornstarch**
> **1 tablespoon margarine *or* butter**
> **1 teaspoon honey**
> **½ teaspoon instant chicken bouillon granules**

Finely shred *1 teaspoon* orange peel. Peel and section *one* orange over a bowl to catch juice; set aside. Squeeze juice from remaining orange. Measure orange juice; add water to equal ⅔ *cup.*

In a small saucepan stir the juice mixture into the cornstarch. Add margarine or butter, honey, and bouillon granules. Cook and stir till thickened and bubbly. Cook and stir for 2 minutes more. Stir in orange sections and orange peel. Heat through. Serve with fish, pork, or poultry. Makes 1 cup (sixteen 1-tablespoon servings).

Microwave directions: Prepare peel and oranges as above. Measure orange juice and add water to equal ⅔ *cup.* In a 2-cup measure stir juice mixture into the cornstarch. Add margarine or butter, honey, and bouillon granules. Microcook, uncovered, on 100% power (high) for 2 to 4 minutes or till thickened and bubbly, stirring every minute till mixture starts to thicken, then every 30 seconds. Stir in orange sections and peel. Cook 30 seconds more.

Zesty Orange-Grape Sauce: Prepare as above, *except* stir in ½ cup seedless *red or green grapes* with the orange sections. Makes about 1⅓ cups (twenty-one 1-tablespoon servings).

Zesty Orange-Raisin Sauce: Prepare as above, *except* omit *one* orange. Finely shred ½ *teaspoon* orange peel. Squeeze juice from the orange and add water to equal ⅔ *cup.* Continue as above, adding ⅓ cup *raisins* to the sauce with the margarine or butter.

Cherry Sauce

In a medium saucepan combine 3 tablespoons *brown sugar,* 4 teaspoons *cornstarch,* ¼ teaspoon ground *cinnamon,* and a dash ground *cloves.* Stir in 1 cup *apple juice,* 1 tablespoon *vinegar,* and, if desired, a few drops red food coloring. Cook and stir over medium heat till thickened and bubbly. Cook and stir 2 minutes more. Stir in one 16-ounce can pitted *tart red cherries* (water pack), drained. Heat through. Serve warm with ham, pork, or poultry. Makes 2¼ cups (thirty-six 1-tablespoon servings).

Pickled Beets

In a medium saucepan combine ⅓ cup *vinegar,* ¼ cup *sugar,* ¼ cup *water,* ½ teaspoon ground *cinnamon,* ¼ teaspoon *salt,* and ¼ teaspoon ground *cloves.* Bring to boiling, stirring occasionally. Add 2 cups sliced, cooked *beets or* one 16-ounce can sliced *beets,* drained. Return to boiling; reduce heat. Cover; simmer 5 minutes. Cool. Chill in liquid at least 8 hours before serving. Cover and store in liquid in the refrigerator up to 1 month. Drain before serving. Makes 8 servings.

Spiced Apple Rings

A tasty and colorful accompaniment to pork.

> **4 small cooking apples**
> **⅓ cup red cinnamon candies***
> **¼ cup sugar**

If desired, peel apples. Core and cut crosswise into ½-inch rings. For syrup, in a large skillet combine candies and sugar. Add 2 cups *water.* Cook and stir over medium heat till liquid boils and candies dissolve. Add apples to syrup. Bring to boiling; reduce heat. Simmer for 10 to 15 minutes or till tender, spooning syrup over apples occasionally. Cool apples in syrup. Cover and store in syrup in the refrigerator up to 1 month. Drain before serving. Makes 6 servings.

***Note:** If desired, substitute 6 inches stick cinnamon, broken, for the cinnamon candies and increase sugar to ¾ *cup.* Cook and stir over medium heat till boiling. Cover and simmer 5 minutes. Add apples to syrup and cook as above.

Cranberry-Orange Relish

> **2 medium oranges**
> **4 cups fresh cranberries (1 pound)**
> **2 cups sugar**
> **¼ cup finely chopped walnuts**

Finely shred *1 tablespoon* orange peel. Peel and section oranges. Using a food processor or food grinder with a coarse blade, process or grind orange sections and cranberries. (If using a food processor, process *half* at a time.) Stir in sugar, walnuts, and orange peel. Cover and store in the refrigerator up to 2 weeks or freeze up to 6 months. Serve with ham or poultry. Makes 3¾ cups (fifteen ¼-cup servings).

Papaya-Apple Chutney

Chutneys are often served as a condiment with highly spiced dishes.

  2 **medium tart cooking apples, peeled, cored, and chopped (2 cups)**
  1 **medium papaya, seeded, peeled, and chopped (1½ cups)**
  ½ **cup packed brown sugar**
  ⅓ **cup chopped green pepper**
  ⅓ **cup vinegar**
  ¼ **cup raisins**
  ¼ **cup water**
  2 **tablespoons chopped onion**
  1 **tablespoon lime *or* lemon juice**
  ¼ **teaspoon salt**
  1 **clove garlic, minced**
  ¼ **cup slivered almonds, toasted (optional)**

In a large saucepan combine apples, papaya, brown sugar, green pepper, vinegar, raisins, water, onion, lime or lemon juice, salt, and garlic. Bring to boiling; reduce heat. Simmer for 30 minutes, stirring occasionally. Cool. Cover and store in the refrigerator up to 4 weeks. Or freeze up to 12 months. Before serving, if desired, stir in almonds. Serve with beef, ham, lamb, pork, or poultry. Makes about 2¼ cups (thirty-six 1-tablespoon servings).

Pineapple-Date Chutney: Prepare as above, *except* omit apples, papaya, and raisins. Combine ½ of a medium *pineapple,* peeled, cored, and chopped (about 2 cups), *or* one 20-ounce can *pineapple chunks,* drained; ¾ cup pitted whole *dates,* snipped; and ¼ teaspoon ground *cinnamon* with vinegar mixture.

Improving Food's Flavor

Just as long, slow simmering improves the flavor of hot foods, so does chilling improve the flavor of many sauces, relishes, and salad dressings. Chill these foods several hours or overnight before serving them so that each ingredient can blend with the others for a full-flavored taste.

Refrigerator Corn Relish

  1 **10-ounce package frozen whole kernel corn**
  ⅓ **cup sugar**
  1 **tablespoon cornstarch**
  ½ **cup vinegar**
  ⅓ **cup cold water**
  ¼ **cup chopped celery**
  ¼ **cup chopped green *or* sweet red pepper**
  2 **tablespoons chopped pimiento**
  1 **tablespoon dried minced onion**
  1 **teaspoon ground turmeric**
  ½ **teaspoon dry mustard**
  ¼ **teaspoon salt**

Cook corn according to package directions; drain. In a saucepan combine sugar and cornstarch. Stir in vinegar and water. Stir in corn, celery, pepper, pimiento, onion, turmeric, mustard, and salt. Cook and stir till thickened and bubbly. Cook and stir for 2 minutes more. Cool. Cover and store in the refrigerator up to 4 weeks. Serve with beef, pork, or poultry. Makes about 2½ cups (ten ¼-cup servings).

Cucumber Relish

  1 **large cucumber (12 ounces)**
  1 **small onion**
  3 **tablespoons vinegar**
  1 **tablespoon sugar**
  1 **tablespoon cooking oil**
  ¼ **teaspoon dried dillweed or dried mint, crushed**
  ⅛ **teaspoon salt**
     Several dashes bottled hot pepper sauce

Slice cucumber in half lengthwise; scoop out seeds and discard. Using a food processor or food grinder with a coarse blade, process or grind cucumber and onion (or finely chop by hand). Drain. Stir in vinegar, sugar, oil, dillweed or mint, salt, and hot pepper sauce. Chill at least 8 hours before serving. Cover; store in the refrigerator up to 1 week. Serve with frankfurters or hamburgers. Makes 1¼ cups (ten 2-tablespoon servings).

Sauerkraut Relish

¼ cup sugar
½ teaspoon prepared mustard
¼ cup vinegar
⅛ teaspoon garlic powder
1 8-ounce can sauerkraut, drained
¼ cup chopped green *or* sweet red pepper
¼ cup chopped cucumber
¼ cup chopped onion

In a mixing bowl combine sugar and mustard. Stir in vinegar, garlic powder, and ⅛ teaspoon *pepper*. Stir in sauerkraut, green pepper, cucumber, and onion. Cover and chill at least 2 hours before serving. Store in refrigerator up to 1 week. Makes 2 cups (thirty-two 1-tablespoon servings).

Salsa

Boost the flavor of omelets or scrambled eggs by spooning this spicy sauce over them.

1 cup finely chopped, peeled tomato
½ cup tomato sauce
1 4-ounce can diced green chili peppers, drained
¼ cup sliced green onion
¼ cup finely chopped green pepper
1 to 2 tablespoons snipped cilantro *or* parsley
2 tablespoons lemon juice
1 clove garlic, minced
 Several dashes bottled hot pepper sauce (optional)

In a mixing bowl combine tomato; tomato sauce; chili peppers; green onion; green pepper; cilantro or parsley; lemon juice; garlic; hot pepper sauce, if desired; and ⅛ teaspoon *pepper*. Place about *half* of the tomato mixture in a blender container or food processor bowl. Cover and blend or process till smooth. Stir in remaining tomato mixture. Cover and chill at least 4 hours before serving, stirring occasionally. Store in refrigerator up to 1 week. Use as a dip for tortilla chips or spoon over main dishes or vegetables. Makes about 2 cups (thirty-two 1-tablespoon servings).

Salsa Verde: Prepare as above, *except* omit tomato and tomato sauce. Add 6 to 8 fresh *tomatillos,* finely chopped, *or* one 13-ounce can *tomatillos,* rinsed, drained, and finely chopped, to chili pepper mixture. Makes about 1¾ cups (twenty-eight 1-tablespoon servings).

Making Flavored Butters

Use these creamy mixtures to dress up vegetables, meats, and breads. Or melt them to pour over popped popcorn.

For a butter base, cut up ½ cup butter or margarine, place in an ovenproof bowl, and set into a cool oven. Turn the oven to 350°. Heat about 3 minutes in an electric oven (4 minutes in a gas oven) or till just softened. *Or,* microcook on 10% power (low) for 1 to 1½ minutes. Transfer butter to a cool bowl and use to make one of the following:

For *garlic butter,* add 2 cloves garlic, minced, *or* ½ teaspoon garlic powder.

For *parsley butter,* add 1 tablespoon snipped parsley; 1 teaspoon lemon juice; ¼ teaspoon dried savory, crushed; and ⅛ teaspoon salt.

For *herb butter,* add ½ teaspoon ground sage and ½ teaspoon dried thyme, crushed.

For *lemon-tarragon butter,* add 1 teaspoon dried tarragon, crushed, and ½ teaspoon finely shredded lemon peel.

For *parmesan butter,* add 2 tablespoons grated Parmesan cheese and ½ teaspoon dried basil, crushed

For *curry butter,* add ½ teaspoon curry powder.

For *Cajun butter,* add ¼ teaspoon ground red pepper, ⅛ teaspoon black pepper, ⅛ teaspoon garlic powder, and ⅛ teaspoon dried thyme, crushed.

For *citrus butter,* add 1 tablespoon powdered sugar and ½ teaspoon finely shredded orange or lemon peel.

For *breakfast butter,* add 2 tablespoons honey or maple-flavored syrup.

Soups &
Stews

Nutrition Analysis

		Per Serving							Percent U.S. RDA Per Serving							
	Servings Per Recipe	Calories	Protein (g)	Carbohydrate (g)	Fat (g)	Cholesterol (mg)	Sodium (mg)	Potassium (mg)	Protein	Vitamin A	Vitamin C	Thiamine	Riboflavin	Niacin	Calcium	Iron
Alphabet-Meatball Soup (p. 373)	4	340	23	37	12	110	1103	972	35	175	34	25	24	24	19	33
Barley-Beef Soup (p. 376)	4	318	25	30	11	65	424	684	39	53	28	14	16	21	7	22
Bean and Sausage Soup (p. 381)	4	426	20	39	22	55	1639	996	30	46	70	37	16	26	17	21
Beef Bourguignonne (p. 374)	6	404	26	35	13	84	381	689	39	271	14	21	27	29	6	26
Beef Broth (p. 372)	8	0	0	0	0	0	266	0	0	0	0	0	0	0	0	0
Beef Stew (p. 371)	4	349	28	31	12	64	952	1410	44	387	85	22	21	39	8	25
Beer Cheese Soup (p. 384)	5	174	9	13	9	28	463	249	14	71	3	6	16	4	25	3
Black Bean Soup (p. 381)	4	440	18	21	32	60	1334	714	28	1	10	45	11	16	7	16
Cheese Dumplings for Stew (p. 378)	4	182	5	17	11	11	209	74	8	5	2	7	7	4	14	4
Cheese Soup (p. 384)	5	159	9	11	9	28	524	241	13	71	3	6	15	3	25	3
Chicken and Sausage Gumbo (p. 380)	4	586	30	41	32	88	874	578	47	9	20	43	14	60	9	19
Chicken Broth (p. 373)	5	0	0	0	0	0	426	0	0	0	0	0	0	0	0	0
Chicken Noodle Soup (p. 377)	4	232	25	21	6	67	754	609	38	85	36	14	16	41	8	15
Chicken Stew with Dumplings (p. 378)	4	357	24	41	11	50	1183	369	36	62	10	21	22	37	8	20
Chicken Vegetable Soup (p. 377)	4	212	24	17	6	62	754	603	37	85	25	11	15	40	8	14
Chili (p. 376)	4	466	34	55	14	58	729	1717	52	37	66	37	22	32	16	52
Cioppino (p. 379)	5	143	12	12	4	50	539	578	19	26	61	8	6	11	8	17
Corn Chowder (p. 384)	4	186	7	28	6	8	286	524	11	11	14	17	15	10	14	5
Cream of Acorn Squash Soup (p. 384)	3	139	4	20	6	6	392	605	6	16	18	16	9	6	15	6
Cream of Asparagus Soup (p. 384)	3	118	7	12	6	6	392	393	10	26	51	8	16	7	13	5
Cream of Broccoli Soup (p. 384)	3	114	6	12	6	6	399	299	9	36	77	9	21	5	22	8
Cream of Brussels Sprout Soup (p. 384)	3	124	6	15	6	6	409	458	9	21	76	11	13	4	14	8
Cream of Carrot Soup (p. 384)	3	131	4	17	6	6	456	372	6	515	5	6	12	4	14	5
Cream of Cauliflower Soup (p. 384)	3	111	5	11	6	6	414	344	8	7	64	7	13	3	13	4
Cream of Celery Soup (p. 384)	3	99	4	10	6	6	694	492	5	9	7	5	10	2	14	2
Cream of Chicken Soup (p. 378)	3	386	23	9	28	115	608	279	36	19	1	8	16	34	9	7
Cream of Green Bean Soup (p. 384)	3	113	5	13	6	6	390	380	7	18	11	7	13	4	14	7
Cream of Mushroom Soup (p. 384)	3	111	5	11	6	6	390	487	8	6	6	8	26	23	11	11
Cream of Onion Soup (p. 384)	3	124	4	15	6	6	417	343	7	6	10	7	9	2	14	2
Cream of Pea Soup (p. 384)	3	174	8	23	6	6	391	420	13	19	27	22	18	12	13	10
Cream of Potato Soup (p. 384)	3	174	5	27	6	6	392	522	8	6	17	11	10	8	11	3
Cream of Spinach Soup (p. 384)	3	109	6	10	6	6	464	637	10	184	13	10	24	4	25	22
Cream of Zucchini Soup (p. 384)	3	103	4	11	5	6	391	434	6	12	7	7	12	4	12	3
Dumplings for Stew (p. 378)	4	144	3	17	7	1	150	49	4	2	2	9	6	6	7	5
Fish Chowder (p. 379)	4	468	39	37	18	136	936	1579	60	189	34	24	33	28	31	35
French Onion Soup (p. 386)	4	270	11	26	14	24	624	184	16	10	8	14	9	6	26	7
Gazpacho (p. 386)	6	57	2	9	3	0	291	389	3	33	46	7	5	5	2	6
Gingered Cream of Chicken Soup (p. 378)	3	386	23	9	28	115	608	279	36	19	1	8	16	34	9	7
Ham and Bean Soup (p. 377)	4	226	18	33	3	19	742	836	28	1	17	40	11	13	10	26
Herbed Lamb Stew (p. 375)	4	451	29	30	19	98	407	1103	44	264	29	22	24	37	10	20
Herbed Tomato Soup (p. 386)	4	93	2	10	6	0	578	441	3	37	29	7	5	6	3	6
Lentil Stew (p. 381)	4	466	26	42	22	39	1261	868	40	94	21	43	17	22	10	31
Manhattan Clam Chowder (p. 380)	4	213	13	32	4	34	970	1060	20	27	55	17	12	20	13	32
Minestrone (p. 382)	5	80	4	12	2	3	230	333	7	41	23	10	4	6	4	8
Mulligatawny (p. 378)	3	323	24	43	6	62	560	579	37	68	20	17	11	43	6	17
New England Clam Chowder (p. 379)	4	393	18	34	20	90	864	1011	28	16	29	16	28	16	29	32
Oyster Stew (p. 379)	4	266	14	13	17	118	496	548	22	15	3	5	29	9	26	47
Quick Minestrone (p. 382)	5	64	3	12	1	0	314	323	5	41	15	7	3	4	4	8
Quick Vegetable-Beef Soup (p. 372)	4	311	23	17	17	77	575	655	35	67	28	12	17	29	6	22
Seafood Gumbo (p. 380)	4	589	32	42	32	144	1271	624	50	9	19	43	13	31	13	25

On the divider: Seafood Gumbo (p. 380).

Nutrition Analysis	Per Serving								Percent U.S. RDA Per Serving							
	Servings Per Recipe	Calories	Protein (g)	Carbohydrate (g)	Fat (g)	Cholesterol (mg)	Sodium (mg)	Potassium (mg)	Protein	Vitamin A	Vitamin C	Thiamine	Riboflavin	Niacin	Calcium	Iron
Shortcut Ham and Bean Soup (p. 377)	4	198	16	29	2	19	738	780	24	1	17	27	8	9	11	25
Shortcut Vegetable-Beef Soup (p. 374)	6	280	22	25	11	57	1138	796	34	133	32	16	16	21	5	20
Split Pea Soup (p. 382)	4	241	20	36	3	19	886	673	31	87	13	44	14	16	4	18
Tomato Ham and Bean Soup (p. 377)	4	244	19	37	3	19	909	1034	29	12	27	42	13	17	11	30
Tortellini-Vegetable Soup (p. 382)	6	74	3	9	3	20	337	176	5	68	11	6	5	5	5	5
Turkey Frame Soup (p. 377)	6	169	17	20	2	55	526	575	26	125	25	14	11	21	7	13
Vegetable-Beef Soup (p. 374)	6	240	22	25	7	57	1138	796	34	133	32	16	16	21	5	20
Vegetable Oyster Stew (p. 379)	4	326	15	15	23	118	594	638	23	97	5	6	30	10	28	48
Vegetable-Pork Soup (p. 376)	4	323	30	22	13	83	514	950	47	35	29	76	21	33	4	12
Vichyssoise (p. 386)	4	208	4	16	15	44	249	438	6	13	17	6	8	5	9	5
Wild Rice Soup (p. 383)	4	194	4	18	12	40	350	185	7	86	4	9	12	6	7	5
Wonton Soup (p. 383)	4	194	7	17	11	16	1106	230	10	95	37	8	7	7	4	7

Soups and Stews

Need a star for a meal? Assign the part to Beef Stew or Chicken and Sausage Gumbo, or any of the other main-dish soups and stews in this chapter. For a partner to a sandwich or salad, choose a side-dish soup like Tortellini-Vegetable Soup or Gazpacho.

Beef Stew

  2 **tablespoons all-purpose flour**
  1 **pound beef or pork stew meat**
  2 **tablespoons cooking oil**
3½ **cups vegetable juice cocktail**
  ½ **cup chopped onion**
  2 **teaspoons instant beef bouillon granules**
  2 **cloves garlic, minced**
  ½ **teaspoon dried basil, crushed**
  ½ **teaspoon dried thyme, crushed**
2¼ **cups cubed, peeled potatoes**
  2 **cups sliced carrots**
  1 **cup sliced celery**

Place flour in a plastic bag. Add meat cubes, a few at a time, shaking to coat. In a large saucepan or Dutch oven brown meat, half at a time, in hot oil. Return meat to saucepan. Add juice cocktail, onion, bouillon granules, garlic, basil, and thyme. Bring to boiling; reduce heat. Cover; simmer 1 to 1¼ hours for beef (30 minutes for pork) or till meat is nearly tender. Add potatoes, carrots, and celery. Cover; simmer 30 minutes more. Skim fat. Makes 4 main-dish servings.

    Crockery-cooker directions: Prepare and brown meat as above. In the bottom of a 3½- or 4-quart electric crockery cooker layer onion, potatoes, carrots, and celery. Sprinkle with bouillon granules, garlic, basil, and thyme; add meat. Pour 2½ *cups* vegetable juice cocktail over meat. Cover; cook on low-heat setting for 10 to 12 hours or till meat and vegetables are tender.

Beef Broth

4 **pounds meaty beef soupbones (shank crosscuts, short ribs, *or* arm bones)**
3 **carrots, cut up**
2 **medium onions, cut up**
2 **stalks celery with leaves, cut up**
8 **sprigs parsley**
10 **whole black peppers**
4 **bay leaves**
1 **tablespoon dried basil *or* thyme, crushed**
2 **cloves garlic, halved**   Oven 450°

Place soupbones in a large shallow roasting pan. Bake in a 450° oven about 30 minutes or till well browned, turning once. Place soupbones in a large Dutch oven. Pour ½ cup *water* into the roasting pan, scraping up crusty browned bits. Add water mixture to Dutch oven. Add carrots, onions, celery, parsley, peppers, bay leaves, basil, garlic, 10 cups *water,* and 1 teaspoon *salt.* Bring to boiling; reduce heat. Cover and simmer 3½ hours. Remove soupbones.

Pour broth through a large sieve or colander lined with 2 layers of cheesecloth. Discard vegetables and seasonings. If desired, clarify broth (see tip, below). If using the broth while hot, skim fat. (Or chill broth, then lift off fat.) If desired, when bones are cool enough to handle, remove meat from bones and reserve meat for another use. Discard bones. Store broth and reserved meat, if any, in *separate* covered containers in the refrigerator up to 3 days or in the freezer up to 6 months. Makes about 8 cups broth.

Clarifying Broth

For crystal-clear soups, use broth that's been clarified. First, separate an egg, Save the yolk for another use. In a Dutch oven or kettle combine strained broth, ¼ cup cold water, and the egg white. Bring to boiling. Remove from the heat and let stand 5 minutes. Strain the broth through a large sieve or colander lined with several layers of damp cheesecloth for cooking.

◀ Strain broth through a sieve lined with cheesecloth to remove the vegetables and seasonings.

Quick Vegetable-Beef Soup

Using ground beef and frozen vegetables yields soup in a jiffy.

1 **pound ground beef**
¼ **cup chopped onion**
4 **cups beef broth (see recipe, left, or tip, opposite)**
1 **10-ounce package frozen mixed vegetables**
1 **7½-ounce can tomatoes, cut up**
⅔ **cup cubed, peeled potato**
½ **cup sliced celery**
½ **teaspoon dried marjoram, crushed**
½ **teaspoon dried oregano, crushed**
¼ **teaspoon salt**
⅛ **teaspoon pepper**
1 **bay leaf**

In a large Dutch oven or kettle cook beef and onion till beef is brown and onion is tender. Drain fat. Stir in beef broth, mixed vegetables, *undrained* tomatoes, potato, celery, marjoram, oregano, salt, pepper, and bay leaf. Bring to boiling; reduce heat. Cover; simmer for 15 to 20 minutes or till vegetables are tender. Discard bay leaf. Makes 4 main-dish servings.

Alphabet-Meatball Soup

    1   beaten egg
    ¼   cup fine dry bread crumbs
    ¼   cup snipped parsley
    2   tablespoons grated Parmesan
          cheese
    ¼   teaspoon garlic salt
    ⅛   teaspoon pepper
    ½   pound ground beef
    4   cups beef broth (see recipe,
          opposite, or tip, below)
    1   15½-ounce can dark red kidney
          beans
    1   8-ounce can stewed tomatoes
    ½   cup thinly sliced carrot
    1   teaspoon dried Italian seasoning
    ¼   cup alphabet pasta *or* other small
          pasta
    8   ounces fresh spinach, coarsely
          chopped, *or* ½ of a 10-ounce
          package frozen chopped spinach,
          thawed and well drained

In a mixing bowl combine egg, bread crumbs, parsley, Parmesan cheese, garlic salt, and pepper. Add ground beef; mix well. Shape meat mixture into sixteen 1-inch balls.

In a medium saucepan combine beef broth, *undrained* beans, tomatoes, carrot, and Italian seasoning. Bring to boiling. Drop meatballs, one at a time, into hot broth mixture. Add pasta. Return to boiling; reduce heat. Cover and simmer for 10 to 12 minutes or till meatballs are no longer pink. Stir in spinach and heat through. Season to taste. Makes 4 main-dish servings.

Broth Substitutions

When you don't have time to make your own beef or chicken broth, try one of these convenience products: ready-to-use canned beef or chicken broth, canned *condensed* beef or chicken broth, or instant beef, chicken, or vegetable bouillon granules or cubes. Mix both the canned condensed broth and bouillon granules or cubes according to package directions before use.

Chicken Broth

For richer color, use an unpeeled yellow onion.

    2½ pounds bony chicken pieces
          (backs, necks, and wings from
          2 chickens)
    3   stalks celery with leaves, cut up
    2   carrots, cut up
    1   large onion, cut up
    2   sprigs parsley
    1   teaspoon salt
    ½   teaspoon dried thyme, sage,
          or basil, crushed
    ¼   teaspoon pepper
    2   bay leaves
    6   cups cold water

In a large Dutch oven or kettle place chicken pieces; celery; carrots; onion; parsley; salt; thyme, sage, or basil; pepper; and bay leaves. Add water. Bring to boiling; reduce heat. Cover and simmer for 2 hours. Remove chicken.

To strain, pour broth through a large sieve or colander lined with 2 layers of cheesecloth. Discard vegetables and seasonings. If desired, clarify broth (see tip, opposite). If using the broth while hot, skim fat. (Or chill broth, then lift off fat.) If desired, when bones are cool enough to handle, remove meat from bones and reserve meat for another use. Discard bones. Store broth and reserved meat, if any, in *separate* covered containers in the refrigerator up to 3 days or in the freezer up to 6 months. Makes about 5 cups broth and 2½ cups meat.

Crockery-cooker directions: In a 3½- or 4-quart electric crockery cooker combine chicken pieces; celery; carrots; onion; parsley; salt; thyme, sage, or basil; pepper; bay leaves; and *4 cups* water. Cover and cook on low-heat setting for 8 to 10 hours. Remove chicken. Strain and store broth and meat as above.

Beef Bourguignonne

A classic French stew flavored with burgundy.

  1 **pound boneless beef chuck roast, cut into ¾-inch cubes**
  2 **tablespoons cooking oil**
  1 **cup chopped onion**
  1 **clove garlic, minced**
  1½ **cups burgundy**
  ¾ **cup beef broth (see recipe, page 372, or tip, page 373)**
  2 **bay leaves**
  1 **teaspoon dried thyme, crushed**
  ¾ **teaspoon dried marjoram, crushed**
  3 **cups fresh mushrooms**
  4 **medium carrots, cut into ¾-inch pieces**
  ½ **pound pearl onions or 2 cups small frozen whole onions**
  2 **tablespoons all-purpose flour**
  ¼ **cup water**
  2 **slices bacon, crisp-cooked, drained, and crumbled**
  3 **cups hot cooked noodles**
    Snipped parsley (optional)

In a large Dutch oven or kettle cook *half* of the meat in *1 tablespoon* of the hot oil till meat is brown. Remove from pan and add remaining oil, remaining meat, the chopped onion, and garlic. Cook till meat is brown and onion is tender. Drain fat. Return all meat to Dutch oven.

Stir in burgundy, beef broth, bay leaves, thyme, marjoram, ½ teaspoon *salt,* and ¼ teaspoon *pepper.* Bring to boiling; reduce heat. Cover and simmer for 45 minutes. Add mushrooms, carrots, and pearl onions. Return to boiling; reduce heat. Cover and cook for 25 to 30 minutes more or till tender. Combine flour and water. Stir into meat mixture. Cook and stir till thickened and bubbly. Cook and stir 1 minute more. Discard bay leaves. Stir in bacon. Serve with noodles and, if desired, garnish with parsley. Makes 6 main-dish servings.

Crockery-cooker directions: Brown meat, chopped onion, and garlic in hot oil as above. In a 3½- or 4-quart electric crockery cooker layer mushrooms, carrots, and pearl onions. Sprinkle with 3 tablespoons *quick-cooking tapioca.* Place meat mixture atop vegetables. Add bay leaves, thyme, marjoram, ½ teaspoon *salt,* and ¼ teaspoon *pepper.* Pour *1¼ cups* burgundy and ½ *cup* broth over meat. Cover; cook on low-heat setting for 10 to 12 hours or till tender. Discard bay leaves. Stir in bacon. Serve with noodles.

Vegetable-Beef Soup

  3 **pounds beef shank crosscuts**
  2 **bay leaves**
  1 **tablespoon salt**
  1 **teaspoon dried oregano, crushed**
  ½ **teaspoon dried marjoram, crushed**
  ¼ **teaspoon pepper**
  1 **10-ounce package frozen whole kernel corn**
  2 **cups chopped, peeled tomatoes or one 16-ounce can tomatoes, cut up**
  1½ **cups cubed, peeled potatoes**
  1 **cup fresh or loose-pack frozen cut green beans**
  1 **cup sliced carrots**
  1 **cup sliced celery**
  ½ **cup chopped onion**

In a large Dutch oven or kettle combine meat, bay leaves, salt, oregano, marjoram, pepper, and 8 cups *water.* Bring to boiling; reduce heat. Cover and simmer for 2 hours. Remove meat. When cool enough to handle, cut meat off bones and coarsely chop. Discard bones. Strain broth through a large sieve or colander lined with 2 layers of cheesecloth. Skim fat and return broth to kettle. Stir in meat, corn, tomatoes, potatoes, beans, carrots, celery, and onion. Return to boiling; reduce heat. Cover and simmer about 30 minutes or till vegetables are crisp-tender. Discard bay leaves. Makes 6 main-dish servings.

Shortcut Vegetable-Beef Soup: Prepare as above, *except* substitute 1 pound *beef stew meat,* cut into ½-inch cubes, for the beef shank crosscuts. Before adding ingredients to Dutch oven, brown meat in 2 tablespoons hot *cooking oil.* Drain fat. If desired, omit straining broth.

Cutting Stew Meat

An economical way to make stew is to cut up your own stew meat. If the recipe calls for beef, buy a beef chuck pot roast; for pork, a pork blade roast; for lamb, a lamb shoulder roast. Trim the separable fat from the meat, then cut the meat into the size cubes the recipe calls for.

Herbed Lamb Stew

- **1 pound lamb *or* pork stew meat, cut into ¾-inch cubes**
- **2 tablespoons cooking oil**
- **2 cups beef broth (see recipe, page 372, or tip, page 373)**
- **1 cup dry red wine *or* beef broth**
- **2 cloves garlic, minced**
- **1 teaspoon dried marjoram, crushed**
- **1 bay leaf**
- **2 cups peeled potatoes cut into ½-inch cubes**
- **1½ cups sliced carrots**
- **1½ cups celery cut into ½-inch slices**
- **½ cup chopped onion**
- **½ cup dairy sour cream**
- **3 tablespoons all-purpose flour**

In a large saucepan brown meat, half at a time, in hot oil. Drain fat. Return all meat to pan. Add broth, wine, garlic, marjoram, bay leaf, ¼ tea-spoon *salt,* and ¼ teaspoon *pepper.* Bring to boiling; reduce heat. Cover; simmer 20 minutes or till nearly tender. Stir in potatoes, carrots, celery, and onion. Return to boiling; reduce heat. Cover; simmer about 30 minutes or till tender. Discard bay leaf. Mix sour cream and flour. Stir ½ *cup* of the hot liquid into sour cream mixture. Return to pan. Cook and stir till bubbly. Cook and stir 1 minute. Makes 4 main-dish servings.

Microwave directions: In a 3-quart casse-role micro-cook meat and onion, covered, on 100% power (high) 6 to 8 minutes or till meat is no longer pink; stir once. Drain. Stir 1¾ *cups* broth, wine, garlic, marjoram, bay leaf, ¼ tea-spoon *salt,* and ¼ teaspoon *pepper* into meat mixture. Cook, covered, on high for 7 to 10 min-utes or till boiling; stir once. Add vegetables. Cook, covered, on 70% power (medium-high) 15 to 20 minutes or till tender; stir once. Discard bay leaf. Mix sour cream and flour. Stir in ½ *cup* hot liquid. Return to casserole. Cook, uncovered, on high 6 to 9 minutes or till bubbly; stir every min-ute. Cook 1 minute more.

Chili

Thick, hearty, and packed with flavor.

    ¾ pound ground beef
    1 cup chopped onion
    ½ cup chopped green pepper
    2 cloves garlic, minced
    1 16-ounce can tomatoes, cut up
    1 16-ounce can dark red kidney beans,
         drained
    1 8-ounce can tomato sauce
    2 to 3 teaspoons chili powder
    ½ teaspoon dried basil, crushed
    ¼ teaspoon salt
    ¼ teaspoon pepper

In a large saucepan cook ground beef, onion, green pepper, and garlic till meat is brown. Drain fat. Stir in *undrained* tomatoes, kidney beans, tomato sauce, chili powder, basil, salt, and pepper. Bring to boiling; reduce heat. Cover; simmer for 20 minutes. Makes 4 main-dish servings.

Microwave directions: In a 2-quart casserole combine beef, onion, green pepper, and garlic. Micro-cook, covered, on 100% power (high) for 6 to 9 minutes or till meat is no longer pink and vegetables are tender, stirring once. Drain. Stir in *undrained* tomatoes, kidney beans, tomato sauce, chili powder, basil, salt, and pepper. Cook, covered, on high for 9 to 11 minutes or till heated through, stirring twice.

Barley-Beef Soup

    ¾ pound beef or lamb stew meat, cut
         into 1-inch cubes
    1 tablespoon cooking oil
    4 cups water
    1 cup chopped onion
    ½ cup chopped celery
    1 tablespoon instant beef bouillon
         granules
    2 cloves garlic, minced
    ¾ teaspoon dried rosemary or basil,
         crushed
    1 bay leaf
    1 cup loose-pack frozen mixed
         vegetables
    1 cup parsnips cut into ½-inch slices
         or peeled potatoes cut into ½-
         inch cubes
    1 7½-ounce can tomatoes, cut up
    ¼ cup quick-cooking barley*

In a large Dutch oven brown meat in hot oil. Drain fat. Add water, onion, celery, bouillon granules, garlic, rosemary, bay leaf, and ¼ teaspoon *pepper.* Bring to boiling; reduce heat. Cover and simmer 1 hour for beef (45 minutes for lamb).

Stir in frozen vegetables, parsnips, *undrained* tomatoes, and barley. Return to boiling; reduce heat. Cover; simmer 15 minutes or till tender. Discard bay leaf. Makes 4 main-dish servings.

Note: If desired, substitute ¼ cup pearl barley for quick-cooking barley. Add with water.

Vegetable-Pork Soup

Making dinner is hassle free when you simmer soup in a crockery cooker during the day.

    1 pound pork stew meat or lamb stew
         meat, cut into ½-inch cubes
    1 tablespoon cooking oil
    ½ cup chopped onion
    1 teaspoon paprika
    3 cups beef broth (see recipe,
         page 372, or tip, page 373)
    1 cup peeled potatoes cut into ½-inch
         cubes
    1 cup loose-pack frozen whole kernel
         corn
    1 cup peeled winter squash or sweet
         potatoes cut into ½-inch cubes
    ⅔ cup chopped tomato
    ½ teaspoon garlic salt
    1 cup torn fresh spinach

In a Dutch oven brown *half* of the meat in hot oil. Remove meat from Dutch oven. Brown remaining meat with onion and paprika. Drain fat. Return all meat to Dutch oven. Add beef broth. Bring to boiling; reduce heat. Cover; simmer for 30 minutes. Add potatoes, corn, squash, tomato, garlic salt, and ⅛ teaspoon *pepper.* Return to boiling; reduce heat. Cover; simmer for 15 to 20 minutes or till vegetables are tender.

Stir in spinach. Simmer for 3 to 5 minutes or till spinach is tender. If necessary, skim fat. Makes 4 main-dish servings.

Crockery-cooker directions: Brown meat, onion, and paprika in oil as above. In a 3½- or 4-quart electric crockery cooker, layer potatoes, corn, squash, and tomato. Place meat-onion mixture atop. Combine *2½ cups* beef broth, garlic salt, and ⅛ teaspoon *pepper.* Pour over mixture in crockery cooker. Cover and cook on low-heat setting for 10 to 12 hours. If necessary, skim fat. Stir in spinach just before serving.

Ham and Bean Soup

1 cup dry navy beans
4 cups water
1 to 1½ pounds smoked pork hocks
   or one 1- to 1½-pound meaty
   ham bone
1½ cups sliced celery
1 cup chopped onion
¾ teaspoon dried thyme, crushed
½ teaspoon salt
¼ teaspoon pepper
1 bay leaf

Rinse beans. In a large saucepan combine beans and water. Bring to boiling; reduce heat. Simmer for 2 minutes. Remove from heat. Cover and let stand for 1 hour. (*Or,* skip boiling the water and soak beans overnight in a covered pan.) Drain and rinse beans. In the same pan combine beans, 4 cups *fresh water,* pork, celery, onion, thyme, salt, pepper, and bay leaf. Bring to boiling; reduce heat. Cover; simmer about 1 hour or till beans are tender. Remove meat. When cool enough to handle, cut meat off bones and coarsely chop. Discard bones and bay leaf. Slightly mash beans in saucepan. Return the meat to saucepan. Heat through. Makes 4 main-dish servings.

Shortcut Ham and Bean Soup: Prepare as above, *except* omit dry beans. In a large saucepan combine *3 cups* water, pork, celery, onion, thyme, salt, pepper, and bay leaf. Cover and simmer for 45 minutes. When cool enough to handle, cut meat off bones and coarsely chop. Discard bones and bay leaf. Return meat to saucepan. Stir in one 15-ounce can *undrained navy or great northern beans.* Heat through.

Tomato Ham and Bean Soup: Prepare as above, *except* add *half* of a 6-ounce can (⅓ cup) *tomato paste* with hocks or ham bone.

Turkey Frame Soup

1 meaty turkey frame
8 cups water
1 large onion, quartered
½ teaspoon garlic salt
   Chopped, cooked turkey
1 16-ounce can tomatoes, cut up
1 tablespoon instant chicken bouillon
   granules
1½ teaspoons dried oregano, basil,
   marjoram, *or* thyme, crushed

¼ teaspoon pepper
3 cups (any combination) sliced
   celery, carrots, parsnips, *or*
   mushrooms; chopped onions *or*
   rutabagas; *or* broccoli *or*
   cauliflower flowerets
1½ cups medium noodles

Break turkey frame or cut in half with kitchen shears. Place in a large Dutch oven or kettle. Add water, onion, and garlic salt. Bring to boiling; reduce heat. Cover; simmer for 1½ hours.

Remove turkey frame. When cool enough to handle, cut meat off bones; coarsely chop. Add additional turkey to equal *2 cups.* Set meat aside. Discard bones. Strain broth through a sieve lined with 2 layers of cheesecloth; discard solids.

Return broth to Dutch oven. Stir in *undrained* tomatoes, bouillon granules, herb, and pepper. Stir in vegetables. Return to boiling; reduce heat. Cover; simmer for 15 minutes. Stir in noodles. Simmer 8 to 10 minutes more or till noodles are done and vegetables are crisp-tender. Stir in turkey; heat through. Makes 6 main-dish servings.

Chicken-Vegetable Soup

Choose the alternate recipe if you are a fan of noodle-filled chicken soup.

4½ cups chicken broth (see recipe or
   tip, page 373)
½ cup chopped onion
½ teaspoon dried basil, crushed
½ teaspoon dried oregano, crushed
1 bay leaf
1 10-ounce package frozen mixed
   vegetables (2 cups)
2 cups cubed, cooked chicken *or*
   turkey
1 16-ounce can tomatoes, cut up

In a large saucepan mix chicken broth, onion, basil, oregano, bay leaf, and ¼ teaspoon *pepper.* Stir in vegetables. Bring to boiling; reduce heat. Cover and simmer for 6 to 8 minutes or till vegetables are crisp-tender. Discard bay leaf. Stir in chicken and *undrained* tomatoes; heat through. Makes 4 to 6 main-dish servings.

Chicken Noodle Soup: Prepare as above, *except,* after chicken broth comes to a boil, stir in ½ cup *uncooked medium noodles or other small pasta.* Return to boiling; reduce heat. Cover and simmer about 8 minutes or till noodles are done and vegetables are crisp-tender.

Cream of Chicken Soup

- **2 tablespoons margarine *or* butter**
- **3 tablespoons all-purpose flour**
- **3 cups chicken broth (see recipe or tip, page 373)**
- **1 cup light cream *or* milk**
- **1½ cups chopped, cooked chicken**

In a large saucepan melt margarine. Stir in flour and dash *pepper*. Add chicken broth and cream or milk. Cook and stir till bubbly. Cook and stir 1 minute more. Stir in chicken; heat through. If desired, garnish with snipped parsley. Makes 3 main-dish servings.

Gingered Cream of Chicken Soup: Prepare as above, *except* cook 1 tablespoon grated *gingerroot* in margarine or butter for 1 minute before adding flour and pepper.

Chicken Stew with Dumplings

If you like, substitute Dumplings for Stew (see recipe, right) for the dumpling mixture.

- **3½ cups chicken broth (see recipe or tip, page 373)**
- **1 10-ounce package frozen mixed vegetables**
- **1 cup small frozen whole onions**
- **½ teaspoon dried basil *or* oregano, crushed, *or* dried dillweed**
- **⅛ teaspoon garlic powder**
- **⅓ cup all-purpose flour**
- **2 5-ounce cans chunk-style chicken *or* turkey *or* 2 cups cubed, cooked chicken *or* turkey**
- **1 cup packaged biscuit mix**
- **⅓ cup milk**
- **½ teaspoon dried parsley flakes**

In a large saucepan combine 2½ cups of the chicken broth, the mixed vegetables, onions, herb, garlic powder, and ⅛ teaspoon *pepper*. Bring to boiling. Combine remaining broth and flour. Stir into vegetable mixture. Stir in chicken. Cook and stir till thickened and bubbly.

Meanwhile, for dumplings, combine biscuit mix, milk, and parsley. Drop dumpling mixture from a tablespoon to make 4 to 8 mounds atop the *bubbling* stew. Cover and simmer over low heat about 13 minutes or till a toothpick inserted in a dumpling comes out clean. Makes 4 main-dish servings.

Dumplings for Stew

Drop these atop Beef Stew or Herbed Lamb Stew (see recipes, pages 371 and 375) or another favorite stew or chili.

- **⅔ cup all-purpose flour**
- **1 tablespoon snipped parsley**
- **1 teaspoon baking powder**
- **⅛ teaspoon dried basil *or* thyme, crushed, *or* dried dillweed**
- **¼ cup milk**
- **2 tablespoons cooking oil**

In a bowl mix flour, parsley, baking powder, herb, and ⅛ teaspoon *salt*. Mix milk and oil. Pour into flour mixture. Stir with a fork till combined. Drop mixture from a tablespoon to make 4 to 6 mounds atop *bubbling* stew. Cover; simmer for 10 to 12 minutes or till a toothpick comes out clean. *Do not lift cover.* Serves 4 to 6.

Cheese Dumplings for Stew: Prepare as above, *except* reduce all-purpose flour to ⅓ cup and add ⅓ cup *cornmeal*. Omit herb. Stir in ⅓ cup shredded *cheddar or Monterey Jack cheese* after stirring in milk-oil mixture.

Mulligatawny

- **2½ cups chicken broth (see recipe or tip, page 373)**
- **1 7½-ounce can tomatoes, cut up**
- **½ cup chopped celery**
- **½ cup chopped, peeled cooking apple**
- **¼ cup chopped carrot**
- **¼ cup chopped onion**
- **1 tablespoon snipped parsley**
- **1 to 1½ teaspoons curry powder**
- **1 teaspoon lemon juice**
- **1½ cups cubed, cooked chicken**
- **2 cups hot cooked rice**

In a saucepan mix broth, *undrained* tomatoes, celery, apple, carrot, onion, parsley, curry powder, lemon juice, and ¼ teaspoon *pepper*. Bring to boiling; reduce heat. Cover; simmer 15 minutes, stirring often. Stir in chicken; heat through. Serve with rice and, if desired, flaked coconut. Makes 3 main-dish servings.

Microwave directions: In a 2-quart casserole mix all ingredients but chicken and rice. Add ¼ teaspoon *pepper*. Micro-cook, covered, on 100% power (high) for 12 to 15 minutes or till tender; stir once. Add chicken. Cook, uncovered, on high for 1 to 2 minutes more. Serve with rice.

Cioppino

California-born, this stew combines three kinds of fish and seafood and a tomatoey broth.

 1 **pound fresh *or* frozen fish fillets**
 ¾ **cup chopped green pepper**
 ½ **cup chopped onion**
 1 **clove garlic, minced**
 1 **tablespoon cooking oil**
 1 **16-ounce can tomatoes, cut up**
 1 **8-ounce can tomato sauce**
 ½ **cup dry white *or* red wine**
 3 **tablespoons snipped parsley**
 ¼ **teaspoon dried oregano, crushed**
 ¼ **teaspoon dried basil, crushed**
 ⅛ **teaspoon salt**
 1 **6½-ounce can minced clams**
 1 **4½-ounce can shrimp, rinsed and drained**

Thaw fish, if frozen. Cut fish into 1-inch pieces. In a large saucepan cook green pepper, onion, and garlic in hot oil till tender. Add tomatoes, tomato sauce, wine, parsley, oregano, basil, salt, and dash *pepper.* Bring to boiling; reduce heat. Cover and simmer 20 minutes. Add fish, *undrained* clams, and shrimp. Bring just to boiling; reduce heat. Cover and simmer 5 to 7 minutes or till fish flakes easily with a fork. Makes 5 main-dish servings.

Oyster Stew

 1 **pint shucked oysters**
 ½ **teaspoon salt**
 2 **cups milk**
 1 **cup light cream**
   Dash bottled hot pepper sauce
   Paprika
   Margarine *or* butter (optional)

In a medium saucepan combine the *undrained* oysters and salt. Cook over medium heat about 5 minutes or till oysters curl around the edges. Stir in milk, cream, and hot pepper sauce. Heat through. Season to taste. Sprinkle each serving with paprika; if desired, top with a pat of margarine or butter. Makes 4 main-dish servings.

Vegetable Oyster Stew: Prepare as above, *except* cook ½ cup shredded *carrot* and ½ cup finely chopped *celery* in 2 tablespoons *margarine or butter* about 3 minutes or till tender. Stir in 1 teaspoon *Worcestershire sauce.* Add vegetable mixture to oysters with milk.

New England Clam Chowder

Serve this creamy chowder as a main dish or a side dish.

 1 **pint shucked clams *or* two 6½-ounce cans minced clams**
 2 **slices bacon, halved**
 2½ **cups finely chopped, peeled potatoes**
 1 **cup chopped onion**
 1 **teaspoon instant chicken bouillon granules**
 1 **teaspoon Worcestershire sauce**
 ¼ **teaspoon dried thyme, crushed**
 ⅛ **teaspoon pepper**
 2 **cups milk**
 1 **cup light cream**
 2 **tablespoons all-purpose flour**

Chop shucked clams, reserving juice; set clams aside. Strain clam juice to remove bits of shell. (*Or,* drain canned clams, reserving juice.) If necessary, add water to clam juice to equal *1 cup.* Set clam-juice mixture aside.

In a large saucepan cook bacon till crisp. Remove bacon, reserving *1 tablespoon* drippings. Drain bacon on paper towels; crumble. Set aside.

In the same saucepan combine reserved bacon drippings, reserved clam juice, potatoes, onion, bouillon granules, Worcestershire sauce, thyme, and pepper. Bring to boiling; reduce heat. Cover and simmer about 10 minutes or till potatoes are tender. With the back of a fork, mash potatoes slightly against the side of the pan.

Combine milk, cream, and flour till smooth. Add to potato mixture. Cook and stir till slightly thickened and bubbly. Stir in clams. Return to boiling; reduce heat. Cook 1 to 2 minutes more. Sprinkle each serving with some of the crumbled bacon. Makes 4 main-dish servings or 6 to 8 side-dish servings.

Fish Chowder: Prepare as above, except substitute 1 pound fresh or frozen *fish steaks,* cut ¾ inch thick, for clams. Thaw fish, if frozen, and cut into ¾-inch cubes. Substitute 1 cup *water* for the reserved clam juice and add ½ cup sliced *carrot* with potatoes and onion. Add fish to chowder with milk mixture. Bring just to boiling; reduce heat. Cover and simmer about 3 minutes more or till fish flakes easily with a fork.

Chicken and Sausage Gumbo

A roux (pronounced roo) adds color and flavor to many basic Cajun dishes like gumbo. (Seafood Gumbo is pictured on page 369.)

- ⅓ **cup all-purpose flour**
- ¼ **cup cooking oil**
- ½ **cup chopped onion**
- ⅓ **cup chopped celery *or* green pepper**
- 4 **cloves garlic, minced**
- ¼ **teaspoon black pepper**
- ¼ **teaspoon ground red pepper**
- 3 **cups chicken broth, heated (see recipe or tip, page 373)**
- 8 **ounces andouille *or* smoked sausage, quartered lengthwise and cut into ½-inch slices**
- 1½ **cups sliced okra *or* one 10-ounce package frozen cut okra, thawed**
- 2 **bay leaves**
- 1 **whole large chicken breast, skinned, boned, and cut into bite-size pieces**
- 2 **cups hot cooked rice**

For roux, in a large heavy saucepan or Dutch oven combine flour and oil till smooth. Cook over medium-high heat for 5 minutes, stirring constantly. Reduce heat to medium. Cook and stir about 15 minutes more or till roux is dark reddish brown.

Stir in onion, celery or green pepper, garlic, black pepper, and red pepper. Cook over medium heat for 3 to 5 minutes or till vegetables are just crisp-tender, stirring often.

Gradually stir in *hot* chicken broth, andouille or smoked sausage, okra, and bay leaves. Add chicken. Bring to boiling; reduce heat. Cover; simmer 20 to 30 minutes or till tender. Discard bay leaves. Serve over rice. If desired, garnish with a carrot top. Makes 4 main-dish servings.

Seafood Gumbo: Prepare as above, *except* substitute 12 ounces frozen shelled *shrimp* and 6 ounces fresh *or* frozen *crabmeat* for the chicken. Thaw shrimp and crab, if frozen. Cut up crab. Cook roux till *light* reddish brown. Add shrimp and crab during last 5 minutes of cooking.

◀ The roux for Chicken and Sausage Gumbo is ready when its color matches that of a penny.

Manhattan Clam Chowder

A full-flavored tomato broth loaded with vegetables and clams.

- 1 **pint shucked clams *or* two 6½-ounce cans minced clams**
- 3 **slices bacon**
- 1 **cup chopped celery**
- 1 **cup chopped onion**
- 1 **28-ounce can tomatoes, cut up**
- 2 **cups finely chopped, peeled potatoes**
- ½ **teaspoon dried basil *or* marjoram, crushed**
- ¼ **teaspoon pepper**

Chop shucked clams, reserving juice; set aside. Strain clam juice to remove bits of shell. (*Or*, drain canned clams, reserving juice.) If necessary, add water to juice to equal *1½ cups.* Set aside.

In a large saucepan cook bacon till crisp. Remove bacon, reserving drippings. Drain bacon on paper towels; crumble. Set aside.

Cook celery and onion in reserved bacon drippings over medium heat about 5 minutes or till tender. Drain. Stir in reserved clam juice, *undrained* tomatoes, potatoes, basil or marjoram, and pepper. Bring to boiling; reduce heat. Cover and simmer for 20 to 25 minutes or till vegetables are tender.

With the back of a fork, slightly mash vegetables against side of pan. Stir in clams. Return to boiling; reduce heat. Cook 1 to 2 minutes more. Sprinkle each serving with bacon. Makes 4 main-dish or 6 to 8 side-dish servings.

Bean and Sausage Soup (FAST)

1 24-ounce can vegetable juice
  cocktail
1 15-ounce can chili beans with chili
  gravy
2 cups loose-pack frozen hash brown
  potatoes with onions and
  peppers
8 ounces fully cooked Polish sausage
  or fully cooked smoked turkey
  sausage, halved lengthwise and
  sliced ¼ inch thick
½ cup shredded cheddar cheese

In a large saucepan combine juice cocktail, *un-drained* beans, potatoes, and sausage. Bring to boiling; reduce heat. Simmer for 10 minutes or till potatoes are tender and mixture is heated through. Sprinkle each serving with some of the cheese. Makes 4 main-dish servings.

Microwave directions: In a 2-quart casserole combine *half* of the vegetable juice and the potatoes. Micro-cook, covered, on 100% power (high) for 10 minutes or till potatoes are tender, stirring once. Add remaining vegetable juice, *undrained* beans, and sausage. Cook, uncovered, on high for 8 to 10 minutes or till heated through. Sprinkle each serving with some of the cheese.

Lentil Stew

This stew is a good choice when you're short on time because the lentils cook in just 35 minutes.

1 cup dry lentils
1 cup sliced leeks or chopped onion
2 cloves garlic, minced
1 tablespoon cooking oil
4 cups beef broth (see recipe, page
  372, or tip, page 373)
1 7½-ounce can tomatoes, cut up
1 tablespoon Worcestershire sauce
¼ teaspoon dried thyme or oregano,
  crushed
¼ teaspoon pepper
⅛ teaspoon ground cumin
1 bay leaf
½ cup chopped carrot
½ cup chopped celery
½ pound fully cooked smoked sausage
  links, sliced

Rinse lentils; set aside. In a large saucepan cook leeks or onion and garlic in hot oil till tender but not brown. Stir in lentils, beef broth, *undrained* tomatoes, Worcestershire sauce, thyme or oregano, pepper, cumin, and bay leaf. Bring to boiling; reduce heat. Cover and simmer for 15 minutes.

Add carrot and celery. Return to boiling; reduce heat. Simmer for 15 to 20 minutes more or till lentils and vegetables are tender. Stir in sausage; heat through. Discard bay leaf. If desired, garnish each serving with snipped parsley. Makes 4 main-dish servings.

Black Bean Soup

1 cup dry black beans
1 cup chopped onion
1 cup chopped celery
4 cloves garlic, minced
2 tablespoons cooking oil
4 cups chicken broth (see recipe or
  tip, page 373)
1 teaspoon ground coriander
¼ teaspoon salt
⅛ to ¼ teaspoon ground red pepper
¾ pound fully cooked smoked turkey
  sausage *or* Polish sausage,
  chopped
3 tablespoons dry sherry (optional)

Rinse beans. In a large saucepan combine beans and 6 cups *water*. Bring to boiling; reduce heat. Simmer for 2 minutes. Remove from heat. Cover and let stand for 1 hour. (*Or,* skip boiling the water and soak beans overnight in a covered pan.) Drain and rinse beans.

In a large saucepan or Dutch oven cook onion, celery, and garlic in hot oil till tender. Add beans, chicken broth, coriander, salt, and red pepper. Bring to boiling; reduce heat. Cover and simmer for 1 to 1½ hours or till beans are tender.

If desired, mash beans slightly with a potato masher. Stir in sausage and, if desired, dry sherry. Cook 2 to 3 minutes more or till heated through. If desired, garnish with dairy sour cream, shredded Monterey Jack cheese, or snipped parsley. Makes 4 main-dish servings.

Split Pea Soup

1 **cup dry split peas**
4 **cups chicken broth (see recipe or tip, page 373)**
1 **to 1½ pounds smoked pork hocks or one 1- to 1½-pound meaty ham bone**
¼ **teaspoon dried marjoram, crushed**
1 **bay leaf**
½ **cup chopped carrot**
½ **cup chopped celery**
½ **cup chopped onion**

Rinse peas. In a large saucepan combine peas, broth, meat, marjoram, bay leaf, and dash *pepper*. Bring to boiling; reduce heat. Cover; simmer for 1 hour. Stir occasionally. Remove meat. When cool enough to handle, cut meat off bone and coarsely chop. Discard bone. Return meat to saucepan. Stir in carrot, celery, and onion. Return to boiling; reduce heat. Cover; simmer for 20 to 30 minutes or till vegetables are crisp-tender. Discard bay leaf. Makes 4 main-dish servings.

Minestrone

¼ **cup dry great northern beans**
¼ **cup chopped carrot**
¼ **chopped celery**
¼ **cup chopped onion**
1½ **teaspoons instant beef bouillon granules**
1 **clove garlic, minced**
½ **teaspoon dried basil, crushed**
¼ **teaspoon dried oregano, crushed**
⅛ **teaspoon pepper**
1 **7½-ounce can tomatoes, cut up**
½ **cup coarsely chopped cabbage**
½ **small zucchini, halved lengthwise and sliced (½ cup)**
½ **ounce thin spaghetti, broken (about 2 tablespoons), or 2 tablespoons tiny shell macaroni**
2 **slices bacon, crisp-cooked, drained, and crumbled**

Rinse beans. In a medium saucepan combine beans and 2½ cups *water*. Bring to boiling; reduce heat. Simmer for 2 minutes. Remove from heat. Cover and let stand for 1 hour. (Or, skip boiling the water and soak beans overnight in a covered pan.) Drain and rinse beans.

In the same saucepan combine beans, 2½ cups *fresh water*, carrot, celery, onion, bouillon granules, garlic, basil, oregano, and pepper. Bring to boiling; reduce heat. Cover and simmer 2 hours or till beans are tender. Add *undrained* tomatoes, cabbage, zucchini, and spaghetti. Bring to boiling; reduce heat. Cover; simmer for 5 to 10 minutes more or till tender. Stir in bacon. If desired, serve with grated Parmesan cheese. Makes 5 side-dish servings.

Quick Minestrone: Prepare as above, ex-cept do not use dry great northern beans. In a large saucepan combine 2½ cups *water*, carrot, celery, onion, bouillon granules, garlic, basil, oregano, and pepper. Bring to boiling; reduce heat. Cover; simmer for 15 minutes. Drain; stir in *half* of one 15-ounce can *great northern beans or* one 8-ounce can *red kidney beans*. Add toma-toes, cabbage, zucchini, and spaghetti. Return to boiling; reduce heat. Cover and simmer for 5 to 10 minutes more or till tender.

Tortellini-Vegetable Soup

Either frozen or dried tortellini works in this soup.

2 **tablespoons snipped basil or 2 teaspoons dried basil, crushed***
2 **cloves garlic, minced***
2 **teaspoons olive oil or cooking oil***
4 **cups beef or chicken broth (see recipes or tip, pages 372 and 373)**
½ **cup beef or cheese tortellini**
¼ **teaspoon salt**
⅛ **teaspoon pepper**
1 **cup chopped, peeled tomatoes**
1 **cup loose-pack frozen cut green beans**
½ **cup sliced carrot**
   Grated Parmesan cheese (optional)

In a medium saucepan cook basil and garlic in hot oil about 1 minute. Add broth, tortellini, salt, and pepper. Bring to boiling; reduce heat. Cover and simmer for 10 minutes. Add tomatoes, green beans, and carrot. Return to boiling; reduce heat. Cover and simmer 10 to 15 minutes more or till tortellini is done and vegetables are tender. If desired, sprinkle each serving with Parmesan cheese. Makes 6 side-dish servings.

***Note:** If desired, substitute 2 tablespoons Pesto for Pasta (see recipe, page 269) for the basil, garlic, and oil. Stir in at the end of cooking.

Wild Rice Soup

A sumptuous side dish with a nutty flavor.

- 3 cups chicken broth (see recipe or tip, page 373)
- ⅓ cup uncooked wild rice
- ½ cup sliced green onions
- ½ cup shredded carrot
- 1 cup light cream or milk
- 2 tablespoons all-purpose flour
- ⅛ teaspoon pepper
- 1 tablespoon dry sherry (optional)
  Snipped parsley or chives

In a medium saucepan combine broth and rice. Bring to boiling; reduce heat. Cover and simmer 45 to 50 minutes or till tender. Stir in onions and carrot during last 5 minutes of cooking. Combine cream or milk, flour, and pepper. Stir into rice mixture. Cook and stir till slightly thickened and bubbly. Cook and stir 1 minute more. If desired, stir in sherry. Garnish with parsley or chives. Makes 4 to 6 side-dish servings.

Wonton Soup

- Wontons (see recipe, page 18)
- 4 cups chicken broth (see recipe or tip, page 373)
- ½ cup thinly bias-sliced carrot
- ½ of a small green pepper, cut into ½-inch pieces, or ½ of a 6-ounce package frozen pea pods, thawed and halved

Prepare wontons as directed, *except* do not fry. Freeze *half* of the wontons for another use.

In a saucepan bring 6 cups *water* to boiling. With a spoon, place wontons, one at a time, into boiling water. Reduce heat. Simmer for 5 minutes. Drain. Rinse with *cool* water; drain again.

In a saucepan combine chicken broth, carrot, and green pepper. (If using the pea pods, add to broth during the last minute of cooking.) Bring to boiling; reduce heat. Cover and simmer for 2 to 4 minutes or till vegetables are crisp-tender. To serve, divide wontons among bowls. Spoon broth mixture atop. Makes 4 to 6 side-dish servings.

Wonton Soup

Cheese Soup

1¾ cups chicken broth (see recipe or
    tip, page 373)
½ cup finely shredded carrot
¼ cup finely chopped celery
¼ cup finely chopped onion
1¾ cups milk
¼ cup all-purpose flour
    Dash pepper
1 cup shredded American cheese
    (4 ounces)

In a medium saucepan combine chicken broth, carrot, celery, and onion. Bring to boiling; reduce heat. Cover and simmer for 6 to 8 minutes or till vegetables are tender. Combine milk, flour, and pepper. Stir into broth mixture. Cook and stir till thickened and bubbly. Cook and stir 1 minute more. Add cheese; stir till melted. Makes 5 side-dish or 3 main-dish servings.

Microwave directions: In a 1½-quart casserole combine ½ cup of the chicken broth, the carrot, celery, and onion. Micro-cook, covered, on 100% power (high) for 6 to 8 minutes or till vegetables are tender. Combine milk, flour, and pepper. Stir into broth mixture. Stir in remaining chicken broth. Cook, uncovered, on high for 8 to 10 minutes or till thickened and bubbly, stirring every 2 minutes till mixture starts to thicken, then every 30 seconds. Stir in cheese. Cook, uncovered, on high about 1 minute or till hot and cheese melts.

Beer Cheese Soup: Prepare as above, *except* reduce chicken broth to *1 cup.* Stir ¾ cup *beer* into soup with the cheese.

Corn Chowder

4 fresh medium ears of corn *or* one
    10-ounce package frozen whole
    kernel corn
½ cup cubed, peeled potato
½ cup chopped onion
⅓ cup water
2 teaspoons instant chicken bouillon
    granules
¼ teaspoon pepper
1¾ cups milk
1 tablespoon margarine *or* butter
2 tablespoons all-purpose flour

If using fresh corn, use a sharp knife to cut off just the kernel tips from the ears of corn, then scrape the cobs with the dull edge of the knife. (You should have 2 cups corn.)

In a large saucepan combine fresh or frozen corn, potato, onion, water, bouillon granules, and pepper. Bring to boiling; reduce heat. Cover and simmer about 10 minutes or till corn and potatoes are just tender, stirring occasionally. Stir in 1½ *cups* of the milk and the margarine or butter. Combine the remaining milk and flour. Stir milk-flour mixture into corn mixture. Cook and stir till thickened and bubbly. Cook and stir 1 minute more. If desired, garnish with snipped chives or snipped parsley and crisp-cooked, crumbled bacon. Makes 4 to 6 side-dish servings.

Cream of Vegetable Soup

    Cooked vegetable (see chart,
      opposite)
1½ cups chicken broth (see recipe or
    tip, page 373)
1 tablespoon margarine *or* butter
1 tablespoon all-purpose flour
    Seasonings (see chart, opposite)
⅛ teaspoon salt
    Dash pepper
1 cup milk *or* light cream

In a blender container or food processor bowl combine the cooked vegetable and ¾ cup of the chicken broth. Cover and blend or process about 1 minute or till smooth. Set aside.

In a medium saucepan melt margarine. Stir in flour, seasonings, salt, and pepper. Add milk all at once. Cook and stir till slightly thickened and bubbly. Cook 1 minute more. Stir in vegetable mixture and remaining broth. Cook and stir till heated through. If necessary, stir in additional milk to make of desired consistency. Season to taste. Makes 3 or 4 side-dish servings.

Microwave directions: Blend or process the vegetable and chicken broth as above. Set aside. In a 1½- or 2-quart casserole micro-cook margarine, uncovered, on 100% power (high) 30 to 60 seconds or till melted. Stir in flour, seasonings, salt, and pepper. Stir in milk all at once. Cook, uncovered, on high for 3 to 5 minutes or till thickened and bubbly, stirring every minute till the sauce starts to thicken, then every 30 seconds. Stir in vegetable mixture and remaining broth. Cook, uncovered, on high 3 to 5 minutes more or till heated through, stirring once. If necessary, stir in additional milk to make of desired consistency.

Making Cream of Vegetable Soup

Use this chart along with the Cream of Vegetable Soup recipe, opposite. Cook vegetables according to the charts on pages 413–416, or according to the package directions. Drain the vegetables well. You should have 2 cups of cooked vegetables to add to the soup.

Vegetables	Seasonings
2 pounds acorn squash *or* pumpkin (scrape flesh from peel after cooking)	¼ teaspoon ground ginger *or* ground cinnamon
3 cups cut asparagus *or* one 10-ounce package frozen cut asparagus	½ teaspoon finely shredded lemon peel and ⅛ teaspoon ground nutmeg
3 cups broccoli flowerets *or* one 10-ounce package frozen cut broccoli	1 teaspoon snipped thyme *or* ¼ teaspoon dried thyme, crushed
2 cups brussels sprouts *or* one 10-ounce package frozen brussels sprouts	1 teaspoon snipped marjoram *or* ¼ teaspoon dried marjoram, crushed
2½ cups sliced carrots *or* loose-pack frozen crinkle-cut carrots	1 tablespoon snipped parsley and 1 teaspoon snipped basil *or* ¼ teaspoon dried basil, crushed
3 cups cauliflower flowerets *or* one 10-ounce package frozen cauliflower	½ to ¾ teaspoon curry powder
2½ cups sliced celery	1 teaspoon snipped dillweed *or* basil, *or* ¼ teaspoon dried dillweed *or* basil, crushed
3 cups cut green beans *or* one 10-ounce package frozen cut green beans	1 teaspoon snipped savory *or* ¼ teaspoon dried savory, crushed
5 cups sliced fresh mushrooms	½ teaspoon snipped thyme *or* ⅛ teaspoon dried thyme, crushed, and, if desired, 1 tablespoon dry sherry
2½ cups chopped onion	1 teaspoon Worcestershire sauce and 1 clove garlic, minced
2½ cups shelled peas *or* one 10-ounce package frozen peas	1 teaspoon snipped sage; ¼ teaspoon dried sage, crushed; 2 teaspoons snipped mint; *or* ¼ teaspoon dried mint, crushed
3 medium potatoes, peeled and cubed, *or* 1¾ cups mashed, cooked potatoes	1 teaspoon snipped dillweed *or* ¼ teaspoon dried dillweed
16 cups fresh spinach *or* one 10-ounce package frozen spinach	½ teaspoon snipped tarragon; ⅛ teaspoon dried tarragon, crushed; *or* ⅛ teaspoon ground nutmeg
3 cups sliced zucchini *or* yellow summer squash	⅛ teaspoon ground nutmeg

French Onion Soup

- 2 tablespoons margarine *or* butter
- 2 cups thinly sliced onions
- 4 cups beef broth (see recipe, page 372, or tip, page 373)
- 2 tablespoons dry sherry (optional)
- 1 teaspoon Worcestershire sauce
- 4 to 6 slices French bread, toasted
- ¾ to 1 cup shredded Gruyère, Jarlsberg, *or* Swiss cheese

In a large saucepan melt margarine or butter. Stir in onions. Cook, covered, over medium-low heat for 8 to 10 minutes or till tender and golden, stirring occasionally. Add beef broth; dry sherry, if desired; Worcestershire sauce; and dash *pepper.* Bring to boiling; reduce heat. Cover and simmer for 10 minutes. Sprinkle toasted bread with cheese. Place bread under broiler till cheese melts and turns light brown. To serve, ladle soup into bowls and float bread atop. Makes 4 to 6 side-dish servings.

Vichyssoise

- ½ cup sliced leeks *or* chopped onion
- 1 tablespoon margarine *or* butter
- 1½ cups sliced, peeled potatoes
- 1 cup chicken broth (see recipe or tip, page 373)
  Dash white pepper *or* pepper
- ¾ cup milk
- ½ cup whipping cream

In a medium saucepan cook leeks in margarine or butter till tender but not brown. Stir in potatoes, broth, pepper, and ⅛ teaspoon *salt.* Bring to boiling; reduce heat. Cover; simmer 20 to 25 minutes or till potatoes are tender. Cool slightly.

Place potato mixture in a blender container or food processor bowl. Cover; blend or process till smooth. Pour into a bowl. Stir in milk and cream. If necessary, add additional milk to make desired consistency. Cover; chill well before serving. If desired, top with snipped chives. Makes 4 side-dish servings.

Microwave directions: Place leeks and margarine or butter in a 1½-quart casserole. Micro-cook, covered, on 100% power (high) for 2 to 3 minutes or till tender. Add potatoes, chicken broth, pepper, and ⅛ teaspoon *salt.* Cook, covered, on high for 8 to 10 minutes or till potatoes are tender, stirring once. Continue as above.

Herbed Tomato Soup

- ½ cup sliced onion
- 2 tablespoons margarine *or* butter
- 2 cups chopped, peeled tomatoes *or* one 14½-ounce can whole, peeled tomatoes, cut up
- 1½ cups chicken broth (see recipe or tip, page 373)
- 1 8-ounce can tomato sauce
- 1 tablespoon snipped basil *or* ½ teaspoon dried basil, crushed
- 1 teaspoon snipped thyme *or* ¼ teaspoon dried thyme, crushed
  Dash pepper

In a large saucepan cook onion in margarine or butter till tender but not brown. Add fresh tomatoes or *undrained* canned tomatoes, broth, tomato sauce, basil, thyme, and pepper. Bring to boiling; reduce heat. Cover and simmer for 30 minutes. Cool slightly. Press mixture through a food mill. (*Or,* place mixture, half at a time, in a blender container or food processor bowl. Cover and blend or process till smooth.) Return mixture to saucepan; heat through. If desired, garnish with lemon slices. Makes 4 side-dish servings.

Gazpacho

Favor your taste buds with this peppy chilled vegetable soup.

- 4 cups chopped, peeled tomatoes
- 1 cup tomato juice *or* vegetable juice cocktail
- 1 cup beef broth (see recipe, page 372, or tip, page 373)
- ½ cup chopped, seeded cucumber
- ¼ cup finely chopped green pepper
- ¼ cup finely chopped onion
- 2 tablespoons snipped basil *or* 1 teaspoon dried basil, crushed
- 1 tablespoon olive oil *or* cooking oil
- 1 tablespoon lemon juice *or* lime juice
- 1 small clove garlic, minced
- ½ teaspoon ground cumin (optional)
- ¼ teaspoon bottled hot pepper sauce

In a bowl mix tomatoes; tomato juice; beef broth; cucumber; green pepper; onion; basil; oil; lemon juice; garlic; cumin, if desired; hot pepper sauce; and ¼ teaspoon *salt.* Cover and chill 2 to 24 hours. If desired, top with croutons. Makes 6 to 8 side-dish servings.

Vegetables

Nutrition Analysis

	Per Serving								Percent U.S. RDA Per Serving							
	Servings Per Recipe	Calories	Protein (g)	Carbohydrate (g)	Fat (g)	Cholesterol (mg)	Sodium (mg)	Potassium (mg)	Protein	Vitamin A	Vitamin C	Thiamine	Riboflavin	Niacin	Calcium	Iron
Acorn Squash Boats (p. 412)	4	249	10	41	6	13	583	599	15	87	30	23	10	14	16	12
Artichokes au Gratin (p. 391)	3	151	6	18	7	6	348	475	9	12	13	9	16	10	14	11
Artichokes with Butter Sauce (p. 390)	2	265	3	15	23	62	326	410	5	22	22	6	5	4	6	11
Artichokes with Sour Cream Sauce (p. 390)	2	191	5	17	13	27	160	485	8	14	27	7	10	5	13	11
Asparagus Dijon (p. 391)	6	118	4	5	10	66	119	338	7	23	40	8	10	6	4	5
Asparagus-Tomato Stir-Fry (p. 408)	4	74	4	8	4	0	227	470	6	24	41	10	14	13	3	7
Baked Bean Quintet (p. 393)	12	306	15	55	4	5	465	921	23	7	10	19	9	9	13	31
Baked Beans (p. 394)	10	282	11	44	7	8	208	782	17	0	4	24	8	8	12	27
Baked Parmesan Cottage Potatoes (p. 404)	4	198	5	21	11	5	224	640	8	8	27	7	4	9	10	5
Baked Potatoes (p. 403)	1	164	3	38	0	0	12	627	5	0	22	11	3	12	2	11
Baked Sweet Potatoes (p. 403)	1	156	2	36	0	0	20	306	4	602	40	7	13	5	3	5
Broccoli-Carrot Stir-Fry (p. 407)	4	97	2	10	6	0	22	279	3	264	37	6	4	3	3	3
Broccoli-Onion Casserole (p. 409)	4	232	7	15	17	34	363	296	11	38	34	9	12	4	13	7
Broccoli Oriental (p. 395)	3	139	5	14	8	0	587	630	8	49	150	9	13	7	7	8
Brown-Sugar-Glazed Carrots (p. 397)	4	75	1	12	3	0	61	262	1	429	12	5	3	4	3	3
Candied Acorn Squash (p. 405)	2	198	1	38	6	0	144	676	2	16	26	16	2	6	8	11
Candied Sweet Potatoes (p. 404)	4	166	2	34	3	0	49	236	3	394	26	4	9	3	3	5
Carrot-Rice Casserole (p. 410)	6	189	9	14	11	75	633	300	15	318	7	8	12	4	24	5
Carrots in Almond Sauce (p. 398)	4	124	2	10	9	0	118	311	3	431	9	6	6	5	4	4
Cauliflower-Broccoli Bake (p. 408)	10	170	7	17	9	20	715	231	11	18	25	5	9	5	14	5
Cauliflower in Cheese Sauce (p. 398)	4	119	6	7	8	16	260	343	9	7	43	6	15	7	14	4
Cheddar-Zucchini Puff (p. 406)	6	143	6	6	11	69	200	246	10	13	8	6	9	3	14	4
Cheese-Frosted Mashed Potatoes (p. 402)	4	258	6	24	16	35	350	479	9	13	18	9	6	8	11	2
Cheese-Topped Parsnips (p. 401)	4	157	3	19	8	7	122	403	5	8	22	6	5	4	9	4
Cheesy Artichoke Casserole (p. 411)	5	282	10	24	17	33	553	455	15	15	13	13	17	10	22	11
Cheesy Bean Combo (p. 393)	4	192	10	21	8	21	240	453	15	12	12	8	10	4	16	11
Cheesy Potato-Carrot Bake (p. 410)	4	217	7	27	9	16	184	579	11	160	23	12	6	11	12	4
Cheesy Scalloped Potatoes (p. 403)	4	291	10	32	14	26	549	616	15	13	19	12	14	9	24	4
Corn on the Cob (p. 399)	1	66	2	15	1	0	12	208	4	4	9	10	3	7	0	2
Cottage Fried Potatoes (p. 404)	4	169	3	21	9	0	241	634	4	7	27	7	3	8	2	5
Creamed Peas and New Potatoes (p. 409)	4	207	7	36	4	5	426	626	11	13	30	20	11	14	10	8
Creamy Brussels Sprouts (p. 396)	4	118	5	12	7	9	163	419	7	21	86	10	9	4	9	7
Creamy Creole Corn (p. 398)	4	157	5	19	9	24	126	346	7	29	50	13	7	8	3	6
Creamy Curried Corn (p. 398)	4	152	5	17	9	24	124	287	7	22	29	12	6	7	3	5
Creamy Green Bean Bake (p. 392)	4	110	2	8	8	7	277	108	3	10	13	2	4	1	5	3
Creamy Spinach (p. 405)	4	67	3	6	4	3	188	330	5	94	7	5	12	2	13	11
Creamy Succotash (p. 411)	3	154	6	23	6	3	424	322	9	9	7	7	9	7	7	6
Creole-Style Green Beans (p. 392)	4	60	3	5	3	5	148	150	5	14	13	7	4	4	3	4
Crumb-Topped Tomatoes (p. 406)	4	64	2	5	4	3	177	144	4	17	11	3	3	3	6	3
Curried Brussels Sprouts (p. 396)	4	121	5	10	8	0	136	433	7	20	85	10	10	10	4	9
Dilled Peas and Walnuts (p. 401)	4	109	3	8	8	0	203	129	5	8	6	10	3	3	2	5
Duchess Potatoes (p. 402)	4	222	4	23	13	69	224	458	6	11	18	9	4	8	2	4
Eggplant Parmigiana (p. 399)	4	315	16	23	19	90	634	486	24	23	10	12	15	10	38	9

On the divider: Asparagus-Tomato Stir-Fry (p. 408).

Nutrition Analysis

	Servings Per Recipe	Calories	Protein (g)	Carbohydrate (g)	Fat (g)	Cholesterol (mg)	Sodium (mg)	Potassium (mg)	Protein	Vitamin A	Vitamin C	Thiamine	Riboflavin	Niacin	Calcium	Iron
	Per Serving								**Percent U.S. RDA Per Serving**							
French Fries (p. 404)	4	285	3	38	14	0	12	627	5	0	22	11	3	12	2	11
Fried Onion Rings (p. 401)	4	550	7	26	47	72	176	241	10	3	10	15	13	7	9	9
Garden-Vegetable Stir-Fry (p. 412)	4	88	3	12	4	0	505	385	4	92	43	7	5	5	4	6
Golden Broccoli Bake (p. 395)	6	87	4	7	5	7	278	171	6	34	40	4	6	2	8	3
Green Beans Amandine (p. 392)	3	85	2	7	6	0	50	196	4	13	15	5	7	4	4	5
Green Pepper Boats (p. 412)	4	213	9	31	6	13	581	272	14	85	134	14	11	11	12	12
Harvard Beets (p. 395)	4	91	1	16	3	0	91	268	2	3	10	3	1	2	1	4
Hashed Brown Potatoes (p. 404)	4	169	3	21	9	0	241	633	4	7	27	7	3	8	1	5
Herb-Buttered Mushrooms (p. 400)	4	97	3	7	6	0	116	464	4	5	6	8	30	24	2	9
Kohlrabi with Honey Butter (p. 400)	4	74	2	12	3	0	61	436	3	105	81	5	2	3	3	3
Lemon-Buttered Turnips (p. 406)	4	81	1	7	6	0	136	217	2	7	29	3	2	2	4	2
Lima Beans and Mushrooms (p. 393)	4	106	5	15	3	0	55	364	8	5	6	5	7	6	3	9
Mashed Potatoes (p. 402)	4	153	2	23	6	1	141	445	4	5	18	8	2	8	2	2
Nutty Cauliflower (p. 398)	4	92	2	5	8	0	42	240	3	20	76	8	3	2	2	4
Orange-Glazed Beets (p. 395)	4	83	1	14	3	0	92	302	2	3	18	4	1	2	2	5
Parsnip Puff (p. 401)	4	187	5	23	9	138	410	493	8	137	32	10	9	5	7	8
Peachy Sweet Potatoes (p. 404)	4	181	2	37	3	0	51	298	3	400	28	5	9	5	3	6
Peas and Mushrooms (p. 401)	4	65	3	7	3	0	202	152	4	8	6	9	7	7	2	5
Pecan-Cabbage Toss (p. 397)	4	103	2	7	8	0	155	266	3	82	41	8	2	2	4	4
Pennsylvania Red Cabbage (p. 397)	3	107	1	17	5	0	186	177	1	1	33	2	1	1	4	4
Potato Chips (p. 404)	4	285	3	38	14	0	12	627	5	0	22	11	3	12	2	11
Potato Patties (p. 402)	4	255	4	25	16	69	259	488	7	13	19	10	5	8	3	4
Ratatouille (p. 408)	4	168	6	12	11	13	243	461	10	12	16	10	6	6	20	7
Saucy Rutabaga-Potato Combo (p. 409)	4	102	3	17	3	1	173	440	4	5	27	8	4	6	6	3
Scalloped Corn (p. 399)	4	200	5	26	9	71	468	243	8	20	28	7	11	7	5	7
Scalloped Potatoes (p. 403)	4	212	5	32	7	6	382	582	8	8	19	12	10	9	11	4
Scalloped Tomatoes (p. 406)	4	136	3	17	7	1	315	243	4	21	18	10	6	6	4	7
Sesame Asparagus (p. 392)	4	59	3	4	4	0	37	307	5	16	31	9	11	9	2	5
Shoestring Potatoes (p. 404)	4	285	3	38	14	0	12	627	5	0	22	11	3	12	2	11
Shortcut Baked Beans (p. 394)	4	385	16	55	12	17	1331	610	24	10	13	16	6	10	14	25
Smothered Okra (p. 400)	4	113	3	13	6	0	348	510	5	38	69	16	6	7	8	8
Spaghetti Squash Marinara (p. 405)	6	84	2	13	3	0	236	331	3	11	18	6	3	9	6	6
Spinach-Green-Bean Casserole (p. 411)	4	188	7	15	12	18	526	473	11	106	16	11	18	5	23	17
Squash-Corn Medley (p. 410)	4	176	5	14	12	12	351	342	8	97	38	8	5	6	15	5
Sweet-and-Sour Carrots (p. 397)	4	14	1	22	6	0	186	357	2	519	13	7	4	5	3	4
Swiss-Cheese-Creamed Peas (p. 402)	4	210	7	12	15	42	348	206	11	16	8	11	9	4	17	5
Turnip Puff (p. 401)	4	141	5	11	9	138	465	316	7	137	27	7	8	4	6	6
Turnip-Zucchini Casserole (p. 411)	6	87	4	7	5	10	211	318	6	11	36	5	5	3	10	4
Twice-Baked Potatoes (p. 403)	4	223	4	38	6	13	138	708	7	5	26	13	5	12	4	3
Vegetables au Gratin (p. 410)	4	203	9	12	14	23	446	237	14	33	57	8	20	5	28	7
Zucchini Boats (p. 412)	4	208	9	30	6	13	581	317	14	83	12	14	10	11	13	9
Zucchini in Dill Sauce (p. 407)	4	96	2	7	7	9	118	333	4	13	13	7	4	3	5	4

Vegetables

On their own or as a team, vegetables make delicious and nutritious side dishes or snacks. The first part of this chapter features recipes for individual vegetables. That's followed by recipes for vegetable combinations. If you need basic preparation and cooking times for fresh vegetables, see pages 412–416.

Artichokes with Butter Sauce

Pluck a leaf and dip it into the sauce. Then savor the flavor as you scrape off the tender flesh with your teeth.

>   2   medium artichokes (about
>   10 ounces each)
>   Lemon juice
>   ¼   cup butter *or* margarine
>   ¼   teaspoon dried dillweed, tarragon,
>   oregano, *or* chervil, crushed
>   1   tablespoon lemon juice

Wash artichokes; trim stems and remove loose outer leaves. Cut 1 inch from each top; snip off the sharp leaf tips. Brush the cut edges with a little lemon juice.

In a large saucepan or Dutch oven bring a large amount of lightly salted water to boiling. Add artichokes. Return to boiling; reduce heat. Cover and simmer for 20 to 25 minutes or till a leaf pulls out easily. Drain upside down.

Meanwhile, for butter sauce, melt butter or margarine. Stir in dillweed, tarragon, oregano, or chervil and the 1 tablespoon lemon juice. Turn artichokes right side up and serve with the butter sauce.* Makes 2 servings.

Microwave directions: Wash and trim artichokes as above. Brush with a little lemon juice. In a 2-quart casserole micro-cook the artichokes, covered, on 100% power (high) for 7 to 9 minutes or till a leaf pulls out easily. For butter sauce, in a 1-cup measure cook butter or margarine and dillweed, tarragon, oregano, or chervil on high about 1 minute or till melted. Stir in the 1 tablespoon lemon juice. Serve as above.

Artichokes with Sour Cream Sauce: Prepare as above, *except* chill cooked artichokes thoroughly. For sauce, omit butter or margarine and the 1 tablespoon lemon juice. Reduce dillweed, tarragon, oregano, or chervil to ⅛ *teaspoon.* Combine ½ cup dairy *sour cream,* 1½ teaspoons *milk,* ½ teaspoon *Dijon-style mustard,* the herb, and dash *onion powder.* Cover and chill the sauce at least 2 hours before serving with chilled artichokes.

*__Note:__ To eat artichokes, pull off one leaf at a time and dip the base of the leaf into the sauce. Turn the leaf upside down and draw it through your teeth, scraping off only the tender flesh at the base of the leaf. Discard the remainder of the leaf. Continue removing leaves until the fuzzy choke appears. Remove the choke by scooping it out with a spoon. Discard the choke. If you have trouble getting the choke out with a spoon, try loosening it with a grapefruit knife and then pulling it out with the spoon. Eat the remaining heart with a fork, dipping each piece into the sauce.

Using kitchen scissors, cut 1 inch from top of artichoke, then cut off tips of sharp leaves.

Artichokes au Gratin

If you like, make this creamy vegetable dish ahead and chill. To heat, just pop the dish into a 350° oven for 25 to 35 minutes or till it's bubbly.

   1   **9-ounce package frozen artichoke hearts**
   1   **tablespooon grated Parmesan cheese**
   1   **tablespoon fine dry bread crumbs**
   ¼   **teaspoon paprika**
   1   **teaspoon margarine *or* butter, softened**
   1   **cup sliced fresh mushrooms**
   1   **tablespoon margarine *or* butter**
   1   **tablespoon all-purpose flour**
   1   **teaspoon Dijon-style mustard**
   ⅛   **teaspoon dried marjoram *or* thyme, crushed**
   ⅔   **cup milk**   Oven 350°

Cook artichokes according to package directions; drain. Combine Parmesan cheese, dry bread crumbs, and paprika; stir in the 1 teaspoon softened margarine or butter. Set aside.

For sauce, in a medium saucepan cook mushrooms in the 1 tablespoon margarine over medium-high heat about 3 minutes or till almost tender. Stir in flour, mustard, marjoram, ⅛ teaspoon *salt,* and dash *pepper.* Add milk all at once. Cook and stir till bubbly. Stir in artichoke hearts. Transfer to a 1-quart casserole. Sprinkle crumb mixture over vegetables. Bake in a 350° oven about 20 minutes or till bubbly. Makes 3 servings.

Microwave directions: Cook artichokes according to package microwave directions. Prepare crumb mixture as above. For sauce, in a 1-quart casserole micro-cook mushrooms and the 1 tablespoon margarine, covered, on 100% power (high) 1½ to 2 minutes or till almost tender; stir once. Add flour, mustard, marjoram, ⅛ teaspoon *salt,* and dash *pepper.* Stir in milk. Cook, uncovered, on high 2½ to 3½ minutes or till bubbly; stir *every* 30 seconds. Stir in artichokes. Cook on high 1 minute more or till heated through. Sprinkle with crumb mixture.

Note: To make 6 servings, double the ingredients and prepare as above, *except* use a *large* saucepan. Transfer to a *1½-quart* casserole. Bake for 25 to 35 minutes. *Or,* in the microwave oven, use a *2-quart* casserole and micro-cook mushroom mixture on high for *2½ to 3* minutes. Cook the sauce on high for *4 to 6* minutes. Bake for 25 to 35 minutes.

Asparagus Dijon

   1½ **pounds asparagus spears *or* two 10-ounce packages frozen asparagus spears**
   ⅓   **cup whipping cream**
   1   **hard-cooked egg, finely chopped**
   2   **tablespoons mayonnaise *or* salad dressing**
   1   **green onion, sliced**
   1   **tablespoon Dijon-style mustard**

Snap off and discard woody bases from fresh asparagus. If desired, scrape off scales. Cook, covered, in a small amount of boiling water for 8 to 10 minutes or till crisp-tender. (*Or,* cook frozen asparagus according to the package directions.) Drain; keep warm.

For sauce, in a mixing bowl beat whipping cream just till stiff peaks form. Fold in chopped egg, mayonnaise or salad dressing, onion, and mustard. Spoon sauce atop asparagus. Serve immediately. Makes 6 servings.

Microwave directions: In a 10x6x2-inch baking dish micro-cook fresh asparagus and 2 tablespoons *water,* covered with vented plastic wrap, on 100% power (high) for 9 to 11 minutes or till crisp-tender, separating and rearranging once. (*Or,* cook frozen asparagus according to package microwave directions.) Drain. Prepare the sauce as above.

Starting at the base and working toward the tip, bend the spear several times until it breaks easily.

Sesame Asparagus

For added lemon flavor, pass lemon wedges.

¾ **pound asparagus spears or one
    10-ounce package frozen cut
    asparagus**
1 **tablespoon margarine or butter**
1 **tablespoon sesame seed**
1 **cup sliced fresh mushrooms**
1 **teaspoon lemon juice**
¼ **teaspoon sesame oil (optional)**

Snap off and discard woody bases from fresh asparagus. If desired, scrape off scales. Cut into 1-inch pieces. Cook, covered, in a small amount of boiling water for 6 to 8 minutes or till crisp-tender. (*Or,* cook frozen asparagus according to package directions.) Drain; remove from pan.

In the same pan melt margarine; add sesame seed. Cook and stir 2 to 3 minutes or till toasted. Add mushrooms; cook and stir till tender. Add lemon juice and, if desired, sesame oil. Add asparagus; toss to coat. Heat through. Serves 4.

Green Beans Amandine

½ **pound green beans or one 9-ounce
    package frozen cut or French-
    style green beans**
2 **tablespoons slivered almonds**
1 **tablespoon margarine or butter**
1 **teaspoon lemon juice**

Cut fresh beans into 1-inch pieces or, for French-style, into lengthwise slices. Cook, covered, in a small amount of boiling water 20 to 25 minutes for cut beans (10 to 12 minutes for French-style beans) or till crisp-tender. (*Or,* cook frozen beans according to package directions.) Drain.

Meanwhile, cook and stir almonds in margarine over medium heat till golden. Remove from heat; stir in lemon juice. Stir almond mixture into beans. Makes 3 servings.

Microwave directions: In a 1½-quart casserole micro-cook fresh beans and 2 tablespoons *water,* covered, on 100% power (high) for 13 to 15 minutes for cut beans (12 to 14 minutes for French-style) or till crisp-tender, stirring once. (*Or,* cook frozen beans according to package microwave directions.) Drain. Return to casserole; keep warm.

Meanwhile, cook almonds in margarine on the range top as above. Continue as above.

Creamy Green Bean Bake

1 **9-ounce package frozen French-
    style green beans or one
    16-ounce can French-style
    green beans**
1 **7½-ounce can semicondensed
    cream of mushroom soup**
¼ **cup dairy sour cream or plain yogurt**
1 **tablespoon diced pimiento**
¼ **of a 3-ounce can (⅓ cup)
    french-fried onions**   Oven 350°

Cook frozen beans according to package directions; drain. (*Or,* drain canned beans.) In a 1-quart casserole combine soup, sour cream, and pimiento. Stir in beans. Bake in a 350° oven 20 to 25 minutes or till bubbly. Sprinkle with onions. Bake 5 minutes more. Serves 4.

Microwave directions: Cook frozen beans according to package microwave directions; drain. (*Or,* drain canned beans.) In a 1-quart casserole combine beans, soup, sour cream, and pimiento. Micro-cook, uncovered, on 100% power (high) for 4 to 6 minutes or till bubbly; stir twice. Sprinkle with onions. Cook on high 30 seconds.

Creole-Style Green Beans

1 **9-ounce package frozen cut or
    French-style green beans, or
    one 16-ounce can cut or
    French-style green beans**
2 **tablespoons finely chopped onion**
¼ **teaspoon dried basil, crushed**
1 **tablespoon margarine or butter**
½ **cup chopped tomato**
¼ **cup diced fully cooked ham**

Cook frozen beans according to package directions; drain. (*Or,* drain canned beans.) Cook onion and basil in margarine till tender, stirring occasionally. Stir in beans, tomato, ham, and dash *pepper.* Cook, covered, 1 to 2 minutes more or till heated through. Serves 4.

Microwave directions: Cook beans according to package microwave directions; drain. (*Or,* drain canned beans.) In a 1-quart casserole micro-cook onion, basil, and margarine, covered, on 100% power (high) 1 to 2 minutes or till onion is tender, stirring once. Stir in drained beans, tomato, ham, and dash *pepper.* Cook on high 1 to 2 minutes more or till heated through.

Cheesy Bean Combo

 1 **10-ounce package frozen baby lima beans (2 cups)**
 ½ **cup chopped onion**
 1 **cup frozen cut green beans *or* whole kernel corn**
 ¼ **cup dairy sour cream *or* plain yogurt**
 1 **tablespoon all-purpose flour**
 ¼ **cup milk**
 ½ **cup shredded American cheese**

In a medium saucepan bring ½ cup *water* to boiling. Add lima beans and onion. Return to boiling; reduce heat. Cover and simmer for 7 minutes. Add green beans or corn and cook 5 minutes more. Drain; return to saucepan.

Meanwhile, in a bowl stir together sour cream and flour; stir in milk. Stir sour cream mixture and cheese into drained vegetables.* Cook and stir till thickened and bubbly, then cook and stir 1 minute more. Makes 4 or 5 servings.

Microwave directions: In a 1½-quart casserole micro-cook lima beans, onion, and ¼ cup *water,* covered, on 100% power (high) for 3 minutes. Add green beans or corn; cook, covered, on high for 6 to 7 minutes or till crisp-tender, stirring once. Drain. Combine sour cream and flour; stir in milk. Stir sour cream mixture and cheese into vegetables.* Cook, uncovered, on high for 3 minutes or till thickened and bubbly, stirring every minute. Cook 30 seconds more.

****Note:** Mixture may appear curdled till cheese is blended.

Lima Beans and Mushrooms

 1 **10-ounce package frozen baby lima beans *or* small peas, *or* one 9-ounce package frozen cut green beans**
 1 **clove garlic, minced**
 ¼ **teaspoon dried basil, crushed**
 1 **tablespoon margarine *or* butter**
 1 **cup sliced fresh mushrooms**

Cook beans or peas according to package directions. Drain; keep warm.

Meanwhile, in a small skillet cook garlic and basil in margarine or butter over medium-high heat for 30 seconds. Add mushrooms and cook for 3 to 4 minutes or till tender. Stir into cooked beans or peas. Season to taste. Makes 4 servings.

Baked Bean Quintet

 1 **cup chopped onion**
 6 **slices bacon, cut up**
 1 **clove garlic, minced**
 1 **16-ounce can lima beans, drained**
 1 **16-ounce can pork and beans with tomato sauce**
 1 **15½-ounce can red kidney beans, drained**
 1 **15-ounce can butter beans, drained**
 1 **15-ounce can garbanzo beans, drained**
 ¾ **cup catsup**
 ½ **cup molasses**
 ¼ **cup packed brown sugar**
 1 **tablespoon prepared mustard**
 1 **tablespoon Worcestershire sauce**
 1 **onion, sliced and separated into rings (optional)**   Oven 375°

In a skillet cook chopped onion, bacon, and garlic till bacon is done and onion is tender but not brown; drain. In a bowl combine onion mixture, lima beans, pork and beans, kidney beans, butter beans, garbanzo beans, catsup, molasses, brown sugar, mustard, and Worcestershire sauce.

Transfer bean mixture to a 3-quart casserole or bean pot. Bake, covered, in a 375° oven for 1 hour. If desired, garnish with onion rings. Makes 12 to 16 servings.

Microwave directions: Halve all ingredients, *except* garbanzo beans. In a 2-quart casserole micro-cook chopped onion, bacon, and garlic, covered, on 100% power (high) for 2 to 3 minutes or till bacon is done and onion is tender but not brown, stirring once. Drain. Stir in lima beans, pork and beans, kidney beans, butter beans, garbanzo beans, catsup, molasses, brown sugar, mustard, and Worcestershire sauce. Cook, covered, on high for 10 to 12 minutes or till mixture is heated through, stirring twice. If desired, garnish with onion rings. Serves 6 to 8.

Crockery-cooker directions: Use main recipe ingredient amounts and assemble as above. Transfer to a 3½- or 4-quart electric crockery cooker. Cover; cook on low-heat setting for 10 to 12 hours or on high-heat setting for 4 to 5 hours. If desired, top with onion rings.

Baked Beans

Boston often gets credit for this dish, but it was popular throughout colonial America.

  1 **pound dry navy beans *or* dry great**
      northern beans (2⅓ cups)
  ¼ **pound bacon *or* salt pork, cut up**
  1 **cup chopped onion**
  ½ **cup molasses *or* maple syrup**
  ¼ **cup packed brown sugar**
  1 **teaspoon dry mustard**
  ½ **teaspoon salt**
  ¼ **teaspoon pepper**   Oven 300°

Rinse beans. In a 4½-quart Dutch oven combine beans and 8 cups *cold water.* Bring to boiling; reduce heat. Simmer for 2 minutes. Remove from heat. Cover and let stand for 1 hour. (*Or,* skip boiling the water and soak beans overnight in a covered pan.) Drain and rinse beans.

In the same pan combine beans and 8 cups *fresh water.* Bring to boiling; reduce heat. Cover and simmer about 1¼ hours or till tender, stirring occasionally. Drain beans, reserving liquid.

In a 2½-quart casserole or bean pot combine the beans, bacon, and onion. Stir in *1 cup* of the reserved bean liquid, the molasses or maple syrup, brown sugar, dry mustard, salt, and pepper.

Bake, covered, in a 300° oven about 2½ hours or to desired consistency, stirring occasionally. If necessary, add additional reserved bean liquid. Makes 10 to 12 servings.

Vegetable Toppings

To dress up buttered, cooked vegetables, sprinkle them with toasted sesame seed; toasted chopped nuts; crumbled, cooked bacon; canned french-fried onions; slightly crushed seasoned croutons; snipped fresh herb; chopped hard-cooked egg; or sieved hard-cooked egg yolk.

Or make a crumb topping. Stir together ¼ cup seasoned fine dry bread crumbs, 1 tablespoon snipped parsley, and 1 tablespoon melted margarine or butter. Sprinkle atop 2 cups of buttered, cooked vegetables.

Shortcut Baked Beans

Easy to whip up for a potluck or picnic.

  3 **slices bacon**
  ½ **cup chopped onion**
  1 **31-ounce can pork and beans**
      in tomato sauce
  ¼ **cup catsup**
  2 **tablespoons brown sugar *or***
      molasses
  2 **teaspoons prepared mustard**
  1 **teaspoon Worcestershire**
      sauce   Oven 350°

In a skillet cook bacon till crisp. Remove bacon, reserving *1 tablespoon* of the drippings. Drain and crumble bacon. Set aside. Cook onion in reserved bacon drippings over medium heat till tender but not brown.

To bake in the oven, in a 1½-quart casserole combine onion, pork and beans, catsup, brown sugar or molasses, mustard, and Worcestershire sauce. Bake in a 350° oven about 1 hour or to desired consistency. Stir bean mixture; top with bacon. Let stand 5 minutes before serving.

To cook on top of the range, in a medium saucepan combine onion, pork and beans, catsup, brown sugar, mustard, and Worcestershire sauce. Cook over low heat about 15 minutes or to desired consistency, stirring frequently. Top with bacon. Makes 4 servings.

Microwave directions: Spoon off and discard about ⅓ *cup* juices from pork and beans. Cut up bacon and micro-cook in a 1½-quart casserole, covered with paper towels, on 100% power (high) for 3 to 4 minutes or till crisp, stirring once. Remove bacon with a slotted spoon, reserving *1 tablespoon* drippings. Drain bacon and set aside. In the casserole cook onion in reserved drippings, uncovered, on high for 2 to 2½ minutes or till tender. Stir in pork and beans, catsup, brown sugar or molasses, mustard, and Worcestershire sauce. Cook, covered, on high for 6 to 8 minutes or till heated through, stirring once. Top with bacon. Let stand 5 minutes.

Crockery-cooker directions: Double all ingredients. Cook bacon and onion as above. In a 3½- or 4-quart electric crockery cooker combine cooked onion, beans, catsup, brown sugar or molasses, mustard, and Worcestershire sauce. Cover and cook on low-heat setting for 10 to 12 hours or on high-heat setting for 4 to 5 hours. Top with crumbled bacon just before serving.

vegetables **395**

Harvard Beets

The sweet-and-sour flavor makes these bright red beets an all-time favorite.

4 medium beets *or* one 16-ounce
    can sliced *or* diced beets
2 tablespoons sugar
2 tablespoons vinegar
2 teaspoons cornstarch
1 tablespoon margarine *or* butter

In a medium saucepan cook fresh whole beets, covered, in boiling water 40 to 50 minutes or till tender. Drain, reserving ⅓ *cup* liquid. Cool slightly. Slip off skins and slice or dice. (*Or,* drain canned beets, reserving ⅓ *cup* liquid.) In a medium saucepan combine reserved liquid, sugar, vinegar, and cornstarch. Cook and stir till thickened and bubbly. Cook and stir 2 minutes more. Stir in beets and margarine. Heat through. Serves 4.

Microwave directions: Prick fresh whole beets. In a 1½-quart casserole micro-cook beets and 2 tablespoons *water,* covered, on 100% power (high) for 10 to 12 minutes or till tender, rearranging once. Drain, reserving ¼ *cup* liquid. Cool slightly. Slip off skins; slice or dice. (*Or,* drain canned beets, reserving ¼ *cup* liquid.)

In a 1½-quart casserole combine reserved liquid, sugar, vinegar, and cornstarch. Cook, uncovered, on high for 1 to 2 minutes or till thickened and bubbly, stirring every 30 seconds. Stir in beets and margarine. Cook on high for 2 to 3 minutes or till heated through.

Orange-Glazed Beets

4 medium beets *or* one 16-ounce
    can sliced beets, drained
1 tablespoon margarine *or* butter
1 tablespoon brown sugar
1 teaspoon cornstarch
¼ teaspoon finely shredded
    orange peel
¼ cup orange juice

In a saucepan cook fresh whole beets, covered, in boiling water 40 to 50 minutes or till tender; drain. Cool slightly; slip off skins and slice.

In a medium saucepan melt margarine or butter. Stir in brown sugar and cornstarch. Stir in orange peel and juice. Cook and stir till thickened and bubbly. Add sliced beets; cook and stir for 3 to 4 minutes or till heated through. Serves 4.

Broccoli Oriental

1 pound broccoli, cut up, *or*
    one 10-ounce package frozen
    cut broccoli
½ cup sliced water chestnuts
2 tablespoons margarine *or* butter
4 teaspoons soy sauce
    Dash ground red pepper

In a medium saucepan cook fresh broccoli and water chestnuts, covered, in a small amount of boiling water for 9 to 11 minutes or till crisp-tender. (*Or,* cook frozen broccoli and water chestnuts according to broccoli package directions.) Drain; transfer to a bowl. Keep warm.

In the same saucepan melt margarine or butter. Stir in soy sauce and red pepper. Heat through. Pour over broccoli. Serves 3.

Golden Broccoli Bake

1½ pounds broccoli, cut up (6 cups),
    or one 16-ounce package frozen
    cut broccoli
1 7½-ounce can semicondensed
    cream of mushroom soup
¼ cup shredded American cheese
2 tablespoons milk
1 tablespoon mayonnaise *or*
    salad dressing
1 tablespoon chopped pimiento
2 tablespoons crushed
    cheese crackers   Oven 350°

Cook fresh broccoli, covered, in a small amount of boiling water for 9 to 11 minutes or till crisp-tender. (*Or,* cook frozen broccoli according to package directions.) Drain. Transfer to a 1½-quart casserole. Combine soup, cheese, milk, mayonnaise, and pimiento. Stir into broccoli. Top with crushed crackers. Bake in a 350° oven about 30 minutes or till heated through. Serves 6.

Microwave directions: In a 1½-quart casserole micro-cook fresh broccoli and 2 tablespoons *water,* covered, on 100% power (high) for 9 to 12 minutes or till crisp-tender, stirring once. (*Or,* cook frozen broccoli according to package microwave directions.) Drain. Combine soup, cheese, milk, mayonnaise, and pimiento. Stir into broccoli. Top with crushed crackers. Cook, uncovered, on high for 3 to 5 minutes or till heated through, giving dish a half-turn once.

Curried Brussels Sprouts

¾ **pound brussels sprouts *or* one
10-ounce package frozen
brussels sprouts**
1 **cup sliced fresh mushrooms**
¼ **teaspoon curry powder**
2 **tablespoons margarine *or* butter**
2 **teaspoons all-purpose flour**
½ **teaspoon instant chicken bouillon
granules**
2 **tablespoons chopped peanuts**

Halve large fresh brussels sprouts. Cook, covered, in a small amount of boiling water 10 to 12 minutes or till crisp-tender. Drain. (*Or,* cook frozen sprouts according to package directions. Drain. Halve large sprouts.) Cook mushrooms and curry powder in margarine 3 to 4 minutes or till tender. Stir in flour and bouillon granules. Add ½ cup *water.* Cook and stir till bubbly. Stir in sprouts; heat through. Top with nuts. Serves 4.

Microwave directions: Halve large fresh brussels sprouts. In a 1½-quart casserole micro-cook fresh brussels sprouts and 2 tablespoons *water,* covered, on 100% power (high) for 4 to 6 minutes or till crisp-tender, stirring once. Drain. (*Or,* cook frozen sprouts according to package microwave directions. Drain. Halve any large sprouts.) Set aside. In the same casserole cook mushrooms and curry powder in margarine, uncovered, on high 2 to 3 minutes or till tender, stirring once. Stir in flour and bouillon granules. Stir in ¼ cup *water.* Cook, uncovered, on high 1 to 3 minutes or till thickened and bubbly, stirring every 30 seconds. Stir in sprouts. Cook on high 30 to 60 seconds more or till hot. Top with nuts.

Easy Herbed Vegetables

To fix up frozen vegetables, cook ¼ cup chopped onion and ¼ teaspoon dried thyme, oregano, basil, marjoram, or rosemary, crushed, or dillweed in 1 tablespoon margarine or butter till onion is tender. Cook one 9- or 10-ounce package (about 2 cups) frozen vegetable according to package directions. Drain. Add onion mixture; toss.

Creamy Brussels Sprouts

Mustard adds a mild but distinctive flavor to the sour cream sauce.

¾ **pound brussels sprouts *or* one
10-ounce package frozen
brussels sprouts**
¼ **cup chopped onion**
1 **tablespoon margarine *or* butter**
½ **cup milk**
¼ **cup dairy sour cream *or* plain yogurt**
2 **teaspoons all-purpose flour**
½ **teaspoon Dijon-style, brown, *or*
horseradish mustard**
⅛ **teaspoon salt**

Halve large fresh brussels sprouts. In a medium saucepan cook fresh sprouts, covered, in a small amount of boiling water for 10 to 12 minutes or till crisp-tender. Drain and remove from pan. (*Or,* cook frozen sprouts according to package directions; drain and remove from pan. Halve any large sprouts.)

In the same saucepan cook onion in margarine or butter till tender. In a bowl combine milk, sour cream or yogurt, flour, mustard, and salt. Add to saucepan. Cook and stir till thickened and bubbly. Stir in brussels sprouts; heat through. Makes 4 servings.

Microwave directions: Halve large fresh brussels sprouts. In a 1½-quart casserole micro-cook fresh brussels sprouts and 2 tablespoons *water,* covered, on 100% power (high) for 4 to 6 minutes or till crisp-tender, stirring once. Drain; remove from casserole. (*Or,* cook frozen brussels sprouts according to package microwave directions; drain and remove from casserole. Halve large sprouts.)

In the same casserole cook onion in margarine or butter, uncovered, on high for 2 to 3 minutes or till tender, stirring once. In a bowl combine milk, sour cream or yogurt, flour, mustard, and salt. Stir into onion mixture. Cook, uncovered, on high for 1½ to 3 minutes or till thickened and bubbly, stirring every 30 seconds. Stir in brussels sprouts. Cook on high for 30 to 60 seconds or till heated through.

Pennsylvania Red Cabbage

Serve this crisp, tangy side dish with baked fish or pot roast.

> 2 tablespoons brown sugar
> 2 tablespoons vinegar
> 1 tablespoon cooking oil
> ¼ teaspoon caraway seed
> 2 cups shredded red *or* green cabbage
> ¾ cup coarsely chopped apple

In a large skillet stir together brown sugar, vinegar, oil, caraway seed, 2 tablespoons *water*, ¼ teaspoon *salt*, and dash *pepper*. Cook for 2 to 3 minutes or till hot, stirring occasionally. Stir in cabbage and apple. Cook, covered, over medium-low heat for 10 to 12 minutes or till crisp-tender, stirring occasionally. Serves 3 or 4.

Microwave directions: In a 1-quart casserole stir together *1 tablespoon* brown sugar, *1 tablespoon* vinegar, 1 tablespoon *water*, *1 teaspoon* cooking oil, *⅛ teaspoon* caraway seed, ⅛ teaspoon *salt*, and dash *pepper*. Micro-cook, uncovered, on 100% power (high) for 1 to 2 minutes or till sugar dissolves, stirring once. Stir in cabbage and apple. Cook, covered, on high for 3 to 5 minutes or till crisp-tender, stirring twice.

Pecan-Cabbage Toss

> 4 cups coarsely shredded cabbage
> ½ cup shredded carrot
> ¼ cup sliced green onion
> 1 tablespoon margarine *or* butter, melted
> 1 teaspoon Dijon-style mustard
> ¼ cup chopped pecans, toasted

In a large saucepan combine cabbage, carrot, onion, 2 tablespoons *water*, ⅛ teaspoon *salt*, and ⅛ teaspoon *pepper*. Toss to mix. Cook, covered, over medium heat for 5 to 7 minutes or till crisp-tender, stirring once. Drain. Combine margarine and mustard. Stir in pecans. Pour over cabbage mixture; toss. Season to taste. Serves 4.

Microwave directions: In a 1½-quart casserole micro-cook cabbage, carrot, onion, 2 tablespoons *water*, ⅛ teaspoon *salt*, and ⅛ teaspoon *pepper*, covered, on 100% power (high) for 5 to 7 minutes or till vegetables are crisp-tender, stirring once. Drain. Combine margarine and mustard. Stir in pecans. Pour over cabbage mixture; toss to mix. Season to taste.

Brown-Sugar-Glazed Carrots

> ¾ pound small *or* medium carrots, parsnips, *or* turnips, peeled
> 1 tablespoon margarine *or* butter
> 1 tablespoon brown sugar

Cut carrots or parsnips in half both crosswise and lengthwise. (*Or,* cut turnips into ½-inch cubes.) In a medium saucepan cook carrots or parsnips, covered, in a small amount of boiling water for 7 to 9 minutes (10 to 12 minutes for turnips) or till crisp-tender. Drain vegetables; remove from pan.

In the same saucepan combine margarine or butter, brown sugar, and dash *salt*. Stir over medium heat till combined. Add carrots, parsnips, or turnips. Cook, uncovered, about 2 minutes or till glazed, stirring frequently. Season to taste with pepper. Makes 4 servings.

Sweet-and-Sour Carrots

> 3 cups sliced carrots *or* frozen crinkle-cut carrots
> 4 green onions, cut into ½-inch pieces
> ¼ cup unsweetened pineapple juice
> 2 tablespoons honey
> 2 tablespoons margarine *or* butter
> 1 tablespoon vinegar
> 1 teaspoon cornstarch
> 1 teaspoon soy sauce

In a medium saucepan cook fresh carrots, covered, in a small amount of boiling water for 7 to 9 minutes or till crisp-tender. (*Or,* cook frozen carrots according to package directions.) Drain; remove from pan. In the same saucepan combine onions, juice, honey, margarine, vinegar, cornstarch, and soy sauce. Cook and stir till bubbly. Add carrots. Cook and stir till heated through. Makes 4 servings.

Microwave directions: In a 1½-quart casserole micro-cook fresh carrots and 2 tablespoons *water*, covered, on 100% power (high) for 7 to 10 minutes or till crisp-tender. (*Or,* cook frozen carrots according to package microwave directions.) Drain; remove from casserole. In the same casserole combine onions, pineapple juice, honey, margarine, vinegar, cornstarch, and soy sauce. Cook, covered, on high for 2 to 3 minutes or till bubbly, stirring every 30 seconds. Stir in carrots. Cook about 1 minute more or till hot.

Carrots in Almond Sauce

¾ **pound baby carrots *or* medium carrots, sliced into 1-inch pieces**
2 **tablespoons margarine *or* butter**
¼ **cup sliced almonds**
¼ **cup sliced green onion**
½ **teaspoon cornstarch**
¼ **teaspoon instant chicken bouillon granules**
¼ **teaspoon dried dillweed**

In a medium saucepan cook carrots, covered, in a small amount of boiling water for 15 to 20 minutes or till crisp-tender. Drain; remove from pan.

In the same pan melt margarine. Add almonds and onion. Cook and stir over medium heat for 3 to 5 minutes or till almonds are golden and onion is tender. Stir in cornstarch. Add bouillon granules, dillweed, ¼ cup *water,* and dash *pepper.* Cook and stir till thickened and bubbly. Stir in carrots; heat through. Makes 4 servings.

Cauliflower in Cheese Sauce

1 **1-pound head cauliflower, broken into flowerets (2 cups)**
1 **tablespoon margarine *or* butter**
1 **tablespoon all-purpose flour**
½ **cup milk**
½ **cup shredded American cheese**
1 **4-ounce can sliced mushrooms, drained**

In a saucepan cook cauliflower, covered, in a small amount of boiling water for 8 to 10 minutes or till crisp-tender. Drain; remove from pan.

In the same pan melt margarine. Stir in flour and dash *pepper.* Add milk all at once. Cook and stir till bubbly. Stir in cheese till melted. Add cauliflower and mushrooms; heat through. Serves 4.

Microwave directions: In a 1½-quart casserole micro-cook cauliflower and 2 tablespoons *water,* covered, on 100% power (high) for 7 to 10 minutes or till crisp-tender; stir once. Drain; remove from casserole. In the same casserole cook margarine on high for 35 to 40 seconds or till melted. Stir in flour and dash *pepper.* Stir in milk. Cook, uncovered, on high 3 to 5 minutes or till thickened and bubbly, stirring every minute till sauce starts to thicken, then every 30 seconds. Cook on high 30 seconds more. Stir in cheese till melted. Add cauliflower and mushrooms. Cook on high 1 minute more.

Nutty Cauliflower

The pecans and garlic butter subtly flavor the sweet pepper and cauliflower.

1 **1-pound head cauliflower, broken into flowerets (2 cups)**
½ **medium green *or* sweet red pepper, cut into bite-size strips**
1 **clove garlic, minced**
1 **tablespoon margarine *or* butter**
¼ **cup broken pecans, toasted**

Cook cauliflower, covered, in a small amount of boiling water for 8 to 10 minutes or till crisp-tender. Drain; transfer to a serving bowl.

Meanwhile, in a medium skillet cook green pepper and garlic in margarine till tender. Pour over cauliflower; toss. Stir in pecans. Serves 4.

Microwave directions: In a 1-quart casserole micro-cook garlic and margarine, uncovered, on 100% power (high) for 30 to 40 seconds or till margarine is melted. Add *uncooked* cauliflower and green pepper. Cook, covered, on high for 6 to 8 minutes or till vegetables are crisp-tender, stirring once. Stir in pecans.

Creamy Curried Corn

In a medium saucepan combine 2 cups cut fresh *corn or* one 10-ounce package frozen whole kernel *corn,* ¼ cup chopped *onion,* ¼ cup chopped green *or* sweet red *pepper,* ½ teaspoon *instant chicken bouillon granules,* ½ teaspoon *curry powder,* and dash *pepper.* Stir in ¼ cup *water.*

Bring to boiling; reduce heat. Cover and simmer for 5 to 7 minutes or till corn is crisp-tender. *Do not drain.* Stir in one 3-ounce package *cream cheese,* cubed. Stir over low heat till melted. If necessary, stir in 1 to 2 tablespoons milk to make of desired consistency. Makes 4 servings.

Microwave directions: In a 1-quart casserole combine corn, onion, green or red pepper, bouillon granules, curry powder, and pepper. Add 1 tablespoon *water.* Micro-cook, covered, on 100% power (high) for 4 to 8 minutes or till corn is crisp-tender. *Do not drain.* Stir in cream cheese. Cook, covered, on high for 1 minute; stir to melt cheese. If necessary, stir in 1 to 2 tablespoons milk to make of desired consistency.

Creamy Creole Corn: Prepare as above, *except* omit curry powder. Add ⅛ teaspoon ground *red pepper* with the corn. Stir in ⅔ cup chopped *tomato* after the cream cheese melts.

Corn on the Cob

Remove the husks from fresh ears of *corn;* scrub with a stiff brush to remove silks. Rinse. Cook, covered, in a small amount of lightly salted boiling water (*or,* uncovered, in enough boiling water to cover) for 5 to 7 minutes or till tender. If desired, serve with margarine or butter.

Microwave directions: Husk, scrub, and rinse corn as above. Wrap each ear in waxed paper; place on paper towels in the microwave. Micro-cook on 100% power (high) 3 to 5 minutes for 1 ear, 5 to 7 minutes for 2 ears, or 9 to 12 minutes for 4 ears.

Oven directions: Husk, scrub, and rinse corn as above. Pat corn dry. Place *each* ear on a piece of heavy foil; spread with ½ tablespoon *margarine or butter.* Wrap corn securely. Bake in a 450° oven about 30 minutes or till tender.

Grill directions: Husk, scrub, and rinse corn as above. Pat corn dry. Place *each* ear on a piece of heavy foil; spread with ½ tablespoon *margarine or butter.* Wrap corn securely. Grill corn on an uncovered grill directly over *hot* coals for 15 to 18 minutes or till tender, turning frequently. (*Or,* in a covered grill arrange *hot* coals around a drip pan. Place corn on grill rack over drip pan but not over coals. Lower grill hood. Grill 20 to 25 minutes or till tender.)

Scalloped Corn

¼ cup finely chopped onion
¼ cup chopped green *or* sweet red
    pepper
2 tablespoons margarine *or* butter
1 beaten egg
½ cup milk
½ cup coarsely crushed saltine
    crackers *or* rich round crackers
1 8¾-ounce can cream-style corn
1 7-ounce can whole kernel
    corn, drained   Oven 350°

Cook onion and sweet pepper in *1 tablespoon* of the margarine till tender. Combine egg, milk, ⅓ *cup* of the crushed crackers, and dash *pepper.* Stir in onion mixture and corn. Pour into a greased 1-quart casserole. Melt remaining margarine; toss with remaining crumbs. Sprinkle crumb mixture atop corn mixture. Bake in a 350° oven about 35 minutes or till a knife inserted near the center comes out clean. Makes 4 servings.

Eggplant Parmigiana

Team this with baked chicken or broiled fish.

1 small eggplant (¾ pound)
1 beaten egg
¼ cup all-purpose flour
2 tablespoons cooking oil
⅓ cup grated Parmesan cheese
1 cup spaghetti sauce
1 cup shredded mozzarella
    cheese   Oven 400°

Peel eggplant and cut crosswise into ½-inch-thick slices. Dip eggplant into egg, then into flour, turning to coat both sides. In a large skillet cook eggplant, *half* at a time, in hot oil for 4 to 6 minutes or till golden, turning once. (If necessary, add additional oil.) Drain on paper towels.

To bake in the oven, place eggplant slices in a single layer in a 12x7½x2-inch baking dish. (If necessary, cut slices to fit.) Sprinkle with Parmesan. Top with spaghetti sauce and mozzarella. Bake in a 400° oven 10 to 12 minutes or till hot.

To heat in the skillet, wipe skillet with paper towels and return eggplant slices. Sprinkle with Parmesan. Top with spaghetti sauce and cheese. Cook, covered, over medium-low heat for 5 to 7 minutes or till heated through. Serves 4.

Grilling Frozen Vegetables

When you're grilling your main dish, try grilling your vegetables, too, for an easy no-mess side dish.

Fold an 18x36-inch piece of heavy foil in half to make an 18-inch square. Bring up the sides to make a pouch, using your fist to form corners. Place the contents of one 10-ounce package frozen vegetables in the pouch. Season to taste with margarine or butter and salt and pepper. Bring two opposite sides of foil together. Leaving space for steam to build, fold edges to seal securely. Seal ends. Grill directly over *medium-hot* coals about 25 minutes for peas or other small vegetables (about 30 minutes for larger vegetables) or till vegetables are tender, turning often.

Kohlrabi with Honey Butter

Kohlrabi is a member of the cabbage family and is similar in flavor and texture to a turnip.

- 4 **small kohlrabies (about 1 pound), peeled and cut into ¼-inch-thick julienne strips (3 cups)**
- 1 **medium carrot, cut into ⅛-inch-thick julienne strips (½ cup)**
- ¼ **teaspoon finely shredded lemon peel**
- 1 **tablespoon lemon juice**
- 1 **tablespoon snipped chives or parsley**
- 2 **teaspoons honey**
- ⅛ **teaspoon pepper**
- 1 **tablespoon margarine or butter**

In a medium saucepan cook kohlrabi and carrot, covered, in a small amount of boiling water for 6 to 8 minutes or till crisp-tender. Drain.

In a bowl combine lemon peel, lemon juice, chives or parsley, honey, and pepper. Pour over hot kohlrabi and carrot; add margarine or butter. Toss to coat. Makes 4 servings.

Microwave directions: In a 1½-quart casserole micro-cook kohlrabi, carrot, and 1 tablespoon *water,* covered, on 100% power (high) for 7 to 9 minutes or till crisp-tender, stirring once. Drain. In a bowl combine lemon peel, lemon juice, chives or parsley, honey, and pepper. Pour over hot kohlrabi and carrot; add margarine or butter. Toss to coat.

Using a sharp knife, pull strips of kohlrabi peel from top to bottom to remove woody fibers.

Herb-Buttered Mushrooms

These basil-and-sherry-flavored mushrooms are delicious with broiled steaks or pork chops.

- 1 **pound fresh mushrooms**
- ¼ **cup chopped onion**
- 2 **cloves garlic, minced**
- 2 **tablespoons margarine or butter**
- 2 **tablespoons dry sherry**
- 1 **tablespoon snipped basil or 1 teaspoon dried basil, crushed**
- ¼ **teaspoon lemon-pepper seasoning or cracked black pepper**

Halve mushrooms (quarter any large mushrooms). In a large skillet cook mushrooms, onion, and garlic in margarine or butter over medium-high heat till mushrooms are tender, stirring occasionally. Stir in sherry, basil, and lemon-pepper seasoning or pepper. Cook for 2 to 3 minutes more or till heated through. Serves 4.

Microwave directions: Halve mushrooms (quarter any large mushrooms). In a 2-quart casserole micro-cook mushrooms, onion, garlic, and *1 tablespoon* of the margarine or butter, covered, on 100% power (high) for 6 to 8 minutes or till mushrooms are tender, stirring twice. Drain. Stir in remaining margarine, sherry, basil, and lemon-pepper seasoning or pepper. Cook, uncovered, on high for 1 to 1½ minutes more or till heated through, stirring once.

Smothered Okra

In a large skillet cook ½ cup chopped *onion;* ½ cup chopped *green pepper;* and 2 cloves *garlic,* minced, in 2 tablespoons *margarine or butter* about 5 minutes or till tender. Stir in 2 cups sliced *okra or* one 10-ounce package frozen cut *okra,* thawed; 2 cups chopped, peeled *tomatoes;* ½ teaspoon *salt;* ⅛ teaspoon *pepper;* and, if desired, ⅛ teaspoon ground *red pepper.* Bring to boiling; reduce heat. Cover and simmer for 20 to 30 minutes for fresh okra (15 minutes for thawed okra) or till okra is very tender. If desired, sprinkle with crumbled, crisp-cooked bacon. Serves 4.

Fried Onion Rings

Keep the fried rings warm in a 300° oven while you're frying the remaining batches.

- **¾ cup all-purpose flour**
- **⅔ cup milk**
- **1 egg**
- **1 tablespoon cooking oil**
   Shortening *or* cooking oil for deep-fat frying
- **4 medium mild yellow *or* white onions, sliced ¼ inch thick**   Oven 300°

In a bowl combine flour, milk, egg, the 1 tablespoon oil, and ¼ teaspoon *salt.* Beat with a rotary beater just till smooth.

In a large skillet heat 1 inch of shortening or oil to 375°. Separate onions into rings. Using a fork, dip onion rings into batter; drain off excess batter. Fry onion rings, a few at a time, in a single layer in hot oil 2 to 3 minutes or till golden, stirring once or twice with a fork to separate rings. Remove from oil; drain on paper towels. Serves 4 to 6.

Parsnip Puff

- **1 pound parsnips, peeled and sliced ½ inch thick (about 3 cups)**
- **¾ cup thinly sliced carrot**
- **¼ cup chopped onion**
- **2 tablespoons margarine *or* butter**
- **⅛ teaspoon ground nutmeg**
- **⅓ cup soft bread crumbs**
- **2 slightly beaten eggs**   Oven 375°

Cook parsnips, carrot, and onion, covered, in a small amount of boiling water for 15 to 18 minutes or till very tender. Drain. Add margarine, nutmeg, ½ teaspoon *salt,* and ¼ teaspoon *pepper.* Mash with a potato masher or beat with an electric mixer on low speed. Add crumbs and eggs; mash or beat till smooth. Transfer to a lightly greased 1-quart casserole. Bake, uncovered, in a 375° oven for 35 to 40 minutes or till a knife inserted near the center comes out clean. Makes 4 to 6 servings.

Turnip Puff: Prepare as above, *except* substitute *turnips,* peeled and cut into ½-inch cubes, for the parsnips. Cook turnips, carrots, and onion in boiling water for 10 to 12 minutes.

Cheese-Topped Parsnips

- **1 pound parsnips, peeled and sliced ¼ inch thick (about 3 cups)**
- **2 tablespoons margarine *or* butter**
- **2 tablespoons snipped parsley**
- **¼ cup shredded cheddar, Swiss, *or* Monterey Jack cheese (1 ounce)**

In a large skillet cook parsnips in margarine or butter over medium-high heat for 7 to 9 minutes or till crisp-tender, stirring frequently. Stir in parsley. Transfer to a serving bowl. Sprinkle with cheese. Let stand, covered, for 1 to 2 minutes or till cheese melts. Makes 4 servings.

Microwave directions: In a 1½-quart casserole micro-cook parsnips and margarine, covered, on 100% power (high) for 5 to 7 minutes or till crisp-tender, stirring once. Continue as above.

Dilled Peas and Walnuts

For variety, experiment with different herbs. After dill, try savory, basil, or mint.

- **2 cups shelled peas *or* one 10-ounce package frozen peas**
- **¼ cup chopped onion**
- **1 tablespoon margarine *or* butter**
- **½ teaspoon dried dillweed**
- **¼ teaspoon salt**
- **¼ teaspoon pepper**
- **¼ cup broken walnuts, toasted**

Cook fresh peas and onion, covered, in a small amount of boiling water for 10 to 12 minutes or till crisp-tender. (*Or,* cook frozen peas and onion according to peas package directions.) Drain well. Stir in margarine, dillweed, salt, and pepper. Heat through. Sprinkle with walnuts. Serves 4.

Microwave directions: In a 1-quart casserole micro-cook fresh peas, onion, and 2 tablespoons *water,* covered, on 100% power (high) 6 to 8 minutes or till peas are crisp-tender, stirring once. (*Or,* cook frozen peas and onion according to peas package microwave directions.) Drain well. Stir in margarine, dillweed, salt, and pepper. Cook, covered, on high 30 to 60 seconds or till heated through. Sprinkle with walnuts.

Peas and Mushrooms: Prepare as above, *except* cook 1 cup sliced fresh *mushrooms* with the peas and onion. Omit dillweed and walnuts. If desired, stir 1 tablespoon diced pimiento into cooked peas and mushrooms. Do not use microwave directions.

Swiss-Cheese-Creamed Peas

Lemon peel and cream make the Swiss cheese sauce extra special.

> 2 **cups shelled peas** *or* **one 10-ounce package frozen peas**
> ¾ **cup sliced green onion**
> 1 **tablespoon margarine** *or* **butter**
> 1 **tablespoon all-purpose flour**
> ⅛ **teaspoon salt**
> ¾ **cup light cream** *or* **milk**
> ½ **cup shredded process Swiss cheese**
> ½ **teaspoon finely shredded lemon peel**
>   **Light cream** *or* **milk (optional)**

Cook fresh peas, covered, in a small amount of boiling water for 10 to 12 minutes or till crisp-tender. (*Or,* cook frozen peas according to package directions.) Drain.

Meanwhile, for sauce, in a medium saucepan cook onion in margarine or butter till tender. Stir in flour and salt. Add cream or milk all at once. Cook and stir till thickened and bubbly. Cook and stir 1 minute more. Add cheese and lemon peel, stirring till cheese melts. Stir in drained peas. If necessary, stir in additional cream or milk to make of desired consistency. Makes 4 servings.

Microwave directions: In a 1-quart casserole micro-cook fresh peas and 2 tablespoons *water,* covered, on 100% power (high) for 6 to 8 minutes or till crisp-tender. (*Or,* cook frozen peas according to package microwave directions.) Drain. Set aside.

In a 2-cup measure cook onion and margarine or butter, covered with vented plastic wrap, on high for 2½ to 3½ minutes or till onion is tender. Stir in flour and salt. Stir in cream.

Cook, uncovered, on high for 2 to 4 minutes or till thickened and bubbly, stirring every minute till sauce starts to thicken, then every 30 seconds. Add cheese and lemon peel; stir till cheese melts. Stir in drained peas. If necessary, stir in additional cream or milk to make of desired consistency.

Mashed Potatoes

> 3 **medium potatoes (1 pound)**
> 2 **tablespoons margarine** *or* **butter**
>   **Milk**

Peel and quarter potatoes. Cook, covered, in a small amount of boiling lightly salted water for 20 to 25 minutes or till tender. Drain. Mash with a potato masher or beat with an electric mixer on low speed. Add margarine and salt and pepper to taste. Gradually beat in enough milk (2 to 4 tablespoons) to make light and fluffy. Serves 4.

Microwave directions: Peel and quarter potatoes. In a 1½-quart casserole micro-cook potatoes and 2 tablespoons *water,* covered, on 100% power (high) for 8 to 10 minutes or till tender, stirring once. Drain. Continue as above.

To make ahead: Prepare as above, *except,* after adding milk, freeze mashed potatoes in ½-cup mounds on a baking sheet. When firm, place in a plastic bag; seal. To reheat, place on a greased baking sheet. If desired, brush with melted margarine or butter. Bake in a 325° oven about 25 minutes or till heated through.

Cheese-Frosted Mashed Potatoes: Prepare as above, *except,* after adding milk, mound mashed potatoes into a greased 8x1½-inch round baking dish. Make a shallow indentation in the top. Whip ¼ cup *whipping cream;* fold in ½ cup shredded *American cheese.* Spread cheese mixture over the indentation in the potatoes. Bake in a 350° oven about 20 minutes or till lightly browned.

Duchess Potatoes: Prepare as above, *except* use *1 to 2 tablespoons* milk. After adding milk, let mashed potatoes cool slightly. With an electric mixer on low speed, beat in 1 *egg.* Using a decorating bag with a large star tip, pipe potatoes into 4 mounds on a greased 15x10x1-inch baking pan. (*Or,* spoon 4 mounds onto the baking pan.) Drizzle with 2 tablespoons melted *margarine or butter.* Bake in a 500° oven for 10 to 12 minutes or till lightly browned.

Potato Patties: Prepare as above, *except,* after adding milk, chill mashed potatoes. In a large skillet cook ⅓ cup sliced *green onion* in 1 tablespoon *margarine or butter.* Remove onion with slotted spoon, reserving drippings. Combine mashed potatoes, onion, and 1 slightly beaten *egg.* Shape into four 3½- to 4-inch-round patties. In the skillet cook patties in reserved drippings and 2 tablespoons melted *margarine or butter* over medium heat about 10 minutes or till golden brown, turning once.

Baked Potatoes and Baked Sweet Potatoes

Oven 425°

Scrub *baking potatoes or sweet potatoes* thoroughly with a brush. Pat dry. If desired, for soft skins, rub with shortening, margarine, or butter; prick potatoes with a fork. (*Or,* if desired, skip rubbing skins. Prick potatoes; wrap each in foil.)

Bake in a 425° oven for 40 to 60 minutes (in a 350° oven for 70 to 80 minutes) or till tender. When done, roll each potato gently under your hand. Cut a crisscross in each top with a knife. Press in and up on the ends of each potato.

Microwave directions: Scrub 6- to 8-ounce baking or sweet potatoes. Pat dry and prick. *Do not rub with shortening, margarine, or butter.* On a plate, arrange potatoes spoke fashion. Microcook, uncovered, on 100% power (high) till tender. Allow 5 to 7 minutes for 1 potato, 7 to 9 minutes for 2 potatoes, or 13 to 16 minutes for 4 potatoes, rearranging and turning potatoes over once. Let stand 5 minutes. Continue as above.

Grill directions: Scrub baking potatoes or sweet potatoes. Pat dry. If desired, for soft skins, rub potatoes with shortening, margarine, or butter. Prick potatoes. Wrap *each* potato in a 7-inch square of heavy foil. Grill potatoes on an uncovered grill directly over *medium-slow* coals for 1 to 2 hours or till tender. Continue as above.

Scalloped Potatoes

¼ cup chopped onion
2 tablespoons margarine *or* butter
2 tablespoons all-purpose flour
1¼ cups milk
3 medium potatoes, peeled and thinly sliced (3 cups)   Oven 350°

For sauce, cook onion in margarine till tender. Stir in flour, ½ teaspoon *salt,* and ⅛ teaspoon *pepper.* Add milk all at once. Cook and stir till thickened and bubbly. Remove from heat. Place *half* the sliced potatoes in a greased 1-quart casserole. Cover with *half* the sauce. Repeat layers.

Bake, covered, in a 350° oven for 35 minutes. Uncover; bake 30 minutes more or till potatoes are tender. Let stand 5 minutes. Serves 4.

Cheesy Scalloped Potatoes: Prepare as above, *except* reduce salt to *¼ teaspoon.* Stir ¾ cup shredded *American cheese* into thickened sauce till melted. If desired, sprinkle ¼ cup shredded American cheese over top before serving.

Twice-Baked Potatoes

4 medium baking potatoes (6 to 8 ounces each)
½ cup dairy sour cream or plain yogurt
¼ teaspoon garlic salt
Milk (optional)
2 slices American cheese, halved diagonally (optional)   Oven 425°

Bake potatoes (see recipe, left). Cut a lengthwise slice from the top of *each* baked potato; discard skin from slice and place pulp in a bowl. Gently scoop out each potato, leaving a thin shell. Add pulp to the bowl.

With an electric mixer on low speed or a potato masher, beat or mash potato pulp. Add sour cream or yogurt, garlic salt, and ⅛ teaspoon *pepper;* beat till smooth. (If necessary, stir in 1 to 2 tablespoons milk to make of desired consistency.) Season to taste. Pile mashed potato mixture into potato shells. Place in a 10x6x2-inch baking dish.

Bake in a 425° oven for 20 to 25 minutes or till lightly browned. If desired, place cheese atop potatoes. Bake for 2 to 3 minutes more or till cheese melts. Makes 4 servings.

Microwave directions: Assemble stuffed potato shells as above. In a 10x6x2-inch baking dish micro-cook stuffed shells, uncovered, on 100% power (high) 4 to 5 minutes or till heated through, rearranging potatoes once. If desired, place cheese atop potatoes. Cook, uncovered, on high 30 to 60 seconds more or till cheese melts.

Using a spoon or pastry bag with tip, fill the potato shells with the mashed potato mixture.

French Fries

Oven 300°

Use 4 medium baking *potatoes*. Peel, if desired. To prevent darkening, immerse peeled potatoes in a bowl of *cold* water till ready to cut. Cut potatoes lengthwise into ⅜-inch-wide strips. Return strips to bowl of water.

In a heavy, deep 3-quart saucepan or deep-fat fryer heat *shortening or cooking oil for deep-fat frying* to 375°. To prevent splattering, pat potatoes dry. With a spoon, carefully add potato strips, a few at a time, to hot oil. Fry for 5 to 6 minutes or till crisp and golden brown; turn once.

With a slotted spoon, carefully remove potatoes from hot oil. Drain on paper towels. If desired, sprinkle with salt or seasoned salt. Keep potatoes hot in a 300° oven while frying remaining potatoes. Makes 4 to 6 servings.

Shoestring Potatoes: Prepare as above, *except* cut potatoes into *long julienne* strips and fry for *3 to 4* minutes.

Potato Chips: Prepare as above, *except* use a food processor or rotary processor to slice potatoes into *thin* slices. (*Or,* use a potato peeler to slice into *very thin* slices.) Fry thin slices *4 to 5* minutes (very thin slices *3 to 4* minutes).

Cottage Fried Potatoes

Also called home fries, these pan-fried potato slices are seasoned with garlic and onion.

  3 **tablespoons margarine *or* butter**
  3 **medium potatoes, thinly sliced**
  ⅛ **teaspoon garlic powder**
  1 **small onion, thinly sliced and separated into rings**

In a large skillet melt margarine. (If necessary, add additional margarine during cooking.) Layer potatoes into skillet. Sprinkle with garlic powder, ¼ teaspoon *salt,* and ⅛ teaspoon *pepper.* Cook, covered, over medium heat for 8 minutes. Add onion rings. Cook, uncovered, 8 to 10 minutes more or till potatoes are tender and browned, turning frequently. Makes 4 servings.

Baked Parmesan Cottage Potatoes: Prepare as above, *except* in a greased 15x10x1-inch baking pan arrange potatoes and onion in a thin layer. Melt margarine; drizzle over potatoes. Combine garlic powder, ¼ cup grated *Parmesan cheese,* and ⅛ teaspoon *pepper.* Sprinkle over potatoes. Bake in a 450° oven about 25 minutes or till browned.

Hashed Brown Potatoes

  3 **medium potatoes (1 pound)**
  ¼ **cup finely chopped onion *or* green onion**
  3 **tablespoons margarine *or* butter**

Peel potatoes; shred to make *3 cups.* Rinse; pat dry with paper towels. Combine potatoes, onion, ¼ teaspoon *salt,* and ⅛ teaspoon *pepper.* In a large skillet melt margarine. With a pancake turner, pat potato mixture into skillet. Cook over medium-low heat about 10 minutes or till bottom is crisp. Cut into 4 wedges; turn. Cook about 10 minutes more or till golden. Makes 4 servings.

Candied Sweet Potatoes

  3 **medium sweet potatoes (about 1 pound) *or* one 18-ounce can sweet potatoes, drained**
  3 **tablespoons brown sugar**
  1 **tablespoon margarine *or* butter**   Oven 375°

Cook fresh sweet potatoes, covered, in enough boiling water to cover for 25 to 35 minutes or till tender. Drain; cool slightly. Peel; cut into ½-inch-thick slices. (*Or,* cut up canned potatoes.)

In a 1-quart casserole layer *half* of the potatoes, *half* of the brown sugar, and *half* of the margarine. Repeat layers. Bake in a 375° oven for 30 to 35 minutes or till potatoes are glazed, spooning liquid over potatoes once or twice.

If desired, sprinkle with nuts or marshmallows. Bake for 5 minutes more. Makes 4 servings.

Microwave directions: Prick whole fresh potatoes in several places. In a 1½-quart casserole micro-cook fresh potatoes and 2 tablespoons *water,* covered, on 100% power (high) for 10 to 12 minutes or till tender, turning potatoes twice. Let stand 5 minutes. Drain, peel, and cut into ½-inch-thick slices. (*Or,* cut up canned potatoes.) In a 1-quart casserole layer ingredients as above. Cook, uncovered, on high for 3 to 5 minutes or till glazed, spooning liquid over potatoes once. If desired, sprinkle nuts or marshmallows on top. Cook, uncovered, on high about 1 minute more or till marshmallows melt.

Peachy Sweet Potatoes: Prepare as above, *except* stir ⅛ teaspoon ground *ginger* into the brown sugar. Drain and cut up one 8¾-ounce can *peach* slices; layer with sweet potatoes. Do not use microwave directions.

Creamy Spinach

1 **10-ounce package frozen chopped spinach**
1 **tablespoon margarine *or* butter**
2 **teaspoons cornstarch**
1 **teaspoon instant chicken bouillon granules**
⅛ **teaspoon ground nutmeg**
¾ **cup milk**

Cook spinach according to package directions. Drain well. In a medium saucepan melt margarine or butter. Stir in cornstarch, bouillon granules, and nutmeg. Add milk all at once. Cook and stir till thickened and bubbly. Cook and stir 2 minutes more. Stir in the cooked spinach; heat through. Makes 4 servings.

Candied Acorn Squash

1 **medium acorn squash (about 1 pound)**
3 **tablespoons brown sugar**
1 **tablespoon margarine *or* butter**
1 **teaspoon lemon juice *or* water**
⅛ **teaspoon ground cinnamon *or* ground nutmeg**   Oven 350°

Cut squash crosswise into 1-inch-thick rings; discard seeds. Arrange in a single layer in an 8x8x2-inch baking dish. If desired, sprinkle with salt and pepper. Bake, covered, in a 350° oven for 40 minutes. Meanwhile, in a small saucepan combine brown sugar, margarine, lemon juice, and cinnamon or nutmeg. Cook and stir till bubbly. Spoon over squash. Bake squash, uncovered, about 10 minutes more or till tender, basting often. Makes 2 or 3 servings.

Microwave directions: Cut squash and arrange in baking dish as above. Micro-cook squash rings and 1 tablespoon *water,* covered with vented plastic wrap, on 100% power (high) for 6 to 9 minutes or till tender, turning dish and rearranging squash after 3 minutes. Drain. Set aside. In a 1-cup measure combine brown sugar, margarine, lemon juice, and cinnamon or nutmeg. Cook, uncovered, on high for 30 to 60 seconds or till bubbly. Pour over squash. Cook squash, uncovered, on high 1 minute more.

Spaghetti Squash Marinara

Marinara sauce is typically served over spaghetti, but spaghetti squash is a tasty, low-calorie, high-vitamin substitute.

1 **medium spaghetti squash (2½ to 3 pounds)**
¼ **cup chopped onion**
2 **cloves garlic, minced**
1 **tablespoon cooking oil**
1 **16-ounce can tomatoes, cut up**
1 **teaspoon dried Italian seasoning**
¼ **teaspoon salt**
¼ **teaspoon pepper**
⅛ **teaspoon fennel seed, crushed (optional)**
  Grated Parmesan cheese (optional)   Oven 350°

Halve squash lengthwise; scoop out seeds. Place squash, cut side down, in a baking dish. With a fork, prick the skin all over. Bake in a 350° oven for 30 to 40 minutes or till tender.

Meanwhile, cook onion and garlic in hot oil till onion is tender but not brown. Stir in *undrained* tomatoes, Italian seasoning, salt, pepper, and, if desired, fennel seed. Bring to boiling; reduce heat. Simmer over medium heat 10 to 15 minutes or to desired consistency, stirring often.

Using a fork, shred and separate the squash pulp into strands. Spoon tomato mixture over squash. If desired, sprinkle with grated Parmesan cheese. Makes 6 servings.

After cooking, scrape the squash from the shells to form spaghettilike strands.

Scalloped Tomatoes

3 slices bread, toasted
2 tablespoons margarine *or* butter
½ cup chopped celery
½ cup chopped onion
3 medium tomatoes, peeled and cut
   up (about 2 cups), *or* one
   16-ounce can tomatoes, cut up
1 tablespoon all-purpose flour
1 teaspoon sugar
½ teaspoon dried marjoram
   or basil, crushed   Oven 350°

Spread toast with *1 tablespoon* maragarine. Cut into cubes. Set aside. Cook celery and onion in remaining margarine till crisp-tender. Add fresh or *undrained* canned tomatoes. Bring to boiling; reduce heat. Cover; simmer 8 minutes. Combine flour, sugar, marjoram, 2 tablespoons *water,* ¼ teaspoon *salt,* and ⅛ teaspoon *pepper.* Stir into tomatoes. Cook and stir till bubbly. Stir *two-thirds* of the toast cubes into tomato mixture. Pour into a 1-quart casserole. Top tomato mixture with remaining toast cubes. If desired, sprinkle with grated Parmesan cheese. Bake in a 350° oven about 20 minutes or till bubbly. Makes 4 servings.

Crumb-Topped Tomatoes

2 large tomatoes
2 tablespoons fine dry bread crumbs
2 tablespoons grated Parmesan
   cheese
1 tablespoon margarine *or* butter,
   melted
½ teaspoon dried basil, oregano, *or*
   thyme, crushed; *or* 1 tablespoon
   snipped parsley *or* chives
⅛ teaspoon pepper
   Dash garlic *or* onion salt   Oven 375°

Remove stems and cores from tomatoes; halve tomatoes crosswise. Place, cut side up, in an 8x8x2-inch baking dish. Combine bread crumbs, Parmesan cheese, margarine or butter, herb, pepper, and garlic or onion salt. Sprinkle atop tomatoes. Bake in a 375° oven for 15 to 20 minutes or till heated through. Makes 4 servings.

Microwave directions: Prepare tomatoes and crumb mixture as above. Micro-cook, uncovered, on 100% power (high) for 2 to 3 minutes or till heated through, giving dish a half-turn once.

Lemon-Buttered Turnips

This easy lemon butter also is good on cooked broccoli, cauliflower, green beans, or asparagus.

3 medium turnips (1 pound)
2 tablespoons margarine *or* butter
1 green onion, sliced, *or*
   2 tablespoons snipped parsley
2 teaspoons lemon juice

Peel turnips and cut into ½-inch cubes or 2x½-inch sticks. Cook, covered, in a small amount of boiling water for 10 to 12 minutes or till crisp-tender. Drain. Stir in margarine or butter, sliced green onion or snipped parsley, and lemon juice. Season to taste. Makes 4 servings.

Cheddar-Zucchini Puff

1 pound zucchini *or* yellow crookneck
   squash, sliced ¼ inch thick
   (4 cups)
½ cup dairy sour cream
1 beaten egg yolk
1 tablespoon all-purpose flour
¼ teaspoon onion salt
⅛ teaspoon pepper
¾ cup shredded cheddar cheese
1 egg white
2 tablespoons seasoned fine dry
   bread crumbs
1 teaspoon margarine *or*
   butter, melted   Oven 350°

In a medium saucepan cook zucchini or yellow crookneck squash, covered, in a small amount of boiling water for 3 to 5 minutes or till tender. Drain well. Spread evenly into an 8x1½-inch round baking dish.

In a bowl combine sour cream, egg yolk, flour, onion salt, and pepper. Stir in cheese. In a bowl beat egg white till stiff peaks form (tips stand straight). Fold beaten egg white into sour cream mixture. Spoon atop squash.

In a small bowl combine bread crumbs and melted margarine or butter; sprinkle over egg mixture. Bake in a 350° oven for 20 to 25 minutes or till golden. Makes 6 servings.

Zucchini in Dill Sauce

  1 **pound zucchini**
  ¼ **cup finely chopped onion**
  2 **tablespoons water**
  1 **tablespoon margarine *or* butter**
  1 **teaspoon snipped dillweed *or***
      ¼ teaspoon dried dillweed
  ¾ **teaspoon instant chicken bouillon**
      granules
  1 **tablespoon all-purpose flour**
  ⅓ **cup dairy sour cream**

Cut zucchini into 2x¼-inch strips. In a large saucepan combine zucchini, onion, water, margarine or butter, dillweed, and bouillon granules. Bring to boiling; reduce heat. Cover and simmer 3 to 5 minutes or till zucchini is almost tender, stirring once. *Do not drain.* Remove from heat.

Stir flour into sour cream. Stir sour cream mixture into zucchini mixture. Cook and stir till thickened and bubbly. Cook and stir 1 minute more. Makes 4 or 5 servings.

Broccoli-Carrot Stir-Fry

  ⅓ **cup orange juice**
  1 **tablespoon dry sherry**
  1 **teaspoon cornstarch**
  1 **tablespoon cooking oil**
  1 **teaspoon grated gingerroot**
 1½ **cups thinly bias-sliced carrots**
  1 **cup broccoli flowerets**
  2 **tablespoons chopped walnuts**

For sauce, in a bowl stir together orange juice, dry sherry, and cornstarch. Set aside.

Preheat a wok or large skillet over high heat. Add cooking oil. (Add more cooking oil as necessary during cooking.) Stir-fry gingerroot in hot oil for 15 seconds. Add carrots and stir-fry for 1 minute. Add broccoli and stir-fry for 3 to 4 minutes or till crisp-tender. Push vegetables from the center of the wok or skillet.

Stir sauce; add to center of wok. Cook and stir till thickened and bubbly. Cook and stir for 1 minute more. Stir in vegetables and walnuts to coat. Serve immediately. Makes 4 servings.

Broccoli-Carrot Stir-Fry

Asparagus-Tomato Stir-Fry

Pictured on page 387.

- ¾ **pound asparagus spears** *or* **one 10-ounce package frozen cut asparagus**
- ¼ **cup chicken broth**
- 2 **teaspoons soy sauce**
- 1 **teaspoon cornstarch**
- 1 **tablespoon cooking oil**
- ½ **teaspoon grated gingerroot**
- 4 **green onions, bias-sliced into 1-inch lengths**
- 1½ **cups sliced fresh mushrooms**
- 2 **small tomatoes, cut into thin wedges (about 1 cup)**

Snap off and discard woody bases from fresh asparagus. If desired, scrape off scales. Bias-slice asparagus into 1-inch pieces. (*Or,* thaw and drain frozen cut asparagus.)

For sauce, combine chicken broth, soy sauce, and cornstarch. Set aside.

Preheat a wok or large skillet over high heat; add oil. Stir-fry gingerroot in hot oil for 30 seconds. Add asparagus and green onions; stir-fry for 3 minutes. Add mushrooms; stir-fry about 1 minute more or till vegetables are crisp-tender.

Push vegetables from center of wok or skillet. Stir sauce; add to center of wok or skillet. Cook and stir till thickened and bubbly. Add tomatoes; heat through. Serve at once. Serves 4.

Cauliflower-Broccoli Bake

- 1 **10-ounce package frozen cauliflower**
- 1 **10-ounce package frozen cut broccoli**
- 1 **17-ounce can cream-style corn**
- 1 **10¾-ounce can condensed cream of celery soup** *or* **cream of mushroom soup**
- 1½ **cups shredded American** *or* **process Swiss cheese (6 ounces)**
- 1 **4-ounce can sliced mushrooms, drained**
- 1 **tablespoon dried minced onion**
- ½ **teaspoon dried thyme, marjoram, or savory, crushed**
- 2 **tablespoons margarine** *or* **butter**
- 1 **cup soft bread crumbs**   Oven 375°

In a large saucepan cook cauliflower and broccoli according to package directions. Drain; remove vegetables from pan.

In the same pan combine corn, soup, cheese, mushrooms, onion, and herb. Cook and stir till bubbly. Stir in cauliflower and broccoli. Transfer mixture to a 2-quart casserole.

Melt margarine; combine with crumbs. Sprinkle crumbs atop vegetable mixture. Bake in a 375° oven for 12 to 15 minutes or till bubbly and crumbs are browned. Serves 10 to 12.

Microwave directions: In a 2-quart casserole micro-cook cauliflower, broccoli, and 2 tablespoons *water,* covered, on 100% power (high) 8 to 10 minutes or till crisp-tender, stirring once. Drain; remove vegetables from casserole. In the same casserole combine corn, soup, cheese, mushrooms, onion, and herb. Stir in cauliflower and broccoli. Cook, uncovered, on high 10 to 12 minutes or till hot, stirring twice. Melt margarine; combine with crumbs. Sprinkle crumbs atop vegetable mixture. Cook on high 30 seconds more.

Ratatouille

Ratatouille (ra-ta-TOO-ee)—a savory mixture of eggplant, summer squash, and tomatoes—is of Mediterranean origin.

- 2 **cups cubed, peeled eggplant**
- 1 **small zucchini** *or* **yellow crookneck squash, halved lengthwise and cut into ¼-inch-thick slices (1 cup)**
- 1 **7½-ounce can tomatoes, cut up**
- ½ **cup finely chopped onion**
- 2 **tablespoons olive oil** *or* **cooking oil**
- 2 **tablespoons dry white wine** *or* **water**
- ½ **teaspoon dried basil, crushed**
- ¼ **teaspoon garlic salt**
- ⅛ **teaspoon pepper**
- ½ **cup shredded Swiss cheese**

In a large skillet combine eggplant, zucchini, *undrained* tomatoes, onion, olive oil, wine, basil, garlic salt, and pepper. Bring to boiling; reduce heat. Cover; simmer about 20 minutes or till tender. Cook, uncovered, 5 to 10 minutes more or till thickened, stirring occasionally. Sprinkle with cheese. Serves 4.

Microwave directions: Do not use tomatoes, oil, and wine. In a 1½-quart casserole combine eggplant, zucchini, ½ cup *tomato sauce,* onion, basil, garlic salt, and pepper. Micro-cook, covered, on 100% power (high) for 8 to 10 minutes or till tender; stir twice. Sprinkle with cheese.

Broccoli-Onion Casserole

The cream cheese in the sauce makes this dish smooth and tangy.

 1 **10-ounce package frozen cut broccoli**
 1 **cup frozen small whole onions *or* 1 medium onion, cut into thin wedges**
 1 **tablespoon margarine *or* butter**
 1 **tablespoon all-purpose flour**
 ½ **teaspoon dried basil, oregano, *or* marjoram, crushed**
 ¼ **teaspoon salt**
 ¼ **teaspoon pepper**
 ⅔ **cup milk**
 ½ **of an 8-ounce package cream cheese, cut up**
 ¾ **cup soft bread crumbs**
 1 **tablespoon margarine *or* butter, melted**   Oven 350°

In a medium saucepan cook broccoli and whole onions or onion wedges, covered, in a small amount of boiling water for 4 minutes. Drain well, removing vegetables from saucepan.

In the same saucepan melt 1 tablespoon margarine or butter. Stir in flour, herb, salt, and pepper. Add milk all at once. Cook and stir till thickened and bubbly. Add cream cheese; stir till melted. Stir in broccoli and onions.

Transfer to a 1-quart casserole. Combine the bread crumbs and melted margarine or butter. Sprinkle over broccoli mixture. Bake in a 350° oven for 15 to 20 minutes or till heated through. Makes 4 servings.

Microwave directions: In a 1-quart casserole micro-cook broccoli, whole onions or onion wedges, and 2 tablespoons *water,* covered, on 100% power (high) for 5 to 7 minutes or till crisp-tender, stirring once. Drain, removing vegetables from casserole. In the same casserole cook 1 tablespoon margarine or butter on high for 30 to 45 seconds or till melted. Stir in flour, herb, salt, and pepper. Stir in milk all at once. Cook, uncovered, on high for 2 to 4 minutes or till thickened and bubbly, stirring every 30 seconds. Add cream cheese; stir till melted. Stir in broccoli and onions. Cook broccoli mixture on high for 2 to 3 minutes or till heated through, stirring once. Combine bread crumbs and melted margarine or butter; sprinkle over broccoli mixture. Cook on high for 30 seconds more.

Creamed Peas and New Potatoes

 1   **pound whole tiny new potatoes**
 1½ **cups shelled peas *or* loose-pack frozen peas**
 ¼   **cup chopped onion**
 1   **tablespoon margarine *or* butter**
 1   **tablespoon all-purpose flour**
 ½   **teaspoon salt**
      Dash pepper
 1   **cup milk**

Scrub potatoes; cut any large potatoes in half. If desired, remove a narrow strip of peel from around the center of each potato. In a medium saucepan cook potatoes in a small amount of boiling salted water for 10 minutes. Add peas and cook 5 to 10 minutes more or till tender. Drain.

In a medium saucepan cook onion in margarine or butter till tender but not brown. Stir in flour, salt, and pepper. Add milk all at once. Cook and stir till thickened and bubbly. Cook and stir 1 minute more. Stir in potatoes and peas; heat through. Season to taste. Serves 4.

Microwave directions: Scrub potatoes; cut any large potatoes in half. Remove a narrow strip of peel from around the center of each potato. In a 2-quart casserole combine potatoes and 2 tablespoons *water.* Micro-cook, covered, on 100% power (high) for 8 minutes. Stir in peas. Cook, covered, on high for 4 to 6 minutes more or till vegetables are tender. Drain. Continue as above.

Saucy Rutabaga-Potato Combo

 1½ **cups cubed, peeled rutabaga**
 1½ **cups cubed, peeled potato**
 ¼   **cup soft-style cream cheese with chives and onion**
 ¼   **cup milk**
 ¼   **teaspoon salt**
 2   **tablespoons snipped parsley**

Cook rutabaga and potato in a small amount of boiling water for 18 to 20 minutes or till tender. Drain, removing vegetables from saucepan.

In the same saucepan combine cream cheese, milk, and salt. Heat and stir till smooth. Add rutabaga, potato, and parsley. Toss to coat. Makes 4 servings.

Cheesy Potato-Carrot Bake

Follow the grill directions, below, when you're serving this dish with grilled meat, poultry, or fish.

  3 **cups thinly sliced potatoes**
  1 **cup shredded carrot**
  ¼ **cup sliced green onion**
  1 **tablespoon margarine *or* butter**
  ¼ **teaspoon caraway seed**
  2 **slices crumbled, crisp-cooked bacon**
  ½ **cup shredded Monterey Jack cheese (4 ounces)**   Oven 350°

In a 1½-quart casserole layer potatoes, carrot, and green onion. If desired, sprinkle with salt and pepper. Dot with margarine. Sprinkle with caraway seed. Bake, covered, in a 350° oven about 45 minutes or till potatoes are tender. Sprinkle with bacon and cheese. Bake, uncovered, 2 to 3 minutes more or till cheese melts. Serves 4.

  Grill directions: Fold an 18x36-inch piece of *heavy* foil in half to make an 18-inch square. In center of foil layer potatoes, carrot, and green onion. If desired, sprinkle with salt and pepper. Dot with margarine. Sprinkle with caraway seed. Bring up opposite edges of foil; seal tightly with a double fold, leaving a little space for steam to build. Fold in remaining sides to seal. Grill in a covered or uncovered grill directly over *medium-hot* coals about 20 minutes or till tender, turning several times. Carefully open package. Sprinkle with bacon and cheese; close package. Grill for 1 to 2 minutes more or till cheese melts.

Vegetables au Gratin

Oven 350°

In a medium saucepan melt 1 tablespoon *margarine or butter*. Stir in 2 teaspoons *all-purpose flour* and dash *pepper*. Add ⅔ cup *milk* all at once. Cook and stir till thickened and bubbly. Cook and stir 1 minute more. Stir in ¾ cup shredded *American cheese* till melted. Stir in 2 cups cooked or canned *vegetables,* drained.

  Transfer to a 1-quart casserole. Combine ¼ cup *fine dry bread crumbs* and 1 tablespoon *margarine or butter,* melted. Sprinkle over vegetables. Bake in a 350° oven for 20 to 25 minutes or till heated through. Makes 4 servings.

Squash-Corn Medley

  2 **cups shredded, peeled butternut squash, carrots, *or* parsnips**
  ¼ **cup chopped onion**
  ¼ **cup chopped green pepper**
  2 **tablespoons margarine *or* butter**
  1 **8-ounce can whole kernel corn, drained**
  ½ **cup shredded process Swiss cheese (2 ounces)**
  2 **tablespoons chopped pimiento**
  2 **tablespoons chopped pecans *or* walnuts**

In a medium saucepan cook squash, onion, and green pepper, covered, in margarine or butter for 3 to 4 minutes or till tender. Stir in corn, shredded cheese, and pimiento. Heat through. Sprinkle with chopped nuts. Makes 4 servings.

  Microwave directions: In a 1-quart casserole combine squash, onion, green pepper, and margarine or butter. Micro-cook, covered, on 100% power (high) for 4 to 6 minutes or till tender. Stir in corn, shredded cheese, and pimiento. Cook, covered, on high for 2 to 4 minutes or till heated through, stirring once. Sprinkle with chopped nuts.

Carrot-Rice Casserole

  3 **cups shredded carrots, peeled sweet potatoes, *or* parsnips**
  1 **cup water**
  ¼ **cup long grain rice**
  ¼ **cup sliced green onion**
  ½ **teaspoon salt**
  ⅛ **teaspoon pepper**
1½ **cups shredded American cheese (6 ounces)**
  ¾ **cup milk**
  1 **beaten egg**   Oven 350°

In a medium saucepan combine carrots, sweet potatoes, or parsnips; water; *uncooked* rice; green onion; salt; and pepper. Bring to boiling; reduce heat. Cover and simmer for 20 minutes. *Do not drain.* Stir in *1 cup* of the cheese, the milk, and the beaten egg.

  Transfer to a 10x6x2-inch baking dish. Bake in a 350° oven for 30 to 35 minutes or till set. Top with remaining cheese. Let stand about 5 minutes to melt cheese. Cut into squares. Serves 6.

Cheesy Artichoke Casserole

- 1 9-ounce package frozen artichoke hearts
- 2 small zucchini, halved lengthwise and sliced ¼ inch thick
- 1 cup sliced fresh mushrooms
- 1 small onion, halved and sliced
- 1 8-ounce carton dairy sour cream
- 2 tablespoons all-purpose flour
- ¼ teaspoon salt
  Dash pepper
- ¼ cup milk
- ½ cup shredded Monterey Jack cheese
- 1 package (4) refrigerated crescent rolls
- 2 tablespoons grated Parmesan cheese   Oven 375°

Cook artichoke hearts according to package directions. Drain and chop; set aside. Place zucchini, mushrooms, and onion in a steamer basket. Place basket over, but not touching, boiling water. Reduce heat. Cover and steam about 8 minutes or till crisp-tender.

Meanwhile, in a bowl mix sour cream, flour, salt, and pepper. Stir in milk. Stir in artichokes, zucchini mixture, and Monterey Jack cheese.

Transfer to a 1½-quart casserole. Unroll crescent rolls; separate into triangles. Arrange on top of casserole. Sprinkle with Parmesan cheese. Bake in a 375° oven for 20 to 25 minutes or till the top is golden and mixture is heated through. Makes 5 or 6 servings.

Creamy Succotash

- 1 10-ounce package frozen succotash
- 1 tablespoon margarine or butter
- 1 tablespoon all-purpose flour
- ¾ teaspoon instant chicken bouillon granules
- ¼ teaspoon onion powder
  Dash pepper
- ½ cup milk

Cook succotash according to package directions. Drain. Stir in margarine or butter till melted. Stir in flour, bouillon granules, onion powder, and pepper. Add milk all at once. Cook and stir till thickened and bubbly. Cook and stir 1 minute more. Makes 3 or 4 servings.

Turnip-Zucchini Casserole

- 2½ cups cubed, peeled turnips
- 1½ cups zucchini cut into ½-inch slices
- 1 cup cauliflower or broccoli flowerets
- ⅓ cup chopped onion
- 1 tablespoon margarine or butter
- ¾ teaspoon dried basil, crushed
- 1 clove garlic
- 1 large tomato, seeded and chopped
- ½ cup shredded cheddar cheese

In a large skillet combine turnips, zucchini, cauliflower, onion, margarine, basil, garlic, 2 tablespoons *water,* ¼ teaspoon *salt,* and ¼ teaspoon *pepper.* Bring to boiling; reduce heat. Cover; simmer 8 to 10 minutes or till tender. Uncover; cook 2 to 3 minutes more or till liquid is evaporated. Stir in tomato; heat through. Remove from heat. Top with cheese. Cover; let stand 1 to 2 minutes or till cheese melts. Makes 6 servings.

Spinach-Green-Bean Casserole

- 1 10-ounce package frozen chopped spinach
- 1 9-ounce package frozen French-style green beans
- ¾ cup chopped onion
- 1 clove garlic, minced
- 1 tablespoon margarine or butter
- 1 tablespoon all-purpose flour
- ⅛ teaspoon ground nutmeg
- ¾ cup milk
- ½ of a 3-ounce package cream cheese
- ½ cup soft bread crumbs
- 2 tablespoons grated Parmesan cheese
- 1 tablespoon margarine or butter, melted   Oven 350°

Thaw spinach and beans; drain well. Cook onion and garlic in 1 tablespoon margarine till tender. Stir in flour, nutmeg, ½ teaspoon *salt,* and dash *pepper.* Add milk. Cook and stir till bubbly. Stir in cream cheese till melted. Stir in spinach and beans. Transfer to a 1-quart casserole. Bake, covered, in a 350° oven for 30 minutes; stir.

Meanwhile, combine bread crumbs, Parmesan cheese, and the melted margarine. Sprinkle crumbs over casserole. Bake, uncovered, 10 to 15 minutes more or till heated through. Serves 4.

Garden-Vegetable Stir-Fry

1½ teaspoons cornstarch
 2 tablespoons soy sauce
 1 tablespoon dry sherry *or*
      orange juice
 2 teaspoons sugar
     Dash pepper
 1 cup green beans bias-sliced into
      1-inch pieces
1½ cups cauliflower cut into ½-inch
      flowerets
 1 tablespoon cooking oil
 1 medium onion, cut into thin wedges
 ½ cup thinly bias-sliced carrot
 1 cup zucchini cut into ¼-inch slices
     Tomato wedges (optional)

For sauce, combine cornstarch and 2 table-spoons *cold water*. Stir in soy sauce, sherry or orange juice, sugar, and pepper. Set aside.

In a medium saucepan cook green beans, covered, in boiling salted water for 2 minutes. Add cauliflower. Return to boiling; reduce heat. Cover and simmer 1 minute more. Drain well.

Preheat a wok or large skillet over high heat; add cooking oil. Stir-fry onion and carrot in hot oil for 2 minutes. Remove from wok or skillet. Add beans, cauliflower, and zucchini; stir-fry 3 to 4 minutes or till vegetables are crisp-tender. Push vegetables from center of wok or skillet.

Stir sauce and pour into center of wok. Cook and stir till thickened and bubbly. Return all vegetables to wok or skillet. Stir vegetables into sauce. Cook and stir 1 minute more. If desired, garnish with tomato wedges. Makes 4 servings.

Green Pepper Boats

 2 medium green peppers
 3 slices bacon, chopped
 ½ cup shredded carrot
 ¼ cup chopped onion
 1 cup corn bread stuffing mix
 3 tablespoons water
 ¼ cup shredded Swiss
      cheese (1 ounce)   Oven 350°

Cut a thin slice from the top of each green pepper. Cut in half lengthwise and remove seeds. In a saucepan cook pepper halves in boiling salted water for 5 minutes. Invert and drain peppers on paper towels.

For stuffing, in a medium saucepan cook bacon, carrot, and onion over medium heat till onion is tender and bacon is crisp. Drain. Stir in stuffing mix and water. Stir in cheese. Spoon stuffing into prepared peppers. Place in a shallow baking dish. Cover loosely. Bake in a 350° oven about 20 minutes or till peppers are tender and stuffing is heated through. Makes 4 servings.

Acorn Squash Boats: Prepare as above, *except* substitute 2 small *acorn squash* (12 to 16 ounces each) for the peppers. Halve squash; remove seeds. Place squash, cut side down, in a shallow baking dish. Bake in a 350° oven 30 minutes. Turn cut side up. Meanwhile, prepare stuffing as above. Spoon stuffing into squash. Cover and bake about 20 minutes more.

Zucchini Boats: Prepare as above, *except* substitute 2 medium *zucchini* for the peppers. Halve zucchini lengthwise. Scoop out pulp, leaving ¼-inch-thick shells. Discard pulp. Place zucchini halves, cut side down, in a large skillet. Add ½ cup *water*. Bring to boiling; reduce heat. Cover and simmer for 5 minutes. Drain on paper towels. Meanwhile, prepare stuffing as above. Spoon stuffing into zucchini. Cover; bake as above.

Cooking Vegetables

Fresh vegetables: Use the charts on the next few pages for range-top, oven, or microwave cooking. Keep in mind, though, that cooking and steaming times for fresh vegetables may vary depending on the ripeness.

Except for the acorn squash and artichoke entries, the amounts given yield enough cooked vegetables for four servings. (The acorn squash and artichoke amounts will yield two servings.) To steam vegetables that have a steaming option, place them in a steamer basket and position over, but not touching, boiling water. Cover and reduce heat. Steam for the time specified in the chart.

Frozen vegetables: Cook according to package directions for range-top or microwave cooking.

Canned vegetables: Heat the vegetables in their own liquid till heated through. If desired, drain.

Cooking Fresh Vegetables

Vegetable and Amount	Preparation	Range-Top and Oven Directions	Microwave Directions
Artichokes Two 10-ounce	Wash; trim stems. Cut off 1 inch from tops and snip off sharp leaf tips. Brush cut edges with lemon juice.	Cook, covered, in a large amount of boiling salted water 20 to 30 minutes or till a leaf pulls out easily. (Or, steam 20 to 25 minutes.) Invert to drain.	Place in a casserole with 2 tablespoons water. Micro-cook, covered, on 100% power (high) for 7 to 9 minutes or till a leaf pulls out easily, rearranging once. Invert to drain.
Asparagus 1 pound	Wash; scrape off scales. Break off woody bases where spears snap easily. Leave spears whole or cut spears into 1-inch pieces.	Cook, covered, in a small amount of boiling salted water for 10 to 15 minutes for spears (7 to 9 minutes for pieces) or till tender. (Or, steam spears or pieces 5 to 8 minutes.)	Place in a baking dish or casserole with 2 tablespoons water. Micro-cook spears or pieces, covered, on 100% power (high) for 7 to 10 minutes or till crisp-tender, rearranging or stirring once.
Beans, green or wax ¾ pound	Wash; remove ends and strings. Leave whole or cut into 1-inch pieces. For French-style beans, slice lengthwise.	Cook, covered, in a small amount of boiling salted water for 20 to 25 minutes for whole or cut beans (10 to 15 minutes for French-style beans) or till crisp-tender. (Or, steam whole, cut, or French-style beans for 18 to 22 minutes.)	Place in a casserole with 2 tablespoons water. Micro-cook, covered, on 100% power (high) for 13 to 15 minutes for whole or cut beans (12 to 14 minutes for French-style beans) or till tender, stirring once.
Beets 1 pound	For whole beets, cut off all but 1 inch of stems and roots; wash. Do not peel. (For micro-cooking, prick the skins of whole beets.) Or, peel beets; cube or slice.	Cook, covered, in boiling salted water for 40 to 50 minutes for whole beets (about 20 minutes for cubed or sliced beets) or till crisp-tender. Slip skins off whole beets.	Place in a casserole with 2 tablespoons water. Micro-cook whole, cubed, or sliced beets, covered, on 100% power (high) for 9 to 12 minutes or till crisp-tender, rearranging or stirring once. Slip skins off whole beets.
Broccoli ¾ pound	Wash; remove outer leaves and tough parts of stalks. Cut length-wise into spears or cut into ½-inch flowerets.	Cook, covered, in a small amount of boiling salted water 8 to 12 minutes or till crisp-tender. (Or, steam for 8 to 12 minutes.)	Place in a baking dish with 2 tablespoons water. Micro-cook, covered, on 100% power (high) 4 to 7 minutes or till crisp-tender, rearranging or stirring once.
Brussels sprouts ¾ pound	Trim stems and remove any wilted outer leaves; wash. Cut large sprouts in half lengthwise.	Cook, covered, in a small amount of boiling salted water 10 to 12 minutes or till crisp-tender. (Or, steam for 10 to 15 minutes.)	Place in a casserole with 2 tablespoons water. Micro-cook, covered, on 100% power (high) for 4 to 6 minutes or till crisp-tender.

Cooking Fresh Vegetables (Continued)

Vegetable and Amount	Preparation	Range-Top and Oven Directions	Microwave Directions
Cabbage Half of a 1- to 1¼-pound head	Remove wilted outer leaves; wash. Cut into 4 wedges or cut into 1-inch pieces.	Cook, uncovered, in a small amount of boiling water 2 minutes. Cover; cook 6 to 8 minutes for wedges (3 to 5 minutes for pieces) or till crisp-tender. (*Or*, steam wedges 10 to 12 minutes.)	Place in a baking dish or casserole with 2 tablespoons water. Micro-cook, covered, on 100% power (high) for 9 to 11 minutes for wedges (4 to 6 minutes for pieces) or till crisp-tender.
Carrots 1 pound	Wash, trim, and peel or scrub. Cut into ¼-inch-thick slices or julienne strips.	Cook, covered, in small amount of salted water 7 to 9 minutes for slices (5 to 7 minutes for julienne strips) or till crisp-tender. (*Or*, steam slices 8 to 10 minutes or strips 6 to 8 minutes.)	Place in a casserole with 2 tablespoons water. Micro-cook, covered, on 100% power (high) 7 to 10 minutes for slices (5 to 7 minutes for julienne strips) or till crisp-tender.
Cauliflower One 1½-pound head	Wash; remove leaves and woody stem. Leave whole or break into flowerets.	Cook, covered, in a small amount of boiling salted water for 10 to 15 minutes for head (8 to 10 minutes for flowerets) or till tender. (*Or*, steam head or flowerets for 8 to 12 minutes.)	Place in a casserole with 2 tablespoons water. Micro-cook, covered, on 100% power (high) 9 to 11 minutes for head (7 to 10 minutes for flowerets) or till tender, stirring once.
Celery 5 stalks	Remove leaves; wash stalks. Cut into ½-inch slices.	Cook, covered, in a small amount of boiling salted water for 6 to 9 minutes or till tender. (*Or*, steam for 7 to 10 minutes.)	Place in a casserole with 2 tablespoons water. Micro-cook, covered, on 100% power (high) for 6 to 10 minutes or till tender, stirring once.
Kohlrabi 1 pound	Cut off leaves; wash. Peel; chop or cut into julienne strips.	Cook, covered, in a small amount of boiling salted water for 6 to 8 minutes or till tender.	Place in a casserole with 2 tablespoons water. Micro-cook, covered, on 100% power (high) for 6 to 8 minutes or till tender.
Mushrooms ½ pound	Rinse gently in cold water; pat dry. Leave whole, slice, or chop.	Cook in 2 tablespoons hot margarine or butter over medium-high heat for 6 to 8 minutes for whole (4 to 5 minutes for sliced or chopped), stirring often. (*Or*, steam whole or sliced for 5 to 7 minutes.)	Place in a casserole with 2 tablespoons margarine or butter. Micro-cook, covered, on 100% power (high) 4 to 5 minutes for whole (3 to 4 minutes for sliced or chopped) or till tender, stirring once.

Cooking Fresh Vegetables (Continued)

Vegetable and Amount	Preparation	Range-Top and Oven Directions	Microwave Directions
Okra ½ pound	Wash; cut off stems.	Cook, covered, in a small amount of boiling salted water for 8 to 15 minutes or till tender.	Place in a casserole with 2 tablespoons water. Micro-cook, covered, on 100% power (high) for 4 to 6 minutes or till tender, stir-ring once.
Onions 1 large (1 cup chopped)	Peel and chop.	Cook, covered, in 2 tablespoons margarine or butter over medium-high heat till tender but not brown, stirring often.	Place in a casserole with 2 tablespoons water, margarine, or butter. Micro-cook, covered, on 100% power (high) for 3 to 4 minutes or till tender, stirring once.
Parsnips ¾ pound	Wash, trim, and peel or scrub. Cut into ¼-inch-thick slices.	Cook, covered, in a small amount of boiling salted water for 7 to 9 minutes or till tender. (Or, steam for 8 to 10 minutes.)	Place in a casserole with 2 tablespoons water. Micro-cook, covered, on 100% power (high) for 4 to 6 minutes or till tender, stir-ring once.
Pea pods ½ pound	Remove tips and strings; wash.	Cook, covered, in a small amount of boiling salted water for 2 to 4 minutes or till crisp-tender. (Or, steam for 2 to 4 minutes.)	Place in a casserole with 2 tablespoons water. Micro-cook, covered, on 100% power (high) for 3 to 5 minutes or till crisp-tender.
Peas, green 2 pounds	Shell and wash.	Cook, covered, in a small amount of boiling salted water for 10 to 12 minutes or till tender. (Or, steam for 12 to 15 minutes.)	Place in a casserole with 2 tablespoons water. Micro-cook, covered, on 100% power (high) for 6 to 8 minutes or till tender, stir-ring once.
Potatoes 1 pound	Wash and peel. Remove any sprouts or green areas. Cut into quarters or cube.	Cook, covered, in a small amount of boiling salted water for 20 to 25 minutes or till tender. (Or, steam about 20 minutes.)	Place in a casserole with 2 tablespoons water. Micro-cook, covered, on 100% power (high) for 8 to 10 minutes or till tender, stir-ring once.
Potatoes, sweet 1 to 1½ pounds	Wash and peel. Cut off woody portions and ends. Cut into quarters or cube. (For micro-cooking, cut into quarters.)	Cook, covered, in enough boiling salted water to cover for 25 to 35 minutes or till tender.	Place in a casserole with ½ cup water. Micro-cook, covered, on 100% power (high) for 10 to 13 minutes or till tender, stirring once.

Cooking Fresh Vegetables (Continued)

Vegetable and Amount	Preparation	Range-Top and Oven Directions	Microwave Directions
Rutabagas 1 pound	Wash and peel. Cut into ½-inch cubes.	Cook, covered, in a small amount of boiling salted water for 18 to 20 minutes or till tender. (Or, steam for 18 to 20 minutes.)	Place in a casserole with 2 tablespoons water. Micro-cook, covered, on 100% power (high) for 11 to 13 minutes or till tender, stirring 3 times.
Spinach 1 pound	Wash and drain; remove stems.	Cook, covered, in a small amount of boiling salted water 3 to 5 minutes or till tender, beginning timing when steam forms. (Or, steam for 3 to 5 minutes.)	Place in a casserole with 2 tablespoons water. Micro-cook, covered, on 100% power (high) for 7 to 9 minutes or till tender, stirring once.
Squash, acorn One 1-pound	Wash, halve, and remove seeds.	Place halves, cut side down, in a baking dish. Bake in a 350° oven 30 minutes. Turn cut side up. Bake, covered, 20 to 25 minutes more or till tender.	Place squash halves, cut side down, in a baking dish with 2 tablespoons water. Micro-cook, covered, on 100% power (high) for 6 to 9 minutes or till tender, rearranging once. Let stand, covered, 5 minutes.
Squash, butternut One 1½-pound	Wash, halve lengthwise, and remove seeds.	Place halves, cut side down, in a baking dish. Bake in a 350° oven 30 minutes. Turn cut side up. Bake, covered, for 20 to 25 minutes more or till tender.	Place squash halves, cut side down, in a baking dish with 2 tablespoons water. Micro-cook, covered, on 100% power (high) for 9 to 12 minutes or till tender, rearranging once.
Squash, spaghetti One 2½- to 3-pound	Wash, halve lengthwise, and remove seeds.	Place halves, cut side down, in a baking dish. Bake in a 350° oven for 30 to 40 minutes or till tender.	Place halves, cut side down, in a baking dish with ¼ cup water. Micro-cook, covered, on 100% power (high) for 15 to 20 minutes or till tender, rearranging once.
Turnips 1 pound	Wash and peel. Cut into ½-inch cubes or julienne strips.	Cook, covered, in a small amount of boiling salted water for 10 to 12 minutes or till tender. (Or, steam for 10 to 15 minutes.)	Place in a casserole with 2 tablespoons water. Micro-cook, covered, on 100% power (high) for 12 to 14 minutes or till tender, stirring once.
Zucchini ¾ pound	Wash; do not peel. Cut off ends. Cut into ¼-inch-thick slices.	Cook, covered, in a small amount of boiling salted water for 3 to 5 minutes or till crisp-tender. (Or, steam for 4 to 6 minutes.)	Place in a casserole with 2 tablespoons water. Micro-cook, covered, on 100% power (high) 4 to 5 minutes or till tender, stirring twice.

Special Helps

Special Helps Table of Contents

Organizing Your Kitchen

A well-organized kitchen will help you cook faster and more efficiently. To make sure your kitchen is in top working order, follow these tips.

Stockpiling Staples

Keep your kitchen running smoothly by always having an ample supply of staple ingredients on hand—items such as flour, sugar, eggs, and milk. Although you shouldn't buy more than you can use in a reasonable period of time, buy enough to avoid extra trips to the grocery store.

Some ingredients, such as sugar and flour, can be bought in quantity and stored in canisters or other airtight containers for several months. Since herbs and spices lose their flavor in about a year, purchase them in small quantities. The staple ingredients you'll want to stock depend on the foods and recipes you prepare. The following list includes ingredients commonly used in recipes in this book. Use this list as a guide when compiling your own list.

All-purpose flour, sugar, brown sugar, shortening, cooking oil, baking powder, baking soda, cornstarch, salt, pepper, spices, herbs, vanilla, mayonnaise or salad dressing, prepared mustard, honey, vinegar, catsup, Worcestershire sauce, bottled hot pepper sauce, bouillon granules, coffee, tea, pasta, cereals, bread, eggs, meat, poultry, fish, milk, margarine or butter, cheese, salad greens, vegetables, fruits, and fruit juices.

Which Form to Buy

When buying meats, vegetables, fruits, and other perishables, choose the form—fresh, canned, dried, or frozen—that best fits your needs and storage facilities. When buying green beans, for example, choose fresh if you plan to cook them in a day or two. But if you're buying them to use at the end of the week, or just to keep on hand, buy frozen or canned. If freezer space is limited, opt for canned or dried items.

Arranging Foods and Utensils

For maximum efficiency, keep in mind where, what, and how you cook. Place food supplies and utensils as close as possible to the spot where you'll use them. Save easy-to-reach shelves and cupboards for the items you use most often. Store less frequently used items in more-out-of-the-way places.

Arrange canned goods and packaged mixes on shelves by types of food so that you can find them quickly and easily. Periodically check the expiration dates on the labels and dispose of foods past their prime. Store the newest cans or packages toward the back and move older items to the front.

Avoid storing foods near appliances that give off heat (such as stoves, refrigerators, and freezers), or in damp areas. Heat and moisture shorten the shelf life of canned and packaged foods.

Common Ingredients

Ever wonder what the difference is between all-purpose flour and self-rising flour, or between light cream and whipping cream? Wonder no more. These notes give the basics on frequently used recipe ingredients.

Flour: *All-purpose flour* is a must in every kitchen because it is used in all kinds of baking and to thicken sauces. For specialty breads or cookies, you also may want to keep *whole wheat flour, rye flour,* or other special flours on hand. Store all-purpose flour in airtight containers either at room temperature or in the freezer. Keep whole wheat and other whole-grain flours in the refrigerator or freezer because they may become rancid quickly.

Self-rising flour is an all-purpose flour that contains leavening and salt. It may be substituted for all-purpose flour in quick breads. Be sure, though, to omit the salt, baking powder, and baking soda from the recipe.

Some cooks prefer *cake flour* in angel and chiffon cakes. Because cake flour is made from a softer wheat, it produces a more delicate cake. If you choose cake flour, sift it before use.

Sugar: *Granulated sugar* is used to sweeten beverages, cereals, and many other foods. *Powdered sugar,* sometimes called *confectioners' sugar,* is crushed granulated sugar with starch added to prevent lumping. It's used in uncooked frostings and for dusting cakes and cookies. *Brown sugar* is a less-refined form of granulated sugar that gets its special flavor and moistness from the molasses that clings to the granules. *Dark brown sugar* has a stronger flavor than light brown sugar. You'll need brown sugar for baking and for some main dishes and vegetable dishes.

Other sweeteners: *Honey* is made from flower nectar by bees. It is sweeter than sugar and adds a characteristic flavor. Honey is used in baking and to sweeten many other foods. *Corn, cane, maple,* and *maple-flavored syrups* are used as toppings and in recipes.

Cooking oils and flavored oils: *Vegetable oil* or *salad oil* is light yellow with a mild flavor. It's often used in baking and for salads. It works well, too, for deep-fat frying. Vegetable oil usually is made from corn, soybeans, sunflowers, or peanuts. *Olive oil,* made from pressed olives, gives a full-bodied flavor and aroma to salad dressings. It's not suitable for deep-fat frying because it smokes easily, and its strong flavor makes it a poor choice for baking. *Nut oil* and *sesame oil* have pronounced flavors and are used in small amounts to add zest to salads or stir-fries.

Shortening: Hydrogenated vegetable shortening is made from oils such as soy or palm. The oils are processed to give the desired consistency and flavor. Shortening is commonly used in baking, but also can be used for deep-fat or shallow frying. Store at room temperature.

Leavenings: *Baking powder* and *baking soda* are used to leaven cakes, quick breads, and cookies. For yeast breads, you'll need either *active dry yeast* or *quick-rising active dry yeast.* Yeast, a microscopic plant, makes bread rise by producing carbon dioxide.

Cornstarch: Cornstarch is used to thicken sauces, puddings, and pie fillings. It gives a more translucent product than flour and has about twice the thickening power.

Tapioca: Tapioca is used to thicken pie fillings and puddings.

Margarine and butter: Margarine and butter give flavor to baked goods and shallow-fried foods. They are not suitable, however, for deep-fat frying. Many people choose margarine over butter because margarine is made from vegetable oils and has no cholesterol.

Milk: *Whole milk, low-fat milk,* and *skim milk* may be used interchangeably in cooking. They differ only in the amount of fat they contain, and in the richness of flavor they lend to foods. Whole milk contains at least 3 percent fat, low-fat milk has from ½ percent to 2 percent fat, and skim milk has less than ½ percent fat.

Milk products: Commercially cultured *buttermilk* is made by adding bacteria to skim milk. *Whipping cream* contains 30 percent to 40 percent fat. *Light cream* (half-and-half) contains 10 percent to 30 percent fat. *Dairy sour cream* is a commercially cultured light cream. *Yogurt* is fermented milk.

Nonfat dry milk is milk with both the fat and water removed. It's sold as a powder that mixes easily with water. *Evaporated milk* is milk with 60 percent of the water removed. It's sold in cans. *Sweetened condensed milk* has about half of the water of regular milk and is sweetened with sugar. It, too, is sold in cans.

Equipment Tips

Cooking is faster, less work, and more fun when you let your kitchen equipment work for you. Here's how to use your blender, food processor, and kitchen thermometers to the best advantage. You'll also find some ideas for makeshift cookware and a chart of basic kitchen tools (see opposite).

Blender

This kitchen helper trims minutes from your cooking time by blending, chopping, and pureeing foods. To make the best use of your blender, follow these guidelines.

● Cut fresh fruits and vegetables, cooked meats, fish, or seafood into ½- to 1-inch pieces before chopping them in your blender.

● Stop your blender often and check the size of the food pieces. Blenders work quickly and can easily overblend or overchop food.

● Cube and soften cream cheese before blending it with liquid ingredients.

● When blending thick mixtures, stop your blender often and use a rubber spatula to scrape the sides of the container.

● For better control of chopping fineness and to avoid overworking the motor, blend large quantities of foods in several small batches.

Food Processor

A food processor not only blends, chops, and purees, as a blender does, but it also slices and shreds. In addition, some food processors mix batters and doughs and knead bread and pastry doughs. Refer to your owner's manual to see if your model can perform these more difficult tasks. Keep these points in mind when using your food processor.

● For even slices, fit the food into the feed tube as tightly as possible. If the food pieces lean to one side, you'll get diagonal slices.

● When slicing foods with peels, place the food pieces in the feed tube so that the peel faces the center of the work bowl. That way, the blade of the slicing disk will hit the peel side first and cut through it, rather than scraping it.

● Store the sharp food processor blades and disks away from other utensils and out of the reach of small children.

Kitchen Thermometers

Meat thermometers: These thermometers tell you when a large piece of meat reaches just the right doneness. The most common type is a needle-shaped instrument with a tube of mercury in the center. For an accurate temperature reading, make sure the tip of the thermometer is touching meat and is not resting on a bone, fat, gristle, or the pan bottom.

Candy/deep-fat-frying thermometers: These thermometers have different temperature ranges from meat thermometers. Some may be used for both deep-fat frying and candy making, others are calibrated specifically for candy making.

Before making candy, always test the thermometer's accuracy in boiling water. If the thermometer registers above or below 212°, add or subtract the same difference in degrees from the temperature given in the recipe. Remember to read the thermometer at eye level. And, if you live more than 1,000 feet above sea level, decrease the temperature given in the recipe 2 degrees for each 1,000 feet of elevation.

Appliance thermometers: Use an oven thermometer to check the temperature of your oven. If your oven cooks too hot or cool, you'll need to adjust the settings you use for recipes. Use a freezer thermometer to make sure that your freezer registers below 0°.

Make-Do Cookware

If you start a recipe and discover that you don't have the recommended cooking equipment, try some of these spur-of-the-moment substitutions.

● Create a covered casserole by covering a baking dish with foil.

● Cook a pizza on a baking sheet instead of a pizza pan. Build up the crust edges to hold the filling.

● Substitute any straight-sided casserole for a soufflé dish as long as the volumes are the same.

● Sieve food through a strainer instead of using a food mill.

● Construct a double boiler by placing a metal or heat-resistant glass bowl in a saucepan. Be sure the bowl is wide enough so that its bottom doesn't touch the bottom of the pan.

● Steam vegetables without a steamer by placing them in a metal colander, then placing the colander over a saucepan of boiling water.

Basic Kitchen Equipment

The equipment needed to prepare food can be broken down into four groups: preparation and cooking utensils, range-top cookware, bakeware, and equipment for food storage. Outfit your kitchen with this basic equipment and you'll be able to make almost any recipe in this book. Purchase other less essential equipment as the need arises or when it fits your budget.

Preparation and Cooking Utensils	Range-Top Cookware	Bakeware	Food Storage Products
Set of mixing bowls	1-quart covered saucepan	Baking sheet	Assorted refrigerator dishes
Set of dry measuring cups	2-quart covered saucepan	6-ounce custard cups	Vapor- and moisture-proof containers for freezing foods
Clear glass liquid measuring cup	3-quart covered saucepan	Muffin pan	Foil
Set of measuring spoons	4- or 6-quart covered Dutch oven or kettle	9-inch pie plate	Clear plastic wrap
Wooden spoons	6- or 8-inch skillet	8x4x2-inch loaf pan or dish	Waxed paper
Rubber spatulas	10-inch skillet with cover	9x5x3-inch loaf pan or dish	Large and small plastic bags
Flexible metal spatulas	12-inch skillet	12x7½x2-inch baking dish	Paper towels
Serrated knife		13x9x2-inch baking dish or pan	Assorted canisters for storing foods
Paring knife		8x8x2-inch baking dish or pan	Juice pitcher
Utility knife		9x9x2-inch baking pan	
Chef's knife		8x1½-inch round baking pans or dishes	
Sharpening steel		9x1½-inch round baking pans	
Vegetable peeler		15x10x1-inch baking (jelly roll) pan	
Meat mallet		10-inch tube pan	
Long-handled fork		Various sizes of casserole dishes	
Long-handled spoon		Roasting pan with rack	
Ladle		Pizza pan	
Slotted spoon			
Pancake turner			
Tongs			
Kitchen scissors			
Bottle opener			
Can opener			
Corkscrew			
Rotary beater			
Grater and/or shredder			
Small and large strainers			
Colanders			
Kitchen timer			
Cutting board			
Rolling pin			
Meat thermometer			
Oven thermometer			
Wire cooling rack			

Food Safety And Storage

Keeping food safe to eat is as simple as keeping hot foods hot, cold foods cold, and all foods clean. The following pointers, and the food-storage timings on the opposite page, tell you how.

Keeping Foods Hot

● To prevent the buildup of illness-causing bacteria, cook foods thoroughly, especially meat, poultry, and dishes containing eggs. *Do not partially cook food, stop, then finish the cooking later.* Bacteria may grow before the second cooking time.

● Since bacteria grow at room temperature, discard any cooked or chilled food that has been left out longer than two hours.

● Cover leftovers while reheating to retain moisture. Be sure, too, to heat the food completely.

Keeping Foods Cold

● Keep your refrigerator at about 40° and your freezer at 0° or less. Check them both periodically with an appliance thermometer.

● Thaw meat and poultry in the refrigerator overnight. For faster thawing, place frozen packages in a watertight plastic bag under cold water. Change the water often. *Do not thaw meat on the kitchen counter.*

● Store leftovers in the refrigerator as soon as possible. *Do not let food cool on the counter.*

● When shopping, pick up perishables last. Be sure frozen foods are solid and refrigerated foods are cold. If you live more than 30 minutes from the store, you may want to stow frozen, refrigerated, and perishable foods in an ice chest for the trip home.

Keeping Foods Clean

● Since bacteria live all around us, always wash and dry your hands with clean cloths before you begin to cook.

● When working with raw meat and poultry, wash hands, counters, and utensils in hot soapy water between *each* recipe step. Bacteria on raw meat and poultry can contaminate other foods. Never put cooked meat or poultry on the same plate that held the raw food.

Shelf Storage

Store staples like flour, sugar, and canned goods in cool, dry, well-ventilated places away from sunlight. The best storage temperature is between 50° and 70°.

Preparing Foods for Storage

● *Cooked foods:* Cover and chill or freeze cooked foods and leftovers promptly. For freezing, use moisture- and vaporproof materials such as heavy foil, freezer paper, freezer bags, freezer plastic wrap, or freezer containers. Keep cooked meat or poultry away from any equipment that was used with the raw meat or poultry.

● *Fresh fruits* and *vegetables:* Store most fresh fruits and vegetables in the refrigerator crisper. Keep items such as potatoes and onions in a cool, well-ventilated place.

● *Meat, poultry,* and *fish:* Chill meat and poultry in the store's packaging. For longer storage, remove the packaging. Wrap tightly in moisture- and vaporproof material—such as heavy foil, freezer paper, freezer bags, freezer plastic wrap, or freezer containers—and freeze. Tightly wrap fresh fish in moisture- and vaporproof material before refrigerating or freezing.

● *Eggs:* Keep eggs in the covered egg carton in the refrigerator. Chill leftover separated eggs in tightly covered containers (cover yolks with cold water). To freeze eggs, break into a bowl and stir to combine. Add 1½ teaspoons sugar or corn syrup, or ⅛ teaspoon salt, per ¼ cup whole eggs (two whole) or ¼ cup yolks (four yolks). Egg whites require no additions. Place eggs in freezer containers or bags and freeze. Thaw in the refrigerator; use within 24 hours. Allow for any added sugar, corn syrup, or salt when using in recipes.

● *Dairy products:* Store cheese, milk, cream, sour cream, yogurt, margarine, and butter tightly covered in the refrigerator. Chill strong-flavored cheese in a tightly covered glass container.

Meat and Poultry Hot Line

For answers to your questions about meat and poultry handling or safety, call the U.S. Department of Agriculture's Meat and Poultry Hotline. The toll-free number is 800/535-4555. (In the Washington, D.C., area, call 447-3333.) Home economists at the hot line take calls from 10 a.m. to 4 p.m. eastern time (the hours usually are extended around Thanksgiving).

Maximum Food-Storage Times

Refer to the information opposite for directions on preparing foods for storage. Then use this chart to see how long you should keep the food in the refrigerator or freezer.

When freezing foods, remember to label the packages with the type of food, quantity or weight, and the date frozen. Place the most recently frozen food to the back.

Food	Refrigerator (36° to 40°)	Freezer (0° or lower)
Fresh Meats		
Roasts (beef)	3 to 5 days	6 to 12 months
Roasts (lamb)	3 to 5 days	6 to 9 months
Roasts (pork, veal)	3 to 5 days	4 to 8 months
Steaks (beef)	3 to 5 days	6 to 12 months
Chops (lamb)	3 to 5 days	6 to 9 months
Chops (pork)	3 to 5 days	3 to 4 months
Ground and stew meats	1 to 2 days	3 to 4 months
Sausage (pork)	1 to 2 days	1 to 2 months
Cooked Meats		
Cooked meat and meat dishes	3 to 4 days	2 to 3 months
Processed Meats		
Bacon	7 days	1 month
Frankfurters	7 days*	1 to 2 months
Ham (whole)	7 days	1 to 2 months
Luncheon meats	3 to 5 days*	1 to 2 months
Sausage (smoked)	7 days	1 to 2 months
Fresh Poultry		
Chicken and turkey (whole)	1 to 2 days	12 months
Chicken pieces	1 to 2 days	9 months
Turkey pieces	1 to 2 days	6 months
Duck and goose (whole)	1 to 2 days	6 months
Cooked Poultry		
Covered with broth, gravy	1 to 2 days	6 months
Pieces not in broth or gravy	3 to 4 days	1 month
Cooked poultry dishes	3 to 4 days	4 to 6 months
Fish		
Fat fish	1 to 2 days	4 months
Lean fish	1 to 2 days	8 months
Eggs		
Whites	2 to 4 days	9 to 12 months
Whole eggs	4 weeks	9 to 12 months
Yolks	2 to 3 days	9 to 12 months
Cheese		
Cottage cheese	5 days	Not recommended
Hard cheese	3 to 4 months	6 months
Soft cheese	2 weeks	4 months
Ice cream		1 to 3 months
Margarine and butter	7 days	3 to 6 months

*Once a vacuum-sealed package is opened. Unopened vacuum-sealed packages can be stored in refrigerator for 2 weeks.

Shopping Tips

Take a few minutes to apply these shopping tips and you'll find that your trips through the grocery store aisles are quicker and cheaper.

Making a List

A grocery list speeds your shopping, ensures that you buy everything you need, and limits impulse buying. Here's how to put a list together.
- Make your list as you plan your weekly menus. Be sure to include how much of each food you need, as well as the can and package sizes.
- Hang a tablet or small notebook in your kitchen for keeping an ongoing shopping list. Jot down items as you use them up and ask the rest of your family to do the same.
- If you're running low on any staples, add them to your list.
- Check newspaper food ads. You may be able to plan several meals around the weekly specials.
- Divide your shopping list into categories, arranging the categories in the order that they appear in your store. Include categories such as produce, dairy products, meat, canned foods, frozen foods, breads and cereals, beverages, baking products, paper products, health and beauty aids, cleaning supplies, and miscellany.
- Besides foods and amounts needed, list advertised specials (note the prices and brands of the specials).
- Mark any items for which you have coupons, and have your coupons ready before you go to the store. When you get to the store, however, compare prices to see if the special or the coupon brand is really the best buy.
- Once you're in the store, stick to your shopping list and avoid impulse purchases. But keep your eyes open for unadvertised specials. Plan to buy fruits and vegetables in season and other needed items on sale at lower-than-usual prices.

Timesaving Strategies

- Save time by doing all your shopping in one store. To save money, plan your menus around the specials in that store.
- Shop only at markets you are familiar with so you don't waste time searching for items. Save trips to new stores for days when you have some time to browse.

- Try to avoid rush hour at the grocery store (from 5 p.m. to 6:30 p.m. on weekdays and anytime on weekends). Shop when the aisles aren't jammed with carts and people and when the checkout lines are short.

Read the Label

The labels on most foods provide a wealth of information. Government regulations stipulate that ingredients in packaged foods be listed on the label in descending order by weight. You'll find the chemical additives used to preserve freshness or to improve flavor or color listed at the end of the ingredients section.

Many products also carry nutrition information on their labels. The U.S. Food and Drug Administration requires that nutrition information be given on foods with added nutrients or those advertised as having special nutritional qualities. The nutrition information must list the serving size and number of servings, along with the amount of protein, fat, and carbohydrates per serving. The percentage of the U.S. Recommended Daily Allowances for protein and seven other vitamins and minerals met by each serving also must be shown. The quantities of sodium, potassium, cholesterol, and saturated and polyunsaturated fats may be listed, too.

Meal Planning

Spending a little time each week planning meals can save you lots of time and money at the grocery store, as well as help you put more nutritious meals on the table faster.

Seven Steps to Nutritious Meals

Paying attention to these seven steps, as well as the Basic Food Groups (see page 428), makes planning delicious, attractive, and nutritious meals easy.

● Select a main dish from the Meat Group, one that includes beef, pork, poultry, or fish.

● Add a bread or cereal, say rolls or a rice pilaf, to complement the main dish.

● Choose a hot or cold vegetable.

● Select a fruit or vegetable salad to complement the main dish.

● Choose a beverage. This is an excellent place for a serving from the Milk Group.

● If desired, add a dessert. Fruits and milk-based desserts, such as pudding, can help you round out your meals and help you meet your quotas from the Basic Food Groups.

● After you've met the first four food group requirements, add extras, if you like, from the fifth group, fats and sweets. Remember to include these foods only in moderation.

As you plan your menus, think of all the meals for the day. Make sure that the foods you choose tally up to include the recommended amounts from each of the Basic Food Groups. If you have an egg for breakfast, for example, you need only one serving of meat, fish, or poultry the rest of the day. Keep in mind, too, that some dishes, such as casseroles and salads, combine foods from two or more food groups.

Meals That Sparkle

Keep meals exciting by planning menus with a variety of colors, forms, flavors, textures, and temperatures. Proper seasoning also is important. To jazz up your meals:

● Choose dishes whose colors complement each other. Avoid choosing foods of the same color. A meal of chicken, fried potatoes, and baked beans, for example, would be pretty drab. Dress up plain foods with sprigs of parsley, bright red radishes, ripe olives, or spiced crab apples.

● Vary the sizes and shapes of the foods you serve. Leave some foods whole and serve others sliced, cubed, mashed, or cut into strips.

● Provide a combination of mild and not-so-mild flavors. For example, serve sweet-and-sour Oriental dishes with rice and chili with corn bread.

● Serve crisp foods with soft ones. Good foods for adding crunch include breadsticks, croutons, and lettuce.

● Plan a balance of hot and cold foods.

Solving the Time Bind

When you're short on time, depend on fast-cooking or convenience foods. Choose one of the recipes in this book marked "fast," then plan the rest of the meal around it. Make the other courses simple. Lettuce with bottled dressing and ice cream or sherbet with prepared toppings are tasty time-savers.

Save the more-involved menus for days when you have the time to spare and feel like cooking. You also may want to set aside a day to prepare several meals at one time to have on hand for future busy days.

Write It Down

Equipped with recipes and newspaper food ads, sit down and write menus for several days or a week at a time. At the same time, write your shopping list. Be sure to list everything you need to make the recipes you've selected, including staples you're low on and nonfood items. The more planning you do, the less time you'll spend at the grocery store and over the stove.

Finally, take note of the menus your family especially likes. Then save your menu plans and use them again. Once you've collected several family favorites, your meal planning will be easier and faster.

The Basics of Good Eating

Good nutrition and good health go hand in hand. Once you understand the basics of good nutrition, you're on your way to planning healthful meals.

Nutrition Know-How

The easiest path to good nutrition is to eat a variety of foods. When planning meals, use the Basic Food Groups as a guide. The chart on page 428 tells which foods are in each group and how much of each you should eat.

The Role of Nutrients

Food nourishes us by supplying our bodies with protein, carbohydrates, fats, vitamins, and minerals. Most foods contain several of these nutrients, but no single food contains them all. That's why a healthy diet includes a variety of foods.

Protein

Protein helps build, maintain, and repair our bodies. It also helps produce antibodies that ward off disease, and it contributes to the production of enzymes and hormones that regulate many of our bodies' processes.

Protein is found in foods of both animal and plant origin. The proteins found in meat, poultry, fish, eggs, cheese, and milk are complete proteins. They can supply the body's need for protein all on their own. Plant forms of protein include legumes, rice, wheat, corn, and nuts. They're called incomplete proteins because, on their own, they can't meet our protein needs. But when two or more plant proteins are combined in one dish or are eaten together in a meal, they add up to a complete protein. Dried beans and rice, for example, combine to equal a complete protein in Meatless Red Beans and Rice (see recipe, page 161).

Carbohydrates

Carbohydrates provide the body with fuel and are an important part of our diets, especially in starch form. Starches exist in potatoes, breads, cereals, and pasta. Besides existing in starch form, carbohydrates also are available as sugars. Sugars are found in fresh fruits, vegetables, some dairy products, honey, corn syrup, brown sugar, molasses, and table sugar.

Fats

Fats provide a highly concentrated form of energy, and, despite all the bad publicity they receive, some fat is essential to our diets. Fats carry certain vitamins through our bodies and help cushion body organs. They give a staying power to our meals that keeps us from getting hungry too soon after we eat.

Vitamins

Various vitamins are needed to spur chemical reactions in our bodies. This list describes some of the vitamins essential for good health:

Vitamin A promotes growth and the development of normal skin. It also contributes to bone and tooth development, aids our night vision, and helps prevent eye disease.

Vitamin C (ascorbic acid) aids the formation of healthy bones, teeth, gums, and blood vessels. It also plays a part in the creation of collagen, which binds our bodies' cells together.

Thiamine helps regulate our appetite and digestion, helps us maintain a healthy nervous system, and helps our bodies use carbohydrates.

Riboflavin helps us use food efficiently, promotes healthy skin, helps our cells use oxygen, and aids our vision in bright light.

Niacin helps convert sugars to energy and keeps our skin, digestive tract, and nervous system healthy.

Minerals

Even though minerals are found in very small amounts in foods, they're vital to good health.

Calcium gives strength and structure to our bones and rigidity and permanence to our teeth. It helps make sure, too, that our blood clots and our muscles contract.

Iron is an important part of every red blood cell. It plays a role in carrying oxygen through the body and also helps the body resist infections.

Sodium helps regulate the passage of water and nutrients in and out of our cells. It also helps us maintain the proper balance of body fluids.

Potassium helps steady our body-fluid balance, too. It also regulates muscular contractions.

Other Dietary Concerns

In addition to nutrients, food supplies our bodies with water, fiber, and cholesterol. Each of these plays an important role in our general health.

Water bathes our tissues, lubricates our joints, carries nutrients, takes waste away from our cells, and is built into the structure of many chemical compounds in our bodies. Water is part of all the foods we eat, but our bodies also need several additional glasses per day.

Fiber is the portion of food that can't be broken down (digested) in the body. Fiber passes through our intestines and carries waste products with it. To add fiber to your diet, eat plenty of fresh fruits and vegetables, grains, and whole-grain foods.

Cholesterol is essential to life, but most of us consume more than we need. Cholesterol makes up cell membranes, builds nerve sheaths, and provides raw materials for hormones. In adults, the liver and other organs manufacture enough cholesterol to meet most needs. Cholesterol usually is most concentrated in foods with saturated fats, such as meats, butters, and egg yolks.

Calories and Dieting

Just as your car needs gas to run, your body needs calories to function. A calorie is the measurement of the energy supplied by food. A certain number of calories is necessary for body functions and activity. This number depends on your body size, sex, and stage of life. When more calories are consumed than the body needs, the excess is stored as body fat. Each pound of excess body fat is produced from 3,500 extra calories.

Ideally the number of calories we consume should match the number we burn. But that's rarely the case. If you're among the many who carry a few extra pounds, try to lose weight through a combination of exercise and dieting. Once you reach your ideal weight, continued exercise will help you maintain it.

Nutrition Analysis

At the beginning of each chapter, you'll find a chart listing the nutrition analyses for all of the recipes in that chapter. The numbers listed are per serving. Protein, carbohydrates, and fat are given in grams; cholesterol, sodium, and potassium are in milligrams. The analyses also give you the percentages of the U.S. Recommended Daily Allowances for vitamin A, vitamin C, thiamine, riboflavin, niacin, calcium, and iron provided by each recipe serving.

Here are some tips to help you best use our nutrition-analysis charts.
● The title, plus the page number, of each recipe is listed alphabetically on the left side of each chart.
● The number of servings in each recipe is listed in the first column.
● If a recipe lists ingredients for a stuffing, sauce, topping, or dressing within the recipe, the analysis for these ingredients was included in the nutrition analysis for the recipe. To calculate the nutrition analyses for cakes, frostings, and fillings, see the tip on page 75.
● Suggested garnishes and optional ingredients were omitted from the nutrition analyses.
● For ingredients of variable weight ("3- to 3½-pound beef chuck pot roast") or for recipes with a serving range ("Makes 4 to 6 servings"), calculations were made using the first figure.
● When a recipe gives options for an ingredient ("1 pound ground beef, pork, or turkey"), calculations were made using the first option.
● The nutrition analyses for recipes calling for fresh ingredients were calculated using measurements for the raw fruits, vegetables, and meats.

The Basic Food Groups

	Foods in Group	Number of Daily Servings	Serving Size	Major Nutrients
Vegetables and Fruits	All vegetables and fruits (fresh, canned, frozen, or dried) and their juices.	4 servings. (For vitamin C, use citrus fruits, melons, berries, tomatoes, or dark green vegetables daily. For vitamin A, use dark green or deep yellow vegetables.)	½ cup or a typical portion such as 1 medium orange, ½ of a medium grapefruit, 1 medium potato, or 1 wedge of lettuce.	Carbohydrates, fiber, and vitamins A and C. Dark green vegetables are good sources of riboflavin, folacin, iron, and magnesium. Some greens contain calcium.
Breads and Cereals	All foods based on whole grains or enriched flour or meal. Includes breads, biscuits, muffins, waffles, pancakes, pasta, rice, and cereals.	4 servings. (For fiber, include some whole-grain bread or cereal every day.)	1 slice bread; 1 biscuit or muffin; 1 pancake or waffle; ½ to ¾ cup cooked pasta, rice, bulgur, or cereal; or 1 ounce ready-to-eat cereal.	Carbohydrates, protein, thiamine, riboflavin, niacin, B vitamins, and iron. Whole-grain products provide magnesium, fiber, and folacin.
Milk and Cheese	All types of milk, yogurt, cheese, ice milk, ice cream, and foods prepared with milk (milk shakes, puddings, and creamed soups).	Children under 9, 2 to 3 servings. Children 9 to 12, 3 servings. Teens, 4 servings. Adults, 2 servings. Pregnant women, 3 servings. Nursing mothers, 4 servings.	1 cup milk or yogurt, 2 cups cottage cheese, 1⅓ ounces cheese, 2 ounces process cheese food or spread, ¼ cup Parmesan cheese, or 1½ cups ice cream.	Protein, calcium, riboflavin, and vitamins A, B_6, and B_{12}. When fortified, these products also provide vitamin D.
Meats, Fish, Poultry, and Beans	Beef, veal, lamb, pork, poultry, fish, shellfish, variety meats, dry beans or peas, soybeans, lentils, eggs, peanuts and other nuts, peanut butter, and seeds.	2 servings.	2 to 3 ounces lean cooked meat, poultry, or fish; 1 to 1½ cups cooked dry beans, peas, or lentils; 2 eggs; ½ to 1 cup nuts or seeds; or ¼ cup peanut butter.	Protein, phosphorus, and vitamin B_6. Foods of animal origin provide vitamin B_{12}. Meats, dry beans, and dry peas provide iron. Liver and egg yolks provide vitamin A.
Fats, Sweets, and Alcohol	All fats and oils; mayonnaise and salad dressings; all concentrated sweets; highly sugared beverages; alcoholic beverages; unenriched, refined flour products.	No serving number is recommended. In moderation, these foods can be used to round out your meals, as long as requirements from the other categories are satisfied.	No specific serving size is recommended.	These foods provide very few nutrients in proportion to the number of calories they contain. Vegetable oils provide vitamin E and essential fatty acids.

Calorie Tally

Keeping track of your daily calorie intake? Use this handy chart to find the per-serving calorie count for more than 175 foods.

A-B

ALFALFA SPROUTS, fresh; 1 cup ——— 10
APPLE; fresh; 1 medium ——— 80
APPLESAUCE, canned
   sweetened; ½ cup——— 98
   unsweetened; ½ cup ——— 53
APRICOTS
   canned, in syrup; ½ cup ———108
   fresh; 3 medium ——— 50
ASPARAGUS
   cooked, drained; 4 spears——— 15
AVOCADO, peeled; ½ avocado———170
BACON
   Canadian-style, cooked; 2 slices ——— 85
   crisp strips, medium thickness;
   3 slices———110
BANANA; 1 medium ———105
BEANS
   baked, with tomato sauce and pork,
     canned; ½ cup———155
   garbanzo, cooked, drained; ½ cup———135
   green snap, cooked, drained;
     ½ cup ——— 23
   navy, dry, cooked, drained; ½ cup———113
   red kidney, canned; ½ cup———115
BEEF, corned, canned; 3 ounces———185
BEEF CUTS, cooked
   flank steak, lean only; 3 ounces———207
   ground beef, lean; 3 ounces ———234
   ground beef, regular; 3 ounces———260
   pot roast, chuck, lean only;
     3 ounces ———196
   rib roast, lean only; 3 ounces———204
   round steak, lean only; 3 ounces———165
   sirloin steak, lean only; 3 ounces———177
BEEF LIVER, braised; 3 ounces———137
BEETS, cooked, diced; ½ cup———28

BEVERAGES
   beer; 12 ounces———150
   cola; 12 ounces ———160
   dessert wine; 3½ ounces———140
   ginger ale; 12 ounces ———125
   gin, rum, vodka (80 proof);
     1½ ounces ——— 95
   table wine, white; 3½ ounces ——— 80
BLUEBERRIES
   fresh; ½ cup——— 40
   frozen, sweetened; ½ cup ——— 93
BREADS
   bagel; 1 (3½-inch diameter)———200
   bun, frankfurter or hamburger; 1 ———119
   English muffin, plain; 1———140
   French; 1 slice (1 inch thick)———100
   pita; 1 (6½-inch diameter)———165
   raisin; 1 slice——— 65
   white; 1 slice——— 65
   whole wheat; 1 slice——— 70
BROCCOLI
   cooked, drained; 1 medium stalk——— 50
   frozen chopped, cooked, drained;
     ½ cup ——— 25
BRUSSELS SPROUTS
   cooked, drained; ½ cup——— 30
BUTTER; 1 tablespoon ———100

C

CABBAGE
   common varieties, raw, shredded;
     1 cup ——— 15
   red, raw, shredded; 1 cup ——— 20
CAKES, baked from mixes
   angel, no icing; 1/12 cake———125
   devil's food or yellow, 2 layers,
     9-inch diameter, chocolate frosting;
     1/16 cake———235
CANDIES
   caramel; 1 ounce ———115
   gumdrops; 1 ounce ———100
   hard; 1 ounce ———110
   milk-chocolate bar; 1 ounce ———145
CANTALOUPE; ½ of a 5-inch-diameter
   melon——— 95
CARROTS
   cooked, drained, sliced; ½ cup ——— 35
   raw; 1 large ——— 30
CATSUP; 1 tablespoon ——— 15
CAULIFLOWER
   cooked, drained; ½ cup——— 15
   raw, whole flowerets; 1 cup——— 25
CELERY, raw, chopped; ½ cup——— 10

CEREALS, ready to eat

bran flakes; about ¾ cup _____ 90

cornflakes; about 1¼ cups _____ 110

granola; about ⅓ cup _____ 125

wheat flakes; about 1 cup _____ 100

CHEESES

American, process; 1 ounce _____ 105

blue; 1 ounce _____ 100

Camembert; 1 ounce _____ 86

cheddar; 1 ounce _____ 115

cottage, cream-style, large curd;

1 cup _____ 235

cottage, low fat (2% fat); 1 cup _____ 205

cream cheese; 1 ounce _____ 100

cream cheese, reduced calorie; 1 ounce _____ 60

Monterey Jack; 1 ounce _____ 106

mozzarella, part skim milk; 1 ounce _____ 72

Neufchâtel; 1 ounce _____ 74

Parmesan, grated; 1 tablespoon _____ 25

ricotta, part skim milk; 1 cup _____ 340

Swiss, natural; 1 ounce _____ 105

CHERRIES

canned, in syrup, sweet;

½ cup _____ 107

canned, water pack, tart, pitted;

½ cup _____ 45

fresh, sweet, whole; 10 cherries _____ 50

CHICKEN

breast, skinned, roasted; ½ breast _____ 142

canned, with broth; 5 ounces _____ 234

dark meat, skinned, roasted; 1 cup _____ 286

light meat, skinned, roasted; 1 cup _____ 242

CHOCOLATE

bitter; 1 ounce _____ 145

semisweet; 1 ounce _____ 143

sweet plain; 1 ounce _____ 150

syrup, fudge-type; 2 tablespoons _____ 125

syrup, thin-type; 2 tablespoons _____ 85

CLAMS, canned; 3 ounces _____ 85

COCONUT, sweetened, shredded;

¼ cup _____ 118

COOKIES

chocolate chip; 1 (2¼-inch diameter) _____ 45

cream sandwich, chocolate; 1 _____ 49

fig bar; 1 _____ 53

sugar; 1 (2½-inch diameter) _____ 59

vanilla wafer; 3 (1¾-inch diameter) _____ 56

CORN

canned, cream-style; ½ cup _____ 93

canned, vacuum pack, whole kernel;

½ cup _____ 83

sweet, cooked; 1 ear (5x1¾ inches) _____ 85

CORNSTARCH; 1 tablespoon _____ 29

CORN SYRUP; 1 tablespoon _____ 59

CRABMEAT, canned; ½ cup _____ 68

CRACKERS

cheese; 1 (1-inch square) _____ 5

graham; 2 (2½-inch square) _____ 60

saltine; 2 (2-inch square) _____ 25

CREAM

half-and-half; 1 tablespoon _____ 20

whipping; 1 tablespoon _____ 50

CUCUMBER; 6 large slices _____ 5

D-G

DATES, fresh or dried, pitted; 10 _____ 230

DOUGHNUTS

cake, plain; 1 (3¼x1 inch) _____ 210

yeast; 1 (3¾x1¼ inches) _____ 235

EGG

fried; 1 large _____ 95

poached, or hard or soft cooked;

1 large _____ 80

scrambled, plain; made with

1 large egg _____ 110

white; 1 large _____ 15

yolk; 1 large _____ 65

EGGNOG; 1 cup _____ 340

EGGPLANT, cooked, diced; ½ cup _____ 13

FISH

haddock, breaded, fried; 3 ounces _____ 175

halibut, broiled; 3 ounces _____ 140

herring, pickled; 3 ounces _____ 190

salmon, broiled or baked; 3 ounces _____ 140

salmon, canned, pink; 3 ounces _____ 120

sardines, canned, in oil, drained;

3 ounces _____ 175

tuna, canned, in oil, drained;

3 ounces _____ 165

tuna, canned, in water, drained;

3 ounces _____ 135

FLOUR

all-purpose; 1 cup _____ 455

whole wheat; 1 cup _____ 400

FRANKFURTER, cooked; 1 _____ 145

GRAPEFRUIT

fresh; ½ medium _____ 40

juice, canned, sweetened; 1 cup _____ 115

juice, fresh; 1 cup _____ 95

GRAPES

green, seedless; 10 _____ 35

H-O

HAM, fully cooked, lean only;
2.4 ounces _____ 105
HONEYDEW MELON; 1/10 of a
6½-inch-diameter melon _____ 45
ICE CREAM, vanilla
ice milk; 1 cup (about 4% fat) _____ 185
regular; 1 cup (about 11% fat) _____ 270
soft serve; 1 cup _____ 223
JAM; 1 tablespoon _____ 55
JELLY; 1 tablespoon _____ 50
KALE, cooked, drained; ½ cup _____ 20
KIWI FRUIT; 1 _____ 45
KOHLRABI, cooked, drained, diced;
½ cup _____ 25
LAMB, cooked
loin chop, lean only; 2.3 ounces _____ 140
roast leg, lean only; 2.6 ounces _____ 140
LEMONADE, frozen concentrate,
sweetened, reconstituted; 1 cup _____ 106
LETTUCE
Boston; ¼ of a medium head _____ 5
iceberg; ¼ of a medium compact head _____ 20
LIMEADE, frozen concentrate,
sweetened, reconstituted; 1 cup _____ 100
LOBSTER, cooked; ½ cup _____ 69
LUNCHEON MEATS
bologna; 1 slice (1 ounce) _____ 90
salami, cooked; 1 slice (1 ounce) _____ 73
MAPLE SYRUP; 1 tablespoon _____ 50
MARGARINE, soft or regular;
1 tablespoon _____ 100
MARSHMALLOWS; 1 ounce _____ 90
MAYONNAISE; 1 tablespoon _____ 100
MILK
buttermilk; 1 cup _____ 100
chocolate drink (2% fat); 1 cup _____ 180
condensed, sweetened, undiluted;
1 cup _____ 980
dried nonfat, instant; 1 cup _____ 245
evaporated, skim, undiluted; 1 cup _____ 200
evaporated, whole, undiluted; 1 cup _____ 340
low fat (2% fat); 1 cup _____ 120
skim; 1 cup _____ 85
whole; 1 cup _____ 150
MOLASSES, light; 2 tablespoons _____ 85
MUFFINS
blueberry; 1 _____ 135
bran; 1 _____ 125
corn; 1 _____ 145
MUSHROOMS
canned, drained; ⅓ cup _____ 12
raw, sliced; 1 cup _____ 20

NUTS
almonds; 1 ounce _____ 165
cashews, roasted in oil; 1 ounce _____ 165
peanuts, roasted in oil, shelled;
1 ounce _____ 165
pecans; 1 ounce _____ 190
walnuts; 1 ounce _____ 170
OIL; 1 tablespoon _____ 125
OLIVES
green; 4 medium _____ 15
ripe; 3 small _____ 15
ONIONS
green, without tops; 6 small _____ 10
mature, raw, chopped; ½ cup _____ 28
ORANGES
fresh; 1 medium _____ 60
juice, canned, unsweetened;
1 cup _____ 105
juice, fresh; 1 cup _____ 110
juice, frozen concentrate,
reconstituted; 1 cup _____ 110
OYSTERS
raw; ½ cup (6 to 10 medium) _____ 80

P-S

PANCAKE; 1 (4-inch diameter) _____ 60
PEACHES
canned, in juice; ½ cup _____ 55
canned, in syrup; ½ cup _____ 95
fresh; 1 medium _____ 35
PEANUT BUTTER; 1 tablespoon _____ 95
PEA PODS, cooked, drained; ½ cup _____ 33
PEARS
canned, in juice; 2 halves _____ 63
canned, in syrup; ½ cup _____ 95
fresh; 1 medium _____ 100
PEAS, green, cooked; ½ cup _____ 63
PEPPERONI; 1 slice (⅛ inch thick) _____ 27
PEPPERS, green, sweet, chopped;
¾ cup _____ 20
PICKLES
dill; 1 medium _____ 5
sweet; 1 small _____ 20
PIES; ⅛ of a 9-inch pie
apple _____ 303
blueberry _____ 286
cherry _____ 308
lemon meringue _____ 268
pumpkin _____ 240

PINEAPPLE
 canned, in juice; ½ cup _____ 75
 fresh, diced; ½ cup _____ 38
 juice, canned, unsweetened; 1 cup _____ 140

PLUMS
 canned, in juice; ½ cup _____ 73
 fresh; 1 (2-inch diameter) _____ 3

POPCORN
 plain, air-popped; 1 cup _____ 30
 plain, popped in oil; 1 cup _____ 55

PORK, cooked
 chop, loin center cut, lean only;
  2½ ounces _____ 165
 sausage, links; 3 ounces _____ 150

POTATO CHIPS; 10 medium _____ 105

POTATOES
 baked; 1 (about 8 ounces) _____ 220
 boiled; 1 (about 5 ounces) _____ 120
 mashed with milk; ½ cup _____ 80
 sweet, baked; 1 medium _____ 115

PRUNE JUICE, canned; 1 cup _____ 180

PRUNES, dried, uncooked, pitted;
 5 large _____ 115

PUDDINGS, cooked
 chocolate; ½ cup _____ 150
 vanilla; ½ cup _____ 145

PUMPKIN, canned; 1 cup _____ 85

RAISINS; 1 cup (not packed) _____ 435

RASPBERRIES
 fresh; ½ cup _____ 30
 frozen, sweetened; ½ cup _____ 128

RHUBARB
 cooked, sweetened; ½ cup _____ 140
 raw, diced; 1 cup _____ 26

RICE
 brown, cooked; ½ cup _____ 115
 white, cooked; ½ cup _____ 113
 white, quick cooking, cooked;
  ½ cup _____ 93

ROLLS
 cloverleaf; 1 (2½-inch diameter) _____ 85
 hard; 1 (3¾-inch diameter) _____ 155
 sweet; 1 medium _____ 220

SALAD DRESSINGS
 blue cheese; 1 tablespoon _____ 75
 French; 1 tablespoon _____ 85
 Italian; 1 tablespoon _____ 80
 mayonnaise; 1 tablespoon _____ 100
 mayonnaise-type; 1 tablespoon _____ 60
 Thousand Island; 1 tablespoon _____ 60

SAUERKRAUT, canned; ½ cup _____ 23
SHERBET, orange; ½ cup _____ 135
SHORTENING; 1 tablespoon _____ 115
SHRIMP, canned; 3 ounces _____ 100

SOUPS, condensed, canned
 (diluted with water unless
  specified otherwise)
 beef bouillon, broth, consommé;
  1 cup _____ 15
 chicken noodle; 1 cup _____ 75
 cream of chicken,
  diluted with milk; 1 cup _____ 190
 cream of mushroom,
  diluted with milk; 1 cup _____ 205
 tomato; 1 cup _____ 85
 tomato, diluted with milk; 1 cup _____ 160

SOUR CREAM, dairy; ½ cup _____ 248

SPINACH
 canned, drained; ½ cup _____ 25
 frozen, cooked, drained; ½ cup _____ 28
 raw, torn; 1 cup _____ 10

SQUASH
 summer, cooked, drained, sliced;
  ½ cup _____ 18
 winter, baked, cubed; ½ cup _____ 40

STRAWBERRIES
 fresh, whole; ½ cup _____ 23
 frozen, sweetened, sliced; ½ cup _____ 123

SUGARS
 brown, packed; ½ cup _____ 410
 granulated; 1 tablespoon _____ 45
 powdered; ½ cup _____ 193

T-Z

TOMATOES
 canned; ½ cup _____ 25
 fresh; 1 medium _____ 25
 juice, canned; 1 cup _____ 40
 paste, canned; 1 cup _____ 220
 sauce; 1 cup _____ 75

TURKEY
 roasted, light and dark; 1 cup _____ 240

TURNIPS, cooked, diced; ½ cup _____ 15
VEAL, cooked, cutlet; 3 ounces _____ 185

WAFFLE; 1 section
 (4½x4½x⅝ inch) _____ 140

WATERMELON; 1 wedge
 (8x4 inches) _____ 155

YOGURT
 low fat, fruit flavored;
  8 ounces _____ 230
 low fat, plain; 8 ounces _____ 145

Seasoning Guide

Use this guide to match spices and herbs with foods. For most spices and dried herbs, start with ¼ teaspoon for every 4 servings, then taste before adding more. Crush dried herbs before using. To substitute fresh for dried, use three times more of the snipped fresh herb.

Allspice: pot roasts, soups, stews, hams, vegetables, baked foods.

Anise: beef, pork, carrots, beets, cakes, cookies, pastries.

Basil: meats, poultry, fish, soups, stews, pasta, stuffings, vegetables, salads, dressings, eggs, dips, sauces.

Bay leaf: corned beef, soups, stews, pot roasts, fish, eggs, dried bean dishes, potatoes, rice, salads, gravies, marinades.

Caraway seed: meat loaves, pot roasts, soups, stews, eggs, stuffings, vegetables, salads, sauerkraut, breads, dips, sauces, spreads.

Cardamom: meats, poultry, fish, fruit salads and dressings, pastries, breads, cookies, cakes.

Celery (seed, flakes, salt): meats, poultry, soups, stews, eggs, salads, sauces, breads, stuffings, spreads, relishes.

Chervil: meats, poultry, fish, eggs, vegetables, salads, dressings.

Chili powder: meats, poultry, fish, Mexican dishes, soups, stews, eggs, cheese dishes, vegetables, spreads, French dressing, snacks.

Chives: eggs, cheese dishes, vegetables, sauces.

Cinnamon: pork, chicken, lamb, soups, fruit, fruit salads, salad dressings, breads, pies, cakes, cookies, beverages, snacks.

Cloves: pork, lamb, vegetables, relishes, pies, cakes, cookies, beverages.

Coriander: poultry, pork, curries, soups, stews, stuffings, fruit salads.

Cumin: Mexican dishes, cheese dishes, soups, stews, vegetable dips, sauces, salad dressings, snacks.

Curry powder: meats, fish, poultry, vegetables, soups, dips, cheese spreads, salads, dressings, chutneys, relishes.

Dill (weed, seed): meats, poultry, fish, seafood, stews, eggs, vegetables, salads, dressings, breads, sauces.

Fennel: meats, poultry, fish, seafood, soups, stews, vegetables, salads, dressings, pickles.

Garlic (clove, powder, salt): meats, poultry, casseroles, soups, stews, vegetables, dressings, sauces, marinades.

Ginger: Oriental dishes, meats, poultry, vegetables, cakes, cookies, pies, pickles.

Mace: veal, fish, soups, fondues, cakes, cookies.

Marjoram: meats, poultry, soups, stews, eggs, salads, sauces.

Mint: lamb, fish, poultry, vegetables, salads, fruits, sauces, marinades, desserts, beverages.

Mustard (dry, seed): corned beef, eggs, sauerkraut, macaroni salads, dressings, marinades, sauces, dips, pickles.

Nutmeg: meat loaves, meatballs, chicken, quiches, fruits, eggnog, cookies, cakes, pies.

Oregano: meats, poultry, fish, seafood, soups, stews, casseroles, eggs, vegetables, salads, breads.

Paprika: meats, fish, soups, stews, eggs, potatoes, sauces.

Parsley: meats, fish, poultry, casseroles, soups, salads, vegetables, sauces, breads.

Pepper: meats, fish, poultry, eggs, salads, vegetables, marinades.

Poppy seed: pasta, breads, desserts.

Red pepper (ground, crushed): Mexican and Cajun dishes, eggs, dips, spreads, cream soups, French dressing.

Rosemary: meats, poultry, fish, casseroles, eggs, soups, stews, vegetables, salads, breads.

Saffron: chicken, fish, seafood, rice, breads, cakes.

Sage: meats, poultry, soups, stews, casseroles, eggs, stuffings, vegetables, sauces, gravies.

Savory: meats, poultry, fish, soups, stews, eggs, vegetables, sauces.

Sesame seed: poultry, fish, vegetables, breads, cookies.

Tarragon: meats, poultry, casseroles, fish, seafood, soups, stews, eggs, cheese dishes, vegetables, salads, dressings, sauces.

Thyme: meats, poultry, meat loaves, meatballs, fish, seafood, eggs, soups, stews, casseroles, vegetables, salads, breads, sauces.

Turmeric: poultry, fish, eggs, soups, salad dressings, sauces, relishes, pickles.

Cutting Techniques

Here's a short explanation of some often-confused cutting terms.

1. Cubing
Cut the food into strips ½ inch or more wide. Line up strips; cut crosswise to form pieces.

2. Dicing
Cut the food into strips ⅛ to ¼ inch wide. Line up and stack strips; cut crosswise to form pieces.

3. Chopping
Cut the food into irregularly sized pieces about pea size.

4. Finely Chopping
Cut the food into irregularly sized pieces smaller than peas.

5. Slicing and Bias-Slicing
To slice, cut food crosswise, making cuts perpendicular to cutting surface. To bias-slice, hold knife at a 45-degree angle to cutting surface.

6. Cutting into Julienne Strips
Cut the food into slices about 2 inches long and ¼ to ½ inch thick. Stack the slices, then cut lengthwise again to make thin, matchlike sticks.

7. Shredding
Push the food across a shredding surface to make long, narrow strips. (Or, use a food processor.) Use for most vegetables and cheeses.

8. Finely Shredding
Push the food across a fine shredding surface to make very thin strips. Use for potent seasonings such as citrus peel or for vegetables and cheeses.

9. Mincing
Cut peeled garlic cloves into tiny, irregularly shaped pieces. (Or, use a garlic press.)

10. Grating
Rub the food across a grating surface to make very fine pieces. Grate potent seasonings such as nutmeg or hard cheeses such as Parmesan.

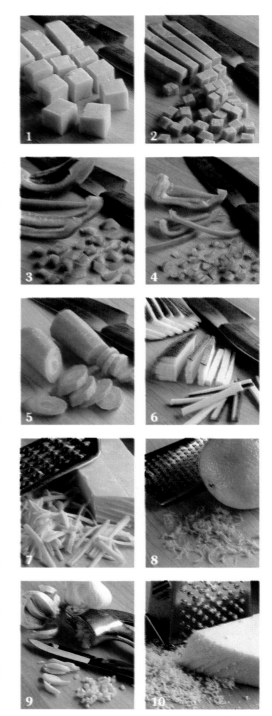

Measuring Techniques

Correctly measuring ingredients is important for consistent results. But not all ingredients are measured the same way. To ensure accuracy, follow these directions.

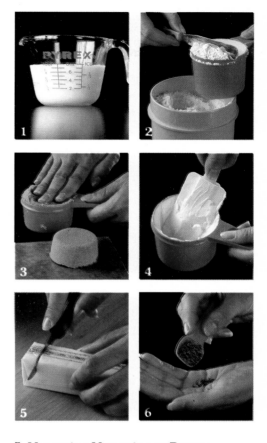

1. Measuring Liquids

Use a glass or clear plastic measuring cup. Place the cup on a level surface and bend down so your eye is level with the marking you wish to read. Fill the cup to the marking. Don't lift the cup off the counter to your eye; your hand is not as steady as the countertop.

When using measuring spoons to measure a liquid, pour the liquid just to the top of the spoon without letting it spill over. Don't measure over the mixing bowl because the liquid could overflow from the spoon into the bowl.

2. Measuring Flour

Stir the flour in the canister to lighten it. (Sifting flours, except cake flour, no longer is necessary.) Then gently spoon the flour into a dry measuring cup and level off the top with the straight edge of a knife or a metal spatula.

3. Measuring Sugar

Press brown sugar firmly into a dry measuring cup so that it holds the shape of the cup when turned out.

To measure granulated sugar, spoon the sugar into a dry measuring cup, then level it off with the straight edge of a knife or a metal spatula.

4. Measuring Solid Shortening

Using a rubber spatula, press the shortening firmly into a dry measuring cup. Level it off with the straight edge of a knife or a metal spatula.

5. Measuring Margarine or Butter

For stick margarine or butter, use an entire ¼ pound stick for ½ cup, half of a stick for ¼ cup, or an eighth of a stick for 1 tablespoon. With a sharp knife, cut off the amount needed, following the guidelines on the wrapper. For unwrapped margarine or butter, soften it, then measure as directed for solid shortening.

6. Measuring Dried Herbs

Lightly fill a measuring spoon just to the top with the dried herb (leveling with a spatula is not necessary). Then empty the spoon into your hand. Crush the herb with the fingers of your other hand. This breaks the leaves and releases their flavor. (Some of the harder dried herbs, such as rosemary and thyme, are best crushed with a mortar and pestle.)

Cooking Techniques

Understanding some basic cooking techniques is essential to preparing successful recipes. Mastering these techniques will make your cooking easier and more enjoyable, too.

1. Simmering
Heat liquids over low heat till bubbles form slowly and burst below the surface.

2. Boiling
Heat liquids till bubbles form and rise in a steady pattern, breaking on the surface.

3. Poaching
Cook food partially or completely submerged in simmering liquid.

4. Steaming
Cook food in the steam given off by boiling water. Place the food in a perforated metal basket, a bamboo steamer, or on a wire rack set just above, but not touching, boiling water. Cover the pan and steam till the food is done.

5. Stir-Frying
Cook food quickly over high heat in a lightly oiled wok or skillet, lifting and turning the food constantly.

6. Deep-Fat Frying
Cook food in enough melted shortening or cooking oil to cover. The fat should be hot enough (365° or 375°) so that the food cooks without absorbing excess grease, but not so hot that the fat smokes or food burns.

7. Baking
Cook food in the indirect, dry heat of an oven. The food may be covered or uncovered.

8. Broiling
Cook food a measured distance from the direct, dry heat of the heat source. A broiler also is used to brown or toast foods or melt cheese.

Preparation Techniques

Glance through the next few pages to find directions for some basic preparation tasks.

1. Using Fresh Herbs
To snip a fresh herb, put the herb in a deep container, such as a 1-cup glass measure, and snip it with kitchen shears. To substitute fresh herbs for dried, use three times more of the fresh.

2. Peeling Tomatoes
Spear a tomato in the stem end with a fork, then plunge the tomato into boiling water for 30 seconds or just till the skin splits. (You also can hold the tomato with a slotted spoon.) Immediately dip the tomato into cold water. Using a sharp paring knife, pull the skin off the tomato. Peel peaches and apricots the same way.

3. Toasting Nuts, Seeds, and Coconut
Spread the desired nuts, seeds, or coconut into a thin layer in a shallow baking pan. Bake in a 350° oven for 5 to 10 minutes or till light golden brown, stirring once or twice.

4. Dissolving Unflavored Gelatin
Place one envelope of unflavored gelatin in a small saucepan. Stir in at least ¼ cup water or other liquid, such as broth or fruit juice. Let stand 5 minutes to soften. Heat and stir over low heat till the gelatin is dissolved. (Softening unflavored gelatin when it's combined with at least ¼ cup sugar is not necessary. Combine the gelatin-sugar mixture with liquid and heat immediately to dissolve the gelatin and sugar.) Once dissolved, the gelatin can be combined with other ingredients. If used undissolved, gelatin forms rubbery lumps.

5. Clarifying Butter
Melt the butter over low heat in a heavy saucepan without stirring. When the butter is completely melted, you will see a clear oily layer atop a milky layer. Slowly pour the clear liquid into a dish, leaving the milky layer in the saucepan. Discard the milky liquid. The clear liquid is the clarified butter. Use as a dipping sauce for lobster, scallops, and other seafood. Clarified butter also is good for panfrying or sautéing because it does not burn as easily as regular butter.

6. Caramelizing Sugar
Place the sugar in a heavy skillet or saucepan. Heat over medium-high heat, without stirring, till the sugar begins to melt; shake skillet occasionally. Reduce heat to low; cook and stir frequently till the sugar is golden brown and completely melted. Use for Caramel Flan (see recipe, page 134) or to give nuts a candy coating.

7. Separating Eggs

Over a bowl, carefully crack open an egg and gently slip the yolk back and forth from one shell half to the other, allowing the white to fall into the bowl. (*Or,* use an egg separator.) Place the egg white in another bowl, then separate the next egg into the first bowl. This procedure prevents any yolk that accidentally spills into the white from spoiling the entire batch of egg whites. Even the smallest amount of egg yolk can prevent whites from beating properly.

8. Slightly Beating Eggs

Use a fork to beat the egg till the white and yolk are combined with no streaks remaining.

9. Beating Egg Whites to Soft Peaks

Place the egg whites in a glass or metal bowl. *Do not use a plastic bowl.* Beat the egg whites with an electric mixer or rotary beater till they form peaks with tips that curl over when the beaters are lifted.

10. Beating Egg Whites to Stiff Peaks

Place the egg whites in a glass or metal bowl. *Do not use a plastic bowl.* Beat the egg whites with an electric mixer or rotary beater till they form peaks with tips that stand straight when the beaters are lifted.

11. Beating Egg Yolks

Place the egg yolks in a mixer bowl. Beat with an electric mixer on high speed about 5 minutes or till thick and lemon colored.

12. Whipping Cream

Using an electric mixer or rotary beater, beat the cream just till it mounds slightly and soft peaks form when the beaters are lifted. For the best volume, chill the utensils about 30 minutes in the refrigerator or 10 minutes in the freezer before using, and use chilled cream. Avoid overbeating the whipping cream or it will turn to butter.

13. Using a Pastry Bag

Fold back the top of the bag several inches. Hold the bag near the tip. Spoon about ½ cup of the desired mixture into the bag. (If you're using whipped cream, you may add more.) Unfold the top and twist closed. Hold the twist between your thumb and forefinger and gently squeeze the bag to release the contents. Guide the bag with your other hand.

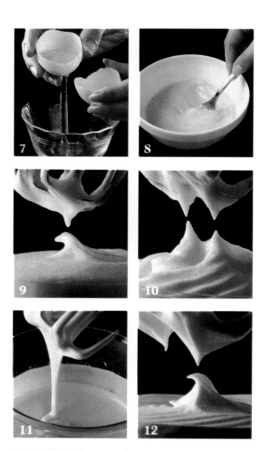

14. Melting Chocolate
Melt unsweetened, semisweet, or sweet chocolate over low heat in a small heavy saucepan, stirring often to avoid scorching. If the recipe calls for cooled chocolate, remove the pan from the heat and let it stand till the chocolate is lukewarm. Scrape the chocolate from the saucepan with a rubber spatula.

15. Sifting Powdered Sugar
Spoon the powdered sugar into a sifter or sieve. Sift into a bowl or directly onto cakes, bars, or cookies. For a patterned look, place a paper doily on top of the food. Lightly sift the powdered sugar over the doily. Remove the doily carefully. Sifting prevents powdered sugar from clumping.

16. Sectioning Oranges or Grapefruit
Cut a thin slice from each end of the fruit. Using a very sharp utility knife or a serrated knife for peeling citrus fruits, and cutting from the top of the fruit down, cut off the peel and the white membrane. (*Or,* cut around the fruit in a spiral.) Working over a bowl to catch the juices, cut between one fruit section and the membrane. Cut to the center of the fruit. Turn the knife and slide it up the other side of the section next to the membrane; repeat. Remove any seeds from the fruit sections.

17. Juicing Citrus Fruits
Cut each piece of fruit in half crosswise. Hold a citrus juicer atop a measuring cup or a bowl. (*Or,* use a freestanding juicer.) Press each half of fruit into the citrus juicer, turning the fruit back and forth till all the juice is out. Discard the pulp and seeds that collect in the juicer.

18. Cutting Fresh Pineapple
First, remove the crown (leaves) by holding the pineapple in one hand and the crown in the other; twist in opposite directions.

Next, trim the top of the pineapple and cut off the base. Set the pineapple upright on a cutting board. Starting at the top of the fruit and working down, cut off wide strips of peel with a knife.

Remove the eyes from the pineapple by cutting narrow wedge-shaped grooves diagonally around the fruit (follow the pattern of the eyes). To serve, cut the fruit into spears, slices, or chunks, removing the hard core from the center of the pineapple.

19. Sieving Berries
In a blender container or food processor bowl, blend or process berries till smooth. Place a sieve over a bowl. Pour the pureed berries into the sieve. Using the back of a wooden spoon, stir and press the fruit through the sieve. Discard any seeds that remain in the sieve.

Microwave Basics

When you're short on cooking time, the microwave oven can be a lifesaver. To better understand micro-cooking, read through these dos and don'ts.

Microwave Cookware

Cookware that's labeled microwave safe by its manufacturer is your best bet for use in the microwave oven. Many other dishes also can be used, however.

To help you decide if a dish is microwave safe, pour ½ cup of cold water into a glass measure. Set the measure into the microwave, inside or beside the dish you wish to test. Micro-cook on 100% power (high) for 1 minute. If the water is warm but the dish remains cool, you can use the dish for micro-cooking. If the water is warm and the dish feels lukewarm, the dish is suitable for heating or reheating food in the microwave, but probably not for micro-cooking food. If the water stays cool and the dish becomes hot, *do not use the dish in the microwave.* Similarly, *do not use a dish or plate that has gold or silver trim or markings.* The metal in the trim or markings may overheat and blacken or crack the dish.

White paper towels and paper plates are fine for micro-cooking if the food is moist and the total cooking time is less than 10 minutes. Never use paper products to cook food in the microwave for more than 10 minutes, or to cook very small amounts of food (¼ cup or less), because the paper could catch fire.

Select paper products labeled microwave safe.

If the Dish Fits

When selecting cookware, remember that the dishes must fit in your microwave oven. The size of oven cavities varies widely. Learn which dishes will fit in your oven and check recipes to be sure that the required dishes won't be too large. If you own an oven with a built-in turntable, choose dishes that are small enough to not bump the oven's walls as they turn.

Hot Spots

Because they have hot spots (places where foods cook faster), microwave ovens don't always cook evenly. Our recipes recommend stirring, rearranging, or turning foods to avoid overcooking in these hot spots (see photos, opposite).

Variable Power

Some microwave ovens have more than one power setting, or variable power. Microwave ovens with variable power can cook at settings lower than 100% power (such as 10%, 30%, 50%, and 70% power). They do this by cycling on and off during the cooking time.

Most of our recipes cook on 100% power (high), or the highest power setting available on your microwave. If a recipe calls for 50% power (medium), and your oven has no such setting, use a setting that is in the middle of the range of power settings available on your oven. If your oven has only high and defrost settings, use defrost for those recipes that call for 50% power. A defrost setting is actually a little lower than 50% power, so plan on your foods taking a minute or two longer to micro-cook.

Check Your Power Source

Make sure you're getting the maximum power from your oven by plugging it into an outlet on a separate circuit from your other appliances, if at all possible.

If you notice that your oven cooks slower at certain times, you may be operating it during peak power periods, when the outlet cannot feed maximum power into the oven. During these times, compensate for the decrease in power by cooking foods a little bit longer.

Your Microwave's Wattage

Microwave ovens vary in wattage according to the manufacturer and model. All of the recipes in this book were tested in high-wattage (600- to 750-watt) ovens. Because individual ovens differ, you may find that your timings vary slightly from the timings given in this book. The best rule of thumb for micro-cooking is to check the food at the end of the minimum time given in the recipe. Then cook the remaining time, if needed.

Microwave Techniques

Our microwave directions tell you when to cover, vent, stir, rearrange, or turn the food. Here's what we mean.

1. Covering
Cover foods with dish lids or microwave-safe plastic wrap to hold in steam and help foods cook faster. Cover vegetables, casseroles, fruits, fish, skinned poultry, and ground meat.

2. Venting
When you use microwave-safe plastic wrap as a cover, vent it by turning back one corner. The unsealed corner allows excess steam to escape.

3. Stirring
Because microwave energy tends to penetrate the edges of food first, stir the hotter portion on the outside into the cooler center.

4. Rearranging
Rearrange foods that can't be stirred so that they'll cook evenly. Move the less-cooked food from the center of the dish or plate to the outside. Some foods that require rearranging are chicken pieces, fish fillets, muffins, cupcakes, and foods in individual dishes.

5. Turning the Dish
Turn foods that can't be stirred or rearranged. Every time a recipe says to turn a food, rotate the dish halfway, unless otherwise specified.

6. Turning Food Over
Turn over large pieces of food, such as burgers, if you notice that they're cooking faster on the bottom than on the top.

7. Testing for Doneness
Always test foods after the minimum cooking time specified in the recipe, using the doneness test given. Some micro-cooked foods may look as if they need more cooking even when they are done. Finished cakes, muffins, and other baked products, for example, still will look wet on the surface. To test these foods for doneness, scratch the surface and see if a cooked texture has formed underneath.

Grilling Techniques

Grilling food can be almost as much fun as eating it, if you follow these simple pointers.

Types of Grills

Covered grills: These grills can be either kettle- or wagon-shaped. They are the most versatile of all grills because you can grill both directly and indirectly in them. The grills come in charcoal, gas, or electric models. Air vents in the bottom and in the grill hood control ventilation, making for very even heat.

Braisers: These shallow uncovered grills are designed for direct-heat grilling only.

Hibachis: These small portable grills work well for appetizers or for grilling one or two servings.

Grilling Options

Although gas and electric grills are easy to use, directions differ by brand. Refer to your owner's manual for operating instructions. To cook with a charcoal grill, read the tips that follow.

Preparing the Firebox

Before using your charcoal grill, check your owner's manual to see if your firebox needs to be protected. If it does, line the box with *heavy* foil. Then add an inch of pea gravel or coarse grit. The gravel lets air under the coals so that they will burn better. It also protects the firebox from intense heat and reduces flare-ups by absorbing meat drippings. Change the foil liner when it's full of drippings. At the same time, replace the gravel, or wash and air-dry it, then reuse.

Adding the Briquettes

Choose either regular or self-lighting briquettes. To determine how many briquettes you'll need, spread them into a single layer, extending them about an inch beyond the area of the food to be cooked. Then mound the briquettes in the center of the firebox (see photo 1, right).

Lighting the Fire

If you're using regular briquettes, light the coals in one of the following ways:

Charcoal starter fluid: Squirt the starter fluid over the coals. Allow the fluid to soak into the briquettes for about a minute before lighting. Don't add more starter once the fire is burning. *Never use gasoline or kerosene.* Gasoline may explode and kerosene gives food an unpleasant taste.

Electric starters: These handy gadgets provide glowing coals in only five to 15 minutes. Pile the briquettes over the starter coil and plug in the starter. When the coals are heated to the correct temperature, remove the coil.

If you are using self-lighting briquettes, simply ignite them with a match.

Arranging the Coals

After lighting the fire, leave the briquettes in a mound until they look ash gray during the daytime or glow red after dark. This usually takes about 20 to 30 minutes for standard briquettes and five to 10 minutes for self-lighting briquettes.

Once the coals are ready, spread them out as follows. (The method you choose will depend on the type of food you're cooking. Check the recipe to determine the appropriate method.)

For *direct-heat grilling,* use long-handled tongs to spread the hot coals into a single layer. For more even heat, arrange the coals about ½ inch apart. Place the food directly over the coals and cook uncovered. Cook burgers, sausages, kabobs, steaks, and chicken pieces this way.

For *indirect-heat grilling,* use either a disposable foil drip pan or make your own. (To make a drip pan, tear off a piece of *heavy* foil twice the length of your grill; fold it in half for a double thickness. Turn the edges up 1½ inches. Miter the corners by pressing the tips of the corners together and folding them toward the inside.) Place the drip pan in the center of the firebox. Then, using long-handled tongs, arrange the hot coals in a circle around the pan. Place the food over the drip pan but not over the coals, and cover the grill. Use this method when cooking roasts, whole chickens or turkeys, and other large pieces of meat.

Judging Coal Temperature
Each grill recipe specifies a temperature for the coals. Recipes for indirect-heat grilling also give a temperature above the drip pan. To check the temperature, hold your hand, palm side down, above the coals, or above the drip pan, at the height the food will be cooked (see photos 2 and 3, opposite). Start counting the seconds, "one thousand one, one thousand two." If you need to remove your hand after two seconds, the coals are *hot;* after three seconds, they're *medium-hot;* after four seconds, they're *medium;* after five seconds, they're *medium-slow;* and after six seconds, they're *slow.*

Adjusting the Heat
If your coals are too hot, raise the grill rack, spread the coals farther apart, close the air vents halfway, or remove some of the hot briquettes.

To increase the temperature in the grill, tap the ashes off the burning coals with tongs, move the coals closer together, add more briquettes, lower the grill rack, or open the vents completely.

Speed Up Cleanup
These tips will make cleanup chores easier.
● Clean the grill rack as soon as possible after cooking. (Check your owner's manual before using any cleaning products or abrasives.)

To clean the grill rack, remove the rack from over the coals. Cover both sides of the rack with wet paper towels or newspapers and let stand while you eat. Later, the burned-on food should wash right off. To remove stubborn burned-on food, sprinkle dry baking soda on a damp sponge and scour lightly. Or use a scouring pad, crumpled foil, or a stiff grill brush.
● For gas grills, clean the inside by first turning the gas burners on high. Close the hood and let the grill burn about 15 minutes. After the grill cools, wipe the rack clean.

Crockery-Cooker Techniques

With an electric crockery cooker, it's easy to work home-style meals into your busy life-style. Start the cooker early in the day to have dinner ready when you get home.

Types of Cookers
There are two main types of crockery cookers available. The recipes for this book were tested in cookers that have a *continuous* slow-cooking cycle. You can identify this type of crockery cooker by the fixed settings on the heat control: low, high, and sometimes automatic (shifts from high to low heat on its own).

Another type of cooker has a dial indicating temperatures in degrees. With this type of cooker, the heating element cycles on and off. Our recipes will not work in these cookers.

Tips for Use
Here's how to use your crockery cooker most efficiently. (To learn about the specific features of your model, check the owner's manual.)
● Do some of the chopping and measuring of ingredients ahead, if possible. Assemble the ingredients in a bowl, cover, and refrigerate till it's time to begin cooking. (If your cooker has a *removable liner,* assemble and refrigerate the food in the liner rather than in a bowl.)
● Keep the lid securely on the crockery cooker during cooking and be sure the food doesn't push up on the lid. Because crockery cooking depends on the heat that builds up in the cooker itself, resist the temptation to take a quick peek or stir frequently.
● To protect the crockery liner, avoid subjecting it to sudden temperature changes. For instance, do not preheat the cooker and then add food.

Cooking Terms

Al dente: Describes spaghetti or other pasta that is cooked only till it offers a slight resistance to the bite.

Baste: To moisten foods during cooking with pan drippings or a special sauce in order to add flavor and prevent drying.

Beat: To make a mixture smooth by briskly whipping or stirring it with a spoon, wire whisk, rotary beater, or electric mixer.

Blanch: To partially cook fruits, vegetables, or nuts in boiling water or steam to prepare for canning or freezing.

Blend: To process foods in an electric blender.

Braise: To cook food slowly in a small amount of liquid in a tightly covered pan on the range top or in the oven.

Butterfly: To split foods such as shrimp or steak through the middle without completely separating the halves, then spreading the halves to resemble a butterfly.

Coat: To evenly cover food with crumbs, flour, or a batter.

Crisp-tender: Describes vegetables cooked until they're just tender but still somewhat crisp.

Cut in: To combine shortening with dry ingredients using a pastry blender or two knives.

Dash: An ingredient measure that equals about half of ⅛ teaspoon.

Dissolve: To stir a dry substance in a liquid, such as sugar in coffee or gelatin in water, till no solids remain. Heating the liquid is sometimes necessary.

Dollop: To place a scoop or spoonful of a semi-liquid food, such as whipped cream or sour cream, on top of another food.

Fillet: To cut lean meat or fish into pieces without bones.

Flake: To break food gently into small pieces.

Fold: To gently mix ingredients, using a folding motion. With a spatula, cut down through the mixture; cut across the bottom of the bowl, then up and over, close to the surface. Turn the bowl frequently for even distribution.

Garnish: To add visual appeal to finished food by decorating it with small pieces of food or edible flowers.

Glaze: To brush a mixture on a food to give it a glossy appearance or a hard finish.

Grind: To use a food grinder or food processor to cut food such as meat or fruit into fine pieces.

Knead: To work dough with the heel of your hand in a pressing and folding motion.

Melt: To heat a solid food, such as margarine or sugar, till it is a liquid.

Mix: To stir, usually with a spoon, till ingredients are thoroughly combined.

Mull: To slowly heat beverages, such as red wine or cider, with spices and sugar.

Panbroil: To cook meats in a skillet without added fat, removing any fat as it accumulates.

Panfry: To cook meats, poultry, or fish in a small amount of hot fat.

Partially set: Describes a gelatin mixture chilled until its consistency resembles unbeaten egg whites.

Peel: To remove the outer layer or skin from a fruit or vegetable.

Pit: To remove the seed from a piece of fruit.

Preheat: To heat an oven to the recommended temperature before cooking in it.

Process: To blend a food in a food processor. Also refers to the technique of canning foods.

Puree: To chop food into a liquid or heavy paste, usually in a blender, food processor, or food mill.

Reduce: To boil liquids such as pan juices or sauces rapidly so that some of the liquid evaporates, thickening the mixture.

Roast: To cook meats, uncovered, in the oven.

Sauté: To cook or brown food in a small amount of hot fat.

Score: To cut narrow grooves or slits partway through the outer surface of a food.

Shuck: To remove the shells or husks from foods such as oysters, clams, or corn.

Sift: To put one or more dry ingredients through a sifter or sieve to incorporate air and break up any lumps.

Skim: To remove melted fat or other substances from the surface of a liquid.

Stew: To cook food in liquid for a long time till tender, usually in a covered pot.

Stir: To mix ingredients with a spoon in a circular or figure-8 motion till combined.

Whip: To beat food lightly and rapidly using a wire whisk, rotary beater, or electric mixer to incorporate air into the mixture and increase its volume.

Garnishing Techniques

Make even the most everyday meal seem special with these easy-to-do garnishes.

1. Radish Accordions
Make 8 to 10 narrow crosswise cuts ⅛ inch apart in long narrow radishes, cutting only partially through each radish. (To keep from cutting through the radishes, place them between two parallel wooden sticks when cutting.) Place the radishes in ice water so the slices fan out. Use with meats or salads.

2. Citrus Twists
Thinly slice lemons, limes, and oranges. Cut into center of each slice; twist ends in opposite directions. Use with fish and citrus or cream pies.

3. Fluted Mushrooms
With a paring knife held at an angle, and beginning at the top of each mushroom cap, make cuts in the form of an inverted V. Turn mushroom slightly; cut another inverted V; repeat around cap. For a similiar effect, make a series of slight indentations in mushroom cap with a punch-type can opener. Use with salads and meats.

4. Tomato Roses
Cut a base from the stem end of each tomato (do not sever). Cut a continuous narrow strip in spiral fashion, tapering end to remove. Curl strip onto its base in a rose shape. Use with salads and dips.

5. Scored Cucumbers
Make a V-shape cut lengthwise down each cucumber (or run the tines of a fork lengthwise down each cucumber, pressing to break the skin). Repeat at regular intervals around cucumber. Slice or bias-slice. Use with salads and dips.

6. Onion Brushes
Slice roots from ends of green onions; remove most of green portion. Make slashes at both ends of the onion pieces to make fringes. Place in ice water to curl the ends. Use with steaks or roasts.

7. Carrot Curls/Zigzags
Using a vegetable peeler, cut thin lengthwise strips from carrots. For curls, roll up; secure with toothpicks. For zigzags, thread on toothpicks accordion-style. Put curls and zigzags in ice water; remove toothpicks before using. Use with salads, sauces, and thickened soups.

8. Chocolate Curls/Grated Chocolate
For curls, use a bar of chocolate at room temperature. Carefully draw a vegetable peeler across the chocolate, making thin strips that curl. To grate, rub a cool, firm square of chocolate across a hand grater. Use to garnish cakes, tortes, custards, or ice-cream drinks.

Cooking at High Altitudes

High-altitude cooking would be a snap if only there were a magic formula for converting all recipes. Unfortunately, since ingredients and proportions vary by recipe, no such formula exists. If you live more than 1,000 feet above sea level, your best bet is to become familiar with how altitude affects food, then experiment with recipe ingredients and amounts to find the balance suitable for your location. Measure amounts carefully and keep a record of the amounts you use and the results you achieve each time you cook. To help you get started, here are some general high-altitude tips.

Baking

For *cakes* leavened by air, such as angel cakes, beat the egg whites only to *soft* peaks. Otherwise, your cakes may expand too much. When making a cake that contains a large amount of fat or chocolate, you may need to reduce the shortening by 1 to 2 tablespoons and add an egg to prevent the cake from falling. The leavening, sugar, and liquid in cakes leavened with baking powder or baking soda may need adjustment, too. Use the chart on page 85 to compensate for altitude.

Cookies, biscuits, and *muffins,* on the other hand, are more stable than cakes and need little adjustment. If necessary, experiment by slightly reducing the sugar and baking powder and increasing the liquid.

For both *cakes* and *cookies,* increase the oven temperature about 20 degrees and decrease the baking time slightly. These steps will keep cakes from expanding too much and cookies from drying out.

For *yeast doughs,* allow the unshaped dough to rise according to the recipe directions, then punch the dough down. Repeat this rising step once more before shaping the dough. Also, if your yeast dough seems dry, add more liquid; and reduce the amount of flour the next time you make the recipe. Flours tend to be drier at high altitudes and sometimes absorb more liquid.

Range-Top Cooking

When *boiling* foods at high altitudes, increase the cooking time. This is necessary because liquids boil at lower temperatures at high altitudes. Also increase the amount of liquid, as it will evaporate more quickly. Do not increase the heat because your food might scorch.

For *deep-fat frying,* fry foods at a lower temperature for a longer time. Since the moisture in the food has a lower boiling point, food fried at the recommended sea-level temperature will be crusty but underdone. Lower the temperature of the fat 3 degrees for each 1,000 feet you live above sea level.

For *candies,* decrease the temperature given in the recipe 2 degrees for each 1,000 feet of elevation. This step is necessary because rapid evaporation causes candies to concentrate more quickly at high altitudes.

When *canning* foods at high altitudes, adjust the processing time or pressure to guard against food contamination. If you plan to use the boiling-water method of canning, contact your county extension agent for detailed instructions. For information on pressure canning at high altitudes, see "Canning at High Altitudes," page 192. If you are unsure about the altitude of your home, contact your county extension agent.

To *blanch* vegetables for freezing, heat 1 minute longer than the sea-level directions if you live more than 5,000 feet above sea level.

Further Information

For more information on cooking at high altitudes, contact your county extension agent or write or call:

Colorado State University
Bulletin Room
Fort Collins, CO 80523
303/491-7334

Broiling Meat/Poultry

Place **meat** on the unheated rack of a broiler pan. For cuts less than 1½ inches thick, broil 3 inches from the heat. For cuts 1½ inches thick or thicker, broil 4 to 5 inches from the heat. Broil for the time given or till done, turning meat over after half of the broiling time.

For **poultry,** remove the broiler pan and preheat the broiler for 5 to 10 minutes. Arrange the poultry on the unheated rack of the broiler pan, bone side up. Place the pan under the broiler so the surface of the poultry is 4 to 5 inches from the heat. Turn chicken quarters and meaty pieces over after 20 minutes. Poultry is done when meat is tender and no longer pink.

	Total Time in Minutes
Beef steaks (top loin, tenderloin, T-bone, porterhouse, sirloin, rib, rib eye)	
1-inch	
Rare	8–12
Medium	13–17
Well-done	18–22
1½-inch	
Rare	14–18
Medium	19–22
Well-done	23–28
Ground-meat patties (beef, pork, lamb)	
¾-inch	
Medium (beef and lamb only)	12–14
Well-done	15–18
Pork chops	
¾-inch	
Well-done	12–14
1¼- to 1½-inch	
Well-done	24–28
Pork blade steaks	
½-inch	
Well-done	12–14
Fully cooked ham center slice	
1-inch	14–18
Lamb chops	
1-inch	
Rare	8–10
Medium	10–12
Well-done	14–16
Chicken	
Quartered or cut up	25–35
Chicken breast halves, thighs, and drumsticks	25–35

Weights and Measures

3 teaspoons = 1 tablespoon	4 cups = 1 quart
4 tablespoons = ¼ cup	2 pints = 1 quart
5⅓ tablespoons = ⅓ cup	4 quarts = 1 gallon
8 tablespoons = ½ cup	1 tablespoon = 15 milliliters
10⅔ tablespoons = ⅔ cup	1 cup = 250 milliliters
12 tablespoons = ¾ cup	1.06 quarts = 1 liter
16 tablespoons = 1 cup	¼ pound = 125 grams
1 tablespoon = ½ fluid ounce	½ pound = 250 grams
1 cup = 8 fluid ounces	¾ pound = 375 grams
1 cup = ½ pint	1 pound = 500 grams
2 cups = 1 pint	

Microwave Timing Tips

Melting chocolate: In a bowl micro-cook chocolate, uncovered, on 100% power (high) 1 to 2 minutes for 1 square (1 ounce) (1½ to 2½ minutes for one 6-ounce package [1 cup] chocolate pieces) or till soft enough to stir smooth, stirring every minute.

Melting margarine or butter: In a bowl micro-cook margarine, uncovered, on 100% power (high) 40 to 50 seconds for 2 tablespoons, 45 to 60 seconds for ¼ cup, or 1 to 2 minutes for ½ cup.

Softening margarine or butter: In a bowl heat margarine, uncovered, on 10% power (low) 1 to 1½ minutes for ½ cup or till softened.

Softening cream cheese: In a bowl heat cream cheese, uncovered, on 100% power (high) 15 to 30 seconds for 3 ounces (45 to 60 seconds for 8 ounces) or till softened.

Reheating muffins and rolls: Place muffins or rolls on a plate. Heat, uncovered, on 100% power (high) 15 to 20 seconds for 1 or 2 muffins (30 to 60 seconds for 4 muffins).

Heating pancake syrup: Heat, uncovered, on 100% power (high) 30 to 60 seconds for ½ cup syrup (1 to 1½ minutes for 1 cup syrup) or till warm.

Heating ice-cream topping: Heat chilled topping, uncovered, on 100% power (high) ½ to 1½ minutes for ½ cup topping (1 to 2 minutes for 1 cup topping).

Warming fruit pie: Place 1 slice of fruit pie on a plate. Heat, uncovered, on 100% power (high) for 45 to 60 seconds or till warm.

Softening ice cream: Heat 1 pint solidly frozen ice cream in a container, uncovered, on 100% power (high) for 15 seconds or till soft.

Heating canned soups: In a bowl combine one 10- to 11-ounce can condensed soup and 1 soup can water. Micro-cook, uncovered, on 100% power (high) for 2½ to 3½ minutes or till hot.

Juicing lemons: Halve or quarter 1 lemon. Heat on 100% power (high) for 30 to 45 seconds. Squeeze out juice.

Emergency Substitutions

For best results, use the ingredients specified in the recipe.

If you don't have:	Substitute:
1 cup cake flour	1 cup *minus* 2 tablespoons all-purpose flour
1 tablespoon cornstarch (for thickening)	2 tablespoons all-purpose flour
1 teaspoon baking powder	½ teaspoon cream of tartar *plus* ¼ teaspoon baking soda
1 package active dry yeast	1 cake compressed yeast
1 cup sugar	1 cup packed brown sugar *or* 2 cups sifted powdered sugar
¼ cup fine dry bread crumbs	¾ cup soft bread crumbs, *or* ¼ cup cracker crumbs, *or* ¼ cup cornflake crumbs
1 cup honey	1¼ cups sugar *plus* ¼ cup liquid
1 cup corn syrup	1 cup sugar *plus* ¼ cup liquid
1 square (1 ounce) unsweetened chocolate	3 tablespoons unsweetened cocoa powder *plus* 1 tablespoon shortening *or* cooking oil
1 cup whipping cream, whipped	2 cups whipped dessert topping
1 cup buttermilk	1 tablespoon lemon juice *or* vinegar *plus* enough whole milk to make 1 cup (let stand 5 minutes before using), *or* 1 cup whole milk *plus* 1¾ teaspoons cream of tartar, *or* 1 cup plain yogurt
1 cup whole milk	½ cup evaporated milk *plus* ½ cup water, *or* 1 cup water *plus* ⅓ cup nonfat dry milk powder
1 cup light cream	1 tablespoon melted butter *plus* enough milk to make 1 cup
2 cups tomato sauce	¾ cup tomato paste *plus* 1 cup water
1 cup tomato juice	½ cup tomato sauce *plus* ½ cup water
1 small onion, chopped (⅓ cup)	1 teaspoon onion powder *or* 1 tablespoon dried minced onion
1 teaspoon dry mustard (in cooked mixtures)	1 tablespoon prepared mustard

Ingredient Equivalents

Food	Amount Before Preparation	Approximate Measure After Preparation	Food	Amount Before Preparation	Approximate Measure After Preparation
Cereals			**Fruits** (continued)		
Macaroni	1 cup (3½ oz.)	2½ cups cooked	Oranges	1 medium	¼ to ⅓ cup juice; 4 tsp. shredded peel
Noodles, medium	3 cups (4 oz.)	3 cups cooked			
Spaghetti	8 oz.	4 cups cooked	Peaches, pears	1 medium	½ cup sliced
Long grain rice	1 cup (7 oz.)	3 cups cooked	Rhubarb	1 pound	2 cups cooked
Quick-cooking rice	1 cup (3 oz.)	2 cups cooked	Strawberries	4 cups whole	4 cups sliced
			Vegetables		
Popcorn	⅓ to ½ cup	8 cups popped	Cabbage	1 pound (1 small)	5 cups shredded
Crumbs			Carrots, without tops	1 pound (6 to 8 medium)	3 cups shredded *or* 2¼ cups chopped
Bread	1 slice	¾ cup soft crumbs *or* ¼ cup fine dry crumbs			
			Cauliflower	1 medium head	4½ cups sliced
			Celery	1 stalk	½ cup chopped
Saltine crackers	14 crackers	½ cup finely crushed	Green beans	1 pound (4 cups)	2½ cups cooked
Rich round crackers	12 crackers	½ cup finely crushed	Green peppers	1 large	1 cup chopped
			Lettuce	1 medium head	6 cups torn
Graham crackers	7 squares	½ cup finely crushed	Mushrooms	½ pound (3 cups)	1 cup cooked
			Onions	1 medium	½ cup chopped
Gingersnaps	7 cookies	½ cup finely crushed	Potatoes	3 medium	2 cups cubed *or* 1¾ cups mashed
Vanilla wafers	11 cookies	½ cup finely crushed			
			Spinach	1 pound	12 cups torn
Fruits			Tomatoes	1 medium	½ cup chopped
Apples	1 medium	1 cup sliced	**Miscellaneous**		
Bananas	1 medium	⅓ cup mashed	Cheese	4 ounces	1 cup shredded
Lemons	1 medium	3 tbsp. juice; 2 tsp. shredded peel	Whipping cream	1 cup	2 cups whipped
			Ground beef	1 pound raw	2¾ cups cooked
Limes	1 medium	2 tbsp. juice; 1½ tsp. shredded peel	Cooked meat	1 pound	3 cups chopped
			Chicken breasts	1½ pounds (2 whole medium)	2 cups chopped cooked chicken

Index

***Recipe includes
microwave directions.**

*Recipe includes
microwave directions.

*Recipe includes
microwave directions.

G

*Recipe includes
microwave directions.

H

*Recipe includes
microwave directions.

**°Recipe includes
microwave directions.**

*Recipe includes
microwave directions.

*Recipe includes
microwave directions.

*Recipe includes
microwave directions.

Have BETTER HOMES AND
GARDENS® magazine delivered
to your door.
For information, write to:
MR. ROBERT AUSTIN
P.O. BOX 4536
DES MOINES, IA 50336

*Recipe includes
microwave directions.

Notes

Notes

Notes

Notes